D1456407

COST-BENEFIT ANALYSIS

Second
Edition

COST-BENEFIT ANALYSIS
Concepts and Practice

Anthony E. Boardman
University of British Columbia

David H. Greenberg
University of Maryland Baltimore County

Aidan R. Vining
Simon Fraser University

David L. Weimer
University of Wisconsin–Madison

Prentice
Hall

UPPER SADDLE RIVER, NJ 07458

Library of Congress Cataloging-in-Publication Data

Cost-benefit analysis : concepts and practice / Anthony E. Boardman ... [et al.]—2nd ed.
   p. cm.
Includes bibliographical references and index.
ISBN 0-13-087178-8
1. Cost effectiveness.   I. Boardman, Anthony E.

HD47.4.C699   2001
658.15'54—dc21

                                        00-058457

Vice President/Editorial Director: James Boyd
Editor-in-Chief: PJ Boardman
Senior Editor: Rod Banister
Managing Editor (Editorial): Gladys Soto
Editorial Assistant: Marie McHale
Assistant Editor: Holly Brown
Media Project Manager: Bill Minick
Marketing Manager: Josh McClary
Production/Manufacturing Manager: Gail Steier de Acevedo
Production Coordinator: Maureen Wilson
Senior Prepress/Manufacturing Manager: Vincent Scelta
Manufacturing Buyer: Natacha St. Hill Moore
Cover Design: Bruce Kenselaar
Composition: Omegatype Typography, Inc.

Prentice
Hall

10 9 8 7 6 5 4 3 2 1
ISBN 0-13-087178-8

To
Barbara, Linda, Melanie, and Ulrike

Brief Contents

CONTENTS

PREFACE

Collaborative academic projects often take longer than originally anticipated, not just because of the normal delays of coordinating the efforts of busy people but also because initially modest goals can become more ambitious as participants delve into their subject. We confess to both these sins with respect to preparing the first edition of this text. Our original plans made in 1990 were very modest. We intended to use an expanded version of the chapter on cost-benefit analysis in the text *Policy Analysis: Concepts and Practice* by David Weimer and Aidan Vining as the conceptual foundation for a collection of cases. Our goal was to produce a book that would be conceptually sound, practically oriented, and easily accessible to both students and practitioners. Though our final product was far different in form and content than we initially planned, we believe that our first edition was such a book.

Our plans evolved for a number of reasons. Perhaps most importantly, through our teaching of undergraduate and graduate students as well as our experiences training government employees, we realized that many topics demanded extended treatment if the essential basics were to be effectively conveyed and solid foundations laid for further learning of advanced topics. We also decided that fully integrating illustrations and examples with concepts and methods is pedagogically superior to presenting independent cases. The result was a series of chapters that develop conceptual foundations, methods of application, and extensions of cost-benefit analysis through numerous practical examples and illustrations.

Our own use of the book in teaching, as well as comments from other teachers and students, helped us identify several areas for improvement in this second edition. In addition to adding new material, including an entire chapter on applying cost-benefit analysis in developing countries, we revised and reorganized many chapters to make the presentation clearer and more effective. For example, we essentially rewrote the chapter on the social discount rate, added considerable new material on obtaining shadow prices from secondary sources, expanded the discussion of the value of information, and divided two long chapters into shorter and more manageable ones.

These improvements were made with our three intended audiences in mind. First, we intend the book for use in courses on public-sector decision making offered in graduate programs in public policy analysis, urban planning, public administration, business, economics, public health, and environmental studies. Second, we envision it being used at the undergraduate level either as a primary text for a course on cost-benefit analysis or as a supplementary text for economics courses in public finance, public-sector economics, and policy analysis. Third, we intend it to be useful to policy analysts and public managers as a general introduction and practical guide to cost-benefit analysis, as well as a starting point for exploring advanced topics. In order to be appropriate for these diverse audiences, the second edition continues to emphasize clear discussion over formal mathematics, and application over abstract theory. Nevertheless, we think that we cover important, if difficult, conceptual issues in adequate detail both as a framework for thoughtful application and as a basis for further study.

The process of preparing the second edition has been a rewarding one for us. As during preparation of the first edition, we were forced to think more deeply about some topics that we thought we had already mastered and to develop others with which none of us was very familiar. We did this enjoyably together through numerous exchanges of drafts and during an intensive work session at the University of British Columbia.

Our project was also made more productive and enjoyable by our many colleagues and students who gave us advice, comments, encouragement, or information. We thank here just a few people who were particularly helpful: Marcus Berliant, Edward Bird, James Brander, Ian Davis, John DeWald, Haynes Goddard, Tim Grindling, Eric Hanushek, Robert Havemen, Stanley Engerman, Doug Landin, Walter Oi, W. G. Waters II, and Michael Wolkoff. We thank Roy I. Gobin, Loyola University, Chicago; George T. Fuller, Wagner Graduate School, New York University; Ruth Shen, San Francisco State University; and Larry Karp, University of California at Berkeley, who wrote thoughtful reviews of the first edition for the publisher, and Laurie T. Johnson, State University of New York, Albany; Roger G. Noll, Stanford University; Terri A. Sexton, California State University, Sacramento; and Nachum Sicherman, Columbia University, who offered valuable comments during preparation of the second edition. We especially thank Mark Moore, whose joint work with two of us helped us substantially improve our discussion of the social discount rate, and Roger Noll, who made extremely valuable suggestions that prompted many other substantial revisions. Of course, they are not responsible for any errors that remain.

NEW INSTRUCTIONAL MATERIALS

We are pleased to provide our users with two new supplements to the textbook. Instructors and students will be able to log on to http://www.prenhall.com/boardman where they will find an Extended Bibliography that complements the textbook. In addition, our new Instructor's Manual will provide instructors with Chapter Summaries, answers to the end-of-chapter exercises, and overheads of the figures and tables in the book. With the increased use of the book for professional, as well as distance education, the manual will be invaluable for teachers in both traditional and nontraditional settings. Instructors should contact their Prentice Hall sales representatives for the user identification number and password to access the faculty resources or call our Faculty and Field Services Department at 1-800-526-0485.

COST-BENEFIT ANALYSIS

1

INTRODUCTION TO COST-BENEFIT ANALYSIS

In the Affair of so much Importance to you, wherein you ask my Advice, I cannot for want of sufficient Premises, advise you what *to determine, but if you please I will tell you* how. *When those difficult Cases occur, they are difficult, chiefly because while we have them under Consideration, all the Reasons* pro and con *are not present to the Mind at the same time; but sometimes one Set present themselves, and at other times another, the first being out of Sight. Hence the various Purposes or Inclinations that alternately prevail, and the Uncertainty that perplexes us.*

To get over this, my Way is, to divide half a Sheet of Paper by a Line into two Columns; writing over the one Pro, *and over the other* Con. *Then during three or four Days Consideration, I put down under the different Heads short Hints of the different Motives, that at different Times occur to me,* for *or against the Measure. When I have thus got them all together in one View, I endeavor to estimate their respective Weights; and where I find two, one on each side, that seem equal, I strike them both out. If I find a Reason* pro *equal to some two Reasons* con, *I strike out the three. If I judge some* two *Reasons* con, *equal to some three Reasons* pro, *I strike out the five; and thus proceeding I find at length where the Balance lies; and if after a Day or two of farther consideration, nothing new that is of Importance occurs on either side, I come to a Determination accordingly. And, tho' the Weight of Reasons cannot be taken with the Precision of Algebraic Quantities, yet, when each is thus considered, separately and comparatively, and the whole lies before me, I think I can judge better, and am less liable to make a rash Step; and in fact I have found great Advantage from this kind of Equation, in what may be* called Moral or Prudential Algebra.

—B. FRANKLIN, London, September 19, 1772.[1]

INDIVIDUAL VERSUS SOCIAL COSTS AND BENEFITS

Benjamin Franklin's advice about how to make a personal decision illustrates many of the features of cost-benefit analysis (CBA). These include a systematic cataloguing of impacts as benefits (pros) and costs (cons), valuing in dollars (assigning weights), and then determining the *net benefits* of the proposal relative to the status quo (net benefits equal benefits minus costs).

When we as individuals talk of costs and benefits, we naturally tend to consider only our *own* costs and benefits. To oversimplify, we choose between alternative courses of action according to which has the largest individual net benefits. Similarly, in evaluating various investment alternatives, firms tend to consider only those costs (expenditures) and benefits (revenues) that flow to them. In cost-benefit analysis we try to consider *all of the costs and benefits to society as a whole.* For this reason, some people refer to CBA as *social* cost-benefit analysis.

Cost-benefit analysis is a policy assessment method that quantifies in monetary terms the value of all policy consequences to all members of society. The net social benefits measure the value of the policy. Social benefits (B) minus social costs (C) equals net social benefits (NSB):

$$NSB = B - C \qquad \textbf{(1.1)}$$

Throughout this book we will use the terms *policy* and *project* interchangeably. CBA applies to policies, programs, projects, regulations, demonstrations, and other government interventions.

Stated at this level of abstraction, it is unlikely that many people would disagree with doing CBA. In practice, however, there are two types of disagreements. First, social critics including some political economists, philosophers, libertarians, and socialists have disputed the fundamental utilitarian assumptions of CBA that the sum of individual utilities should be maximized and that it is possible to trade off utility gains for some against utility losses for others. These critics are not prepared to make trade-offs between one person's benefits and another person's costs. Second, participants in the public policy-making process (analysts, bureaucrats, and politicians) may disagree about such practical issues as whether certain given impacts are costs or benefits, what those impacts will be over time, how to monetize (attach a dollar value to them), and how to make trade-offs between the present and the future.

Our purpose in this chapter is to provide a nontechnical but reasonably comprehensive overview of CBA. Though we introduce a number of key concepts, we do so informally, returning to discuss them thoroughly in subsequent chapters. Therefore, this chapter is best read without great concern about definitions and technical details.

THE PURPOSE AND USES OF CBA

The broad purpose of CBA is to help social decision making. More specifically, the objective is to facilitate more efficient allocation of society's resources. As we will see, where markets work well, individual self-interest leads to an efficient allocation of resources. Consequently, government analysts and politicians bear the burden of providing a rationale for any governmental interference with private choice. Economists lump these rationales under the general heading of *market failures.* Where markets fail, there is a prima facie rationale for government intervention. But, and this is important to emphasize, it is no more than that. One must be able to demonstrate the superior efficiency of a particular intervention relative to the alternatives, including the status quo. For this purpose, we use CBA.

There are two major types of cost-benefit analysis. *Ex ante* CBA, which is just standard CBA as the term is commonly used, is conducted while a project or policy is under consideration, before it is started or implemented. *Ex ante* CBA assists in the decision about whether scarce resources should be allocated by government to a specific project or policy. Thus, its contribution to public policy decision making is direct, immediate, and bureau specific. *Ex post* analysis is conducted at the end of a project. At this time, all of the costs are "sunk" in the sense that they have already been given up to do the project. The value of *ex post* analyses is broader but less immediate as they provide information not only about the particular intervention but also about the "class" of such interventions. In other words, they contribute to "learning" by government managers, politicians, and academics about whether particular classes of projects are worthwhile.

Some CBA studies are performed during the course of the life of a project, that is, *in medias res*. Some elements of such studies are similar to an *ex ante* analysis, whereas others are similar to an *ex post* analysis.

There is also a fourth type of CBA—one that compares an *ex ante* CBA with an *ex post* (or *in medias res*) CBA *of the same project*. This comparative type of CBA is most useful to policymakers for learning about the efficacy of CBA as a decision-making and evaluative tool. Unfortunately, there are almost no disinterested published examples of this type of CBA.[2] (In Chapter 19 we provide an example of such a comparison.) The paucity of this type of CBA is not as surprising as it may appear because the constituencies for *ex ante* CBA are frequently different from those for *ex post* or *in medias res* CBA.

It is useful to elaborate on the values of these four types of CBAs. Table 1.1 summarizes the important ways in which the different types of analysis aid government decision making.

Project-Specific Decision Making

Ex ante analysis is most useful for deciding whether resources should be allocated to a particular project that is under consideration. For ongoing projects an *in medias res* analysis can also be used for decision-making purposes when it is potentially feasible to shift resources to alternative uses. It is rare that such analysis will lead to termination of an investment project nearing completion because a large share of the costs will have been incurred, and benefits subsequent to the analysis will usually exceed the remaining costs. However, it can happen. For example, a Canadian Environmental Assessment Panel recently recommended the decommissioning of a just completed dam on the basis of an *in medias res* analysis that showed that, with use, future environmental costs would exceed future benefits.[3] Because *ex post* analysis is conducted at the end of the project, it is obviously too late to reverse resource allocation decisions with respect to that particular project.

Learning about the Net Social Benefits of a Specific Project

In the early stages of a project there is considerable uncertainty about the project's actual impacts and, consequently, about the true net social benefits. As time goes by, more is known about the impacts, and CBA studies conducted later can estimate the

4 PART I *Overview*

TABLE 1.1   Value of Different Classes of CBA

Value	Ex Ante	In Medias Res	Ex Post	Ex Ante/Ex Post or Ex Ante/In Medias Res Comparison
Resource allocation decision for this project	Yes—helps to select best project or make "go" versus "no-go" decisions, if accurate	If low sunk costs, can still shift resources. If high sunk costs, usually recommends continuation	Too late—the project is over	Same as *in medias res* or *ex post* analysis
Learning about actual value of specific project	Poor estimate—high uncertainty about future benefits and costs	Better—reduced uncertainty	Excellent—although some errors may remain. May have to wait long for study	Same as *in medias res* or *ex post* analysis
Contributing to learning about actual value of similar projects	Unlikely to add much	Good—contribution increases as performed later. Need to adjust for uniqueness.	Very useful—although may be some errors and need to adjust for uniqueness. May have to wait long for project completion.	Same as *in medias res* or *ex post* analysis
Learning about omission, forecasting, measurement and evaluation errors in CBA	No	No	No	Yes, provides information about these errors and about the accuracy of CBA for similar projects

Source: Anthony E. Boardman, Wendy L. Mallery, and Aidan R. Vining, "Learning from *Ex Ante/Ex Post* Cost-Benefit Comparisons: The Coquihalla Highway Example," *Socio-Economic Planning Sciences,* 28, no. 2 (1994), 69–84, Table 1, p. 71. Reprinted with kind permission from Elsevier Science Ltd., The Boulevard, Langford Lane, Kidlington OX5 1GB, UK.

net benefits of the project more accurately. In general, *ex post* studies are more accurate than *in medias res* studies, which are more accurate than *ex ante* studies.

Learning about the Potential Benefits of Similar Projects

Ex post analyses not only provide information about a particular policy intervention but, more importantly, about similar interventions as well. They help analysts who are currently conducting *ex ante* CBAs of similar policies. Furthermore, *ex post* analyses (and *in medias res* analyses) potentially contribute to learning by political and bureaucratic decision makers, as well as policy researchers, about whether particular kinds of projects are worthwhile. The U.S. federal government has explicitly induced learning by sponsoring and requiring evaluation of a variety of "pilot tests," "demonstration projects," and "social experiments" including, for example, various welfare reform demonstrations that were conducted by different states during the 1980s.[4] Eventually the weight of evidence may lead to a policy change; these welfare demonstrations contributed to the passage of a new federal welfare law, the Family Support Act of 1988.[5] Similarly, a whole range of CBAs in the 1960s and 1970s of industry-specific economic regulations showed that the costs of regulation often exceeded the benefits, thereby paving the way for deregulation initiatives in the 1980s in the trucking, airline, and telecommunications industries.[6]

The amount of societal learning from *in medias res* and *ex post* analyses depends on the *generalizability* of a particular project. This is crucial for realistic assessment of the usefulness of CBA.[7] For example, CBAs of experiments involving the efficacy of new surgical procedures or new pharmaceutical products are usually generalizable to larger populations. Lessons from many experiments, however, are not as generalizable as they appear.[8] For example, if the proposed intervention is several orders of magnitude larger than the experiment, there may be unknown nonlinear scale effects.[9] Also, if the proposed program has a more extended time frame than the experiment, this may increase the incentives for behavioral changes that increase costs or reduce benefits unpredictably.

Learning about the Efficacy of CBA

Comparison of an *ex ante* with either an *in medias res* or an *ex post* analysis is most useful for learning about the value of CBA itself. Most importantly, a comparison CBA provides information about the accuracy of the earlier *ex ante* CBA, which, in turn, provides guidance about the accuracy of subsequent similar *ex ante* CBAs. Information about the predictive capability of CBA is useful for decision-making purposes. Comparison studies also help analysts understand the reasons for any divergence between predicted and actual benefits or costs. In Chapter 19 we discuss four important potential types of errors: omission errors, forecasting errors, measurement errors, and valuation errors. Understanding the reasons for these errors helps to reduce them in the future.

THE DEMAND FOR CBA

The U.S. federal government first mandated the general use of CBA in Executive Order 12291, issued by President Reagan in early 1981. This order requires a regulatory impact analysis (RIA) for every major regulatory initiative. (An RIA is essentially a cost-benefit analysis that also takes into account distributional and fairness considerations.) President Clinton confirmed the federal government's commitment to CBA in Executive Order No. 12866, 3 C.F.R. 638 (1994).

Although Congress, in spite of many recent attempts, has failed to pass a comprehensive act requiring the application of cost-benefit analysis, there are several pieces of legislation that mandate *ex ante* CBA. The Unfunded Mandates Reform Act of 1995 passed by the 104th Congress requires agencies, except for independent regulatory boards and commissions, to prepare cost-benefit analyses for any regulation likely to result in costs of $100 million or more in any year. The CBA must also consider reasonable alternatives and select the least costly, most cost-effective, or least burdensome of the alternatives, or explain why such alternatives were not selected. The Treasury and General Government Appropriations Act of FY 2000 (HR 2000), which President Clinton signed into law in September 1999, requires the Office of Management and

Budget to issue a report providing information on the costs and benefits of federal regulations and to issue guidelines to standardize measures of costs and benefits. Previous appropriation acts have contained identical provisions.

Nearly all other Western industrialized countries have similar protocols covering broad ranges of programs or specific program areas. For example, Canada's Federal-Provincial Fraser River Flood Control Agreement recognizes that before any dike construction can take place projects have to be determined to have sound engineering and be economically viable. Economic viability is determined by CBA.

The demand for *ex post* analysis is not so explicit; there are no mandatory requirements that it be done. Nonetheless, resource allocation decisions often draw heavily on such analyses. For example, President Clinton's State of the Union Address on February 17, 1993, emphasized the relationship between *ex post* CBAs of specific Head Start programs (i.e., educational programs for low-income preschool children) and his intention to increase funding and expand the scope of such programs.

As public officials face citizen resistance to raising taxes or pressure to reduce taxes, they are increasingly forced to ensure that government works more efficiently and effectively. In practice, this provides an impetus toward the increased use of CBA and related methods to make more efficient resource allocation decisions. Such trends are contemporaneous with greater concern for the environment, which calls for the valuation of environmental and other social impacts, in addition to consideration of government expenditures.

THE COST OF CBA

Although the demand for CBA is increasing, we should keep in mind that it takes many resources (time, skill, and money) to do CBA well, especially when the projects are large, complex, and have unique features. The costs of conducting CBAs can be very large. For example, Thomas Hopkins reported in 1992 that a CBA of reducing lead in gasoline cost the Environmental Protection Agency (EPA) roughly $1 million.[10] On average, the EPA spends approximately $700,000 for a major CBA, that is, for the analysis of projects with compliance costs in excess of $100 million annually.[11] Large-scale evaluations of training programs, of which CBA is one component, often run into the millions of dollars.

READERS OF THIS BOOK

This book is primarily for people who want to know how to do CBA. Second, it is for people who want to know how to interpret CBAs—in other words, clients of CBAs. Clients can be helped in two ways. In the narrow sense, clients should be well enough informed to evaluate a specific CBA and to judge whether it has been conducted well. In the broad sense, clients may need to evaluate CBA studies well enough to have a sense of the conclusions of the literature in a specific area, such as employment training or environmental regulation. In order to do this well, one has to understand the basic principles of CBA.

THE BASIC STEPS OF CBA: COQUIHALLA HIGHWAY EXAMPLE

CBA may look intimidating and complex. To help make the process of conducting a CBA more manageable, we break it down into nine basic steps, which are listed in Table 1.2. We describe and illustrate these steps using a relatively straightforward highway example. For each step, we also point out some practical difficulties of performing CBA. The conceptual and practical issues that we broach are the focus of the rest of this book. Do not worry if the concepts are unfamiliar to you; this is a dry run. Subsequent chapters fully explain them.

Imagine that in 1986 a cost-benefit analyst, who works for the Province of British Columbia, Canada, has been asked to perform a CBA of a proposed highway between the town of Hope in the south-central part of the province and Merritt, which is more or less due north. This highway would be called the Coquihalla Highway. The analyst's CBA is presented in Table 1.3.[12] How did she get these results? What were the difficulties? We will go through the nine steps, one at a time. One factor that helps us identify the difficulties is the fact that the Coquihalla Highway was actually built in 1987.

1. **Specify the set of alternative projects.** Step 1 requires the analyst to specify the set of alternative projects. In this example, the provincial government required the analyst to consider only two alternative highways, one with tolls and one without. The provincial Department of Transportation decided that the toll, if applied, would be $40 for large trucks and $8 for cars. Thus, the analyst has a tractable set of alternatives to analyze.

In practice, however, there are often difficulties even at this stage. For many projects, including this one, the number of potential alternatives is huge. This highway could vary on many dimensions including:[13]

Road surface: It could be surfaced in bitumen or concrete.
Routing: It could take different routes.
Size: It could have two, four, or six lanes.
Tolls: The tolls could be higher or lower.
Wild animal friendliness: The highway could be built with or without "elk tunnels."
Timing: It could be delayed until a later date.

TABLE 1.2 The Major Steps in CBA

1. Specify the set of alternative projects.
2. Decide whose benefits and costs count (standing).
3. Catalogue the impacts and select measurement indicators (units).
4. Predict the impacts quantitatively over the life of the project.
5. Monetize (attach dollar values to) all impacts.
6. Discount benefits and costs to obtain present values.
7. Compute the net present value (*NPV*) of each alternative.
8. Perform sensitivity analysis.
9. Make a recommendation based on the *NPV* and sensitivity analysis.

TABLE 1.3	Coquihalla Highway CBA (1986 $ Million)			
	No Tolls		**With Tolls**	
	A	**B**	**C**	**D**
	Global Perspective	**Provincial Perspective**	**Global Perspective**	**Provincial Perspective**
Project Benefits:				
Time and Operating Cost Savings	389.8	292.3	290.4	217.8
Terminal Value of Highway	53.3	53.3	53.3	53.3
Safety Benefits (Lives)	36.0	27.0	25.2	18.9
Alternative Routes Benefits	14.6	10.9	9.4	7.1
Toll Revenues	—	—	—	37.4
New Users	0.8	0.6	0.3	0.2
Total Benefits	494.5	384.1	378.6	334.7
Project Costs:				
Construction	338.1	338.1	338.1	338.1
Maintenance	7.6	7.6	7.6	7.6
Toll Collection	—	—	8.4	8.4
Toll Booth Construction	—	—	0.3	0.3
Total Costs	345.7	345.7	354.4	354.4
Net Social Benefits	148.8	38.4	24.2	−19.7

Source: Adapted from Anthony Boardman, Aidan Vining, and W. G. Waters II, "Costs and Benefits through Bureaucratic Lenses: Example of a Highway Project," *Journal of Policy Analysis and Management,* 12, no. 3 (1993), 532–555, Table 1, p. 537.

Changing the highway on just one of these dimensions would generate at least one new alternative. Changing two or three simultaneously greatly increases the number of alternatives. In general, if there were n dimensions, each with k possible values, there would be k^n alternatives. For example, if there were three dimensions, each with three possible values, there would be 27 mutually exclusive alternatives. With four dimensions, each with three possible values, there would be 81 alternatives! Neither decision makers nor analysts can cognitively handle comparisons among such a large number of alternatives.[14]

CBA compares the net social benefits of investing resources in a particular project with the net social benefits of a hypothetical project that would be displaced if the project under evaluation were to proceed. The displaced hypothetical project is sometimes called the *counterfactual.* Usually, the counterfactual is the status quo, which means there is no change in government policy. In Table 1.3 the analyst compares the net social benefits if the highway were built either with or without tolls to the net social benefits under the status quo—if the highway were not built.

Sometimes the status quo is not a viable alternative. *If a project would displace a specific alternative rather than a hypothetical one, it should be evaluated relative to the specific alternative.* Thus, if government has committed resources to either the highway project or a health care project, without any prospect of reconsideration, then the highway project should be compared with the health care project, not the status quo.

This CBA pertains to a specific highway between Hope and Merritt. There is no attempt to compare this highway project to alternative highway projects in British Columbia, although one could do so. Rarely does the analyst compare a highway project more broadly to completely different types of projects, such as health care, antipoverty, or national defense projects. As a practical matter, full optimization is impossible. The limited nature of the comparisons sometimes frustrates politicians and decision makers who imagine that CBA is a *deus ex machina* that will rank *all* policy alternatives. On the other hand, as we mentioned earlier, the weight of CBA evidence can and does help in making broad social choices across policy areas.

2. **Decide whose benefits and costs count (standing).** Next, the analyst must decide who has standing, that is, whose benefits and costs should be counted. In this example, she was not in a position to decide this; her superiors in the provincial government were. They wanted the analysis done from the provincial perspective but also asked her to take a global perspective. The provincial perspective measures only the benefits and costs that affect British Columbian residents, including costs and benefits borne by the British Columbian government. The global perspective includes the benefits and costs that affect everyone, irrespective of where they reside. Thus, it includes benefits and costs to Albertans, U.S. residents, and even tourists from the United Kingdom. Combining these two perspectives on standing with the no-tolls and with-tolls alternatives gives the four columns in Table 1.3 labeled A through D.

It is often contentious whether an analysis should be performed from the global, national, state (provincial), or local perspective. Although the federal government usually performs analyses taking only national costs and benefits into account, critics argue that many issues should be analyzed from a global perspective. Recent environmental issues that fall into this category include ozone depletion, global climate change, and acid rain. At the other extreme, local governments typically want to ignore costs and benefits that occur in adjacent municipalities or are borne by higher levels of government. Our highway example deals with this issue by analyzing costs and benefits from both the global and the British Columbian perspectives.

3. **Catalogue the impacts and select measurement indicators (units).** Step 3 requires the analyst to list the physical impacts of the alternatives as benefits or costs and to specify the impacts' measurement units. We use the term *impacts* broadly to include inputs (required resources) and outputs. For this proposed highway, the anticipated beneficial impacts are time saved and reduced vehicle operating costs for travelers on the new highway ("Time and Operating Cost Savings" in Table 1.3); the residual value after the discounting period of 20 years ("Terminal Value of Highway"); accidents avoided (including lives saved) due to drivers switching to the shorter, safer new highway ("Safety Benefits"); reduced congestion on the existing alternative routes—the old road ("Alternative Routes Benefits"); revenues collected from tolls ("Toll Revenues"); and benefits accruing to new travelers ("New Users"). The anticipated cost impacts are construction costs ("Construction"); additional maintenance and snow removal ("Maintenance"); toll collection ("Toll Collection"); and toll booth construction and maintenance ("Toll Booth Construction").

Specification of impact category measurement indicators usually occurs at the same time as specification of the impact categories. There are no particular difficulties in specifying measurement indicators of each impact category in this illustration. For example, number of lives saved per year, person-hours of travel time saved, and dollar value of gasoline saved are reasonably natural.

In this example, identifying most impacts is relatively straightforward, although critics might argue that some relevant impacts were omitted. Health impacts from automobile emissions, impacts on the elk population and other wildlife, and changes in scenic beauty were not considered.

From a CBA perspective, analysts are only interested in project impacts that affect the utility of individuals with standing. In CBA, so-called impacts that do not have any value to human beings are not counted. (The big caveat is that this applies only when human beings have the relevant knowledge and information to make rational valuations.) Politicians often state the purported impacts of projects in very general terms. For example, they might say that a project will promote "community capacity building." CBA requires analysts to identify explicitly the ways in which the project would make some individuals better off through, for example, improved skills and better education. Similarly, politicians have a strong tendency to regard "growth" and "regional development" as beneficial impacts. In CBA analysts should identify the people who may have higher incomes or may consume more goods and services. Of course, analysts should also include the negative environmental and congestion impacts of growth.

Put another way, in order to treat something as an impact, we have to know there is a cause-and-effect relationship between some physical outcome of the project and the utility of human beings with standing. For some impacts, this relationship is so obvious that we do not think about it explicitly. For example, we do not question the existence of a causal relationship between motor vehicle usage and accidents involving human morbidity and mortality. For other impacts, the causal relationships may not be so obvious. What about the impact of exhaust fumes from vehicle usage of the highway on residents' blood pressure? Or the impact of more airborne lead on blood pressure? Demonstrating such cause-and-effect relationships often requires an extensive review of scientific research.

Some potentially very important impacts may depend on unresearched, preliminary, or contradictory scientific or biological knowledge. For example, controversy surrounds the effect of chlorinated organic compounds in bleached pulp mill effluent on wildlife. Although an earlier Swedish study found such a link, a more recent Canadian study found none.[15] The highly publicized controversy surrounding the northern spotted owl demonstrates how widely opinions can vary. Although some experts feel the social costs of logging that eliminate the owl from some areas are relatively minor, Jonathan Rubin and his colleagues have argued the costs may be very large:

> Biologically, the owl is an indicator for old-growth temperate ecosystems: the trees, associated plant communities, and wildlife species that find their optimal habitat in these forests. If the spotted owl cannot survive, its extinction could represent a lack of viability for old-growth habitat itself. Elimination of an ecosystem, itself a unique resource, clearly has greater costs for society than mere extinction of the owl.[16]

Watch out for impacts where different groups of people view what is apparently the same impact in opposite ways. Consider, for example, "flooded land" as a potential impact category. Residents of a flood plain generally view floods as a cost because flood waters damage homes, whereas duck hunters regard floods as a benefit because ducks like them. Even though opposing valuations of the same impact could be aggregated in one category, it is usually more useful to have two impact categories—one for damaged homes, another for recreation benefits.

Due to data limitations, it may not be feasible to measure some impacts using natural measurement units. For example, an analyst may wish to measure the number of crimes avoided due to a policy intervention but may not have such estimates. Instead, the analyst may have access to some indicators, such as changes in arrest rates or changes in conviction rates. The analyst can use one of these surrogates or some combination of them. Remember that valuation of the impact at step 5 should be consistent with the chosen measurement indicator. For example, the valuation of an arrest would be lower than the valuation of a conviction so that the analyst would obtain similar estimates of the benefits of reduced crime from using either indicator. Also, bear in mind that all indicators involve some loss of information.

4. **Predict the impacts quantitatively over the life of the project.** The proposed highway project, like almost all projects, has impacts that extend over time. The fourth task is to quantify all impacts for each alternative over the life of the project. The analyst needs to predict for the no-tolls and with-tolls alternatives, for each year, and for each category of vehicle (trucks, passenger cars on business, passenger cars on vacation):

- the number of vehicle-trips on the new highway
- the number of vehicle-trips on the old roads
- the proportion of travelers from British Columbia

With estimates of these impacts, knowing the highway is 195 kilometers, and with other information the analyst can estimate:

- the total vehicle operating costs that users save
- the number of accidents avoided
- the number of lives saved

For example, the analyst estimated the new highway would save 6.5 lives each year:

> **SHORTER DISTANCE:**
> 130 vkm $\times$ 0.027 lives lost per vkm   = 3.5 lives/year
>
> **SAFER (4-LANE VERSUS 2-LANE):**
> 313 vkm $\times$ 0.027 lives lost per vkm $\times$ 0.33   = 3.0 lives/year
> Total lives saved.[17]   = 6.5 lives/year

Lives would be saved for two reasons. First, the new highway is shorter than existing alternative routes. It is expected that travelers will avoid 130 million vehicle-kilometers (vkm) of driving and evidence suggests that, on average, there are 0.027 deaths per million vehicle-kilometers. The shorter distance is expected, therefore, to save 3.5 lives per year. The new highway is also predicted to be safer per kilometer driven. It is expected that 313 million vehicle-kilometers will be driven each year on the new highway. Based on previous traffic engineering evidence, the analyst estimated that the new highway would lower the fatal accident rate by one-third. Consequently, the new highway is expected to save 3.0 lives per year due to being safer. Combining the two components, 6.5 lives are saved per year.

Now we turn to difficulties of predicting impacts. One odd feature of the cost-benefit literature is that hardly anybody discusses the fact that prediction is both essential and very difficult! Most textbooks focus on theoretical issues, assuming that market demand and supply curves are known. But often they are not. Surprisingly, as we discussed earlier, there are almost no published examples of CBA comparison studies that provide information about the predictive accuracy of CBAs. This issue is so important that Chapter 19 is devoted largely to it. As discussed there, the actual usage levels of the Coquihalla Highway and, therefore, the benefits are considerably higher than predicted, and so are costs. Even this understates the problem as there are errors within benefit categories, which do not show up in the aggregate dollar benefit figure because they offset each other. Prediction is especially difficult when projects are unique, have long time horizons, or relationships among variables are complex.

Many of the realities associated with actually doing steps 3 and 4 are brilliantly summarized by Kenneth Boulding's poem on dam building in the Third World, presented in Exhibit 1.1. Many of his points deal with omission of impact categories due to misunderstanding or ignorance of cause-and-effect relationships and to prediction errors. He also makes points about the distribution of costs and benefits, which we discuss later.

EXHIBIT 1.1 A Ballad of Ecological Awareness

The cost of building dams is always underestimated,
There's erosion of the delta that the river has created,
There's fertile soil below the dam that's likely to be looted,
And the tangled mat of forest that has got to be uprooted.

There's the breaking up of cultures with old haunts' and habits' loss,
There's the education programme that just doesn't come across,
And the wasted fruits of progress that are seldom much enjoyed
By expelled subsistence farmers who are urban unemployed.

There's disappointing yield of fish, beyond the first explosion;
There's silting up, and drawing down, and watershed erosion.
Above the dam the water's lost by sheer evaporation;
Below, the river scours, and suffers dangerous alteration.

For engineers, however good, are likely to be guilty
Of quietly forgetting that a river can be silty,
While the irrigation people too are frequently forgetting
That water poured upon the land is likely to be wetting.

Then the water in the lake, and what the lake releases,
Is crawling with infected snails and water-borne diseases.
There's a hideous locust breeding ground when water level's low,
And a million ecologic facts we really do not know.

There are benefits, of course, which may be countable, but which
Have a tendency to fall into the pockets of the rich,
While the costs are apt to fall upon the shoulders of the poor.
So cost-benefit analysis is nearly always sure
To justify the building of a solid concrete fact,
While the Ecologic Truth is left behind in the Abstract.

—Kenneth E. Boulding

Reprinted with the kind permission of Mrs. Boulding.

5. **Monetize (attach dollar values to) all impacts.** The analyst next has to monetize each of the impacts. *Monetization* means assigning value in dollars. Specifically, the analyst has to monetize time saved, lives saved, and accidents avoided. For this, the analyst needs the monetary value of an hour saved by each type of traveler, the value of a statistical life saved, and the value of an avoided accident. Ideally, these estimates should be specific to British Columbia in 1986. Some of the dollar values used in this CBA are:

- leisure time saved per vehicle (25 percent of gross wage times the average number of passengers) = $6.68 per vehicle-hour
- business time saved per vehicle = $12 per vehicle-hour
- truck drivers' time saved per vehicle = $14 per vehicle-hour
- value of a life saved = $500,000 per life

These estimates are based on studies conducted prior to 1986. Recent estimates of the value of a life saved are much higher, closer to $2 million in 1986 dollars.[18]

Sometimes the most intuitively important impacts are very difficult to value in monetary terms. The value of environmental impacts is especially contentious. In CBA, value is measured in terms of willingness-to-pay. As we discuss in Chapter 4, when markets exist and work well (they don't "fail"), willingness-to-pay can be determined from the appropriate demand curve. Naturally, problems arise when markets do not exist or do not work well. Obtaining values for such impact categories can be a life's work. Scholars have spent many person-years trying to determine the appropriate value of a saved life. In practice, most CBA analysts do not reinvent these wheels but instead draw on previous research: They use plug-in values whenever possible. Although catalogues of impact values are not comprehensive, considerable progress has been made in this regard, as we show in Chapter 15.

If no person is willing to pay a strictly positive amount for some impact, then that impact would have zero value in a CBA. Thus, for example, if construction of a dam would lead to the extermination of a species of small fish, but if no one with standing was willing to pay a positive amount to save that species, then the extermination of this fish would have zero value in a CBA of the dam.

Some government agencies and critics of CBA are unwilling to attach a monetary value to life. This forces them to use an alternative method of analysis, such as *cost-effectiveness analysis* or *multigoal analysis,* which we discuss in Chapters 2 and 17.

6. **Discount benefits and costs to obtain present values.** For a project that has costs or benefits that arise over extended periods (years), we need a way to aggregate the benefits and costs that occur in different years. Usually, future benefits and costs are *discounted* relative to present benefits and costs in order to obtain their *present values, PV.* The need to discount arises due to most people's preference to consume now rather than later and because if we consume now we usually give up the opportunity to consume more in the future. Discounting has nothing to do with inflation per se, although inflation must be taken into account.

A cost or benefit that occurs in year t is converted to its present value by dividing it by $(1 + s)^t$, where s is the social discount rate. Suppose a project has a life of n years and let B_t and C_t denote the benefits and costs in year t, respectively. The present value of the benefits, $PV(B)$, and the present value of the costs, $PV(C)$, of the project are, respectively:

$$PV(B) = \sum_{t=0}^{n} \frac{B_t}{(1+s)^t} \qquad (1.2)$$

$$PV(C) = \sum_{t=0}^{n} \frac{C_t}{(1+s)^t} \qquad (1.3)$$

In the highway example the analyst used a real (inflation-adjusted) social discount rate of 7.5 percent.

As we discuss in Chapter 10, the choice of the appropriate social discount rate is still contentious. Different theories suggest different values. Unfortunately for the practically oriented analyst, there is still some theoretical disagreement. The value of the social discount rate is, thus, a good candidate for sensitivity analysis. For government analysts the discount rate is usually mandated by a government agency with authority (e.g., the Office of Management and Budget, the General Accounting Office, Ministry of Finance, or Treasury Board). Often, for example, the specified real (inflation-adjusted) discount rate is 7 percent. But most economists regard this rate as too high.

7. **Compute the net present value of each alternative.** The *net present value* of an alternative, *NPV*, equals the difference between the present value of the benefits and the present value of the costs:

$$NPV = PV(B) - PB(C) \qquad (1.4)$$

The basic decision rule for a single alternative (relative to the status quo) is simple: *Adopt the project if its NPV is positive.* In short, the analyst should recommend proceeding with the project if its $NPV = PV(B) - PV(C) > 0$; that is, $PV(B) > PV(C)$.

When there is more than one alternative to the status quo, the rule is slightly more complicated: *Select the project with the largest NPV.* This rule assumes implicitly that at least one *NPV* is positive. If no *NPV* is positive, then none of the specified alternatives are superior to the status quo, which should remain in place.

Earlier we emphasized the net social benefits of a project. We show in Chapter 6 that the *NPV* of a project or policy is identical to the present value of the net social benefits (*NSB*):

$$NPV = PV(NSB) \qquad (1.5)$$

Thus, selecting the project with the largest *NPV* is equivalent to selecting the project with the largest present value of the net social benefits.

In the highway example, the no-tolls alternative has a higher net present value than the with-tolls alternative. Thus, the analyst is inclined to recommend the highway should be constructed without tolls. However, the *NPV* of the no-tolls alternative from the provincial perspective is quite small, although positive. Earlier, we emphasized that conducting CBA requires prediction and monetization, which are not always completely accurate. It is important to remember that the net present values presented in Table 1.3 are estimates and that sensitivity analysis should be conducted before making a final recommendation. However, before turning to sensitivity analysis (step 8), we discuss decision making in a bit more detail.

In fact, there is some confusion about the appropriate decision rule. Both the *internal rate of return*, which is discussed in Chapter 6, and the *benefit-cost ratio,* which is discussed in Chapter 2, have both been proposed as decision rules. The appropriate criterion to use is the *NPV* rule. Other methods may give incorrect answers; the *NPV* rule does not.

An obvious caveat about the *NPV* criterion is that it is only applies to the actual alternatives specified. Other alternatives might conceivably be better. Although the *NPV* criterion results in a *more efficient* allocation of resources, it does not necessarily recommend *the most efficient* allocation of resources. This point is illustrated in Figure 1.1. Consider a project for which the alternatives vary along an output scale (Q). The benefits and costs associated with alternative scales are represented by the functions $B(Q)$ and $C(Q)$, respectively. The benefits increase as the scale increases but at a decreasing rate. In contrast, costs increase at an increasing rate. A small-scale project

FIGURE 1.1 CBA Seeks More Efficient Resource Allocation

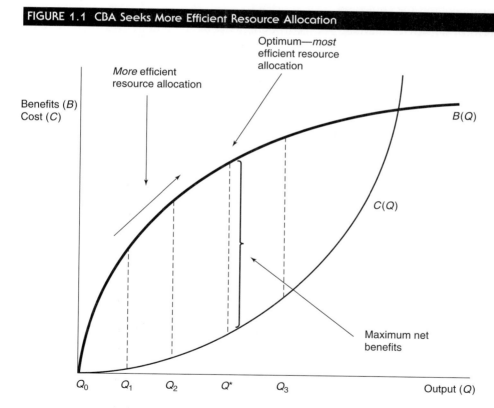

Moving from Q_0 toward Q^* increases efficiency; that is: $NPV(Q^*) > NPV(Q_2) > NPV(Q_1) > NPV(Q_0)$

Moving beyond Q^* reduces efficiency, but Q_3 is more efficient than Q_0: $NPV(Q^*) > NPV(Q_3) > NPV(Q_0)$

(for example, Q_1) has positive net benefits relative to the status quo, Q_0. As the scale increases, the net benefits increase up to the optimal scale, $Q*$.[19] As the scale increases beyond $Q*$, the net benefits decrease. Net benefits are positive as long as the benefit curve is above the cost curve, they are zero where the cost curve and benefit curve intersect and are negative for larger-scale projects.

Suppose that the analyst evaluates only two alternative output levels, Q_1 and Q_2, relative to the status quo. Clearly, output level Q_2 is preferred to output level Q_1, which, in turn, is preferred to the status quo, Q_0. The analyst would, therefore, recommend Q_2. However, as the figure shows, net social benefits are maximized at output level $Q*$. This optimal output level was not recommended because it was not among the set evaluated. In this example, use of the *NPV* criterion leads to a more efficient alternative to the status quo but not to the most efficient alternative.

The analyst may not have included the optimum output level in the set of alternatives for a number of reasons. The analyst may have not known the optimum output level, even approximately, until after performing the analysis. Cognitive capacity limitations, often summarized as *bounded rationality* problems, may hinder the analyst from considering the optimal alternative.[20] Additionally, budgetary or political constraints may limit the choice set.

8. **Perform sensitivity analysis.** As the foregoing discussion emphasizes, there may be considerable uncertainty about both the predicted impacts and the appropriate monetary valuation of each unit of the impact. For example, the analyst may be uncertain about the predicted number of lives saved and about the appropriate dollar value to place on a statistical life saved. The analyst may also be uncertain about the appropriate social discount rate and about the appropriate level of standing. Sensitivity analysis, which we discuss in Chapter 7, attempts to deal with these uncertainties. As shown in Table 1.3, the analyst performed sensitivity analysis on the standing issue by computing the net present values from both the global perspective and the provincial perspective.

There are practical limits to the amount of sensitivity analysis that is feasible. Potentially, every assumption in a CBA can be varied infinitely. In practice, one has to use judgment and focus on the potentially most important assumptions. Although this can mean that CBA is vulnerable to the judgment biases of the analyst, carefully thought-out scenarios are usually more informative than a mindless varying of assumptions.

9. **Make a recommendation based on the *NPV* and sensitivity analysis.** Generally, the analyst should recommend adoption of the project with the largest *NPV*. In the highway example, one of the alternative projects has a negative *NPV* from a British Columbian perspective, suggesting that from this perspective it would be more efficient not to build the Coquihalla Highway at this time than to build it and charge tolls. Sometimes the status quo is the best alternative. Here, however, from a global perspective both the with-tolls and no-tolls alternatives are preferable to the status quo. Based on selecting the alternative with the largest *NPV,* the analyst would recommend the selection of A above C, and B above D. In short, the no-tolls alternative is superior. This result gives a flavor of the possibly counterintuitive recommendations that CBA can support. In this case, tolls lower the *NPV* because they deter people from using the highway, and so fewer people enjoy the benefits.[21]

As we have emphasized, however, the net present values are expected values. Sensitivity analysis, which we have not shown in detail, might suggest that the alternative with the largest expected *NPV* is not necessarily the best alternative under all circumstances.

Finally, it is important to note that analysts make recommendations, not decisions. CBA concerns how resources *should* be allocated; it is *normative*. It does not claim to be a *positive* (i.e., descriptive) theory of how resource allocation decisions are actually made. Such decisions are made in political and bureaucratic arenas. CBA is only one input to this political decision-making process—one that attempts to push it toward more efficient resource allocation. CBA does not always succeed. Politicians are often reluctant to be upstaged by economic arguments. Indeed, the highway was built with tolls!

BUREAUCRATIC AND POLITICAL "LENSES"[22]

Thus far, we have assumed that CBA is not influenced by bureaucratic or political processes. This approach is reasonable given that CBA concerns how resource allocation decisions should be made. In practice, however, CBA frequently gets distorted when bureaucrats and politicians get their hands on it. Government bureaucrats have a tendency to see costs and benefits differently depending on their position and their agency. A bureaucrat's role has a strong influence on what he or she thinks CBA is, or should be, about. Specifically, their perception of what constitutes benefits and costs are based on whether they are "analysts," "spenders," or "guardians."[23] These labels are indicative of three different perspectives bureaucrats bring to project evaluation in government. The analysts' perspective is standard CBA, which we have already presented in Table 1.3. Guardians and spenders have quite different perspectives.

Most students of CBA and most government employees have not taken, and will not take, formal courses in CBA analysis. They believe that what they think is CBA is, in fact, CBA, even if it is not. This section describes the perspectives of guardians and spenders and shows how these perspectives differ from CBA. This helps clarify what CBA actually is in contrast to what one may think it is. This section also identifies many of the common mistakes in CBA. These mistakes often vary systematically according to one's background and experiences. Even those trained in CBA may modify their orientation toward those of guardians or spenders as a consequence of the immediacy of their daily bureaucratic roles. When you are in a government job, you should make sure you are not unconsciously adopting a guardian or spender perspective. We also hope that by understanding these different perspectives, analysts may be better able to communicate with guardians and spenders, and guardians and spenders may be better able to communicate with each other. Finally, this section helps students understand better why decisions are often not consistent with CBA—they are often made by guardians or spenders, not analysts.

We recognize that the following *bureaucratic lenses* are caricatures. In practice, a bureaucrat may not exhibit all of the characteristics associated with a particular lens. From time to time, bureaucrats exhibit schizophrenic tendencies—sometimes they adopt one perspective, sometimes another. In particular, guardians in line agencies are prone to cognitive dissonance because they have dual allegiances. They are quite likely to describe themselves as being unsure of whether they are guardians, spenders, or both. In practice, though, most bureaucrats with whom we have discussed this recognize that they have a tendency to frequently adopt a guardian or spender perspective.

Guardians

Guardians are often found in central budgetary agencies, such as the U.S. Office of Management and Budget, and in controllership or accounting functions within line agencies. They tend to have a bottom-line budgetary orientation. Their natural tendency is to equate benefits with revenue inflows to their agency or other governmental coffers and to equate costs with revenue outflows from their agency or other governmental coffers. Thus, they engage in *revenue-expenditure analysis.*[24] Guardians have a natural tendency to regard CBA as naive, impractical, and, worst of all in their eyes, a tool whereby spenders can justify whatever it is they want to do.

The conceptual lens of "pure" guardians can be illustrated by the way they tend to look at the costs and benefits of the Coquihalla Highway. Table 1.4 summarizes how a provincially based guardian would evaluate the no-tolls highway alternative and the corresponding with-tolls alternative. These evaluations can be compared to the analyst's evaluations, which appear in columns B and D of Table 1.3, respectively.

To guardians, all toll revenues are regarded as benefits, whether paid by provincial residents or by nonresidents. Construction costs are a cost because they are an outlay by provincial government. Because guardians seek to minimize net budgetary expenditures, their preference, not surprisingly, is for the with-tolls alternative. Indeed, their gut reaction is to consider raising tolls, irrespective of its effect on levels of use or its impact on social benefits.

How does the guardians' perspective differ from CBA? Most importantly, guardians ignore nonfinancial social benefits, in this case $384.1 million for the no-tolls al-

TABLE 1.4 Coquihalla Highway from a Provincial Guardian's Perspective (1986 $ Million)

	No Tolls	With Tolls
Revenues ("Benefits"):		
Toll revenues from British Columbia residents	0	112.1
Toll revenues from non–British Columbia residents	0	37.4
	0	149.5
Expenditures ("Costs"):		
Construction	338.1	338.1
Maintenance	7.6	7.6
Toll collection	—	8.4
Toll booth construction	—	0.3
	345.7	354.4
Net Revenue-Expenditure "Benefits"	−345.7	−204.9

Source: Adapted from Anthony Boardman, Aidan Vining, and W. G. Waters II, "Costs and Benefits through Bureaucratic Lenses: Example of a Highway Project," *Journal of Policy Analysis and Management,* 12, no. 3 (1993), 532–555, Table 2, p. 539.

ternative and $297.3 million for the with-tolls alternative. In general, they ignore impacts valued by consumers and producers such as time saved and lives saved. When guardians are in control of a government service, it is easy to understand why one has to wait so long for the service. Neither your time nor anyone else's figures into their calculations. Similarly, guardians tend to ignore nonfinancial social costs, such as congestion and pollution.

In the Coquihalla Highway example, all social costs happen to represent governmental budgetary costs and so there is no difference between the CBA cost figures and the guardians' cost figures. In other situations, however, there might be considerable differences between correct social costs and guardians' costs. Consider, for example, the cost of labor in job-creation programs. Guardians would treat the full financial remuneration to labor as a cost, whereas CBA analysts would consider only the loss of other opportunities (such as lost leisure time). Another manifestation of the same mistake concerns the treatment of resources currently owned by the government, such as offices or land. Guardians tend to treat these resources as free because using them for a project does not entail additional budgetary outlay. They ignore the value of these resources in other uses.

Guardians ignore costs not borne by their level of government. Thus, they ignore the loss suffered by British Columbians from paying tolls and treat toll revenues as a benefit. In CBA tolls are a transfer from travelers to the government: Offsetting costs and benefits results in net benefits of zero. On the other hand, guardians automatically treat subsidies from the federal government as a benefit because they are revenue inflows. However, if the federal government has earmarked a certain amount of money to transfer to British Columbia and if funds used for one purpose reduce the amount available for other purposes, then federal funds for this highway should not be treated as a benefit from the provincial perspective.

Finally, guardians generally want to use a high social discount rate. Because of their financial background or their agency's culture, they naturally prefer to use a financial market discount rate, which is generally higher than the appropriate social discount rate. They also know that using a high discount rate will make it more difficult to justify most projects because costs usually occur before benefits. Thus, it is easier to limit spenders who, in their view, overestimate benefits, underestimate costs, and generally use money less efficiently than the private sector.

Spenders

Spenders are usually in service or line departments. Some service departments, such as transportation, may be involved with physical projects, whereas social service departments, such as health, welfare, or recreation, make human capital investments. Some service departments, such as housing, make both types of expenditures. The views of spenders are somewhat more variegated than those of guardians because the constituencies of particular agencies are more varied. Nevertheless, there are several major commonalities.

Most importantly, spenders have a natural tendency to regard expenditures on constituents as benefits rather than as costs. Thus, for example, they typically see expenditures on labor as a benefit rather than a cost. Spenders regard themselves as builders or professional deliverers of government-mandated services. As spenders focus on providing projects or services to particular groups in society, we characterize them as engaging in *constituency-support analysis*. Table 1.5 summarizes how spenders in the provincial highway department view the no-tolls and with-tolls alternatives.

Spenders treat social benefits received by and monetary payments to their constituents (residents of British Columbia in this example) as benefits. Thus, time saved, lives saved, and vehicle operating costs saved by British Columbians are benefits. However, they also treat money received by construction workers who build the highway as a benefit. Thus, spenders think of both project benefits *and* project costs as benefits. With this method of accounting, both the with-tolls and no-tolls highway alternatives generate huge net constituency benefits. In general, spenders tend to support *any* alternative rather than the status quo (no project). Thus, the mistrust of spenders by guardians is perfectly understandable. Guardians and spenders almost always oppose one another.

Spenders view monetary outlays by British Columbian highway users (also their constituents) as costs; for example, they treat tolls paid by British Columbians as costs. Table 1.5 shows that spenders favor the no-tolls alternative primarily because a toll is a cost for some of their constituents. Indeed, spenders normally do not favor "user pay" fees unless their agency keeps the toll revenue within its own budget or the payers are nonconstituents. If spenders could collect and keep the tolls, they would face a dilemma: Tolls would reduce constituency benefits but would increase the agency's budget. Thus, they would face a trade-off between constituency-support maximization and budget maximization.[25]

In general, as Robert Haveman and others have pointed out, politicians prefer projects that concentrate benefits on particular interest groups and camouflage costs or diffuse them widely over the population.[26] Spenders are similar. They tend to weight each impact category by the strength of the connection that constituents make between the impact and their agency. They focus on impacts that their constituents will give them a lot of credit for and will ignore others. Because people almost always notice expenditures on themselves, such "benefits" are invariably weighted more heavily than social benefits.[27] Thus, for example, construction jobs are more heavily weighted than diffuse social benefits.

TABLE 1.5 Coquihalla Highway from a Provincial Spender's Perspective (1986 $ Million)

	No Tolls	With Tolls
Constituency "Benefits":		
Project Costs (from CBA)	345.7	354.4
Project Benefits (from CBA)	384.1	334.7
	729.8	689.1
Constituency "Costs":		
Toll Revenues from British Columbia Residents	—	112.1
Net Constituency "Benefits"	729.8	577.0

Source: Adapted from Anthony Boardman, Aidan Vining, and W. G. Waters II, "Costs and Benefits through Bureaucratic Lenses: Example of a Highway Project," *Journal of Policy Analysis and Management,* 12, no. 3 (1993), 532–555, Table 3, p. 542.

Spenders are also similar to politicians in their determination to complete partially completed projects. Congress, for example, decided to complete the Tellico Dam when it was 90 percent complete, even though the incremental costs exceeded the incremental benefits.[28]

Presumably, the politicians believed that continuation of the project bought ongoing political support. Even though sunk costs are, by definition, sunk, and it may not be efficient to finish a partially completed project, spenders tend to believe that there are positive constituency-support benefits from completion of projects.

Spenders treat some inputs as neither benefits nor costs. Currently owned government assets may simply be ignored. In support of the Tellico Dam, for example, the Tennessee Valley Authority (TVA) argued that "since the farmland behind the dam had already been purchased, the value of this land should be considered a sunk cost, even though the land has yet to be flooded and could be resold as farmland if the project was not completed."[29]

Spenders tend to favor large, irreversible, capital-intensive projects. For example, spenders tend to favor urban rail systems over buses. Once the infrastructure is in place, it cannot be easily redeployed to other uses so the system will almost certainly remain in operation and constituents are guaranteed to receive some benefits. Furthermore, the normally lower operating costs for such projects allow for lower prices and relatively high usage levels, thereby further increasing constituency support.

The perspective of spenders concerning market efficiency has a bearing on the way they view many aspects of CBA. To spenders, markets are almost always inefficient. Spenders act as if unemployment is high in all labor markets. They believe that unemployment will be reduced by the number of people used on a government project. Even if some workers switch from other employment, these workers' vacated jobs will be filled by an unemployed worker. Thus, even if the job created did not go directly to an unemployed worker, there would eventually be a job "created" for an unemployed worker. Spenders do not recognize that project resources are diverted from other potentially productive uses that would also involve jobs.

Furthermore, spenders believe there are indirect benefits of creating jobs and making other project expenditures—there is a multiplier effect.[30] In the extreme, spenders have a "Midas touch" view of project evaluation: First declare the expenditures (costs) to be a "benefit," and then multiply these expenditures by a multiplier. As a result, any government project would be seen as producing "benefits" greater than "costs."

Spenders generally favor using a low (even zero) social discount rate. For some, this is because they are not familiar with the concept of discounting. For others, they know this tends to raise the project's *NPV* and, therefore, the probability of its adoption. Other ways spenders generate support for their projects is to choose a poorly performing counterfactual (a straw man) or to overestimate project usage levels and, therefore, benefits.[31]

CONCLUSION

This chapter provides a broad overview of many of the most important issues in CBA. We deal with these issues in detail in subsequent chapters. At this point, do not worry if you can only see CBA "through the glass, darkly." Do not worry if you cannot entirely follow the highway analysis. Our aim was to give you a taste of the practical realities. We think that it is important to provide readers with a sense of these realities before dealing with the technical issues.

CBA is often taught in a way that is completely divorced from political reality. We wish to avoid this mistake. CBA is a normative tool, not a description of how political and bureaucratic decision makers actually make decisions. Because CBA disregards the demands of politicians, spenders, guardians, and interest groups, it is not surprising that there are tremendous pressures to ignore it or, alternatively, to adapt it to the desires of various constituencies or interest groups. In practice, correct CBA is no more than a voice for rational decision making.

Exercises for Chapter 1

1. Imagine that you live in a city that currently does not require bicycle riders to wear helmets. Furthermore, imagine that you enjoy riding your bicycle without wearing a helmet.
    a. From your perspective, what are the major costs and benefits of a proposed city ordinance that would require all bicycle riders to wear helmets?
    b. What are the costs and benefits from society's perspective?
2. The effects of a tariff on imported kumquats can be divided into the following categories: tariff revenues received by the treasury ($8 million); increased use of resources to produce more kumquats domestically ($6 million); the value of reduced consumption by domestic consumers ($4 million); and increased profits received by domestic kumquat growers ($5 million). A CBA from the national perspective would find costs of the tariff equal to $10 million—the sum of the costs of increased domestic production and forgone domestic consumption ($6 million + $4 million = $10 million). The increased profits received by domestic kumquat growers and the tariff revenues received by the treasury simply reflect higher prices paid by domestic consumers on the kumquats that they continue to consume and, hence, count as neither benefits nor costs. Thus, the net benefits of the tariff are negative (−$10 million). Consequently, the CBA would recommend against adoption of the tariff.
    a. Assuming the agriculture department views kumquat growers as its primary constituency, how would it calculate net benefits if it behaves as if it is a spender?
    b. Assuming the treasury department behaves as if it is a guardian, how would it calculate net benefits if it believes that domestic growers pay profit taxes at an average rate of 20 percent?

Notes

1. "Letter to Joseph Priestley," in *Benjamin Franklin: Representative Selections, with Introduction, Bibliography and Notes,* Frank Luther Mott and Chester E. Jorgenson, eds., (New York: American Book Company, 1936), pp. 348–349. We would like to thank Ken MacCrimmon for bringing this quote to our attention.
2. But see Linda R. Cohen and Roger G. Noll, eds., *The Technology Pork Barrel* (Washington, DC: The Brookings Institution, 1991). We do not include CBAs by the World Bank of its own projects because they are neither disinterested nor published. In fact, evidence suggests that the World Bank does not actually use CBA much; see Nathaniel H. Leff, "The Use of Policy-Science Tools in Public-Sector Decision Making: Social Benefit-Cost Analysis in the World Bank," *Kyklos,* 38, no. 1 (1985), 60–76.

3. Federal Environmental Assessment Review Office, *Oldman River Dam: Report of the Environmental Assessment Panel,* Ottawa, Ontario, May 1992.

4. For summaries of the workfare evaluations, see Judith M. Gueron and Edward Pauly, *From Work to Welfare* (New York: Russell Sage Foundation, 1991), and Daniel Friedlander, David H. Greenberg, and Philip K. Robins, "Evaluating Government Training Programs for the Economically Disadvantaged," *Journal of Economic Literature,* 35, no. 4 (1997), 1089–1855.

5. See Martha Derthick and Paul J. Quirk, *The Politics of Deregulation* (Washington, DC: The Brookings Institution, 1985), and Carol H. Weiss, "Evaluation for Decisions: Is Anybody There? Does Anybody Care?" *Evaluation Practice,* 9, no. 1 (1988), 5–20.

6. See Robert Hahn and John A. Hird, "The Costs and Benefits of Regulation: Review and Synthesis," *Yale Journal of Regulation,* 8, no. 1 (1991), 233–278.

7. Of course, other criteria may determine whether evaluative research actually gets used; see the preceding paragraph. For a review of evaluative research utilization in policy analysis, see David H. Greenberg and Marvin B. Mandell, "Research Utilization in Policymaking: A Tale of Two Series of Social Experiments," *Journal of Policy Analysis and Management,* 10, no. 4 (1991), 633–656.

8. Robinson G. Hollister, Peter Kemper, and Rebecca A. Maynard, eds., *The National Supported Work Demonstration* (Madison, WI: University of Wisconsin, 1984).

9. See Thomas K. Glennan, Jr., "Evaluating Federal Manpower Programs: Notes and Observations," in *Evaluating Social Programs: Theory, Practice and Politics,* Peter H. Rossi and Walter Williams, eds. (New York: Seminar Press, 1972).

10. Thomas D. Hopkins, "Economic Analysis Requirements as a Tool of Regulatory Reform: Experience in the United States," Statement presented to the Sub-Committee on Regulations and Competitiveness Standing Committee on Finance, House of Commons, Ottawa, September 15, 1992, p. 10.

11. U.S. Environmental Protection Agency, *EPA's Use of Benefit-Cost Analysis: 1981–1986,* EPA-230-05-87-028, Office of Policy, Planning and Evaluation, August 1987, pp. 1–3.

12. This example is based on W. G. Waters II and Shane Meyers, "Benefit-Cost Analysis of a Toll Highway: British Columbia's Coquihalla," *Journal of Transportation Research Forum,* 28, no. 1 (1987), 434–443.

13. In fact, the divided highway was made of concrete with four lanes, and with tunnels for animals to be able to safely reach the other side.

14. G. A. Miller, "The Magical Number Seven, Plus or Minus Two: Some Limits on Our Capacity for Processing Information," *Psychological Review,* 65, no. 1 (1956), 81–97.

15. These studies are discussed by Robert Williamson, "Pulp Cleanup May Be Waste of Money," *Toronto Globe and Mail,* December 23, 1992, pp. A1, A6.

16. Jonathan Rubin, Gloria Helfand, and John Loomis, "A Benefit-Cost Analysis of the Northern Spotted Owl," *Journal of Forestry,* 89, no. 12 (1991), 25–30, at p. 26.

17. Of course, some additional deaths will occur as a result of more people traveling by road. This additional cost is netted out against the generated traffic benefits.

18. Ted R. Miller, "The Plausible Range for the Value of Life—Red Herrings Among the Mackerel," *Journal of Forensic Economics,* 3, no. 3, (1990), 17–39.

19. Note that at the optimum output level, marginal benefits equal marginal costs: $dB/dQ = dC/dQ$. One can see that the slope of the benefit curve at Q^* equals the slope of the cost curve at Q^*.

20. For the seminal writing on this topic, see Herbert A. Simon, *Models of Man* (New York: Wiley, 1957). Although this problem is unlikely to be of major importance in situations similar to that depicted in Figure 1.1, cognitive factors become an increasingly important issue when (1) project benefits and costs vary simultaneously on many dimensions, (2) the benefit and cost functions are discontinuous or complex (e.g., with interaction terms), or (3) there is uncertainty about the interactions or the functional forms.

21. As we will discuss in Chapter 4, tolls on congested highways generally increase net social benefits.

22. This section draws heavily on Anthony Boardman, Aidan Vining, and W. G. Waters II, "Costs and Benefits through Bureaucratic Lenses: Example of a Highway Project," *Journal of Policy Analysis and Management,* 12, no. 3 (1993), 532–555.

23. This terminology was introduced by Sanford Borins and David A. Good, "Spenders, Guardians and Policy Analysts: A Game of Budgeting Under the Policy and Expenditure Management System," Toronto, Case Program in Canadian Administration, Institute of Public Administration of Canada, 1987 (revised 1989).

24. In practice, revenue-expenditure analysis is similar to *cash flow analysis* and *budget impact analysis*. For certain purposes cash flow analysis and budget impact analysis are very helpful. A problem arises when an analyst does this type of analysis while thinking or maintaining that he or she is performing CBA.

25. See, for example, William A. Niskanen, "Bureaucrats and Politicians," *Journal of Law and Economics*, 18, no. 3 (1975), 617–643, and André Blais and Stéphane Dion, eds., *The Budget-Maximizing Bureaucrat: Appraisals and Evidence* (Pittsburgh, PA: University of Pittsburgh Press, 1991). For various reasons, senior spenders may be more interested in the discretionary budget or "budget shaping" than in budget maximizing; see Patrick Dunleavy, *Democracy, Bureaucracy and Public Choice* (Englewood Cliffs, NJ: Prentice Hall, 1992). They may, therefore, be willing to support projects that involve considerable "contracting out" and other activities that may not be budget maximizing per se.

26. Robert H. Haveman, "Policy Analysis and the Congress: An Economist's View," *Policy Analysis*, 2, no. 2 (1976), 235–250.

27. Barry R. Weingast et al. refer to this phenomenon as the "Robert Moses effect" after the "famous New Yorker who appreciated it and exploited it so effectively." See Barry R. Weingast, Kenneth A. Shepsle, and Christopher Johnsen, "The Political Economy of Benefits and Costs: A Neoclassical Approach to Distributive Politics," *Journal of Political Economy*, 89, no. 4 (1981), 642–664, at p. 648.

28. R. K. Davis, "Lessons in Politics and Economics from the Snail Darter," in *Environmental Resources and Applied Welfare Economics: Essays in Honor of John V. Krutilla*, Vernon K. Smith, ed., (Washington, DC: Resources for the Future, 1988), pp. 211–236.

29. Robert D. Behn, "Policy Analysis and Policy Politics," *Policy Analysis*, 7, no. 2 (1981), 199–226, at p. 213, n. 27.

30. One reason some bureaucrats attach so much importance to multipliers is because they have a basic grounding in input-output analysis, but they do not clearly understand the fundamental distinction between impact analysis and evaluation analysis; see W. G. Waters II, "Impact Studies and the Evaluation of Public Projects," *Annals of Regional Science*, 10, no. 1 (1976), 98–103.

31. See, for example, John F. Kain, "The Use of Straw Men in the Economic Evaluation of Rail Transport Projects," *American Economic Review, AEA Papers and Proceedings,* 82, no. 2 (1992), 487–493, and Linda R. Cohen and Roger G. Noll, eds., *The Technology Pork Barrel* (Washington, DC: The Brookings Institution, 1991).

CHAPTER
2

CONCEPTUAL FOUNDATIONS OF COST-BENEFIT ANALYSIS

It seems only natural to think about the alternative courses of action we face as individuals in terms of their costs and benefits. Is it appropriate to evaluate public policy alternatives in the same way? The CBA of the highway sketched in the first chapter suggests some of the practical difficulties analysts typically encounter in measuring costs and benefits. Yet, even if analysts can measure costs and benefits satisfactorily, evaluating alternatives solely in terms of their net benefits may not always be appropriate. An understanding of the conceptual foundations of CBA provides a basis for determining when CBA can be appropriately used as a decision rule, when it can usefully be part of a broader analysis, and when it should be avoided.

The goal of *allocative,* or *Pareto, efficiency* provides the conceptual basis for CBA. In this chapter we provide a nontechnical introduction to Pareto efficiency. We then explain its relationship to *potential Pareto efficiency,* which provides the practical basis for actually doing CBA. Our exploration of the roles of Pareto efficiency and potential Pareto efficiency in CBA provides a basis for distinguishing it from other analytical frameworks. It also provides a basis for understanding the various philosophical objections commonly made against the use of CBA for decision making.

CBA AS A FRAMEWORK FOR MEASURING EFFICIENCY

CBA can be thought of as providing a framework for measuring efficiency.[1] Though we develop a more formal definition of efficiency in the following section, it can be thought of as a situation in which resources, such as land, labor, and capital, are deployed in their highest valued uses in terms of the goods and services they create. In situations in which analysts care only about efficiency, CBA provides a method for making direct comparisons among alternative policies. Even when goals other than efficiency are important, CBA serves as a yardstick that can be used to provide information about the relative efficiency of alternative policies. Indeed, analysts rarely encounter situations in which efficiency is not one of the relevant goals. Critical evaluation of these assertions requires a more precise definition of efficiency.

Pareto Efficiency

A simple and intuitively appealing definition of efficiency, referred to as *Pareto efficiency,* underlies modern welfare economics and CBA. *An allocation of goods is Pareto efficient if no alternative allocation can make at least one person better off without making anyone else worse off.* An allocation of goods is inefficient, therefore, if an alternative allocation can be found that would make at least one person better off without making anyone else worse off. One would have to be malevolent not to want to achieve Pareto efficiency—why forgo gains to persons that would not inflict losses on others?

Figure 2.1 illustrates the concept of Pareto efficiency in a simple situation involving the allocation of a fixed amount of money between two persons. Imagine that the two persons will receive any total amount of money of up to $100 if they agree on how to split it between themselves. Assume that if they do not agree, then each person receives just $25. The vertical axis measures the amount of money received by person 1 and the horizontal axis measures the amount of money received by person 2. The point labeled $100 on the vertical axis represents the outcome in which person 1 gets the entire $100. Similarly, the point labeled $100 on the horizontal axis represents the outcome in which person 2 gets the entire $100. The line connecting these two extreme points, which we call the *potential Pareto frontier,* represents all the feasible splits between the two persons that allocate the entire $100. Splits involving less than $100 lie within the triangle formed by the potential Pareto frontier and the axes. The one labeled ($25, $25) is such a point. This point represents the status quo in the sense that it gives the amounts the two persons receive if they do not reach an agreement about splitting the $100. The segment of the potential Pareto frontier that gives each person at least as much as the status quo is called the *Pareto frontier.*

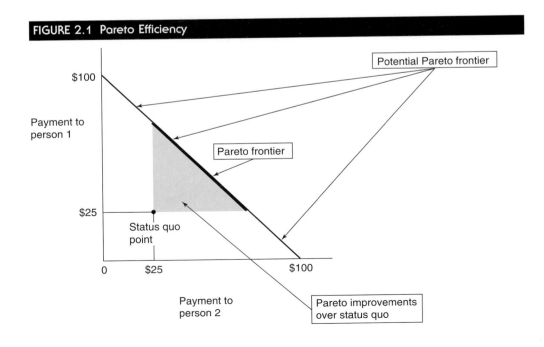

FIGURE 2.1 Pareto Efficiency

The lightly shaded triangle formed by the lines through the status quo point and the Pareto frontier represents all the alternative allocations that would make at least one of the persons better off than the status quo without making the other worse off. The existence of these points, which are feasible alternatives to the status quo that make at least one person better off without making the other worse off, means that the status quo is not Pareto efficient. Movement to any one of these points is called a Pareto improvement. Any Pareto improvement that does not lie on the potential Pareto frontier would leave open the possibility of further Pareto improvements and, thus, not provide a Pareto efficient allocation. Only on the potential Pareto frontier is it impossible to make a feasible reallocation that makes one person better off without making the other person worse off.

It should be clear that the segment of the potential Pareto frontier that guarantees at least $25 to each person represents all the Pareto efficient allocations relative to the status quo. Each of these points makes a Pareto improvement over the status quo and leaves no opportunity for further improvements. The segment of the potential Pareto frontier that represents actual Pareto improvements depends on the status quo. In other words, implicit in the concept of Pareto efficiency is the initial starting positions of the members of society. We return later to the significance of the difference between the potential and actual Pareto frontiers in our discussion of criticisms of CBA.

Net Benefits and Pareto Efficiency

The link between positive net benefits and Pareto efficiency is straightforward: *If a policy has positive net benefits, then it is possible to find a set of transfers, or side payments, that makes at least one person better off without making anyone else worse off.* A full understanding of this link requires some reflection on how one measures benefits and costs in CBA. In particular, as illustrated in Figure 2.2, it requires one to consider willingness-to-pay as the method for valuing the outputs of a policy and opportunity cost as the method for valuing the resources required to implement the policy. Though we develop these important concepts more fully in the next three chapters in the context of market exchange, the simple introductions that follow provide the basis for understanding the link between net benefits and Pareto efficiency.

Willingness-to-Pay   Consider a proposed policy that would produce outputs of relevance to three people. Assume that these people make honest revelations of their assessments of the values of the outputs. Through a series of questions, we elicit the

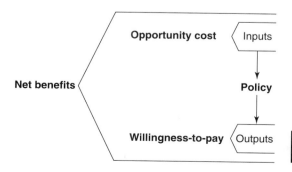

FIGURE 2.2 Categorization of Net Benefits of Projects

payments that each person would have to make or to receive under the policy so that he or she would be indifferent between the status quo on one hand and the policy with the payments on the other. So, for example, imagine that person 1 honestly reveals that she would be indifferent between the status quo and paying $100 to have the policy implemented. Similarly, person 2 might say that he is indifferent between the status quo and paying $200 to have the policy implemented. These values are the willingness-to-pay of persons 1 and 2 for the policy. Unlike persons 1 and 2, assume that person 3 does not like the impacts of the proposed policy and would have to receive a payment of $250 if the policy were implemented to feel just as well off as he did under the status quo; it is the amount that would have to be given to the person in conjunction with the proposed policy so that he is indifferent between it and the status quo. The negative of this amount (−$250) would be the willingness-to-pay of person 3 for the policy.

The algebraic sum of these willingness-to-pay values is the appropriate measure of the net benefits of the impacts of the policy. In this example, the willingness-to-pay amounts can be divided into $300 of benefits ($100 + $200) accruing to persons 1 and 2 and $250 of costs (−$250) accruing to person 3. The net benefits are, thus, positive and equal to $50. If these were the only three persons affected by the policy, and if the policy required no resources to implement, then the $50 would be the appropriate measure of net benefits from the perspective of CBA. Simple implementation of the policy would not be Pareto efficient because person 3 would be made worse off with respect to the status quo.

Yet we can easily imagine altering the policy so that it would be Pareto efficient. For example, imagine that person 3 receives $75 from person 1 and $175 from person 2 as part of the policy. Now person 1 is better off than the status quo ($100 of benefits minus $75 given to person 3), person 2 is better off ($200 of benefits minus $175 given to person 3), and person 3 is no worse off ($250 of costs from the policy minus $250 of benefits in the form of compensation from persons 1 and 2).

The key point is that if and only if the aggregate net benefits of the policy as measured by the willingness-to-pay of all affected individuals are positive, then there exist sets of contributions and payments that would make the policy a Pareto improvement over the status quo.

Opportunity Cost   The implementation of policies almost always requires the use of some inputs that could be used to produce other things of value. For example, implementing a policy to build a bridge across a river would require the use of labor, steel, concrete, construction machinery, and land that could be used to produce other things of value to people. The concept of opportunity cost is used in CBA to place a dollar value on the inputs required to implement policies. *The opportunity cost of using an input to implement a policy is its value in its best alternative use.* Opportunity cost measures the value of what society must forgo to use the input to implement the policy.

Return to the example of the three persons whose aggregate willingness-to-pay for the policy was $50. Imagine that the policy requires inputs that have an opportunity cost of $75. That is, if the policy were implemented, then some other members of society would have to give up goods valued at $75. In this case, the policy does not generate enough net benefits to the three persons to allow them to compensate those who must forgo the $75 of goods—the net benefits to society as a whole are negative $25 ($50 of net benefits to the three persons minus $75 in opportunity costs to the rest of society). Thus, the policy could not be made Pareto efficient because it does not produce enough benefits to permit all those who bear costs to be compensated fully. If the opportunity cost were only $20 instead of $75, then net benefits to society would be $30 and it would be possible to compensate all those who bear costs so that no one is made worse off, and some people are made better off, by the policy. In general, if the net benefits of a policy are positive, then it is potentially Pareto improving.

USING CBA FOR DECISION MAKING

The connection between net benefits and Pareto efficiency should now be clear. *As long as analysts value all impacts in terms of willingness-to-pay and all required inputs in terms of opportunity costs, then the sign of the net benefits indicates whether or not it would be possible to compensate those who bear costs sufficiently so that no one is made worse off.* Positive net benefits indicate the potential for compensation to make the policy Pareto efficient; negative net benefits indicate the absence of this potential.

One could imagine the following decision rule for CBA: Adopt only policies that are actually Pareto efficient. In other words, only policies that yielded some positive benefits after actually providing full compensation to all those who bear costs would be adopted so that there would be no losers, only winners. Though very appealing conceptually, such a rule would be extremely difficult to apply in practice for a number of reasons. First, it would place great informational burdens on analysts not just to measure aggregate costs and benefits, which can often be inferred from observing prices and quantities in markets, but also to measure costs and benefits for each person—a task that would generally render CBA too costly to use. Second, once the distribution of costs and benefits at the individual level were known, the administrative costs of actually making specific transfers for each government policy would almost certainly be high. Third, it is very difficult to operate a practical system of compensation payments that does not distort the investment and work behavior of households. Fourth, the requirement that everyone be fully compensated would create a strong incentive for people to find ways to overstate the costs and understate the benefits that they expect to receive from policies, complicating the already difficult task of inferring how much each person is willing to pay for the outputs produced by the policy. The actual Pareto efficiency principle in practice would, thus, result in society forgoing many policies that offer positive net benefits and the diversion of much effort toward the seeking of unjustified compensation.

Potential Pareto Efficiency

CBA utilizes an alternative decision rule with somewhat less conceptual appeal, but much greater feasibility, than the actual Pareto efficiency rule. It is based on what is known as the *Kaldor-Hicks criterion:* A policy should be adopted if and only if those who will gain *could* fully compensate those who will lose and still be better off.[2] The Kaldor-Hicks criterion provides the basis for the *potential Pareto efficiency rule,* or, more commonly, the *net benefits criterion: Adopt only policies that have positive net benefits.* As long as net benefits are positive, it is at least possible that losers could be compensated so that the policy potentially could be Pareto improving. In terms of Figure

2.1, any point on the potential Pareto frontier would pass the potential Pareto efficiency rule whereas only those points on the potential Pareto frontier that guarantee at least $25 to each person (the heavily shaded segment of the potential Pareto frontier) pass the actual Pareto efficiency rule.

Several justifications, aside from feasibility, are commonly offered in defense of the potential Pareto efficiency rule. First, by always choosing policies with positive net benefits, society maximizes aggregate wealth. This indirectly helps those who are worse off in society because richer societies have greater capability for helping their poorest members and, if redistribution is a normal good (i.e., other things equal, people want more of it as their wealth increases), members of society have a greater willingness to help.[3] Second, it is likely that different policies will have different sets of winners and losers. Thus, if the rule is consistently applied to government activity, then costs and benefits will tend to average out across people so that each person is likely to realize positive net benefits from the full collection of policies. Third, as we discuss later in this chapter, the rule stands in contrast to the incentives in representative political systems to give too much weight to costs and benefits that accrue to organized groups (so-called *stakeholders*) and too little weight to costs and benefits that accrue to unorganized interests. Its use in public discourse may thereby reduce the chances that Pareto inefficient policies will be adopted. Fourth, if a more equal distribution of wealth or income is an important goal, then it is possible to address it directly through transfers after a large number of efficiency-enhancing policies have been adopted. In other words, redistribution can at least in theory be done "wholesale" with a single redistribution program rather than "retail" with each of many policies.

Application of the Decision Rule in Practice

Two polices can be thought of as independent if the adoption of one does not influence the costs and benefits of the other. When all relevant projects are independent, the CBA decision rule is simple: *Adopt all policies that have positive net benefits.* A more general version of the rule applies in situations involving multiple policies that may enhance or interfere with each other: *Choose the combination of policies that maximizes net benefits.* Physical, budgetary, and other constraints may limit the combinations of policies that are feasible.

Consider the list of projects in Table 2.1. Interpret the costs and benefits as being expressed in terms of present values, so that they can be directly compared with dollars of current consumption. Suppose we could choose any combination of projects; then we should simply choose all those with positive net benefits—namely, projects A, B, C, and D.

Policies are sometimes *mutually exclusive,* however. For example, we cannot drain a swamp to create agricultural land and simultaneously preserve it as a wildlife refuge. When all the available policies are mutually exclusive, efficiency is maximized by choosing the one with the largest net positive benefits—project B, with net benefits of $20 million. Assume, however, that all projects are mutually exclusive, except C and D, which can be built together to obtain synergistic gains. By taking the combination of C and D to be a separate project, we can consider all the projects on the list to be mutually exclusive. Looking down the column labeled "Net Benefits," we see that project B still offers the largest net benefits and, therefore, should be the one selected, but the combination of C and D offers the next highest net benefits.

TABLE 2.1 Choosing among Projects: Net Benefits versus Benefit-Cost Ratios

	Costs (mllions of dollars)	Benefits (millions of dollars)	Net Benefits (millions of dollars)	Benefits/Costs
No project	0	0	0	—
Project A	1	10	9	10
Project B	10	30	20	3
Project C	4	8	4	2
Project D	3	5	2	1.7
Projects C and D	7	21	14	3
Project E	10	8	−2	0.8

No constraints: Choose A, B, and combination C and D (net benefits equal $43 million).
All projects mutually exclusive: Choose B (net benefits equal $20 million).
Costs cannot exceed $10 million: Choose A and combination C and D (net benefits equal $23 million).

Source: Adapted from David L. Weimer and Aidan R. Vining, *Policy Analysis: Concepts and Practice,* 3rd edition, (Upper Saddle River, NJ: Prentice Hall, 1999), Figure 12.2.

Analysts often compare programs in terms of *benefit-cost ratios.* Note that project B, which offers the largest net benefits, does not have the largest ratio of benefits to costs. Project A has a benefit-cost ratio of 10, whereas project B has a benefit-cost ratio of only 3. Nevertheless, project B should be selected because it offers larger net benefits than project A. This comparison shows how the benefit-cost ratio can sometimes confuse the choice process when the projects under consideration are of different scale (i.e., project B involves substantially higher costs than project A). Furthermore, the benefit-cost ratio is sensitive to whether negative willingness-to-pay amounts are subtracted from benefits or added to costs. For example, imagine that the cost of $10 million for project B was opportunity costs and the benefits of $30 million consisted of $40 million for one group and −$10 million for another. Treating the negative willingness-to-pay as a cost rather than as a negative benefit would leave the net benefits unchanged but lower the benefit-cost ratio from 3 to 2. Thus, benefit-cost ratios are subject to manipulation. For these reasons, we recommend that analysts avoid using benefit-cost ratios and rely instead on net benefits to rank policies.

Note that projects C and D are shown as synergistic. That is, the net benefits from adopting both together exceed the sum of the net benefits from adopting each one independently. Such might be the case if project C were a dam that created a reservoir that could be used for recreation as well as hydroelectric power and D were a road that increased access to the reservoir. Of course, projects can also interfere with each other—for instance, the dam might reduce the benefits of a downstream recreation project. The important point is that care must be taken to determine interactions among projects so that the combinations of projects providing the greatest net benefits in aggregate can be readily identified.

Return to Table 2.1 and interpret the listed costs as public expenditures exactly equal to opportunity costs and the listed benefits as the willingness-to-pay values for all project effects. Now assume that, although none of the projects are mutually exclusive in a physical sense, total public expenditures (costs) cannot exceed $10 million because of a budget constraint that is binding for political reasons. If project B is selected, then the budget constraint is met and net benefits of $20 million result. If project A and the combination of projects C and D are selected instead, then the budget constraint is also met, but net benefits of $23 million result. No other feasible combination offers larger net benefits. Thus, under the budget constraint, net benefits are maximized by choosing project A and the combination of projects C and D.

FUNDAMENTAL ISSUES RELATED TO WILLINGNESS-TO-PAY

Three sets of fundamental issues arise with respect to the interpretation of willingness-to-pay as a measure of benefits in the assessment of the efficiency of policies. First, a theoretical limitation in the aggregation of willingness-to-pay amounts across individuals opens the possibility that the net benefits criterion will not lead to fully satisfactory rankings of policies. Second, normative issues arise because of the dependence of willingness-to-pay on the distribution of wealth in society. Third, normative issues also arise with respect to the issue of *standing*, which concerns whose willingness-to-pay counts in the aggregation of benefits.

The Theoretical Limitation of Willingness-to-Pay as a Basis for Social Orderings

Although using net benefits as a basis for choosing efficient public policies is intuitively appealing, its implementation through the aggregation of the willingness-to-pay amounts of the members of society confronts a fundamental theoretical limitation: Ranking policies in terms of net benefits does not guarantee a *transitive* social ordering of the policies.

A transitive ordering requires that if X is preferred to Y, and Y is preferred to Z, then X is preferred to Z. The logic of transitivity seems so clear that it is usually taken as an axiom of rationality in the preferences of individuals. We would certainly be skeptical about the mental state of someone who tells us he prefers apples to oranges, and he prefers oranges to peaches, but he prefers peaches to apples. This violation of transitivity implies a cyclical and, therefore, ambiguous ordering of the alternatives: the ordering—apples, oranges, peaches, apples—leaves us uncertain as to whether this person ranks apples lowest or highest in his preferences. Clearly, transitivity is a desirable property of any preference ordering.

If every member of a society has transitive preferences, does it follow that reasonable procedures for aggregating their preferences will always produce a transitive social ordering? An example makes clear that the answer is no. Consider a very common aggregation procedure: majority rule voting over pairs of alternatives. Imagine that society consists of three voters who have preferences over three alternatives, X, Y, and Z as displayed in Table 2.2. Specifically, voter 1 prefers X to Y to Z; voter 2 prefers Z to X to Y; and voter 3 prefers Y to Z to X. If the voters express their sincere preferences in each round of voting, then we would find that given the choice between X and Y, a majority of voters (voters 1 and 2) would vote for X because they each prefer it to Y. Similarly, given the choice between Y and Z, a majority would vote for Y. Yet in a choice between X and Z, a majority would vote for Z. Thus, the implied social ordering is intransitive because X is preferred to Y, Y is preferred to Z, but Z is preferred to X!

TABLE 2.2 Cyclical Social Preferences under Pairwise Majority Rule Voting

Preference Ordering	Voter 1	Voter 2	Voter 3
First Choice	X	Z	Y
Second Choice	Y	X	Z
Third Choice	Z	Y	X

Pairwise Voting Outcomes: *X* versus *Y*, *X* wins; *Y* versus *Z*, *Y* wins; *X* versus *Z*, *Z* wins.

Implied Social Ordering: *X* is preferred to *Y*, *Y* is preferred to *Z*, but *Z* is preferred to *X*!

   Is the possibility of obtaining an intransitive social ordering peculiar to the use of pairwise majority rule voting to produce rankings alternatives? Surprisingly, it can result from any rule for creating a social ordering that satisfies certain minimal requirements. We cannot expect any rule for creating a social ranking of policy alternatives to be fully satisfactory. In 1951, Kenneth Arrow proved that any *social choice rule* that satisfies a basic set of fairness conditions could produce an intransitive social ordering.[4] Arrow's *General Possibility Theorem* applies to any rule for choice in which two or more persons must select a policy from among three or more alternatives. It requires any such scheme to satisfy at least the following conditions to be considered fair: First, each person is allowed to have any transitive preferences over the possible policy alternatives (*axiom of unrestricted domain*). Second, if one alternative is unanimously preferred to a second, then the rule for choice will not select the second (*axiom of Pareto choice*). Third, the ranking of any two alternatives should not depend on what other alternatives are available (*axiom of independence*). Fourth, the rule must not allow any one person dictatorial power to impose his or her preferences as the social ordering (*axiom of nondictatorship*). Arrow's theorem states that any fair rule for choice (one that satisfies the four preceding axioms) will not guarantee a transitive *social ordering* of policy alternatives. That is, it is possible that individual preferences are such that the social ordering will be cyclical. Thus, unless the net benefit rule, which is a social choice rule, violates one of the axioms, it cannot guarantee a transitive social ordering of policies.

   In order to ensure that the use of willingness-to-pay in the implementation of the net benefit rule will produce a transitive social ordering of policies, some restrictions, violating the axiom of unrestricted domain, must be placed on the preferences that individuals are allowed to hold.[5] Economic models commonly assume that individual preferences are represented by utility functions (numerical representations of preference orderings) that exhibit positive but declining marginal utility—other things equal, incremental consumption of any good increases utility but not by as much as the previous incremental unit. Unfortunately, this relatively weak restriction of the domain of preferences (it rules out preference that cannot be represented by such utility functions) is not enough to guarantee that the net benefit rule based on willingness-to-pay will *always* produce a transitive social ordering. Two additional restrictions are required: The utility functions of individuals must be such that the individual demand curves that they imply can be aggregated into a market demand curve with the sum of individual incomes as an argument; and all individuals must face the same set of prices.[6] The first restriction is quite strong in that it requires every individual's demand for each good to increase linearly with increasing income and have the same rate of increase for each individual. The second restriction, generally satisfied when all goods are traded in markets, may be violated when policies allocate quantities of goods to individuals who cannot resell them in markets.

The necessity of restricting the allowed preferences of individuals to guarantee a transitive social ordering from the use of willingness-to-pay in the implementation of the net benefits criterion makes clear that it is an imperfect criterion for assessing the relative efficiency of alternative policies.[7] Of course, analysts can avoid this theoretical problem by assuming that the preferences of individual consumers conform to restrictive assumptions consistent with the existence of an appropriate aggregate demand function. Alternatively, analysts can avoid the problem by assuming that policies affect the price of only a single good so that choice is over a single dimension. Indeed, as discussed in the next three chapters, analysts seeking to estimate willingness-to-pay typically work with an aggregate, or market, demand schedule for a single good, implicitly assuming away price effects in the markets for other goods.

Despite its theoretical imperfection as a measure of efficiency, willingness-to-pay is an intuitively appealing and practical concept for guiding the implementation of the net benefits criterion. As discussed next, however, its dependence on the distribution of wealth raises a serious normative concern about its use.

Dependence of Willingness-to-Pay on the Distribution of Wealth

The willingness of a person to pay to obtain a desired policy impact will tend to be higher the greater the wealth that she or he has available. Consequently, the sum of the willingness of persons to pay, the benefit measure in CBA, depends on their levels of wealth. If the distribution of wealth in society were to be changed, then it would be likely that the sum of individuals' willingness-to-pay amounts would change as well, perhaps altering the ranking of alternative policies in terms of their net benefits.

The dependence of net benefits on the distribution of wealth would not pose a conceptual problem if losers from adopted policies were *actually* compensated so that the adopted polices would produce actual, rather than potential, Pareto improvements. From a utilitarian perspective, Pareto improvement guarantees that the sum of utilities of individuals in society increases. In application of the potential Pareto principle, however, it is possible that an adopted policy could actually lower the sum of utilities if people with different levels of wealth had different *marginal utilities of money*.[8] As an illustration, consider a policy that gives $10 of benefits to a person with high wealth and inflicts $9 of costs on a person with low wealth. If the low-wealth person's marginal utility of money is higher than that of the high-wealth person, then it is possible that the utility loss of the low-wealth person could outweigh the utility gain of the high-wealth person. Thus, although the Pareto principle allows us to avoid interpersonal utility comparisons by guaranteeing increases in aggregate utility for policies with positive net benefits, the potential Pareto principle does not do so.

The implication of the dependence of willingness-to-pay on wealth is that the justification for the potential Pareto principle weakens for policies that concentrate costs and benefits on different wealth groups. Policies with positive net benefits that concentrate costs on low-wealth groups may not increase aggregate utility; moreover, policies with negative net benefits that concentrate benefits on low-wealth groups may not decrease aggregate utility. However, if the potential Pareto principle is consistently applied, and adopted policies do not produce consistent losers or winners, then the overall effects of the policies taken together will tend to make everyone better off. Hence, concerns about reductions in aggregate utility would be unfounded.

Critics of CBA sometimes question the validity of the concept of Pareto efficiency itself because it depends on the status quo distribution of wealth. Returning to Figure 2.1, note that the location of the Pareto frontier would change if the location of the status quo point were changed. Some have advocated the formulation of a social welfare function that maps the utility, wealth, or consumption of all individuals in society into an index that ranks alternative distributions of goods.[9] In this broader framework incorporating distributional values, an efficient policy is one that maximizes the value of the social welfare function. But how does society determine the social welfare function? Unfortunately, Arrow's General Possibility Theorem, as well as practical difficulties in obtaining needed information, preclude the formulation of a social welfare function through any fair collective choice procedure.[10] In practice, it must, therefore, be provided subjectively by the analyst. We believe that it is usually better to keep the subjective distributional values of analysts explicit by comparing policies both in terms of efficiency and the selected distributional criteria, as illustrated in the discussion of multigoal analysis and distributionally weighted CBA later in this chapter. As an alternative, analysts can report net benefits by wealth or income group as well as for society as a whole.

Dependence of Net Benefits on Assumptions about Standing

The question of whose willingness-to-pay should count in the aggregation of net benefits has come to be known as the issue of standing.[11] It has immediate practical importance in at least three contexts: the jurisdictional definition of society, the exclusion of socially unacceptable preferences, and the inclusion of the preferences of future generations. A recognition of social constraints, rights, and duties often helps answer the question of standing.

Jurisdictional Definition of Society   The most inclusive definition of society encompasses all people, no matter where they live or to which government they owe allegiance. Analysts working for the United Nations or some other international organization might very well adopt such a universalistic, or global, perspective. Yet for purposes of CBA, most analysts define society at the national level. The basis for this restriction in jurisdiction is the notion that the citizens of a country share a common constitution, formal or informal, that sets out fundamental values and rules for making collective choices. In a sense, they consent to being a society. Furthermore, they accept that the citizens of other countries have their own constitutions that make them distinct societies.

The distinction between universal and national jurisdiction becomes relevant in the evaluation of policies whose impacts spill over national borders. For example, if U.S.

analysts adopt the national-level jurisdiction as defining society, then they would not attempt to measure the willingness of Canadian residents to pay to avoid pollution originating in the United States that exacerbates acid rain in Canada. Of course, the willingness of U.S. citizens to pay to reduce acid rain in Canada should be included in the CBA, though in practice it would be very difficult to measure.

As in the highway example discussed in Chapter 1, a similar issue arises with respect to subnational units of government. As an illustration, consider a city that is deciding whether to build a convention center. Assume that a CBA from the national perspective (giving standing to everyone in the country) predicts that the project will generate $1 million in benefits (which all accrue to city residents), $2 million in costs (which are also borne by city residents) and, therefore, negative $1 million in net benefits (or $1 million in net costs). Also assume, however, that through an intergovernmental grants program, the national government will repay the city $2 million for costs resulting from this particular project. The grant appears to the city residents as a $2 million benefit offsetting $2 million in local costs. Thus, from the perspective of the city, the convention center generates $1 million in net benefits rather than $1 million in net costs.

One can make an argument that the city should treat its residents as the relevant society and, hence, should not give standing to nonresidents. The city government has a charter to promote the welfare of its residents. The city by itself can do relatively little to affect national policy—even if it does not take advantage of all the opportunities offered by the national government, other cities probably will. Furthermore, analysts who do not adopt the city's perspective, but instead employ only the broader national perspective, risk losing influence, a possibility of special concern to analysts who earn their living by giving advice to the city.

Adopting the subnational perspective, however, makes CBA a less valuable decision rule for public policy. We believe that analysts should generally conduct CBA from at least the national perspective. They may, of course, also conduct a parallel CBA from the subnational perspective as a response to the narrower interests of their clients. If major impacts spill over national borders, then the CBA should be done from the global as well as the national perspective.

Jurisdictional Membership   Deciding the jurisdictional definition of society leaves open a number of questions about who should be counted as members of the jurisdiction. For example, almost all analysts agree that citizens of their country living abroad should have standing. With respect to noncitizens in their country, most analysts would probably give standing to those who are in the country legally. Less consensus exists with respect to the standing of other categories of people: Should illegal aliens have standing? What about the children of illegal aliens?

One source of guidance for answering these sorts of questions is the system of legally defined rights.[12] For example, a ruling by the courts that the children of illegal aliens are entitled to access publicly funded education might encourage the analyst to give these children standing in CBA. Reliance on legally defined rights to determine standing, however, is not always morally acceptable. It would not have been right to deny standing in CBA to slaves in the antebellum United States, nonwhites in apartheid South Africa, or Jews in Nazi Germany simply because they lacked legal rights. Therefore, legal rights alone cannot fully resolve the issue of standing in CBA—they provide a presumption, but one that analysts may sometimes have an ethical responsibility to challenge. Democratic polities usually provide mechanisms for challenging such presumptions, but often with personal cost to individual analysts.

One other issue of membership deserves brief mention. CBA is anthropocentric. Only the willingness-to-pay of people counts. Neither flora nor fauna have standing. That is not to say that their "interests" have no representation. Many people are willing to pay to preserve species, and some are even willing to pay to preserve individual animals or plants. As discussed in Chapter 9, it is conceptually correct within the CBA framework to take account of these willingness-to-pay amounts, though effectively doing so is very often beyond our analytical reach.

Exclusion of Socially Unacceptable Preferences   People sometimes hold preferences that society seeks to suppress through widely supported legal sanctions. For instance, though some people would be willing to pay for the opportunity to have sexual relations with children, most countries attempt to thwart the expression of such preferences through very strict criminal penalties. Should such socially unacceptable preferences be given standing in CBA?

One approach to answering this question adds duties and prohibitions to legal rights as sources of guidance about social values. Together they can be thought of as social constraints that should be taken into account in CBA just as the analyst takes account of physical and budgetary constraints.[13] Clear and widely accepted legal sanctions may help identify preferences that should not have standing.

An important application arises in estimating the net benefits of policies that are intended to reduce the amount of criminal behavior in society. Some analysts count reductions in the monetary returns to crime as a cost borne by criminals, offsetting the benefits of reduced criminal activity enjoyed by their victims.[14] As the returns from crime are illegal and widely viewed as wrong, however, the social constraint perspective argues against treating them in this manner.

The issue of the standing of preferences can be especially difficult for analysts to resolve when they are dealing with foreign cultures. Consider, for instance, the CBA of a program to bring water to poor communities in Haiti.[15] Analysts found that husbands had a negative willingness-to-pay for the time that their wives saved from easier access to water. By contemporary standards in most urban settings, people would generally regard these preferences as unworthy. Yet in the cultural context of rural Haiti at the time, they were quite consistent with prevailing norms. Should these preferences of husbands have standing? In practice, lack of data to estimate willingness-to-pay amounts for this sort of impact usually spares analysts from having to answer such difficult questions.

Inclusion of the Preferences of Future Generations   Some policies adopted today, such as the disposal of nuclear wastes or the restoration of wilderness areas, may have impacts on people not yet born. Though we believe that these people should have standing in CBA, there is no way to measure their willingness-to-pay directly because they are not yet here to express it.[16] How serious a problem does this pose for CBA?

The absence of direct measures of the willingness of future generations to pay for policy impacts is unlikely to be serious in most circumstances for two reasons. First, because few policies involve impacts that appear only in the far future, the willingness-to-pay of people alive today can be used to predict how future generations will value them. Second, as most people alive today care about the well-being of their children, grandchildren, and great-grandchildren, whether or not they have yet been born, they are likely to include the interests of these generations to some extent in their own valuations of impacts. Indeed, because people cannot predict with certainty the place that their future offspring will hold in society, they are likely to take a very broad view of future impacts.

In Chapters 9 and 10, we return to the question of the standing of future generations when we discuss existence value and social discounting.

CONCERNS ABOUT THE ROLE OF CBA IN THE POLITICAL PROCESS

The most vocal critics of CBA fear that it subverts democratic values. Some see the monetizing of impacts as a profane attempt to place a price on everything. Others see CBA as undermining democracy. Though these fears are largely unfounded, they deserve explicit consideration by advocates of CBA.

Does CBA Debase the Terms of Public Discourse?

A number of objections have been raised to the effort made in CBA to value all policy impacts in terms of dollars: Pricing goods not normally traded in markets—for example, life itself—decreases their perceived value by implying that they can be compared to goods that are traded in markets; pricing such goods reduces their perceived value by weakening the claim that they should not be for sale in any circumstance; and pricing all goods undercuts the claim that some goods are "priceless."[17] The language and conceptual frameworks that people use almost certainly affect the nature of debate to some extent. It is not clear, however, how influential the technical concepts of economics are in actually shaping public discourse. In any event, the correct interpretation of how nonmarket goods are monetized largely undercuts the charge that CBA debases public discourse.

Consider the issue of the monetization of the value of life. On the surface it may appear that economists are implying that a price can be put on someone's life. A closer look, which we provide in Chapters 13 and 15, indicates that the value of life estimated by economists is a measure of how much people are willing to pay to reduce their risk of death; in other words, it is the value of a *statistical life,* the willingness-to-pay to avoid risks that will result in one less death in a population. Although it may not be appropriate to place a dollar value on the life of any particular person, it is appropriate to use the value of a statistical life in assessing proposed policies that change the risk of death that people face.

Every day people voluntarily make trade-offs between changes in the risk of death and other values: driving faster to save time increases the risk of being involved in a fatal traffic accident; eating fatty foods is pleasurable but increases the risk of fatal heart disease; skiing is exhilarating but risks fatal injury. Is it profane to take account of these preferences in valuing the impacts of public policies? Most economists would answer no. Indeed, valuing statistical lives seems less profane than attempting to place a dollar value on a specific person by estimating the person's forgone future earnings, a procedure employed by courts in cases of wrongful death.

Does CBA Undermine Democracy?

Some critics of CBA charge that it undermines democracy by imposing a single goal, efficiency, in the assessment of public policies. Their charge would be justified if the appropriate comparison were between a world in which public policy is determined solely through democratic processes that give equal weight to all interests and a world in which public policy is determined strictly through the application of CBA. But this is an inappropriate comparison for two reasons. First, actual governmental processes fall far short of "ideal democracy." Second, at most, CBA has modest influence in public policy making.[18]

The interests of vocal constituencies, often those who can organize themselves in anticipation of obtaining concentrated benefits or avoiding concentrated costs, typically receive great attention from those in representative governments who wish to be reelected or advance to higher office. Less vocal constituencies usually have their interests represented less well. The interests of many of these less vocal constituencies are often better reflected in CBA. For example, CBA takes account of the individually small, but in aggregate large, costs borne by consumers because of government price-support programs that raise prices to the benefit of a small number of well-organized agricultural producers. But CBA rarely serves as the decisive decision rule for public policy. Indeed, it is difficult to identify important public policies selected solely on the basis of CBA.

A realistic assessment of representative democracy and the current influence of CBA should allay concerns that the latter is subverting the former. To the extent it is influential, CBA probably contributes to more democratic public policy by paying attention to diffuse interests typically underrepresented in a representative democracy. It would have to become very much more influential before it could possibly be viewed as undermining democratic processes. Despite our hopes that the readers of this book will help make the use of CBA more prevalent, we have no concerns about it being too influential in the near future.

LIMITATIONS OF CBA: OTHER ANALYTICAL APPROACHES

It is important for analysts to realize the limitations of CBA. Two types of circumstances make the net benefits criterion an inappropriate decision rule for public policy. First, technical limitations may make it impossible to quantify and then monetize all relevant impacts as costs and benefits. Second, goals other than efficiency are relevant to the policy. For example, some policies are intended to affect the equality of outcomes or opportunity. Nevertheless, even when the net benefits criterion is not appropriate as a decision rule, CBA usually provides a useful yardstick for comparing alternative policies in terms of efficiency.

Technical Limitations to CBA

CBA in its pure form requires that all impacts relevant to efficiency be quantified and made commensurate through monetization. Only when all the costs and benefits are expressed in dollars can the potential Pareto principle be applied through the calculation of net benefits. Limitations in theory, data, or analytical resources, however, may make it impossible for the analyst to measure and value all impacts of a policy as commensurate costs and benefits. Nonetheless, it may still be desirable to do a qualitative cost-benefit analysis, or, if all but one important effect can be monetized, to switch from CBA to cost-effectiveness analysis. A brief description of each of these alternative approaches follows.

Qualitative CBA   The advice given by Benjamin Franklin at the beginning of Chapter 1 can be thought of as a prescription for qualitative CBA. In conducting qualitative CBA, the analyst monetizes as many of the impacts as possible. The analyst then makes qualitative estimates of the relative importance of the remaining costs and benefits. Consider, for instance, a program to plant trees along an urban highway. The cost of the program, which consists only of the expenditures that must be made to hire a contractor to plant and to maintain the trees, can be directly monetized. The benefits, however, include a number of effects that are likely to be very difficult to monetize: the visual pleasure the trees give to motorists, the reduction of noise in adjoining neighborhoods, and the filtering of pollutants from the air. With sufficient resources, the analyst would be able to estimate these benefits through a variety of techniques such as surveys of motorists and comparisons with the effects of other noise reduction programs on property values. But because the program involves relatively small costs, it is unlikely that such efforts would be justified. Instead, a reasonable approach would be to list these benefits with rough estimates of their order of magnitude.

Analysts who lack the time, data, or other resources needed to value all relevant impacts directly may be able to make use of estimates found in other CBAs or economic research. For example, most analysts doing CBA do not directly estimate people's willingness-to-pay for reductions in mortality risk. Instead, as discussed in Chapters 12, 13, and 15, they rely on econometric studies investigating how people trade such things as money, wages, and time for changes in levels of risk.

Generally, when possible, analysts should quantify the impacts, that is, estimate the numeric values of the nonmonetized impacts of the policy. For example, consider the CBA of a proposed regulation to restrict commercial fishing practices so that fewer dolphins will be killed per ton of tuna harvested. The regulation produces a benefit because some people have a positive willingness-to-pay for dolphin deaths avoided. Actually monetizing, that is, measuring the willingness-to-pay, is a difficult task that very well might not be feasible for the analyst conducting the CBA. Even if monetization is unfeasible, however, it is useful to attempt to predict the number of dolphins saved by the regulation. Doing so increases the usefulness of the qualitative CBA for others by conveying the magnitude of the impact of the regulation. Additionally, the client or other users of the analysis may be able to provide estimates of the willingness of people to pay for each dolphin saved so that a fully monetized CBA becomes feasible.

Analysts often face a more complicated choice than simply whether or not to quantify a category of costs or benefits. Empirical measures can have varying degrees of accuracy, ranging from very precise estimates in which we have great confidence to very imprecise estimates in which we have little confidence. The decision to quantify, and with what degree of effort, should reflect the value of the increased precision that can be obtained and the costs of obtaining it. In other words, we should make such decisions within a CBA framework!

Cost-Effectiveness Analysis   Analysts can often quantify impacts but not monetize them all. If the analyst is unable or unwilling to monetize the major benefit, then cost-effectiveness analysis may be appropriate. Because not all of the impacts can be monetized, it is not possible to estimate net benefits. The analyst can, however, construct a ratio involving the quantitative, but nonmonetized, benefit and the total dollar costs. A comparison allows the analyst to rank policies in terms of the cost-effectiveness criterion. However, unlike the net benefits criterion of CBA, it does not directly allow the analyst to conclude that the highest-ranked policy contributes to greater efficiency.

Return to the qualitative CBA of the fishing regulation discussed earlier. Imagine that, except for the benefit from avoided dolphin deaths, all the impacts could be monetized to a net cost of c dollars. If the number of avoided dolphin deaths were n_d, then the analyst could construct a cost-effectiveness ratio for the regulation, n_d/c, which can be interpreted as the average number of dolphins saved per dollar of opportunity cost borne. (Alternatively, the analyst could construct the cost-effectiveness ratio as c/n_d, which would be interpreted as the average dollar cost per dolphin saved.) Now imagine a number of alternative regulations, each of which involves different net costs and a different number of dolphins saved. A cost-effectiveness ratio can be calculated for each of these programs to facilitate comparison across alternative regulations.

Using cost-effectiveness analysis for decision making usually requires that some additional information be considered. If the objective is to save as many dolphins as possible at a net cost of no more than c^*, then the analyst should select the most effective regulation from among those with net costs of less than c^*. Alternatively, if the objective is to save at least n_d^* dolphins, then the analyst should select the regulation with the lowest cost from among those regulations saving at least n_d^*. This is not necessarily the alternative with the best cost-effectiveness ratio. For example, if $n_d^* = 1,000$, one would choose a regulation that saved 1,000 dolphins at a cost of $1 million ($1,000 per dolphin saved) over an alternative regulation that saved 500 dolphins at a cost of $50,000 ($100 per dolphin saved).

Analysts often encounter situations in which they themselves or their clients are unable or unwilling to monetize impacts such as human lives saved, injuries avoided, and the acres of old-growth forest preserved. Because cost-effectiveness analysis may be useful in these situations, we consider it in greater depth in Chapter 17.

The Relevance of CBA When Goals Other Than Efficiency Matter

One goal, efficiency, underlies CBA. The general public, politicians, and even economists, however, very often consider goals reflecting other values to be relevant to social problems and the public policies proposed to solve them. Though efficiency almost always is one of the relevant goals in policy analysis, other goals such as equality of opportunity, equality of outcome, expenditure constraints, political feasibility, and national security, for instance, may be as, or even more, important. Indeed, the spenders and guardians we met in Chapter 1 behave as if they are responding to goals other than efficiency. When goals in addition to efficiency are relevant, as well as when efficiency is the only goal, but relevant impacts cannot be confidently monetized, *multigoal analysis* provides the appropriate framework. In the special case in which efficiency and equality of outcome are the only relevant goals, *distributionally weighted* CBA may be an appropriate technique.

Multigoal Analysis   The most general analytical framework is multigoal analysis. At the heart of multigoal analysis lies the notion that all policy alternatives should be compared in terms of all the relevant goals. Though multigoal analysis can be prescribed as a number of distinct steps,[19] three of its aspects are especially important. First, the analyst must move from relevant social values to general goals to specific criteria that can be used as yardsticks for evaluating alternative policies. For example, Exhibit 2.1 shows how government analysts in Hong Kong translated general goals for infrastructure projects into specific objectives (criteria) for assessing port and airport expansion strategies. Second, the analyst must evaluate each alternative policy, including the status quo, with respect to each of the criteria. Third, as no policy alternative is likely to dominate the others in terms of all the objectives, the analyst usually can only make a recommendation to adopt one of the alternatives by carefully considering and making a subjective judgment concerning the trade-offs in the achievement of objectives it offers relative to the other alternatives.

As a simple example, consider a multigoal analysis of alternative income transfer policies intended to help poor families. The analyst might construct the worksheet shown in Table 2.3 as a checklist for keeping track of the relevant goals. Increasing efficiency and improving the quality of life of poor families are appropriate substantive goals. The goal of achieving political feasibility might be added to take account of the fact that a consensus on the relative importance of the substantive goals among politicians is unlikely—in this example, it can be thought of as an instrumental goal that is valuable not for its own sake but because it helps achieve the substantive goals. The major efficiency impacts are likely to be work disincentives for the recipients of aid and

EXHIBIT 2.1

In its evaluation of alternative strategies for improving ports and airports, the Hong Kong government developed the following goals and associated objectives:

Goal	*Subsumed Objectives*
Economic Performance	• Maximize net benefits • Maximize confidence in Hong Kong's future • Minimize detrimental impact on Hong Kong's economy • Ensure strategies fall within limits of government's resource availability
Environmental and Social Impact	• Minimize disturbance to existing communities (including noise) • Minimize disturbance to local economies • Minimize detrimental impact on recreational opportunities • Minimize detrimental impact on landscape and ecology • Minimize detrimental impact on water quality • Minimize detrimental impact on air quality • Maximize opportunities for replanning of and improvement to existing urban areas
Programming	• Provide facilities in line with forecast demand • Minimize uncertainty of program

Goal	*Subsumed Objectives*
Flexibility and Robustness	• Minimize detrimental impact of the following eventualities: Port demand not reaching forecast levels Airport demand growth not reaching forecast levels Port demand growth exceeding forecast rates Delays in provision of facilities or other transport infrastructure Siltation of North Lantau Channel more serious than forecast Closure of a major transportation link • Optimize capacity to accommodate expansion in port, airport, and associated uses: As forecast for the period 2006 to 2011 Beyond 2011
Financial Performance	• Maximize net present value of public sector investment • Maximize the opportunity for major project packages to be financially viable

The government evaluated three combinations of airport and port facilities in terms of these goals and objectives. The maximization of net economic benefits, the first objective under the goal of "Economic Performance," was a CBA that included the opportunity costs of land and capital, revenues from non–Hong Kong users, and the benefits of accommodating greater air passenger demand as its major components. The objectives under "Financial Performance" were addressed by comparing government expenditures and revenues under each of the alternatives.

Source: Government Secretariat, *Land and Works Branch, Ports & Airport Development Strategy* (Hong Kong: Government Printer, December 1989).

TABLE 2.3 Evaluation Matrix Worksheet for Alternative Family Aid Policies

		Policy Alternatives		
Goals	*Criteria*	*Policy A (status quo)*	*Policy B*	*Policy C*
Increase efficiency	Increase work incentives			
	Reduce administrative costs			
Improve quality of life of poorest families	Reduce number of families below poverty line			
	Reduce number of one-parent families			
	Increase educational achievement of family members			
Achieve political feasibility	Maximize probability of adoption of required legislation			

the real resource costs of administering the aid policy. If both of these impacts could be monetized, then the criterion for measuring efficiency would simply be the sum of the net benefits of these two impacts as measured in CBA. If either one of them could not be monetized, however, then efficiency would be stated in terms of two criteria corresponding to the two impacts. The goal of improving the quality of life of poor families would probably be expressed in terms of such criteria as reducing the number of families below the poverty line, reducing the number of one-parent families, and increasing the educational achievement of family members. The criterion associated with the additional goal of political feasibility might be maximizing the probability of passage of legislation required to implement the policy.

Before selecting among the alternative policies, the analyst should fill in all the cells of a matrix such as the one shown in Table 2.3. Each cell would contain a prediction of the effect of a particular policy in terms of a particular criterion. By filling in *all* the cells, the analyst seeks to gain a comprehensive comparison of the alternatives across all the criteria.

Note that one can think of CBA, qualitative CBA, and cost-effectiveness analysis as special cases of multigoal analysis. In the case of CBA, there is one goal (increase efficiency) with one criterion (maximize net benefits) so that the evaluation matrix has only one row and the choice among alternatives is trivial (simply select the policy with the largest net benefits). In the case of qualitative CBA, there is also one goal but, because all relevant impacts cannot be monetized, it corresponds to several criteria, one for each impact. In the case of cost-effectiveness analysis, the goal of efficiency is often combined with some other goal such as satisfying a constraint on monetary costs or achieving some target level of reduction in the quantified but nonmonetized impact.

Distributionally Weighted CBA   If both efficiency and equality of income are relevant goals, and their relative importance can be quantified, then distributionally weighted CBA provides an alternative decision rule to the maximization of net benefits. Instead of considering aggregate net benefits as in standard CBA, net benefits are first calculated for each relevant group distinguished by income, wealth, or some similar characteristic of relevance to a distributional concern. As discussed in more detail in Chapter 18, the net benefits of each group are then multiplied by a weighting factor, selected by the analyst to reflect some distributional goal, and finally summed to arrive at a number that can be used to rank alternative policies.

The major problem analysts encounter in doing distributionally weighted CBA is arriving at an appropriate and acceptable set of weights. One general approach, which takes as a desirable social goal increasing equality of wealth, involves making the weights inversely proportional to wealth (or income) to favor policies that tend to equalize wealth (or income) in the population.[20] Another general approach, which takes as a desirable social goal the raising of the position of the least advantaged in society, involves placing a higher weight on the net benefits of those with incomes or wealth below some threshold level than on those with incomes or wealth above the threshold. As reasonable arguments can be made in support of each of these approaches, the absence of a consensus about appropriate weights is not surprising.[21]

Obviously, developing weights that allow a single quantitative criterion for ranking alternative policies makes the choice among policy alternatives very easy. Yet this ease is achieved only by making an assumption that forces efficiency and equality of outcome to be fully commensurate. Dissatisfaction with the strong assumptions required to do this has led a number of analysts to suggest that distributionally weighted CBA should always be done in conjunction with standard CBA to make clearer the efficiency implications of the selected weights.[22] In doing so, the study becomes in effect a multigoal analysis, raising the question of whether an explicit treatment of efficiency and equality as separate goals might not be a more appropriate framework when both efficiency and distributional concerns are important. Cost-effectiveness analysis might also provide a more reasonable approach than distributionally weighted CBA by posing the question in terms of achieving the most desirable redistribution possible for some fixed level of net cost.[23]

CONCLUSION

CBA is a method for determining if proposed policies could potentially be Pareto improving: Positive net benefits make it at least possible to compensate those who bear costs so that some people are made better off without making anyone else worse off. Willingness-to-pay and opportunity cost are the guiding principles for measuring benefits and costs. Much of the rest of this book deals with how to make use of the concepts in practice.

Part II sets out the conceptual foundations for CBA in more depth. It begins by reviewing supply and demand analytics (Chapter 3) and then uses these analytics to show how information revealed in markets can be used to estimate willingness-to-pay and opportunity cost (Chapters 4 and 5). Subsequent chapters consider how to take account of policy effects that accrue in different time periods (Chapters 6 and 10) or with uncertainty (Chapters 7 and 8), and impacts on goods that have value beyond their direct use (Chapter 9).

Part III considers empirical approaches for predicting and valuing policy impacts. Three chapters demonstrate estimation methods based on observed behavior. Policy demonstrations sometimes provide information of direct relevance to CBA, especially in terms of predicting policy impacts (Chapter 11). More often, however, analysts face the task of making inferences about demand schedules from data revealed in markets (Chapter 12) or through other behaviors (Chapter 13). In some circumstances, especially those arising in the context of environmental policy, the unavailability of data from observed behavior forces analysts to rely on survey responses as a basis for estimation (Chapter 14). Analysts can often make use of existing research to find values needed to monetize impacts as costs and benefits (Chapter 15), though some special care must be taken in transferring these values to CBAs of policies in developing countries (Chapter 16).

Part IV further develops two of the analytical methods introduced in this chapter that can be used as alternatives to CBA: cost-effectiveness analysis (Chapter 17) and distributionally weighted cost-benefit analysis (Chapter 18). Chapter 19 concludes by investigating the accuracy of CBAs done in conjunction with the highway project described in Chapter 1.

Exercises for Chapter 2

1. Many experts claim that, although VHS is now dominant, Betamax is a superior video recorder technology. Assume that these experts are correct, so that, all other things equal, a world in which all video recorders were Betamax technology would be Pareto superior to a world in which all video recorders were VHS technology. Yet it seems implausible that a policy that forced a switch in technologies would be even potentially Pareto improving. Explain.

2. Let's explore the concept of willingness-to-pay with a thought experiment. Imagine a specific sporting, entertainment, or cultural event that you would very much like to attend—perhaps a World Cup match, the seventh game of the World Series, a Garth Brooks concert, or Kathleen Battle performance.
   a. What is the most you would be willing to pay for a ticket to the event?
   b. Imagine that you won a ticket to the event in a lottery. What is the minimum amount of money that you would be willing to accept to give up the ticket?
   c. Imagine that you had an income 50 percent higher than it is now, but that you didn't win a ticket to the event. What is the most you would be willing to pay for a ticket?
   d. Do you know anyone who would sufficiently dislike the event so that he or she would not use a free ticket unless he or she were paid to do so?
   e. Do your answers suggest any possible generalizations about willingness-to-pay?

3. How closely do government expenditures measure opportunity cost for each of the following program inputs?
   a. Time of jurors in a criminal justice program that requires more trials.
   b. Land to be used for a nuclear waste storage facility, which is owned by the government and located on a military base.
   c. Labor for a reforestation program in a small rural community with high unemployment.
   d. Labor of current government employees who are required to administer a new program.
   e. Concrete that was previously poured as part of a bridge foundation.

4. Three mutually exclusive projects are being considered for a remote river valley: Project R, a recreational facility, has estimated benefits of $10 million and costs of $8 million; project F, a forest preserve with some recreational facilities, has estimated benefits of $13 million and costs of $10 million; project W, a wilderness area with restricted public access, has estimated benefits of $5 million and costs of $1 million. In addition, a road could be built for a cost of $4 million that would increase the benefits of project R by $8 million, increase the benefits of project F by $5 million, and reduce the benefits of project W by $1 million. Even in the absence of any of the other projects, the road has estimated benefits of $2 million.
   a. Calculate the benefit-cost ratio and net benefits for each possible alternative to the status quo. Note that there are seven possible alternatives to the status quo: R, F, and W, both with and without the road, and the road alone.
   b. If only one of the seven alternatives can be selected, which should be selected according to the CBA decision rule?

5. An analyst for the Navy was asked to evaluate alternatives for forward-basing a destroyer flotilla. He decided to do the evaluation as a CBA. The major categories of costs were related to obtaining and maintaining the facilities. The major cate-

gory of benefit was reduced sailing time to patrol routes. The analyst recommended the forward base with the largest net benefits. The admiral, his client, rejected the recommendation because the CBA did not include the risks to the forward bases from surprise attack and the risks of being unexpectedly ejected from the bases because of changes in political regimes of the host countries. Was the analyst's work wasted?

6. Because of a recent wave of jewelry store robberies, a city increases police surveillance of jewelry stores. The increased surveillance costs the city an extra $500,000 per year, but as a result, the amount of jewelry that is stolen falls. Specifically, without the increase in surveillance, jewelry with a retail value of $1 million would have been stolen. This stolen jewelry would have been fenced by the jewelry thieves for $600,000. What is the net social benefit resulting from the police surveillance program?

Notes

1. Unless otherwise stated, we intend efficiency to mean *allocative efficiency*, as defined in this section. A broader interpretation of efficiency, which we discuss in a later section, is the maximization of a specific social welfare function that explicitly ranks alternative allocations.

2. Nicholas Kaldor, "Welfare Propositions of Economics and Interpersonal Comparisons of Utility," *Economic Journal*, 49, no. 195 (1939), 549–552; John R. Hicks, "The Valuation of the Social Income," *Economica*, 7, no. 26 (1940), 105–124. The principle can also be stated as suggested by Hicks: Adopt a policy if and only if it would not be in the self-interest of those who will lose to bribe those who will gain not to adopt it.

3. Those who are worse off in society may or may not have been the ones who have borne the net costs of public policies. This argument thus shifts the focus from fairness with respect to particular policies to the relative position of those in society who are worse off for whatever reason.

4. Kenneth Arrow, *Social Choice and Individual Values,* 2nd ed. (New Haven, CT: Yale University Press, 1963). For a treatment that can be followed with minimal mathematics, see Julian H. Blau, "A Direct Proof of Arrow's Theorem," *Econometrica*, 40, no. 1 (1972), 61–67.

5. For an overview, see Charles Blackorby and David Donaldson, "A Review Article: The Case Against the Use of the Sum of Compensating Variation in Cost-Benefit Analysis," *Canadian Journal of Economics*, 23, no. 3 (1990), 471–494.

6. Charles Blackorby and David Donaldson, "Consumers' Surpluses and Consistent Cost-Benefit Tests," *Social Choice and Welfare*, 1, no. 4 (1985), 251–262.

7. Even if one does not demand that the potential Pareto principle always produce a transitive social ordering of policies, the most commonly used measure of willingness-to-pay, *compensating variation*, can produce what are called *Scitovsky reversals* [Tibor Scitovsky, "A Note on Welfare Propositions in Economics," *Review of Economic Studies*, 41, no. 1 (1941), 77–88]. Compensating variation, which is discussed in Appendix 3A, is the change in income that would be needed to make the consumer indifferent between the new policy with the income change and the old policy without it. For example, if the price of a good increases, compensating variation is the amount of income needed to compensate the consumer so that he or she would be indifferent between the original price and the new price with the compensation. A Scitovsky reversal results when the sum of compensating variations for a group of individuals is positive for a move from one Pareto efficient policy to another *and* is also positive for a move from the new policy back to the original! More generally, the sum of compensating variations can be positive for moves among Pareto efficient allocations, so that it being positive is a necessary but not a sufficient condition for a potential Pareto improvement (Blackorby and Donaldson, "A Review Article: The Case Against the

Use of the Sum of Compensating Variation in Cost-Benefit Analysis," 471–494).

8. The marginal utility of money is how much a person's utility changes for a small increase in the person's wealth. Economists generally assume declining marginal utility of money. That is, as a person's wealth increases, each additional dollar produces smaller increases in utility.

9. Abram Bergson [as Burk], "A Reformulation of Certain Aspects of Welfare Economics," *Quarterly Journal of Economics*, 52, no. 2 (1938), 310–334.

10. Tibor Scitovsky, "The State of Welfare Economics," *American Economic Review*, 51, no. 3 (1951), 301–315; Kenneth Arrow, *Social Choice and Individual Values*, 2nd ed. (New Haven, CT: Yale University Press, 1963).

11. The seminal work is Dale Whittington and Duncan MacRae Jr., "The Issue of Standing in Cost-Benefit Analysis," *Journal of Policy Analysis and Management*, 5, no. 4 (1986), 665–682.

12. Richard O. Zerbe Jr., "Comment: Does Benefit-Cost Analysis Stand Alone? Rights and Standing," *Journal of Policy Analysis and Management*, 10, no. 1 (1991), 96–105.

13. For a development of the notion of social constraints in CBA, see William N. Trumbull, "Who Has Standing in Cost-Benefit Analysis?" *Journal of Policy Analysis and Management*, 9, no. 2 (1990), 201–218; and Richard O. Zerbe Jr., "Is Cost-Benefit Analysis Legal? Three Rules," *Journal of Policy Analysis and Management*, 17, no. 3 (1998), 419–456. For a more general treatment of institutional constraints and social welfare, see Daniel W. Bromley, *Economic Interests and Institutions: The Conceptual Foundations of Public Policy* (New York: Basil Blackwell, 1989).

14. David A. Long, Charles D. Mallar, and Craig V. D. Thornton, "Evaluating the Benefits and Costs of the Job Corps," *Journal of Policy Analysis and Management*, 1, no. 1 (1981), 55–76.

15. For a discussion of this case from the perspective of a number of issues of standing of preferences, see Duncan MacRae Jr. and Dale Whittington, "Assessing Preferences in Cost-Benefit Analysis: Reflections on Rural Water Supply Evaluation in Haiti," *Journal of Policy Analysis and Management*, 7, no. 2 (1988), 246–263.

16. See Daniel W. Bromley, "Entitlements, Missing Markets, and Environmental Uncertainty," *Journal of Environmental Economics and Management*, 17, no. 2 (1989), 181–194.

17. Steven Kelman, "Cost-Benefit Analysis: An Ethical Critique," *Regulation* (January/February 1981), 33–40.

18. Alan Williams, "Cost-Benefit Analysis: Bastard Science? And/Or Insidious Poison in the Body Politick?" *Journal of Public Economics*, 1, no. 2 (1972), 199–226; Aidan R. Vining and David L. Weimer, "Welfare Economics as the Foundation for Public Policy Analysis: Incomplete and Flawed But Nevertheless Desirable," *Journal of Socio-Economics*, 21, no. 1 (1992), 25–37.

19. For a detailed presentation of multigoal analysis, see David L. Weimer and Aidan R. Vining, *Policy Analysis: Concepts and Practice* 3rd edition (Englewood Cliffs, NJ: Prentice Hall, 1999), Chapter 10.

20. For a demonstration of the application of various measures of vertical and horizontal equality, see Marcus C. Berliant and Robert P. Strauss, "The Horizontal and Vertical Equity Characteristics of the Federal Individual Income Tax," in *Horizontal Equity, Uncertainty, and Economic Well-Being*, eds. Martin David and Timothy Smeeding (Chicago: University of Chicago Press, 1985), 179–211.

21. The fact that people routinely donate to charities suggests that, other things being equal, most people would be willing to pay something to obtain a distribution of wealth that is more favorable to the currently poor. Ironically, CBA provides a conceptual way to place a dollar value on alternative distributions of wealth: the sum of the willingness of the individual members of society to pay for moving from the status quo distribution of wealth to an alternative one. Unfortunately, it is usually impractical to elicit willingness-to-pay amounts of this sort.

22. For example, Harberger proposes that a dual test be applied: The policy should have positive weighted and unweighted net benefits. Arnold C. Harberger, "On the Use of Distributional Weights in Social Cost-Benefit Analysis," *Journal of Political Economy*, 86, no. 2, part 2 (1978), S87-S120.

23. For an excellent development of this approach, see Edward M. Gramlich and Michael Wolkoff, "A Procedure for Evaluating Income Distribution Policies," *Journal of Human Resources*, 14, no. 3 (1979), 319–350.

3

BASIC MICROECONOMIC FOUNDATIONS OF COST-BENEFIT ANALYSIS

Microeconomic theory provides the basic conceptual foundation for CBA. In this chapter, we review the major concepts of microeconomic theory as they apply to the measurement of costs and benefits. Most of these concepts should be at least somewhat familiar from your previous exposure to economics. Although we assume that most readers have some familiarity with the concepts, we seek to provide as simple an overview of the topics relevant to CBA as possible.

For purposes of simplicity, the presence of perfect competition is assumed throughout this chapter. Specifically, it is assumed that there are so many buyers and sellers in each market that no one can individually affect prices, that buyers and sellers can easily enter and exit from each market, that the goods sold in each market are homogeneous (i.e., identical), that there is an absence of transaction costs in buying and selling in each market, that information is perfect, and that private costs and benefits are identical to social costs and benefits (i.e., there are no externalities). Measuring benefits and costs when some of these assumptions do not hold and, consequently, various forms of market failure are present is considered in Chapter 4.

DEMAND SCHEDULES

A demand schedule, or demand curve, indicates the quantities of a good that individuals purchase at various prices. A single person has an individual demand schedule; all individuals in a market contribute to the market demand schedule. A standard assumption in economics is that demand schedules slope downward. The reasoning behind, and the importance of, this assumption to CBA will become clear as we proceed. A downward-sloped demand schedule is illustrated as line D in Figure 3.1.

The rationale for the downward slope is based on the principle of *diminishing marginal utility;* each additional unit of the good is valued slightly less by each consumer than the preceding unit. And for that reason, each consumer is willing to pay less for another unit than for the preceding unit. Indeed, at some point, each consumer would be unwilling to pay anything for an additional unit; his or her demand would be sated.

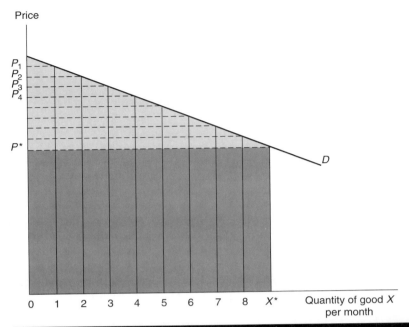

FIGURE 3.1 Consumer Gross Benefits and Consumer Surplus

This notion that demand schedules indicate how much people are willing to pay for various quantities of a good is absolutely critical to understanding the role of demand schedules in CBA. The key is the link between demand schedules and willingness-to-pay (WTP), a concept that was originally introduced in Chapter 2. To explore this link, we consider market demand schedules, which convey information about how all the potential consumers of the good in an economic society value it in aggregate. Figure 3.1 illustrates the demand schedule for these consumers.

Figure 3.1 indicates that there is at least one member of society who is willing to pay a price of P_1 for one unit of good X. Similarly, there is at least one person who would pay a price of P_2 for the second unit of X, and there is someone who would pay P_3 for the third unit of X, and so forth.[1] The message from this exercise should be obvious: The area under the demand schedule—in other words, the sum of all the unit-wide rectangles—closely approximates the willingness-to-pay for X by all the members of society. Each additional unit is valued at a price given by the height of the demand schedule; summing these prices over the units corresponds approximately to adding the unitwide rectangles (the rectangles are approximate because they miss the small triangles at the top of the trapezoids). Thus, the lightly shaded area plus the darkly shaded area in Figure 3.1 approximate society's willingness-to-pay for a given amount of X—say, X^*. To put it just a little differently, the sum of the lightly and darkly shaded areas approximates the total gross benefits society would receive from consuming X^* units of good X.

Now, under most circumstances, people actually have to pay something to consume good X. Let us assume that the competitive market sets the price of X at P^*. Thus, consumers pay P^*X^*, the darkly shaded area, to the producers of the good. In this case, the net benefits from consuming X^* units—that is, gross benefits less the required purchase payments—equal the area below the demand schedule but above the price line. This lightly shaded area is called *consumer surplus.*

When demand schedules are known, consumer surplus is one of the basic concepts used in CBA to value impacts. The reason why consumer surplus is so important to CBA is that, under most circumstances, changes in consumer surplus can appropriately be used as reasonable approximations of society's willingness-to-pay for policy changes. That is, as stated in Chapter 2, the algebraic sum of willingness-to-pay values is the appropriate measure of the benefits of a policy. In the Appendix to this chapter, we examine the circumstances under which changes in consumer surplus do provide close approximations to willingness-to-pay values and the circumstances under which they do not. The major conclusion is that in most instances such approximations are sufficiently accurate for CBA purposes.

Changes in Consumer Surplus

To see how the concept of consumer surplus can be used in CBA, consider a policy that results in a price change. For example, as shown in Figure 3.2(a), a policy that reduces the price of good X from P^* to P_1 would result in a benefit to consumers (i.e., an increase in consumer surplus) equal to the area of the shaded trapezoid P^*ABP_1—it results both because consumers gain from paying a lower price for the X^* units they previously purchased and because they gain from the consumption of $X_1 - X^*$ additional units. Similarly, as shown in Figure 3.2(b), a policy that increases the price of good X from P^* to P_2 would impose a "cost" on consumers (i.e., a loss in consumer surplus) equal to the area of the shaded trapezoid P_2ABP^*.

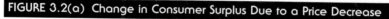

FIGURE 3.2(a) Change in Consumer Surplus Due to a Price Decrease

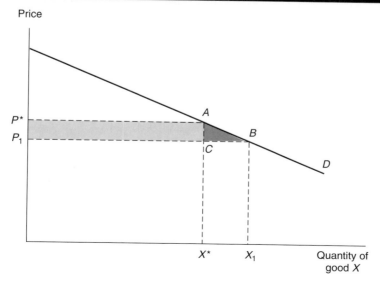

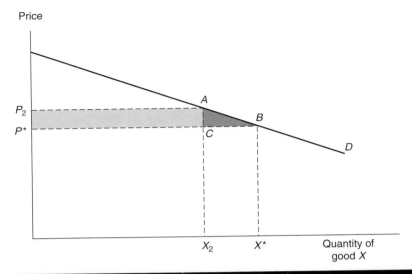

Price

P_2

P^*

A

B

C

D

X_2 X^* Quantity of good X

FIGURE 3.2(b) Change in Consumer Surplus Due to a Price Increase

If the change in the price of X, ΔP, and the change in the quantity of good X consumed, ΔX, are both known, and the demand schedule is linear, then the change in consumer surplus, ΔCS, can be readily computed by the following formula:

$$\Delta CS = (\Delta P)(X^*) + \tfrac{1}{2}(\Delta X)(\Delta P) \qquad (3.1)$$

Sometimes after a known price change, the change in quantities consumed, ΔX, is not directly known, but an estimate of the price elasticity of demand is available. The price elasticity of demand, ε_d, is defined as the percentage change in quantity that results from a 1 percent change in price. It can be computed as follows:[2]

$$\varepsilon_d = (\Delta X/\Delta P)(P^*/X^*) \qquad (3.2)$$

Although the computation of ε_d will produce a negative value because demand curves are negatively sloped, the negative sign is usually ignored in discussing the price elasticity of demand. When the change in the quantity is not known, but the price elasticity of demand is known, the change in consumer surplus can be computed by using a slight modification of equation (3.1).[3]

$$\Delta CS = \Delta P(X^*) + \tfrac{1}{2}[(\Delta X/\Delta P)(P^*/X^*)][(\Delta P)(X^*)(\Delta P/P^*)]$$
$$= \Delta P(X^*)[1 + \tfrac{1}{2}(\Delta P/P^*)\varepsilon_d] \qquad (3.3)$$

Taxes

Now, let us assume that the price increase from P^* to P_2 shown in Figure 3.2(b) results from a government-imposed excise tax, where each unit of X has been taxed by an amount equal to the difference between the old and the new price $(P_2 - P^*)$. In this case, the rectangular part of the trapezoid in Figure 3.2(b), P_2ACP^*, represents the tax revenue collected. It can be viewed as a *transfer*—money that is transferred from consumers of X to the government. It is called a transfer because from the perspective of society as a whole its net impact is zero. The transfer of tax revenue imposes a cost on consumers of X, but this cost is offset by an identical benefit received by the government.[4]

The triangular part of the trapezoid, *ABC,* is a pure cost of the tax, however. That is, consumers lose consumer surplus, but there is no offsetting benefit to some other part of society. This pure loss in consumer surplus is an example of *deadweight loss.*[5] It results from the distortion in economic behavior from the competitive equilibrium. The tax causes some consumers to purchase less output than they would in the absence of the tax because, inclusive of the tax, the price now exceeds these consumers' willingness-to-pay. Those consumers, who in the absence of the tax would collectively have purchased $X^* - X_2$ of the good and received the consumer surplus represented by the triangular area, *ABC,* lose this consumer surplus.

In general, there will always be a deadweight loss if a government imposes a tax on a good sold in a competitive market. The implications of this for cost-benefit analysis are further discussed in Chapter 4.

Individual versus Market Demand Schedules

Just one more basic point concerning demand schedules remains to be mentioned—the relationship between the demand schedules of individual consumers in a market and the demand schedule for the entire market. The market demand schedule for a private good is simply the horizontal sum of the individual demand schedules. Individual demand schedules indicate the amount of the good each consumer wants to purchase at each price. By adding together all these quantities at each price, which graphically corresponds to summing the demand schedules for individuals horizontally, the market demand schedule is obtained. This is important for cost-benefit purposes because it implies that a market demand schedule can appropriately be used to measure the effect of a price change on the total consumer surplus of all buyers in the market. In other words, total consumer surplus is just the sum of the surpluses of each of the individual consumers in the market and, consequently, changes in total consumer surplus approximate the sum of all the willingness-to-pay values associated with a given price change.

SUPPLY SCHEDULES

Figure 3.3 presents a standard U-shaped *marginal cost curve* for an individual firm. The curve pertains to costs in the short run, when at least one factor of production, say, capital, is fixed. Thus, as output expands and increasing amounts of the variable factors of production, such as labor, are used with the fixed factor, diminishing returns must eventually occur. This implies that at least part of the marginal cost curve must slope upward, as is shown in the diagram.[6]

It is important to recognize that the upward-sloping segment of the firm's marginal cost curve above the firm's average variable cost curve (AVC) corresponds to the firm's supply schedule or supply curve.[7]

If the price were lower than the firm's average variable cost curve, the firm could not cover its average variable cost and would shut down rather than produce any output. At a price above average variable cost, however, the upward-sloping segment of the marginal cost curve determines how much output the firm will produce per period at any given price. For example, at a price of P^*, the firm would maximize profit by

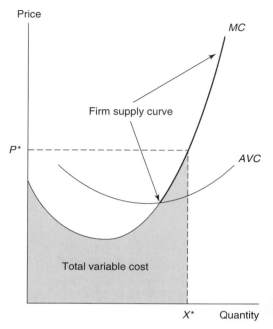

Price

MC

Firm supply curve

P*

AVC

Total variable cost

X*   Quantity

FIGURE 3.3 Individual Firm Supply Curve

producing at X^*. If it produced more output than X^*, it would take in less in additional revenue than the additional cost it would incur. And if it produced less output than X^*, it would lose more in revenue than it would save in costs.

Just as the demand schedule indicates the willingness-to-pay for each additional unit of a good consumed, the marginal cost curve indicates the additional cost incurred to produce each additional unit of a good. This means that the area under the marginal cost curve represents the total variable cost of producing a given amount of good X, say, X^*.

It is important to emphasize that the variable costs we are considering are opportunity costs, the value of what is given up to produce X^*, not accounting costs. For example, if the owner of the firm represented in the diagram could earn $80,000 a year working for someone else but actually withdraws a salary of only $50,000 a year from the firm, it is the $80,000 figure that should be counted as costs incurred by the firm. This amount is the appropriate measure of opportunity costs—the value to society of what the owner could produce in alternative employment.

As indicated in Chapter 2, the notion of opportunity cost is critical to CBA. The cost of a policy or project includes the opportunity costs incurred by various members of society so that it can command the resources it requires. Consequently, the cost curve in Figure 3.3 should be viewed as drawn under the assumption that the owners of all the resources the firm uses are paid prices equal to the opportunity costs of the resources. In competitive markets, they could not receive more; and rather than accept less, they would sell to some other firm. For such factors as capital and entrepreneurship, these opportunity costs include a *normal return*[8] because, under perfect competition, these factors would receive such a return in their best alternative use.[9]

Market Supply Schedule

Similar to the case of demand schedules, a market supply schedule, or supply curve, can be derived by summing horizontally the individual supply schedules of all the individual firms in a market. These individual supply schedules indicate how much output each firm in a market is willing to sell at each price. Thus, the individual supply schedules provide the information required to determine the total supply available to the market at each price.

A market supply schedule is illustrated in Figure 3.4. As in the case of the marginal cost curves for individual firms, the area under this curve indicates the total variable costs, that is, the opportunity costs incurred in producing a given amount of output, say, X^*. The area $0abX^*$ is the additional cost of supplying X^*. Put another way, it is the minimum total revenue that firms must receive before they would be willing to produce output X^*.

Producer Surplus

Although area $0abX^*$ is the minimum total revenue that firms in the market represented in Figure 3.4 must receive before they would be willing to produce X^* at a price of P^*, these firms actually receive total revenues equal to the area represented by the rectangular area, $0P^*bX^*$. The difference between this rectangular area and the area under the supply schedule, that is, the area aP^*b, is called *producer surplus*. Thus, producer surplus equals the revenues from selling X^* less the variable costs required to produce X^*. Or viewed slightly differently, the sum of total producer surplus and opportunity costs—that is, areas $aP^*b + 0abX^*$—corresponds to total revenues.

Producer surplus is the supply-side equivalent to consumer surplus. Just as changes in prices resulting from government policies have impacts on consumers that can be

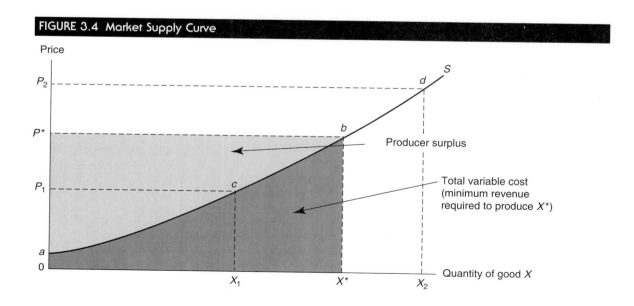

FIGURE 3.4 Market Supply Curve

valued in terms of changes in consumer surplus, price changes also result in impacts on producers that can be valued in terms of changes in producer surplus (or stated slightly differently, as changes in the economic profits of firms in the market). For example, a decrease in price from P^* to P_1 decreases producer surplus (or economic profits) by P^*bcP_1 and an increase in price to P_2 increases producer surplus (or economic profits) by P^*bdP_2.[10]

Project Length: Fixed versus Variable Costs

In conducting an actual CBA, the costs considered should be appropriate to the specific study context. Although we have been emphasizing short-run supply schedules, the appropriate time period for the CBA could correspond to either the short run (where labor is free to vary, but capital is fixed) or the long run (where all inputs can vary). For example, if the government is considering a one-time purchase of concrete to build a road extension, then certain expenditures by firms in the industry from which the government makes the purchase (e.g., their purchases of trucks) may be unaffected. Such costs are best viewed as fixed costs, not variable costs. Thus, they would not be included in the area under the industry's short-run supply schedule and should be ignored in the cost-benefit analysis. On the other hand, if the appropriate time-horizon is long or the project is large (e.g., the Three Gorges Dam in China), then all the factors of production (such as the number of trucks) are free to vary. Such changes should be included in measuring project costs in a CBA.

Finally, consider a change to an existing program. For example, the government wants to examine the possibility of eliminating price supports in a competitive agricultural market. In this instance, the measured opportunity costs must reflect the value of assets at the time the policy change is made. Some assets may have depreciated in value (e.g., although the tractors owned by farmers who would be driven out of business by the fall in prices could be sold, their value would be less than their original purchase price because of depreciation). It is their current economic value that should be considered in the cost-benefit analysis, not their purchase price or their current accounting book value. Other assets may have no remaining value because their costs are *sunk* (barns owned by the farmers who would be driven out of business may have no scrap value) and would, therefore, be ignored in the cost-benefit analysis.

SOCIAL SURPLUS AND ALLOCATIVE EFFICIENCY

The sum of consumer surplus and producer surplus is called *social surplus.* Social surplus is illustrated in Figure 3.5, which depicts both a market demand schedule and a market supply schedule in the same graph. In this graph, which once again is drawn under an assumption of perfect competition, equilibrium occurs at a price of P^* and a quantity of X^*. Social surplus, given this equilibrium, is the large triangular area, *abc,* between the demand and supply schedules. Viewed slightly differently, social surplus can be defined as the difference between the area under the demand schedule (i.e., the gross benefits received by consumers of output X^*) and the area under the supply schedule (the opportunity cost of the resources required to produce X^*) from zero to X^*. If the equilibrium output, X^*, is produced, social surplus—that is, benefits less costs—is maximized.

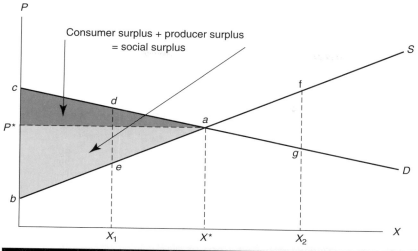

FIGURE 3.5 Social Surplus

To reiterate a point made earlier, under well-functioning, perfectly competitive markets and in the absence of market failures, the market equilibrium maximizes social surplus. In fact, Pareto efficiency will be obtained: It is not possible to make someone better off without making someone else worse off. Indeed, an equilibrium point, such as X^*, is said to be *allocatively efficient* because anything that interferes with the competitive process and causes too few or too many resources to be allocated to the production of a good will reduce social surplus. For example, anything that causes output to be different from this equilibrium level—for instance, to be at either X_1 or X_2—is an *economic distortion* that shrinks the area of social surplus. Therefore, at least some people will be worse off relative to output level X^*.

The losses in social surplus (which at X_1 would equal the triangular area ade and at X_2 would equal the triangular area afg) are deadweight losses, reductions in allocative efficiency. Deadweight losses represent net costs to society because they reduce social surplus. Thus, any government policy that tends to move the market away from the perfectly competitive equilibrium (e.g., imposition of a tax) imposes a social cost by increasing deadweight loss and, thereby, reducing social surplus. And a government policy that moves a distorted market toward the perfectly competitive equilibrium produces a social benefit by reducing deadweight loss and, hence, increasing social surplus.

This simple model of economic welfare can also be used to examine how the social benefits or costs that result from government policies are distributed among different economic groups in society. For example, suppose that the perfectly competitive market shown in Figure 3.6 is initially in equilibrium at a price of P^* and a quantity of X^*. At the point of equilibrium, b, the price paid by consumers equals the marginal cost of producing the good because the supply schedule corresponds to the marginal cost curve. *Allocative efficiency can be obtained only when the price paid by consumers for a good equals the marginal cost to society of producing the good.*[11]

Now assume that a law is passed guaranteeing sellers a price of P_T. Such a policy has been utilized in otherwise competitive agricultural markets in the United States,

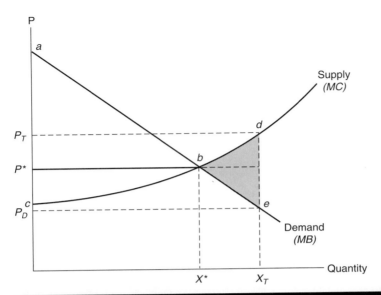

FIGURE 3.6 The Efficiency of Perfect Markets

such as those for corn and cotton, and is known as *target pricing.* At a target price of P_T, sellers desire to sell a quantity of X_T. However, buyers are willing to pay a price of only P_D for this quantity so this becomes the effective market price. Under target pricing, the gap between P_T and P_D is filled by subsidies paid to sellers by the government. As the marginal cost of producing X_T exceeds the willingness of consumers to pay for this quantity of X, a deadweight loss, corresponding to area *bde,* results from the policy. Thus, target pricing with subsidies causes a loss in social surplus by moving the market away from the perfectly competitive equilibrium.

The policy, however, affects buyers, sellers, and taxpayers differently. Because buyers pay a price of only P_D under the policy, total consumer surplus increases from area abP^* to area aeP_D, a gain of P^*beP_D. Sellers receive an effective price of P_T, causing total producer surplus to increase from area P^*bc to area P_Tdc, a gain of P_TdbP^*. Taxpayers, through government-provided subsidies, pay for these benefits to buyers and sellers. The cost of these subsidies to taxpayers is represented by area P_TdeP_D. Note that these subsidies exceed the combined gains of the buyers and sellers by the area *bde,* the deadweight loss resulting from the policy. Although area *bde* represents the net social loss resulting from the policy, the remainder of the subsidies—areas P^*beP_D and P_TdbP^*—represent *transfers* from taxpayers to buyers and to sellers, respectively. Although these transfers are a cost to taxpayers, they are benefits to both buyers and sellers in this market. Because the benefits and costs associated with transfers are fully offsetting, they are typically treated in CBA as having no net impact on society.

The proportion of each dollar given up by one group in society (e.g., taxpayers) that as a result of deadweight loss (or administrative costs) does not accrue as transfers to any other group (e.g., consumers or producers) is sometimes called *leakage.* In the target pricing example illustrated in Figure 3.6 (in which administrative costs are ignored), leakage is bde/P_TdeP_D.

CONCLUSION

This chapter has reviewed some of the major principles from microeconomics that provide the conceptual foundation for cost-benefit analysis. The key concept is that in conducting a CBA one must estimate the changes in social surplus and government revenues that result when new policies, programs, or projects are implemented. The chapter, however, mainly focuses on simple changes in prices and tax rates and on markets that are operating under perfect competition. The direction and size of surplus and revenue changes depend on the specific nature of the policy under consideration and also on the sorts of markets that are affected by the policy. Chapters 4 and 5 make use of the principles reviewed in this chapter to develop measures of benefits and costs that are conceptually appropriate under numerous different circumstances.

Appendix 3A

CONSUMER SURPLUS AND WILLINGNESS-TO-PAY

Earlier in this chapter, we assert that under most circumstances, estimates of changes in consumer surplus, as measured by demand schedules, can be used in CBA as reasonable approximations of individuals' willingness-to-pay to obtain or to avoid the effects of policy changes. In this appendix, we examine the circumstances under which measured changes in consumer surplus do in fact provide a close approximation to willingness-to-pay and the circumstances under which they do not. For purposes of illustration, we specifically focus on the link between the amount a consumer would be willing to pay to avoid a given price increase and estimates based on the demand schedule of the loss in the consumer's surplus resulting from the price increase.

COMPENSATING VARIATION

The maximum amount of money that a consumer would be willing to pay to avoid a price increase is the amount required to return her to the same level of utility she enjoyed prior to the change in price, an amount called *compensating variation*.[1] If the consumer had to spend any more than the value of her compensating variation, then she would be worse off paying to avoid the increase than allowing it to occur. If she could spend any less, then she would be better off paying to avoid the increase rather than allowing it to occur. Hence, for a loss in consumer surplus resulting from a price increase to equal the consumer's willingness-to-pay to avoid the price increase, it has to correspond exactly to the compensating variation value associated with the price increase.

These assertions are most readily demonstrated by an indifference curve analysis. Such an analysis is presented in panel (a) of Figure 3A.1. This diagram represents a consumer who faces a world with only two goods, *X* and *Y*. The straight lines in the

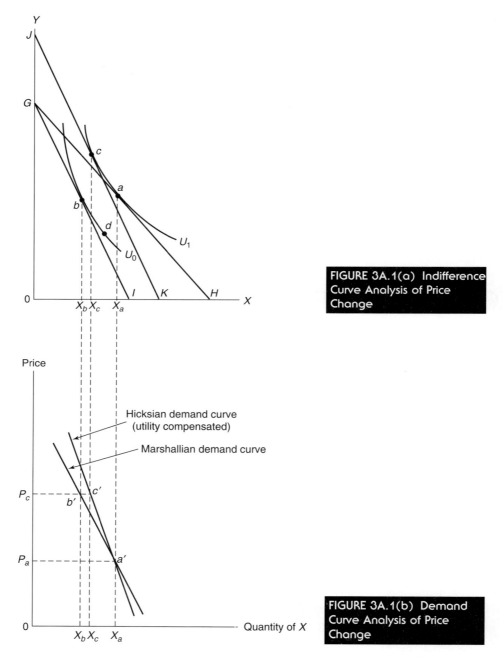

FIGURE 3A.1(a) Indifference Curve Analysis of Price Change

FIGURE 3A.1(b) Demand Curve Analysis of Price Change

diagram are budget constraints. The particular budget constraint that the consumer faces depends on the consumer's income level and on the relative prices of goods X and Y. The greater the consumer's income, the more of X and Y she can afford and, consequently, the greater the distance the budget constraint will be from the origin, O. Thus, for example, the budget constraint JK represents a higher income level than the budget constraint *GI*. The slope of the consumer's budget constraint indicates how many additional units of *Y* can be obtained if one less unit of *X* is purchased. Thus, holding everything else constant, the slope of the budget constraint is negative and depends on the price of *X* relative to the price of *Y*. Consequently, if the price of *X* rises relative to that of *Y*, the consumer's budget constraint will become more steeply sloped, changing, for example, from budget constraint *GH* to budget constraint *GI*. As can be seen, such a change indicates that a larger number of units of *Y* can be purchased in exchange for each unit of *X* that the consumer gives up.

The curved lines in Figure 3A.1(a) are *indifference curves*. All points along a single indifference curve represent combinations of goods *X* and *Y* that provide the consumer with equal levels of utility. Thus, the consumer is indifferent between points *b* and *d* on U_0 or points *a* and *c* on U_1. The further an indifference curve is from the origin, the greater the level of utility. Thus, the consumer would prefer any point on indifference curve U_1 (e.g., point *a*) to any point on indifference curve U_0 (e.g., point *b*). This is not surprising in this case because more of both good *X* and good *Y* would be consumed at point *a* than at point *b*.

The indifference curves in Figure 3A.1(a) are negatively sloped because any movement along an indifference curve definitionally represents a situation whereby an increase in the consumption of one good is offset by a sufficient reduction in the consumption of the other good such that the consumer's level of utility is left unchanged.[2] Were the individual to consume either more of both goods or less of both goods, her level of utility would obviously change. The fact that the indifference curves are convex in shape (i.e., they bend inward toward the origin) reflects *diminishing marginal utility*—as the consumer consumes more of one good, she becomes increasingly less willing to give up consumption of an additional unit of the other good. For example, the convex shape of indifference curve U_0 implies that at point *b* the consumer would be willing to give up more units of *Y* in order to consume one additional unit of *X* than she would at point *d*.

Now let us assume that good *X* in Figure 3A.1(a) is a product on which the consumer spends only a small fraction of her total income—for example, movie tickets—and good *Y* is a composite good on which the consumer spends all the rest of her income. Under these circumstances, good *Y* is a reasonable approximation of the consumer's total money income. Consequently, the slope of a budget constraint in the figure would indicate the price of good *X*—that is, the amount of money income (i.e., good *Y*) the consumer would have to give up to obtain one more unit of *X*.

Assume that the consumer initially faces budget constraint *GH*. She will then choose point *a* on indifference curve U_1. Point *a* represents an equilibrium because the consumer cannot increase her utility by moving to any alternative point and, hence, has no incentive to do so.[3] Now assume that as a result of a government policy, the price of good *X* is doubled.[4] This changes the consumer's equilibrium to point *b* on a more steeply sloped budget constraint, *GI,* and a lower indifference curve, U_0. Thus, the consumer's consumption of good *X* falls from X_a to X_b.[5]

If the consumer were paid a lump sum of money sufficient to compensate her entirely for the price increase in *X*, this would shift the budget constraint in a parallel movement from *GI* to *JK,* allowing her to move back to the original indifference curve, U_1. However, the consumer would now choose point *c* (rather than *a*) and would consume X_c of the good (rather than X_a). As the vertical distance between the two parallel budget constraints (i.e., the difference between points G and J on the vertical axis) represents the amount of good Y—that is, money income—that the consumer would have to be paid in order to lose no utility as a result of the price increase, this distance measures the compensating variation associated with the price increase.

As asserted previously, this compensating variation value is the maximum amount that the consumer would be willing to pay to avoid the price increase. To see this, suppose that the price increase occurs and that the consumer is fully compensated for it. Now imagine that if she is willing to pay all the compensation she received—that is, the full value of her compensating variation—the price increase will be revoked. Will she accept or reject this offer? She will, in fact, be indifferent to it. If she accepts the offer, then she will return to her initial equilibrium at point a on indifference curve U_1; and if she rejects it, then she will remain at point c, which is also on U_1. Thus, the compensation value represents the maximum amount the consumer would be willing to pay to avoid the price increase. If she could pay a bit less to revoke the price increase, then she would definitely do so. If she had to pay a bit more, then she would prefer to accept the increase.

INCOME AND SUBSTITUTION EFFECTS

Given the information contained in Figure 3A.1(a), the total effect of the increase in the price of X on the consumer's demand for good X—that is, the change from X_a to X_b—can be decomposed into two separate effects: a *compensated substitution effect* and an *income effect*.[6] The compensated substitution effect is represented in Figure 3A.1(a) as the change in demand from X_a to X_c. It allows us to examine the effect of a change in the price of X on the demand for X if the individual were exactly compensated for any losses of utility she suffers as a result of the price increase and, as a consequence, remained on indifference curve U_1. The compensated substitution effect always causes the demand for a good to change in the opposite direction from a change in the price of the good. For example, holding the consumer's level of utility constant, an increase in the price of good X causes her to substitute some of the now relatively less expensive good Y for good X. Hence, as shown in the figure, X_c is smaller than X_a.

The income effect is represented in Figure 3A.1(a) as the change in demand from X_c to X_b and results because the increase in the price of good X reduces the consumer's disposable income. If, as the diagram implies, X is a *normal good*—that is, if purchases of the good and disposable income are positively related—the consumer will purchase less of it. Hence, X_b is smaller than X_c. Thus, like the substitution effect, the income effect associated with the price increase will also cause the consumer to reduce her demand for the good.

DEMAND SCHEDULES

Because the slopes of the budget constraints in Figure 3A.1(a) indicate both the old and the new prices of good X and the points tangent to these budget constraints with indifference curves indicate the amount of the good that the consumer wants at each price, the figure provides information about two points along the consumer's demand schedule for X. Indeed, as we know the quantity of output the consumer would demand after the price increase, both if her utility were held constant and if it were not, we can actually determine the location of pairs of points along two different demand schedules. These two pairs of points appear in Figure 3A.1(b) as points a' and c' and as points a' and b', respectively. We can approximate the demand schedules with straight lines by simply drawing straight lines between the two points in each pair.

The line in Figure 3A.1(b) that connects points a' and b' is a conventional demand schedule of the sort usually emphasized in textbooks. This demand schedule, which is known as a *Marshallian demand schedule,* incorporates both the substitution and income effects associated with changes in the price of good X. Statistical efforts by economists to estimate relations between the price of a good and quantities purchased, holding income, other prices, and other factors constant, are attempts to estimate Marshallian demand schedules empirically.

The demand schedule in Figure 3A.1(b) that connects points a' and c' keeps utility constant as the price of good X changes and, thus, incorporates only the compensated substitution effect associated with price changes. This demand schedule is sometimes called the *utility-compensated* or the *Hicksian demand schedule.* Because Hicksian demand schedules are unaffected by income effects, they are usually, as is the case in Figure 3A.1(b), more steeply sloped than Marshallian demand schedules. Because of the difficulty of holding utility constant, unlike Marshallian demand schedules, Hicksian demand schedules cannot usually be directly estimated using statistical techniques.

EQUIVALENCE OF CONSUMER SURPLUS AND COMPENSATING VARIATION

Movements up the Hicksian demand schedule, say, from P_a to P_c, are equivalent to allowing the price to increase while compensating the consumer with a lump-sum payment of just sufficient size to permit her to remain on her original indifference curve. This lump-sum payment can be measured graphically as either the vertical distance between the two parallel budget constraints in Figure 3A.1(a) (i.e., as the difference between money income at points G and J) or as the change in consumer surplus indicated by the Hicksian demand schedule in Figure 3A.1(b) (the area $P_a a' c' P_c$). Thus, the change in consumer surplus resulting from a price change measured with a Hicksian demand schedule exactly equals the consumer's compensating variation—that is, the maximum amount the consumer would be willing to pay to avoid the price increase.

Hence, it is Hicksian demand schedules that permit measurement of the compensating variation associated with price changes. However, as pointed out earlier, it is Marshallian schedules that are more often available for use in actually conducting CBA. To the extent these two demand schedules differ, using a Marshallian demand schedule to measure consumer surplus will result in a biased estimate of compensating variation and, therefore, of willingness-to-pay. As can be seen from Figure 3A.1(b), the two alternative demand schedules do produce different measures of consumer surplus, one that differs by the triangular area $a'b'c'$. For a price increase, the change in consumer surplus is smaller if measured with the Marshallian demand schedule than with a Hicksian demand schedule; for a price reduction, it is larger.

As previously suggested, the difference between the two types of demand schedules is that the Marshallian schedule incorporates the income effects associated with price changes, as well as the substitution effects, whereas the Hicksian schedule incorporates only the latter. Thus, the biased estimate of willingness-to-pay that results from using Marshallian rather than Hicksian demand schedules to measure consumer surplus depends on the size of the income effect associated with a price change. *Usually this income effect and, hence, the bias are small and can be safely ignored in CBA.*[7] This, at least, is the case if the price change is moderate and the good in question accounts for a fairly small part of total consumption. Thus, CBAs of government policies that affect corn, cotton, tobacco, and gasoline prices will generally be little affected by use of Marshallian rather than Hicksian demand schedules. However, *the bias could be of some importance for a CBA of a government policy that would result in large price changes in such consumption goods as housing or automobiles or in big changes in wage rates.*[8] Consequently, except for a few instances when it clearly seems inappropriate to do so, throughout the rest of this book, we shall assume that the income effects associated with various policy changes are sufficiently small that consumer surpluses that are measured by using Marshallian demand schedules provide reasonable approximations of willingness-to-pay.

Exercises for Chapter 3

1. A person's demand for gizmos is given by the following equation:

$$q = 6 - 0.5p + 0.0001I$$

where q is the quantity demanded at price p when the person's income is I. Assume initially that the person's income is $40,000.
   a. At what price will demand fall to zero? (This is sometimes called the choke price because it is the price that chokes off demand.)
   b. If the market price for gizmos is $10, how many will be demanded?
   c. At a price of $10, what is the price elasticity of demand for gizmos?
   d. At a price of $10, what is the consumer surplus?
   e. If price rises to $12, how much consumer surplus is lost?
   f. If income were $60,000, what would be the consumer surplus loss from a price rise from $10 to $12?

2. At the current market equilibrium, the price of a good equals $30 and the quantity equals 10 units. At this equilibrium, the price elasticity of supply is 1.5. Assume that the supply schedule is linear.
   a. Use the price elasticity and market equilibrium to find the supply schedule. (Hint: the supply schedule has the following form: $q = a + (\Delta q / \Delta p)p$. First, find the value of $\Delta q / \Delta p$, and then find the value of a.)
   b. Calculate the producer surplus in the market.
   c. Imagine that a policy results in price falling from $30 to $20. By how much does producer surplus fall?
   d. What fraction of the lost producer surplus is due to the reduction in the quantity supplied and what fraction is due to the fall in price received per unit sold?

Notes

1. Note that viewed in this fashion the relation depicted in Figure 3.1 is called an *inverse demand curve*; that is, price is viewed as a function of quantity, rather than the other way around, as is more ordinarily the case. One can envision deriving an inverse demand curve through an auction in which bids are taken on the first unit of a good offered for sale, then on the second unit, then on the third unit, and so forth, with successively lower bids obtained for each additional unit of the good that is offered. This kind of auction is called a Dutch auction. Apparently, in years past, it was common in Holland to have a mechanical "clock" with hands that started at the bid made on the previous unit and swept through successively lower bids until stopped by an individual who wished to make a bid.

2. This is an approximation. More accurately, $\varepsilon_d = (dX/dP)(P^*/X^*) < 0$. If the absolute value of ε_d is greater than one and, hence, the percentage change in quantity demanded is greater than the percentage change in price, then demand is said to be *relatively elastic*. On the other hand, if the absolute value of ε_d is less than one and, hence, the percentage change in quantity demanded is smaller than the percentage change in price, then demand is said to be relatively inelastic. If the value approaches infinity (i.e., the demand schedule is horizontal), then demand is said to be *perfectly elastic*, whereas if the value is zero (the demand schedule is vertical), then demand is said to be *completely inelastic*.

3. The use of elasticity estimates in conducting CBAs is further described in Chapter 12.

4. The government is not, of course, the ultimate beneficiary of the tax revenues. This depends on the projects and programs that are funded by the tax revenues.

5. Deadweight loss (*DWL*) may be defined more formally in terms of Figures 3.2(a) and (b) as follows:

$$DWL = \int_{x^*}^{x_1} (MSB - MSC)\,dx, \qquad \text{if } x^* < x_1$$

$$DWL = \int_{x_2}^{x^*} (MSB - MSC)\,dx, \qquad \text{if } x_2 < x^*$$

where *MSB* is marginal social benefits and *MSC* is marginal social costs.

When the elasticity of demand (ε_d) is known, the change in deadweight loss resulting from a price change—for example, one imposed by a tax—can be computed by using the formula:

$$\Delta DWL = -\tfrac{1}{2}[P^*X^*(\Delta P/P^*)^2 \varepsilon_d]$$

Notice that this formula is similar to equation (3.3).

6. Over longer periods of time, fewer factors of production are fixed so that supply schedules tend to be flatter.

7. In the absence of perfect competition (e.g., in the case of monopoly), the upward-sloping segment of a firm's marginal cost curve is not its supply schedule. This point is further discussed in Chapter 4.

8. By normal return, we simply mean the market price or rate of return that each unit of a resource commands under perfect competition.

9. Thus, because we are presently assuming the existence of perfect competition and well-functioning markets, social opportunity costs, as we have defined them, correspond to private economic costs. In the absence of perfect competition (or if externalities exist), private economic costs may differ from the costs that using resources imposes on society. These latter costs, *social opportunity costs*, are the relevant cost measure for purposes of CBA. The use of shadow pricing to obtain appropriate measures of social opportunity costs when markets are distorted is discussed in Chapter 4.

10. The longer the time period being considered in cost-benefit analysis, the flatter the market supply schedule (i.e., more elastic) is likely to be, both because more of the factors of production are free to vary and because firms can enter and exit from the market. Consequently, the larger will be the impacts of price increases on producer surplus and the smaller will be the impacts of price decreases.

11. In this discussion, we are assuming perfect competition and, hence, that marginal private costs equal marginal social costs. In Chapter 4, we consider situations in which marginal private costs do not equal marginal social costs—for example, when externalities exist.

Appendix Notes

1. An alternative to compensating variation as the money metric for measuring welfare changes is equivalent variation, the amount of money that if paid by the consumer would cause her to lose just as much utility as the price increase. The major points made in this appendix are valid for either measure. We focus on compensating variation because it has a somewhat more natural interpretation than equivalent variation. George W. McKenzie argues, however, that only equivalent variation satisfies all the desirable properties of a money metric for social welfare. See George W. McKenzie, *Measuring Economic Welfare: New Methods* (New York: Cambridge University Press, 1983).

   Although compensating variation and equivalent variation are appropriate measures of the welfare changes resulting from price increases or decreases, it has been argued that either compensating surplus or equivalent surplus is more appropriately used when the quantity of a good, rather than its price, increases or decreases. In this appendix, we focus on price rather than quantity changes. For a discussion of when each of the four welfare change measures are most appropriately used, as well as a useful graphical presentation of each, see V. Kerry Smith and William H. Desvousges, *Measuring Water Quality Benefits* (Boston: Kluwer-Nijhoff Publishing, 1986), Chapter 2.

2. The slope of an indifference curve is called the marginal rate of substitution, where the marginal rate of substitution $= \frac{\partial Y}{\partial X}\big|_{U} < 0$ and $\overline{U}$ indicates that utility is being held constant.

3. At equilibrium, the marginal rate of substitution will equal the ratio of the price of good X to the price of good Y.

4. Thus, in Figure 3A.1(a), $0I = \frac{1}{2}OH$.

5. Depending on the slopes of the indifference curves, the consumption of good Y could either increase or decrease. As shown in Figure 3A.1(a), it slightly decreases in this particular example.

6. In calculus notation, this decomposition can be represented as follows:

$$\frac{dX}{dP} = \frac{dX}{dP}\bigg|_{\overline{U}} - X\frac{dX}{dY}\bigg|_{\overline{P}}$$

   This equation is known as the *Slutsky equation*. The first term to the right of the equal sign is the substitution effect, where utility is held constant. The second term is the income effect, where prices are held constant and X is the amount of the good consumed prior to the price change.

7. For analyses of the size of the bias, see Ian J. Irvine and William A. Sims, "Measuring Consumer Surplus with Unknown Hicksian Demands," *The American Economic Review*, 88, no. 1 (1998), 314–322; Robin W. Boadway and Neil Bruce, *Welfare Economics* (Oxford, United Kingdom: Basil Blackwell Ltd., 1984), pp. 216–219; Julian M. Alston and Douglas M. Larson, "Hicksian vs. Marshallian Welfare Measures: Why Do We Do What We Do?" *American Journal of Agricultural Economics*, 75 (1993), 764–769; and Robert D. Willig, "Consumer's Surplus Without Apology," *American Economic Review*, 66, no. 4 (1976), 589–597.

8. In situations in which the bias should not be ignored, it is often possible to use estimates of Marshallian demand schedules to obtain close approximations of the Hicksian measure of consumer surplus. Doing this first requires obtaining estimates of the relation between quantity purchased and prices and the relation between quantity purchased and income and then (as implied by footnote 6) using the Slutsky equation to derive the income-compensated (rather than the utility-compensated) relation between prices and quantity purchased. A fairly simple procedure for using the Slutsky equation to approximate the Hicksian measure of consumer surplus is described by Irvine and Sims ("Measuring Consumer Surplus . . . "). In practice, however, it is not always feasible to estimate the relation between quantity purchased and income and, hence, to use the Slutsky equation.

CHAPTER

4

VALUING BENEFITS AND COSTS IN PRIMARY MARKETS

A cost-benefit analysis of a government policy sums all the benefits resulting from the policy and subtracts all the associated costs. Doing this requires that the values of all these benefits and costs are measured in monetary terms. Although in practice, as suggested in Chapter 1, this is often difficult to accomplish, in principle, it would be relatively straightforward if all the changes in consumer and producer surplus resulting from a government policy, as well as the policy's effects on government revenues, could be determined. Under most circumstances, as indicated in Chapter 3, it is changes in these values that provide conceptually correct measures of the monetary value of a government policy's benefits and costs. Because these values are in monetary terms, they can be summed. Specifically, the net social benefits (*NSB*) from a government policy equal:

$$NSB = \Delta CS + \Delta PS + \Delta GR$$

where ΔCS, ΔPS, and ΔGR are the total changes in consumer surplus, producer surplus, and (net) government revenues, respectively, resulting from the policy. Because each of these components can be either positive or negative, *NSB* itself can be either positive or negative.

This chapter and the next illustrate how ΔCS, ΔPS, and ΔGR could be readily estimated if all the pertinent market demand and supply schedules were known. The current chapter focuses on demand and supply schedules in *primary markets,* whereas the following chapter examines demand and supply schedules in *secondary markets.* Primary markets refer to markets that are directly affected by a policy or project; for example, if a city builds a new subway system, the primary markets are the market for public transportation and the market for materials used to build the subway. Secondary markets are markets that are indirectly affected—for example, the market for gasoline if more commuters use the new subway and fewer use automobiles.

This chapter begins with a brief discussion of why actual studies often fail to use conceptually correct measures of benefits and costs and what the implications are of this. We then examine how the effects of government policies in primary markets can be valued. In doing this, we emphasize the concept of willingness-to-pay and, thus, demand schedules and consumer surplus. We next describe the valuation of resources purchased in primary markets as inputs for government projects, stressing the concept of opportunity costs and, hence, the use of supply schedules and producer surplus. Following this, we discuss costs that result from the need to raise tax revenues to pay for government projects.

This chapter also provides brief explanations of common types of market failures including monopoly, externalities, information asymmetries, and public goods. The reason for discussing market failures is that their presence provides the prima facie rationale for most, although not all, proposed government interventions that are assessed through CBA. If markets worked perfectly, then Pareto efficiency would be obtained without government intervention: A set of prices would arise that distributes resources to firms and goods to individuals in such a way that it would not be possible to find a reallocation that would make at least one person better off without also making at least one other person worse off. Indeed, doing so could not pass a cost-benefit test. It is only when markets fail that there are grounds for government interventions. However, no more than a prima facie case exists. It is up to CBA to demonstrate that a specific intervention is worthwhile. CBA may also be needed to assess already existing government policies. In this case, the analyst is essentially attempting to determine whether the current policy is inefficient and, therefore, exhibits "government failure."[1] These two rationales for CBA, market failure and government failure, are summarized in Figure 4.1.

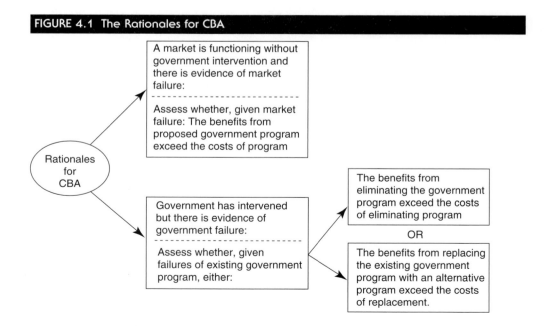

FIGURE 4.1 The Rationales for CBA

Rationales for CBA

A market is functioning without government intervention and there is evidence of market failure:
- -
Assess whether, given market failure: The benefits from proposed government program exceed the costs of program

Government has intervened but there is evidence of government failure:
- -
Assess whether, given failures of existing government program, either:

The benefits from eliminating the government program exceed the costs of eliminating program

OR

The benefits from replacing the existing government program with an alternative program exceed the costs of replacement.

ACTUALLY USED VERSUS CONCEPTUALLY CORRECT MEASURES OF BENEFITS AND COSTS

In most CBAs, the measures of benefits and costs actually used differ from the conceptually correct measures to some extent. One purpose of examining the conceptually correct measures of the benefits and costs of a government policy is so they can serve as a benchmark against which the measures used in actual CBAs can be compared. So that we can focus on this objective in this and the next chapter, we ignore the problems inherent in actually deriving demand and supply schedules needed to measure benefits and costs, an issue we take up in detail in Part III. Instead, we focus on how the conceptually correct measures of benefits and costs would be obtained if the necessary schedules were known.

Before turning to the conceptually correct measures, it is helpful to examine briefly why they often differ from the measures used in actual CBAs. A fundamental reason is that it is often convenient to use observed prices in valuing benefits and costs. However, as illustrated later in this chapter, whenever a government policy involves the production of a public good, or an externality or monopoly power is present, market prices may not provide good indicators of the social value of benefits and costs. There are other situations in which a market price does not even exist. To mention just one example: Persons entering parks in the U.S. National Park system pay a fee, but this fee is set by the Park Service, not by the market. Consequently, it is unlikely that it bears a very strong relation to the value of the benefits visitors actually receive from visiting the parks. Thus, a continuum exists. At one end of this continuum are values that can be measured in terms of prices that are set in well-functioning, competitive markets. At the other end is the complete absence of markets that can be used to value benefits and costs resulting from a government policy.

When observed prices fail to reflect the social value of a good accurately or observed prices do not exist, an approach called *shadow pricing* is often used to measure benefits and costs. That is, analysts adjust observed prices or assign values when appropriate observed prices do not exist. They attempt to come as close as possible to measuring the value that those receiving benefits from a government project place on them or the lost value to those who incur costs. For example, prices charged by paper factories may understate the true social cost of paper if the production process generates pollution. Given such circumstances, an analyst conducting a CBA may adjust the market price upward to account for the negative externality resulting from the pollution. Another important example of shadow pricing is the considerable effort that economists have put into attempting to place an appropriate value or price on human life. Similarly, economists have also put much effort into trying to determine the social value of recreational areas such as public parks.

We indicate numerous other situations in this chapter when shadow pricing is required and at several junctures suggest approaches that can be taken toward obtaining shadow prices. In Chapters 13–15, we describe additional techniques that are used to obtain shadow prices for purposes of CBA.

Although numerous shadow pricing techniques exist, it is still frequently the case that the measures of benefits and costs used in actual studies differ from their conceptually correct counterparts. There are several reasons for this:

1. As discussed in Chapter 19, errors are sometimes made in CBA. In some instances, for example, the distinction between the measure being used and the conceptually correct measure is sufficiently subtle that it is inadvertently overlooked. In such instances, those conducting the study may be unaware that their results are incorrect and do not even attempt to utilize appropriate shadow pricing techniques.

2. It is often difficult to derive an appropriate shadow price. In some studies, consequently, the difference between the actual and the correct measure may be potentially serious, but it is technically infeasible or beyond the time and resources available to those conducting the study to do much about it. In the most extreme instances, even determining the conceptually correct measures of value is so complex and daunting as to put it beyond the grasp of analysts. But even when shadow prices are used, the resulting measures of benefits and costs may still vary from their conceptually correct counterparts. When this is the case, it is at least incumbent upon those conducting the study to point out why and how the study results may be biased.

3. There may be reason to think that differences between the actual and the correct measures are sufficiently minor that the study results are not very much affected. In such instances, shadow pricing may not be necessary.

VALUING OUTCOMES: WILLINGNESS-TO-PAY

The valuation of policy outcomes should be based on the concept of willingness-to-pay: *Benefits are the sums of the maximum amounts that people would be willing to pay to gain outcomes that they view as desirable; costs are the sums of the maximum amounts that people would be willing to pay to avoid outcomes that they view as undesirable.*[2] Estimating changes in social surpluses that occur in relevant markets enables us to take account of these costs and benefits. In the discussion that follows, we distinguish between changes in surplus that take place in efficient markets and those that occur in inefficient or distorted markets where market or government failures are found. This discussion also focuses on *gross benefits,* rather than *net benefits,* because it usually ignores the inputs the government must purchase to carry out policies. Measurement of the social cost of these resources is discussed in the following section. Net benefits would be obtained by subtracting these costs from gross benefits.

Valuing Benefits in Efficient Markets

Valuation of gross benefits is relatively straightforward when a policy affects the supply schedules of goods in efficient markets. Under these circumstances, the rule is that *the gross social benefits of a policy equal the net revenue generated by the policy plus the resulting change in social surplus.* We examine two common situations in which this rule is applicable. First, we consider policies that directly affect the quantity of a good available to consumers. For example, a publicly operated day care center shifts the supply schedule to the right, as it results in more day care being offered to consumers at each price. This often (but not always) reduces prices, resulting in direct reductions in costs to consumers. Second, we consider policies that shift the supply schedule down by altering the price or availability of some input used to produce the good. For example, deepening a harbor so that it accommodates larger, more efficient ships, reducing the cost of transporting bulk commodities to and from the port for shipping companies. Here, there are direct reductions in costs to producers.

Direct Reductions in Costs to Consumers   Figure 4.2 shows the gross benefits that result when a project directly increases the available supply of a good in a well-functioning market, but the increase is so small that the price of the good is unaffected. If the government sells the additional units of the good at the market price, it may be treated like other competitors in an efficient market. Hence, as shown in the figure, it faces a horizontal demand schedule, D, for the good at the market price, P_0. If the project directly adds a quantity, q', to the market, then the supply schedule as seen by consumers shifts from S to $S + q'$.[3] Because the demand schedule is horizontal, the price of the good and, hence, social surplus are unaffected by the shift in the supply schedule. However, if consumers purchase the additional units of the good, the government receives revenue equal to P_0 times q', the area of rectangle $q_0 abq_1$. The rectangle $q_0 abq_1$ also, of course, represents a cost to those consumers who purchase the good. This "cost," however, is exactly

FIGURE 4.2 Measuring Benefits in an Efficient Market with No Price Effects

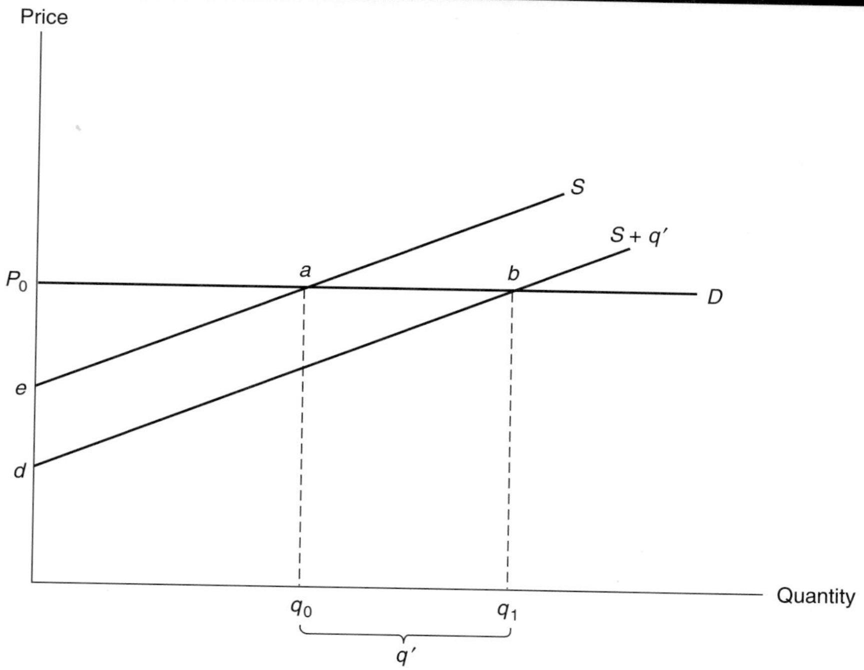

Social surplus change:

(a) Direct supply of q' by project: gain of project revenue equal to area of rectangle $q_0 abq_1$
(b) Supply schedule shift through cost reduction: gain of trapezoid $abde$

offset by benefits that these persons enjoy in consuming the good and, consequently, can be ignored in our analysis. Therefore, the revenues received by the government are the only gross benefits that accrue from the project selling q' units in the market. The project does not provide net benefits to consumers.

If the government adds a sufficiently large quantity of a good to a market to reduce the price of the good, however, then it will benefit consumers because they can now pay less. Figure 4.3 illustrates this possibility by showing the demand schedule, D, as downward sloping. The intersection of the demand schedule and the supply schedule, S, indicates the equilibrium price, P_0, prior to the project. The equilibrium price of the good falls to P_1 after the government enters the market by providing the q' units of the good. This time, because of the reduction in costs to consumers, there is a change in social surplus. If consumers pay for the additional units of the good from the project at the new market price, then the gain in consumer surplus corresponds to the area of trapezoid P_0abP_1. Because private-sector suppliers continue to operate on the original supply schedule, S, they suffer a loss of producer surplus equal to the area of trapezoid P_0acP_1. Thus, the net gain in social surplus equals the area of triangle *abc*, which is lightly shaded. In addition, the government receives revenues from the project equal to the area of rectangle q_2cbq_1. The sum of project revenues and the gain in social surplus in the market equals area q_2cabq_1, which is the total gross benefits from the project selling q' units in the market.

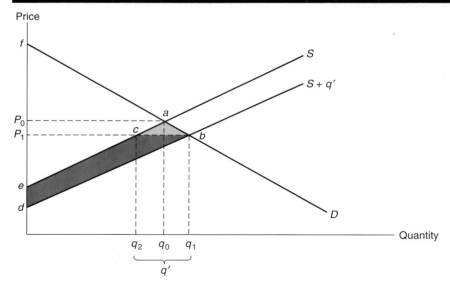

FIGURE 4.3 Measuring Benefits in an Efficient Market

Social surplus change:

(a) Direct supply of q' by project: gain of triangle *abc*
   plus project revenue equal to area of rectangle q_2cbq_1
(b) Supply schedule shift through cost reduction: gain
   of trapezoid *abde*

What benefits would accrue if q' units of the good were instead distributed free to selected consumers? If the price of the good does not change, as in the situation depicted in Figure 4.2, the answer is straightforward: As a result of receiving q' units of the good free, consumers gain surplus equal to the area of rectangle q_0abq_1, an area that exactly corresponds to the revenues that would have accrued had the project's output been sold.

The answer is more complex if the q' units of the good are distributed free, but the increase in supply causes its price to fall. This situation is shown in Figure 4.3. Under these circumstances, if the q' units are given only to those consumers who would have valued these units at P_1 or higher, then the project's gross benefit measure is again exactly the same as it would have been had the output been sold. As before, the reduction in price from P_0 to P_1 results in an increase in social surplus equal to area abc. With free distribution, however, no revenue accrues to the project. Instead, as a result of receiving q' units of the good free, consumers enjoy an additional surplus equal to the area of rectangle q_2cbq_1. Thus, total gross benefits from the project once again equal the area of q_2cabq_1.

It is more likely, however, that if q' units of the good are distributed for free, some would go to consumers who are located below point b on the market demand schedule shown in Figure 4.3. In other words, some units would be distributed to some consumers in greater quantities than they would have purchased at price P_1. If these consumers keep the excess units, then area q_2cabq_1 overestimates the project's benefit because these persons value their marginal consumption of these units at less than P_1. Area q_2cabq_1 approximates project benefits, however, if recipients of the excess units sell them to others who would have been willing to buy them at a price of P_1 (provided the transaction costs associated with the sale of the excess units are zero).

Suppose, for example, that a project provides previously stockpiled gasoline free to low-income consumers during an oil supply disruption (an in-kind subsidy). Some low-income households will find themselves with more gasoline than they would have purchased on their own at price P_1; therefore, they will try to sell the excess. Doing so will be relatively easy if access to the stockpiled gasoline is provided through legally transferable coupons; it would obviously be more difficult if the gasoline had to be physically taken away by the low-income households. If the gasoline coupons could be costlessly traded among consumers, then we would expect the outcome to be identical to one in which the gasoline is sold in the market and the revenue given directly to low-income consumers.

Reductions in Costs to Producers   We now turn to a different type of public-sector project: those, such as harbor deepening, that lower the private sector's cost of supplying a market. Figure 4.3 can again be used to analyze this situation. In this case, however, the supply schedule shifts to $S + q'$, not because the project directly supplies q' to the market but rather because reductions in their marginal costs allow private-sector firms to offer q' additional units profitably at each price.[4] As in the case of direct supply of q', the new equilibrium price is P_1. Thus, the gain in consumer surplus corresponds to the area of trapezoid P_0abP_1. The change in producer surplus corresponds to the difference in the areas of triangle P_0ae (the producer surplus with supply schedule S) and triangle P_1bd (the producer surplus with supply schedule $S + q'$). Area P_1ce is common to the two triangles and, therefore, cancels. Hence, producers enjoy a net gain in surplus equal to area $ecbd$ minus area P_0acP_1. Adding this gain to the gain in consumer surplus, area P_0abP_1, means that the gain in social surplus resulting from the project equals the area of trapezoid $abde$. (That is, area $ecbd$ + area P_0abP_1 − area P_0acP_1 = area $ecbd$ + area abc = area $abde$.[5]) Because no project revenue is generated, area $abde$ alone is the gross benefit of the project. Notice that because we once again ignore expenditures the government incurs in purchasing inputs needed to undertake the project, we are again measuring gross benefits rather than net benefits.

Valuing Benefits in Distorted Markets

If market or government failures distort the relevant product market, then project benefits should continue to be measured as changes in social surplus resulting from the project plus net revenues generated by the project. However, complications arise in determining the correct social surplus changes. We illustrate these complications by examining four different types of market failures: monopoly (including natural monopoly), information asymmetry, externalities, and public goods. We do not attempt to provide a comprehensive discussion of market failures in this chapter, just an overview. For a comprehensive discussion, we recommend a book by David Weimer and Aidan Vining.[6]

Monopoly   It is useful to examine monopoly first because it is an excellent example of a topic discussed in Chapter 3: a deviation from the competitive equilibrium that results in a deadweight loss and, hence, reduces social surplus.[7] One key to understanding monopoly is to recognize that because, by definition, a monopolist is the only firm in its market, it views the market demand curve as the demand schedule for its output. Because market demand schedules slope downward, if the monopolist sells all its output at the same price, then it can sell an additional unit of output only by reducing the price on every unit it sells. Consequently, the monopolist's marginal revenue—the additional revenue it receives for each additional unit of output it sells—is less than the selling price of that output. For example, if a monopolist could sell four units of output at a price of $10 but must reduce its price to $9 in order to sell five units, its revenue would increase from $40 to $45 as a result of selling the fifth unit. Therefore, the $5 in marginal revenue it receives from the fifth unit is less than the $9 selling price of the unit.

Thus, as shown in Figure 4.4, the monopolist's marginal revenue curve is located below its demand schedule.[8] Given this situation, the monopolist would maximize profit by producing at Q_m, where its marginal cost equals its marginal revenue.[9] At this output level, the price it can charge, P_m, is determined by the demand schedule it faces.

As in the competitive case, the social surplus generated by the output produced and sold by the monopolist is represented graphically by the area between the demand schedule and the marginal cost curve that is to the left of the intersection of the marginal revenue and marginal cost curves. The social surplus above the price line (i.e., the consumer surplus) is captured by buyers. And that below the price line (the producer surplus) is captured by the monopolist.

Although the term *monopolist* is sometimes used pejoratively, in a CBA any increase in producer surplus received by a monopolist that results from a government policy is counted as a benefit of the policy. The rationale is that owners of monopolies, like consumers and the owners of competitive firms, are part of society; therefore, benefits accruing to them "count."[10]

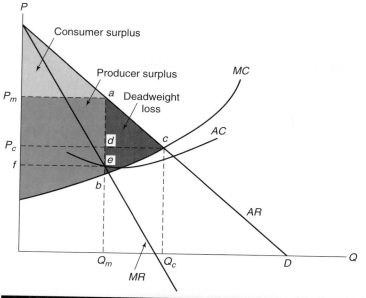

FIGURE 4.4 Monopoly

Notice that, unlike the perfectly competitive case, social surplus is not maximized if the monopolist is left to its own devices. This is because the monopolist does not produce at the "competitive level," Q_c, where the marginal cost curve intersects the demand schedule, and does not charge the competitive price, P_c. This lost social surplus, which is represented in Figure 4.4 by the triangular area *abc,* is the deadweight loss that results from monopolistic behavior. Were it possible for the government to break the monopoly represented in Figure 4.4 into a large number of competing firms so that a competitive outcome resulted,[11] two things would happen: First, the deadweight loss would disappear and social surplus would increase by the area *abc.* In CBA, this is counted as a benefit of the government's actions. Second, because the competitive price, P_c, is less than the monopolistic price, P_m, consumers would capture that part of the monopolist's producer surplus that is represented by the rectangular area $P_m a d P_c$. In CBA, this is viewed as a transfer.

Natural Monopoly   So far, we have been focusing on a general form of monopoly. We now turn to a specific type of monopoly: *natural monopoly.* The essential characteristic of a natural monopoly is that its fixed costs are very large relative to its variable costs; public utilities, roads, and bridges all provide good examples. As shown in Figure 4.5, these large fixed costs cause average costs to be very large at low levels of output and, as the fixed component of costs becomes spread over increasing units of output, they continue to fall over a large range of output. This, in turn, means that over this wide range of output, average costs will exceed marginal costs. Indeed, in Figure 4.5, average costs exceed marginal costs over what we shall term the *relevant range of output,* which is the range between the first unit of output and the amount consumers would demand at a zero price, Q_0.

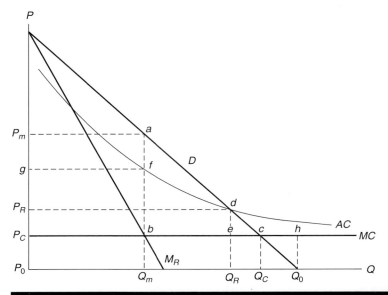

FIGURE 4.5 Natural Monopoly

In principle, marginal costs could be rising or falling over the relevant output range, but for the sake of simplicity, we have drawn the marginal cost curve as horizontal. The important point is that the marginal cost curve is below the average cost curve over the relevant range of output, so that it pulls average cost down as output increases. Hence, average costs continue to fall over the relevant range of output. As a result, one firm, a natural monopoly, can provide a given amount of output at a lower average cost than could two or more firms.

Given these circumstances, it is reasonable for the government to permit a monopoly to exist. But if it does, it must decide on whether or not to regulate the monopoly, and if it does regulate it, what sort of policies to invoke. To make our discussion of these policies as concrete as possible, we will assume that the natural monopoly represented in Figure 4.5 is a road and that output is the number of cars that travel the road. Although most roads are built under government contract and operated by the government, they could instead be built and operated by private-sector firms under various regulatory frameworks. In fact, several privately owned roads, including one to Dulles Airport near Washington, D.C., have been built in recent years.

There are at least four policies the government could follow. The first is simply to allow the road operating authority, whether a private-sector firm or a government agency, to maximize profits. As discussed previously, profits are maximized at output Q_m, where marginal cost equals marginal revenue. The road operating authority could obtain this output level by charging a toll (i.e., a price) of P_m. However, under this policy, output is restricted below the competitive level of Q_c, and willingness-to-pay (WTP), P_m, exceeds marginal costs, P_c. This results in a deadweight loss equal to area *abc*. The policy is also unattractive politically because it typically permits substantial monopoly profits. These profits would correspond to area $P_m afg$.

An alternative policy that is often used in regulating natural monopolies is to require the road operating authority to set its price at P_R, where the average cost curve crosses the demand schedule. This policy eliminates monopoly profits by transferring social surplus from the road operating authority to persons using the road. It also expands output, increasing social surplus and reducing deadweight loss from area *abc* to area *dec*. Thus, as compared to allowing the road operating authority to maximize profits, society receives a benefit from the policy that corresponds to area *adeb*. But deadweight loss is not completely eliminated. In other words, society could potentially benefit still further if output could be expanded somewhat more.

The third policy alternative does this by requiring the road operating authority to set its price at P_C, where the marginal cost curve intersects the demand schedule—in other words, by requiring competitive market pricing. This completely eliminates the deadweight loss, thereby maximizing net social benefits. But there is a problem with this policy: Price is below average costs; hence, revenues no longer cover costs. As a result, tax money must be used to subsidize the construction and operation of the road.

Yet another policy is the one most often used in the case of roads: to allow free access. In other words, to charge a zero price. In this case, output would expand to Q_0, the point at which the demand schedule intersects the horizontal axis. The problem with this policy is that output expands to a level at which marginal costs exceed WTP. This results in a deadweight loss equal to the triangular area chQ_0, a social cost of making the road free. Moreover, because no tolls are collected directly from road users, the entire construction and operating costs of the road must be paid through government subsidies obtained from taxes.

Information Asymmetry   The term *information asymmetry* implies that information about a product or a job may not be equal on both sides of a market. For example, sellers may have more information concerning how well made or safe a product is than buyers, doctors may know more about needed care than patients, or employers may know more about job-related health risks than their workers.

The implications of information asymmetry are easy to show in a diagram. To do this, we focus on the case in which sellers of a product have more information than buyers. Such a situation is represented by the two demand schedules that appear in Figure 4.6. One of these schedules, D_i, represents how much of the product buyers would desire if they had full information concerning it, whereas the other demand schedule, D_u, indicates how much they actually desire, given their lack of full information.[12] In other words, the two demand schedules represent, respectively, WTP with and without full information concerning the product. They indicate that if buyers had full information, their WTP would diminish.[13]

Figure 4.6 shows that there are two effects of information asymmetry. First, by raising the price and the amount of the good purchased, information asymmetry increases producer surplus and reduces consumer surplus, resulting in a transfer from consumers to sellers. This transfer is shown in Figure 4.6 by the trapezoidal area P_uacP_i. Second, by increasing the amount of the good sold relative to the full information case, information asymmetry results in deadweight loss, which is shown in the figure as the triangular area *abc*.

These two effects, especially the second one, suggest a rationale for the government to intervene by providing the missing information. If the government does this

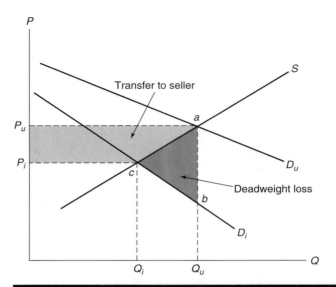

FIGURE 4.6 Information Asymmetry

effectively, society will benefit because deadweight loss is reduced. In addition, there will be a transfer of surplus (back) from sellers to buyers. However, there are also costs associated with the government obtaining and disseminating information. These costs may be sizable even though they do not explicitly appear in the diagram.[14] Hence, for a government information program to have positive net benefits, and not just positive gross benefits, the deadweight loss associated with the lack of information in the absence of government intervention usually must be substantial.

It is useful to discuss the circumstances under which information asymmetry is sufficiently important that the benefits from government intervention are likely to exceed the costs. This largely depends on two factors: first, the ease with which consumers can obtain the information for themselves; and second, whether third parties that could provide the missing information are likely to arise through market forces. To discuss these factors, it is helpful to distinguish among three types of products: (1) search goods, (2) experience goods, and (3) postexperience goods.[15]

Search goods are products with characteristics that consumers can learn about by examining them prior to purchasing them. For example, a student who needs a notebook for a class can go to the bookstore and easily learn pretty much everything he or she wants to know about the characteristics of alternative notebooks. Under such circumstances, information asymmetry is unlikely to be a serious problem.

Experience goods are products about which consumers can obtain full knowledge but only after purchasing and experiencing them. Good examples are tickets to a movie, a meal at a new restaurant, a new television set, and a house. At least to a degree, information asymmetry concerning many such products takes care of itself. For example, once consumers have been to a restaurant, they acquire some information concerning the expected quality of the meal should they eat there again. Warranties, which are typically provided for televisions and many other major consumer durables, serve a similar purpose. In addition, market demand for information about experience goods often prompts third parties to provide information for a fee. This reduces information asymmetry. For example, newspaper reviews provide information about movies and restaurants; in the United States, *Consumer Reports* provides information about many goods; and inspection services examine houses for prospective buyers.

In the case of *postexperience goods,* consumption does not necessarily reveal information to consumers. Government intervention to reduce information asymmetry associated with postexperience goods is most likely to be efficiency enhancing because learning through individual action does not always occur. Examples of this situation include adverse health effects associated with a prescription drug and a new automobile with a defective part. Employee exposure to an unhealthy chemical at work is similar. In these cases, information asymmetry may persist for long periods of time, even until after the health of some people has been ruined. Moreover, because the needed information is often expensive to gather and individuals may be unwilling to pay for it, third parties may not provide the necessary information. Under these circumstances, there may be a strong rationale for government intervention.

Externalities   An *externality* is an effect that production or consumption has on third parties—people not involved in the production or consumption of the good. It is a by-product of production or consumption for which there is no market. Indeed, externalities are sometimes referred to as the problem of "missing markets." Standard examples include pollution caused by a factory and the pleasure derived from a neighbor's beautiful garden. Externalities may occur for a wide variety of reasons; for example, some result because a particular type of manufacturing technology is used (e.g., air pollution caused by smokestack industry). Others arise because of interdependencies (or synergies) between producers and consumers or different groups of producers (e.g., beekeepers who provide pollination services for nearby fruit growers). Still other externalities occur because of networking (e.g., the larger the number of persons who purchase a particular type of automobile, the greater the number of qualified service garages available to each owner).[16] Because the number of externalities is enormous, a careful CBA should first be conducted before the government intervenes to correct any specific externality.

We first examine a negative externality (i.e., one that imposes social costs) and then a positive externality (i.e., one that produces benefits). Figure 4.7 illustrates a market in which the production process results in a negative externality, such as air or water pollution. The supply schedule, S^*, reflects only the private marginal costs incurred by the suppliers of the good, whereas the second supply schedule, $S^{\#}$, incorporates the costs that the negative externality imposes on third parties, as well as the private marginal costs incurred by suppliers. For purposes of simplicity we are assuming that these two curves are parallel, although they may not be in practice. The vertical distance between the two supply curves, measured over the quantity of the good purchased, can be viewed as the amount those subjected to the negative externality would be willing to pay to avoid it. In other words, it represents the costs imposed by the externality on third parties.

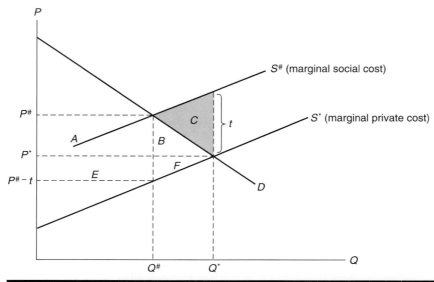

FIGURE 4.7 Negative Externality

The amount of these costs depends in part on whether the market somehow compensates third parties for the negative externality. For example, the costs would be smaller if homeowners were able to purchase their houses at lower prices because of pollution in their neighborhood than if they were not.

Figure 4.7 indicates that, if left to its own devices, the market sets too low a price for the good (P^* versus $P^{\#}$) because it fails to take account of the cost to third parties of producing the good. As a result, too much output is produced (Q^* instead of $Q^{\#}$). This causes deadweight loss, which is represented by the shaded triangular area labeled C. This deadweight loss reflects the fact that for each unit of additional output produced in excess of $Q^{\#}$, marginal social costs (shown by the supply schedule $S^{\#}$) increasingly exceed marginal social benefits (shown by the demand schedule D).

The standard technique for reducing deadweight loss resulting from negative externalities is to impose taxes.[17] For example, the suppliers of the good represented in Figure 4.7 could be required to pay a tax, t, on each unit they sell, with the tax set equal to the difference between marginal social costs and marginal social benefits (shown in the figure as the vertical distance at Q^* between the two supply schedules). As production costs would now include the tax, the supply schedule of sellers, S^*, would shift upward to $S^{\#}$. Consequently, the price paid by consumers would increase from P^* to $P^{\#}$, the net price received by producers would fall from P^* to $P^{\#} - t$, and output produced and sold would fall from Q^* to $Q^{\#}$. Note that pollution associated with the good would be reduced, but not be completely eliminated, because the good would continue to be produced, although in smaller amounts.[18]

Figure 4.7 implies that the benefits and costs of the government's tax policy are distributed unequally among different groups in the economy. These are displayed in the social accounting ledger that follows:

	Benefits	**Costs**
Consumers of Good		$A + B$
Producers of Good		$E + F$
Third Parties	$B + C + F$	
Government Revenue	$A + E$	
Social Benefit	C	

Because the policy causes consumers to pay a higher price for less of the good, they lose surplus equal to areas A and B. Similarly, because the tax causes producers to sell less of the good, but increases their production costs, they lose producer surplus equal to areas E and F. On the other hand, because of the reduction in production of the good and, hence, in pollution, third parties receive benefits from the policy corresponding to areas B, C, and F. Finally, the government receives tax revenues equal to areas A and E. Because areas A, B, E, and F represent transfers from one group to another, only area C can be counted as a gain to society as a whole from the tax policy. This area corresponds to the deadweight loss eliminated by the tax policy. To compute the *net* gain to society from the tax, the cost of administering the tax would have to be subtracted from the reduction in deadweight loss.

Now let us look at an example of a positive externality, a program that subsidizes the purchase of rodent extermination services in a poor neighborhood. One mechanism for doing this is to provide residents of the neighborhood with vouchers that are worth a certain number of dollars, v, for each unit of extermination services they purchase. After subtracting the face value of these vouchers from what they charge neighborhood residents for their services, exterminators would then be reimbursed the face value of the voucher by the government.

By increasing the use of extermination services, such a program may result in a positive externality: The fewer rodents in the neighborhood, the easier it is for residents in adjoining neighborhoods to control their own rodent populations. This situation is illustrated in Figure 4.8, where the market demand schedule, D_M, is shown as understating the social demand schedule, D_S. The area between these two demand schedules represents the WTP for the extermination voucher program by residents of adjoining neighborhoods, assuming they had knowledge of the potential benefits from the program to them. Thus, the market equilibrium price, P_0, and quantity, q_0, are both too low from the social perspective.

What are the social benefits of a program that distributes vouchers worth v per unit of extermination service to the residents of a poor neighborhood? As implied by Figure 4.8, when the vouchers become available, residents of the poor neighborhood face a supply schedule that is below the original market supply schedule, S, by v. As a consequence of a voucher-induced shift in the supply schedule, neighborhood residents increase their purchases of extermination services from q_0 to q_1, paying an effective price of P_1. Consumers in the targeted neighborhood enjoy a surplus gain equal to the area of trapezoid $B + E$; producers, who now receive a higher supply price of $P_1 + v$, enjoy a surplus gain equal to the area of trapezoid $A + C$; and people in the surrounding neighborhoods, who enjoy the positive externality, gain surplus equal to the area of parallelogram $C + G + F$, the area between the market and social demand schedules over the increase in consumption. The program must pay out v times q_1 in subsidies,

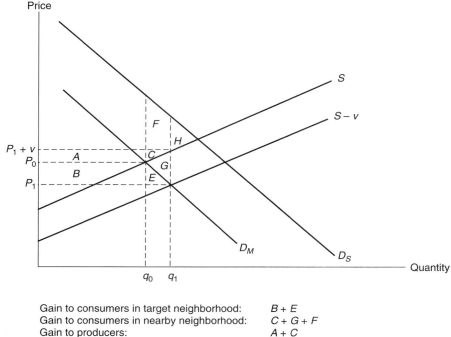

Gain to consumers in target neighborhood:	$B + E$
Gain to consumers in nearby neighborhood:	$C + G + F$
Gain to producers:	$A + C$
Program costs:	$A + B + C + G + E$
Net benefits:	$C + F$

FIGURE 4.8 Social Benefits for Direct Supply of a Good with a Positive Externality

which equals the area of rectangle $A + B + C + G + E$. Subtracting this program cost from the gains in social surplus in the market yields gross program benefits: the area of trapezoid $C + F$.[19] This benefit results because the program succeeds in eliminating part (although not all) of the deadweight loss in the market for extermination services.

Public Goods   Once produced, *public goods*—for example, flood control projects or national defense—are there for everyone. No one can or, indeed, should be excluded from enjoying their benefits. In this sense, public goods may be regarded as a special type of positive externality. Similar to other positive externalities, private markets, if left to their own devices, tend to produce less public goods than is socially optimal. Pure public goods have two key characteristics: They are *nonexcludable* and they are *nonrivalrous.*

A good is nonexcludable if it is impossible, or at least highly impractical, for one person to prevent others from consuming it.[20] If it is supplied to one consumer, it is available for all consumers, a phenomenon sometimes called *jointness in supply*. For example, it would be very difficult for a user of the light emitted from a particular streetlight to prevent others from using that light. In contrast, most private goods are excludable. For instance, a purchaser of a hamburger can exclude others from taking a bite unless overcome by physical force.

The reason nonexcludability causes market failure is easy to see. Once a nonexcludable good such as street lighting or national defense exists, it is there for everyone to use. Because there is no way to exclude people from its use, a *free-rider problem* results. As a consequence, there is not sufficient incentive for the private sector to provide it. Usually it must be publicly provided, if it is going to be provided at all.

Nonrivalry implies that one person's consumption of a good does not prevent someone else from also consuming it; consequently, more than one person can obtain benefits from a given level of supply at the same time. For example, one person's use of a streetlight to help her see at night does not diminish the ability of another person to use the same light. But if one person eats a hamburger, another cannot consume the same hamburger. The hamburger is rivalrous; streetlight is nonrivalrous. Thus, unlike the hamburger, even if it were feasible to exclude a second person from using street lighting, it would be inefficient to do so because the marginal cost of supplying lighting to the second person is zero.

The reason nonrivalry causes market failure can be examined by contrasting how a *total marginal benefit curve,* a curve that reflects the incremental benefits to consumers from each additional unit of a good that is available for their consumption, is derived for a rivalrous good with how such a curve is derived for a nonrivalrous good. To do this graphically as simply as possible, we assume that there are only two potential consumers of each of the two goods. Thus, Figure 4.9 displays two graphs: one for the rivalrous good (hamburgers) and one for the nonrivalrous good (streetlight). Each graph contains three curves: a demand schedule representing consumer A's WTP (d_A); a demand schedule representing consumer B's WTP (d_B); and a total marginal benefit (MB) curve, which is derived from the demand schedules for the two consumers.

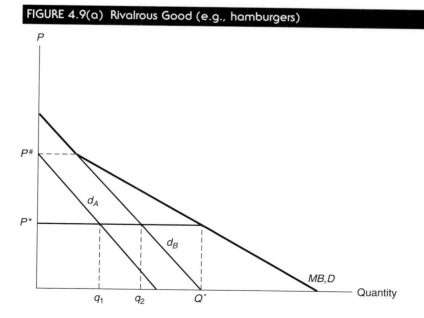

FIGURE 4.9(a) Rivalrous Good (e.g., hamburgers)

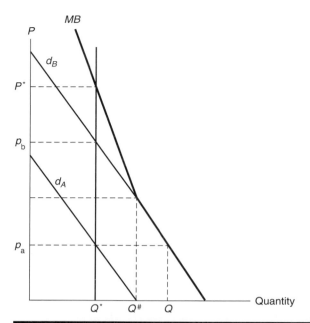

FIGURE 4.9(b) Nonrivalrous Good (e.g., streetlight)

The total marginal benefit curve for the rivalrous good is equivalent to a market demand schedule. To derive this curve, the two demand schedules for individual consumers are summed horizontally. For example, at a price of P^*, consumer A would want to consume q_1 and consumer B would want q_2 of the good. Total market demand for the good at a price of P^* is equal to $q_1 + q_2$, a total of Q^*. Thus, WTP for (or equivalently, marginal benefits from) the last unit of the total of Q^* units consumed is P^*. Notice that until the price falls below $P^\#$, the marginal benefit curve would correspond to B's demand schedule because A would not demand any of the good.

In contrast, the total marginal benefit curve for the nonrivalrous good is derived by adding the demand schedules for individual consumers vertically rather than horizontally. At an output level of Q^*, for example, total WTP (i.e., the total marginal benefits from the last unit of good that is made available) is equal to $p_a + p_b$ or P^*. Notice that at output levels above $Q^\#$, consumer A's WTP falls to zero and, consequently, the marginal benefit curve corresponds to consumer B's demand schedule.

The reason the demand schedules for individual consumers must be summed horizontally in the presence of rivalry and vertically in its absence can be clarified through use of a numerical example. If at a price of $2 consumer B wanted to buy two hamburgers and consumer A one, total demand would equal three hamburgers—the horizontal sum. But if at a price of $1,000, B wanted two streetlights on the block on which he and A both lived, but A wanted only one, two streetlights would completely satisfy the demands of both. Thus, the total demand for a nonrivalrous good cannot be determined by summing the quantity of the good each consumer desires at a given price. It must be determined instead by summing each consumer's WTP for a given quantity of the good. Hence, although A and B have a different WTP for the two streetlights, their total WTP for the two streetlights can be determined by adding A's WTP for two lights to B's.

The distinction between how the total demand for rivalrous and nonrivalrous goods is determined has an important implication. In the case of the rivalrous good, customers will reveal to the market how much they want. For example, if the price of hamburgers is set at P^*, consumer A will actually purchase q_1 of the good and consumer B will purchase q_2. But in the case of a nonrivalrous good, there is no market mechanism that causes consumers to reveal how many units they would purchase at different prices. For example, if the price of streetlight is at p_b, consumer B would be willing to purchase Q^* of the good. But if B did that, A would not purchase any because, as a result of B's purchase, he could consume all he wanted. In other words, A would free ride on B. Because of this free-rider problem, B might refuse to make any purchase until A agreed to make some sort of contribution.[21]

When only a small group of people is involved, they may be able to work out the free-rider problems caused by the nonexcludability and nonrivalry of public goods through negotiations. For example, a neighborhood association might make arrangements for installing and paying for streetlights. But too much or too little of the good may be produced. For example, if consumers A and B are to be charged for streetlight on the basis of their WTP, each will probably try to convince the other that he places a low value on streetlights regardless of how he actually values them. It is, therefore, difficult to determine where the total marginal benefit curve for a public good is located, even if only a small group of people is involved. When a large group of people share a good that is nonexcludable and nonrivalrous, such as national defense, negotiations become impractical. Consequently, if the good is going to be produced at all, the government must almost certainly intervene by either producing the good itself or subsidizing its production.

Because streetlighting is both nonrivalrous in consumption and nonexcludable, it is close to being a pure public good. Other goods are either nonrivalrous or nonexcludable, but not both. For example, an uncrowded road is essentially nonrivalrous in nature. One person's use of it does not keep another from using it. Yet, it is excludable. Individuals could be required to pay a toll to use it. So, it is sometimes called a *toll good*.[22] Fish in international waters provide an example of a good that is rivalrous but nonexcludable. Fish and fishers move around so it is difficult to preclude fishers from catching a particular type of fish, say, tuna. But if a fisher catches a tuna, then that tuna is no longer available to other fishers. This type of good is called an *open access resource*.[23] Goods that are either nonrivalrous or nonexcludable, but not both, do not exhibit all of the characteristics of public goods, but do exhibit some of these characteristics.[24] However, for the sake of brevity, we have focused on pure public goods, which are both nonrivalrous and nonexcludable. Examples of goods that are close to being pure public goods are streetlight, flood control, national defense, and the crime deterrence resulting from police on the streets.

As suggested by the preceding analysis, because of both nonrivalry and nonexcludability, actual markets for pure public goods are unlikely to exist. However, marginal benefit and marginal cost curves, which are analogous to market demand and supply schedules, do exist. We have already shown how to derive a marginal benefit curve for a public good. And, as in the case of a private good, the marginal cost curve for a public good simply reflects the costs of producing each incremental unit of the good.

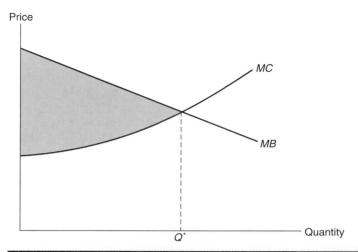

FIGURE 4.10 Marginal Benefit and Marginal Cost Curves for a Public Good

The marginal benefit and cost curves for a pure public good are illustrated in Figure 4.10. Social welfare is maximized when marginal benefits equal marginal costs, whereas deadweight loss results at either smaller or larger output amounts. Thus, the diagram implies that society would be best off if Q^* of the good were produced and consumed. However, because of the absence of a true market, little or none of the public good represented in the diagram would be produced without government intervention, or at least some sort of negotiation process. Thus, in the absence of government intervention or negotiations, society would forgo most or all the social surplus represented by the shaded triangular area. Even if the government does intervene or negotiations do take place, however, there is no guarantee that output of the good will be at Q^*. Instead, because the marginal benefit curve for a pure public good is inherently unknowable, too much or too little of it may be produced. However, as described in Chapter 14, there are techniques that can be used to obtain information about WTP for public goods.

VALUING INPUTS: OPPORTUNITY COSTS

Public policies usually require resources (i.e., inputs) that could be used to produce other goods or services instead. Public works projects such as dams, bridges, highways, and subway systems, for example, require labor, materials, land, and equipment. Similarly, social service programs typically require professional employees, computers, telephones, and office space; and wilderness preserves, recreation areas, and parks require at least land. The resources used for these purposes obviously cannot be used to produce other goods and services. Almost all public policies incur opportunity costs. Conceptually, these costs equal the value of the goods and services that would have been produced had the resources used in carrying them out been used instead in the best alternative way. These opportunity costs, as seen in Chapter 3, are represented by areas under supply schedules. These areas are the theoretically appropriate measures of the costs of the inputs.

As a practical matter, the most obvious and natural way to measure the value of the resources used by a project is simply as the direct budgetary outlay needed to purchase them. Under certain circumstances the direct budgetary outlay is also identical to the conceptually appropriate opportunity cost measure, but under other circumstances it is not. To determine when it is and when it is not permissible to use budgetary outlays, we compare the conceptually appropriate measure of costs with the direct budgetary outlay measure of costs in three alternative market situations: (1) when the market for a resource is efficient (i.e., there are no market failures) and purchases of the resource for the project will have a negligible effect on the price of the resource; (2) when the market for the resource is efficient, but purchases for the project will have a noticeable effect on prices; and (3) when the market for the resource is inefficient (i.e., there is a market failure). As will be seen, in the first of these situations, budgetary expenditures usually accurately measure project opportunity costs; in the second situation, budgetary outlays often only slightly overstate project opportunity costs; and in the third situation, expenditures may substantially overstate or understate project opportunity costs.

Before beginning, it may be helpful to make a general point concerning opportunity costs: The relevant determination is what must be given up today and in the future, *not* what has already been given up. The latter costs are *sunk* and, unlike variable costs, are not represented by the area under supply schedules. In CBA, the extent to which costs are sunk depends importantly on whether an *ex ante, ex post,* or *in medias res* analysis is being conducted. For instance, suppose that you are asked to evaluate a decision to complete a bridge after construction has already begun. What is the opportunity cost of the steel and concrete that are already in place? It is not the original expenditure made to purchase them. Rather, it is the value of these materials in their current best alternative use. This value is most likely measured by the maximum amount for which the steel and concrete could be sold as scrap. Conceivably, the cost of scrapping the materials may exceed their value in any alternative use so salvaging them would not be justified. Indeed, if salvage is still necessary, say, for environmental or other reasons, then the opportunity cost of the materials will be negative (and, thus, counted as a benefit, an avoided cost) when calculating the net gains of *continuing* construction. In situations in which resources that have already been purchased have exactly zero scrap value (the case of labor already expended, for instance), the costs are entirely sunk and are not relevant to decisions concerning future actions.

Measuring Opportunity Costs in Efficient Markets with Negligible Price Effects

Perfectly Elastic Supply Schedules   An example of this is when a government agency running a training program for unemployed workers purchases pencils for trainees. Assuming an absence of failures in the market for pencils, and that the agency buys only a small proportion of the total pencils sold in the market, the agency is realistically viewed as facing a horizontal supply schedule for pencils. Thus, the agency's purchases will have a negligible effect on the price of pencils; it can purchase additional pencils at the price they would have cost in the absence of the training program.

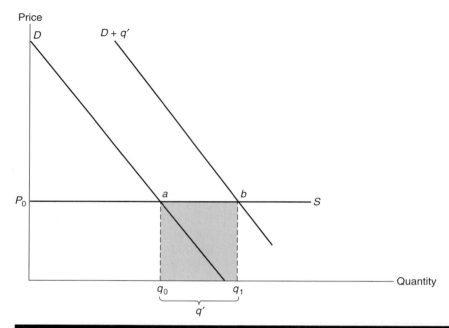

FIGURE 4.11 Opportunity Costs with No Price Effects

This situation is depicted in Figure 4.11. If a project purchases q' units of the input factor represented in the diagram (e.g., pencils), the demand schedule, D, would shift horizontally to the right by q'. As implied by the horizontal supply schedule, marginal costs remain unchanged and, hence, the price remains at P_0. The area under the supply schedule represents the opportunity cost of the factor, and P_0 is the opportunity cost of one additional unit of the factor. Consequently, the opportunity cost to society of the q' additional units of the factor needed by the project is simply the original price of the factor times the number of units purchased (i.e., P_0 times q'). In Figure 4.11, this is represented by the shaded rectangle abq_1q_0. Thus, the amount that the agency must pay to purchase additional pencils equals the opportunity cost of the resources used to produce them. In other words, if the q' units of the factor were not used for purposes of the project, then P_0 times q' worth of goods could be produced elsewhere in the economy.

What is important about the situation just described is that the social cost of the units of the factor needed by the project, the shaded rectangular area in Figure 4.11, is identical to the budgetary outlay required to purchase the units; both are equal to P_0 times q'. *Because most factors have neither steeply rising nor declining marginal cost curves, it is often reasonable to presume that expenditures required for project inputs equal their social costs.* This at least is the case when the quantity of the resource purchased makes only a small addition to the total demand for the resource, and when, in addition, there is no reason to suspect the existence of significant market failures.

Perfectly Inelastic Supply Schedules   In contrast to pencils, let us now examine a government purchase of a parcel of land for a park. We assume that, unlike the pencils,

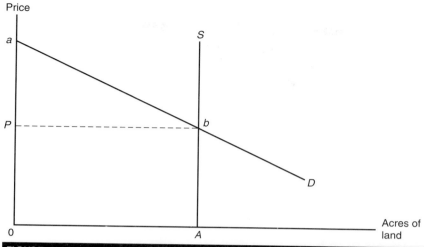

FIGURE 4.12 Opportunity Costs with Inelastic Supply

the quantity of land in a specified area is fixed at *A* acres. Thus, the government faces a vertical rather than horizontal supply schedule. In addition, in this example, we assume that if the government does not purchase the land, it will be sold in one-acre parcels to private buyers who will build houses on it.

This situation is represented in Figure 4.12, where *S* is the supply schedule and *D* the private-sector demand schedule. If the owners of the land sell it in the private market, they receive the amount represented by the rectangle *PbA0*. Now let us assume that the government secures all the units of the land in the parcel, *A*, at the market price through its eminent domain powers, paying owners the market price of *P*. Thus, the government's budgetary cost is represented in Figure 4.12 by area *PbA0*.

Here, however, the government's budgetary outlay understates the opportunity cost of removing the land from the private sector. The reason is that the potential private buyers of the land lose consumer surplus (triangle *aPb* in Figure 4.12) as a result of the government taking away their opportunity to purchase land, a real loss that is not included in the government's purchase price. The full cost of the land if it is purchased by the government is represented in Figure 4.12 by all of the area under the demand schedule to the left of the vertical supply schedule, area *abA0*, not only the rectangular area below the price line.[25]

Measuring Opportunity Costs in Efficient Markets with Noticeable Price Effects

It is possible that even when a resource required by a project is purchased in an essentially efficient market, such a large quantity is required that its price is bid up. This could occur, for example, if the construction of a very large dam requires massive amounts of concrete. In such a situation, the project should be viewed as facing an upward-sloping supply schedule for the resource input. Such a supply schedule is illustrated in Figure 4.13. In this example, project purchases of *q'* units of the resource

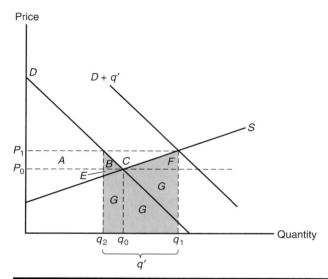

FIGURE 4.13 Opportunity Costs with Price Effects

would shift the demand schedule, D, to the right. Because the supply schedule, S, is upward sloping, the equilibrium price rises from P_0 to P_1, indicating that the large purchase causes the marginal cost of the resource to rise. The price increase causes the original buyers in the market to decrease their purchases from q_0 to q_2. However, total purchases, including those made by the project, expand from q_0 to q_1. Thus, the q' units of the resource purchased by the project come from two distinct sources: (1) units bid away from their previous buyers; and (2) additional units sold in the market.

Total project expenditures on the resource are equal to P_1 times q'. In Figure 4.13, these expenditures are represented by areas $B + C + G + E + F$, which together form a rectangle. Unlike the case in which the price of the resource does not change, however, this expenditure does not correspond to the opportunity cost of using q' units of the resource. The price change must be taken into account in computing the opportunity cost. In doing this, *the general rule is that opportunity cost equals expenditure less (plus) any increase (decrease) in social surplus occurring in the factor market.* In other words, budgetary outlays on a resource do not equal opportunity costs when the outlays cause a change in social surplus in the market for the resource.

To understand why, first look at the areas labeled A and B in Figure 4.13. These two areas represent a decrease in the consumer surplus of the original buyers because of the price increase. However, sellers gain more in producer surplus as a result of the price increase than the original buyers lose—a gain represented by areas $A + B + C$. Part of the gain in producer surplus, namely the area represented by $A + B$, merely offsets the loss in consumer surplus and, hence, is a transfer from buyers to sellers. However, area C represents a gain in social surplus that partially offsets the social cost resulting from increased government expenditure on the resource.[26] To measure the social cost of the project's purchase of the resource, this net gain in social surplus must be subtracted from the project's total budgetary outlay on the resource, areas

$B + C + G + E + F$. Thus, the net social cost of the project's purchase of q' units of the resource is represented by areas $B + G + E + F$. The effects of the purchase are summarized in the following accounting ledger:

	Benefits	**Costs**
Original Buyers		$A + B$
Sellers	$A + B + C$	
Project Expenditures		$B + C + G + E + F$
Net Social Cost		$B + G + E + F$

The basic point is that when prices change, the budgetary outlay does not equal the social cost. In the example shown in Figure 4.13, they differ by area C. As an examination of the figure suggests, however, unless the rise in prices is quite substantial, this area will be small relative to total budgetary cost. This suggests that in many instances budgetary outlay will provide a good approximation of true social cost.

If the price of an input does go up substantially, however, the budgetary cost must be adjusted for CBA purposes. If the demand and supply schedules are linear (or can be reasonably assumed to be approximately linear), the amount of this adjustment, which is the area represented by C, can be readily calculated. It equals the amount of the factor purchased for the project, q', multiplied by $\frac{1}{2}(P_1 - P_0)$, half the difference between the new and the old prices.[27] The opportunity cost of purchasing the resource for the project can also be computed directly by multiplying the amount purchased by the average of the new and old prices, $\frac{1}{2}(P_1 + P_0)(q')$.[28] The average of the new and old prices is a shadow price; it reflects the social opportunity cost of purchasing the resource more accurately than either the old price or the new price alone.

It is useful to recognize that the social cost of using a resource for a project or program does not necessarily depend on the mechanism that a government uses to obtain it. Suppose, for example, that instead of paying the market price for q' units of the resource represented in Figure 4.13, the government instead first orders supplying firms to increase their prices to the original buyers in the market from P_0 to P_1, thereby causing sales to these buyers to fall from q_0 to q_2. Next suppose that the government orders these firms to supply q' units to the government at the additional cost required to produce them. The social surplus loss resulting from the price increase to the original buyers is area $B + E$, which is the deadweight loss attributable to the increase. The social opportunity cost of producing the additional q' units of the resource for the government, which in this case corresponds to the government's budgetary expenditure, is the trapezoidal area $G + F$. Thus, the total social cost that results from the government's directive is $B + G + E + F$. This social cost is exactly the same as the social cost that results when the government purchases the resource in the same manner as any other buyer in the market. Notice, however, that this time the government's budgetary outlay, $G + F$, is smaller, rather than larger, than the social opportunity cost of using the resource.

Measuring Costs in Inefficient Markets

As indicated in Chapter 3, in an efficient market, price equals marginal social cost. Whenever price does not equal marginal social cost, allocative inefficiency results. A variety of circumstances can lead to inefficiency: absence of a working market; market failures (e.g., public goods, externalities, natural monopolies, markets with few sellers, and information asymmetries); and distortions due to government interventions (such as taxes, subsidies, regulations, price ceilings, and price floors). Any of these distortions can arise in factor markets, complicating the estimation of opportunity cost.

Because of space limitations, it is possible to examine only three distortions here. First, we consider the situation in which the government purchases an input at a price below the factor's opportunity cost. Second, we examine the case in which the government hires from a market in which there is unemployed labor. Third, we explore the situation in which the government purchases inputs for a project from a monopolist. In each of these situations, shadow pricing is needed to measure accurately the opportunity cost of the input.

Purchases at Below Opportunity Costs   Consider a proposal to establish more courts so that more criminal trials can be held. Budgetary costs include the salaries of judges and court attendants, rent for courtrooms and offices, and perhaps expenditures for additional correctional facilities (because the greater availability of trial capacity leads to more imprisonment). For these factors, budgetary costs may correspond well to social opportunity costs. However, the budget may also include payments to jurors, payments that typically just cover commuting expenses. The commuting expenses estimate should obviously include the actual resource costs of transporting jurors to the court, not just out-of-pocket payments. More important, the jurors may not be compensated for their time. If they are, the payment is usually set at a nominal per diem not related to the value of their time as, say, reflected by their wage rates. Thus, budgetary outlay to jurors almost certainly understates the opportunity cost of jurors' time. Consequently, some form of shadow pricing is necessary. A better estimate of jurors' opportunity cost is, for example, their commuting expenses plus the number of juror-hours times either the average or the median pretax hourly wage rate for the locality. The hourly pretax wage rate times the hours spent on jury duty provides a measure of the value of goods forgone because of lost labor, although several criticisms of it are discussed in Chapter 13.

Hiring Unemployed Labor   We have stressed that assessing opportunity costs in the presence of market failures or government interventions requires a careful accounting of social surplus changes. Analysis of the opportunity cost of workers hired for a government project who would otherwise be unemployed illustrates the kind of effort that is required.

Let us examine the opportunity costs of labor in a market in which minimum wage laws, union bargaining power, or some other factor creates a wage floor that keeps the wage rate above the market clearing level and, consequently, there is unemployed labor.[29] Notice that we are focusing here on a very specific form of unemployment: that which occurs when the number of workers who desire jobs at the wage paid in a particular labor market exceed the number of workers employers are willing to hire at that wage. Workers who are unemployed for this reason are sometimes said to be *in surplus*. We focus on surplus workers so that we can examine their opportunity costs when they are hired for a government project. This issue is of particular importance because there are some government projects that are specifically designed to put surplus workers to work and numerous other projects that are likely to hire such workers. Of course, there are other forms of unemployment than the type considered here. For example, some persons are briefly unemployed while they move from one job to another.

Before discussing how the opportunity cost of surplus labor might be measured, it may be useful to consider more explicitly the extent to which the labor hired to work on a government project reduces the number of unemployed workers.[30] Say, for example, a project hires 100 workers. How many fewer workers will be unemployed as a result? In considering this question, it is important to recognize that the project does not have to hire directly from the ranks of the unemployed. Even if the project hires 100 previously employed persons, this will result in 100 job vacancies, some of which may be filled by the unemployed. If the unemployment rate for the type of workers hired for the project (as determined by their occupation and geographic location) is very high (say, over 10 or 15 percent), the number of unemployed workers may fall by nearly 100. But if the unemployment rate for the workers is low (say, below 4 percent), most of the measured unemployed are probably between jobs rather than in surplus. As a consequence, the project is likely to cause little reduction in the number of persons who are unemployed. Instead the project will draw its workforce from those employed elsewhere or out of the labor force. At rates of unemployment between 4 and 10 percent, the reduction in the number of unemployed persons will probably be well under 100 but substantially above zero.

Figure 4.14 depicts a situation in which a government project reduces unemployment in a labor market with a wage floor. This wage floor could result from a legal minimum wage, union wage agreements, or other reasons. In this figure, the preproject demand schedule for labor, D, and the supply schedule for labor, S, intersect at P_e, the equilibrium price in the absence of the wage floor, P_m. At the wage floor, L_s workers desire employment, but only L_d workers are demanded so that $L_s - L_d$ workers are unemployed. Now, imagine that L' workers are hired for a government project at a

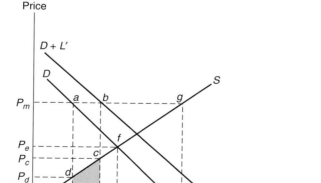

FIGURE 4.14 Opportunity Costs with a Price Floor

wage of P_m. This shifts the demand schedule to the right by L'. As long as L' is less than the number of unemployed laborers, the wage rate remains at the floor.

We now consider five alternative measures of the social cost of hiring the L' unemployed workers. All five of these measures are subject to criticism. Indeed, it is not obvious that, as a practical matter, it is possible to obtain an accurate value of the social cost of hiring the unemployed. However, some of the alternative measures described here are far better approximations of the true social cost than others.

1. **Measure A.** It is sometimes suggested that because the unemployed are not working, there are zero opportunity costs in putting them to work. This treats the unemployed, however, as if their time is valueless. This is clearly inappropriate on two grounds. First, many unemployed persons are in fact engaged in productive enterprises such as job search, child care, and home improvements. Second, even if they were completely at leisure, leisure itself has value to those who are enjoying it. Consequently, few, if any, unemployed persons are willing to work at a zero wage. Indeed, the supply schedule in Figure 4.14 represents the value that various individuals, both those who are employed and those who are unemployed, place on their time when they are not employed. For example, an individual located at point f would only be willing to accept employment at a wage of P_e or greater. Thus, P_e provides a measure of the value that this person places on his or her time. In other words, his or her opportunity cost of giving up leisure time to work is P_e. Similarly, individuals located on the supply schedule at points c and d value their time at P_c and P_d, respectively. No individual is willing to work at a wage below P_r, and, as P_r has a positive value, Figure 4.14 implies that the opportunity cost of hiring the unemployed must be above zero.

2. **Measure B.** Figure 4.14 indicates that total budgetary expenditure on labor for this project is P_m times L', which equals the area of rectangle abL_tL_d. This budgetary outlay for labor, however, is likely to overstate substantially the true social cost of hiring workers for the project. As implied by the supply schedule in Figure 4.14, although employed workers are paid a wage of P_m, most would be willing to work for less. This difference between the value they place on their time, as indicated by the supply schedule, and P_m, the wage they are actually paid while employed, is producer (i.e., worker) surplus, which may be viewed as a transfer to the workers from the government agency hiring them. To obtain a measure of the social cost of hiring workers for the project, this producer surplus must be subtracted from the budgetary expenditure on labor. Measure B fails to do this.

3. **Measure C.** As the project expands employment in the market represented by Figure 4.14 from L_d to L_t, one might assume that the trapezoid $abcd$ represents producer surplus enjoyed by the newly hired. Given this assumption, one would subtract area $abcd$ from area abL_tL_d to obtain a measure of the social cost of hiring workers for the project. Thus, the social cost would be measured as the shaded trapezoid cdL_dL_t, the shaded area under the supply schedule between L_d and L_t. This area would equal the opportunity cost of the newly hired workers—that is, the value of the time they give up when they go to work.

4. **Measure D.** One shortcoming of measure C is that it is implicitly based on an assumption that all the unemployed persons hired for the project value their time at less than P_c and at greater than P_d. In other words, this approach assumes that these work-

ers are all located between points c and d on the supply schedule. However, there is no basis for such an assumption. Indeed, it is quite likely that some of the hired unemployed persons value their time at well above P_c and that others value their time at well under P_d. In fact, the figure implies that unemployed persons who value their time as low as P_r or as high as P_m would be willing to work on the project because the project would pay them a wage of P_m. Thus, perhaps, a better assumption is that the unemployed persons who would actually get hired for the project are distributed more or less equally along the supply schedule between points e and g, rather than being confined between points d and c. This assumption implies that the unemployed persons who are hired for the project value their time by no more than P_m, by no less than P_r, and, on average, by $(\frac{1}{2})(P_m + P_r)$. Thus, the social cost of hiring L' workers for the project would be computed as equal to $(\frac{1}{2})(P_m + P_r)(L')$.

5. **Measure E.** One practical problem with using measure D in an actual CBA is that the value of P_r, the lowest wage at which any worker represented in Figure 4.14 would be willing to accept employment, is unlikely to be known. Given this, some assumption about the value of P_r must be made. One possible, and perhaps not unreasonable, assumption is that the supply schedule passes through the origin and, hence, the value of P_r equals zero. The fact that the probabilities of illness, divorce, and suicide all increase with unemployment, while job skills deteriorate, suggest that P_r could, in practice, be very low for at least some unemployed persons. If we once again assume that the unemployed persons who are hired for the project are distributed more or less equally along the supply schedule between the point at which it intersects the vertical axis and point g, this implies that the unemployed persons who are hired for the project value their time by no more than P_m, by no less than zero, and, on average, by $(\frac{1}{2})(P_m + 0) = \frac{1}{2}P_m$. Hence, the social cost of hiring workers for the project would be computed as $\frac{1}{2}P_m(L')$. Note that the estimate provided by this computation is equal to half the government's budgetary outlay. Although this cost estimate would be smaller and almost certainly less accurate than that computed using measure D, it is usually easier to obtain.

Given our preceding argument that nonwork time has a positive value, measure E is probably best viewed as providing an easily obtainable lower-bound estimate of the true project social costs for labor, whereas the project budgetary cost for labor, measure B, provides an upper-bound estimate.

Purchases from a Monopoly   We now turn to a final example of measuring the social cost of project or program purchases in an inefficient market—the purchase of an input supplied by a monopoly. In this circumstance, a government agency's budgetary outlay overstates the true social costs resulting from the purchase. This overstatement occurs because the price of the input exceeds the social cost of producing it. As a consequence, a substantial share of the revenues a monopolist receives are transfers or *monopoly rents*. Thus, in principle, a CBA should not use the budgetary outlay as a measure of social cost.

Figure 4.15 illustrates a government agency's purchase of an input from a monopoly. Prior to the purchase, the input is produced at level Q_1, where the monopolist's marginal cost and marginal revenue curves intersect. The price at Q_1, as determined by the demand schedule, is P_1. Now, as a result of the agency's purchase of Q_1 units, the

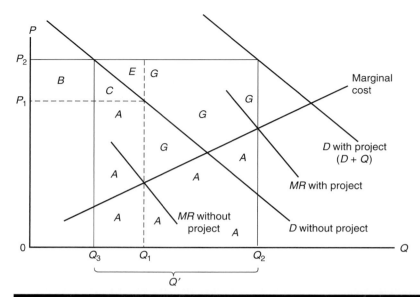

FIGURE 4.15 Opportunity Costs When Buying from a Monopoly

monopolist's demand schedule and the marginal revenue curve shift to the right. The price of the input increases to P_2 and the quantity sold increases to Q_2. At the new price, the agency purchases a quantity equal to the distance between Q_3 and Q_2, while the original buyers in the market reduce the quantity they purchase by an amount equal to the distance between Q_1 and Q_3.

As in our previous examples, the direct budgetary cost of the agency's purchase equals the price times the quantity purchased: $P_2(Q_2 - Q_3)$. In Figure 4.15, this is represented by the rectangle between Q_3 and Q_2 and bounded by P_2 (i.e., areas $A + C + G + E$). However, these budgetary costs overstate the true social cost. To find the true social cost of the agency's purchase, one must examine the effects of the purchase on the monopolist and the original buyers of the input, as well as on the agency's revenues.

Because the monopolist sells more of the input at higher prices, its producer surplus increases. This increase has two parts: (1) that resulting from the higher price the monopolist now receives for the units that it previously sold (which is represented in Figure 4.15 by areas $B + C + E$); and (2) that resulting from the additional units that the monopolist now sells (area G). Thus, as can be seen from Figure 4.15, part of the cost to the agency—areas $C + G + E$—is a transfer to the monopolist.

Original buyers in the market are clearly worse off as a result of the agency's purchase because they now have to pay a higher price for the input. In measuring their loss of consumer surplus, it is the original demand schedule that is pertinent because this is the schedule that reflects the original buyers' willingness-to-pay for the input. Thus, the total loss in consumer surplus by the original buyers, all of which is a transfer to the monopolist, is equal to areas $B + C$.

The following distributional accounting ledger summarizes the effects of the purchase:

	Benefits	*Costs*
Original Buyers		$B + C$
Monopolistic Seller	$B + C + G + E$	
Project Expenditures		$A + C + G + E$
Net Social Cost		$A + C$

The major conclusion of this analysis is that in the case of input purchases from a monopolist, budgetary expenditures are larger than the social costs. The reason is that the price the monopoly charges exceeds the marginal cost of producing the input. Consequently, in conducting a CBA, the government's budgetary cost should, in principle, be adjusted downward through shadow pricing. In practice, however, the error that would result from using the unadjusted budgetary expenditures would often not be very large. As an examination of Figure 4.15 suggests, the size of the bias, areas $G + E$, depends on the extent to which the price the monopoly charges exceeds its marginal costs—in other words, on how much monopoly power it actually has. And this, in turn, depends on how steeply sloped the demand schedule is. Thus, before an analyst develops shadow prices, a sometimes difficult undertaking, he or she should ask whether it is really necessary to do so.

The General Rule   Other market distortions also affect opportunity costs in predictable ways. It is useful to summarize the direction of the bias created by some of these distortions. In factor markets in which supply is taxed, direct expenditure outlays overestimate opportunity cost; in factor markets in which supply is subsidized, expenditures underestimate opportunity cost. In factor markets exhibiting positive externalities of supply, expenditures overestimate opportunity cost; in factor markets exhibiting negative externalities of supply, expenditures underestimate opportunity costs. To determine opportunity costs in such cases, apply the general rule: *Opportunity cost equals direct expenditures on the factor minus (plus) gains (losses) in social surplus occurring in the factor market.*

PROJECT EFFECTS ON GOVERNMENT REVENUES

As illustrated in this chapter, government projects affect government revenues in a wide variety of ways. In principle, by affecting government revenues, these projects either require taxes to increase or allow them to decrease. At least conceptually, changes in government revenues increase or decrease the amount of taxes that, other things equal, would be required for the government to achieve the same aggregate financial position.

In Chapter 3, we indicated that a tax on a good, such as an excise tax, usually results in deadweight loss. Typically, a project that is funded through additional taxes increases deadweight loss, whereas a project that increases government revenues and thereby allows reductions in taxes decreases deadweight loss. As suggested earlier in this chapter, however, there are important exceptions. If prior to being taxed, for example, a good was overconsumed due to a negative externality, then the introduction of a tax could increase efficiency by reducing the overconsumption. The key point, however, is that whenever there is a behavioral response to a change in taxes—for instance, an increase in excise taxes on a consumption good causes purchases of the good to fall somewhat or an increase in taxes on earnings causes workers to reduce their work hours somewhat—deadweight loss will change. Although these changes in deadweight loss are typically ignored in conducting CBAs, they should not be.

Because there are numerous sources of deadweight loss in addition to taxes, economists refer to deadweight loss specifically resulting from a tax as *excess burden* and the change in deadweight loss resulting from raising an additional dollar of tax revenue as the *marginal excess tax burden* (METB). In Chapter 12 estimation of the marginal excess tax burden is discussed further. Estimates of the METB under different types of taxes are presented in Chapter 15. The size of the METB is usually measured as a percentage of the additional tax dollars collected as a result of an increase in tax rates. As will be seen in Chapter 15, this percentage is positive and substantial for most types of taxes, although it is larger for some types of taxes than others.

In principle, if a government project is funded through additional taxes that increase excess burden, then this increase should be counted as part of the cost of the project. Symmetrically, project revenues that allow the government to reduce taxes and thereby reduce excess burden provide a social benefit. Consequently, *project expenditures and project revenues that affect the government's financial position should be translated into social costs and benefits by multiplying them by the marginal excess tax burden.*

To be more specific, in conducting a cost-benefit analysis, an analyst should first take account of all project costs and benefits, exclusive of effects on the marginal excess burden. Some, but not all, of these costs and benefits will result in decrements and increments to the government's financial position. The analyst should compute the additional costs and benefits that result from these changes in the government's financial position by multiplying them by the estimated value of the METB. For purposes of doing this, it is useful to distinguish among five categories of project costs and benefits. First, *project costs that represent expenditures on the project by the government should be multiplied by the METB.* Second, *project benefits that accrue as revenue to the government should also be multiplied by the METB.* Third, *costs that accrue as losses in social surplus exclusive of government expenditures should not be multiplied by the METB.* Fourth, *benefits that accrue as gains in social surplus exclusive of government revenue should not be multiplied by the METB.* Fifth, *transfers, which otherwise either would not be recorded as costs and benefits or would be recorded as exactly offsetting costs and benefits, should be recorded and multiplied by the METB if they represent increments or decrements to government cash flow.* In other words, project-specific taxes or subsidies must be multiplied by the METB; they do not "cancel out." Thus, care should be taken to enumerate all costs and benefits, including transfers.

CONCLUSION

This chapter has shown that the benefits and costs associated with government programs and projects are appropriately determined by valuing the resulting changes in net government revenue flows and producer and consumer surplus. Even when the relevant demand and supply schedules are known, great care must be exercised in order to measure the changes appropriately, especially when the relevant markets are distorted. Two types of relevant markets were considered: the market in which the policy intervention takes place and factor markets in which the government purchases the inputs required by the program or project. These markets, primary markets, are the ones that are directly affected by a particular policy. Markets that are indirectly affected—secondary markets—are the focus of the following chapter.

Exercises for Chapter 4

1. Consider a low-wage labor market. Workers in this market are not presently covered by the minimum wage, but the government is considering implementing such legislation. If implemented, this law would require employers in the market to pay workers a $5 hourly wage. Suppose that all workers in the market are equally productive, that the current market clearing wage rate is $4 per hour, and that at this market clearing wage there are 600 employed workers. Further suppose that under the minimum wage legislation, only 500 workers would be employed and 300 workers would be unemployed. Finally, assume that the market demand and supply schedules are linear and that the market reservation wage, the lowest wage at which any worker in the market would be willing to work, is $1. Compute the dollar value of the impact of the policy on employers, workers, and society as a whole.

2. Suppose the government is considering an increase in the toll on a certain stretch of highway from $.40 to $.50. At present, 50,000 cars per week use that highway stretch; after the toll is imposed, it is projected that only 40,000 cars per week will use the highway stretch.

   a. Assuming that the marginal cost of highway use is constant (i.e., the supply schedule is horizontal) and equal to $.40 per car, what is the net cost to society attributable to the increase in the toll? (Hint: The toll increase will cause the supply schedule, not the demand schedule, to shift.)

   b. Because of the reduced use of the highway, the government would reduce its purchases of concrete from 20,000 tons per year to 19,000 tons per year. Thus, if the price of concrete were $25 per ton, the government's cost savings would be $25,000. However, the government's reduced demand for concrete causes its market price to fall from $25 per ton to $24.50 per ton. Moreover, because of this reduction in price, the purchases of concrete by nongovernment buyers increase by 300 tons per year. Assuming that the factor market for concrete is competitive, can the government's savings of $25,000 be appropriately used as the measure of the social value of the cost savings that result from the government purchasing less concrete? Or is it important to use shadow pricing?

3. A country imports 3 billion barrels of crude oil per year and domestically produces another 3 billion barrels of crude oil per year. The world price of crude oil is $18 per barrel. Assuming linear schedules, economists estimate the price elasticity of domestic supply to be 0.25 and the price elasticity of domestic demand to be 0.1 at the current equilibrium.

   a. Consider the changes in social surplus that would result from imposition of a $6 per barrel import fee on crude oil that would involve annual administrative costs of $50 million. Assume that the world price will not change as a result of the country imposing the import fee, but that the domestic price will increase by $6 per barrel. Also assume that only producers, consumers, and taxpayers within the country have standing. Determine the quantity consumed, the quantity produced domestically, and the quantity imported after the imposition of the import fee. Then estimate the annual social net benefits of the import fee.

b. Economists have estimated that the marginal excess burden of taxation in the country is 0.25. Reestimate the social net benefits assuming that 20 percent of the increase in producer surplus is realized as tax revenue under the existing tax system. In answering this question, assume that increases in tax revenues less the cost of administrating the import fee are used to reduce domestic taxes.

c. The reduction in the country's demand for imports may affect the world price of crude oil. Assuming that the import fee reduces the world price from $18 to $16 per barrel and, thus, the after-tax domestic price is $16 + $6 = $22 per barrel, a net increase in domestic price of $4 per barrel, repeat the analysis done in parts a and b.

Notes

1. For a detailed examination of government failures, see David L. Weimer and Aidan R. Vining, *Policy Analysis: Concepts and Practice*, 3rd ed. (Upper Saddle River, NJ: Prentice Hall, 1998), Chapter 8.

2. As mentioned in Chapter 1, sometimes in a CBA a policy outcome that people would be willing to pay to avoid is referred to as a *negative benefit* rather than as a *cost*. These two terms can be viewed as equivalent.

3. A change in price only causes a movement along the supply schedule, a change in quantity supplied. But a project that provides more of a good increases the supply of the good, resulting in a shift of the supply schedule.

4. This assumes, of course, that the market is sufficiently competitive and the firms in it are efficient enough that all of the cost savings are passed on to consumers in the form of a price decrease.

5. An alternative method of measuring the gain in social surplus is simply to compare total social surplus with and without the project. In the absence of the project, total social surplus would be represented by the triangular area *fae*, whereas in the presence of the project, total social surplus would be represented by the triangular area *fbd*. Subtracting the smaller triangle from the larger triangle, we again find that the net gain in social surplus equals the trapezoidal area *abde*.

6. Weimer and Vining, *Policy Analysis: Concepts and Practice*. For a theoretical treatment of externalities, public goods, and club goods, see Richard Cornes and Todd Sandler, *The Theory of Exter-*

nalities, Public Goods, and Club Goods (New York: Cambridge University Press, 1986).

7. There are, of course, other types of markets in which individual firms have market power—for example, those characterized by oligopoly or monopolistic competition. We focus on markets characterized by monopoly, and especially natural monopoly, because government intervention is most likely to occur in these markets.

8. If the demand schedule is linear, the marginal revenue curve will also be linear and will be located halfway between the demand schedule and the vertical axis. That is, given a linear demand curve, $p = a - bq$:

$$TR = pq = (a - bq)q = aq - bq^2$$

Therefore, marginal revenue $= dTR/dq = a - 2bq$. Hence, the slope of the marginal revenue curve $(-2b)$ is twice the slope of the demand curve $(-b)$.

9. To maximize its profit (π), the monopolist would produce where the difference between total revenues (TR) and total costs (TC) are as large as possible, that is, where $\pi = TR - TC$ is at a maximum. At this point, $d\pi/dQ = dTR/dQ - dTC/dQ$. Hence, $MR = MC$. However, although quantity is determined by the intersection of the monopolist's marginal cost and marginal revenue curves, price is not. Thus, unlike a perfectly competitive firm's marginal cost curve, a monopolist's marginal cost curve cannot be interpreted as its supply schedule.

10. Of course, foreign-owned firms, regardless of whether they are competitive or monopolistic,

usually would not be given standing. Therefore, their benefits would not be counted in a CBA.

11. There are, of course, alternative policies that the government might adopt in response to the monopoly. For example, it might tax the monopolist's profits, regulate the prices the monopolist charges, or operate the monopoly as a state-owned enterprise.

12. In principle, it is possible that D_u could be to the left of D_i, rather than to the right of it as shown in Figure 4.6. This would occur if instead of desiring more of the product in the absence of information concerning it than they would with the information, consumers desire less of it. In practice, however, such situations are unlikely to continue for long because strong incentives would exist for sellers to eliminate such information asymmetry by providing buyers with the needed information, thereby increasing their demand for the product. But when the actual demand schedule is to the right of the fully informed demand schedule, the incentive, in contrast, is for sellers to withhold the information.

13. The two demand schedules are drawn closer together at high prices than at low prices to imply that at higher prices buyers would go to more trouble to obtain additional information about the product than at lower prices. Whether or not this is actually the case, however, is not essential to the analysis.

14. This is discussed more fully in Aidan R. Vining and David L. Weimer, "Information Asymmetry Favoring Sellers: A Policy Framework," *Policy Sciences,* 21, no. 4 (1988), 281–303.

15. For a more extensive discussion of these three types of products, see Vining and Weimer, "Information Asymmetry Favoring Sellers: A Policy Framework."

16. For an entertaining discussion of possible misuses of the term *externality* and when intervention may or may not be appropriate for correcting externalities, see Virginia Postrel, "External Cost: The Dangers of Calling Everything Pollution," *Reason Magazine,* 1999.

17. This tax can be levied either in the traditional manner—that is, on the good itself—or, alternatively, by the government issuing transferable permits that, in effect, tax effluents emitted by firms rather than the goods they produce. Under the latter approach, which is currently being used in the

United States to control sulphur dioxide emissions, firms that have found ways to control their pollution relatively inexpensively can sell their permits to pollute to firms for which pollution control would be relatively more costly. In principle, the advantage of this approach is that a market would be established that places responsibility for pollution control on those firms that can do it most efficiently. For a detailed description and critique of the permit approach, see Karl Hausker, "The Politics and Economics of Auction Design in the Market for Sulfur Dioxide Pollution," *Journal of Policy Analysis and Management,* 11, no. 4 (1992), 553–572.

18. Indeed, when, as in the case illustrated in Figure 4.7, the tax is levied on the good, there is no special incentive for firms to reduce the amount of pollution resulting from their production process. However, when the effluent itself is taxed—for example, through use of the transferable pollution permits discussed in the previous note—such incentives do exist.

19. In this example, gross program benefits only differ from net program costs by the administrative costs required to operate the program. Also notice that in the context of the example the rule that gross project benefits equal changes in social surplus net revenues generated by the project continues to hold once it is recognized that in this instance net revenues are actually negative.

20. When it is feasible to do so, private firms attempt to make nonexcludable goods excludable. One example of this is scramblers used by certain television cable networks.

21. The free-rider problem is also closely linked to difficulties in remedying problems resulting from externalities. For example, because clean air is both nonrivalrous and nonexcludable, in the absence of government intervention, there is limited incentive for the private sector to produce clean air by reducing air pollution.

22. In some circumstances, toll goods may be provided by clubs, which are voluntary organizations with the capability to exclude nonmembers from consuming goods provided by the club, including those that are nonrivalrous. See James M. Buchanan, "An Economic Theory of Clubs," *Economica,* 32, no. 1 (1965), 1–14; and Richard Cornes and Todd Sandler, *The Theory of Externalities, Public Goods, and Club Goods* (New York: Cambridge University Press, 1986).

23. Open access implies that anyone who has the physical capability to use units of the good may do so. When the set of possible users of the good is restricted, then the good is considered a *common property resource*. For example, fish in international waters are an open access good, whereas fish in coastal waters may be available only to denizens of the country enforcing sovereignty over the waters and are, thus, a common property good. Although economists tend to use the terms interchangeably, the distinction is worth making because restriction of the set of possible users seems to be a prerequisite for self-regulation that may emerge to limit the extent of overconsumption. See Elinor Ostrom, *Governing the Commons: The Evolution of Institutions for Collective Action* (New York: Cambridge University Press, 1990).

24. Common property resources are similar to open access goods except that the set of potential users is clearly defined. For an extensive discussion of such goods, see Weimer and Vining, *Policy Analysis: Concepts and Practices,* pp. 88–94. Two additional publications that focus on common property resource goods are Elinor Ostrom, *Governing the Commons,* and Glenn Stevenson, *Common Property Economics* (New York: Cambridge University Press, 1991).

25. If the government were to purchase only a small part of the fixed supply of land on the open market, its budgetary outlay would very closely approximate the opportunity cost of removing the land from the private sector. In this case, the government's entry into the market would bid up the price of the land slightly, crowding potential private-sector land buyers who are just to the left of point *b* on the demand schedule out of the market. These buyers would lose a negligible amount of surplus. In addition, those private-sector buyers who remain in the market would pay a slightly higher price. Hence, surplus would be transferred between these buyers and the sellers of the land.

26. There is a natural tendency of those who are promoting a particular government project (e.g., a dam or a recreational area) to emphasize the potential benefits to those who must supply resources to the project. Our analysis suggests that in well-functioning markets these benefits only occur if the price of these resources increases, and even then, part of the benefits to the suppliers of the resources is offset by increases in costs to the original buyers of the resources. Note, however, that the analysis is based on the assumption that the resources used in the project would be fully employed even in the absence of the project. As will be seen later in this chapter, if this assumption does not hold, additional benefits can then accrue to suppliers of the resources used in the project.

27. This formula is based on a bit of geometry. The triangular area C equals one-half the rectangular area from which it is formed, $B + C + F$. Thus, area C is equivalent to $\frac{1}{2}(P_1 - P_0)(q')$.

28. This amount is derived as follows:

$$P_1 q' - \frac{1}{2}(P_1 - P_0)q' = \frac{1}{2}(P_0 + P_1)(q')$$

29. For a discussion of various forms of wage rigidity that result in unemployment, see Ronald G. Ehrenberg and Robert S. Smith, *Modern Labor Economics: Theory and Public Policy*, 6th ed. (Reading, MA: Addison Wesley Longman, Inc., 1997), Chapter 15.

30. For more detailed discussions of these issues, see Robert H. Haveman, "Evaluating Public Expenditure Under Conditions of Unemployment," in *Public Expenditure and Policy Analysis*, 3rd ed., Robert H. Haveman and Julius Margolis, eds. (Boston: Houghton Mifflin Company, 1983), pp. 167–182, and E. J. Mishan, *Cost-Benefit Analysis*, 4th ed. (London: Unwin Hyman, 1988), pp. 325–329.

CHAPTER
5

VALUING BENEFITS AND COSTS IN SECONDARY MARKETS

In conducting CBAs of government policies, there is a natural tendency to list as many effects of the policies as one's imagination permits. For example, an improvement in public transportation in a particular city may increase bus usage and reduce car usage. It may also reduce downtown pollution and congestion. In addition, it may reduce the demand for automobile repairs, parking places, and gasoline.

To assess these effects, one must first determine which occur in primary markets and which occur in secondary markets. Primary markets refer to markets that are directly affected by a policy, whereas secondary markets are markets that are indirectly affected. The change in bus usage just mentioned clearly occurs in the primary market for public transportation. The reductions in pollution and congestion also occur in the primary market for public transportation, a market that is distorted due to externalities. Any effect that occurs in a primary market should be accounted for in a CBA. On the other hand, effects on the demand for auto repairs, parking places, and gasoline occur in secondary markets and, as will be seen, often can (and indeed should) be ignored in conducting CBA. This last group of effects are often referred to as *secondary, second-round, spillover, pecuniary, indirect,* or *side effects.*

Whereas Chapter 4 examined the benefits and costs of government policies that occur in primary markets, this chapter focuses on policy impacts in secondary markets. As in Chapter 4, we distinguish between efficient and distorted markets. In addition, the chapter takes a brief look at the special implications of secondary market effects for local communities, as the benefits of such effects are often touted by advocates of local infrastructure projects such as sports stadiums and convention centers.

VALUING BENEFITS AND COSTS IN EFFICIENT SECONDARY MARKETS

Complements and Substitutes

Secondary market effects result because government policies affect the prices of goods in primary markets, and this, in turn, noticeably affects the demand for other goods. These latter goods are referred to as *complements* and *substitutes.*

Consider the following example. Stocking a lake near a city with fish lowers the effective price of access to fishing grounds for the city's residents. They not only fish more often, but they also demand more bait and fishing equipment. We say that access to fishing grounds and fishing equipment are complements because a decrease (increase) in the price of one will result in an increase (decrease) in the demand for the other. In contrast, fishing is a substitute for golfing because as the price of fishing goes down (up), the demand for golfing goes down (up).

If government policies affect the demand for goods in secondary markets, then prices in these secondary markets may or may not change as a result. We first discuss the simpler situation in which prices do not change. We then analyze the more complex situation in which prices do change in secondary markets.

Efficient Secondary Market Effects without Price Changes

Because most goods have substantial numbers of complements and substitutes, many government projects cause effects in large numbers of secondary markets. Accounting for all these effects would obviously impose an enormous burden on analysts. Fortunately, however, such effects can often be ignored in CBA without substantially biasing the estimates of net benefits. When can we ignore secondary market effects? *We can and indeed should ignore impacts in undistorted secondary markets as long as changes in social surplus in the primary market resulting from a government project are measured* and *prices in the secondary markets do not change.* The reason for this is that in the absence of price adjustments in undistorted secondary markets in response to price changes in primary markets, impacts are typically fully measured as surplus changes in primary markets. Measuring the same effects in both markets will, therefore, result in double counting. Thus, for example, if the prices in the fishing equipment market do not change and the market is undistorted, then the increased consumption of fishing equipment is not relevant to the CBA of a project that increases access to fishing grounds.

A closer look at the fishing example should make the rule for the treatment of secondary markets clearer. For simplicity, we assume that the price of fishing equals the marginal social cost of fishing and that marginal social costs are constant. This, in turn, implies that there are no producer surplus or externalities in the primary market (e.g., highway congestion does not result because of increased travel to the newly stocked lake).

Panel (a) in Figure 5.1 shows the market for "fishing days." Prior to the stocking of the nearby lake, the effective price of a day of fishing (largely the time costs of travel) was P_{F_0}, the travel cost to a lake much farther away. Once fishing is available at the nearby lake, the effective price falls to P_{F_1} and, as a consequence, the number of days spent fishing by local residents rises from q_{F_0} to q_{F_1}. The resulting increase in social surplus equals the area of trapezoid $P_{F_0}abP_{F_1}$, the gain in consumer surplus. We measure this gain in consumer surplus using the demand schedule for fishing, D_F. As is customary in textbooks, this demand schedule should be viewed as the relation between price and quantity that would exist in the primary market if the prices of all secondary goods were held constant. Later we discuss the importance of this assumption.

Now consider the market for fishing equipment. The decline in the effective price of fishing days shifts the demand schedule for fishing equipment from D_{E_0} to D_{E_1} as

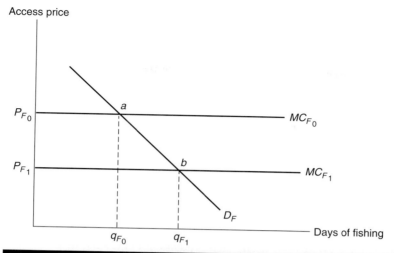

FIGURE 5.1(a) Primary Market: Market for Fishing Days

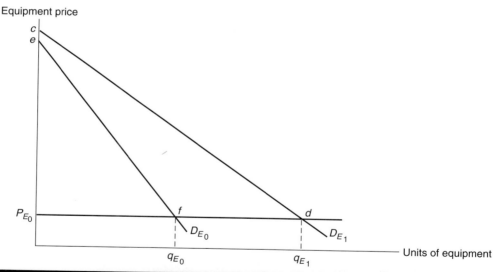

FIGURE 5.1(b) Secondary Market: Market for Fishing Equipment (No Price Effect)

shown in panel (b) of Figure 5.1. If the supply schedule is perfectly elastic, which is likely when the local market accounts for only a small fraction of regional or national demand, then the shift in demand will not increase the price of fishing equipment.

Does this shift in demand for fishing equipment represent a change in consumer welfare that should be counted in a CBA of the fish stocking project? In other words, should the gap between the old and new demand schedules that is above the price line be counted as an additional increase in consumer surplus? It is tempting to treat the increase in consumer surplus from efP_{E_0} to cdP_{E_0} in panel (b) as an additional increase in social benefits that should be added to $P_{F_0}abP_{F_1}$ in panel (a), but this should *not* be done. As discussed next, doing so would result in double counting. As long as price does not change in the equipment market as a result of stocking the lake, the social surplus change in the fishing market measures the entire benefit from the stocking project.

To see this, first consider fishers who already own all the fishing equipment they need at the time the lake is stocked and, hence, presently contribute no demand to the market for fishing equipment. The value that these persons place on their existing fishing equipment will tend to increase as a result of stocking the nearby lake. However, because they are not in the market for new fishing equipment, the gap between the old and new demand schedules for new fishing equipment does not reflect this increase. Of course, these persons' willingness-to-pay for fishing days will presumably be higher than it otherwise would have been as a result of the fact that they will not have to incur further expenditures for fishing equipment. But any additional increase in consumer surplus that these fishers enjoy as a result of already owning fishing equipment at the time the nearby lake is stocked will already be reflected by the primary market demand schedule for fishing days, which will be further to the right than it otherwise would be. It cannot show up in the secondary market for fishing equipment.

Now consider individuals who do not own fishing equipment at the time the lake is stocked but are now induced to make such purchases. The gap between the two demand schedules in panel (b) of Figure 5.1 does accurately reveal the increased value that these persons place on fishing equipment. That is, these people are now willing to pay more for fishing equipment, and indeed they will buy more fishing equipment. It is the only way they can fully realize surplus gains from the stocking project. But this expenditure is obviously not an additional benefit from the stocking project. Just like the fishers who already own fishing equipment, the increase in consumer surplus that these persons receive from the stocking project is fully reflected by the primary market demand schedule for fishing days. This includes any consumer surplus that they receive from their purchases of fishing equipment. Thus, counting the gap between the two demand schedules in panel (b) as benefits, and also counting the increase in consumer surplus shown in panel (a) as benefits, would result in counting the same benefits twice.

Persons who do not own fishing equipment at the time the lake is stocked would be even better off if, like the current owners of fishing equipment, they did not have to buy new equipment in order to take advantage of the newly stocked lake. Thus, everything else being equal, willingness-to-pay for fishing days is presumably greater among those who already own fishing equipment than among those who must purchase it. The increase in consumer surplus that results from the stocking project for both groups, even if different from one another, will be fully reflected in the primary market demand schedule for fishing days.

It is important to stress that secondary market effects can only be ignored if social surplus in the primary market is measured directly. As discussed in greater detail in Chapter 13, in situations in which cost-benefit analysts are unable to measure social surplus changes in primary markets, they may infer them instead from the demand shifts in secondary markets. For example, imagine that analysts have no information about the demand schedule for fishing days, but they do know how the demand schedule for fishing equipment will change. With no direct measure of the benefits from stocking the lake, they might take the difference between the social surplus in the fishing equipment market after the project (based on demand schedule D_{E_1}) and the social surplus in the equipment market prior to the project (based on demand schedule D_{E_0}). They would then apply some scaling factor to correct for underestimation that results from the fact that not all the consumer surplus from fishing will be reflected in the equipment market. (Some fishers will use old equipment and collect their own bait—their surplus will not appear in the equipment market. Moreover, equipment and bait comprise only some of the inputs to fishing.)

Efficient Secondary Market Effects with Price Changes[1]

The situation is more complex when the supply schedule in the secondary market is upward sloping. To see this, we examine the effect of stocking the lake on the demand for golfing. In Figure 5.2, panel (a) once again shows the demand for fishing days, whereas panel (b) now shows the demand for golfing days. As before, the reduction in the price of fishing days from P_{F_0} to P_{F_1} as a result of stocking the lake causes an increase in social surplus equal to the area $P_{F_0}abP_{F_1}$ (for the moment ignore demand schedules D_{F_1} and D^*).

As fishing and golf are presumed to be substitutes, a reduction in the price of fishing days from P_{F_0} to P_{F_1} would cause the demand for golfing to fall. Thus, the demand schedule for golfing in panel (b) would shift to the left from D_{G_0} to D_{G_1}. As previously emphasized, by itself, this shift does not represent a change in consumer surplus that is not already fully accounted for in measuring the change in consumer surplus in the primary market. Golfers are obviously not made worse off by stocking the lake, although some may now place a lower valuation on golf. Instead, by itself, the shift in demand merely indicates that in the absence of golf, the consumer surplus gains from stocking the lake would have been even larger. The existence of golf is reflected in the location of the demand schedule for fishing days, which is further to the left than it would have been if golf were not available as a substitute for fishing.

The shift of demand from D_{G_0} to D_{G_1}, however, causes the fees for golf course use to fall from P_{G_0} to P_{G_1}. This, in turn, results in an increase in consumer surplus, one represented by the area $P_{G_0}efP_{G_1}$, which has not previously been taken into account. In addition, the fall in golfing fees also causes a reduction in producer surplus equal to area $P_{G_0}gfP_{G_1}$. As the reduction in producer surplus exceeds the increase in consumer surplus, a net loss in social surplus equal to the area of triangle *efg* results.[2]

Should this loss in social surplus in the golfing market be subtracted from the social surplus gain in the fishing market in measuring net gains from the project? It is frequently unnecessary to do so. The reason is that the increase in consumer surplus gain in the fishing market is often likely, in practice, to be measured as the area $P_{F_0}acP_{F_1}$ rather than as the area $P_{F_0}abP_{F_1}$. If measured in this way, the increase in consumer surplus in the fishing market would be understated by the triangular area *abc*, but this triangle typically closely approximates triangle *efg*, the net loss in social surplus in the golfing market.

To see why the consumer surplus gain in the fishing market may, in practice, be measured as the area $P_{F_0}acP_{F_1}$ rather than as the area $P_{F_0}abP_{F_1}$, one must recognize

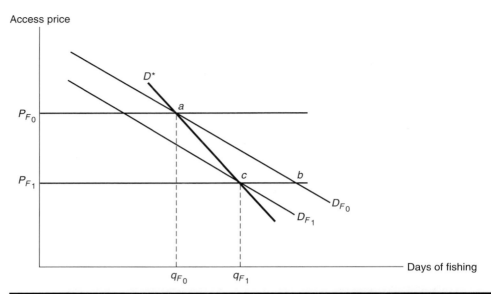

FIGURE 5.2(a) Primary Market: Market for Fishing Days

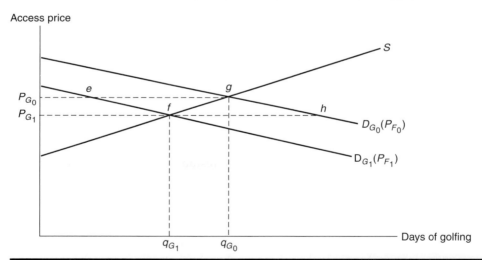

FIGURE 5.2(b) Secondary Market: Market for Golfing Days (Price Effects)

that our fishing story does not end with the shift in the demand schedule in the secondary market. If golf and fishing are substitutes, the reduction in golf course fees will cause people to switch from fishing to golf and the demand for fishing days will fall. This is shown in panel (a) as a leftward shift in the demand schedule for fishing days from D_{F_0} to D_{F_1}. By itself, this shift does not cause any further changes in social surplus; because we have assumed that the supply of fishing days is perfectly elastic, prices in the market for fishing days are unaffected. Note, however, that by drawing a line between the original and the final equilibrium points in panel (a) of Figure 5.2—that is, between points *a* and *c*—one can derive a special type of demand schedule, D^*.

This demand schedule, which is sometimes called an *observed* or an *equilibrium* demand schedule,[3] indicates what the demand for fishing days will be once prices in other markets, including the market for golfing days, have fully adjusted to the change in prices in the market for fishing days. Thus, D^* differs from the demand schedules D_{F_0} and D_{F_1}, which as mentioned earlier, indicate the number of fishing days demanded at each price for fishing days, *holding the prices of all other goods constant*. As it is frequently difficult statistically to hold the prices of secondary goods constant while measuring the relation between price and quantity demanded in a primary market, empirically estimated demand schedules—the ones actually observed and available for use in a CBA—often more closely resemble equilibrium demand schedules such as D^* instead of "textbook-style" demand schedules such as D_{F_0} and D_{F_1}.[4]

Thus, the equilibrium demand schedule, D^*, is the one that may be used in practice to obtain a measure of the increase in social surplus resulting from the reduction in the price of fishing days. However, the resulting measure, $P_{F_0} ac P_{F_1}$, understates the true measure of the gain in social surplus in the primary market, $P_{F_0} ab P_{F_1}$, by the triangular area *abc*. But, as previously suggested, area *abc* provides a good approximation of area *efg* in panel (b),[5] the area that should be subtracted from area $P_{F_0} ab P_{F_1}$ to obtain an accurate measure of the overall net gains from stocking the lake. In other words, area *abc* represents part of the benefits from the fish stocking project and area *efg* an approximately offsetting cost of the project. Hence, by using the equilibrium demand schedule to measure the change in social surplus, we incorporate social surplus changes that occur in the market for golfing days, as well as those that occur in the market for fishing days. We do not need to obtain separate measures of the surplus changes that occur in secondary markets.[6]

This is significant because it illustrates an important general point: By using an equilibrium demand schedule for the primary market—the type of demand schedule that is often empirically estimated, and hence, available—one can capture the effects of policy interventions both in the primary market in which they were initiated and in all secondary markets. Thus, we can restate our earlier rule concerning project impacts in secondary markets: *We should ignore effects in undistorted secondary markets, regardless of whether or not there are price changes, if we are measuring benefits in the primary market using empirically measured demand schedules that do not hold prices in secondary markets constant.* Some interesting implications of this rule are illustrated in an international trade context in Exhibit 5.1, where an equilibrium demand schedule is used in assessing the effects of a policy that restrained automobile imports.

EXHIBIT 5.1

In 1981, under strong pressure from the Reagan administration and the U.S. Congress, the Japanese government agreed to limit the number of automobiles shipped to the United States. This so-called voluntary restraint agreement (VRA) was motivated by the notion that, because Japanese imports were close substitutes for U.S.-produced automobiles, a reduction in the number of imports would increase the sales of domestically produced cars.

A CBA of the VRA for automobiles, as well as other similar import restraint agreements, can be conducted with the aid of the model illustrated in Figures A and B in this exhibit. In this model, the U.S. market for cars imported from Japan is viewed as the primary market, as it is the market at which the policy action was directed, whereas the market for

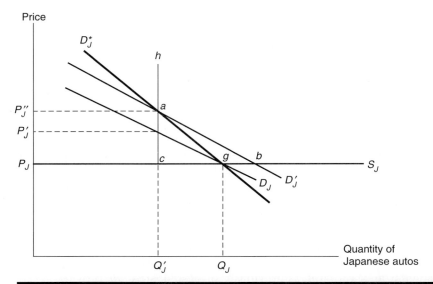

FIGURE A Japanese Automobiles (Primary Market)

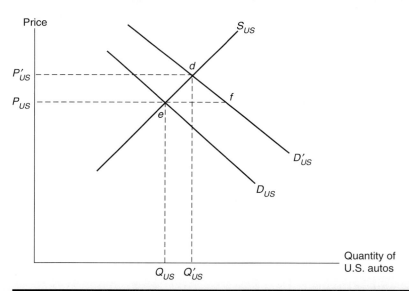

FIGURE B U.S. Automobiles (Secondary Market)

U.S.-produced automobiles is viewed as the secondary market. In the diagrams, D_J and S_J represent the demand and supply schedules for Japanese imports in the absence of the VRA, whereas D_{US} and S_{US} represent their counterparts in the market for domestically produced automobiles. Thus, in the absence of the VRA, Q_J cars would have been imported from Japan to the United States and sold at price of P_J, whereas Q_{US} domestically produced autos would have been purchased at a price of P_{US}. The diagrams reflect the fact that in 1981 Japanese imports were considerably less expensive, on average, than their U.S. counterparts. The flat supply schedule for Japanese automobiles is based on the assumption that the Japanese were willing to supply as many cars as U.S. consumers were willing to purchase at a price of P_J.

The VRA set a ceiling on the number of cars the Japanese could export to the United States at Q'_J, thereby substantially reducing the number of Japanese automobiles available to U.S. consumers. Thus, the new supply schedule for Japanese imports corresponded to $P_J ch$. As a result, the price of Japanese imports increased to P'_J. Because imported automobiles and domestic automobiles are substitutes, the higher price of Japanese automobiles caused an upward shift in the demand for domestic automobiles to D'_{US}, increasing their price to P'_{US} and their quantity to Q'_{US}. The increased price of domestic autos, in turn, caused the demand schedule for Japanese imports to shift to D'_J, prompting an additional increase in their price to P''_J.

It can be seen that the VRA resulted in deadweight loss equal to the triangular area *abc*. In addition, because of the higher prices paid for Japanese automobiles, Japanese automobile producers received a transfer from U.S. consumers corresponding to the rectangular area $P'_J acP_J$. Based on information about the prices and sales of imported and domestic automobiles under the VRA and empirical estimates of the slopes of the relevant supply and demand schedules, David G. Tarr and Morris E. Morkre calculated that in 1981 the deadweight loss equaled \$155 million and the transfer equaled \$753 million. If Japanese automobile producers are not given standing, and the very nature of the VRA suggests that they should not be, the sum of these two figures, \$908 million, was the total social cost of the VRA in 1981. Similar costs also occurred in each of the following years until 1985, when the policy was dropped.

Tarr and Morkre used an estimate of the equilibrium demand schedule, D^*_J, to compute the value of the deadweight loss resulting from the VRA. Thus, their estimate corresponded to area *agc,* rather than area *abc.* As pointed out in the text, by using the equilibrium demand schedule, we need focus only on the primary market to determine the effects of a policy on social surplus. By doing this, however, we ignore the domestic beneficiaries of the VRA—U.S. auto producers and workers. Indeed, producer surplus in the market for U.S. automobiles, the secondary market in our analysis, increased by area $P'_{US} deP_{US}$. This increase, however, was more than offset by the decrease in consumer surplus that occurred in the secondary market, area $P'_{US} dfP_{US}$. (As suggested in the text, the difference between the increase in producer surplus and the decrease in consumer surplus in the secondary market, area *def,* is taken into account by using the equilibrium demand schedule to measure the VRA's impacts in the primary market.) Thus, although U.S. auto producers gained surplus, a VRA policy must decrease overall domestic social surplus. In fact, as pointed out by Jose A. Gomez-Ibanez, Robert A. Leone, and Stephen A. O'Connell, over the long run a VRA can even hurt domestic auto producers and workers by, for example, encouraging Japanese producers to circumvent limits on the number of imports by selling high-price rather than low-price autos and by setting up production plants in the United States.

Source: David G. Tarr and Morris E. Morkre, "Aggregate Costs to the United States of Tariffs and Quotas on Imports: General Tariff Cuts and Removal of Quotas on Automobiles, Steel, Sugar, and Textiles," (Washington, DC: Bureau of Economics Staff Report to the Federal Trade Commission, 1984), pp. 54–74, and Jose A. Gomez-Ibanez, Robert A. Leone, and Stephen A. O'Connell, "Restraining Auto Imports: Does Anyone Win?" *Journal of Policy Analysis and Management,* 2, no. 2 (1983), 196–219.

VALUING BENEFITS AND COSTS IN DISTORTED SECONDARY MARKETS

Unfortunately, use of equilibrium demand schedules in primary markets misses part of the effects that occur in distorted secondary markets—that is, secondary markets in which prices do not equal social marginal costs. To see why, examine Figure 5.3, a slightly altered version of panel (b) of Figure 5.1. This new figure is based on the assumption that because of negative externalities the market price of fishing equipment, P_{E_0},

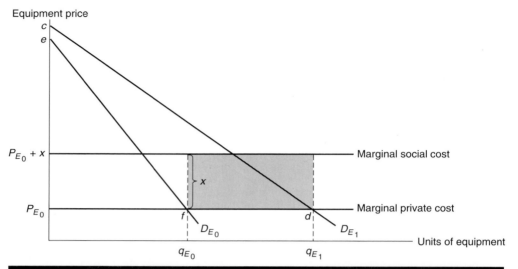

Equipment price

FIGURE 5.3 **Distorted Secondary Market: Market for Fishing Equipment (No Price Effect)**

underestimates the marginal social cost by x cents. (Think of the equipment as lead sinkers, some of which eventually end up in the lake, where they poison ducks and other wildlife. The x cents would then represent the value of the expected loss of wildlife from the sale of another sinker.) In this case, the expansion of consumption involves a social surplus loss equal to x times $(q_{E_1} - q_{E_0})$, which is represented in Figure 5.3 by the shaded rectangle. This loss, which is not reflected at all by market demand or supply schedules in the fishing market, should be subtracted from the benefits occurring in that market in order to obtain an accurate measure of net gains from the program.

Another type of distortion in secondary markets is imposed by the presence of taxes. For example, Figure 5.4 illustrates local produce markets for beef and chicken, which are substitutes for one another. For simplicity, the supply schedules in both markets are assumed to be perfectly elastic. In the absence of any taxes on these products, the price of beef (the primary good) would be P_B and the price of chicken (the secondary good) would be P_C.

For purposes of our illustration, let us assume that chicken is currently subject to a tax of t_C cents per pound, but beef is not presently taxed. Given this situation, the existing demand schedules for beef and chicken are represented by D_{B_0} and D_{C_0}, respectively. As panel (b) of Figure 5.4 indicates, the tax on chicken provides the government with revenue equal to the rectangular area *fgji* but reduces consumer surplus by the area of trapezoid *fgki*. Thus, the tax on chicken results in deadweight loss equal to the triangular area *gkj*.

Now assume that the government is considering imposing a tax of t_B cents per pound on beef. As indicated in panel (a), if the new tax is adopted, the government will collect revenue represented by the rectangular area *abde*, but consumers of beef will lose surplus equal to the area of trapezoid *abce*. Consequently, imposition of the new tax will result in deadweight loss in the beef market equal to the triangular area *bcd*.

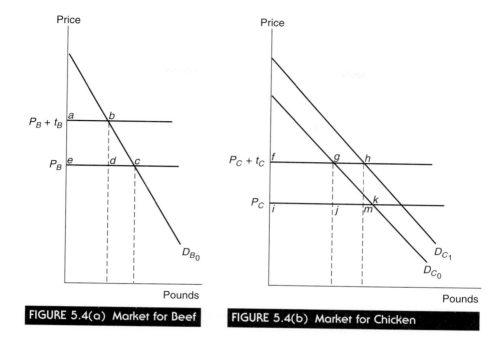

FIGURE 5.4(a) Market for Beef   **FIGURE 5.4(b) Market for Chicken**

Yet, the increase in the market price of beef shifts the demand schedule for chicken, a substitute, from D_{C_0} to D_{C_1}. For reasons discussed previously, this shift does not represent a change in consumer surplus. But the shift does cause an increase in the sale of chicken, resulting in an increase in tax revenues collected by the government. This increase, which is represented in panel (b) by area *ghmj,* is a benefit from the tax imposed on beef that could conceivably more than offset the deadweight loss occurring in the beef market.

The important lesson from this illustration is that, unlike situations in which there are no distortions in secondary markets, benefits and costs of a policy intervention cannot be fully measured by observing only the effects that occur in primary markets. Effects that occur in distorted secondary markets should, in principle, be valued separately. Yet, in practice, it may be very difficult to do so. Estimation problems usually preclude accurate measurement of welfare changes that occur in secondary markets. Estimating own-price effects (how quantity demanded of a good changes as its price changes) is often difficult; estimating cross-price effects (how the quantity demanded of good Y changes as the price of good Z changes) is more difficult yet. Consequently, we are rarely very confident of predictions of demand shifts in secondary markets. Moreover, when secondary markets are distorted, it is also very difficult to measure the size of the distortions. (Recall the x-cent loss of wildlife from the sale of another sinker. How is the value of x to be estimated?) But such measures are usually needed if program effects in distorted secondary markets are to be taken into account.

Fortunately, price changes in most secondary markets are likely to be small. Most pairs of goods are neither strong complements nor strong substitutes. Hence, large price changes in the primary markets are usually necessary to produce noticeable demand shifts in the secondary markets. Thus, even when secondary markets are distorted, ignoring these markets may result in relatively little bias to CBA.

SECONDARY MARKET EFFECTS FROM THE PERSPECTIVE OF LOCAL COMMUNITIES

Advocates of localized recreational facilities—for example, advocates of new sports stadiums, museums, and parks—frequently contend that major benefits will occur in secondary markets. For example, they predict that the demand for the services of local restaurants, hotels, and other businesses will increase. In addition they often claim that such projects result in *multiplier effects;* that is, as purchases from nearby businesses increase, these businesses will, in turn, also spend their newly gained revenues nearby, and this, in turn, will generate still more revenues that will be spent locally, and so forth.

As long as secondary markets in a community are not distorted, one should be very cautious in counting revenues from local projects that are generated by secondary market effects and multiplier effects as project benefits. There are several reasons for exercising this caution.

First, absent market distortions, these revenues are relevant only when standing is restricted to some group smaller than society as a whole, such as to residents of a specific geographic area. As discussed in this chapter, when society is broadly defined such claims cannot be justified unless the secondary market is distorted. For example, in evaluating the fish stocking project from the narrow perspective of the local county, one might count as a benefit increases in revenues received by local businesses resulting from nonresidents buying fishing equipment in the county or frequenting local hotels or restaurants. From the broader social or national perspective, they simply represent a transfer from nonresidents to residents because they only occur as a result of consumers shifting their spending from one geographic area to another.

Second, when standing is restricted to residents of a local community, any social surplus gains that accrue to nonresidents as a result of a local project can no longer be counted as project benefits. For example, surplus gains enjoyed by sports team fans or owners who reside outside the community no longer count. Thus, the case for a local project could actually be stronger if standing is not restricted to the local community than if it is.

Third, as indicated earlier in this chapter, even if the demand for local products and services increases as a result of a local project, suppliers do not receive increases in surplus unless prices increase. And even when prices do increase, the resulting increase in producer surplus is at least partially offset because consumers who are residents of the local community must now pay more for goods and services and, as a result, lose consumer surplus. However, some residents may value the growth that occurs in the local economy in and of itself. Moreover, expansions in local businesses may provide some opportunities for taking advantage of economies of scale and, therefore, could produce benefits in the form of lower production costs.

Fourth, localized multiplier effects generally tend to be relatively small because local businesses are often owned by nonresidents. Moreover, many of the purchases by local businesses are made outside the local area. Thus, expenditures made within a local area readily dissipate elsewhere, and this becomes increasingly true as standing is restricted to a smaller geographic area.

It is only when secondary markets are distorted that effects in these markets can potentially generate important benefits for the community. However, negative impacts can also occur, such as increases in pollution and congestion that result when nonresidents use local roads to reach a recreational facility. Local projects are most likely to generate significant positive benefits in secondary markets when local rates of unemployment are high or other local resources are idle, and there are substantial barriers to resource mobility. Under such circumstances, increases in demand in secondary markets and the multiplier effects that accompany these demand increases could significantly reduce levels of unemployment and increase the utilization of other idle resources such as empty buildings. The utilization of such idle resources as empty buildings obviously has very low opportunity costs, and, as discussed in Chapter 4, large increases in surplus accrue to many unemployed workers when they are hired. However, as also pointed out in Chapter 4, it is only when the rate of unemployment is fairly high that a substantial fraction of those hired is likely to be drawn from the ranks of the unemployed.

CONCLUSION

Most of the key concepts from Chapters 4 and 5 are summarized in Table 5.1. As the table indicates, changes in social surplus serve as the basis for measuring the costs and benefits of policies. The concept of opportunity cost helps us value the inputs that policies divert from other uses; the concept of willingness-to-pay helps us value policy outputs. The key to valuing outputs is to identify the primary markets in which they occur. When the outputs are not traded in organized markets, ingenuity is often needed to infer supply and demand schedules (remember the market for fishing days). For this purpose, various shadow pricing techniques, such as those discussed in Part III of this book are often needed. Costs and benefits that occur in undistorted secondary markets are typically very difficult to value but generally need not, indeed, should not, be added to costs and benefits that are measured in primary markets. Doing so will usually result in double counting.

The rules that appear in Table 5.1 cannot be used without first determining the type of market in which the various potential impacts of a project or program occur—primary, secondary, or factor market—and then determining whether the market is efficient or inefficient. In practice, this is sometimes difficult. To illustrate the sorts of judgments that must be made in practice, we conclude by listing selected impacts of a hypothetical street-widening project that would substantially increase traffic along the route and ask the reader to consider what type of market each occurs in and, hence, whether each should be included in a cost-benefit analysis of the project. Our own judgment concerning each, which is based on the assumption that surplus gains by those who drive on the street are measured using an equilibrium demand schedule for trips, appears in Exhibit 5.2.

1. The increased traffic would cause vibrations that crack the walls of adjacent houses.
2. Profits of gasoline at filling stations that are located along the route would increase.

TABLE 5.1 Rules for Measuring Social Benefits and Costs of Government Interventions

Type of Intervention	Efficient Markets	Inefficient Markets
Purchases from factor markets	If supply schedule is flat, value cost as direct budgetary expenditure (example: purchase materials from a competitive national market)	Value costs as direct budgetary expenditure less (plus) any increase (decrease) in social surplus in market
(concept: value costs as the opportunity cost of the purchased resources)	If supply schedule is not flat, value cost as direct budgetary expenditure less (plus) any increase (decrease) in social surplus in market (example: purchases of materials from a competitive local market)	(examples: hiring unemployed labor; purchases of materials from a monopoly)
Changes in costs to consumers or producers in primary markets	Value change as net change in social (i.e., consumer and producer) surplus plus (less) any increase (decrease) in government revenues	Value change as net change in social (i.e., consumer, producer and third-party) plus (less) increase (decrease) in government revenues
(concept: value benefits as willingness-to-pay for the change and costs as willingness-to-pay to avoid the change)	(example: government provision of goods and services to consumers or producers)	(example: tax or subsidy in market with externality)
Changes in quantities exchanged in secondary markets as a result of government intervention in primary or factor markets	If prices do not change in secondary market, ignore secondary market impacts	Costs or benefits resulting directly from increases in the size of the distortion should, in principle, be measured. Other impacts in secondary market should be ignored if prices do not change
(concepts: commodities exchanged in secondary markets are typically complements of or substitutes for commodities exchanged in primary markets; most impacts in secondary markets can be valued in primary markets)	If prices do change but benefits in primary market are measured using a demand schedule with other market prices held constant, then social surplus changes in the secondary market will always represent reductions in social surplus that should be subtracted from changes in the primary market. But if benefits in the primary market are measured using a demand schedule that does not hold other prices constant, ignore secondary market impacts (example: price changes in primary market cause demand schedule shifts in competitive secondary market)	(example: price changes in primary market cause demand schedule shift in secondary market with externality)

These rules pertain only to measuring impacts of government interventions on society as a whole. Issues associated with standing are ignored in the rules.

3. The property values of these stations would also increase.
4. Traffic on adjacent streets would decline. Therefore, the remaining motorists would experience quicker and cheaper journeys.
5. Air pollution along the route would increase.
6. The increased auto traffic would require the city to hire three more police officers to enforce traffic regulations.

7. The greater number of motorists would lead to an increased number of traffic violations and the resulting fines would mean that the city receives increased revenue.
8. Fewer people would ride buses; as a consequence the bus company would lay off ten bus drivers.
9. Widening the road would necessitate cutting down a number of trees. These trees would then be sold to a nearby sawmill.

EXHIBIT 5.2

1. The cracked walls in houses that would result from the increased traffic is a negative externality. Although the externality would occur in the secondary market for housing, it should be taken into account in the study.
2. The increased purchases of gasoline would occur in a secondary market. If this market is not seriously distorted (e.g., by externalities or monopoly power), the increase in gasoline purchases should be ignored in the study because any effects on social surplus will be captured by measuring surplus in the primary market. (Notice, however, that doing this neglects the fact that it is the owners of the filling stations, rather than automobile drivers, who receive the increase in surplus from increased purchases of gasoline; it also ignores the possibility that filling station owners who are located on other streets may face reductions in surplus.)
3. The property market is also a secondary market. Hence, these effects should also be ignored.
4. The decrease in traffic on adjacent streets can be viewed as a reduction in a negative externality, congestion, that distorts a secondary market (the adjacent streets are presumably substitutes for the street that would be widened). This is a real benefit that should be taken into account in the study.
5. Air pollution is a negative externality that distorts the primary market. Hence, it should be taken account of in the CBA.
6. The hiring of three additional police officers would take place in a factor market for labor and should be viewed as a direct cost of the project.
7. The increase in traffic fines would simply be a transfer between motorists and the city and, except for their distributional implications, can be ignored by the CBA.
8. The ten laid-off bus drivers would lose their jobs because the demand schedule in the secondary market for public transportation would shift to the left. Unless this market or the factor markets that serve this market are distorted, the shift in demand can be ignored in the CBA. Examples of such distortions are the loss of monopoly profits by the bus company or the inability of the bus drivers to find new jobs because of high rates of unemployment. Otherwise, the bus drivers would simply find new jobs at a similar level of compensation, implying that widening the road would have no effect on the social value of the output they produce.
9. The benefits and costs of cutting down the trees and selling them to a sawmill can be assessed independently of the street-widening project. If the benefits from cutting down the trees exceed the costs, then the trees should be cut regardless of whether the street-widening project is undertaken. However, if the costs exceed the benefits, then the costs and benefits of cutting the trees should be included in the CBA of the street-widening project.

Exercises for Chapter 5

1. Recall question 2 from the exercises for Chapter 4 in which an increase in the toll on a highway from $.40 to $.50 would reduce use of the highway by 10,000 cars per week.

a. Because of the reduced use of the highway, demand in the secondary market for subway rides increases. Assuming that the price of subway rides is set equal to the marginal cost of operating the subway and marginal costs are constant (i.e., the supply schedule is horizontal), and no externalities result from the reduced use of the highway and the increased use of the subway, are there additional costs or benefits due to the increased demand for subway rides? Why or why not?

b. Because of the reduced use of the highway, demand in the secondary market for gasoline falls—indeed, by 30,000 gallons per year. As we realize, there is a stiff tax on gasoline, one that existed prior to the new toll. Assuming that the marginal cost of producing gasoline is $1 per gallon, that these marginal costs are constant (i.e., the supply schedule is horizontal), that no externalities result from the consumption of gasoline, and that the gasoline tax adds 30 percent to the supply price, are there any additional costs or benefits due to this shift? If so, how large are they?

2. Recall question 3 from Chapter 4 in which a country imposes an import fee on the crude oil it imports. Assume that prior to the imposition of the import fee, the country annually consumed 900 million short tons of coal, all domestically mined, at a price of $22 per short ton. How would the CBA of the import fee change if, after imposition of the import fee, the following circumstances are assumed to result from energy consumers switching from crude oil to coal?

a. Annual consumption of coal rises by 40 million short tons, but the price of coal remains unchanged.

b. Annual consumption of coal rises by 40 million short tons and the price of coal rises to $23 per short ton. In answering this question, assume that the prices of other goods, including coal, were not held constant in estimating the demand schedule for crude oil.

c. Annual consumption of coal rises by 40 million short tons and the price of coal rises to $23 per short ton. In answering this question, assume that the prices of other goods, including coal, were held constant in estimating the demand schedule for crude oil. Also assume that the demand schedule for coal is completely inelastic.

d. The market price of coal underestimates its marginal social cost by $5 per short ton because the coal mined in the country has a high sulphur content that produces smog when burned. In answering this question, assume that, as in question 2.a, the annual consumption of coal rises by 40 million short tons, but the price of coal remains unchanged.

3. Recall question 3 from Chapter 4 in which a country imposes an import fee on the crude oil it imports. Imagine that all the crude oil imports to the country are made by ships owned by its nationals. The Association of Petroleum Shippers argues that the reduction in imports resulting from the import fee discussed in question 3 in Chapter 4 will drive down the price of shipping services and thereby inflict a loss on them. The Committee for Energy Independence, which favors the import fee, argues that the reduction in shipping prices will benefit consumers of shipping services. Which argument is correct? In preparing an answer, make the following assumptions: The import fee will reduce the quantity of imported crude oil from 3 billion to 2.5 billion barrels per year; the reduction in barrels shipped will drive per barrel shipping costs down from $1 per barrel to $.75 per barrel; and the elasticity of demand in the shipping market at the new equilibrium ($.75, 2.5 billion barrels) is −0.3. Also assume that the shipping market is undistorted and that the prices of other goods, including shipping services, were held constant in estimating the demand schedule for crude.

Notes

1. For a useful analysis that uses a somewhat different approach than the one presented in this subsection but reaches very similar conclusions, see Herbert Mohring, "Maximizing, Measuring, and Not Double Counting Transportation-Improvement Benefits: A Primer on Closed- and Open-Economy Cost-Benefit Analysis," *Transportation Research,* 27, no. 6 (1993), 413–424.

2. As advocates of a policy often claim benefits in secondary markets, it is somewhat ironic that demand shifts in undistorted secondary markets that cause price changes always involve losses in social surplus. This can be seen by using panel (b) in Figure 5.2 to illustrate the case of an outward shift in demand in a secondary market, as well as the case of an inward shift in demand. Simply take D_{G_1} as the original demand schedule and D_{G_0} as the postproject demand schedule. Using the postproject demand schedule for measuring social surplus changes, we see that the price increase from P_{G_1} to P_{G_0} results in a producer surplus increase equal to the area of trapezoid $P_{G_1}fgP_{G_0}$ and a consumer surplus loss equal to the area of $P_{G_1}hgP_{G_0}$ so that social surplus falls by the area of triangle *fgh*.

3. See Richard E. Just, Darrell L. Hueth, and Andrew Schmitz, *Applied Welfare Economics and Public Policy* (Englewood Cliffs, NJ: Prentice Hall, 1982), Chapter 9.

4. For greater detail concerning this point, see ibid., pp. 200–213.

5. Indeed, under certain assumptions, areas *abc* and *efg* will almost exactly equal one another. The most important of these assumptions is that the price changes in the two markets represented in Figure 5.2 are small and that no income effects result from these price changes. If there are no income effects, there will be symmetry in substitution between the two goods. In other words, their cross-substitution effects will be equal. That is, $\partial q_F/\partial P_G = \partial q_G/\partial P_F$. Given this equality, $\Delta P_F \cdot \Delta q_F \approx \Delta P_G \cdot \Delta q_G$. Hence, area *abc* approximately equals area *efg*. Typically, income effects do occur as a result of price changes, but as discussed in Appendix 3A, these effects tend to be very small for most goods. Consequently, one would anticipate that area *abc* would generally closely approximate area *efg*.

6. Separate measures would have to be obtained, however, to examine how benefits and costs were distributed among various groups. For example, area *abc* is a gain to consumers, whereas area *efg* is a loss to producers. To the extent these two areas are equal, they represent a transfer of surplus from producers to consumers. In addition, surplus corresponding to area $P_{G_0}efP_{G_1}$ is also transferred from producers to consumers.

CHAPTER

6

DISCOUNTING FUTURE BENEFITS AND COSTS

Both private and public decisions can have important consequences that extend over time. When consumers buy houses, automobiles, or education, they generally expect to derive benefits and incur costs over a number of years. When the government builds a dam, subsidizes job training, regulates carbon dioxide emissions, or leases the outer continental shelf for oil exploration, it sets in motion impacts that extend over many years. Often analysts have to compare projects with benefits and costs that arise in different time periods. Formally, they have to make intertemporal (across time) comparisons. To do this, analysts *discount* future costs and benefits so that all costs and benefits are in a common metric—the present value. Thus, they can measure and compare the net social benefits of each policy alternative using the *net present value* criterion.

This chapter deals with the practical issues one must know in order to compute the net present value of a project (or policy).[1] It assumes that the *social discount rate,* the rate at which analysts should discount future benefits and costs of a project, is known. As we discuss in Chapter 10, in practice the discount rate is often set for analysts by an oversight agency, such as the Congressional Budget Office in the United States, or the Treasury Board in Canada.

The sections of this chapter cover the following topics: the basics of discounting; compounding and discounting over multiple years; the timing of benefits and costs; long-lived projects and terminal values; comparing projects with different time frames; real versus nomimal dollars; relative price changes; and sensitivity analysis in discounting. Appendix 6A presents some shortcut methods for calculating the present value of annuities and perpetuities. Appendix 6B demonstrates how to calculate present values when interest is compounded more frequently than once per period. The topics covered in this chapter are essentially uncontroversial. Readers who are familiar with capital budgeting techniques may want to skip this chapter.

BASICS OF DISCOUNTING

Projects with Lives of One Year

Technically speaking, discounting takes place over *periods* rather than years. But because the period of discounting is a year in almost all applications, and it is easier to think of years rather than periods, we generally use the term *years*. To begin we consider projects that last for exactly one year. In the next section we consider projects that last for longer than one year. In Appendix 6B we discuss how to discount with multiple compounding during a period.

Suppose a state government has the opportunity to buy a parcel of land for $10 million. It knows that if it buys the land, then the land will be sold for $11 million one year from now. Should the state buy the land now?

Before proceeding further, it is often useful to lay out the annual benefits and costs of the project on a *time line* as shown in Figure 6.1. A time line is really useful to clarify the timing of the benefits and costs of a project. The horizontal axis represents time measured in years. Benefits appear above the time line, whereas costs are below the time line.

The state should compare the project that has a cost of $10 million now and a benefit of $11 million in one year to the most likely alternative—the status quo. There are three ways to do this, each of which gives the same answer.

Future Value Analysis   This method compares what the state will receive in the future if it invests in the project with what it will receive in the future if it invests the money in the best alternative. Suppose that if the state does not buy the land it will invest the money in treasury bills (T-bills) at an interest rate of 7 percent.[2] If it buys the T-bills, it will have $10.7 million in a year—the principal amount of $10 million plus interest of $10 million × 0.07 = $700,000. This amount, $10.7 million, is called the *future value (FV)* of the T-bills because it represents the amount the state will have in a future period if it buys the T-bills. The state can compare this future value with the future value it will receive if it invests in the land, $11 million, and choose the alternative that has the highest future value. In this example, the state should buy the land.

FIGURE 6.1 A Time Line Diagram

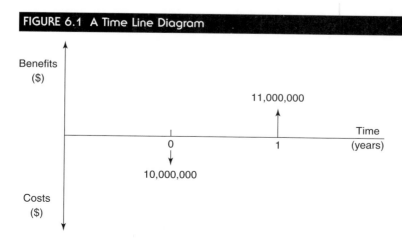

In general, the future value in one year of some amount X is given by the following formula:

$$FV = X(1 + i) \qquad \textbf{(6.1)}$$

where i is the annual rate of interest. The future value is also called the *compound value*. Equation (6.1) illustrates the basic idea of *simple compounding*. We present this method first because the idea of simple compounding is intuitively appealing for anyone who has ever had a savings account. For example, if one invests \$1,000 in a savings account at 5 percent, one will have $\$1,000(1 + 0.05) = \$1,050$ in a year.

Note that interest rates are often stated as percentages, such as 5 percent. This corresponds to an interest rate, i, equal to 0.05.

Present Value Analysis   We now switch from compounding to discounting and from future values to present values. Present value analysis compares the amount of money the state must invest today in T-bills in order to have the same amount in a year that it will have if it buys the land with the amount it will invest in T-bills now if it does not buy the land. The *present value* (*PV*) of the land is the amount the state must invest today in T-bills that yield 7 percent in order to obtain the value of the land in a year, \$11 million. Setting $X = PV$ and $i = 0.07$ in equation (6.1) gives:

$$PV(1 + 0.07) = \$11,000,000$$

Solving this equation for *PV* gives:

$$PV = \frac{\$11,000,000}{1.07} = \$10,280,374$$

The present value of buying the land is \$10,280,374. In contrast, the present value of the best available alternative, buying the T-bills now, is \$10 million.[3] Comparing these two present values shows that the state will be \$280,374 better off in present value terms if it buys the land.

The present value, *PV*, of an amount that will be received in the future is the current equivalent value of that amount given prevailing interest rates. In general, if the prevailing interest rate is i, then the present value of an amount received in one year is given by:

$$PV = \frac{Y}{1 + i} \qquad \textbf{(6.2)}$$

The process of calculating the present value of future amounts is called *discounting*. Comparing equations (6.1) and (6.2) shows that discounting is the opposite of compounding.[4] As is evident from equation (6.2), the present value of a future amount decreases as the interest rate increases.

Net Present Value Analysis   This method calculates the present values of all the benefits and costs of a project, including the initial investment, and sums them to obtain the *net present value* (*NPV*) of the project. For the land purchase example, the *NPV* is the difference between the present value of the land and the current cost of the land:

$$NPV = \$10,280,374 - \$10,000,000 = \$280,374$$

These calculations are represented graphically on a time line in Figure 6.2. As the *NPV* of buying the land is positive, the state should invest in this project. The state will be \$280,374 better off in present value terms if it buys the land.

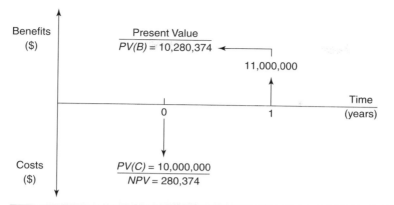

FIGURE 6.2 *NPV Calculation*

The *NPV* of a project equals the difference between the present value of the benefits, *PV(B)*, and the present value of the costs, *PV(C)*:

$$NPV = PV(B) - PV(C) \tag{6.3}$$

As mentioned in Chapter 1, the *NPV* method provides a simple criterion for deciding whether to undertake a project. If the *NPV* of a project is positive, then one should proceed with it; if the *NPV* is negative, then one should not. The positive *NPV* decision rule assumes implicitly that there is no other alternative with a higher *NPV*. *If there are multiple, mutually exclusive alternatives, then one should select the alternative with the highest NPV.*

The foregoing example assumes that the state has $10 million available that could be used either to buy the land or to invest at interest rate *i*. Sometimes analysts calculate *NPV*s of projects for which the government may not have all the cash immediately available and it may have to borrow some funds. *Implicitly, analysts assume that the government can borrow or lend funds at the same interest rate* i. *Under this assumption it does not matter whether the government currently has the money or not: The NPV rule still holds.* In Chapter 10 we discuss how the source of funding for a project may affect the choice of the discount rate. However, even in these situations, analysts should select the project with the largest *NPV.*

COMPOUNDING AND DISCOUNTING OVER MULTIPLE YEARS

We now generalize these results across many years. As before we first discuss future values, then present values, and finally net present values.

Future Value over Multiple Years   Suppose that the state could invest the $10 million for five years with interest at 7 percent per annum compounded annually. Using equation (6.1), at the end of the first year the state would have $10 million $\times$ 1.07 = $10.7 million. Again using equation (6.1), at the end of the second year the state would have $10.7 million $\times$ 1.07 = $11.449 million. Notice that the interest in the second year, $0.749 million, is more than the interest in the first year, $0.700 million. In the second and subsequent years, interest is earned on the principal amount and on the interest that has been reinvested (*interest on the interest*). Interest on reinvested interest is called *compound interest,* and the process is called *compounding interest.*

Table 6.1 illustrates that when interest is compounded annually, the principal amount can grow quickly. For example, after only five years, the original capital amount has increased by over 40 percent. During this five-year period, the total interest is $4.026 million. If, instead, interest had been computed using *simple interest* (i.e., without compounding), then the annual interest would have been $0.700 million, which amounts to only $3.5 million in total. Over longer periods (ten years or more), the divergence between compound interest and simple interest becomes quite large. This gap increases with time, thereby lending credence to the adage of many pension funds sales agents who exhort young adults "to invest early and leave it there."

In general, if an amount, denoted X, is invested for n years and interest is compounded annually at i percent per annum, then the future value is:[5]

$$FV = X(1 + i)^n \tag{6.4}$$

For example, if $10 million is invested for four years with interest compounded annually at 7 percent, then the future value is:

$$FV = \$10(1 + 0.07)^4 = \$13.108 \text{ million}$$

The term $(1 + i)^n$, which gives the future value of $1 in n years at annual interest rate i, is called the *compound interest factor.* In this example, the compound interest factor is 1.3108. Most finance textbooks include an appendix of compound interest factors. Many pocket calculators have this function, as do most computer spreadsheet programs.[6]

There is a handy rule for computing approximate future values called the rule of 72. Capital roughly doubles when the interest rate (expressed in percentage points) times the number of years equals 72: $100 \times i \times n = 72$. For example, if the interest rate is 8 percent, then your capital doubles in $72/8 = 9$ years. Similarly, in order to double your capital in ten years, you need an interest rate of at least $72/10 = 7.2$ percent.

Present Value over Multiple Years   Now consider present values, which require discounting rather than compounding. Suppose that a branch of the federal government wants to undertake an organizational restructuring in three years, which is expected to cost $100,000 at that time. If interest rates are 6 percent, then the amount needed now

TABLE 6.1 Investment of $10 Million with Interest Compounded Annually at 7 Percent			
Year	*Beginning of Year Balance ($ millions)*	*Annual Interest ($ millions)*	*End of Year Balance ($ millions)*
1	10.000	0.700	10.700
2	10.700	0.749	11.449
3	11.449	0.801	12.250
4	12.250	0.858	13.108
5	13.108	0.918	14.026

to yield $100,000 in three years, denoted by *PV*, can be found by substituting into equation (6.4):

$$PV(1 + 0.06)^3 = \$100,000$$

Solving this equation for *PV* gives:

$$PV = \frac{\$100,000}{(1 + 0.06)^3} = \frac{\$100,000}{1.19102} = \$83,962$$

Consequently, the government branch would need $83,962 now to have $100,000 in three years.

In general, the present value of an amount received in *n* years, denoted *Y*, with interest compounded annually at rate *i* is:

$$PV = \frac{Y}{(1 + i)^n} \tag{6.5}$$

The term $1/(1 + i)^n$, which equals the present value of $1 received in *n* years when the interest rate is *i*, is called the *present value factor* or the *discount factor*. For example, the present value factor in the foregoing example equals $1/(1 + 0.06)^3 = .8396$. Again, these factors are available in most finance textbooks, on handheld calculators, and in computer spreadsheet programs.

If a project yields benefits in many periods, then we can compute the present value of the whole stream by adding the present values of the benefits received in each period. Specifically, if B_t denotes the benefits received in period *t* for $t = 0, 1, ..., n$, then the present value of a stream of benefits, denoted *PV(B)*, is:

$$PV(B) = \frac{B_0}{(1 + i)^0} + \frac{B_1}{(1 + i)^1} + \cdots + \frac{B_{n-1}}{(1 + i)^{n-1}} + \frac{B_n}{(1 + i)^n}$$

$$PV(B) = \sum_{t=0}^{n} \frac{B_t}{(1 + i)^t} \tag{6.6}$$

Similarly, if C_t denotes the costs incurred in period *t* for $t = 0, 1, ..., n$, then the present value of a stream of costs, denoted *PV(C)*, is:

$$PV(C) = \sum_{t=0}^{n} \frac{C_t}{(1 + i)^t} \tag{6.7}$$

To illustrate the use of equation (6.6), consider a government agency that has to choose between two alternative projects. Project I yields a benefit of $10,500 four years from now whereas project II yields $5,500 four years from now and an additional $5,400 five years from now. Assume the interest rate is 8 percent. Which is the better project? The present values of each project are:

$$PV(I) = \frac{\$10,500}{(1 + 0.08)^4} = \$7,718$$

$$PV(II) = \frac{\$5,000}{(1 + 0.08)^4} + \frac{\$5,400}{(1 + 0.08)^5} = \$4,043 + \$3,675 = \$7,718$$

In this example, the present values of the two projects happen to be identical. Time lines for these projects are shown in Figure 6.3.

Net Present Value of a Project   We have now introduced all of the material on basic discounting needed for CBA. As discussed earlier, the *NPV* of a project is the difference between the present value of the benefits and the present value of the costs, as represented in equation (6.3). Substituting equations (6.6) and (6.7) into equation (6.3) gives the following useful expression:

$$NPV = \sum_{t=0}^{n} \frac{B_t}{(1+i)^t} - \sum_{t=0}^{n} \frac{C_t}{(1+i)^t} \tag{6.8}$$

To illustrate the mechanics of computing the *NPV* of a project using this formula, suppose a district library is considering purchasing a new information system that will give users access to a number of online databases for five years. The benefits of this system are estimated to be $100,000 per annum, including both cost savings to the library and user benefits. The information system costs $325,000 to purchase and set up initially and $20,000 to operate and maintain each year. After five years, the system will be dismantled and sold for $20,000.[7] Assume the appropriate discount rate is 7 percent and there are no other costs or benefits.

A time line for this project is shown in Figure 6.4. It shows the timing of each of the benefits and costs, their present values, the present value of all the benefits, the pre-

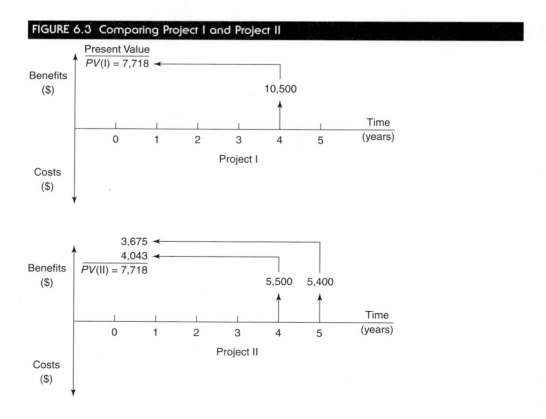

FIGURE 6.3 Comparing Project I and Project II

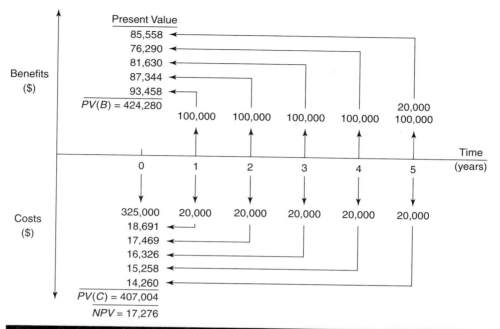

FIGURE 6.4 Time Line of the Benefits and Costs of the Library Information System

sent value of all the costs, and the *NPV* of the project. The present value of the benefits is $424,280, the present value of the costs is $407,004, and the *NPV* of the project is $17,276. As the *NPV* is positive, the library should purchase the new information system.

An alternative way to compute the *NPV* of a project is to compute the present value of the annual *net benefits (NB)*. Let $NB_t = B_t - C_t$ denote the annual net benefits arising in year t ($t = 0, 1, 2, ..., n$). It follows from equation (6.8) that the *NPV* of a project equals the present value of the net benefits:[8]

$$NPV = \sum_{t=0}^{n} \frac{NB_t}{(1 + i)^t} \tag{6.9}$$

To illustrate that equation (6.9) and equation (6.8) produce the same *NPV*, Table 6.2 contains the annual benefits, annual costs, and annual net benefits of the library information system project. Using equation (6.9), the present value of the net benefits of the project is $17,276, as shown in the last column of Table 6.2. This is the same value as the *NPV* obtained earlier by taking the difference between the present value of the benefits and the present value of the costs.

In many respects, tables and time lines are interchangeable. For comparison purposes a time line using net benefits appears in Figure 6.5. Tables and time lines present key information succinctly and facilitate computation of project *NPV*s. Neither is necessary. Analysts can experiment with them and use them whenever they are helpful. An advantage of time lines is that they indicate precisely when impacts occur during a year.

TABLE 6.2 The Net Present Value of the Library Information System

Year	Event	Annual Benefits	Annual Costs	Annual Net Benefits
0	Purchase and install	0	325,000	−325,000
1	Annual benefits and costs	100,000	20,000	80,000
2	Annual benefits and costs	100,000	20,000	80,000
3	Annual benefits and costs	100,000	20,000	80,000
4	Annual benefits and costs	100,000	20,000	80,000
5	Annual benefits and costs	100,000	20,000	80,000
5	Liquidation	20,000	0	20,000
	PV	$424,280	$407,004	$ 17,276

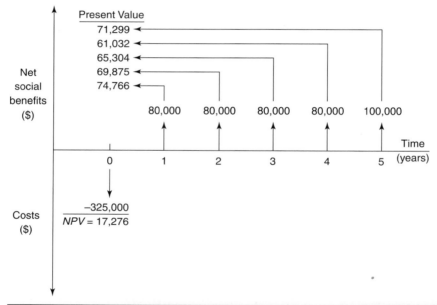

FIGURE 6.5 Time Line of the Net Social Benefits of the Library Information System

Two special situations are worth discussing briefly. For some projects all of the costs occur immediately ($t = 0$) and only benefits occur in the ensuing years ($t = 1, 2, ..., n$). In this situation, equation (6.8) simplifies to:

$$NPV = \sum_{t=0}^{n} \frac{B_t}{(1 + i)^t} - C_0$$

For a project with some impacts that last indefinitely, we replace n in equation (6.8) or (6.9) with infinity, ∞. Alternatively, we discount over some finite period and use a terminal value to capture the present value of subsequent net benefits. Estimation of terminal values is discussed later in this chapter.

TIMING OF BENEFITS AND COSTS

The compounding and discounting formulas presented so far assume that all benefits and costs occur at the end of each period (year). Impacts are assumed to arise immediately ($t = 0$), or at the end of the first year ($t = 1$), or at the end of the second year ($t = 2$), and so on. For many projects this is a reasonable assumption. Furthermore, when most of the costs occur early in the project and most of the benefits occur late in the project, this assumption is conservative in the sense that the *NPV*s are lower than they would be if they were computed under alternative assumptions.

To illustrate this point, reconsider the library information system example, but now assume that the annual benefits of $100,000 all occur at the beginning of each year instead of at the end of each year, and assume the timing of all other benefits and costs is unchanged. A time line under these assumptions is given in Figure 6.6. The present value of the benefits has increased by $28,702 from $424,280 to $452,982, and the *NPV* of the project has increased by $28,702 from $17,276 to $45,978, more than two and a half times the initial amount. Clearly, the *NPV* can vary considerably according to the assumption made about the timing of benefits or costs.

FIGURE 6.6 Time Line of Benefits and Costs of the Library Information System Assuming User Benefits Occur at the Beginning of Each Year

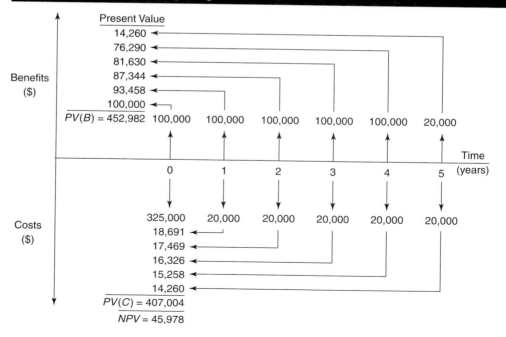

A more reasonable assumption might be to assume that the benefits occur through-out the year. The average of the two *NPVs*, ($17,276 + $45,978)/2 = $31,627, provides an estimate of the *NPV* under this assumption.

LONG-LIVED PROJECTS AND TERMINAL VALUES

Earlier we stated that analysts should discount benefits and costs over "the life of the project" using equation (6.8) or, equivalently, equation (6.9). These equations imply that all of the impacts attributable to the project have occurred during the first *n* years—the life of the project. Subsequent benefits and costs are assumed to equal zero.

Even though a project may be finished from an engineering or administrative per-spective after a relatively short period of time, the benefits (and some costs) may con-tinue to flow from the project for many years. In England, for example, cars travel on roads that were laid out by the Romans—more than 15 centuries ago. The Great Wall of China continues to generate tourism benefits even though it was built many cen-turies ago. The same issue also arises in human capital investment programs, especially training and health programs. For example, preschool training programs may benefit participants throughout their entire lives, years after they participated in the program; some benefits may even accrue to their children. All of these impacts should be in-cluded in a CBA. In practice, it is not clear how to handle costs and benefits that arise far in the future.

One option is to estimate the benefits and costs (or the net benefits) in each and every period and to calculate the *NPV* using the following formula:

$$NPV = \sum_{t=0}^{\infty} \frac{NB_t}{(1 + i)^t} \qquad (6.10)$$

It is practical to use this method if it is reasonable to assume that the net benefits are constant or grow at a constant rate; see Appendix 6A. But these assumptions may not be appropriate. Furthermore, as analysts are likely to be more confident about predict-ing the "near future" than the "far future," it is often useful to distinguish between them.

For most long-lived projects, analysts prefer to select a *relatively* short discounting period (often the *useful life* of the project), include a *terminal value* to reflect all sub-sequent benefits and costs, and perform *sensitivity analysis* on the terminal value. Thus, analysts distinguish between "near future" impacts and "far future" impacts. The latter are reduced to a single number, the terminal value. Formally, if *k* denotes the number of discounting periods and *T(k)* denotes the terminal value, then we use the following formula to compute the *NPV*:

$$NPV = \sum_{t=0}^{k} \frac{NB_t}{(1 + i)^t} + T(k) \qquad (6.11)$$

The terminal value is the net present value of all the benefits and costs that occur after the discounting period.[9] Because of uncertainty concerning the actual magnitude of the terminal value, sensitivity analysis is often conducted by selecting alternative terminal values and seeing how this affects the findings.[10]

When using terminal values, the length of the discounting period, *k,* is arbitrary in theory.[11] In practice, the discounting period is usually determined by the nature of each project. For example, it is common to use a 20-year discount period for highways because they tend to last about 20 years before they require major repairs.

Alternative Methods for Estimating Terminal Values

There is a variety of methods for estimating terminal values. One method is based on simple projections, another uses scrap values or liquidation values, a third uses (economic) depreciated values, a fourth is based on initial construction costs, and a fifth assumes the terminal value is zero.

Terminal Values Based on Simple Projections   One theoretically appropriate method estimates the terminal value based on simple extrapolations of benefits and costs (or net benefits). This is similar to estimating equation (6.10) directly, but it distinguishes between the "near future" and the "far future." Consider, for example, the construction of a new dike and suppose the annual net benefits have been calculated for the first 35 years. It is necessary to estimate a terminal value for the period after 35 years. One possibility is to make an assumption about the growth in future net benefits. Suppose analysts expect net benefits will be $1 million in the 36th year and they will grow at 1.5 percent per annum indefinitely. Using equation (6A.7) in Appendix 6A, the formula for the *PV* of a perpetuity that grows at a constant rate, and an interest rate of 8 percent, the value at the end of the 35th year of the subsequent net benefits is $1/(0.008 − 0.015) million = $15.38 million. The present value of these net benefits is $1.04 million.

For many government projects, especially training programs, it is reasonable to assume that the annual net benefits decay at a constant rate after some date. In this case equation (6A.7) can be used with a negative growth rate.

Terminal values obtained by this method are usually very sensitive to the discount rate and the growth rate, again emphasizing the importance of sensitivity analysis. However, there is strong evidence that, for medium- to long-term periods, simple forecasting models predict better than more complicated models. Thus, this method may estimate the *NPV* at least as well as more complicated direct estimation of equation (6.10).

Terminal Values Based on Salvage Value or Liquidation Value   For some projects, the scrap value, residual value, liquidation value, or salvage value of the plant and equipment may be used as the terminal value. For example, a school board may buy some buses that will last 25 years at which time they will be sold at market value for use by someone else or for scrap. This liquidation value or scrap value may be used as the terminal value. This method is appropriate when no other (social) costs or benefits arise beyond the discounting period, when there is a well-functioning market in which to value the asset, and when the market value reflects the asset's social value (e.g., no negative externalities).

Notice that many short projects have terminal values. For example, the library information system would be sold for $20,000 after only five years. This amount is a terminal value. Analysts should consider whether $20,000 is an accurate measure of the net social benefits of the equipment at liquidation. For example, if the equipment would be used in schools where its social value (less new set-up costs) would be more than $20,000, then a higher terminal value should be used.

In practice, it may be very difficult to determine the liquidation value of an asset. Consider estimating a terminal value for a highway project at the end of its useful life of, say, 20 years. Clearly there is no market for used highways and, even if there was one, it would probably not reflect the discounted value of future net social benefits.

Estimating Terminal Values Based on Depreciated Value   The third method recognizes that the stream of benefits and costs from a capital-oriented project is directly related to its depreciated value. Indeed, by definition, the value of an asset equals the present value of the net benefits that it generates. However, rather than focus on estimating the stream of benefits and costs, this method focuses on estimating the depreciated value.[12]

It is important to emphasize that we are referring to real (i.e., economic) depreciation, not accounting depreciation. There may be a huge difference. Economic depreciation concerns the decline in the economic value of an asset over time. In contrast, accounting depreciation is largely determined by tax or reporting requirements. Tax authorities may allow companies to take 100 percent depreciation in one year, in which case a company can write off 100 percent of the cost of an investment, even though the investment itself may yield benefits that extend over decades. Thus, the depreciated accounting value may bear no relationship to the reduced usefulness or the amount of wear and tear of an asset. *Accounting depreciation should never be included as a cost (expense) in CBA.*

Using economic depreciation value is applicable where there is no market for some capital item so that it remains in the public sector. However, this method suffers from three problems:

1. Estimating economic depreciation rates can be very difficult. Different assets depreciate at different rates. For example, aircraft are maintained at near 100 percent efficiency until they fall apart; in contrast, the efficiency of railroads initially declines very quickly and then decreases at a decreasing rate.
2. The amount of economic depreciation is often endogenous: Depreciation is affected by how the asset is used and maintained in the project. If usage is low and maintenance is high, then an asset may continue to perform at 100 percent efficiency for many years. If usage is high and maintenance is low, then it may start to fall apart quickly. Thus, a capital asset's value depends on the project itself.
3. The rate at which a piece of equipment or a project actually declines may bear no relationship to the stream of social benefits and costs that it generates. For example, an aircraft may be maintained at 100 percent efficiency but, if it is in "mothballs" and nobody flies in it, the social benefits may be zero.

Estimating Terminal Values Based on the Initial Construction Cost   This method estimates the terminal value based on initial construction costs. In the highway example we present in Chapter 1, we discount the annual benefits over 20 years, the expected useful life of the project before major repairs. The terminal value of the highway *at the end of the discounting period* was assumed to equal 75 percent of initial construction costs: $0.75 \times \$338.1$ million $= \$253.58$ million. That is, the future value of the highway in 21.5 years (20 years after construction *was completed*) was assumed to equal $253.58 million, which has a present value in 1986 dollars of $53.3 million. Consequently, according to the method basing terminal values on initial construction cost, the terminal value is $53.3 million.

In effect, this method is a special case of using depreciated values. When using this method, the analyst must select some proportion of the initial construction costs to use as a terminal value. However, there is no evidence to suggest that the present value of the net social benefits of a highway after 20 years is related to initial construction costs at all. The 75 percent figure is quite arbitrary. This method then is not intuitively appealing.

Setting the Terminal Value Equal to Zero   A final method chooses a fairly long discounting period and ignores subsequent benefits and costs. In effect, this is a special case of the first method we discussed—it is equivalent to assuming that after k periods the net benefits in each subsequent period are zero. In private-sector decision making, this may be a reasonable assumption because project evaluation requires only the consideration of private benefits and costs that may approach zero fairly quickly. But the social impacts of government projects may last many years. Analysts may omit important benefits or costs if they use a time horizon that is too short.

Conclusion Concerning Terminal Values

The analyst must decide on both the discounting period and the method for calculating the terminal value. *We suggest analysts discount over the useful life of the project and estimate the terminal value on the basis of simple projections that rely on reasonable assumptions.* The other methods that are used for computing terminal values are more difficult in practice or are more ad hoc. Thus, in practice, the estimated terminal value may bear little relation to the theoretically correct amount. *One should usually perform sensitivity analysis on the terminal value.*

The length of the discounting period and the method for calculating the terminal value may be interdependent. If, for example, the analyst is going to assume the terminal value is zero, then he or she should use a relatively long discounting period. If the analyst is using one of the other methods, then it makes sense to discount over the project's useful life. For physical projects this information is usually provided by engineers.

COMPARING PROJECTS WITH DIFFERENT TIME FRAMES

Projects with different time frames are not directly comparable. They should always be compared over the same discounting period.

Lack of Comparability between Projects with Different Time Frames

Suppose an electric utility company is considering two alternative proposals for new sources of energy. One is a major hydroelectric dam (*HE*), which would last 75 years; the other is a cogeneration plant, which would last 15 years. After considering all relevant social benefits and costs, and assuming a discount rate of 8 percent, the *NPV* of the 75-year hydroelectric project is $30 million and the *NPV* of the 15-year cogeneration project is $24 million. Is the hydroelectric project preferable simply because it has the larger *NPV*? The answer is "no." These projects are not commensurable because they have different life spans. The smaller project could be "rolled over" five times within the life of the hydro project.

There are two methods for evaluating projects with different time frames: rolling over the shorter project and the *equivalent annual net benefit method.* They always lead to the same conclusion, as we now illustrate.

Rolling Over the Shorter Project

Suppose that the utility decides to build the cogeneration power plant. Further suppose that in 15 years it builds a new cogeneration plant, in 30 years it builds another new cogeneration plant, and again in years 45 and 60. If so, the length of these five sequential cogeneration plants will be the same as the length of the hydroelectric project. This makes the projects comparable.[13]

The *NPV* of five back-to-back cogeneration power plants is:

$$NPV(5CP) = \$24 + \frac{\$24}{(1 + 0.08)^{15}} + \frac{\$24}{(1 + 0.08)^{30}} + \frac{\$24}{(1 + 0.08)^{45}} + \frac{\$24}{(1 + 0.08)^{60}}$$

$$= \$34.94 \text{ million}[14]$$

As this *NPV* is higher than the *NPV* of the hydroelectric project, the utility should build the cogeneration plant.

Equivalent Annual Net Benefit Method

An often easier way to compare projects of unequal lengths is the *equivalent annual net benefit (EANB) method.* The *EANB* of an alternative equals its *NPV* divided by the *annuity factor* that has the same life as the project (i.e., the present value of an annuity of $1 per year for the life of the project, discounted at the rate used to calculate the *NPV*):

$$EANB = \frac{NPV}{a_i^n} \tag{6.12}$$

where a_i^n is the annuity factor, which is defined by equation (6A.2). The *EANB* is the amount which, if received each year for the life of the project, would have the same *NPV* as the project. For example, the *EANBs* for the hydroelectric (*HE*) and the cogeneration (*CG*) projects equal:[15]

$$EANB(HE) = \$30/12.4611 = \$2.407$$

$$EANB(CG) = \$24/8.559 = \$2.804$$

The *EANB* of the cogeneration project is $2.804 million, which implies that this project is equivalent to an annuity of $2.804 million per year for 15 years. In contrast, the net benefit of the hydroelectric alternative is equivalent to an annuity of $2.407 million per year for 75 years. If one could continuously replace each project at the end of its life with a similar project, the cogeneration project would yield net annual benefits equivalent to $2.804 million per year indefinitely and the hydroelectric project would yield annual net benefits equivalent to $2.407 million per year indefinitely. Consequently, the cogeneration alternative is preferable, assuming continuous replacement is possible.

An Additional Advantage of the Cogeneration Project

In fact, if the utility chooses the cogeneration project, it may not be desirable to replace it with an identical cogeneration plant in 15 years. At that time a more efficient alternative may be available. In contrast, if the utility builds the hydroelectric project, then it is locked in for 75 years. Thus, the cogeneration project has an additional benefit because of its flexibility in allowing the introduction of more efficient technology if it becomes available during the 75-year period. Chapter 7 discusses such benefits, called quasi-option value, in more depth. Here, it is sufficient to recognize that this alternative has an additional benefit that is not incorporated in the *EANB*.

REAL VERSUS NOMINAL DOLLARS

Conventional private-sector financial analysis measures revenues, expenditures, net income, assets, liabilities, and cash flows in terms of historical monetary units. Such units are referred to as *nominal dollars* (sometimes called *current dollars*). However, if you have ever listened to an older person reminisce, then you probably know that a dollar purchased more in 1970 than it does now—"a dollar's not worth a dollar anymore!" For example, nominal per capita disposable personal income in the United States was four-and-one-half times higher in 1990 than in 1970 ($3,521 versus $16,236), but you could not buy four-and-one-half times as many goods and services on an average income in 1990 as you could on an average income in 1970. The purchasing power of a dollar declines with price inflation. In order to control for the declining purchasing power of a dollar due to inflation, we convert nominal dollars to *real dollars* (sometimes called *constant dollars*).

To obtain real, or constant, dollar measures, analysts adjust for changes in inflation. In effect, analysts *deflate* dollars to account for higher prices. The consumer price index (CPI) is the most commonly used *deflator*.[16] It is expressed as the ratio of the cost of purchasing a standard market basket of goods in a particular year to the cost of purchasing the same (or very similar) basket of goods in some base year, multiplied by 100. The CPI for the United States since 1970 is shown in Table 6.3.[17] Currently, the base year in the United States is 1982–84; thus, for the period 1982–84 the *CPI* = 100. Because the CPI for 1970 was 38.8, this implies that the cost of a basket of goods in 1970 was only 38.8 percent of the price of a similar basket of goods in 1982–84. Similarly, because the CPI for 1990 was 130.7, this implies that the price of a basket of goods in 1990 was 130.7 percent of the price in 1982–84 for a similar basket. Thus, the price of a basket of goods was 130.7/38.8 = 3.37 times higher in 1990 than in 1970. Consequently, returning to our example, a person on a salary of $3,521 in 1970 would be able to purchase in 1990 the same (or similar) basket of goods as a person on a salary of $3,521 × 3.37 = $11,865. Because the average income was $16,236 in 1990, we can conclude that effective (i.e., real) incomes increased by ($16,236 − $11,865)/$11,865 = 0.37, or 37 percent from 1970 to 1990.

In order to convert amounts measured in nominal dollars for some year into amounts measured in real dollars for the base year (1982–84), we simply divide by the CPI for that year (divided by 100). For example, the average real income of people in 1970 measured in 1982–84 dollars was $3,521/0.388 = $9,074, and the average real income of people in 1990 measured in 1982–84 dollars was $16,236/1.307 = $12,422.

TABLE 6.3 The U.S. Consumer Price Index (CPI)
All items
1982–84 = 100

Year	CPI	% Change	Year	CPI	% Change	Year	CPI	% Change
1970	38.8	5.7	1980	82.4	13.5	1990	130.7	5.4
1971	40.5	4.4	1981	90.9	10.3	1991	136.2	4.2
1972	41.8	3.2	1982	96.5	6.2	1992	140.3	3.0
1973	44.4	6.2	1983	99.6	3.2	1993	144.5	3.0
1974	49.3	11.0	1984	103.9	4.3	1994	148.2	2.6
1975	53.8	9.1	1985	107.6	3.6	1995	152.4	2.8
1976	56.9	5.8	1986	109.6	1.9	1996	156.9	3.0
1977	60.6	6.5	1987	113.6	3.6	1997	160.5	2.3
1978	65.2	7.6	1988	118.3	4.1	1998	163.0	1.6
1979	72.6	11.3	1989	124.0	4.8	1999	166.6	2.2

Source: ftp://ftp.bls.gov/pub/special.requests/cpi/cpiai.txt

To convert these amounts from base-year dollars to, say, 1994 dollars, they are multiplied by the CPI for 1994, which is 148.2 (divided by 100):

$$(\$3,521/0.388) \times 1.482 = \$13,449$$
$$(\$16,236/1.307) \times 1.482 = \$18,410$$

Thus, the average real incomes of people in 1970 and 1990, expressed in 1994 dollars, were $13,449 and $18,410, respectively. More generally, as the preceding example illustrates, to convert amounts expressed in year *a* nominal dollars into amounts expressed in year *b* real dollars, the year *a* dollar amounts are divided by the CPI for year *a* and multiplied by the CPI for year *b*.

Past Problems with the CPI

Although the CPI is the most widely used measure of inflation, it has historically overstated the rate of increase in the cost of living. Recently, a commission set up by the Senate Finance Committee and chaired by Michael Boskin estimated that in the United States the CPI overestimated inflation by about one percentage point per annum, with a range between 0.8 percentage point and 1.6 percentage points.[18] As a result, people receiving entitlements with increases linked to the CPI were, in effect, receiving more than was originally intended.

There were many reasons for the upward bias in the CPI in the past.[19] One problem was that the CPI did not accurately reflect consumers' purchases. In the pharmaceutical area, for example, when patents expire some consumers switch to generic drugs, which are often as effective as patented drugs but considerably less expensive. As this switch was not immediately picked up by the CPI, the cost of living was overestimated.[20] A second problem was that the CPI did not reflect changes in product quality or improvements in the quality of living due to new products.

Economists and statisticians are correcting these problems. In 1998 the U.S. CPI underwent some major revisions.[21] Nonetheless, we suggest that, when using historical

CPI data, *analysts should convert amounts measured in nominal dollars to amounts measured in real dollars in two ways: using the official CPI as suggested earlier in this section and using a price deflator that increases at one percentage point per annum less than the CPI.* For example, someone with an income of $100,000 in 1994 would have a real income in 1999 dollars of $112,416 using the official CPI, but an income of $107,018 using a price deflator that increases at one percentage point per annum less than the CPI.[22]

Analyzing Future Benefits and Costs in CBA

Analysts may project benefits and costs in either real dollars or nominal dollars. Also, they may use a real interest rate or a nominal interest rate. Care must be taken to ensure that the units of measurement of benefits and costs are consistent with the units of measurement of the discount rate. *If benefits and costs are measured in nominal dollars, then the analyst should use a nominal discount rate; if benefits and costs are measured in real dollars, then the analyst should use a real discount rate.* Both methods result in the same numerical answer.[23]

In the private sector, it is more natural to work in nominal dollars. Interest rates and other market data are expressed in nominal dollars, *pro forma* income and cash flow projections make more sense in nominal dollars, and the tax system is based on nominal amounts. However, for analysis of public policy projects, *it is usually easier and more intuitively appealing to express all benefits and costs in real dollars and to discount using a real discount rate.* Returning to our library example, it makes more sense to think about the current and future annual benefits in terms of cost savings to the library at today's prices and to think about user benefits in terms of the number of hours of use at today's value per hour than it does to think about these benefits in terms of future prices or values. If one expects user benefits will actually increase over time, for example, due to more people using the system or because each person uses it more often as he or she learns its capabilities, then the projected real annual benefits will increase. This would be clear if annual benefits and costs were in real dollars. If, alternatively, the annual benefits were expressed in nominal dollars, and they were increasing, it might not be immediately obvious whether the increases were due to increases in real benefits or were due to inflation.

If the analyst prefers to work in real dollars, but benefits, costs, or the interest rate are expressed in nominal dollars, then the amounts in nominal dollars must be converted to real dollars. To convert future benefits and costs from nominal dollars to real dollars, we use the formula for computing present values, equation (6.5), but discount at rate m, where m is the expected rate of inflation during the project.[24] To convert a nominal interest rate, i, to a real interest rate, r, with an expected inflation rate, m, we use the following equation:[25]

$$r = \frac{i - m}{1 + m} \qquad \textbf{(6.13)}$$

For example, if the nominal interest rate is 10 percent and inflationary expectations are 4 percent, then the real interest rate is $[(0.10 - 0.04)/1.04] \times 100 = 5.77$ percent.

If expected inflation is quite low (m is small), the real interest rate *approximately* equals the nominal interest rate minus the expected rate of inflation: $r \simeq i - m$. For example, if the nominal interest rate is 10 percent and inflationary expectations are 4 percent, then the real interest rate is approximately 6 percent.

In order to convert benefits or costs from real dollars to nominal dollars, analysts can use the formula for computing future values, equation (6.4), but compound at the expected rate of inflation. To convert a real interest rate to a nominal interest rate, solve equation (6.13) for *i*.

Estimates of Expected Inflation

Moving from real interest rates or dollars to nominal interest rates or dollars, or vice versa, requires an estimate of the *expected* rate of inflation *during the life of the proposed project*. Analysts often use the current CPI as an estimate of future inflation. However, this estimate will be too low when inflation is increasing and too high when inflation is decreasing. It would be better to use one of a number of widely available forecasts, although these are often available only for one-year or two-year forecasts.[26]

Inflation forecasts are available from reputable investment firms, branches of the federal government, a Federal Reserve Bank, or the OECD (Organization for Economic Cooperation and Development). Each week *The Economist* presents recent changes in consumer prices and the results of a poll of consumer price forecasts for the current year and the following year.

In the United States there are three easily accessible survey measures of inflationary expectations: the Livingston survey of professional economists, the Michigan survey of households, and the Survey of Professional Forecasters (SPF).[27] In a recent article, Lloyd Thomas compares the one-year predictive performance of these surveys and two simple naive alternatives, one using the latest 12-month CPI figure and the other based on the Fisher model of interest rates, equation (6.13).[28] He finds that the surveys perform better than the naive models, with the *median* household forecasts performing best. He notes that the forecasts of professional economists have improved over time, and he suggests that the SPF is likely to become increasingly popular. Of particular interest, SPF respondents have been asked to provide 10-year-ahead inflation forecasts of the CPI since 1991.

A Practical Example: Garbage Trucks

A practical example illustrates the basic issues in moving from market interest rates, which are nominal rates, to real interest rates. Consider a city that uses a rural landfill to dispose of solid refuse. By adding larger trucks to the refuse fleet, the city would save $100,000 in disposal costs during the first year, and *equivalent amounts* in each successive year. The trucks would be purchased today for $500,000 and would be sold after four years when the city will open a resource recovery plant that will obviate the need for landfill disposal. The real liquidation value of the trucks (i.e., the current market value of four-year-old trucks of the same type and quality as the city would buy) is $200,000. The city can currently borrow money at a market interest rate of 10 percent. Analysts generally expect that inflation will be 4 percent during the next four years. Should the city buy the trucks? As usual, the answer should be "yes" if the *NPV* is positive. Is it?

Using Real Dollars

The annual benefits and costs in real dollars are given in column 3 of Table 6.4. It is assumed that the annual savings are the same in real terms each year. This assumption is based on several implicit assumptions, for example, the amount of vehicle operating maintenance does not change over the period, and, if the city does not buy the larger trucks, it will not have to pay for overtime. Furthermore, it implicitly assumes that the *relative valuations* (prices) of wages, gasoline, and other components that figure into the benefit calculations do not change over time.

As benefits and costs are expressed in real dollars, we need to use a real discount rate. As the market interest rate is 10 percent and inflationary expectations are 4 percent, the real interest rate is approximately 6 percent. More precisely, using equation (6.13), the real interest rate is 5.77 percent.[29] Applying this real discount rate to the real annual costs and benefits yields an *NPV* equal to $8,155. Thus, as long as no alternative equipment configuration offers a greater *NPV*, the city should purchase the larger trucks.

Using Nominal Dollars

If analysts take the nominal market interest rate facing the city as the appropriate discount rate, then they must predict future costs and benefits in nominal dollars. The right-hand column of Table 6.4 shows the anticipated benefits and costs of this project in nominal dollars, assuming a 4 percent annual inflation rate. As mentioned earlier, this example assumes that wage rates, gasoline prices, and other prices that figure into the benefit calculations increase at the same rate as the general price level. To convert amounts in real dollars to nominal dollars, simply inflate them by the expected rate of inflation, m. Notice that the city expects to receive $233,972 when it sells the trucks at the end of the fourth year. This is called the *nominal liquidation value* of the trucks.

Discounting the benefits and costs measured in nominal dollars using a nominal (market) interest rate gives an *NPV* of the project equal to $8,155, as shown in Table 6.4. Thus, the two methods give the same answer.

TABLE 6.4   The Net Preset Value of Investment in New Garbage Trucks

Year	Event	Annual Benefits and Costs (In real dollars)	Annual Benefits and Costs (In nominal dollars)
0	Purchase	−500,000	−500,000
1	Annual savings	100,000	100,000
2	Annual savings	100,000	104,000
3	Annual savings	100,000	108,160
4	Annual savings	100,000	112,486
4	Liquidation	200,000	233,972
	NPV	8,155[a]	8,155[b]

[a]Using a real discount rate of 5.769231 percent.
[b]Using a nominal discount rate of 10 percent.

RELATIVE PRICE CHANGES

The preceding section discusses how to handle expected price changes due to inflation (i.e., general price increases). It assumes relative prices do not change. This section discusses how to handle relative price changes.

The importance of relative price changes is well illustrated by a CBA of a coal development project in British Columbia to supply Japanese customers.[30] Consider Table 6.5. The second, third, and fourth columns contain the proposed project's benefits, costs, and net benefits, respectively, according to a CBA prepared by the provincial government of British Columbia (roughly equivalent to a state government in the United States).[31] Overall, the net benefits were estimated to be $330 million. The main beneficiaries of this project were expected to be the Canadian National Railway (CNR), which was the state-owned railway company at that time, and the Canadian federal

TABLE 6.5   CBA of North East Coal Development Project

	Benefits ($ million)	Costs ($ million)	Net Benefits Base Case ($ million)	90% Base Price ($ million)	90% Base Price and Quantity ($ million)
Mining Sector	3,316	3,260*	56	−146	−240
Transport Sector					
Trucking	33	33	0	0	0
Canadian National Railway	504	358	146	146	121
B.C. Railway	216	202	15	15	6
Port Terminal	135	150	−15	−15	−23
Analysis and Survey	11	11	0	0	0
British Columbia**					
Royalties	77	0	77	69	62
Corporate Taxes	154	0	154	125	107
Producer Surplus (Labor)	25	0	25	25	25
Environment	10	5	5	5	5
Highways***	0	88	−88	−88	−88
Tumbler Ridge Branchline	91	267	−176	−176	−185
Canada					
Corporate Taxes	132	0	132	107	92
Highways, Port Navigation	0	26	−26	−26	−26
Producer Surplus (Labor)	25	0	25	25	25
Totals	4,729	4,400	330	66	−119

* Includes taxes and royalties.
** Excluding impacts included elsewhere.
*** Highways, electric power, townsite.
Source: Based on W. G. Waters II, "A Reanalysis of the North East Coal Development," (undated), Tables 2 & 3. All figures in millions of 1980 dollars, assuming a 10 percent real discount rate with the discounting period ending in 2003 and no terminal value.

government, which would receive corporate taxes. Here corporate taxes and royalties are a benefit to government but a cost to the mining sector; thus, they are a transfer and they "net out." The British Columbian government was also expected to benefit from royalties and higher corporate taxes, but it would pay for the Tumbler Ridge Branchline, an extension of the provincially owned railway system to the North East Coal Development Project. The mining sector would benefit in terms of increased producer surplus. Also, this project was expected to create jobs for unemployed workers in British Columbia and the rest of Canada. The present value of the producer surplus to labor was estimated to be $25 million. Notice that the analysis does not include any consumer surplus because all of the coal would be exported.

The fifth column contains the expected net benefits to each sector if the price of coal were to fall to 90 percent of the base price. Under this assumption, the aggregate net benefits would fall by $264 million from $330 million to $66 million, a substantial change. The sixth column contains the expected net benefits to each sector if the price of coal were to fall to 90 percent of the base price and Japanese customers were to cut back their purchases of coal to 90 percent of their expected orders. Under this assumption, the overall net benefits would fall by $449 million from $330 million to −$119 million.[32] Thus, relatively small changes in relative prices and in quantities purchased have a huge impact on the *NPV* of this project.

In this example the benefits and costs are broken down by sector to illustrate distributional impacts. The main anticipated "winners" were the CNR and the federal government of Canada. If the price of coal fell by 10 percent, then the mining sector would lose money. Also, the residents of British Columbia would switch from being marginal "winners" to marginal "losers," largely because royalties and corporate taxes would decrease while the costs of highways and the Tumbler Ridge Branchline are fixed. If the price and quantity levels were to fall to 90 percent of the anticipated levels, then the mining sector would lose badly.

SENSITIVITY ANALYSIS IN DISCOUNTING

This chapter assumes that the rate that should be used to discount future benefits and costs is known. However, for reasons discussed in Chapter 10, there are significant differences of opinion about the correct social discount rate. Also, for reasons discussed earlier in this chapter, there is frequently considerable uncertainty about the magnitude of the terminal value. Because the discount rate and the terminal value often "drive" a CBA, analysts frequently conduct sensitivity analyses with respect to these two parameters.

Varying the Discount Rate and the Terminal Value

As discussed more fully in Chapter 7, the most straightforward way to perform sensitivity analysis is to systematically vary each parameter about which there is uncertainty and recalculate the *NPV*. This is very easy to do on a spreadsheet. If the policy recommendations are robust (i.e., the *NPV* remains either positive or negative) to plausible alternative values of the parameters, we can have greater confidence in them.

Figure 6.7 plots the *NPV* of the library project against the discount rate for two different terminal values, one with a terminal value of $20,000 and the other with a terminal value of $0. Clearly, the choice of the discount rate is important. As the discount rate increases, the *NPV* of the project decreases. This common pattern arises for investment projects whose costs occur early and whose benefits occur late. Using a higher discount rate results in a lower *NPV* because the future benefits are discounted more than are the more immediate costs.

The top curve corresponds to a terminal value of $20,000. The *NPV* equals $17,276 if the discount rate equals 7 percent. The *break-even* discount rate is 8.9 percent, which can be read off the graph where the *NPV* = 0 or found exactly by trial and error.[33] As long as the appropriate discount rate is less than 8.9 percent, the project offers a positive *NPV* and should be adopted. If the appropriate discount rate is more than 8.9 percent, then the project has a negative *NPV* and it should not be approved. Most analysts agree that the appropriate real social discount rate is less than 8.9 percent—see Chapter 10. Consequently, we can be reasonably confident that if the project goes ahead it will have a positive *NPV*.

If the terminal value is zero, the curve shifts down by the discounted value of $20,000. As this value decreases as the discount rate increases, the curve shifts down less for high interest rates than for low interest rates. Thus, it is flatter than the curve with a terminal value of $20,000. Although the *NPV* is smaller at every interest rate, it is still positive as long as the social discount rate is less than 7.35 percent. As most analysts believe that the appropriate real social discount rate is less than 7.35 percent, we would still recommend the project should proceed.

Of course, we can also compute the *break-even terminal value*—the terminal value at which the *NPV* equals zero. Assuming the appropriate discount rate is 7 percent, the break-even terminal value is −$4,230, which implies the city would just break even on the project if it *cost* $4,230 to dismantle the project at the end.[34]

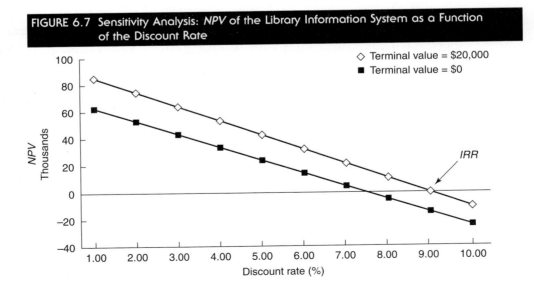

FIGURE 6.7 Sensitivity Analysis: *NPV* of the Library Information System as a Function of the Discount Rate

The Internal Rate of Return

The discount rate at which the *NPV* is zero is also called the *internal rate of return* (*IRR*). The *IRR* of the library information system is 8.9 percent, which implies that it is equivalent to a project of similar size that provides annual benefits equal to 8.9 percent of the original amount for five years (the length of the project) and returns all of the initial invested capital at the end of the 5th year.

The *IRR* can be used to express the decision rule for selecting projects *when there is only one alternative to the status quo.* If the *IRR* of a project is greater than the appropriate discount rate, then one should proceed with the project; if the *IRR* is less than the appropriate discount rate, one should not proceed with it. In this example, the library should proceed with the project because the *IRR* of 8.9 percent is greater than the appropriate discount rate of 7 percent. The basic idea, which we discuss in depth in Chapter 10, is that society should only invest in projects that earn a higher return than could be earned by investing the resources elsewhere. In other words, the appropriate discount rate should reflect the opportunity cost of the funds.

There are, however, a number of potential problems with using the *IRR* for decision making. First, it may not be unique; that is, there may be more than one discount rate at which the *NPV* is zero. This problem only arises when annual net benefits change more than once from positive to negative (or vice versa) during the discount period. Second, *IRR*s are percentages (i.e., ratios), not dollar values. Therefore, they should not be used to select one project from a group of mutually exclusive projects that differ in size. This scale problem always arises with the use of ratios, including *IRR*s and benefit-cost ratios. Nonetheless, if it is unique, the *IRR* conveys useful information to decision makers or other analysts who want to know how sensitive the results are to the discount rate.[35]

CONCLUSION

This chapter presents the main issues concerning the mechanics of discounting in CBA. It assumes that the appropriate discount rate is known. In fact, determination of the appropriate discount rate to use in CBA is a contentious issue, which we discuss in Chapter 10.

Appendix 6A

SHORTCUT METHODS FOR CALCULATING THE PRESENT VALUE OF ANNUITIES AND PERPETUITIES

In many practical situations the benefits or costs of a project can be treated as annuities or perpetuities. The present value of an annuity or perpetuity is relatively easy to compute.

An *annuity* is an equal, fixed amount received (or paid) each year for a number of years. A *perpetuity* is an annuity that continues indefinitely. Suppose, for example, that in order to finance a new highway, a state government issues $100 million worth of 30-year bonds with an interest rate of 7 percent paid annually. The annual interest payments of $70,000 are an annuity. If, at the end of *each* 30-year period, the state government refinances the debt by issuing another 30-year bond that also has an interest rate of 7 percent, then the annual interest payments of $70,000 would continue indefinitely, which is a perpetuity. Sometimes an annuity or perpetuity grows or declines at a constant rate. In any of these situations, using equation (6.6) or (6.7), the method described in the main body of this chapter to compute the present value, can be extremely time consuming. Fortunately, some simple formulas enable analysts to compute present values easily.

PRESENT VALUE OF AN ANNUITY

The library information system problem contains two annuities: the annual benefits of $100,000 per year for five years, which we refer to as annuity A1, and the annual costs of $20,000 per year for five years, which we refer to as annuity A2. From Figure 6.4 we see that the present value of A1 is $410,020 and the present value of A2 is $82,004. But there is an easier way to obtain the present values.

Using equation (6.6), the present value of an annuity of A per annum (with payments received at the end of each year) for n years with interest at i percent is given by:

$$PV = \sum_{t=1}^{n} \frac{A}{(1 + i)^t}$$

This is the sum of n terms of a geometric series with the common ratio equal to $1/(1 + i)$. Consequently:

$$PV = A \times a_i^n \qquad \text{(6A.1)}$$

where:

$$a_i^n = \frac{1 - (1 + i)^{-n}}{i}. \qquad \text{(6A.2)}$$

The term, a_i^n, which equals the present value of an annuity of $1 per year for n years when the interest rate is i percent, is called an *annuity factor*. Tables of annuity factors are contained in most finance textbooks and are also built into many handheld calculators and computer spreadsheets.

Returning to our library example, the present value of annuity A1 computed using equations (6A.1) and (6A.2) is:

$$PV(A1) = \$100,000 \times \frac{1 - (1 + 0.07)^{-5}}{0.07}$$

$$PV(A1) = \$100,000 \times 4.1002$$

$$PV(A1) = \$410,020$$

Similarly:

$$PV(A2) = \$20,000 \times 4.1002 = \$82,004$$

Although this example deals with only a five-year annuity, it is easy to compute the present value of annuities that extend over much longer periods.

When working with annuities it is important to get the timing of the cash flows exactly right. Equation (6A.1) assumes that the benefits or costs occur at the end of each year, with the first payment occurring one year from now. This type of annuity is called an *ordinary annuity*. Care is required when the annuity payments start now or when they begin more than one year from now.

An *annuity due* is an annuity with payments that occur at the beginning of each year. Many spreadsheets allow one to compute the present values of ordinary annuities and of annuities due. If the spreadsheet (or calculator) computes only ordinary annuities, then one can calculate the *PV* of an annuity due for n years by computing the *PV* of an ordinary annuity for $n - 1$ years and adding the value of one initial payment or receipt made today.

A *deferred annuity* is an annuity whose first payment is deferred until after the first year. Suppose, for example, a government agency is considering refinancing some of its debt. Currently, it is scheduled to make debt payments of $150,000 per year for seven years with the first payment in three years. Assuming interest rates are 8 percent, what is the present value of this obligation? A time line for this problem is shown in Figure 6A.1. The first step is to treat the seven annual payments as an ordinary annuity and compute its present value using equations (6A.1) and (6A.2) or a calculator. The *PV* of the annuity is $780,956. The second and most important step is to recognize that this amount is the value of an ordinary annuity *in two years' time*—one year before payments are scheduled to begin. The third and final step is to discount the $780,956 back two years to obtain the present value of $669,543.

It is informative to note how the present value of an annuity varies with time and the interest rate. *The present value of an annuity decreases as interest rates increase, and vice versa.* This is a partial explanation for why bond prices rise as interest rates fall, as they did in the United States between 1988 and 1993.

Another important observation is that when there is a relatively constant annuity stream, *annuity payments received after about the twentieth year add little to the present value when interest rates are 10 percent or higher.* Thus, private companies are often reluctant to make very long-term investments such as reforestation.

FIGURE 6A.1 Present Value of $150 per Year (in Thousands) for Seven Years, Starting in Three Years

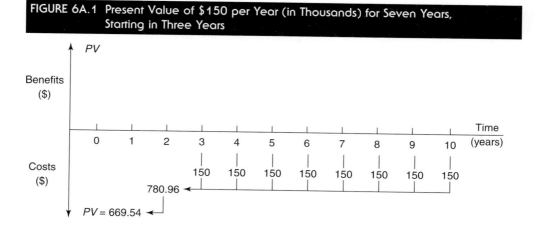

PRESENT VALUE OF A PERPETUITY

A *perpetuity* is an annuity that continues indefinitely. Taking the limit of equation (6A.2) as n goes to infinity, the annuity factor reduces to $1/i$, if $i > 0$. Consequently, the present value of an amount, denoted by A, received (at the end of) each year in perpetuity is given by:

$$PV = \frac{A}{i} \qquad \text{if } i > 0 \qquad\qquad \textbf{(6A.3)}$$

To provide some intuition for this formula, suppose that a municipality has an endowment of \$10 million. If interest rates are 6 percent, then this endowment will provide annual interest payments of \$600,000 indefinitely. More generally, if the municipality has an endowment of X and if the interest rate is i, then the perpetual annual income from the endowment, denoted by A, is given by $A = iX$. Rearranging this equation, the present value of the perpetual annuity is given by $X = A/i$, which is equation (6A.3).

Equation (6A.3) is easy to apply. For example, the present value of a perpetuity of \$150,000 per year when interest rates are 8 percent is:

$$PV = \frac{\$150,000}{0.08} = \$1,875,000$$

When interest rates are 10 percent, the present value of a perpetuity is especially easy to calculate: It equals the perpetuity multiplied by 10. For example, the present value of a perpetuity of \$150,000 per year is \$1,500,000 when interest rates are 10 percent.

THE PRESENT VALUE OF AN ANNUITY THAT GROWS OR DECLINES AT A CONSTANT RATE

Sometimes a project's benefits (or costs) grow at a constant rate. Let B_t denote the benefits in year t. If the annual benefits grow at a constant rate, g, then the benefits in year t will be:

$$B_t = B_{t-1}(1 + g) = B_1(1 + g)^{t-1} \qquad t = 2, \ldots, n \qquad \textbf{(6A.4)}$$

Under these circumstances, and if $i > g$, then the present value of the total benefits—the stream over n years—can be shown to be:[1]

$$PV(B) = \frac{B_1}{(1 + g)} \times a_{i_0}^n, \qquad\qquad \textbf{(6A.5)}$$

where, $a_{i_0}^n$ is defined by equation (6A.2) and:

$$i_0 = \frac{i - g}{1 + g} \qquad\qquad \textbf{(6A.6)}$$

Comparing equation (6A.1) with (6A.5) shows that the PV of a benefit stream that starts at B_1 in year 1 and grows at a constant rate g for $n - 1$ additional years, when the interest rate is i, equals the PV of an annuity of $B_1/(1 + g)$ for n years when the interest rate is i_0, where i_0 is given by equation (6A.6).

To illustrate how to calculate the present value of a stream of benefits that grows at a constant rate, return again to the library example. Suppose we now assume that, due to increased use, annual benefits grow at 2 percent per annum (and, as before, $i = 0.07$). From equation (6.A5), the present value of the stream of benefits equals the present value of an annuity of $\$100,000/1.02 = \$98,039$ per annum for five years, discounted at the following rate:

$$i_0 = \frac{i - g}{1 + g} = \frac{0.07 - 0.02}{1.02} = 0.049$$

which amounts to $\$425,636.$[2] In contrast, when annual benefits are constant ($\$100,000$), the present value equals $\$410,020$, a difference of $\$15,616$. This increase would be carried straight to the bottom line as the *NPV* would also increase by $\$15,616$; in fact, it almost doubles from $\$17,276$ to $\$32,892$. This example illustrates that even quite small growth rates can have large impacts on *NPV*s.

If the growth rate is small, then $B_1/(1 + g) \approx B_1$ and $i_0 \approx i - g$. Therefore, from equation (6A.5), the present value of a benefits stream that starts at B_1 and grows at rate g for $n - 1$ additional years approximately equals the present value of an annuity of B_1 for n years discounted at rate $i - g$. This approximation makes it clear that when benefits grow at a positive rate, the annuity is discounted at a lower rate, which will yield a higher *PV*. On the other hand, if the benefits are declining at a constant rate, then the annuity is discounted at a higher rate, which will yield a lower *PV*.

To illustrate this approximation, note that the present value of a stream of benefits that starts at $\$100,000$ per year and grows at 2 percent per annum for four additional years with $i = 0.07$ is approximately equal to the present value of an annuity of $\$100,000$ per year for five years discounted at $i - g = 5$ percent, which equals $\$432,949.$[3] This value is slightly higher than the correct amount of $\$425,634$, but it is within 2 percent of the right answer and it is easier to calculate.

Equation (6A.5) only holds if the interest rate exceeds the growth rate: $i > g$. If $i \leq g$, then it should not be used. Importantly, though, it can be used if g is negative, that is, if benefits decline at a constant rate. Of course, equation (6A.5) pertains to costs that change at a constant rate as well as to benefits that change at a constant rate.

PRESENT VALUE OF BENEFITS (OR COSTS) THAT GROW OR DECLINE AT A CONSTANT RATE IN PERPETUITY

If initial benefits, B_1, grow indefinitely at a constant rate g and if the interest rate equals i, then the *PV* is found by taking the limit of equation (6A.5) as n goes to infinity, which gives:

$$PV(B) = \frac{B_1}{i - g}, \qquad \text{if } i > g \qquad \textbf{(6A.7)}$$

Some finance students will recognize this model as the Gordon growth model, which is also called the dividend growth model. This model can be used to value a stock that yields a constant flow of dividends that grow at a constant rate.[4] As before, this formula holds only if $i > g$.

Appendix 6B

DISCOUNTING WITH MULTIPLE COMPOUNDING IN EACH PERIOD

FUTURE VALUE WITH MULTIPLE COMPOUNDING IN A YEAR

Thus far we have assumed that interest is calculated only once each period, with a period being a year. In practice, mortgages, savings accounts, and other investments compound interest more frequently than once a year.

Suppose we can invest $1,000, the annual interest rate is 8 percent, but interest is compounded semiannually, that is, every six months. How much will we have at the end of the year? With an annual interest rate of 8 percent but with semiannual compounding, we earn 4 percent interest every six months. Therefore, at the end of the first six-month period, we will have:

$$\$1,000(1 + 0.04) = \$1,000(1.04) = \$1,040$$

If we leave the money in the bank for another six months, at the end of the year we will have:

$$\$1,040(1.04) = \$1,081.60$$

Clearly, investing for one year at 8 percent annual interest with semiannual compounding is equivalent to investing for two years at 4 percent per annum with annual compounding:

$$\$1000\left(1 + \frac{0.08}{2}\right)^2 = \$1,000(1.04)^2 = \$1,081.60$$

When interest is compounded semiannually, there are twice as many periods as before. However, *during each period* the interest rate is only half the annual rate.

A comparison of the amount realized with semiannual compounding to the amount obtained with annual compounding shows that as interest is compounded more frequently, the future value increases more quickly. This occurs because as interest is compounded more frequently, interest on the interest is earned sooner. Thus, the effective annual interest rate with multiple compounding is higher than the effective annual rate with single compounding. In this example, the *effective annual interest rate,* which is the interest rate that one would have to obtain if interest were compounded annually in order to yield the same amount as multiple compounding, is 8.16 percent.

In general, the future value of *X in one year* at interest rate *i* compounded *k* times a year is:

$$FV = X\left(1 + \frac{i}{k}\right)^k$$

Thus, the future value of X in n years with interest rate i compounded k times per year is:

$$FV = X\left[\left(1 + \frac{i}{k}\right)^k\right]^n$$

$$= X\left(1 + \frac{i}{k}\right)^{kn} \tag{6B.1}$$

To illustrate the application of equation (6B.1) suppose, for example, your local bank offers two savings accounts: one provides interest of 8 percent calculated daily (*DIS*), the other provides interest of 9 percent calculated monthly (*MS*). If you deposit $1,000 to each account, how much would accumulate in each account in two years?

$$FV(DIS) = \$1,000\left(1 + \frac{0.08}{365}\right)^{2\times365} = \$1,173.49$$

$$FV(MS) = \$1,000\left(1 + \frac{0.09}{12}\right)^{2\times12} = \$1,196.41$$

FUTURE VALUE WITH CONTINUOUS COMPOUNDING

If interest is compounded continuously, then the future value of X in n years with interest rate i is given by:

$$FV = Xe^{in} \tag{6B.2}$$

where e is the base of the natural logarithm, which equals 2.71828 to five decimal places.[5]

For example, suppose you put $1,000 into a savings account for two years. If interest is compounded continuously and the interest rate is 8 percent, then the future value will be:

$$FV = \$1,000e^{(0.08\times2)} = \$1,173.51$$

If the interest rate is 9 percent, then the future value will be:

$$FV = \$1,000e^{(0.09\times2)} = \$1,197.22$$

As one would expect, continuous compounding yields slightly larger amounts than daily or monthly interest compounding, which we computed earlier. However, over a two-year period, the difference is not very much.

PRESENT VALUE WITH MULTIPLE COMPOUNDING IN A YEAR

Suppose your parents want you to visit them in a year and at that time the trip will cost $1,000. How much do you need to set aside now in order to buy the ticket in a year's time if the current interest rate is 5 percent, and interest is compounded twice a year? If you had X now, then with semiannual compounding you would have $X(1 + \frac{0.05}{2})^2$ in a year, so you should set this amount equal to $1,000 and solve for X:

$$X\left(1 + \frac{0.05}{2}\right)^2 = \$1,000$$

$$X = \frac{1,000}{\left(1 + \frac{0.05}{2}\right)^2} = \$951.81$$

Thus, the present value of $1,000 in a year with interest at 5 percent compounded semi-annually is $951.81. This is how much you would need to have now.

In general, the present value of Y received *in one year* with interest rate i compounded k times a year is:

$$PV = \frac{Y}{\left(1 + \frac{i}{k}\right)^k}$$

The present value of Y received in n years at interest rate i compounded k times a year is:

$$PV = \frac{Y}{\left(1 + \frac{i}{k}\right)^{nk}} \tag{6B.3}$$

To illustrate use of this formula, imagine that a coupon-clipped bond with $10,000 face value will mature two years from today. The market interest rate is 10 percent and interest is compounded twice a year. Using equation (6B.3), the present value of the bond is:

$$PV = \frac{10,000}{\left(1 + \frac{0.10}{2}\right)^{2\times 2}} = \frac{10,000}{(1.05)^4} = \$8,227.02$$

PRESENT VALUE WITH CONTINUOUS COMPOUNDING

If interest is compounded continuously, then the present value of Y received in n years' time with interest rate i is given by:

$$PV = \frac{Y}{e^{in}} \tag{6B.4}$$

For example, the present value of $10,000 received in 12 years' time with interest at 8 percent, compounded continuously, is:

$$PV = \frac{\$10,000}{e^{0.08 \times 12}} = \frac{\$10,000}{2.612} = \$3,829$$

Exercises for Chapter 6

1. A highway department is considering building a temporary bridge to cut travel time during the three years it will take to build a permanent bridge. The temporary bridge can be put up in a few weeks at a cost of $740,000. At the end of three years, it would be removed and sold for scrap at a net cost of $81,000, estimated as the net cost of a similar operation done today. Based on estimated time savings and wage rates, fuel savings, and reductions in risks of accidents, department analysts predict that the benefits in real dollars would be $275,000 during the first year, $295,000 during the second year, and $315,000 during the third year. Departmental regulations require use of a real discount rate of 6 percent.
    a. Calculate the present value of net benefits assuming that the benefits are realized at the end of each of the three years.
    b. Calculate the present value of net benefits assuming that the benefits are realized at the beginning of each of the three years.
    c. Calculate the present value of net benefits assuming that the benefits are realized in the middle of each of the three years.
    d. Calculate the present value of net benefits assuming that half of each year's benefits are realized at the beginning of the year and the other half at the end of the year.
    e. Does the temporary bridge pass the net benefits test?

2. A government data processing center has been plagued in recent years by complaints from employees of back pain. Consultants have estimated that upgrading office furniture at a net cost of $425,000 would reduce the incidence and severity of back injuries, allowing the center to avoid medical care that currently costs $68,000 each year. They estimate that the new furniture would also provide yearly benefits of avoided losses in work time and employee comfort worth $18,000. The furniture would have a useful life of five years, after which it would have a positive salvage value equal to 10 percent of its initial net cost. The consultants made their estimates of avoided costs assuming that they would be treated as occurring at the beginning of each year. In its investment decisions, the center uses a nominal discount rate of 9.5 percent and an assumed general inflation rate of 4 percent. It expects the inflation rate for medical care to run between 4 percent and 6 percent but is uncertain as to the exact rate. In other words, it is uncertain as to whether the cost of medical care will inflate at the same rate as other prices or rise 2 percent faster. Should the center purchase the new furniture?

3. A town's recreation department is trying to decide how to use a piece of land. One option is to put up basketball courts with an expected life of eight years. Another is to install a swimming pool with an expected life of 24 years. The basketball courts would cost $180,000 to construct and yield net benefits of $40,000 at the end of each of the eight years. The swimming pool would cost $2.25 million to construct and yield net benefits of $170,000 at the end of each of the 24 years. Each project is assumed to have zero salvage value at the end of its life. Using a real discount rate of 5 percent, which project offers larger net benefits?

4. The environmental protection agency of a county would like to preserve a piece of land as a wilderness area. The current owner has offered to lease the land to the county for 20 years in return for a lump-sum payment of $1.1 million, which would be paid at the beginning of the 20-year period. The agency has estimated that the land would generate $110,000 per year in benefits to hunters, bird watchers, and hikers. Assume that the lease price represents the social opportunity cost of the land and that the appropriate real discount rate is 6 percent.

   a. Assuming that the yearly benefits, which are measured in real dollars, accrue at the end of each of the 20 years, calculate the net benefits of leasing the land.

   b. Some analysts in the agency argue that the annual real benefits are likely to grow at a rate of 2 percent per year due to increasing population and county income. Recalculate the net benefits assuming that they are correct.

5. Imagine that the current owner of the land in the previous exercise was willing to sell the land for $2 million. Assuming this amount equaled the social opportunity cost of the land, calculate the net benefits if the county were to purchase the land as a permanent wildlife refuge. In making these calculations, first assume a zero annual growth rate in the $110,000 of annual real benefits; then assume that these benefits grow at a rate of 2 percent per year.

Notes

1. Parts of this chapter draw on Anthony E. Boardman and David H. Greenberg, "Discounting and the Social Discount Rate," in *Handbook of Public Finance,* Fred Thompson and Mark T. Green, eds. (New York: Marcel Dekker, 1998), pp. 269–318.

2. A T-bill is a short-term bond issued by the Treasury Department of the U.S. government. Usually, the minimum size is $100,000. It yields an interest rate that is slightly higher than the rate of interest offered by banks on personal savings accounts. Some banks offer a T-bill account, which enables customers with less than $100,000 (but more than some specified minimum) to earn almost the same rate as that given on T-bills.

3. $PV = \dfrac{\$10,280,374}{1.07} = \$10,000,000$

4. The following equation summarizes the relationship between discounting and compounding for projects of one year's duration:

$$PV = \frac{FV}{1+i}$$

5. At the end of the first year one would have $FV = X(1 + i)$. At the end of the second year, one would have $FV = [X(1 + i)](1 + i) = X(1 + i)^2$, and so on.

6. One should be aware, however, that different sources may give slightly different answers due to rounding error. For example, the more accurate answer to the foregoing question, without rounding, is $13,107,960. In practice, rounding errors are not material.

7. The $20,000 figure includes the dismantling costs.

8. $NPV = \displaystyle\sum_{t=0}^{n} \frac{B_t}{(1+i)^t} - \sum_{t=0}^{n} \frac{C_t}{(1+i)^t}$
$= \displaystyle\sum_{t=0}^{n} \frac{B_t - C_t}{(1+i)^t} = \sum_{t=0}^{n} \frac{NB_t}{(1+i)^t}$

9. Comparing equation (6.11) with equation (6.9) implies:

$$T(k) = NPV - \sum_{t=0}^{k} \frac{NB_t}{(1+i)^t} = \sum_{t=k+1}^{n} \frac{NB_t}{(1+i)^t}$$

10. Terminal values are well understood in the context of the private-sector capital budgeting literature. See, for example, Peter Lusztig and Bernhard Schwab, *Managerial Finance in a Canadian Setting* (Toronto, Ontario: Butterworths, 1988), Chapter 8: Capital Budgeting, especially pp. 310–311. See also pp. 976–979.

11. For example,

$$NPV = \sum_{t=0}^{20} \frac{NB_t}{(1+i)^t} + T(20) = \sum_{t=0}^{30} \frac{NB_t}{(1+i)^t} + T(30)$$

12. For a discussion about how to measure depreciated capital, see Charles R. Hulten, "The Measurement of Capital," Chapter 4 in *Fifty Years of Economic Measurement: The Jubilee of the Conference on Research in Income and Wealth*, Ernst R. Berndt and Jack E. Triplett, eds. (Chicago: The University of Chicago Press, 1990), pp. 119–152.

13. If project A were two-thirds the length of project B, then the analyst should compare three project As back-to-back with two project Bs back-to-back.

14. The difference between the *NPV* of five back-to-back cogeneration plants and the *NPV* of only one cogeneration plant is $10.94 million. We would have arrived at the same figure if we had evaluated building only one cogeneration plant but assigned a terminal value of $10.94 million to this project.

15. The annuity factor for the hydroelectric project is the present value of an annuity of $1 per year for 75 years using an interest rate of 8 percent, which, using equation (6A.2) or a calculator, equals

12.4611. Similarly, the annuity factor for the co-generation project equals the present value of $1 per annum for 15 years at an interest rate of 10 percent.

16. A broader measure is the implicit deflator for gross national product (GNP), which is the ratio of GNP measured at current prices to GNP measured at prices in some base year. Whereas CPI is based on a standard market basket of consumer goods, the implicit deflator for GNP is a comprehensive price index.

17. The most recent CPI figures for the United States as well as CPI figures back to 1913 are available from the Bureau of Labor Statistics at its Web site: www.bls.gov. The most recent CPI figures for Canada are available from Statistics Canada at its Web site: www.statcan.ca. For long-term historical Canadian data, see F. H. Leacy, ed., *Historical Statistics of Canada* (Ottawa, Ontario: Statistics Canada, 1983).

18. See Michael J. Boskin, Ellen R. Dulberger, Robert J. Gordon, Zvi Griliches, and Dale W. Jorgenson, *Toward a More Accurate Measure of the Cost of Living,* Final Report to the Senate Finance Committee from the Advisory Committee to Study the Consumer Price Index (Washington, DC: Senate Finance Committee, 1996). In Canada, the CPI was overestimated by about 0.7 percentage points per annum.

19. For a recent summary, see Brent R. Moulton, "Bias in the Consumer Price Index: What Is the Evidence?" *Journal of Economic Perspectives,* 10, no. 4 (1996), 159–177.

20. See Zvi Griliches and Iain Cockburn, "Generics and New Goods in Pharmaceutical Price Indexes," *American Economic Review,* 84, no. 5 (1994), 1213–1232.

21. For more information about the CPI revisions see http://stats.bls.gov/cpihome.htm.

22. To covert the $100,000 in 1994 dollars into an amount in 1999 dollars, we divide by the CPI for 1994 and multiply by the CPI for 1999: ($100,000/148.2) $\times$ 166.6 = $112,416. Between 1994 and 1999, the CPI increased by 2.34 percentage points per annum, on average. If the actual CPI increased by one percentage point per annum less than the reported CPI, it would have increased by 1.34 percentage points per annum, from 148.2 to 158.62. Consequently, the $100,000 in 1994 would equal ($100,000/148.2) $\times$ 158.6 = $107,018 in 1999 dollars.

23. Recall that the *NPV* for a project is given by equation (6.8), and suppose that these benefits, B_t, and costs, C_t, are in nominal dollars and i is the nominal interest rate. Let b_t denote real benefits, c_t denote real costs, and suppose the rate of inflation is m, then, using equation (6A.4), $B_t = b_t(1 + m)^t$ and $C_t = c_t(1 + m)^t$.

Consequently:

$$NPV = \sum_{t=0}^{n} \frac{B_t - C_t}{(1 + i)^t} = \sum_{t=0}^{n} \frac{(b_t - c_t)(1 + m)^t}{(1 + i)^t}$$

Now, setting $1/(1 + r) = (1 + m)/(1 + i)$, where r is the real interest rate, gives:

$$NPV = \sum_{t=0}^{n} \frac{b_t - c_t}{(1 + r)^t}$$

24. The expected CPI in t periods in the future equals $(1 + m)^t$ times the current CPI. Therefore, dividing the future amounts measured in nominal dollars by $(1 + m)^t$, in accordance with equation (6.5), is exactly the same as the method implied at the end of the previous subsection for converting amounts expressed in year b dollars into amounts expressed in year a dollars, namely, dividing by the expected CPI in t periods in the future and multiplying by the CPI for the current year.

25. This relationship is known as the Fisher effect. For derivation of this expression, rewrite the equation that introduces r in note 23. Alternatively, note that $1 invested today at a nominal interest rate of i yields $(1 + i)$ one year later. However, with an inflation rate of m during the year, $(1 + i)$ one year from now buys only as much as $(1 + i)/(1 + m)$ does today. The real interest rate, r, is, therefore, defined by $(1 + r) = (1 + i)/(1 + m)$. Rearranging this expression gives equation (6.13).

26. An alternative procedure draws on the Fisher model and assumes the real yield on bonds of a particular duration is constant over time. Specifically, this estimate of expected inflation during the life of the project equals the current yield on bonds that have the same term as the project minus the historical real yield on bonds of this term. For example, if the life of the project is 20 years, if the yield on bonds that mature in 20 years is currently 10 percent, and if 20-year bonds typically yield a real return of 2 percent, then the expected annual rate of inflation over this period is about 8 percent. If the life of the project is only

three years, if the yield on bonds that mature in three years is 9 percent, and if the historical real yield on bonds that mature in three years is 1.5 percent, then the expected annual rate of inflation over the next three years is about 7.5 percent. Notice that in this example, the market expects inflation will be higher in years 4 to 20 than in the first three years. For historical nominal and real returns on stocks, corporate bonds, government bonds, and treasury bills, see Ibbotson Associates, *Stocks, Bonds and Inflation: 1989 Yearbook* (Chicago: Ibbotson Associates, 1989), and their more recent publications.

27. For more information about the Livingston survey and the SPF, see the Web site of the Federal Reserve Bank of Philadelphia at http://phil.frb.org. For more information about the Michigan survey of households, see the Institute for Social Research's Survey of Consumer Attitudes Web site at http://athena.sca.isr.umich.edu.

28. Lloyd B. Thomas Jr., "Survey Measures of Expected U.S. Inflation," *Journal of Economic Perspectives*, 13, no. 4 (1999), 125–144.

29. From equation (6.13), $r = (0.10 - 0.04)/(1 + 0.04)$ = 5.77 percent. More accurately, the real discount rate is 5.769231 percent, which is the rate used in the *NPV* calculations in this example in order to ensure that the results for the real and nominal methods are identical.

30. An initial study was prepared by the government of British Columbia, "A Benefit-Cost Analysis of the North East Coal Development" (Victoria, BC: Ministry of Industry and Small Business, 1982). The sensitivity analyses were prepared by W. W. Waters II, "A Reanalysis of the North East Coal Development" (Working paper, University of British Columbia, undated).

31. The initial study made shadow price adjustments for foreign exchange earnings. These are excluded from Table 6.5 because, according to Bill Waters, the author of the reanalysis, they are probably inappropriate.

32. This scenario of declining prices and declining quantities sold is quite plausible for this project. The major Japanese customers were simultaneously encouraging development of Australian and other sources. If these sources came on line at the same time, there would be a worldwide excess supply, internationally determined coal prices would fall, and demand for BC coal would fall.

33. By definition, the break-even discount rate can be found by setting the left-hand side of equations (6.8) or (6.9) equal to zero and solving for i. In practice, this can be quite difficult. Usually, trial and error is much easier. Some spreadsheet programs allow this to be done quite readily.

34. The *NPV* is $17,276, which has a future value in year 5 of $24,230. Thus, one would obtain an *NPV* equal to zero if the terminal value were reduced by $24,230 from $20,000 to −$4,230.

35. If expenditures equal social costs and if the total amount of expenditures is constrained, then ranking projects on the basis of the *IRR* criterion may maximize the total *NPV*s. For example, if three projects cost a *total* of $1 billion and, in addition, each has a higher *IRR* than a fourth project that costs $1 billion by itself, then the first three projects will also have a larger *combined NPV* than the *NPV* of the fourth project. In effect, the *IRR* provides an estimate of the average annual net benefit per unit of (constrained) expenditure. Problems with ranking projects in terms of their *IRR*s only arise when the total expenditure on the projects with the highest *IRR*s does not exactly equal the total amount available. Even if the first, second, and third projects have higher *IRR*s than the fourth project, the fourth project *may* still have a higher *NPV* than the three smaller projects combined if its total cost is larger (but still no more than $1 billion). In any constrained project choice setting, the optimal set of projects can always be found readily by using linear programming.

Appendix Notes

1. $$PV(B) = \sum_{t=1}^{n} \frac{B_1(1+g)^{t-1}}{(1+i)^t}$$

$$= \sum_{t=1}^{n} \frac{B_1}{(1+g)} \times \left(\frac{1+g}{1+i}\right)^t$$

Setting $i_0 = (i - g)/(1 + g)$ implies $1/(1 + i_0) = (1 + g)/(1 + i)$. Consequently:

$$PV(B) = \sum_{t=1}^{n} \frac{B_1}{(1+g)} \times \frac{1}{(1+i_0)^t} = \frac{B_1}{(1+g)} \times a_{i_0}^n$$

2. Alternatively, substituting equation (6A.2) into equation (6A.5) gives the following formula for computing the *PV* of the benefits:

$$PV(B) = \frac{B_1}{1+g} \times \frac{1 - (1+i_0)^{-n}}{i_0}$$

Therefore, for this example:

$$PV(B) = \frac{100{,}000}{(1+0.02)} \times \frac{1 - (1+0.049)^{-5}}{0.049}$$
$$= \$98{,}039 \times 4.3415 = \$425{,}636$$

3. That is:

$$PV(B) = \sum_{t=1}^{n} \frac{B_1}{(1+i-g)^t}$$

$$= \sum_{t=1}^{5} \frac{100{,}000}{(1+0.07-0.05)^t} = \$432{,}948$$

4. See M. Gordon, *The Investment, Financing and Valuation of the Corporation* (Homewood, IL: Richard D. Irwin, 1962), pp. 46–47.

5. Formally, $e = \lim(1 + 1/n)$ as $n \to \infty$.

7

DEALING WITH UNCERTAINTY

*Expected Value, Sensitivity
Analysis, and the Value
of Information*

Cost-benefit analysis often requires us to predict the future. Whether or not it is desirable to begin a project depends on what we expect will happen after we have begun. But, as mere mortals, we rarely are able to make precise predictions about the future. Indeed, in many situations analysts can be certain that circumstances largely beyond their clients' control, such as epidemics, floods, bumper crops, or fluctuations in international oil prices, will greatly affect the benefits and costs that would be realized from proposed policies. How can analysts reasonably take account of these uncertainties in CBA?

In this chapter, we consider three topics relevant to uncertainty: *expected value* as a measure reflecting risks, *sensitivity analysis* as a way of investigating the robustness of net benefit estimates to different resolutions of uncertainty, and the *value of information* as a benefit category for CBA and as a guide for allocating analytical effort. Expected values take account of the dependence of benefits and costs on the occurrence of specific contingencies, or "states of the world" to which analysts are able to assign probabilities of occurrence. Sensitivity analysis is a way of acknowledging uncertainty about the values of important parameters in our predictions—it should be a component of almost any CBA. When analysts have opportunities for gaining additional information about costs or benefits, they may be able to value the information by explicitly modeling the uncertainty inherent in their decisions. A particular type of information value, called *quasi-option value,* is relevant when assessing currently available alternatives that have different implications for learning about the future.

EXPECTED VALUE ANALYSIS

One can imagine several types of uncertainty about the future. At the most profound level, one might not be able to specify the full range of relevant circumstances that may occur. Indeed, the human and natural worlds are so complex that one cannot hope to anticipate every possible future circumstance. Yet, in many situations of relevance to one's daily life and public policy, it is reasonable to characterize the future in terms of a number of distinct contingencies. For example, in deciding whether or not to take an umbrella to work, one might reasonably divide the future into two contingencies: Either it will or will not rain sufficiently to make the umbrella useful. Of course, other relevant contingencies can be imagined as well—it will be a dry day, but one may or may not be the victim of an attempted mugging in which the umbrella would prove valuable in self-defense! Yet if these additional contingencies are extremely unlikely, it is often reasonable to leave them out of one's model of the future. Modeling the future as a set of relevant contingencies involves yet another narrowing of uncertainty: How likely is each of the contingencies? If one is willing to assign probabilities of occurrence to each of the contingencies, then uncertainty about the future becomes a problem of dealing with risk. In relatively simple situations, risk can be readily incorporated into CBA through expected value analysis.

Contingencies and Their Probabilities

Modeling uncertainty as risk begins with the specification of a set of *contingencies* that are *exhaustive* and *mutually exclusive*. Contingencies can be thought of as possible events, outcomes, or states of the world such that one and only one of the relevant set of possibilities will actually occur. What makes a set of contingencies the basis of an appropriate model for conducting a CBA of a policy?

One important consideration is that the contingencies capture the full range of likely variation in net benefits of the policy. So, for example, in evaluating an oil stockpile for use in the event of an oil price shock sometime in the future, one would want to consider at least two contingencies: There never will be an oil price shock (a situation in which the policy is likely to result in net losses), and there will be a major price shock (a situation in which the policy is likely to result in net gains).

Another consideration is how well the contingencies represent the possible outcomes between the extremes. In some circumstances, the possible contingencies can be listed exhaustively so that they are fully representative. More often, however, they sample an infinite number of possibilities. In these circumstances, each contingency can be thought of as a *scenario*—a description of a possible future. Do the specified contingencies provide a sufficient variety of scenarios to convey the possible futures adequately? If so, then the contingencies are representative.

Figure 7.1 illustrates the representation of a continuous scale with discrete contingencies. The horizontal axis gives the number of inches of summer rainfall in an agricultural region. The vertical axis gives the net benefits of a water storage system, which increase as the amount of rainfall decreases. Imagine that an analyst represents uncertainty about rainfall with only two contingencies: "excessive" and "deficient." The excessive contingency assumes 22 inches of rainfall, which would yield zero net benefits from the storage system. The deficient contingency assumes zero inches of rainfall, which would yield $4.4 million in net benefits. If the relationship between rainfall and net benefits follows the straight line labeled *A,* and all the rainfall amounts between zero and 22 are equally likely, then the average of net benefits over the full continuous range would be $2.2 million. If the analyst assumed that each of the contingencies were equally likely, then the average over the two contingencies would also be $2.2 million so that using two scenarios would be adequately representative.[1]

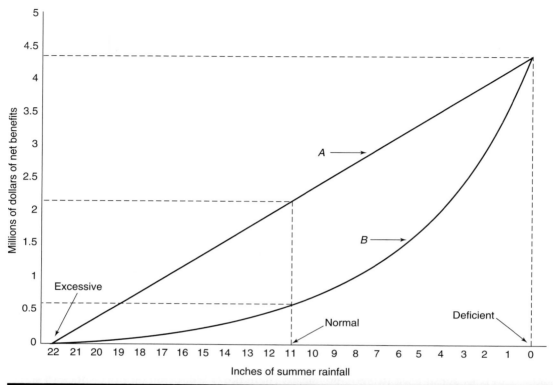

FIGURE 7.1 Representativeness of Contingencies

Now imagine that the net benefits follow the curved line labeled *B*. Again assuming that all rainfall amounts between zero and 22 inches are equally likely, the average of net benefits over the full continuous range would only be about $1.1 million, so that using only two contingencies would grossly overestimate the average net benefits from the storage system. Adding "normal" as a contingency that assumes 11 inches of rainfall and averaging net benefits over all three contingencies yields net benefits of $1.6 million, more representative than the average calculated with two contingencies but still considerably larger than the $1.1 million calculated over the full continuous range. Even more contingencies are desirable. For example, moving to five equally spaced contingencies gives an average of $1.3 million, much closer yet to the average over the continuous range.[2]

EXHIBIT 7.1

Being explicit about contingencies, their probabilities, and their consequences can help structure complex decision problems. Consider the following letter that President Abraham Lincoln wrote to Major General George B. McClellan on February 3, 1862:

My dear Sir:

You and I have distinct, and different plans for a movement of the Army of the Potomac—yours to be down the Chesapeake, up the Rappahannock to Urbana, and across land to the terminus of the Railroad on the York River—, mine to move directly to a point on the Railroad South West of Manassas.

If you will give me satisfactory answers to the following questions, I shall gladly yield my plan to yours.

First. Does not your plan involve a greatly larger expenditure of time and money than mine?

Second. Wherein is a victory more certain by your plan than mine?

Third. Wherein is a victory more valuable by your plan than mine?

Fourth. In fact, would it not be less valuable, in this, that it would break no great line of the enemy's communications, while mine would?

Fifth. In case of disaster, would not a safe retreat be more difficult by your plan than by mine?

Yours truly, Abraham Lincoln

Source: John G. Nicolay and John Hay, eds., *Abraham Lincoln: Complete Works, Volume Two* (New York: The Century Company, 1894), p. 120.

Once we have specified a tractable but representative set of contingencies, the next task is to assign probabilities of occurrence to each of them. To be consistent with the logical requirement that the contingencies taken together are exhaustive and mutually exclusive, the probabilities that we assign must each be nonnegative and sum to exactly one. Thus, if there are three contingencies, C_1, C_2, and C_3, we must assign corresponding probabilities p_1, p_2, and p_3 such that $p_1 + p_2 + p_3 = 1$.

EXHIBIT 7.2

In their evaluation of alternative government oil stockpiling programs in the early 1980s, Glen Sweetnam and colleagues at the U.S. Department of Energy modeled the uncertainty surrounding oil market conditions with five contingencies: *slack market*—oil purchases for the U.S. stockpile of up to 1.5 million barrels per day (mmb/d) could be made without affecting the world oil price; *tight market*—oil purchases increase world price at the rate of $3.60 per mmb/d; *minor disruption*—loss of 1.5 mmb/d to the world market (say, caused by a revolution in an oil-exporting country); *moderate disruption*—loss of 6.0 mmb/d to the world market (say, caused by a limited war in the Persian Gulf); *major disruption*—loss of 12.0 mmb/d to the world market (say, caused by a major war in the Persian Gulf). For each of the 24 years of their planning horizon, they assumed that the probabilities of each of the contingencies occurring depended only on the contingency that occurred in the previous year. For each year, they calculated the social surplus in the U.S. oil market conditional on each of the five market contingencies and change in the size of the stockpile.

The model they constructed allowed them to answer the following questions: For any current market condition and stockpile size, what change in stockpile size maximizes the present value of expected net benefits? How much storage capacity should be constructed? How fast should it be added? The model and the answers it provided were influential in policy debates concerning expansion of the U.S. stockpile, the Strategic Petroleum Reserve.

Sources: Glen Sweetnam, "Stockpile Policies for Coping with Oil-Supply Disruptions," in *Policies for Coping with Oil-Supply Disruptions,* George Horwich and Edward J. Mitchell, eds. (Washington, DC: American Enterprise Institute for Public Policy Research, 1982), pp. 82–96. On the role of the model in the policy-making process, see Hank C. Jenkins-Smith and David L. Weimer, "Analysis as Retrograde Action: The Case of Strategic Petroleum Reserves," *Public Administration Review,* 45, no. 4 (1985), 485–494.

The probabilities may be based solely on historically observed frequencies, on subjective assessments by clients, analysts, or other experts based on a variety of information and theory, or on both. For example, return to the contingencies in Figure 7.1: agriculturally "excessive," "normal," and "deficient" precipitation in a river valley for which a water storage system has been proposed. The National Weather Service may be able to provide data on average annual rainfall over the last century that allows an analyst to estimate the probabilities of the three levels of precipitation from their historical frequencies. If such data were not available, then the analyst would have to base the probabilities on expert opinion, comparison with similar valleys in the region for which data are available, or some other subjective assessment. Because such subjective assessments are rarely made with great confidence, it is especially important to investigate the sensitivity of the results to the particular probabilities chosen.

Calculating the Expected Value of Net Benefits

The specification of contingencies and their respective probabilities allows us to calculate the *expected net benefits* of a policy. We do so by first predicting the net benefits of the policy under each contingency and then taking the weighted average of these net benefits over all the contingencies, where the weights are the respective probabilities that the contingencies occur. Specifically, for n contingencies, let B_i be the benefits under contingency i, C_i be the costs under contingency i, and p_i be the probability of contingency i occurring. Then the expected net benefits, $E[NB]$, are given by the formula:

$$E[NB] = p_1(B_1 - C_1) + \cdots + p_n(B_n - C_n) \qquad \textbf{(7.1)}$$

which is just the expected value of net benefits over the n possible outcomes.[3]

When facing complicated risk problems, analysts often find it useful to model them as *games against nature*. A game against nature assumes that nature will randomly, and nonstrategically, select a particular state of the world. The random selection of a state of the world is according to assumed probabilities. The selection is nonstrategic in the sense that nature does not alter the probabilities of the states of the world in response to the action selected by the analysts. A game against nature in *normal form* has the following elements: *states of nature* and their *probabilities of occurrence; actions* available to the decision maker facing nature; and *payoffs* to the decision maker under each combination of state of nature and action.

Table 7.1 shows the analysis of alternatives for planetary defense against asteroid collisions as a game against nature in normal form. It considers three possible states of nature over the next 100 years: exposure of Earth to collision with an asteroid larger than one kilometer in diameter, which would have enough kinetic energy to have severe regional or even global effects on society (10 on the Torino Scale); exposure of Earth to collision with an asteroid smaller than one kilometer but larger than 20 meters in diameter, which would have severe local or regional effects on society (8 or 9 on the Torino Scale); and no exposure of Earth to an asteroid larger than 20 meters in diameter. The game shows three actions: build a forward-based asteroid defense, which would station nuclear devices sufficiently deep in space to give a good possibility of their timely use in diverting asteroids from collision courses with Earth; build a near-Earth asteroid defense, which would be less expensive but not as effective as the forward-based defense; and build no asteroid defense.

Although actually estimating the payoffs for this game would be a monumental and controversial analytical task, Table 7.1 displays some hypothetical figures. The payoffs, shown as the present value of net costs over the next century, range from $30 trillion (Earth is exposed to a collision with an asteroid larger than one kilometer in diameter in the absence of any asteroid defense) to $0 (Earth is not exposed to collision with an asteroid larger than 20 meters and no defense system is built). Note that

TABLE 7.1 A Game against Nature: Expected Values of Asteroid Defense Alternatives

State of Nature	*Exposure to a Collision with an Asteroid Larger Than One Kilometer in Diameter*	*Exposure to a Collision with an Asteroid between 20 Meters and 1 Kilometer in Diameter*	*No Exposure to Collision with an Asteroid Larger Than 20 Meters in Diameter*	
Probabilities of states of nature (over next century)	.001	.004	.995	
Actions (alternatives)	*Payoffs (net costs in billions of 2000 dollars)*			*Expected Value*
Forward-Based Asteroid Defense	5,060	1,060	60	69
Near-Earth Asteroid Defense	10,020	2,020	20	**38**
No Asteroid Defense	30,000	6,000	0	54

Choose Near-Earth Asteroid Defense: Expected net cost = $38 billion.

estimating the costs of a collision between Earth and an asteroid would itself involve expected value calculations that take account of size, composition, and point of impact of the asteroid. The $30 trillion figure is a bit larger than the world's annual gross domestic product.

The last column of Table 7.1 shows expected values for each of the three alternatives. The expected value for each alternative is calculated by summing the products of its payoff conditional on states of nature with the probabilities of those states. For example, the expected value of payoffs (present value of net costs) for no asteroid defense is:

$$(0.001)(\$30,000 \text{ billion}) + (0.004)(\$6,000 \text{ billion}) + (0.995)(\$0) = \$54 \text{ billion}$$

Similar calculations yield $69 billion for forward-based asteroid defense and $38 billion for near-Earth asteroid defense. As the maximization of expected net benefits is equivalent to minimizing expected net costs, the most efficient alternative is the near-Earth asteroid defense. Alternatively, one could think of the near-Earth asteroid defense as offering expected net benefits of $16 billion relative to no defense ($54 billion in expected costs minus $38 billion in expected costs equals $16 billion in expected net benefits) whereas forward-based asteroid defense offers negative $15 billion in expected net benefits relative to no defense ($54 billion in expected net costs minus $69 billion in expected net costs equals negative $15 billion in expected net benefits).

In CBA, it is common practice to treat expected values as if they were certain amounts. For example, imagine that a perfect asteroid defense system would have a present value cost of $100 billion under each of the states of nature. In this case, assuming accurate prediction of costs, the $100 billion *would be certain* because it does not depend on which state of nature actually results. CBA generally treats a certain amount such as this as fully commensurate with expected values, even though the latter will not actually result in its expected value. In other words, although the expected net cost of no asteroid defense is $54 billion, assuming accurate prediction of payoffs, the actually realized net cost will be $30 trillion, or $6 trillion, or $0. If the perfect defense system cost $54 billion, CBA would rank it and no defense as equally efficient.

Chapter 8 considers the appropriateness of treating expected values and certain equivalents as commensurate. It explains that doing so is not conceptually correct in measuring willingness-to-pay in circumstances in which individuals face uncertainty. Nevertheless, it argues that, in practice, *treating expected values and certain amounts as commensurate is generally reasonable when either the pooling of risk over the collection of policies, or the pooling of risk over the collection of persons affected by a policy, will make the actually realized values of costs and benefits close to their expected values.* For example, a policy that affects the probability of highway accidents involves reasonable pooling of risk across many drivers (some will have accidents, others will not) so that realized values will be close to expected values. In contrast, a policy that affects the risk of asteroid collision does not involve pooling across individuals (either everyone suffers from the global harm if there is a collision or no one does if there is no collision) so that the realized value of costs may be very far from their expected value. As discussed in Chapter 8, such unpooled risk may require an adjustment to expected benefits called *option value.*

EXHIBIT 7.3

Hepatitis B poses a serious risk to health care workers. A CBA of a proposed regulation that would require employers to offer free vaccination to workers exposed 12 or more times per year to the hepatitis B virus involved the estimation of a large number of probabilities, including rates of exposure, vaccination effectiveness, postexposure treatment effectiveness, natural immunity, worker turnover, and voluntary participation. The estimated expected cost to an individual who develops hepatitis B ($21,000) was based on the probabilities of various acute and chronic conditions involving different medical costs, lost employment, and reduced life expectancy:

Acute Disease	*Probability*	*Cost/Case ($)*
Subclinical	.330	0
Mild, not hospitalized	.420	380
Moderate, not hospitalized	.200	3,900
Severe, hospitalized	.050	30,000
Chronic Disease		
No chronic symptoms	.956	0
Chronic persistent hepatitis	.020	2,000
Chronic active hepatitis	.020	865,000
Primary hepatic cancer	.004	300,000

Measuring benefits as avoided costs of medical care, prophylaxis, and lost productivity yields annual net benefits for the regulation of $63.6 million.

Source: Josephine A. Mauskopf, Cathy J. Bradley, and Michael T. French, "Benefit-Cost Analysis of Hepatitis B Vaccine Programs for Occupationally Exposed Workers," *Journal of Occupational Medicine*, 33, no. 6 (1991), 691–698.

Decision Trees and Expected Net Benefits

The basic procedure for expected value analysis, taking weighted averages over contingencies, can be directly extended to situations in which costs and benefits accrue over multiple years, as long as the risks in each year are independent of the realizations of risks in previous years. Consider, for example, a CBA of a dam with a 20-year life. Assume that the costs and benefits of the dam depend only on the contingencies of below-average rainfall and above-average rainfall in the current year. Additionally, if the analyst is willing to make the plausible assumption that the amount of rainfall in any year does not depend on the rainfall in previous years, then the analyst can simply calculate the present value of expected net benefits for each year and calculate the present value of this stream of net benefits in the usual way.

The basic expected value procedure cannot be so directly applied when either the net benefits accruing under contingencies or the probabilities of the contingencies depend on the contingencies that have previously occurred. For example, above-average rainfall in one year may make the irrigation benefits of a dam less in the next year because of accumulated ground water. In the case of a policy to reduce the costs of earthquakes, the probability of a major earthquake may change each year depending on the mix of earthquakes that occurred in the previous year.

Such situations require a more flexible framework for handling risk than basic expected value analysis. *Decision analysis* provides the needed framework.[4] Though it takes us too far afield to present decision analysis in any depth here, we sketch its general approach and present simple illustrations that demonstrate its usefulness in CBA. A number of book-length treatments of decision analysis are available for those who wish to pursue this topic in more depth.[5]

Decision analysis can be thought of as a *sequential,* or *extended form,* game against nature. It proceeds in two basic stages. First, one specifies the logical structure of the decision problem in terms of sequences of decisions and realizations of contingencies using a diagram, called a *decision tree,* that links an initial decision (the trunk) to final outcomes (branches). Second, one works backward from final outcomes to the initial decision, calculating expected values of net benefits across contingencies and pruning dominated branches (i.e., eliminating branches with lower expected values of net benefits).

Consider a vaccination program against a particular type of influenza that involves various costs.[6] The costs of the program result from immunization expenditures and possible adverse side effects; the benefits consist of the adverse health effects that are avoided if an epidemic occurs. This flu may infect a population over the next two years before sufficient immunity develops worldwide to stop its spread. Figure 7.2 presents a simple decision tree for a CBA of this vaccination program. The tree should be read from left to right to follow the sequence of decisions, denoted by ❏, and random selections of contingencies, denoted by ◯. The tree begins with a decision node, the square labeled 0 at the extreme left. The upper bough represents the decision to implement the vaccination program this year; the lower bough represents the decision not to implement the program this year.

Upper Bough: The Vaccination Program   Follow the upper bough first. If the program is implemented, then it will involve direct administrative costs, C_a, and the costs of adverse side effects, such as contracting the influenza from the vaccine itself, suffered by those who are vaccinated, C_s. Note that C_s, like most of the other costs in this example, is itself an expected cost based on the probability of the side effect, the cost to persons suffering the side effect, and the number of persons vaccinated. The solid vertical line on the bough can be thought of as a toll gate at which point the program costs,

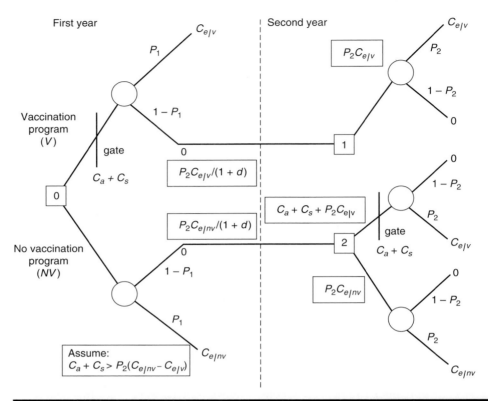

FIGURE 7.2 Decision Tree for Vaccination Program Analysis

$C_a + C_s$, are incurred. A chance node, represented by a circle, appears next. Either the influenza infects the population (the upper branch, which occurs with probability P_1 and results in costs $C_{e|v}$, where the subscript should be read as "epidemic occurs given the vaccination program has been implemented") or the influenza does not infect the population (the lower branch, which occurs with probability $1 - P_1$ and results in zero costs at that time). If the influenza does occur, then the population will be immune in the next year. Thus, the upper branch does not continue. If the influenza does not occur, then there is still a possibility that it might occur in the next year. Therefore, the lower branch continues to the second year, where the square labeled 1 notes the beginning of the second year. It leads directly to another chance node that specifies the two contingencies in the second year: The influenza infects the population (the upper subbranch, which occurs with probability P_2 and results in costs $C_{e|v}$) or the influenza does not infect the population (the lower subbranch, which occurs with probability $1 - P_2$ and results in zero costs).[7] We assume that P_2 is known at the time of the initial decision.[8]

Lower Bough: No Vaccination Program   We now return to the initial decision node and follow the lower bough representing no vaccination program in the first year. Initially there is no cost associated with this decision. A chance node follows with two branches: Either the influenza infects the population (the lower branch, which occurs with probability P_1 and results in costs $C_{e|nv}$) or the influenza does not infect the population (the upper branch, which occurs with probability $1 - P_1$ and results in zero costs).[9] If the influenza does occur, then there is no need to consider the next year. If it does not occur, then the tree continues to decision node 2: Either implement the vaccination program in the second year (the upper subbranch crossing the gate where program costs $C_a + C_s$ are incurred) or do not implement it (the lower subbranch).

If the program is implemented, then a chance node occurs: The influenza infects the population (the lower twig, which occurs with probability P_2 and results in costs $C_{e|v}$) or the influenza does not infect the population (the upper twig, which occurs with probability $1 - P_2$ and results in zero costs). We complete the tree by considering the parallel chance node following the decision not to implement the program: The influenza infects the population (the lower twig, which occurs with probability P_2 and results in costs $C_{e|nv}$) or the influenza does not infect the population (the upper twig, which occurs with probability $1 - P_2$ and results in zero costs).

Solving the Decision Tree   To solve the decision problem, we work from right to left, replacing chance nodes with their expected costs and pruning off parallel nodes that are dominated. Consider the chance node following decision node 1. Its expected cost, calculated by the expression $P_2 C_{e|v} + (1 - P_2)0$, equals $P_2 C_{e|nv}$.

Now consider the chance nodes following decision node 2. The lower chance node, following a decision not to implement the vaccination program, has an expected cost of $P_2 C_{e|nv}$. The upper chance node has an expected cost of $P_2 C_{e|v}$, to which must be added the certain payment of program costs so that the full expected cost of implementing the vaccination program in the second year is $C_a + C_s + P_2 C_{e|v}$. We can now compare the expected cost of the two possible decisions at node 2: $P_2 C_{e|nv}$ versus $C_a + C_s + P_2 C_{e|v}$. Assume that program costs are greater than the expected cost reduction from the vaccine; that is, $C_a + C_s > P_2(C_{e|nv} - C_{e|v})$, then $P_2 C_{e|nv}$ is smaller than $C_a + C_s + P_2 C_{e|v}$ so that not implementing the program dominates implementing it.[10] We can now prune off the upper subbranch. If we reach decision node 2, then we know that we can obtain expected second-year costs of $P_2 C_{e|nv}$.

At decision node 0 the expected costs of implementing the vaccination program (i.e., following the upper bough) consist of direct costs plus the expected costs of the following chance node, which now has the payoffs $C_{e|v}$ if there is an epidemic and the discounted expected value of node 1, $P_2 C_{e|v}/(1 + d)$ if there is not an epidemic. Note that because this latter cost occurs in the second year, it is discounted using rate d. Thus, the present value of expected costs from implementing the vaccination program is given by:

$$E[C_v] = C_a + C_s + P_1 C_{e|v} + (1 - P_1)P_2 C_{e|v}/(1 + d) \tag{7.2}$$

where the last term incorporates the expected costs from the second year.

The expected costs of not implementing the vaccination program are calculated in the same way: The payoff if there is not an epidemic becomes the discounted expected costs from decision node 2, $P_2 C_{e|nv}/(1 + d)$; the payoff if there is an epidemic is still $C_{e|nv}$. Therefore, the expression:

$$E[C_{nv}] = P_1 C_{e|nv} + (1 - P_1)P_2 C_{e|nv}/(1 + d) \tag{7.3}$$

gives the present value of expected costs of not implementing the program.

The final step is to compare the present values of expected costs for the two possible decisions at node 0. We prune the bough with the larger present value of expected costs. The remaining bough is the optimal decision.

As an illustration, suppose that we have gathered data suggesting the following values for parameters in the decision tree: $P_1 = .4$, $P_2 = .2$, $d = .05$, $C_{e|v} = .5C_{e|nv}$ (the vaccination program cuts the costs of influenza by half), $C_a = .1C_{e|nv}$ (the vaccination costs 10 percent of the costs of the influenza), and $C_s = .01C_{e|nv}$ (the side-effect costs are 1 percent of the costs of the influenza). For these values, $E[C_v] = .367C_{e|nv}$ and $E[C_{nv}] = .514C_{e|nv}$. Therefore, the vaccination program should be implemented in the first year because $E[C_v] < E[C_{nv}]$.

Calculating Expected Net Benefits of the Vaccination Program   Returning explicitly to CBA, we can recognize the benefits of the vaccination program as the costs it avoids. Thus, the present value of expected net benefits of the vaccination program is simply $E[C_{nv}] - E[C_v]$, which in the numerical illustration presented in the preceding paragraph equals $0.147C_{e|nv}$. In Chapter 8, we return to the question of the appropriateness of expected net benefits as a generalization of net benefits in CBA.

Extending Decision Analysis

Decision analysis can be applied to both public- and private-sector issues, and it can be used to structure much more complicated analyses than the CBA of the vaccination program. Straightforward extensions include more than two alternatives at decision nodes, more than two contingencies at chance nodes, more than two periods of time, and different probabilities of events in different periods. For example, analyses of the U.S. oil stockpiling program typically involve trees so large that they can only be fully represented and solved by computers.[11] Even in less complex situations, however, decision analysis can be very helpful in showing how risk should be incorporated into the calculation of expected net benefits.

SENSITIVITY ANALYSIS

Whether or not we structure a CBA explicitly in terms of contingencies and their probabilities, we always face some uncertainty about the magnitude of the impacts we predict and the values we assign to them. Our basic analysis usually submerges this uncertainty by using our most plausible estimates of these unknown quantities. These estimates comprise what is called the *base case*. The purpose of sensitivity analysis is to acknowledge the underlying uncertainty. In particular, it should convey how sensitive predicted net benefits are to changes in assumptions. If the sign of net benefits does not change when we consider the range of reasonable assumptions, then our analysis is robust and we can have greater confidence in its results.

Large numbers of unknown quantities, the usual situation in CBA, make the brute force approach of looking at all combinations of assumptions unfeasible. For example, the vaccination program analysis, which we further develop in the next section, involves 17 different uncertain numerical assumptions. If we looked at just three different values for each assumption, there would still be over 129 million different combinations of assumptions to consider.[12] Even if we could compute net benefits for all these combinations, we would still face the daunting task of sorting through the results and communicating them in an effective way.

Instead, we illustrate three more manageable approaches to doing sensitivity analysis. First, we demonstrate partial sensitivity analysis: How do net benefits change as we vary a single assumption while holding all others constant? Partial sensitivity is most appropriately applied to what the analyst believes to be the most important and uncertain assumptions. It can be used to find the values of numerical assumptions at which net benefits equal zero, or just break even. Second, we consider worst- and best-case analysis: Does any combination of reasonable assumptions reverse the sign of net benefits? Analysts are generally most concerned about situations in which their most plausible estimates yield positive net benefits, but they want to know what would happen in a worst case involving the least favorable, or most conservative, assumptions. Third, we present Monte Carlo sensitivity analysis: What distribution of net benefits results from treating the numerical values of key assumptions as draws from probability distributions? The mean and variance, or spread, of the distribution of net benefits convey key information about the riskiness of the project.

A Closer Look at the Vaccination Program Analysis

We illustrate these techniques by considering a more detailed specification of the costs relevant to the decision analysis of the hypothetical vaccination program presented in Figure 7.2. This program would vaccinate some residents of a county against a possible influenza epidemic.[13]

Consider the following general description of the program. Through an advertising and outreach effort by its Department of Health, the county expects to be able to recruit a large fraction of older residents in poor health who are at high mortality risk from influenza and a much smaller fraction of the general population for vaccination. As the vaccine is based on a live virus, some fraction of those vaccinated will suffer an adverse reaction that, in effect, converts them to high-risk status and gives them influenza, a cost included in C_s. As the vaccine does not always confer immunity, often because it is not given sufficiently in advance of the exposure to the influenza virus, its effectiveness rate is less than 100 percent. Everyone who contracts the influenza must be confined to bed rest for a number of days. Analysts can value this loss as the average number of hours of work lost times the average wage rate for the county, though this procedure might overestimate the opportunity costs of time for older persons and underestimate the cost of the unpleasantness of the influenza symptoms for both younger and older persons. They can place a dollar value on the deaths caused by the influenza by multiplying the number of expected deaths times the dollar value of life. The various numerical assumptions for the analysis appear in Table 7.2. Notice, for example, that the base-case value used for each saved life is $3 million. That is, it is assumed that people make decisions about how much value they place on changes in risks of death as if they valued their lives at $3 million.

The benefits of vaccination arise through two impacts. First, those effectively vaccinated are immune to the influenza. Thus, the program targets persons with high mortality risk because they benefit most from immunity. Second, through what is known as

TABLE 7.2 Base-Case Values for Vaccination Program CBA

Parameter	Value [Range]	Comments
County Population (N)	380,000	Total population in the county
Fraction High Risk (r)	.06 [.04,.08]	One-half population over age 64
Low-Risk Vaccination Rate (v_l)	.05 [.03,.07]	Fraction of low-risk persons vaccinated
High-Risk Vaccination Rate (v_h)	.60 [.40,.80]	Fraction of high-risk persons vaccinated
Adverse Reaction Rate (α)	.03 [.01,.05]	Fraction vaccinated who become high risk
Low-Risk Mortality Rate (m_l)	.00005 [.000025,.000075]	Mortality rate for low-risk infected
High-Risk Mortality Rate (m_h)	.001 [.0005,.002]	Mortality rate for high-risk infected
Herd Immunity Effect (θ)	1.0 [.5,1.0]	Fraction of effectively vaccinated who contribute to herd immunity effect
Vaccine Effectiveness Rate (e)	.75 [.65,.85]	Fraction of vaccinated who develop immunity
Hours Lost (t)	24 [18,30]	Average number of work hours lost to illness
Infection Rate (i)	.25 [.20,.30]	Infection rate without vaccine
First-Year Epidemic Probability (p_1)	.40	Chance of epidemic in current year
Second-Year Epidemic Probability (p_2)	.20	Chance of epidemic next year
Vaccine Dose Price (q)	$9/dose	Price per dose of vaccine
Overhead Cost (o)	$120,000	Costs not dependent on number vaccinated
Opportunity Cost of Time (w)	$12/hour	Average wage rate in the county
Value of Life (L)	$3,000,000	Assumed value of life
Discount Rate (d)	.05	Real discount rate
Number High-Risk Vaccinations (V_h)	13,680	High-risk persons vaccinated: $v_h rN$
Number Low-Risk Vaccinations (V_l)	17,860	Low-risk persons vaccinated: $v_l(1-r)N$
Fraction Vaccinated (v)	.083	Fraction of total population vaccinated: $rv_h + v_l(1-r)$

the *herd immunity effect,* a positive externality, vaccinated persons reduce the risks of infection to those not vaccinated—thus, some low-risk persons are recruited for vaccination to increase the total fraction of the population that is vaccinated.[14] These two effects cause the expected costs of the epidemic with vaccination, $C_{e|v}$, to be less than the expected costs of the epidemic without the vaccination program, $C_{e|nv}$.

TABLE 7.3 Formulas for Calculating the Net Benefits of Vaccination Program

Variable	Value (millions of dollars)	Formula
C_a	0.404	$o + (V_h + V_l)q$
C_s	3.111	$\alpha(V_h + V_l)(wt + m_h L)$
$C_{e|nv}$	57.855	$i[rN(wt + m_h L) + (1 - r)N(wt + m_l L)]$
$C_{e|v}$	36.014	$(i - \theta ve)\{(rN - eV_h)(wt + m_h L) + [(1 - r)N - eV_l](wt + m_l L)\}$
EC_v	22.036	$C_a + C_s + p_1 C_{e|v} + (1 - p_1)p_2 C_{e|v}/(1 + d)$
EC_{nv}	29.754	$p_1 C_{e|nv} + (1 - p_1)p_2 C_{e|nv}/(1 + d)$
$E[NB]$	7.718	$EC_{nv} - EC_v$

Table 7.3 relates the specific numerical assumptions in Table 7.2 to the parameters in Figure 7.2. From Table 7.3, we see that the direct program costs, C_a, depend on the overhead (i.e., fixed) costs, o, and cost per vaccination, q, times the number of vaccinations given $(V_h + V_l)$. The costs of side effects, C_s, depend on the adverse reaction rate, α, the number vaccinated, and the cost per high-risk infection, $wt + m_h L$, where wt is the opportunity cost of lost labor and $m_h L$ is the cost of loss of life. The epidemic's costs without the vaccination program, $C_{e|nv}$, depend on the infection rate, i, the number of high-risk susceptibles, rN, and low-risk susceptibles, $(1 - r)N$, and the costs per high- and low-risk infections. Finally, the cost of the epidemic with the vaccination program, $C_{e|v}$, depends on the postvaccination infection rate, $i - \theta ve$, the number of high-risk individuals remaining susceptible, $rN - eV_h$, the number of low-risk individuals remaining susceptible, $(1 - r)N - eV_l$, and the costs per low- and high-risk infections. Working through these formulas yields expected net benefits equal to $7.718 million (see Table 7.3) for the base-case assumptions presented in Table 7.2.

Partial Sensitivity Analysis   An important assumption in the analysis is the probability that the epidemic occurs. In the base case, we assumed that the probability of the epidemic in the next year, given no epidemic in the current year, p_2, is one-half the probability of the epidemic in the current year, p_1. To investigate the relationship between net benefits and the probability of epidemic, we vary p_1 (and, hence, p_2) holding all other base-case values constant. Specifically, we vary p_1 from 0 to 0.5 by increments of 0.05. We thereby isolate the marginal partial effect of changes in probability on net benefits.

The results of this procedure are displayed as the line labeled $L = \$3$ million in Figure 7.3. This label reminds us of another base-case assumption, the value of life equals $3 million, which we vary next. Because the equations underlying the calculation of net benefits were embedded in a spreadsheet on a personal computer, it was easy to generate the points needed to draw this line by simply changing the values of p_1 and recording the corresponding net benefits.

As expected, this line is upward sloping: The higher the probability of the epidemic, the larger the net benefits of the vaccination program. Note that for values of p_1 less than about .11, net benefits become negative (i.e., it lies below the solid horizontal

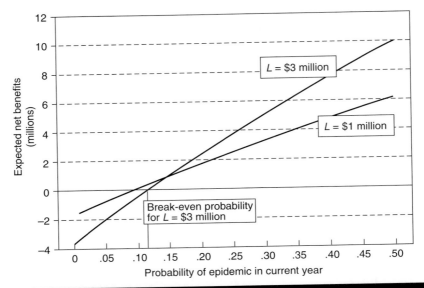

FIGURE 7.3 Expected Net Benefits of Vaccination

line). In other words, if we think that the probability of the epidemic in the current year is less than .11, and we are willing to accept the other base-case assumptions, then we should not implement the program. The probability at which net benefits switch sign is called the *break-even value*. Finding and reporting break-even values for various parameters is often a useful way to convey their importance.

The line labeled $L = \$1$ million repeats the procedure, changing the base-case assumption of the value of life from $3 million per life to $1 million per life.[15] The graph, thus, conveys information about the impact of changes in two assumptions: Each line individually gives the marginal impact of epidemic probability; looking across lines conveys information about the impact of changes in the assumed value of life. As this illustration suggests, we can easily consider the sensitivity of net benefits to changing two assumptions at the same time by constructing families of curves in a two-dimensional graph. Though computers make it feasible to produce graphs that appear three-dimensional, the added information that these graphs convey may confuse the viewer.

Figure 7.4 considers one more example of partial sensitivity analysis. It repeats the investigation of the marginal impact of epidemic probability on net benefits for two different assumptions about the size of the herd immunity effect, θ. The upper curve is for the base case that assumes a full herd immunity effect ($\theta = 1$). The lower curve assumes that only one-half of the effect occurs ($\theta = .5$), perhaps because the population does not mix sufficiently uniformly for the simple model of herd immunity assumed in the base case to apply. (Both cases return to the base-case assumption of $3 million per life saved.) Note that the break-even probability rises to over .15 for the weaker herd immunity effect. Of course, we could instead give primary focus to the herd immunity effect by graphing net benefits against the size of the herd immunity effect, holding epidemic probability constant.

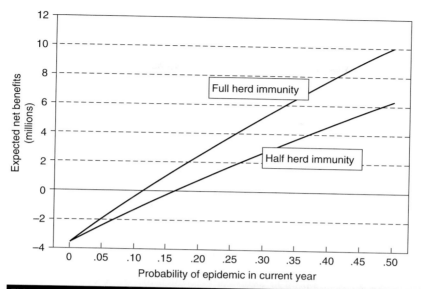

FIGURE 7.4 Expected Net Benefits of Vaccination

A thorough investigation of sensitivity ideally considers the partial marginal impacts of changes in each of the important assumptions. However, there is a "chicken and egg" problem: Identifying the important assumptions often cannot be done before actually doing the sensitivity analysis because importance depends on the marginal response of net benefits to changes in assumptions, as well as the plausible range of the assumptions. In the analysis of the vaccination program, for example, partial sensitivity analysis might well be warranted for most of the assumptions presented in Table 7.2.

Worst- and Best-Case Analysis The base-case assumptions, which generally assign the most plausible numerical values to unknown parameters, produce an estimate of net benefits that we think is most representative. In the vaccination program example, these assumptions yield fairly large positive net benefits. We can put a plausible lower bound on net benefits by considering the least favorable of the plausible range of values for each of the assumptions. In this way, we can calculate a pessimistic prediction of net benefits. Also, we can calculate an optimistic prediction of net benefits by using the most favorable assumptions. As we discuss later in the chapter, information usually has value in decision making to the extent it can potentially lead us to make a different choice. Therefore, worst-case analysis is generally most valuable when the expected net benefits are positive; best-case analysis is generally most valuable when the expected net benefits are negative. It should be kept in mind, however, that if the ranges really are plausible, then the probability of actually realizing net benefits as extreme as either the worst or the best case gets very small as the number of parameters gets large.

Worst-case analysis acknowledges that society, or specific decision makers, may be risk averse. That is, they often care not just about expected net benefits, the appropriate consideration in most cases, but also about the possible downside. Furthermore, as we point out in Chapters 1 and 19, there are often cognitive limitations and bureaucratic incentives to generate optimistic forecasts. Worst-case analysis provides a useful check against these biases.

As a demonstration of worst-case analysis, we take the lower end of each of the ranges presented in Table 7.2 for $r, v_l, v_h, m_l, m_h, \theta, e, t,$ and i, and the higher end of the range for α. For example, we assume that r, the fraction of the population at high mortality risk, equals .04 rather than the base-case value of .06. (For the time being, we keep $p_1, p_2, q, o, w, L,$ and d at their base-case values.) With worst-case assumptions, net benefits fall to $0.101 million. Though still positive, this more conservative estimate is almost two orders of magnitude (10^2) less than under the base-case assumptions.

Return to the question of the sensitivity of net benefits to the probability of epidemic. The break-even probability rises from about 11 percent under the base-case assumptions to almost 37 percent under the more conservative worst-case assumptions. In other words, expected net benefits would no longer be positive if we assessed the probability of an epidemic to be only slightly less likely than .4, the assumed value under the base case.

Care must be taken in determining which are the most conservative assumptions. Under the base-case assumptions, for example, net benefits increase as our assumed value of life increases. Under the conservative assumptions, however, net benefits decrease as the value of life increases. This reversal in the direction of the marginal impact of the value of life occurs because the higher rate of adverse reactions, α, under the conservative case is sufficiently large so that the expected number of deaths is greater with the vaccination program (1.8 deaths) than without it (1.7 deaths).

More generally, caution is warranted when net benefits are a nonlinear function of a parameter. In such cases, the value of the parameter that either minimizes or maximizes net benefits may not be at the extreme of its plausible range. Close inspection of partial sensitivity graphs generally gives a good indication of the general nature of the relationship, though they can sometimes be misleading because they depend on the particular assumed values of all other parameters. A more systematic approach is to inspect the functional form of the model used to calculate net benefits. When a nonlinear relationship is present, extreme values of assumptions may not necessarily result in extreme values of net benefits. Indeed, inspection of Table 7.3 indicates that net benefits are a quadratic function of vaccination rates v_l and v_h because they depend on $C_{e|v}$, which involves the product of direct effects and the herd effect. Under the base-case assumptions, for instance, net benefits would be maximized if all high-risk persons were vaccinated and 46 percent of low-risk persons were vaccinated. As these rates are well above those that could realistically be obtained by the program, we can reasonably treat the upper and lower bounds of vaccination rates as corresponding to extreme values of net benefits.

If the base-case assumptions generate negative net benefits, then it would have been reasonable to see if more optimistic, or best-case, assumptions produce positive net benefits. If the best-case prediction of net benefits is still negative, then we can be very certain that the policy should not be adopted. If it is positive, then we may want to see if combinations of somewhat less optimistic assumptions can also sustain positive net benefits.

Monte Carlo Sensitivity Analysis   Partial and extreme case sensitivity analyses have two major limitations. First, they may not take account of all the available information about assumed values of parameters. In particular, if we believe that values near the base-case assumptions are more likely to occur than values near the extremes of their plausible ranges, then the worst and best cases are highly unlikely to occur because they require the joint occurrence of a large number of independent low-probability events. Second, these techniques do not directly provide information about the variance, or spread, of the statistical distribution of realized net benefits. If we cannot distinguish between two policies in terms of expected values of net benefits, we may be more confident in recommending the one with the smaller variance because it has a higher probability of producing realized net benefits near the expected value.

Monte Carlo analysis provides a way of overcoming these problems. The name suggests the casinos of that famous gambling resort. It is apt because the essence of the approach is playing games of chance many times to elicit a distribution of outcomes. Monte Carlo analysis has played an important role for many years in the investigation of statistical estimators whose properties cannot be adequately determined through mathematical techniques alone. The falling opportunity cost of computing, especially the greater availability of flexible spreadsheet software for microcomputers, makes Monte Carlo analysis feasible for an ever increasing number of practicing policy analysts. As it is a method that very effectively takes account of uncertainty about assumed parameters in complex analyses, it should be in every analyst's tool kit.

The basic steps for doing Monte Carlo analysis are as follows. First, specify probability distributions for all the important uncertain quantitative assumptions. For the Monte Carlo analysis of the vaccine program, we focus on the 10 parameters with expressed ranges in Table 7.2. If we do not have theory or empirical evidence that suggests a particular distribution, then it is sometimes reasonable to specify a uniform distribution over the range. That is, we assume that any value between the upper and lower bounds of plausible values is equally likely. For example, we assume that the distribution of the fraction of the population at risk, r, is uniformly distributed between .04 and .08. Often, though, we believe that values near the most plausible estimate should be given more weight. For example, assume that analysts believe that hours lost due to influenza follows a normal distribution. They could then center it at the best estimate of 24 hours and set the standard deviation at 3.06 so that there is only a 5 percent chance of values falling outside the plausible range of 18 to 30 hours. (See Appendix 7.A for a brief discussion of working with probability distributions on spreadsheets.) As discussed in Chapter 12, analysts can sometimes estimate unknown parameters statistically using regression analysis. They might then wish to use their 95 percent confidence intervals as their ranges. Commonly used regression models allow analysts to approximate the distribution of an unknown parameter as normal with mean and standard deviation given by their empirical estimates.

Second, we execute a trial by taking a random draw from the distribution for each parameter to arrive at a set of specific values for computing realized net benefits. For example, in the case of the vaccination program analysis, analysts have to determine which contingencies occur in each of the two periods. To determine if an epidemic occurs in the current year, they take a draw from a Bernoulli distribution with probability p_1 of yielding "epidemic" and $(1 - p_1)$ of yielding "no epidemic." That is, it is as if we were to flip a coin that has a probability of p_1 of landing with "epidemic" face up. Although not all computer spreadsheets allow users to take draws directly from a Bernoulli distribution, almost all spreadsheets allow users to take draws from random variables uniformly distributed between 0 and 1—a draw from the uniform distribution produces an outcome within this range that is as likely to occur as any other outcome in the range. There is, thus, a p_1 probability of a value between 0 and p_1 occurring. To implement a draw from a Bernoulli distribution that has a probability of p_1 of yielding "epidemic," one simply compares the draw from the uniform distribution to p_1: If the random draw from the uniform distribution is smaller (larger) than p_1, then assume that an epidemic does (not) occur in the current year; if an epidemic does not occur in the current year, then follow a similar procedure to determine if an epidemic occurs in the second year. Three mutually exclusive realizations of net benefits are possible:

Epidemic in neither year:	$NB = -(C_a + C_s)$
Epidemic in current year:	$NB = -(C_a + C_s) + (C_{e\|nv} - C_{e\|v})$
Epidemic in next year:	$NB = -(C_a + C_s) + (C_{e\|nv} - C_{e\|v})/(1 + d)$

where the value of NB depends on the particular values of the parameters drawn for this trial.

Note that these estimates of NB no longer involve expectations with respect to the contingencies of epidemics, though the cost estimates themselves are expected values. For each random draw, only one combination of contingencies can actually occur. (As discussed in Chapter 8, the epidemic poses a collective risk to the population, whereas the costs result from the realizations of independent risks to individuals in the population.)

Third, we repeat the trial described in the second step many times to produce a large number of realizations of net benefits. The average of the trials provides an estimate of the expected value of net benefits. An approximation of the probability distribution of net benefits can be obtained by breaking the range of realized net benefits into a number of equal increments and counting the frequency with which trials fall into each one. The resulting histogram of these counts provides a picture of the distribution. The more trials that go into the histogram, the more likely it is that the resulting picture gives a good representation of the distribution of net benefits. Underlying this faith is the law of large numbers, which tells us that, as the number of trials approaches infinity, the frequencies will converge to the true underlying probabilities.

Figure 7.5 presents a histogram of 1,000 replications of random draws from the bracketed assumptions in Table 7.2. The assumed distributions are all uniform except that for hours lost, t, which follows a normal distribution, and whether or not the epidemic occurs, which, although a Bernoulli distribution, is implemented with the readily available uniform distribution. The height of each bar is proportional to the number of trials that had net benefits falling in the corresponding increment.

The average of net benefits over the 1,000 trials is $5.48 million. This differs from our base-case calculation of $7.72 million because the base-case value of the herd immunity factor, θ, was set at 1 rather than at the middle of the plausible range. Repeating the Monte Carlo procedure with the herd immunity factor set to 1 yields an average of realized net benefits of $7.47 million, which is very close to the base-case calculation of expected net benefits.[16]

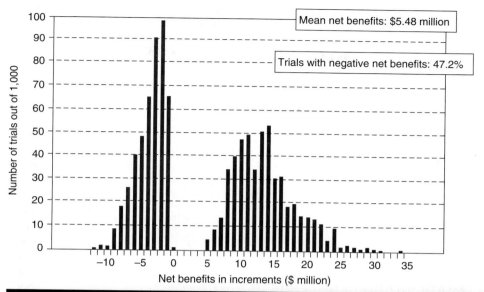

FIGURE 7.5 Histogram of Realized Net Benefits

The histogram provides a visual display of the entire distribution of net benefits so that its spread and symmetry can be easily discerned. The trials themselves can be used to calculate directly the sample variance, standard error, and other summary statistics describing net benefits.

The most striking feature of the histogram is that it portrays a bimodal distribution. If an epidemic occurs in either year, then the vaccination program in the first year has positive net benefits and it is as if we are drawing only from the right-most hump of the distribution. If an epidemic occurs in neither year, then the vaccination program has negative net benefits and it is as if we are drawing from the left-most hump of the distribution. The assumed probabilities of epidemic in the two years lead us to expect positive net benefits 52 percent of the time $[p_1 + (1 - p_1)p_2]$, which is close to the 52.8 percent of trials with positive net benefits in the Monte Carlo analysis.

The Monte Carlo results presented in Figure 7.5 treated several parameters as if they were certain. Most importantly, it treated the values of time and life as certain. As suggested in Chapter 15, we are in fact uncertain about these values. One approach would be to repeat the Monte Carlo analysis treating these parameters as random variables as well. In effect, we would be mixing uncertainty about predicted effects with uncertainty over how we value those effects. In some situations, this may be appropriate, but here it would probably be clearer to distinguish between these two types of uncertainty. To take account of our uncertainty about how we should value effects, we can simply repeat the original Monte Carlo analysis for a number of combinations of fixed values of time and life. Our results would be a collection of histograms such as Figure 7.5 that would provide the basis for assessing how sensitive our assessment of net benefits is to changes in these critical values.

EXHIBIT 7.4

Research and development projects typically have very uncertain costs and benefits when they are initiated. Based on an assessment of detailed case studies of six research and development projects (Supersonic Transport, Applications Technology Satellite Program, Space Shuttle, Clinch River Breeder Reactor, Synthetics Fuels from Coal, and Photovoltaics Commercialization), Cohen and Noll concluded: "The final success of a program usually hinges on a few key technical objectives and baseline economic assumptions about demand or the cost of alternative technologies, or both. The results of the research that addressed the key technical issues, and realizations a few years after that program was started of the key unknown economic parameters, typically made the likely success of a project very clear" (p. 82).

For example, Susan Edelman prepared CBAs of the supersonic transport project with the information that would have been available to conscientious analysts in each of a number of years. She reports that the plausible range of benefit-cost ratios fell from 1.97 to 4.97 in 1963 to 0.84 to 1.32 in 1971. They declined as it became clear that either higher operating costs or reduced loads would result from failures to achieve technical objectives and that operations over land would likely be restricted to reduce the impacts of sonic booms on people (pp. 112–121).

Source: Linda R. Cohen and Roger G. Noll, eds., *The Technology Pork Barrel* (Washington, DC: The Brookings Institution, 1991).

INFORMATION AND QUASI-OPTION VALUE

The various analytical techniques developed in the previous sections provide a basis for assessing information in CBA. In this section we demonstrate the use of games against nature to place value on information itself. We use the normal form to illustrate the basic concepts. We then use decision trees to explicate a particular information value, the quasi-option value, which arises in the context of delaying irreversible decisions to allow time for the gathering or revelation of information about the future.

Introduction to the Value of Information

The value of information in the context of a game against nature answers the following question: By how much would the information increase the expected value of playing the game? As an example of how to answer this question, return to the asteroid defense game presented in Table 7.1. Imagine that scientists have proposed developing a detection device that would allow them to determine with certainty whether or not Earth would actually be exposed to a collision with a large asteroid (diameter greater than one kilometer) in the next 100 years. What is the maximum investment that should be made to develop this device?

If the device were to be built, then it would tell us which of two possible futures were true: First, with a probability of .001, it would tell us that there would be a collision with a large asteroid. Second, with a probability of .999, it would tell us that there would be no collision with a large asteroid. Each of these two futures implies a different game against nature. These are shown in Table 7.4.

Game One, shown on the left side of Table 7.4, results if the detection device indicates that Earth will be exposed to collision with a large asteroid. Not surprisingly, in this game the best action is to choose the forward-based asteroid defense, which has the smallest net costs of the three actions ($5,060 billion). Game Two, shown on the right side of Table 7.4, results if the detection device indicates that Earth will not be exposed to collision with a large asteroid. As exposure to collision with a large asteroid

TABLE 7.4	Reformulated Games against Nature: Value of Device for Detecting Large Asteroids					
	Game One $p = .001$			*Game Two* $p = .999$		
State of Nature	*Exposure to a Collision with an Asteroid Larger Than 1 Kilometer in Diameter*			*Exposure to a Collision with an Asteroid between 20 Meters and 1 Kilometer in Diameter*	*No Exposure to Collision with an Asteroid Larger Than 20 Meters in Diameter*	
Probabilities of states of nature (over next century)	1			.004004	.995996	
Actions (alternatives)	*Payoffs (net costs in billions of 2000 dollars)*	*Expected Value*		*Payoffs (net costs in billions of 2000 dollars)*		*Expected Value*
Forward-based asteroid defense	5,060	**5,060**		1,060	60	64.01
Near-Earth asteroid defense	10,020	10,020		2,020	20	28.01
No asteroid defense	30,000	30,000		6,000	0	**24.02**

Game One: Choose forward-based asteroid defense: Expected net cost = $5,060 billion.

Game Two: Choose no asteroid defense: Expected net cost = $24.02 billion.

Expected net cost of decision with detection device: (.001)($5,060 billion) + (.999)($24.02 billion) = $29.06 billion.

Value of information provided by detection device: $38 billion − $ 29.06 billion = $8.94 billion.

is ruled out, the probabilities of the other two possible states of nature are adjusted upward so that they sum to one (.004/.999 and .995/.999). In this game, the best action is to choose no asteroid defense, which has the smallest net costs of the three actions ($24.02 billion).

Prior to developing the detection device, we do not know which of these two games it will give us to play. We do know, however, that it will indicate Game One with probability .001 and Game Two with probability .999. Thus, we can compute an expected net cost over the two games as (.001)($5,060 billion) + (.999)($24.02 billion) = $ 29.06 billion. In order to place a value on the information provided by the device, we compare the expected net cost of the optimal choice in the game without it ($38 billion as shown in Table 7.1) with the expected net cost resulting from optimal choices in the games with it ($29.06 billion). The difference between these net costs ($38 billion − $29.06 billion) equals $8.94 billion, which is the value of the information provided by the device. Consequently, as long as the detection device costs less than $8.94 billion, it would be efficient to develop it.

Note that the value of the information derives from the fact that it leads to different optimal decisions. The optimal choice without the device is the near-Earth asteroid defense. The optimal choice with the device is either the forward-based asteroid defense if collision exposure is confirmed, or no asteroid defense if the absence of collision exposure is confirmed.

In practice, analysts rarely face choices requiring them to value perfect information of the sort provided by an asteroid detection device. They do, however, routinely face choices involving the allocation of resources—time, energy, budgets—toward reducing uncertainty in the values of the many parameters used to calculate net benefits. For example, a statistical estimate based on a random sample of size 600 will be much more precise than one based on a sample of 300. How can the analyst determine if the investment in the larger sample size is worthwhile?

In a CBA involving many assumed parameters, Monte Carlo analysis may provide especially useful information. For example, suppose an agency is deciding whether or not it is worthwhile to invest analytical resources in conducting a study that would reduce the estimate of the variance of hours lost from the influenza described in the previous section. One could replicate the analysis presented in Figure 7.5 with a smaller assumed variance of hours lost and compare the resulting distribution of net benefits to that resulting with the larger variance. A necessary condition for the investment of analytical resources to be worthwhile is a meaningful change in the distribution of realized net benefits.

Quasi-Option Value

It may be wise to delay a decision if better information relevant to the decision will become available in the future. This is especially the case when the costs of returning to the status quo once a project has begun are so large that the decision is effectively irreversible. For example, consider the decision of whether or not to develop a virgin wilderness area. We may be fairly certain about the costs and benefits of development to the current generation. We may be very uncertain of the opportunity cost to future generations of losing the virgin wilderness, however. If information will become available over time that will reduce our uncertainty about how future generations will value the wilderness area, then it may be desirable to delay a decision about irreversible development so that we have the opportunity to incorporate the new information into our decision. The expected value of information gained by delaying an irreversible decision is called *quasi-option value*.[17]

Quasi-option value can be quantified by explicitly formulating a multiperiod decision problem that allows for the revelation of information about the value of options in later periods.[18] Though some environmental analysts see quasi-option value as a distinct benefit category for policies that preserve unique assets such as wilderness areas, scenic views, and animal species, it is more appropriately thought of as a correction to the calculation of expected net benefits through an inappropriate one-period decision problem. As the calculation of quasi-option value itself requires specification of the proper decision problem, whenever quasi-option value can be quantified, the correct expected net benefits can and should be calculated directly.

As background for an illustration of quasi-option value, Table 7.5 sets out the parameters for a CBA of alternatives for use of a wilderness area. The value of net benefits from full development (*FD*) and limited development (*LD*) are measured relative to no development (*ND*) for two contingencies. Under the contingency labeled "Low Value," which will occur with a probability p, future generations place the same value as current generations on preservation of the wilderness area. Under the contingency labeled "High Value," which will occur with a probability $1 - p$, future generations place a much higher value than current generations on preservation of the wilderness

TABLE 7.5 *Ex ante* Benefits and Costs of Alternative Development Policies

	Preservation Contingencies	
	Low Value	**High Value**
Full development (*FD*)	B_F	$-C_F$
Limited development (*LD*)	B_L	$-C_L$
No development (*ND*)	0	0
Probability of contingency	p	$1 - p$

Expected value of full development:	$E[FD] = pB_F - (1 - p)C_F$
Expected value of limited development:	$E[LD] = pB_L - (1 - p)C_L$
Expected value of no development:	$E[ND] = 0$
Adopt full development if:	$pB_F - (1 - p)C_F > pB_L - (1 - p)C_L$ and $pB_F - (1 - p)C_F > 0$

area. If the Low Value contingency occurs, then *FD* yields a positive present value of net benefits equal to B_F and *LD* yields a positive present value of net benefits equal to B_L. If instead the High Value contingency occurs, then *FD* yields a negative present value of net benefits equal to $-C_F$ and *LD* yields a negative present value of net benefits equal to $-C_L$. Assume that $B_F > B_L > 0$ and $C_F > C_L > 0$ so that *FD* yields greater net benefits under the Low Value contingency and greater net costs under the High Value contingency than *LD*.

Imagine that we conduct a CBA assuming that no learning will occur over time. That is, we assume that no useful information will be revealed in future periods. The expected net benefits of *FD* equal $pB_F - (1 - p)C_F$; the expected net benefits of *LD* equal $pB_L - (1 - p)C_L$; and the expected net benefits of *ND* equal 0. We would simply choose the alternative with the largest expected net benefits.

Now consider the case of *exogenous learning*. That is, we assume that after the first period we discover with certainty which of the two contingencies will occur. Our learning is exogenous in the sense that the information is revealed to us no matter what actions we take.

Figure 7.6 presents a decision tree for the case of exogenous learning. The square box at the extreme left-hand side of the figure represents our initial decision. If we select *FD*, then we have the same expected value as in the case of no learning—we have made an irreversible decision and, hence, knowing the contingency has no value because we have no decision left to make in period 2. If we select either *LD* or *ND* in the first period, then we do have a decision left to make in period 2 after we know which contingency has occurred. The expected values of the *LD* and *ND* decisions in period 1 can be found by the method of backward induction introduced in the vaccine example developed earlier in the chapter.

Consider *LD* first. If the Low Value contingency is revealed at the beginning of period 2, then the optimal decision will be to complete the development to obtain net benefits $B_F - B_L$. The present value of this amount is obtained by discounting at rate d. It is then added to B_L, the period 1 net benefits, to obtain the net benefits of *LD* conditional on the Low Value contingency occurring. If the High Value contingency is

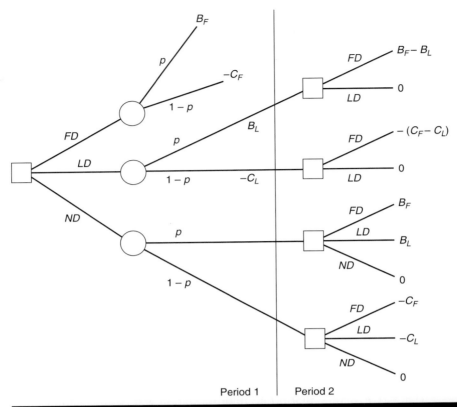

Period 1 | Period 2

FIGURE 7.6 Exogenous Learning

revealed at the beginning of period 2, then the optimal decision is to forgo further development so that the net benefits conditional on the High Value contingency occurring consist only of the $-C_L$ realized in period 1. Multiplying these conditional net benefits by their respective probabilities yields the expected net benefits for limited development in period 1 of $p[B_L + (B_F - B_L)/(1 + d)] - (1 - p)C_L$. Note that it differs from the expected value in the no-learning case by the expected net benefits of the period 2 option, $p(B_F - B_L)/(1 + d)$, which is the quasi-option value of LD.

Next consider the decision ND in period 1. If the Low Value contingency is revealed at the beginning of period 2, then the optimal decision is FD, which has a present value of $B_F/(1 + d)$. If the High Value contingency is revealed at the beginning of period 2, then the optimal decision is ND, which has a present value of 0. Consequently, the expected net benefits from choosing ND in period 1 are $pB_F/(1 + d)$, which equal the quasi-option value of ND.

The middle column of Table 7.6 summarizes the expected values of the period 1 alternatives for the case of exogenous learning.

Figure 7.7 presents a decision tree for the case of endogenous learning. Unlike the case of exogenous learning, information is generated only from development itself. For example, the value placed on preservation by future generations may depend on the risk that development poses to a species of bird that feeds in the wilderness area dur-

TABLE 7.6   Expected Values for Decision Problems: Quasi-Option Values (QOV) Measured Relative to No Learning Case

	No Learning	Exogenous Learning	Endogenous Learning
$E[FD]$	$pB_F - (1-p)C_F$	$pB_F - (1-p)C_F$	$pB_F - (1-p)C_F$
		$QOV = 0$	$QOV = 0$
$E[LD]$	$pB_L - (1-p)C_L$	$p[B_L + (B_F - B_L)/(1+d)] - (1-p)C_L$	$p[B_L + (B_F - B_L)/(1+d)] - (1-p)C_L$
		$QOV = p(B_F - B_L)/(1+d)$	$QOV = p(B_F - B_L)/(1+d)$
$E[ND]$	0	$pB_F/(1+d)$	0
		$QOV = pB_F/(1+d)$	$QOV = 0$

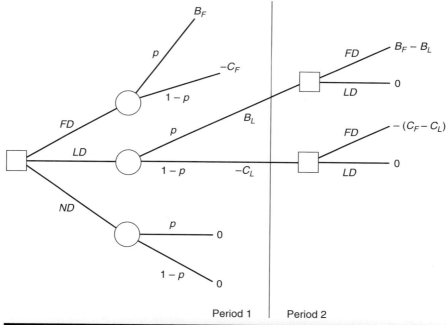

FIGURE 7.7 Endogenous Learning

ing its migration. The effect of limited development on the species may provide enough information to permit a reliable prediction of the effect of full development. If no development is undertaken, then no new information will be available at the beginning of the second period. If full development is undertaken, then new information will be generated but there will be no decision for it to affect.

As shown in the last column of Table 7.6, the expected net benefits for the *FD* and *LD* alternatives in the case of endogenous learning are identical to those for the case of exogenous learning. The expected net benefits of *ND* are zero, however, because there will be no new information to alter the decision not to develop in the future.

TABLE 7.7 Numerical Illustration of Quasi-Option Value ($ million)			
Assumptions:			
$B_F = 100$ $C_F = 80$			
$B_L = 50$ $C_L = 40$	*No*	*Exogenous*	*Endogenous*
$p = .5$ $d = .08$	*Learning*	*Learning*	*Learning*
$E[FD]$	10.00	10.00	10.00
$E[LD]$	5.00	28.15	28.15
$E[ND]$	0.00	46.30	0.00

Table 7.7 compares the different learning cases for a specific set of parameter values. If we specify the decision problem as one of no learning, then *FD* has the largest expected net benefits. Imagine that instead we specify the decision problem as the exogenous learning case. Now *ND* has the largest expected net benefits. Furthermore, relative to the case of no learning, the quasi-option value of *ND* is $46.3 million (46.30 − 0) and the quasi-option value of *LD* is $23.15 million (28.15 − 5).

Now imagine that we specify the decision problem as the case of endogenous learning. *LD* has the largest expected net benefits. Relative to the case of no learning, the quasi-option value of *LD* is $23.15 million (28.15 − 5) and the quasi-option value of *ND* is 0 (0 − 0).

This simple numerical illustration conforms to the common wisdom about quasi-option value: *It tends to be large for no development in cases of exogenous learning and large for limited development in cases of endogenous learning.* It is important to keep in mind, however, that the illustration is based on very stylized models of learning. Differently specified models could yield different rankings and different quasi-option values for the alternatives. Even with this simple model, different numerical assumptions could lead to different rankings of alternatives.

Note that our numerical estimates of quasi-option values in the illustration depend on expected values calculated by comparing what was assumed to be the correct two-period decision problem to a one-period decision problem that incorrectly fails to take account of learning. Of course, if we knew the correct decision problem, then there would be no need to concern ourselves with quasi-option value as a separate benefit category because solving the decision problem would lead to the appropriate calculations of expected net benefits.

Quasi-Option Value and Discounting

In recent years economists have developed a "new" investment theory based on models of investment projects that have three characteristics: First, they are irreversible in the sense that they involve large initial costs that cannot be recovered if they are abandoned. Second, they can be delayed. And third, information about their likely consequences will be revealed during the delay.[19] Of course, these are just the characteristics that make quasi-option value relevant. The innovative contribution of the new investment theory is that it links very general assumptions about the nature of uncertainty in project benefits to appropriate adjustments in the discount rate.

The approach is best illustrated with a specific example.[20] First, consider a project that requires an irreversible initial investment of C and that yields current benefits of B_0. Assume further that benefits are expected to grow over time, say because of increases in population or wealth, so that the benefits at any time t in the future are given by $B_t = B_0 e^{gt}$, where g is the rate of growth of benefits.[21] As shown in Chapter 6, if there is an infinite time horizon, then the stream of benefits has a present value of $B_0/(i - g)$ where i is the discount rate. Thus, the present value of net benefits will be positive if $B_0/(i - g) > C$, or $B_0 > (i - g)C$.

Now imagine that the future benefits of this project are not certain—in addition to the underlying growth trend, they include a random component. By making some specific assumptions about the nature of the random component, it is possible to show that the proper decision rule is to implement the project *now* only if $B_0 > OVM(i - g)C$, where *OVM* is called the *option value multiple*.[22] *OVM* is always greater than 1; therefore, this decision rule will reject immediate adoption of some projects that have positive net benefits. As annual benefits have both an upward trend and a random component, they may turn out in some year in the future to be sufficiently large so that a project that was initially rejected under the stringent *OVM* decision rule can later pass it and appropriately be adopted.

Table 7.8 shows *OVM*s for assumed values of g, i, and σ, the annual standard deviation of benefits, for a specific model of future benefits.[23] For example, the *OVM* entry for a zero growth rate, a discount rate of 0.04, and an annual standard deviation of 0.05 is 1.19. Under these assumptions, the magnitude of observed annual benefits must be 19 percent larger than under the standard net benefits rule to justify the project. Note that these *OVM* values are for a specific model of future benefits; other plausible models could produce different *OVM* values.

Three patterns emerge from inspection of Table 7.8. First, looking down columns, it is clear that the *OVM* is larger for higher growth rates in benefits. Higher growth rates have the effect of reducing the opportunity cost of delaying the project—with a

TABLE 7.8 Option Value Multiples for Specific Growth Rates (g), Standard Deviations (σ), and Discount Rates (i)[a]

g \ σ	$i = 0.04$					$i = 0.07$				
	0.05	0.10	0.15	0.20	0.25	0.05	0.10	0.15	0.20	0.25
0.000	1.19	1.42	1.69	2.00	2.36	1.14	1.31	1.49	1.70	1.93
0.005	1.30	1.55	1.84	2.19	2.60	1.19	1.36	1.56	1.78	2.03
0.010	1.46	1.73	2.06	2.46	2.92	1.27	1.44	1.64	1.88	2.14
0.015	1.72	2.00	2.38	2.84	3.38	1.36	1.53	1.75	2.00	2.28
0.020	2.12	2.43	2.86	3.14	4.07	1.48	1.65	1.88	2.15	2.45
0.025	2.80	3.15	3.69	4.39	5.24	1.63	1.80	2.04	2.33	2.67
0.030	4.01	4.64	5.38	6.37	7.60	1.82	2.00	2.26	2.57	2.93
0.035	8.28	9.12	10.48	12.4	14.7	2.07	2.26	2.53	2.88	3.28

[a]Assumes geometric Brownian motion with drift: $dB = gBdt + \sigma B\varepsilon_t(dt)^{1/2}$ where B is benefits, dB is the differential of benefits, dt is the differential of time, and ε_t is a normally distributed random variable with mean zero and unit variance.

positive growth rate the present value of benefits falls less over time than the present value of costs, reducing the cost of delay. Second, looking across rows for a particular discount rate, the *OVM* is larger for larger standard deviations in annual benefits. Greater uncertainty makes the information about the magnitude of benefits revealed through delaying the project more valuable. Third, the *OVM* is smaller for higher discount rates. Higher discount rates raise the cost of forgoing immediate benefits.

Unless analysts face a problem for which one of the particular models, such as the one underlying Table 7.8, that have already been analyzed is appropriate, they must use quite demanding analytical techniques to find the *OVM*. Additionally, they must make estimates of the parameters of the model, a task for which little information is likely to be available. Consequently, they are unlikely to be able to make confident assessments about the appropriate *OVM*. Nevertheless, the concept of *OVM* urges caution in applying the standard net benefits test to projects involving large irreversible investments and the potential for learning about future benefits through delay.

Quasi-Option Value in Practice

How should we treat quasi-option value in practice? Two heuristics seem warranted. First, *quantitative quasi-option values should be based on an explicit decision problem that structures the calculation of the expected net benefits.* An explicit decision problem focuses attention on the key assumptions that determine the magnitude of quasi-option value. It also makes it unnecessary to consider quasi-option value as a distinct benefit category. Second, *when insufficient knowledge is available to formulate a decision problem for explicitly calculating the magnitude of quasi-option value or, alternatively, the OVM, it should be discussed as a possible source of bias rather than added as an arbitrary quantitative adjustment to expected net benefits.* As with other biases, one can ask the question: How big would quasi-option value have to be to affect the ranking of policies?

CONCLUSION

Uncertainty inheres to some degree in every CBA. Through expected value analysis, we attempt to average over the possible contingencies to arrive at expected net benefits as a plausible prediction of net benefits. In situations not explicitly involving risk, we often assume parameter values that are more appropriately thought of as draws from probability distributions rather than as certainties. The purpose of sensitivity analysis is to determine how net benefits change if these parameters deviate from their assumed values. Partial sensitivity analysis, the most commonly used approach, focuses attention on the consequences of alternative assumptions about key parameters. Extreme-case analysis examines whether combinations of plausible assumptions exist that reverse the sign of net benefits. Monte Carlo analysis attempts to estimate the distribution of net benefits by explicitly treating assumed parameter values as random variables. It is especially useful when the risk of the policy is of particular concern and the parameters have nonuniform distributions or the formula for the calculation of net benefits involves the parameters in other than simple sums. Although the nature of the policy under consideration and the resources available to the analysts attempting to estimate its benefits and costs determine the appropriate form of sensitivity analysis, every CBA should be subjected to tests of its sensitivity to the assumptions it employs.

Explicit decision analysis frameworks, including games against nature in both normal and extensive form, provide a basis for assessing the value of information in risky circumstances. It allows an explicit calculation of quasi-option value, which is sometimes treated as a separate benefit category in CBAs. Quasi-option values take account of the value of being able to act upon future information. As solving a correctly specified decision problem naturally incorporates quasi-option values, they need not be treated as distinct benefits. Quantitative claims about quasi-option values should be based on an explicit decision problem.

Appendix 7A

DOING MONTE CARLO SENSITIVITY ANALYSIS WITH A SIMPLE SPREADSHEET

Spreadsheets greatly reduce the labor needed to conduct sensitivity analysis. Usually the calculation of net benefits can be organized so that partial sensitivity analysis can be done by simply changing the value of a single spreadsheet cell. Though specialized software is available for doing Monte Carlo analysis, with a bit of effort it can be done with any simple spreadsheet that provides a random number generator.

Generating Random Variables

Most spreadsheets provide a function for generating random variables that are distributed uniformly from zero to one. To generate uniform random variables with other ranges, one simply multiplies the draw from the random variable uniformly distributed from zero to one by the desired range and then adds the minimum value. So, for example, to get the appropriate random variable for the fraction of high-risk persons in the population, r in Table 7.2, use the following formula: $.04 + (.08 - .04)z$ where z is the uniform random variable with range zero to one.

Some other distributions can be generated directly from the uniform distribution. For example, to obtain draws from an exponential distribution, one would simply take the natural logarithm of the uniformly distributed random variable and multiply it by the negative of the desired expected value of the exponential distribution. Yet the most useful distribution, the normal, cannot be directly generated by a simple formula in some spreadsheets.

The Central Limit Theorem motivates a procedure for generating normally distributed random variables. Very loosely speaking, sums of almost any sort of random variables tend to look normal. One can obtain fairly good approximations of draws from a standardized normal random variable through the Teichroew procedure.[1] First, sum 12 uniform random variables. Second, subtract six from the resulting sum to center it at zero. Third, divide the resulting difference by four to get a random variable we will call y. Fourth, the following polynomial yields a standardized normal random variable:

$$3.949846138y + 0.252408784y^3 + 0.076542912y^5 + 0.008355968y^7 + 0.029899776y^9$$

These steps can be implemented as a formula in a single cell and copied to other cells as needed. For spreadsheets with macro capability, a macro can be written to implement this procedure. Indeed, macros that generate columns of normally distributed and other random variables make Monte Carlo analysis much faster.

The standardized normal distribution can be given any expected value and variance through simple transformations: Add a constant equal to the desired expected value and multiply by the square root of the desired variance. A range of 3.92 standard deviations includes 95 percent of the area of the normal distribution. To get the random variable we used in the Monte Carlo analysis for hours lost, t in Table 7.2, we added 24 to the standardized normal and multiplied it by $(30 - 18)/3.92$ so that there was only a 5 percent chance that a value of t would be generated outside the range 18 to 30.

Most books on mathematical statistics indicate how random variables distributed as Chi-square, Student's t, F, and multivariate normal can be generated using combinations of normally distributed random variables. Similarly, the gamma distribution and the discrete Poisson distribution can be generated from exponential distributions. Discussion of these methods here would take us too far afield.

Steps in Monte Carlo Sensitivity Analysis

Once procedures have been developed for generating appropriately distributed random variables, the conduct of Monte Carlo analysis is straightforward, though, depending on the capabilities of the spreadsheet and the hardware upon which it operates, perhaps tedious. A simple approach follows.

First, construct a row of appropriate random variables and the formulas that use them to compute net benefits. The last cell in the row should contain net benefits.

Second, copy the entire row a number of times so that the last column of the resulting block contains different realizations of net benefits. Most spreadsheet and hardware arrangements should be able to handle blocks of about 100 rows without memory or time problems.

Third, save the realizations in a separate location.

Fourth, repeat steps 2 and 3 until an adequate number of realizations have been accumulated. In some spreadsheets, step 2 can be accomplished by simply entering a "recalculate" command. The adequate number depends on the variances of the random variables and the degree of confidence desired in the distribution of realized net benefits.

Fifth, analyze the accumulated realizations along the lines of Figure 7.5.

Exercises for Chapter 7

1. The initial cost of constructing a permanent dam (i.e., a dam that is expected to last forever) is $425 million. The annual net benefits will depend on the amount of rainfall: $18 million in a "dry" year, $29 million in a "wet" year, and $52 million in a "flood" year. Meteorological records indicate that over the last 100 years there have been 86 "dry" years, 12 "wet" years, and 2 "flood" years. Assume the annual benefits, measured in real dollars, begin to accrue at the end of the first year. Using the meteorological records as a basis for prediction, what are the net benefits of the dam if the real discount rate is 5 percent?

2. Use several alternative discount rate values to investigate the sensitivity of the present value of net benefits of the dam in exercise 1 to the assumed value of the real discount rate.
3. The prevalence of a disease among a certain population is .40. That is, there is a 40 percent chance that a person randomly selected from the population will have the disease. An imperfect test that costs $250 is available to help identify those who have the disease before actual symptoms appear. Those who have the disease have a 90 percent chance of a positive test result; those who do not have the disease have a 5 percent chance of a positive test. Treatment of the disease before the appearance of symptoms costs $2,000 and inflicts additional costs of $200 on those who do not actually have the disease. Treatment of the disease after symptoms have appeared costs $10,000.

The government is considering the following possible strategies with respect to the disease:

   S1. Do not test and do not treat early.
   S2. Do not test and treat early.
   S3. Test and treat early if positive and do not treat early if negative.

Find the treatment/testing strategy that has the lowest expected costs for a member of the population.

In doing this exercise, the following notation may be helpful: Let D indicate presence of the disease, ND absence of the disease, T a positive test result, and NT a negative test result.

Thus, we have the following information:

$$P(D) = .40, \text{ which implies } P(ND) = .60$$
$$P(T\,|\,D) = .90, \text{ which implies } P(NT\,|\,D) = .10$$
$$P(T\,|\,ND) = .05, \text{ which implies } P(NT\,|\,ND) = .95$$

This information allows calculation of some other useful probabilities:

$$P(T) = P(T\,|\,D)P(D) + P(T\,|\,ND)P(ND) = .39 \text{ and } P(NT) = .61$$
$$P(D\,|\,T) = P(T\,|\,D)P(D)/P(T) = .92 \text{ and } P(ND\,|\,T) = .08$$
$$P(D\,|\,NT) = P(NT\,|\,D)P(D)/P(NT) = .07 \text{ and } P(ND\,|\,NT) = .93$$

4. In exercise 3 the optimal strategy involved testing. Does testing remain optimal if the prevalence of the disease in the population is only .05? Does your answer suggest any general principle?
5. (Use of a spreadsheet program to do this exercise is strongly recommended.) A town with a population of 164,250 persons who live in 39,050 households is considering introducing a recycling program that would require residents to separate paper from their household waste so that it can be sold rather than buried in a landfill like the rest of the town's waste. Two major benefits are anticipated: revenue from the sale of waste paper and avoided tipping fees (the fee that the town pays the owners of landfills to bury its waste). Aside from the capital costs of specialized collection equipment, household containers, and a sorting facility, the program would involve higher collection costs, inconvenience costs for households, and disposal costs for paper that is collected but not sold. The planning period for the project has been set at eight years, the expected life of the specialized equipment.

The following information has been collected by the town's sanitation department:

Waste Quantities: Residents currently generate 3.6 pounds of waste per person per day. Over the last 20 years, the daily per capita amount has grown by about 0.02 pounds per year. Small or no increases in the last few years, however, raise the possibility that levels realized in the future will fall short of the trend.

Capital Costs: The program would require an initial capital investment of $1,688,000. Based on current resale values, the scrap value of the capital at the end of eight years is expected to be 20 percent of its initial cost.

Annual Costs: The department estimates that the separate collection of paper will add an average of $6/ton to the cost of collecting household waste. Each ton of paper collected and not sold would cost $4 to return to the landfill.

Savings and Revenues: Under a long-term contract, tipping fees are currently $45 per ton with annual increases equal to the rate of inflation. The current local market price for recycled paper is $22/ton but has fluctuated in recent years between a low of $12 per ton and a high of $32 per ton.

Paper Recovery: The fraction of household waste made up of paper has remained fairly steady in recent years at 32 percent. Based on the experience of similar programs in other towns, it is estimated that between 60 and 80 percent of paper included in the program will be separated from other waste and 80 percent of the paper that is separated will be suitable for sale, with the remaining 20 percent of the collected paper returned to the waste stream for landfilling.

Household Separation Costs: The sanitation department recognized the possibility that the necessity of separating paper from the waste stream and storing it might impose costs on households. An average of 10 minutes per week per household of additional disposal time would probably be needed. A recent survey by the local newspaper, however, found that 80 percent of respondents considered the inconvenience of the program negligible. Therefore, the department decided to assume that household separation costs would be zero.

Discount Rate: The sanitation department has been instructed by the budget office to discount at the town's real borrowing rate of 6 percent. It has also been instructed to assume that annual net benefits accrue at the end of each of the eight years of the program.

a. Calculate an estimate of the present value of net benefits for the program.
b. How large would annual household separation costs have to be per household to make the present value of net benefits fall to zero?
c. Assuming that household separation costs are zero, conduct a worst-case analysis with respect to the growth in the quantity of waste, the price of scrap paper, and the percentage of paper diverted from the waste stream.
d. Under the worst-case assumptions of part (c), how large would the average yearly household separation costs have to be to make the present value of net benefits fall to zero?
e. Investigate the sensitivity of the present value of net benefits to the price of scrap paper.
f. Discuss how you would structure a Monte Carlo analysis of the present value of net benefits of the program.

6. Assume that the net present value of a hydroelectric plant with a life of 70 years was given as $25.73 million. The net present value of a thermal electric plant with a life of 35 years was found to be $18.77 million. Rolling the thermal plant over twice to match the life of the hydroelectric plant had a net present value of ($18.77 million) + ($18.77 million)/$(1 + 0.05)^{35}$ = $22.17 million.

Now assume that at the end of the first 35 years, there will be an improved second 35-year plant. Specifically, there is a 30 percent chance that an advanced solar or nuclear alternative will be available that will increase the net benefits by a factor of three; a 60 percent chance that a major improvement in thermal technology will increase net benefits by 50 percent; and a 10 percent chance that more modest improvements in thermal technology will increase net benefits by 10 percent.
a. Should the hydroelectric or thermal plant be built today?
b. What is the quasi-option value of the thermal plant?

Notes

1. A more realistic assumption (e.g., rainfall amounts closer to the center of the range are more likely) would not change this equality as long as the probability density function of rainfall is symmetric around 11 inches.
2. The representativeness is very sensitive to the particular shape of the probability density function of rainfall. The use of two contingencies would be even less representative if amounts of rainfall near 11 inches were more likely than more extreme amounts.
3. In the case of a continuous underlying dimension, such as price, the expected value of net benefits is calculated using integration, the continuous analog of addition. Let $NB(x)$ be the net benefits given some particular value of x, the underlying dimension. Let $f(x)$ be the probability density function over x. Then:

$$E[NB] = \int NB(x)f(x)dx$$

where the integration is over the range of x.
4. The term *decision analysis* was originally used to include both choice under risk (statistical decision analysis) and games against strategic opponents (game theory). Now it is commonly used to refer only to the former.
5. We recommend Howard Raiffa, *Decision Analysis: Introductory Lectures on Choices under Uncertainty* (Reading, MA: Addison-Wesley, 1969); Morris H. DeGroot, *Optimal Statistical Decisions* (New York: McGraw-Hill, 1970); Robert L. Winkler, *Introduction to Bayesian Inference and Decision* (New York: Holt, Rinehart and Winston, 1972); and Robert D. Behn and James W. Vaupel, *Quick Analysis for Busy Decision Makers* (New York: Basic Books, 1982) as general introductions. For more direct application to CBA, see Miley W. Merkhofer, *Decision Science and Social Risk Management: A Comparative Evaluation of Cost-Benefit Analysis, Decision Analysis, and Other Formal Decision-Aiding Approaches* (Boston: D. Reidel Publishing Company, 1987).
6. This example is hypothetical, though concern about influenza epidemics has been the subject of public policy debate in recent years. See, for example, Richard E. Neustadt and Harvey V. Fineberg, *The Swine Flu Affair: Decision-Making on a Slippery Disease* (Washington, DC: U.S. Government Printing Office, 1978), and David S. Fedson, "The Influenza Vaccination Demonstration Project: An Expanded Policy Goal," *Infection Control and Hospital Epidemiology*, 11, no. 7 (1990), 357–361.
7. Note that in this example the probability of an epidemic in the second year is conditional on whether or not an epidemic occurred in the first year. If an epidemic has occurred in the first year, then the population gains immunity and there is zero probability of an epidemic in the second year. If an epidemic has not occurred, then there is some probability, p_2, that one will occur in the second year.
8. Instead, we might have allowed the estimate of P_2 to be adjusted after information was revealed, or gathered, during the first year. If this were the case, then we might use *Bayes' theorem* to update the initial beliefs about P_2 in the face of the new information. Bayes' theorem provides a rule for updating subjective probability estimates on the basis of new information. Let A and B be events. A basic axiom of probability theory is that:

$$P(A \text{ and } B) = P(A|B)P(B) = P(B|A)P(A)$$

where $P(A \text{ and } B)$ is the probability of both A and B occurring, $P(A)$ is the probability of A occurring, $P(B)$ is the probability of B occurring, $P(A|B)$ is the conditional probability that A occurs given that B has occurred, and $P(B|A)$ is the conditional probability of B occurring given that A has occurred. It follows directly from the axioms that:

$$P(A|B) = P(B|A)P(A)/P(B)$$

which is the simplest statement of Bayes' rule.

Its application is quite common in diagnostic tests. For example, we may know the frequency of a disease in the population, $P(A)$, the probability that a test will yield a positive result if randomly given to a member of the population, $P(B)$, and the conditional probability that, given the disease, the test will be positive, $P(B|A)$. We would, thus, be able to calculate, $P(A|B)$, the conditional probability that someone with a positive test has the disease.

Discussions of Bayes' rule can be found in almost any introductory text on probability and statistics. For a more advanced treatment, see S. James Press, *Bayesian Statistics: Principles, Models, and Applications* (New York: John Wiley and Sons, 1989).

9. Note the assumption that the probability of the influenza reaching the population, p_1, is independent of whether or not this particular population is vaccinated. This would not be a reasonable assumption if the vaccination were to be part of a national program that reduced the chances that the influenza would reach this population from some other vaccinated population.

10. In this particular problem, it will never make sense to wait until the second year to implement the program if it is going to be implemented at all. If, however, the risk of side effects were expected to fall in the second year, say, because a better vaccine would be available, then delay could be optimal. In terms of the decision tree, we could easily model this alternative scenario by using different values of C_s in the current and next years.

11. For a discussion of the application of decision analysis to the stockpiling problem, see David L. Weimer and Aidan R. Vining, *Policy Analysis: Concepts and Practice,* 3rd ed. (Englewood Cliffs, NJ: Prentice Hall, 1999), Chapter 14.

12. Calculating the number of combinations: $3^{17} = 129,140,163$.

13. For examples of CBA applied to hepatitis vaccine programs, see Josephine A. Mauskopf, Cathy J. Bradley, and Michael T. French, "Benefit-Cost Analysis of Hepatitis B Vaccine Programs for Occupationally Exposed Workers," *Journal of Occupational Medicine,* 33, no. 6 (1991), 691–698; Gary M. Ginsberg and Daniel Shouval, "Cost-Benefit Analysis of a Nationwide Neonatal Inoculation Programme against Hepatitis B in an Area of Intermediate Endemicity," *Journal of Epidemiology and Community Health,* 46, no. 6 (1992), 587–594; and Murray Krahn and Allan S. Detsky, "Should Canada and the United States Universally Vaccinate Infants against Hepatitis B?" *Medical Decision Making,* 13, no. 1 (1993), 4–20.

14. Call the basic reproductive rate of the infection R_0. That is, each primary infection exposes R_0 individuals to infection. If i is the fraction of the population no longer susceptible to infection because of previous infection, then the actual reproductive rate is $R = R_0(1 - i - v)$, where v is the fraction of the population effectively vaccinated. If R falls below 1, then the infection dies out because, on average, each infection generates less than one new infection. Assuming that the population is homogeneous with respect to susceptibility to infection and that infected and noninfected individuals uniformly mix in the population, a rough estimate of the ultimate i for the population is given by the formula $i = 1 - (1/R_0) - v$ where $1 - 1/R_0$ is the estimate of the infection rate in the absence of the vaccine. For an overview, see Roy M. Anderson and Robert M. May, "Modern Vaccines: Immunisation and Herd Immunity," *The Lancet,* no. 8690 (1990), 641–645; and Joseph W. G. Smith, "Vaccination Strategy," in *Influenza, Virus, Vaccines, and Strategy,* Philip Selby, ed. (New York: Academic Press, 1976), pp. 271–294.

15. The $L = \$3$ million and $L = \$1$ million lines cross because lives are at risk both from the vaccination side effects and from the epidemic. At low probabilities of epidemic, the expected number of lives saved from vaccination is negative so that net benefits are higher for lower values of life. At higher probabilities of epidemic, the expected number of lives saved is positive so that net benefits are higher for higher values of life.

16. In general, if the calculation of net benefits involves sums of random variables, using their expected values yields the expected value of net benefits. If the calculation involves sums and products of random variables, then using their expected values yields the expected value of net benefits only if the random variables are uncorrelated. In the Monte Carlo approach, correlations

among variables can be taken into account by drawing parameter values from either multivariate or conditional distributions rather than from independent univariate distributions as in this example. Finally, if the calculation involves ratios of random variables, then even independence (i.e., an absence of correlations) does not guarantee that using their expected values will yield the correct expected value of net benefits. In this latter situation, the Monte Carlo approach is especially valuable because it provides a way of estimating the correct expected net benefits.

17. The concept of quasi-option value was introduced by Kenneth J. Arrow and Anthony C. Fisher, "Environmental Preservation, Uncertainty, and Irreversibility," *Quarterly Journal of Economics,* 88, no. 2 (1974), 312–319.

18. Jon M. Conrad, "Quasi-Option Value and the Expected Value of Information," *Quarterly Journal of Economics,* 44, no. 4 (1980), 813–820; Anthony C. Fisher and W. Michael Hanemann, "Quasi-Option Value: Some Misconceptions Dispelled," *Journal of Environmental Economics and Management,* 14, no. 2 (1987), 183–190.

19. For overviews, see Robert S. Pindyck, "Irreversibility, Uncertainty, and Investment," *Journal of Economic Literature,* 29, no. 3 (1991), 1110–1148; Avinash Dixit and Robert Pindyck, *Investment Under Uncertainty* (Princeton, NJ: Princeton University Press, 1994); and Gilbert E. Metcalf and Donald Rosenthal, "The 'New' View of Investment Decisions and Public Policy Analysis: An Application to Green Lights and Cold Refrigerators," *Journal of Policy Analysis and Management,* 14, no. 4 (1995), 517–531.

20. This example is based on Anthony Edward Boardman and David H. Greenberg, "Discounting and the Social Discount Rate," in *Handbook of Public Finance,* Fred Thompson and Mark T. Green, eds. (New York: Marcel Dekker, 1998), pp. 269–318.

21. More generally, the same analysis follows if B_t is interpreted as net benefits in time t exclusive of the initial sunk cost C.

22. The assumption, common in models of the prices of securities, is that benefits follow a geometric Brownian motion with drift. This implies future benefits are distributed according to a lognormal distribution with an expected value growing at the trend rate g.

23. Assuming geometric Brownian motion with drift, $OVM = \beta / (\beta - 1)$ where:

$$\beta = .5 - g/\sigma^2 + \sqrt{(g/\sigma^2 - .5)^2 + 2i/\sigma^2}$$

and σ^2 is the variance of the random component.

Appendix Notes

1. For an explanation of the Teichroew procedure and methods for generating many other distributions from uniform random variables, see Thomas H. Naylor, Joseph L. Balintfy, Donald S. Burdick, and Kong Chu, *Computer Simulations Techniques* (New York: John Wiley & Sons, 1966).

CHAPTER

8

OPTION PRICE
AND OPTION VALUE

In the actual practice of CBA in circumstances involving significant risks, analysts almost always apply the Kaldor-Hicks criterion to expected net benefits. They typically estimate changes in social surplus conditional on particular contingencies occurring, and then they compute an expected value over the contingencies as demonstrated in Chapter 7. Economists, however, now generally consider *option price,* the amount that individuals are willing to pay for policies prior to the realization of contingencies, to be the theoretically correct measure of willingness-to-pay in circumstances of uncertainty. Whereas social surplus can be thought of as an *ex post* measure of welfare change in the sense that individuals value policies as if contingencies have already occurred, option price is an *ex ante* welfare measure in the sense that consumers value policies without knowing which contingency will actually occur. These measures generally differ from one another. In this chapter, we consider the implications of the common use of expected social surplus, rather than option price, as the method for measuring benefits.

The central concern of this chapter is the conceptually correct measure of willingness-to-pay in circumstances in which individuals face uncertainty. Individuals may face uncertainties about their demand for a good, the supply of a good, or both. With respect to demand, one may be uncertain about one's future income, utility function (tastes), and the prices of other goods. For example, one's utility from skiing may depend on the sturdiness of one's knees, a physical condition that cannot be predicted with certainty. With respect to supply, one may be uncertain about the future quantity, quality, or price of a good. For example, the increase in the quality of fishing that will result from restocking a lake with game fish depends on such circumstances as weather and spills of toxic chemicals and, hence, is uncertain to some degree.

In contrast to Chapter 7, we limit our attention to uncertainties of direct relevance to individuals. We ignore uncertainties that are not of direct individual relevance but instead arise because analysts must make predictions about the future to estimate measures of willingness-to-pay. In the context of the CBA of the vaccination program discussed in Chapter 7, for example, the probability of epidemic, the probability an unvaccinated individual will be infected, the probability a vaccinated individual will be infected, and the probability a vaccinated individual will suffer a side effect are exactly the sort of uncertainties considered in this chapter. The analyst's uncertainties about the magnitude of these probabilities, the appropriate shadow price of time, or the number of people who will choose to be vaccinated were adequately addressed in the discussion of sensitivity analysis presented in Chapter 7. Though these analytical uncertainties are usually of greatest practical concern in CBA, we seek here to provide the conceptual foundation required for understanding the appropriate measure of costs and benefits when individuals face significant uncertainties. We are especially interested in how to assess appropriately government policies that increase or reduce the uncertainties that individuals face.

This chapter has three major sections. The first introduces option price and clarifies its relationship to expected surplus. The second section introduces the concept of *option value,* the difference between option price and expected surplus, and reviews the theoretical literature that attempts to determine its sign. Although sometimes thought of as a conceptually distinct category of benefits, option value is actually an adjustment to measured benefits to account for the fact that they are usually measured in terms of expected surplus rather than in terms of option price. The third section provides a general assessment of the appropriateness of the use of expected surplus as a proxy for option price.

EX ANTE WILLINGNESS-TO-PAY: OPTION PRICE[1]

Viewing benefits (or costs) in terms of the willingness of individuals to pay to obtain desirable (or avoid undesirable) policy impacts provides a clear perspective on the appropriateness of treating expected net benefits as if they were certain amounts. By identifying the conceptually correct method for valuing uncertain costs and benefits, we can better understand the circumstances under which the use of expected net benefits is more or less appropriate.

There is now a near consensus among economists that the conceptually correct way to value the benefits of a policy in circumstances involving risk is to sum the *ex ante* amounts that the individuals affected by the policy would be willing to pay to obtain it.[2] To see this, imagine that each person, knowing the probabilities of each of the contingencies that would occur under the policy, would give a truthful answer to the following question: *Prior to knowing which contingency will actually occur, what is the maximum amount that you would be willing to pay to obtain the policy?* Each individual's answer to this question is what economists call the person's *option price* for the policy. If we think of the policy as a lottery having probabilities of various payoffs to the person, then the individual's option price is a *certainty equivalent* of the lottery—that is, an amount the person would pay for a ticket without knowing the payoff (or contingency) that is actually realized. (It is called a certainty equivalent because the amount paid for a lottery ticket is certain even if the payoff is not.)

By summing the option prices of all persons, we obtain the aggregate benefits of the policy, which can then be compared to its opportunity cost in the usual way. If the opportunity cost is not dependent on which contingency actually occurs, then we have fully taken account of risk by comparing the aggregate willingness-to-pay, which is independent of the contingency that actually occurs, with the certain opportunity cost.

Illustrations of Option Price

To illustrate the concept of option price, return to the asteroid defense policies set out in Table 7.1 in the previous chapter. Assume that the United Nations wishes to evaluate the forward-based asteroid defense alternative from the perspective of humankind.

Analysts might employ a contingent valuation survey of the sort described in Chapter 14. It would require surveyors to explain to each person (or more likely to a representative of each household) the possible contingencies (exposure to collision with an asteroid larger than one kilometer in diameter, exposure to collision with an asteroid between 20 meters and one kilometer in diameter, and no exposure to collision with an asteroid larger than 20 meters in diameter), the probabilities of each contingency, and the consequences to Earth under each contingency with and without the forward-based asteroid defense. Each person would then be asked questions to elicit the maximum amount that he or she would be willing to pay to have the forward-based asteroid defense. These amounts would be summed over all earthlings to arrive at the social benefits of the forward-based asteroid defense. As this sum represents aggregate willingness-to-pay before people know which contingency occurs and, therefore, is the willingness-to-pay irrespective of which one actually occurs, it can be thought of as a certainty equivalent. Let us assume that the social net benefits, the sum of individual option prices, equaled $100 billion. The net benefits of the forward-based asteroid defense program would then be calculated as this amount minus the certain program costs of $60 billion, or $40 billion.

Recall that in actual CBA, analysts more commonly measure benefits by first estimating the social surplus under each contingency and then taking the expected value of these amounts using the probabilities of the contingencies. For example, the information in Table 7.1 indicates that the expected benefits of the forward-based asteroid defense program relative to no program to be −$15 billion (the expected value of net costs of no program, $54 billion, minus the expected value of net costs of the program, $69 billion). Thus, in this example, the expected surplus would underestimate net benefits by $55 billion ($40 billion minus negative $15 billion). This difference between option price and expected surplus is the option value of the forward-based asteroid defense program. In this case, the option value can be thought of as an additional "insurance benefit" of the program. It is the maximum amount beyond expected benefits that individuals are willing to pay to have the defense program available to reduce the risk of the catastrophic consequences that would result from an undefended collision with a large asteroid.

In general, how does this expected surplus measure compare to the option price? Assuming that individuals are risk averse, *expected surplus can either underestimate or overestimate option price depending on the sources of risk.* For an individual who is risk averse and whose utility function depends only on income, expected surplus will underestimate option price for policies that reduce income risk and overestimate option price for policies that increase income risk. In order to understand how these possibilities can arise, it is necessary to look more carefully at the relationship between option price and expected surplus from the perspective of an individual consumer. The following diagrammatic expositions illustrate cases in which option price exceeds expected surplus (a temporary dam) and expected surplus exceeds option price (a bridge).

Table 8.1 shows the contingent payoffs for a policy, building a temporary dam that provides water for irrigation. With or without the dam, the farmer can be viewed as facing two contingencies: It rains a lot or it does not rain very much. If it is wet, he will always produce more crops than if it is dry. Without the dam, the farmer would receive an income of $100 if it rains a lot and only $50 if it does not rain very much. As a result of the dam, his income will increase by $50 if it is dry, but by only $10 if it is wet. These $50 and $10 figures are the surpluses that the farmer receives from the dam under each con-

TABLE 8.1 Example of a Risk-Reducing Project

Contingency	Policy Dam	No Dam	Probability of Contingency
Wet	110	100	.5
Dry	100	50	.5
Expected value	105	75	
Variance	25	625	

Surplus point: $U(110 - S_w) = U(100)$ implies $S_w = 10$

$U(100 - S_d) = U(50)$ implies $S_d = 50$

Expected surplus: $E(S) = .5S_w + .5S_d = 30$

Expected utility of no dam: $EU = .5U(100) + .5U(50)$

Willingness-to-pay locus: (δ_w, δ_d) such that

$.5U(110 - \delta_w) + .5U(100 - \delta_d) = EU$

Option price: $.5U(110 - OP) + .5U(100 - OP) = EU$

$EU = 4.26$ and $OP = 34.2$

for $U(c) = \ln(c)$, where c is net income

Comparison: $OP > E(S)$

tingency. In expected value terms, assuming that the dry and wet contingencies are equally likely, this surplus equals $30. This $30 expected surplus figure corresponds to the measure of benefits that is used in CBA when option price is not estimated.[3]

Notice that this example, rather realistically, implies that the dam will store water that can be used for irrigation purposes if it is dry. Consequently, the dam will do more for the farmer if it turns out to be dry than if it turns out to be wet. As a result, his income depends much less on which contingency actually occurs once the dam is built than it did without the dam. In other words, the dam reduces the income risk faced by the farmer by reducing the variation in his income. A useful summary measure of this reduction in income risk is provided by the effect of the dam on the variance of the farmer's income, which is $625 without the dam, but only $25 with the dam.[4]

To determine the farmer's benefits from the dam, we first calculate his expected utility, *EU,* without the dam. We then find his option price—that is, the maximum amount he would be willing to pay for the dam or, equivalently, the amount that gives him the same expected utility as he would have without the dam. To compute these amounts, we need to know the farmer's utility function. Normally, we would not have this information, which is why, in practice, expected surplus, rather than option price, is usually used to determine net benefits. For purposes of our illustration, however, we assume that the farmer's utility is given by the natural log of his income as in Table 8.1.

The curved line in Figure 8.1 shows this utility function. In the absence of a dam, the farmer realizes income of $50 if it is dry and $100 if it is wet. Because the probabilities

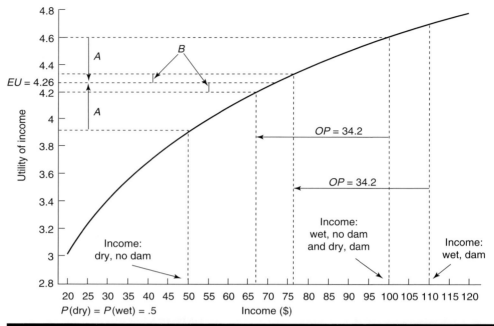

FIGURE 8.1 Utility Function and Option Price for Risk-Decreasing Project

of wet and dry are each one-half, the expected utility without the dam can be found as the point midway between the utilities of these no-dam incomes. The point on the vertical axis labeled $EU = 4.26$ is exactly A away from each of the contingent utilities. As it is midway between them, it equals the expected utility.

If the dam is built, then the farmer receives an income of $100 if it is dry and $110 if it is wet. The option price for the dam is the maximum amount of income the farmer would be willing to give up to have the dam—in other words, the amount that would allow him to obtain the same expected utility with the dam as he would obtain without it. The arrows marked $OP = 34.2$ shift the contingent incomes with the dam by subtracting $34.2 from each so that the net contingent incomes are $65.8 and $75.8. The utilities of these net incomes are each B away from 4.26 so that their expected utility equals the expected utility of no dam. Thus, either no dam or a dam with a certain payment of $34.2 gives the farmer the same expected utility.

The farmer's option price for the dam of $34.20 exceeds his expected surplus of $30. Thus, if the opportunity cost of the project were $32 and the farmer were the only beneficiary, the common practice of using expected surplus would result in rejecting building the dam when, in fact, the option price indicates that building the dam would increase the farmer's utility.

Figure 8.2 provides an alternative graphical representation of the relationship between expected surplus and option price for the farmer. The vertical axis indicates the farmer's willingness-to-pay amounts if it is dry; the horizontal axis represents his willingness-to-pay amounts if it is wet. Thus, point A represents his surplus under each contingency, $50 if it is dry and $10 if it is wet.

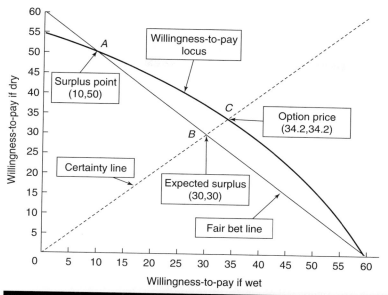

FIGURE 8.2 Risk-Reducing Project: Expected Surplus and Option Price

There is a slightly different way to view point *A*. Imagine that before the government will build the dam, the farmer would be required to sign a contract, contract A, that stipulates that he will pay the government an amount equal to X_w if it turns out to be wet and an amount equal to X_d if it turns out to be dry. This is called a *contingent contract* because its terms depend on events that will not be known until sometime in the future. Although the government is unlikely to require a contingent contract in practice, it is a useful device for thinking about how much the farmer values the dam—in other words, his benefits from the dam. These benefits correspond to the maximum value that the government could assign to X_w and X_d and still get the farmer to sign contract A, $10 and $50, respectively. The farmer would be willing to sign at these amounts because he would be exactly back to the situation he faced without the dam, when his income equaled $100 if it rained and $50 if it was dry. In other words, $10 and $50 are his maximum willingness-to-pay under contract A.

Notice that because the $10 payment if it is wet and the $50 payment if it is dry put the farmer back to where he would be without the dam, they measure the surplus he receives because the dam increases his income but not the utility he receives because the dam reduces the income risk he faces. If the farmer makes these payments, his income variability would be exactly what it was without the dam. To examine the change in income risk resulting from the dam, imagine now that the government is also willing to let the farmer choose an alternative contract, contract B, that allows him to pay the same amount, $30, regardless of which contingency actually occurs. If the government does this, the expected value of the payment it will receive would be equal under the two contracts. However, contract B would place the farmer on a line that bisects the origin of Figure 8.2. This line is called the *certainty line* because payment amounts along it are the same regardless of which contingency actually occurs. Thus, any point along this line, including *B*, represents a certainty equivalent.

The certainty line intersects another line. This one passes through the surplus point, but every point along it has the same expected value. For example, in the case of our illustration, the expected value would always be equal to $30 along this line. This line is called the *fair bet line*. To see why, imagine flipping a coin. A payoff of $10 if you get heads and $50 if you get tails would have exactly the same expected value as $20 if you get heads and $40 if you get tails. Thus, the slope of the fair bet line, −1, is equal to the negative of the ratio of the probabilities of the contingencies. As one moves along the fair bet line toward the certainty line, the expected value always remains the same, but the variation in income decreases. Finally, at point *B* on the certainty line, the payoff is equal regardless of which contingency, heads or tails, actually occurs.[5] In our example, this payoff is $30.

We now return to our farmer and the dam and ask whether he would be indifferent between signing contract A under which he must pay $10 if it is wet and $50 if it is dry and contract B under which he must pay $30 regardless of whether it is wet or dry, noting that the expected value of his income would be equal under the two contracts. To answer this, we look at what his income would be under the two contracts:

Contingency	Probability	Income under Contract A	Income under Contract B
Wet	.5	$100	$80
Dry	.5	$50	$70
EV		$75	$75

Although the expected value (*EV*) of income under the two contracts would be identical, the variation in income between the two contingencies is obviously much less under contract B. Thus, by comparing contracts A and B, we can examine the effect of the dam on the risk facing the farmer, while holding the expected value of his income constant. If the farmer is risk averse and, hence, would prefer a more stable to a less stable income from year to year, then he will not be indifferent between the two contracts, but will prefer B to A because with B he will face less risk.

Now, recall that at point *A* in Figure 8.2 the farmer was willing to sign a contract that would require him to pay $10 if it is wet and $50 if it is dry and that the expected value of these payments was $30. Because the farmer prefers point *B* to point *A,* this suggests that in order to reach the certainty line, the farmer would be willing to sign a contract requiring him to pay a certainty equivalent greater than $30. The maximum such amount that he would pay is represented by point *C* in Figure 8.2, a point that is further northeast along the certainty line than point *B.* Point *C* represents the farmer's option price, the maximum amount that he would be willing to pay for *both* the increase in expected income and the reduction in income risk resulting from the dam. In other words, it incorporates the full value of the dam to the farmer. Conceptually, it is the correct measure of benefits that the farmer would receive from the dam. But in CBAs, it is point *B*—the expected value of the surpluses resulting from the dam—that is typically measured. Although point *B* captures the effect of the dam on expected income, it does not incorporate the effect of the dam on income variability or risk.

Although the farmer would prefer point *B* to point *A,* he would be indifferent between points *A* and *C.* Indeed, a curve drawn between these points is very similar to an indifference curve. This curve, the *willingness-to-pay locus,*[6] shows all of the combinations of contingent payments for the dam that give the farmer the same expected utility with the dam as without it.[7] It is based on knowledge of the probabilities of the contingencies prior to knowing which one will actually occur.

If the cost of the project does not depend on the contingency that occurs, then it would also be represented as a point on the certainty line. If the option price lies further to the northeast along the certainty line than does the cost, the project would increase the farmer's welfare.

Table 8.2 describes a policy involving constructing a bridge in an area where the probability of an earthquake is 20 percent. The bridge would increase the expected value of income the individual described in the table receives, but at the same time, it would make her income more dependent on whether or not a quake actually occurs. In other words, the bridge increases the income risk facing the individual. Consequently, as shown in the table, the expected surplus of $84 exceeds the option price of $71.10. Thus, if the opportunity cost of the bridge were a certain $75 and the person were the only beneficiary, the option price indicates that building it would reduce her expected utility if she actually had to pay the opportunity cost of its construction. Hence, the bridge should not be built even though the expected surplus from building it is positive.

This situation is illustrated in Figure 8. 3. The bridge can be viewed as initially placing the individual at point A. Once again, we can imagine the government requiring the individual to sign a contingent contract, contract A. In this case, the individual

TABLE 8.2 Example of a Risk-Increasing Project

| | Policy | | |
	Bridge	No Bridge	Probability of Contingency
Contingency			
No earthquake	200	100	.8
Earthquake	100	80	.2
Expected value	180	96	
Variance	1600	64	

Surplus point: $\quad U(200 - S_n) = U(100)$ so $S_n = 100$

$\qquad\qquad\qquad\quad U(100 - S_e) = U(80)$ so $S_e = 20$

Expected surplus: $\quad E(S) = .8S_n + .2S_e = 84$

Expected utility of no bridge: $\quad EU = .8U(100) + .2U(80)$

Willingness-to-pay locus: $\quad (\delta_n, \delta_e)$ such that

$\qquad\qquad\qquad\qquad .8U(200 - \delta_n) + .2U(100 - \delta_e) = EU$

Option price: $\qquad .8U(200 - OP) + .2U(100 - OP) = EU$

$\qquad\qquad\qquad EU = 4.56$ and $OP = 71.1$

$\qquad\qquad\qquad$ for $U(c) = \ln(c)$, where c is net income

Comparison: $\qquad OP < E(S)$

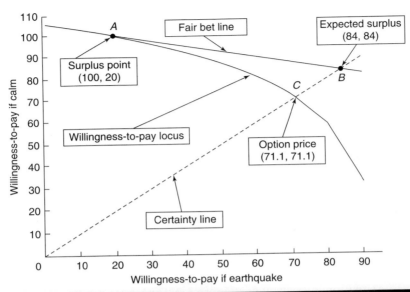

FIGURE 8.3 Risk-Increasing Project: Expected Surplus and Option Price

would be willing to pay up to $100 in the event that there is not a quake, but only $20 if there is a quake. By signing such a contract, she would be no worse off than she was without the bridge.

Again, we have taken account of the fact that the bridge would increase expected surplus but not the fact that it would also affect income risk. Thus, as before, we imagine that the government is also willing to sign a different contract, contract B, as long as the expected value of the payments continues to equal $84, their expected value under contract A.

Which contract would she prefer? If she is risk averse, she would prefer contract A to contract B, because, as shown in the following table, even though the expected value of her income is identical under the two contracts, her income would be subject to less risk.

Contingency	Probability	Income under Contract A	Income under Contract B
No quake	.8	$100	$116
Quake	.2	$80	$16
EV		$96	$96

Because a risk-averse individual would prefer contract A to contract B, her willingness-to-pay locus for the bridge would be below her fair bet line. Consequently, her option price, which is represented by point *C*, is less than $84. As in the previous illustration, the individual would be indifferent between points *A* and *C* but not between points *A* and *B*.

Is Option Price the Best Measure of Benefits?

The illustrations just described demonstrate that, in general, option price does not equal expected surplus in circumstances of uncertainty. In the first illustration, option price was larger than the expected value; in the second illustration, it was smaller. We have implicitly taken option price to be the correct benefit measure. Is this generally the case? The answer to this question requires a clearer specification of the institutional environment of policy choice.

The key consideration concerns the availability of insurance against the risks in question. *If complete and actuarially fair insurance is unavailable against the relevant risks, then option price is the conceptually correct measure of benefits.* Insurance is complete if individuals can purchase sufficient coverage to eliminate their risks entirely. It is actuarially fair if its price depends only on the true probabilities of the relevant contingencies. In the case of two contingencies, with the probability of contingency 1 equal to p and the probability of contingency 2 equal to $1 - p$, actuarially fair insurance would allow the individual to trade contingent income in contingency 1 for contingent income in contingency 2 at a price of $p/(1 - p)$. For example, if p equals .2, then the price of insurance equals .25 (.2/.8) so that to increase income in contingency 1 by $100, the individual would have to give up $25 in contingency 2. Graphically, the availability of actuarially fair insurance means that individuals could move along the fair bet lines toward the certainty lines shown in Figures 8.2 and 8.3 through purchases of insurance.

Complete and actuarially fair insurance is rarely available in the real world.[8] The problem of *moral hazard,* the changes in risk-related behavior of insurees induced by insurance coverage, encourages profit-maximizing insurers to limit coverage through copayments.[9] Insurers may be unwilling to provide full insurance against losses to unique assets that cannot be easily valued in markets.[10] *Adverse selection* occurs when insurees have better information about their true risks than do insurers. Adverse selection may result in either the combining of low- and high-risk persons in the same price pool or the limiting of the extent of coverage to induce high risks to reveal themselves.[11] The pooling of high- and low-risk persons implies that one or both groups receive an actuarially unfair price; limiting available coverage to high-risk persons means that complete insurance is unavailable. Routine administrative costs, as well as efforts to control moral hazard and adverse selection, inflate prices above the actuarially fair levels. Limited pools of insurees or uncertainty about the magnitudes of risks may require a further increment in prices to reduce the risk of bankruptcy.[12] Finally, some risks are so correlated across individuals that risk pooling does not sufficiently reduce aggregate risk to allow actuarially fair prices.[13] In order to manage the risk of going bankrupt, insurers facing correlated risks must charge an amount above the actuarially fair price to build a financial cushion or buy reinsurance to guard against the possibility of having to pay off on many losses at the same time.

Imagine that, despite these practical limitations, complete and actuarially fair insurance were available for the risk in question. It would then be possible for the sponsor of the project to trade the contingent surplus amounts for a certain payment by purchasing sufficient insurance to move along the fair bet line, which represents actuarially fair insurance, to the certainty line. In this way, a certain payment corresponding to the expected surplus could be achieved. For example, returning to Figure 8.3, the project sponsor could guarantee a certain payment of $84, which is larger than the option price of $71.10. Notice, however, that if the option price exceeds the expected surplus (the situation illustrated in Figure 8.2), then the latter will understate the conceptually correct measure of project benefits even if complete and actuarially fair insurance can be purchased. In general, therefore, *if complete and actuarially fair insurance is available, then the larger of option price or expected surplus is the appropriate measure of benefits.*

This generalization ignores one additional institutional constraint: It is not practical to specify contingency-specific payments that would move an individual from his or her contingent surplus point to other points on his or her willingness-to-pay locus. The impracticality may arise from a lack of either information about the shape of the entire willingness-to-pay locus or the administrative capacity to write and execute contingent contracts—actual taxes and subsidies whose magnitudes depend on the occurrence of events. Yet, if such contracts were administratively feasible *and* the analyst knew the entire willingness-to-pay locus, then the policy could be designed with optimal contingent payments so that the person's postpayment contingent surpluses would have the greatest expected value, which could then be realized with certainty through insurance purchases.

Figure 8.4 illustrates this possibility. In the absence of payments, the person realizes either S_1 or S_2 depending on which contingency occurs. If, in addition to the direct

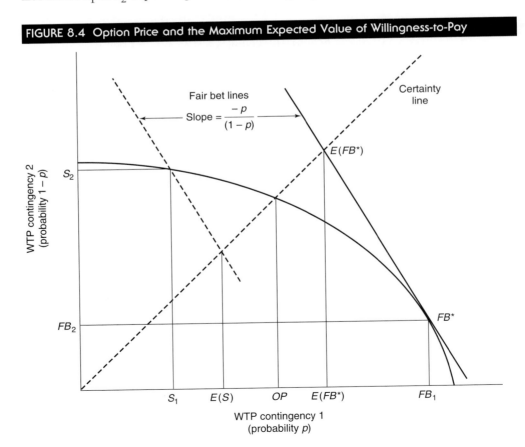

FIGURE 8.4 Option Price and the Maximum Expected Value of Willingness-to-Pay

effects of the policy, the person were given a payment equal to $FB_1 - S_1$ if contingency 1 occurred or paid a fee of $S_2 - FB_2$ if contingency 2 occurred, then the person's post-payment contingent surpluses would be given by point FB^*. Because FB^* is the point of tangency between the willingness-to-pay locus and a fair bet line, it has the largest expected value of any point on the willingness-to-pay locus. Starting at this point, complete and actuarially fair insurance would allow the policy sponsors to move along the fair bet line to the certainty line. The resulting certain payment, $E(FB^*)$ would be the maximum certain amount of benefit produced by the payment-adjusted policy.[14]

Thus, *in the exceedingly unlikely circumstance that optimal contingent payments are feasible, **and** complete and actuarially fair insurance is available, the expected value of the point on the willingness-to-pay locus that is just tangent to the fair bet line is the appropriate measure of benefits.*

In summary, if the policy under consideration involves costs that are certain and complete and actuarially fair insurance is unavailable, then option price is the appropriate measure of benefits because it allows us to compare certain willingness-to-pay amounts with certain costs. In practice, however, option prices are difficult to measure. Indeed, as will be evident from the discussion of option values in the next section, very specific assumptions about the nature of risks must be made to be able to determine whether option price is larger or smaller than the commonly measured expected surplus.

DETERMINING THE BIAS IN EXPECTED SURPLUS: SIGNING OPTION VALUE

Early attempts to apply CBA to recreational resources such as national parks raised uneasiness about the appropriateness of expected surplus as a benefit measure. In a seminal article dealing with the issue, Burton Weisbrod pointed out that estimates of the benefits of preserving a national park based solely on the benefits accruing to actual visitors do not capture its value to those who anticipate visiting it sometime in the future but actually never do.[15] He argued that these nonvisitors would be willing to pay something to preserve the option of visiting. He called this amount *option value*, which has been interpreted by many as a separate benefit category of relevance to valuing assets, such as natural resources, that offer opportunities for future consumption.

Yet CBA requires a more precise definition of option value.[16] The key to formulating it lies in the recognition that option price fully measures a person's *ex ante* willingness-to-pay for a policy in the presence of uncertainty about the benefits that will accrue *ex post*. The uncertainty may arise from a variety of sources, including not only uncertainty about the demand the person will actually have for the goods produced by the policy if it is implemented (Weisbrod's point) but also uncertainty about the quantities, qualities, and prices of the goods, as well as the prices of other goods. Because, even with such uncertainties, it is a full measure of willingness-to-pay: *Option price includes option value.*

It is now standard to define *option value* as the difference between option price and expected surplus:

$$OV = OP - E(S) \tag{8.1}$$

where *OV* is option value, *OP* is the option price, and *E*(*S*) is expected surplus. For example, the option value for the dam presented in Table 8.1 is $4.20—the option price of $34.20 minus the expected surplus of $30. The option value of the bridge presented in Table 8.2 is −$12.90—the option price of $71.10 minus the expected surplus of $84.

Rearranging the equation defining option value gives the practical interpretation of option value as an adjustment to expected surplus required to make it equal to option price:

$$OP = E(S) + OV \tag{8.2}$$

where the left-hand side is the certain amount a person is willing to pay, the conceptually correct measure of benefits, and the right-hand side consists of expected surplus, which is what is typically measurable, and option value, which is the amount that would have to be added to expected surplus to make it equal to option price. Though it may seem natural to interpret option value as a distinct benefit category, it is probably better to interpret it as the bias in benefits resulting from measurement by expected surplus rather than option price. Unfortunately, either interpretation requires caution because the sign, let alone the magnitude, of option value is often difficult to determine.

EXHIBIT 8.1

In 1980 Richard G. Walsh, John B. Loomis, and Richard A. Gillman combined survey and recreational use data in an effort to estimate the willingness of Colorado households to pay for increments of land designated for wilderness. They estimated that residents of the state were willing to pay a total of $41.6 million annually for 2.6 million acres. Approximately $6.0 million, or almost 15 percent, of this total was option value.

Source: Richard G. Walsh, John B. Loomis, and Richard A. Gillman, "Valuing Option, Existence, and Bequest Demands for Wilderness," *Land Economics*, 60, no. 1 (1984), 14–29.

Determining the Sign of Option Value

The sign of option value may be positive or negative, depending on a variety of assumptions concerning the source and nature of risk, the characteristics of the policy being analyzed, and the underlying structure of individual utility. With only a few exceptions, the sign of option value has proven to be theoretically ambiguous. This raises the issue of the usefulness of the concept of option value for even determining the direction of bias when expected surplus is used as an approximation of option price.

The earliest studies (see Appendix 8A) attempted to determine the sign of option price when the change in the price or quantity of the good being valued is certain but the demand for the good is uncertain. For example, in the earliest effort to sign option value, Charles J. Cicchetti and A. Myrick Freeman III assumed that there is some probability that a person will have positive demand for the good.[17] Their conclusion that option price is always positive when demand is uncertain was later contradicted by Richard Schmalensee, who showed that the sign was ambiguous under general assumptions.[18]

Subsequent efforts to sign option value without making specific assumptions about individuals' utility functions has produced an unequivocal result only with respect to uncertainty in income. Specifically, in valuing a certain change in the price or quantity of a normal good (quantity demanded increases with increases in income), option value will be negative for a risk-averse person with uncertain income. (Option price is less than expected surplus because the change in price or quantity of the good accentuates the income uncertainty.) Conversely, in valuing a certain change in the price or quantity of an inferior good (quantity demanded decreases with increases in income), option value will be positive for a risk-averse person. Because CBA typically involves valuing normal goods, this general result cautions against the tendency to think of option value as a positive adjustment to expected surplus.

On the other hand, with the imposition of a variety of different restrictive assumptions, it appears that for risk-averse persons uncertainty about the quantity, quality, or price of a normal good (supply-side uncertainty) will usually result in a positive option value. For example, Douglas M. Larson and Paul R. Flacco show that if the demand for a normal (inferior) good is linear, semilog, or loglinear in price, then option price is positive (negative) for uncertainty in the price or quality of the good being valued.[19] They also show that uncertainty about the prices of other goods and tastes (demand-side uncertainty) similarly yields positive (negative) option values for normal (inferior) goods for these demand functions.[20]

Over all, the theoretical studies of option value suggest the following general heuristic: *With risk-averse individuals and normal (inferior) goods, treat option value as negative (positive) for income uncertainty, ambiguous for other demand-side uncertainties, and generally positive (negative) for supply-side uncertainties.* Of course, the assumed sign of option value should be consistent with the specific assumptions employed. So, for example, if the empirically estimated demand for the good employs a loglinear functional form with a positive income elasticity, then option value would be negative for income uncertainty, positive for other demand-side uncertainties, and positive for supply-side uncertainties.

It should not be surprising that in view of the difficulty in establishing the sign of option value, even less progress has been made in putting bounds on its size relative to expected surplus. Calculations by V. Kerry Smith suggest that the size of option value relative to expected surplus is likely to be greater for assets that have less perfect substitutes.[21] Larson and Flacco derived expressions for option value for the specific demand functions that they investigated, but their implementation is computationally very difficult.[22] Consequently, it is generally not possible to quantify option value using the information from which estimates of expected surplus are typically made.

RATIONALES FOR EXPECTED SURPLUS AS A PRACTICAL BENEFIT MEASURE

Though option price is generally the conceptually correct measure of benefits in circumstances of uncertainty, analysts most often estimate benefits in terms of expected surpluses. As indicated in the preceding discussion of option value, determining even the sign of the bias that results from the use of expected surplus rather than option price is not always possible. In this section we consider the reasonableness of expected surplus as a practical benefit measure.

We present two arguments often made in defense of the use of expected surplus. One argument is based on the consideration of benefits at the aggregate social level. Another argument applies at the level of the individual policy when people face independent risks so that realized net benefits are likely to be close to expected net benefits. We consider each of these arguments in turn.

Expected Values and Aggregate Social Benefits

If society were risk neutral, then choosing policies that individually maximized expected net benefits would be efficient in the sense of maximizing the expected value of society's entire portfolio of policies.[23] If we assume that projects spread costs and benefits broadly over a large population, then the effect of any particular project on the net income of any person is likely to be small. Even if people are risk averse, their preferences can be reasonably approximated as being risk neutral for such small changes in income. Therefore, aggregation of individual preferences would lead to risk neutrality at the social level so that expected surplus would be an appropriate measure of benefits.[24]

The variable magnitudes and uneven distribution of costs and benefits that often arise from public policies undercut this line of argument, however. Policies of great import may involve large costs and benefits that remain significant at the individual level, even when spread over a large population. Policies that are targeted at specific groups, such as the unemployed, or at geographical regions often impose substantial costs on and provide substantial benefits to specific individuals. Thus, because social risk neutrality is a questionable assumption, this aggregate-level argument for the use of expected surplus is weak.

A related line of argument is based on the assumption that society holds a fully diversified portfolio of policies that allows it to self-insure against the risk of any particular project. In other words, society is able to pool risk across projects so that it effectively has complete and actuarially fair insurance. (As previously noted, insurance is complete if it is available against all risks; it is actuarially fair if it is offered at a premium equal to the expected values of the risks.) As discussed earlier, with the availability of such insurance, the larger of option price and expected surplus is the appropriate benefit measure. Thus, benefits would always be at least as large as expected surplus so that any project with positive expected net benefits would be potentially Pareto improving. Of course, the comparison of mutually exclusive policies in terms of expected surpluses could be misleading if any of the projects have option prices larger than expected surpluses.

It is worth noting that this version of the argument does not rely on the collection of policies effectively averaging costs and benefits across individuals as does the first version of the argument. Rather, it relies on an averaging of aggregate net benefits across policies so that the potential Pareto criterion can be met overall, if not at the level of the individual project.

The weakness of this argument is that diversification does not eliminate all risk. As noted in the discussion of the capital asset pricing model in Appendix 10A, a portfolio of policies as broad as even the whole stock market would still involve some systematic risk. For example, imagine adding independent policies with positive expected net benefits to the portfolio. Though the variance of the average net benefits of the policies would approach zero, the variance in total net benefits would actually increase. The variance in total net benefits means that society cannot guarantee that it will realize the total expected value of net benefits. Because diversification does not permit fully effective self-insurance, it does not provide a fully satisfactory rationale for the practical use of expected net benefits.

Expected Values and Pooling Risks across Individuals: Collective and Individual Risk

We next consider the possibility of risk pooling at the level of the individual policy. It is important to make a distinction between collective risk and individual risk.

By *collective risk,* we simply mean that the same contingency will result for all individuals in society. For example, in the context of doing a CBA for a nuclear power plant, the contingencies might be "no accident" and "nuclear accident"—everyone in the geographic area experiences the same realized contingency. The actual realized net benefits can differ substantially from the expected net benefits because all individuals share either the favorable or the unfavorable outcome rather than the weighted average of the two. In such circumstances, the world does not offer us a "middle" outcome corresponding to the expected value. Realized net benefits will, therefore, differ substantially from expected net benefits.

In contrast, consider the case of a large number of individuals who have identical preferences and who face the same probabilities of realizing each of the contingencies, but the contingency that each individual realizes is independent of the contingency realized by any other individual. This is a case of *individual risk.* This might occur, for instance, in the context of evaluating an automobile safety device using a model of traffic accidents in which there is some probability that a driver will have a potentially fatal accident for each mile driven. Multiplying the expected net benefits for one individual by the number of individuals yields a measure of expected net benefits for the policy that can appropriately be treated as approximately certain. The reason is that in circumstances of individual risk with large numbers of individuals exposed to the risk, the proportion of individuals realizing each contingency approximates the probability associated with that contingency. In other words, the averaging process tends to produce realizations of net benefits close to those calculated by the expected value procedure.

This averaging is analytically equivalent to the availability of actuarially fair insurance—it effectively translates, through a movement along a fair bet line, any contingent surplus point to a point on the certainty line. Thus, *in cases of individual risk, the larger of option price and expected surplus is the appropriate benefit measure.* As with complete diversification, the use of expected surplus as a benefit measure would guarantee that adopted policies were potentially Pareto improving but would not necessarily lead to the adoption of the most efficient policies in comparisons of mutually exclusive alternatives.

Summary: Expected Surplus as a Practical Measure

How reasonable is the use of expected surplus as a practical benefit measure? Though social risk neutrality argues for expected surplus as the correct benefit measure, its underlying assumptions are not plausible. Somewhat more plausibly, diversification across policies argues for expected surplus as a conservative measure of benefits. That is, benefits can be no smaller than expected surplus. The pooling of individual risks among those affected by a policy argues convincingly for treatment of expected surplus as a conservative measure of benefits. *Overall, these arguments suggest that when neither option prices nor option values can be estimated, and risks are individual rather than collective, analysts can reasonably use expected surplus as an approximate measure of benefits. When dealing with cases involving collective risk, they should take special care to consider the potential bias in this approach.*

CONCLUSION

We rarely have much opportunity to infer option prices directly from observable behavior, though insurance premiums and self-protection investments may convey some useful information about people's willingness-to-pay for reductions in risk. Contingent valuation surveys provide an alternative approach for directly eliciting option prices through structured conversations with respondents, but they are prone to the problems we discuss in Chapter 14. Consequently, we often have no alternative but to predict policy effects under the specified contingencies, value them with shadow price estimates from observed market behavior, and calculate expected net benefits. In cases of individual risk, it is unlikely that this procedure will result in an overestimation of net benefits. In cases of collective risk, however, these expected net benefits may either understate or overstate the conceptually correct benefits based on option price by an amount called the option value. Unfortunately, confidently signing, let alone quantifying, option price is often not possible.

Appendix 8A

SIGNING OPTION VALUE

The following table shows the progression of theoretical investigations of the sign of option value:

Study	*Assumptions and Conclusions*	*Comments*
Douglas M. Larson and Paul R. Flacco, "Measuring Option Prices from Market Behavior," *Journal of Environmental Economics and Management*, 22, no. 2 (1992), 178–198.	(1) Linear, semilog, or loglinear demand functions; uncertainty in own price, other prices, quality, or tastes: Option value positive for normal goods; option price negative for inferior goods. (2) Linear demand; uncertainty about income; normal or inferior goods: Option value is zero. (3) Semilog or loglinear demand; uncertainty about income; normal or inferior goods: Option value is negative.	Assumption of specific functional forms for demand allow signing of option value for nonincome uncertainty. Linear demand implies risk neutrality; semilog and loglinear demands imply risk aversion for normal goods and risk seeking for inferior goods.
Richard C. Hartman and Mark L. Plummer, "Option Value under Income and Price Uncertainty," *Journal of Environmental Economics and Management*, 14, no. 3 (1987), 212–225.	(1) Uncertainty in income: Option value is negative for normal goods. (2) Uncertainty in own price and other prices: Sign of option value is ambiguous.	General in the sense that preferences may depend on contingencies.

Study	Assumptions and Conclusions	Comments
Mark L. Plummer and Richard C. Hartman, "Option Value: A General Approach," *Economic Inquiry,* 24, no. 3 (1986), 455–471.	(1) Uncertainty in income and risk aversion: Option value is negative for normal goods. (2) Uncertainty in quality and risk aversion: Option value is positive for normal goods. (3) Uncertainty in tastes and risk aversion: Option value ambiguous for more than two contingencies.	Sign of option value for uncertain parameter depends on signs of the changes in surplus and marginal utility with respect to the parameter.
A. Myrick Freeman III, "The Sign and Size of Option Value," *Land Economics,* 60, no. 1 (1984), 1–13.	(1) Uncertainty in demand due to exogenous factors; risk aversion: Option value is positive. (2) If probability of demand is low, expected consumer surplus is large, and person is highly risk averse, then option value may be large.	Depends on assumption that marginal utilities and attitudes toward risk independent of exogenous factors; demonstrated for only two contingencies.
Richard C. Bishop, "Option Value: An Exposition and Extension," *Land Economics,* 58, no. 1 (1982), 1–15.	(1) Uncertainty in demand: Sign of option value is ambiguous. (2) Uncertainty in supply (price uncertainty): Option value is positive.	Supply-side case demonstrated for only two contingencies.
Richard Schmalensee, "Option Demand and Consumer's Surplus: Valuing Price Changes under Uncertainty," *American Economic Review,* 62, no. 5 (1972), 813–824.	Uncertainty in demand: Sign of option value is ambiguous.	Sign depends on risk aversion and whether surplus is measured by equivalent or compensating variation.
Charles J. Cicchetti and A. Myrick Freeman III, "Option Demand and Consumer Surplus: Further Comment," *Quarterly Journal of Economics,* 85, no. 3 (1971), 528–539.	Uncertainty in demand: Option value is positive.	Overly strong assumptions imply the same utility results under each contingency.

Exercises for Chapter 8

1. A large rural county is considering establishing a medical transport unit that would use helicopters to fly emergency medical cases to hospitals. Analysts have attempted to estimate the benefits from establishing the unit in two ways. First, they surveyed a random sample of residents to find out how much they would be willing to pay each year for the unit. Based on responses from the sample, the analysts estimated a total willingness-to-pay of $8.5 million per year. Second, the analysts estimated the dollar value of the improvements in health outcomes and avoided medical costs of users of the unit to be $6.2 million per year.

Taking the analysts' estimates at face value, specify the following:
   a. The aggregate of individuals' annual option prices for the unit.
   b. The annual total expected gain in social surplus from use of the unit.
   c. The annual aggregate option value for the unit.
2. Imagine that we want to value a cultural festival from the point of view of a risk-averse person. The person's utility is given by $U(I)$ where I is her income. She has a 50 percent chance of being able to get vacation time to attend the festival. If she gets the vacation time, then she would be willing to pay up to S to attend the festival. If she does not get the vacation time, then she is unwilling to pay anything for the festival.
   a. What is her expected surplus if the cultural festival takes place?
   b. Write an expression for her expected utility if the festival does not take place.
   c. Write an expression incorporating her option price, OP, for the festival if the festival takes place. (To do this, equate her expected utility if the festival takes place to her expected utility if the festival does not take place. Also, assume that if the festival does take place, then she makes a payment of OP whether or not she is able to attend the festival.)
   d. Manipulate the expression for option price to show that the option price must be smaller than her expected surplus. (In doing this, begin by substituting $0.5S - e$ for OP in the equation derived in 2(c). Also keep in mind that because the person is risk averse, her marginal utility declines with income.)
   e. Does this exercise suggest any generalizations about the benefits of recreational programs when individuals are uncertain as to whether or not they will be able to participate in them?

Notes

1. Our discussion in this section is based on Daniel A. Graham, "Cost-Benefit Analysis Under Uncertainty," *American Economic Review*, 71, no. 4 (1981), 715–725; V. Kerry Smith, "Uncertainty, Benefit-Cost Analysis, and the Treatment of Option Value," *Journal of Environmental Economics and Management*, 14, no. 3 (1987), 283–292; and Charles E. Meier and Alan Randall, "Use Value Under Uncertainty: Is There a 'Correct' Measure?" *Land Economics*, 67, no. 4 (1991), 379–389. The latter is the best overview of this topic despite a pedagogically relevant typographical error (the slope of the fair bet line is misstated in several diagrams).
2. Measuring benefits by persons' *ex ante* willingness-to-pay assumes that they correctly assess and process risks. Lack of information about risks, or biases in processing the information, muddies the comparison between this approach and the expectational approach if the latter involves more accurate risk assessments. For overviews, see Colin F. Camerer and Howard Kunreuther, "Decision Processes for Low Probability Risks: Policy Implications," *Journal of Policy Analysis and Management*, 8, no. 4 (1989), 565–592; and W. Kip Viscusi, *Fatal Trade-offs: Public and Private Responsibilities for Risk* (New York: Oxford University Press, 1992).
3. Formally, let m_i be the person's wealth under contingency i and let Z be an indicator of whether or not the policy under consideration is adopted ($Z = 0$ if not adopted; $Z = 1$ if adopted). The person's utility under contingency i can be written as $U(m_i, Z)$. The person's surplus (willingness-to-pay) for the project given that contingency i occurs, S_i, satisfies the equation:

$$U(m_i - S_i, 1) = U(m_i, 0)$$

The expected value of the person's contingent surpluses is $E(S) = p_1 S_1 + p_2 S_2$ in the case of two contingencies with probabilities p_1 and p_2, respectively.
4. Variance is defined as: $\text{Var}[X] = E\{(X - E[X])^2\}$. For a discrete random variable with possible outcomes x_i, $i = 1, 2, \ldots, n$,

$$E[X] = \Sigma x_i p(x_i) \text{ and}$$
$$\text{Var}[X] = \Sigma(x_i - E[X])^2 p(x_i)$$

where $p(x_i)$ is the probability of the ith outcome occurring. In the case of the payoffs from the dam given in Table 8.1:

$$E[X] = (.5)(110) + (.5)(100) = 105 \text{ and}$$
$$\text{Var}[X] = (.5)(110 - 105)^2 + (.5)(100 - 105)^2 = 25$$

5. The intersection of the fair bet line and the certainty line corresponds to the solution of the following equations:

$$E(S) = p_1 x_1 + p_2 x_2 \text{ (expected value line)}$$
$$x_1 = x_2 \text{ (certainty line)}$$
$$p_1 = 1 - p_2$$

where x_1 defines the location of points on the vertical axis and x_2 defines the location of points on the horizontal axis. Solving these equations gives $E(S) = x$, where x is the point of intersection.

6. Two aspects of the relation among the fair bet line, the certainty line, and the willingness-to-pay locus are worth noting. First, if insurance were available in unlimited quantity at an actuarially fair price, then the person could actually move from any point on the willingness-to-pay locus along the fair bet line to the certainty line by buying insurance. The near consensus that option price is the appropriate benefit measure is based on the reasonable assumption that complete and actuarially fair insurance markets generally do not exist in the real world. Second, a fair bet line can be drawn through any point. Thus, for example, if we wanted to know which point on the willingness-to-pay locus has the largest expected value, then we would find the point that is just tangent to a fair bet line.

7. Continuing with the notation from note 3, points on the willingness-to-pay locus, (w_1, w_2), satisfy the following equation:

$$p_1 U_1 (m_1 - w_1, 1) + p_2 U_2 (m_2 - w_2, 1) = EU$$

where $EU = p_1 U_1 (m_1, 0) + p_2 U_2 (m_2, 0)$ is the person's expected utility without the project.

8. For a general introduction to the theory of insurance, see Isaac Ehrlich and Gary S. Becker, "Market Insurance, Self-Insurance, and Self-Protection," *Journal of Political Economy,* 80, no. 4 (1972), 623–648.

9. Mark V. Pauly, "The Economics of Moral Hazard: Comment," *American Economic Review,* 58, no. 3 (1968), 531–537.

10. Philip J. Cook and Daniel A. Graham, "The Demand for Insurance and Protection: The Case of Irreplaceable Commodities," *Quarterly Journal of Economics,* 91, no. 1 (1977), 141–156.

11. One way to get high-risk persons to reveal themselves is to offer two insurance options: one that gives full coverage at a premium that is actuarially fair for high risks and another that gives only limited coverage at a premium that is actuarially fair for low risks. If the level of coverage under the latter option is sufficiently low, then high risks will be better off revealing themselves to get the full coverage. The result is a so-called *separating equilibrium* in which both risk groups honestly reveal themselves. The information is gained, however, at the cost of limiting coverage to low-risk persons. See Michael Rothschild and Joseph Stiglitz, "Equilibrium in Competitive Insurance Markets: An Essay on the Economics of Imperfect Information," *Quarterly Journal of Economics,* 90, no. 4 (1976), 629–650. An extension of the Rothschild-Stiglitz model incorporating contracting costs allows for the possibility that low-risk persons receive more favorable coverage. See Joseph P. Newhouse, "Reimbursing Health Plans and Health Providers: Efficiency in Production versus Selection," *Journal of Economic Literature,* 34, no. 3 (1996), 1236–1263.

12. J. David Cummins, "Statistical and Financial Models of Insurance Pricing and the Insurance Firm," *Journal of Risk and Insurance,* 58, no. 2 (1991), 261–301.

13. Jack Hirshleifer and John G. Riley, *The Analytics of Uncertainty and Information* (New York: Cambridge University Press, 1992).

14. The difference between $E[FB^*]$ and $E[S]$ is called the *option premium.* Unlike option value, it is always nonnegative. See Dennis C. Cory and Bonnie Colby Saliba, "Requiem for Option Value," *Land Economics,* 63, no. 1 (February 1987), 1–10. Unfortunately, the extreme assumptions of complete and actuarially fair insurance, knowledge of the entire willingness-to-pay locus, and the feasibility of contingent-specific payments give the notion of option premium little practical relevance to CBA.

15. Burton A. Weisbrod, "Collective Consumption Services of Individual Consumption Goods," *Quarterly Journal of Economics,* 78, no. 3 (1964), 71–77.

16. The possibility of double counting benefits with this formulation was soon pointed out by Millard F. Long, "Collective-Consumption Services of Individual-Consumption Goods," *Quarterly Journal of Economics,* 81, no. 2 (1967), 351–352.

17. Charles J. Cicchetti and A. Myrick Freeman III, "Option Demand and Consumer Surplus: Further Comment," *Quarterly Journal of Economics,* 85, no. 3 (1971), 528–539.

18. Richard Schmalensee, "Option Demand and Consumer's Surplus: Valuing Price Changes under Uncertainty," *American Economic Review,* 62, no. 5 (1972), 813–824. Robert Anderson later showed that the contradictory results arose because of additional assumptions made by Cicchetti and Freeman that had the unattractive consequence of guaranteeing the option buyer a certain utility level no matter which contingency arose. Robert J. Anderson Jr., "A Note on Option Value and the Expected Value of Consumer's Surplus," *Journal of Environmental Economics and Management,* 8, no. 2 (1981), 187–191.

19. Douglas M. Larson and Paul R. Flacco, "Measuring Option Prices from Market Behavior," *Journal of Environmental Economics and Management,* 22, no. 2 (1992), 178–198.

20. Larson and Flacco, "Measuring Option Prices from Market Behavior." As discussed in Chapter 12, empirical estimation of demand equations usually involves at least income and own price as explanatory variables for quantity. If the sign of the estimated coefficient of income is positive (negative), then the good is normal (inferior).

21. V. Kerry Smith, "A Bound for Option Value," *Land Economics,* 60, no. 3 (1984), 292–296.

22. Their expressions require not only estimates of the parameters of the demand equations but also fairly complicated expectations over the parameters that are treated as uncertain.

23. To say that society is risk neutral implies that there is a social welfare function that ranks alternative distributions of goods among individuals. That is, it gives a "score" to each possible distribution such that a distribution with a higher score is preferred by society to a distribution with a lower score. Aggregation of individual preferences, however, cannot guarantee a social welfare function that satisfies minimally desirable properties. See Tibor Scitovsky, "The State of Welfare Economics," *American Economic Review,* 51, no. 3 (1951), 301–315. More generally, see Kenneth J. Arrow, *Social Choice and Individual Values,* 2nd ed. (New Haven, CT: Yale University Press, 1963).

24. Kenneth J. Arrow and Robert C. Lind, "Uncertainty and the Evaluation of Public Investment Decisions," *American Economic Review,* 60, no. 3 (1970), 364–378.

CHAPTER
9
EXISTENCE VALUE

Within the CBA framework, people's willingness-to-pay for a policy change comprehensively measures its social benefits. Though analysts sometimes attempt to elicit willingness-to-pay amounts through contingent valuation surveys (see Chapter 14), they more often make inferences about them from observations of people's behaviors (see Chapters 11, 12, and 13). The behaviors usually involve changes in consumption of a good whose price or quantity is affected by the policy change, or changes in consumption of substitutes for or complements of the good—observed responses to price changes permit inferences about demand curves that, in turn, allow willingness-to-pay to be estimated. For many, perhaps most, applications of CBA, analysts can reasonably assume that social surplus changes estimated on the basis of observable changes in the consumption or prices of goods conceptually capture the entire willingness-to-pay. Yet in some applications of CBA, especially those involving changes in unique natural resources, people may be willing to pay for the existence of goods that they themselves will never "consume." Correctly conceptualizing and measuring such *existence values* poses an extremely difficult challenge to the application of CBA.

In this chapter, we consider existence value as a category of benefit. It is often lumped together with option value and quasi-option value under the heading of *passive use* or *nonuse* benefits. As discussed in Chapters 7 and 8, however, option and quasi-option values are better thought of as adjustments to standard benefit measures to take account of various aspects of uncertainty rather than as distinct categories of benefits. In contrast, existence value is a meaningful benefit category, though one that poses definitional problems. After framing existence value as a benefit category, we discuss the theoretical and empirical problems analysts face in measuring it.

ACTIVE AND PASSIVE USE VALUE

The notion that people may place a value on the very existence of "unique phenomena of nature" that they neither visit, nor anticipate ever visiting, was introduced into the CBA literature over 30 years ago by John V. Krutilla.[1] Consider, for example, a wilderness area that provides habitat for rare game animals. Hunters might be willing to pay to preserve the wilderness area because it either lowers the price or increases the quality of hunting. Naturalists might be willing to pay to preserve the area because it provides a desirable area for hiking or bird watching. Nearby residents may be willing to pay to preserve the area because it provides scenic beauty and prevents commercial development that they find undesirable. People who enjoy nature films may be willing to pay to preserve the area because it provides a unique setting for filming rare species. All of these people value the area because they make use of it in some way. Yet one can imagine that some other people might be willing to pay to preserve the area even though they do not use it in any of these ways. In commonly used terminology, this latter group of people is said to derive *nonuse value* from the wilderness area.

Although most economists accept the general idea that people may derive value from mere knowledge of the existence of unique assets such as scenic wilderness, animal species, or works of art, clearly defining nonuse value has turned out to be so very complicated that there is as yet no clear consensus on its precise meaning.

One complication is the difficulty of drawing a sharp line between use and nonuse. In terms of standard consumer theory, any good that a person values is an argument in his or her utility function. The good need not involve any observable activity by the person to secure its value. The quantity of a pure public good such as national defense, for instance, is "consumed" by individuals, however passively. Existence value can also be thought of as a pure public good.[2] It is nonrivalrous—the value one person derives from it does not diminish the values derived by others. It is nonexcludable—no one can be excluded from deriving value from the quantity of the good, which is provided commonly to all. Viewed as a public good, it seems more appropriate to describe existence value as *passive use* rather than nonuse.

Yet, how passive must the "consumption" be to distinguish use from nonuse? It is probably safe to say that merely thinking about the good does not constitute use as the term is commonly understood. What about discussing the good with other people? Consumption now involves observable behavior, the consumption of a complementary good, time, but most economists would probably consider it nonuse. Consuming films and photobooks based on the good, however, probably crosses the line between use and nonuse because it leaves a behavioral trace in the markets for these complementary goods. These distinctions hinge not just on the intrinsic attributes of the good but also on our ability to observe and value behavior. Thus, in actual application, distinguishing between use and nonuse is not a purely conceptual issue with a clear resolution.

A second complication, which we consider in more detail in Appendix 9A, arises because individuals can derive both use and nonuse value from an asset. A person's willingness-to-pay for preservation of the wilderness area may be motivated by the anticipation of hunting and the pleasure of knowing that future generations will be able to enjoy it as well. Although the person's total willingness-to-pay is conceptually clear, the division between these two categories of value is ambiguous because the order of valuation is generally relevant. One ordering in this case is to elicit first the person's willingness-to-pay for use and then, taking this amount as actually paid, to elicit the person's willingness-to-pay for nonuse. The other possible ordering is to elicit first the person's willingness-to-pay for nonuse and then, taking this amount as actually paid, elicit the person's willingness-to-pay for use. The orderings will yield the same total willingness-to-pay, but they probably will yield different values for use and nonuse. Obviously, the ordering problem blurs the boundary between use and nonuse.

A third complication has to do with differences in the way quantity changes affect use and nonuse benefits. In general, nonuse benefits tend to be less quantity sensitive than use benefits. For example, consider a species of mammal that will remain viable as long as its population numbers more than 20,000. Someone may very well have a nonuse value for the existence of this species that is the same for populations of 25,000 and 25 million because each population is large enough to avoid extinction. Hikers who wish to see this species in its natural habitat, however, may have a use value that is substantially larger for larger populations because the larger population offers a greater likelihood of an encounter with the species.

Finally, the nonuse category raises issues of motivation typically avoided by economists. If nonuse does not leave a behavioral trace, then its value can only be discovered empirically through stated rather than revealed preferences.

A theory about the motivations behind nonuse value can help guide the formulation and interpretation of questions for eliciting stated preferences. For example, a possible motivation for nonuse value is altruism toward either current people or future generations. Yet, it makes a difference whether the altruism is either individualistic or paternalistic. A concern about the general utility levels of others is *individualistic altruism;* a concern about the consumption of specific goods by others is *paternalistic altruism.* For example, giving money to homeless alcoholics is consistent with individualistic altruism, whereas contributing to a program that gives them only meals is consistent with paternalistic altruism. If the analyst believes that individualistic altruism is the motivation for existence value, then it is important that respondents be given sufficient context to understand the implications of provision of the good on the overall wealth of others. Because the targets of altruism generally bear some share of the costs of the provided goods, individualistic altruism generally results in lower existence values than paternalistic altruism.[3] For example, altruism might motivate someone to want to bequeath the current world climate to subsequent generations. If the altruism is paternalistic rather than altruistic, then, in determining willingness-to-pay for current policies, the person ignores the possibility that members of future generations might prefer some climate change and a higher endowment of capital to no climate change and a lower endowment of capital.

With these caveats in mind, we offer Table 9.1 as a framework for thinking about existence value as a benefit category.

Consider first benefits that arise from active use of a good. The most obvious benefit category is *rivalrous consumption* of goods, such as trees for wood products, water for irrigation, and grasslands for cattle grazing. As markets usually exist for rivalrous goods, they are the category most amenable to valuation through the estimation of demand schedules and consumer surplus.

The other use categories are for nonrivalrous goods. Those consumed on-site, such as hiking and bird watching that do not interfere with other users or uses, are labeled *direct nonrivalrous consumption.* Though rarely traded in markets, such goods can often be valued by observing the travel and time costs people are willing to bear to consume them. (See Chapter 13.) In alternative taxonomies of benefits, this category is sometimes labeled *nondestructive consumption.*

Indirect nonrivalrous consumption takes place off-site. For example, a person may derive value from watching a film about wildlife in a particular wilderness area. Expenditures of time and money on off-site nonrivalrous consumption provide some information for estimating its value, though much less reliably than for the other use categories.

Consider next passive use benefits. Four categories of existence value can be distinguished in terms of motivation. The first category, *option value,* was discussed in

TABLE 9.1 Taxonomy of Benefits: Possible Partitioning of Willingness-to-Pay

Type of Use	Benefit Category	Example
Active use	Rivalrous consumption	Logging of old-growth forest
	Nonrivalrous consumption: direct	Hiking in wilderness
	Nonrivalrous consumption: indirect	Watching a film of wilderness area
Passive use (nonuse)	Option value	Possibility of visiting wilderness area in the future
	Pure existence value: good has intrinsic value	Perceived value of natural order
	Altruistic existence value: gift to current generation	Others hiking in wilderness
	Altruistic existence value: bequest to future generation	Future others hiking in wilderness

Chapter 8. It is the amount that someone is willing to pay to keep open the option of use, active or passive, in the future. It is passive in the sense that it would not be fully captured by estimates of willingness-to-pay based on observations of active use.

The second category, *pure existence value,* arises because people believe the good has intrinsic value apart from its use. For example, some people might be willing to pay to preserve a wilderness area because they think that it is right that some natural habitats exist for rare animal species.

The remaining two categories are based on altruism. Some people may be willing to pay to preserve a wilderness area, for instance, because they get pleasure from knowing that it is used by others. Generally, the motivation for such *altruistic existence value* is paternalistic in the sense that it is driven by the desire for others to consume this particular good rather than by the desire to increase their consumption overall. It may be based on the belief that exposure to nature, art, or historical sites is intrinsically good, or perhaps on the desire to share with others a type of experience one has found to be emotionally enriching. When the altruism is directed toward future generations, the good is said to have a *bequest value.* People get pleasure from knowing that those not yet born will be able to use (and not use!) the good. Just as people often wish to leave their children a share of the wealth they have accumulated, they may want to bequeath them access to unique goods as well.

The distribution of benefits across these categories obviously depends on the specific attributes of the project being valued. By their very nature, projects involving the conservation of wilderness areas are likely to derive a high fraction of their benefits from nonuse values. For example, based on survey data, K. G. Willis estimated existence values for three nature sites of special scientific interest in Great Britain.[4] Consumer surplus associated with use of the sites appeared to account for only about 10 to 12 percent of people's total willingness-to-pay. Option value accounted for a comparable percentage. The remaining portion of willingness-to-pay consisted of existence (pure and bequest) value. Only if the nonuse benefits were included did conservation of these areas appear to have positive net benefits.

THE MEASUREMENT OF EXISTENCE VALUE

Despite the difficulty economists have in clearly defining existence value as a benefit category, few economists would deny that sometimes people are willing to pay a total amount for the preservation of assets that exceeds their willingness-to-pay for their use or anticipated possible future use. Yet, many economists believe that the method of measurement currently available, the contingent value survey, lacks sufficient reliability for existence values to be reasonably included in CBA. As we consider contingent valuation in detail in Chapter 14, our discussion here raises only the general issues most relevant to the measurement of existence value.

EXHIBIT 9.1

Public opinion and economic analysis frequently conflict in the evaluation of public subsidies for the construction and operation of stadiums for professional sports teams. Valid CBAs of sports stadiums based only on use benefits almost never find positive social net benefits, especially if done from the national perspective. One possible exception is the baseball stadium built for the Baltimore Orioles at Camden Yards, which appears to have increased average attendance from about 30,000 to about 45,000 per game. Furthermore, about 70 percent of the increase in attendance consists of residents from outside Maryland, suggesting the possibility of positive net benefits if the CBA is done from a state rather than a national perspective.

Bruce W. Hamilton and Peter Kahn conducted a detailed CBA from the perspective of the residents of Maryland. They reported the following annual benefits and costs:

Annual Benefits:		$3.36 million
Job creation	$0.48 million	
Out-of-stadium incremental taxes	$1.25 million	
Incremental admission tax	$1.20 million	
Sales tax on incremental stadium spending	$0.43 million	
Annual Costs:		$14.00 million
Annual Net Benefits:		–$10.64 million

The net cost of the stadium to Maryland taxpayers is $10.64 million per year, which is equivalent to about $14.20 per Baltimore household per year. Hamilton and Kahn note that building the stadium was probably necessary to keep the Orioles from eventually moving to another city, and that citizens of Maryland, even if they never attend Orioles games, may place a value on the stadium because they get pleasure from simply having the Orioles in Baltimore. Hamilton and Kahn call these values "public consumption benefits," which can be thought of as passive use benefits, consisting of some combination of option value and existence value. Only if the annual value of public consumption benefits exceed $10.64 million would Oriole Park at Camden Yards pass the net benefits test.

Source: Bruce W. Hamilton and Peter Kahn, "Baltimore's Camden Yards Ballparks," in Roger G. Noll and Andrew Zimbalist, eds., *Sports, Jobs, and Taxes: The Economic Impact of Sports Teams and Stadiums* (Washington, DC: The Brookings Institution, 1997), 245–281. Corrections to original provided by Bruce W. Hamilton.

Directly Eliciting Total Value

One way to avoid some of the conceptual problems in defining existence value is to measure willingness-to-pay for a policy change holistically rather than disaggregating it into component parts. In the context of contingent valuation, the analyst poses questions aimed at getting respondents to state their willingness-to-pay amounts based on consideration of *all* their possible motivations for valuing policy changes. The total value revealed through this *structured conversation* is each respondent's benefit from the policy change.

The viability of this approach obviously depends on the analyst's ability to structure a meaningful conversation. The analyst must convey a full description of the policy effect being valued. Considerably more context must be provided in the valuation of effects on passive than active use. People typically know their own current levels of use as a starting point for valuing marginal changes. They are less likely to know the total stock of a good that has nonuse value to them. Yet their valuation of marginal changes in the good is likely to depend on how much they think is currently available. For example, people who think that a particular species lives only in one particular wilderness area are likely to place a much higher value on the preservation of that area than if they knew that the species lived in several other already protected areas. Indeed, one can imagine that, given enough information and time for reflection, some people may place a zero or negative value on the existence of more of some good when its quantity is above some threshold. One may place a negative value on policies that increase the number of deer in an area, for instance, if their number is already so large as to threaten the survival of other species.

Existence value based on altruism poses special problems for the conversation. When individuals are concerned only about their own consumption, it is reasonable to separate costs from benefits. Each can be estimated separately and combined to find net benefits. Altruistic values, however, may depend on the distribution of both costs and benefits. Respondents, thus, need to know who is likely to use the good being valued and who is likely to bear the costs of preserving it. Failure to include the latter may inflate existence values if it leads to respondents not taking into account all the effects on others.

Let us assume that these concerns, along with the more general problems of contingent valuation discussed in Chapter 14, are adequately addressed so that analysts can be confident that they have correctly elicited individuals' total willingness-to-pay amounts for the policy change under consideration. If their sample of respondents included all the people with standing, then these total valuations would suffice for completing the CBA. Often, however, analysts wish to combine benefits estimated from behavioral data with existence value estimates from a relatively small sample drawn from people with standing. As already noted, partitioning respondents' total willingness-to-pay into use and nonuse values is sensitive to the ordering of categories. If nonuse values from the sample are to be added to use values estimated by other methods to get total benefits, then it is important that questions be asked so as to elicit nonuse values after respondents have considered and reported their use values.

In contrast to use, nonuse does not occur in easily defined geographic markets. Aggregate existence values are very sensitive to the geographic assumptions made in extrapolating from survey samples to the population with standing.[5] People appear to place a higher existence value on resources in closer proximity.[6] Using average existence values estimated from local samples to obtain aggregate existence values for a more geographically extensive population may be inappropriate. Indeed, the question of geographic extrapolation appears to be one of the most controversial aspects of the use of existence values in damage assessment cases.[7]

As a final point, note that as long as the conversation leads respondents to consider all the sources of uncertainty relevant to their valuation of the policy change, their total willingness-to-pay amount is an option price. It is, thus, fully inclusive of option value so that no adjustments for uncertainty are required.

Behavioral Traces of Existence Value?

Many economists would be more comfortable measuring existence value through the observation of related behavior. As a pure public good, however, its behavioral trace is likely to be so very weak that considerable ingenuity will be required to find ways of measuring it through nonconversational methods. Nevertheless, the history of the development of increasingly sophisticated methods for measuring benefits offers some hope that a way will be found.

Bruce Madariaga and Kenneth McConnell suggest one line of investigation.[8] They note that people are willing to pay to join such organizations as the Nature Conservancy and the Audubon Society. Some part of their membership fees can be thought of as voluntary contributions for a public good, the preservation of wilderness areas. Ways of making inferences about existence values from the patterns of contributions to such organizations have yet to be developed. Doing so is complicated by the problem of *free riding*—some who benefit from the public good will not voluntarily contribute to its provision.

More sophisticated models of individual utility may also provide some leverage on the measurement of existence value. Douglas Larson notes that public goods are sometimes complements of, or substitutes for, private goods.[9] If investigators are willing to impose assumptions about the form of the demand for market goods and the nature of the complementarity between market goods and existence values, then they may be able to make inferences about the magnitudes of the existence values from observation of the consumption of the market goods. Larson also suggests that explicitly treating time as a constraint in utility maximization may open up possibilities for measurement based on people's allocations of time. For example, the time people spend watching films or reading books about habitats of endangered species might, with sufficient cleverness, provide a basis for estimating their existence values for the habitats.

Should Existence Value Be Included in CBA?

A growing number of efforts to estimate existence values through surveys can be found in the literature.[10] The particular estimates are often controversial. More generally, the desirability of the effort to incorporate existence values has been debated.[11]

Should existence values be used in CBA? The answer requires a balancing of conceptual and practical concerns. On the one hand, recognizing existence values as pure public goods argues for their inclusion. On the other hand, given the current state of practice, estimates of existence values are very uncertain. This trade-off suggests the following heuristic: *Although existence values for unique and long-lived assets should be estimated whenever possible, costs and benefits should be presented with and without their inclusion to make clear how they affect net benefits.* When existence values for such assets cannot be measured, analysts should supplement CBA with discussion of their possible significance for the sign of net benefits.

CONCLUSION

As CBA is increasingly applied to environmental policies, concern about existence values among analysts will almost certainly grow. Unless methods of measurement improve substantially, however, deciding when and how to include existence values in CBA will continue to be difficult. By being aware of the limitations of these methods, analysts can be better producers and consumers of CBA.

Appendix 9A

EXPENDITURE FUNCTIONS AND THE PARTITIONING OF BENEFITS

Policies that have multiple effects pose conceptual problems for the aggregation of benefits. In most situations, we approximate willingness-to-pay by summing the changes in social surplus associated with each of the effects. In general, however, this procedure tends to overestimate total willingness-to-pay. In this appendix, we introduce some notation for formally representing the measurement of utility changes from policies with multiple effects with expenditure functions, an analytical approach commonly used in more theoretical treatments of social welfare.[1] A stylized numerical example follows to show the ambiguity in the partitioning of benefits among the various effects.

Imagine that a person has a budget B and also has a utility function U that depends on the quantities of goods $X_1, X_2, ..., X_n$. Assume that the prices of these goods are $p_1, p_2, ..., p_n$, respectively. The problem facing the consumer is to choose the quantities of the goods that maximize U such that $p_1 X_1 + p_2 X_2 + \cdots + p_n X_n \leq B$. Let U^* be the maximum utility that the person can obtain given B and the prices of the goods. We can construct an expenditure function, $e(p_1, p_2, ..., p_n; U^*)$, which is defined as the minimum dollar amount of budget necessary to obtain utility U^* at the given prices. Obviously, for the original set of prices that we used to find U^*, $e(p_1, p_2, ..., p_n; U^*) = B$.

Assume that we instituted a policy that *increased* the price of the first good from p_1 to q_1. Associated with this new price is the expenditure function $e(q_1, p_2, ..., p_n; U^*) = B'$, where B' is greater than B because the person must be given more budget to keep the utility equal to U^* in the face of the higher price. A measure of the consumer surplus loss from the price increase is given by:

$$e(q_1, p_2, ..., p_n; U^*) - e(p_1, p_2, ..., p_n; U^*)$$

which equals $B' - B$. This amount equals the compensating variation for the price change as discussed in Chapter 3.[2]

Imagine now that X_1 and X_2 are goods, perhaps existence value and hiking, provided to the person by a particular wilderness area. How would we use the expenditure function to value the wilderness area, given the original budget and set of prices?

We want to know how much compensation we would have to give to the person to restore his or her utility level to U^* after making X_1 and X_2 equal zero. In terms of the expenditure function, we do this by setting p_1 and p_2 sufficiently high so that the person's demand for X_1 and X_2 is "choked off" at zero quantities. Assume that p_{1c} and p_{2c} choke off demand. To get the total value of the wilderness area to the individual, TV, we calculate how much additional budget we would have to give the person to return him or her to the original utility level:

$$TV = e(p_{1c}, p_{2c}, ..., p_n; U^*) - e(p_1, p_2, ..., p_n; U^*)$$

which is an unambiguous and correct measure of the person's willingness-to-pay for the wilderness area.

Now consider how we might partition TV into its two components associated with X_1 and X_2. One way would be to first value X_1 and then X_2. We can express this by adding and subtracting $e(p_1, p_{2c}, ..., p_n; U^*)$ to the equation for TV to get the following equation:

$$TV = [e(p_{1c}, p_{2c}, ..., p_n; U^*) - e(p_1, p_{2c}, ..., p_n; U^*)]$$
$$+ [e(p_1, p_{2c}, ..., p_n; U^*) - e(p_1, p_2, ..., p_n; U^*)]$$

where the first line represents the willingness-to-pay to obtain X_1 at price p_1 and the second line represents the willingness-to-pay to obtain subsequently X_2 at price p_2.

The other possible partition is to first restore X_2 at price p_2 and then restore X_1 at price p_1. It is expressed by the following equation:

$$TV = [e(p_{1c}, p_{2c}, ..., p_n; U^*) - e(p_{1c}, p_2, ..., p_n; U^*)]$$
$$+ [e(p_{1c}, p_2, ..., p_n; U^*) - e(p_1, p_2, ..., p_n; U^*)]$$

where the first line represents the willingness-to-pay to obtain X_2 at price p_2 and the second line represents the willingness-to-pay to subsequently obtain X_1 at price p_1.

These alternative partitionings will not in general yield the same willingness-to-pay amounts for X_1 and X_2. Typically, the willingness-to-pay for a good will be greater if the good is introduced in the partitioning sequence earlier rather than later. The rough intuition behind this result is that a good will be relatively less valuable at the margin if it is added to an already full bundle of goods.

If one can measure TV directly, then this ambiguity in partitioning is of little concern.[3] In most circumstances, however, analysts attempt to construct TV from independent estimates of separate benefit categories. In terms of expenditure functions, what is commonly done can be expressed as follows:

$$TB = [e(p_{1c}, p_{2c}, ..., p_n; U^*) - e(p_1, p_{2c}, ..., p_n; U^*)]$$
$$+ [e(p_{1c}, p_{2c}, ..., p_n; U^*) - e(p_{1c}, p_2, ..., p_n; U^*)]$$

where the first line is the compensating variation for making only X_1 available, the second line is the compensating variation for making only X_2 available, and TB is the total estimated benefits. In general, TB does not equal TV. TB systematically overestimates TV. The overestimation tends to increase as the number of benefit components increases.[4]

We next illustrate these concepts with the stylized numerical example presented in Table 9A.1. The model assumes that the person's utility, U, depends on three goods: E, the size of the wilderness area (existence); X, a particular use of the wilderness area such as hiking; and Z, a composite good that represents all goods other than E and X. It also depends on the parameter Q, an index of the quality of the wilderness area. The person has a budget of $B = 100$ and faces prices for E, X, and Z of $p_e = \$.50$, $p_x = \$1$, and $p_z = \$2$, respectively.[5] The quantities of E, X, and Z that maximize utility for the parameter values listed in the table can be found through numerical methods to be $E = 9.89$, $X = 30.90$, and $Z = 32.08$.[6] The utility from this combination of goods, U^*, equals 38.93.

TABLE 9A.1 An Illustration of the Benefits Partitioning Problem

Utility function	$U(E, X, Z; Q) = QE^\gamma + QX^\beta + Z^\theta$ where E is the quantity of wilderness that exists, X is the use level of the wilderness, Z is a market good, and Q is an index of quality of the wilderness
Budget constraint	$B = p_e E + p_x X + p_z Z$ where B is the available budget, and p_e, p_x, and p_z are the respective prices of E, X, and Z
Optimization problem	Maximize $L = U + \lambda[B - p_e E - p_x X - p_z Z]$ where λ is the marginal utility of money
Numerical assumptions	$Q = 1$; $\gamma = 0.5$; $\beta = 0.75$; $q = 0.9$; $p_e = 0.5$; $p_x = 1$; $p_z = 2$; $B = 100$
Solution values	$E = 9.89$; $X = 30.90$; $Z = 32.08$; $\lambda = .318$ $U(9.89, 30.90, 32.08; 1) = 38.93 = U^*$ $e(p_e, p_x, p_z; Q; U^*) = e(0.5, 1, 2; 1; 38.93) = 100$
Expenditure functions	Wilderness area not available: $e(\infty, \infty, 2; 1; 38.93) = 116.95$ Wilderness existence, no use: $e(0.5, \infty, 2; 1; 38.93) = 111.42$ Wilderness use only: $e(\infty, 1, 2; 1; 38.93) = 105.04$
Existence-use partition TV = 16.95	Existence value $= e(\infty, \infty, 2; 1; 38.93) - e(0.5, \infty, 2; 1; 38.93)$ $= 116.95 - 111.42 = 5.53$ Use value $= e(0.5, \infty, 2; 1; 38.93) - e(0.5, 1, 2; 1; 38.93)$ $= 111.42 - 100 = 11.42$
Use-existence partition TV = 16.95	Use value $= e(\infty, \infty, 2; 1; 38.93) - e(\infty, 1, 2; 1; 38.93)$ $= 116.95 - 105.04 = 11.91$ Existence value $= e(\infty, 1, 2; 1; 38.93) - e(0.5, 1, 2; 1; 38.93)$ $= 105.04 - 100 = 5.04$
Independent summation TB = 17.44	Existence value $= e(\infty, \infty, 2; 1; 38.93) - e(0.5, \infty, 2; 1; 38.93)$ $= 116.95 - 111.42 = 5.53$ Use value $= e(\infty, \infty, 2; 1; 38.93) - e(\infty, 1, 2; 1; 38.93)$ $= 116.95 - 105.04 = 11.91$

The expenditure function follows directly. Obviously, the budget that gives $U^* = 38.93$ is just the budget of $100 in the optimization. Therefore, we can write the expenditure function for the initial position as:

$$e(p_e = 0.5, p_x = 1, p_z = 2; Q = 1; U^* = 38.93) = 100$$

Before illustrating the partitioning problem, it may be helpful to consider how expenditure functions can be used to find compensating variations for independent policy effects. Consider, for instance, how one can find the compensating variation for a reduction in the price of X from $1 to $.50. The procedure involves finding the expenditure function:

$$e(p_e = 0.5, p_x = 0.5, p_z = 2; Q = 1; U^* = 38.93) = 63.25$$

by asking what budget amount would allow the person to obtain the original utility at the lower price. The compensating variation for the price reduction is just the difference between the values of the expenditure function with the lower price, $63.25, and the value of the original expenditure function, $100. That is, the person would be indifferent between facing the original price of $1 with a budget of $100 and facing the reduced price of $.50 with a budget of $63.25. Therefore, the willingness-to-pay for the price reduction is the difference between $100 and $63.25, or $36.75.

Now consider how one could value a policy that would increase the quality index, Q, by 10 percent. The expenditure function for the quality improvement relative to the initial position is:

$$e(p_e = 0.5, p_x = 1, p_z = 2; Q = 1.1; U^* = 38.93) = 94.45$$

which indicates that the compensating variation for the quality improvement is $-$5.55 ($94.45 - $100), indicating that the original utility could be obtained with a smaller budget.

Returning to the initial position, let us now consider the total value of wilderness, TV, and the two ways of partitioning it between existence and use. We choke off consumption of E and X by setting their prices at infinity. This yields the expenditure function:

$$e(p_e = \infty, p_x = \infty, p_z = 2; Q = 1; U^* = 38.93) = 116.95$$

which implies that the wilderness area has a total value of $16.95 ($116.95 - $100). If we partition first by existence and then by use, we calculate:

$$e(p_e = 0.5, p_x = \infty, p_z = 2; Q = 1; U^* = 38.93) = 111.42$$

which implies an existence value of $5.53 ($116.95 - $111.42) and a use value of $11.42 ($111.42 - $100).[7] If instead we partition first by use and then by existence, we calculate:

$$e(p_e = \infty, p_x = 1, p_z = 2; Q = 1; U^* = 38.93) = 105.04$$

which implies a use value of $11.91 ($116.95 - $105.04) and an existence value of $5.04 ($105.04 - $100).[8] Thus, we see that the sequence of valuation makes a difference: Existence and use are each larger when they are valued first rather than second.[9]

Finally, consider the independent summation of benefits. Existence is valued as in the existence-use sequence and use is valued as in the use-existence sequence. Thus, we would estimate the total value of the wilderness to be $17.44 ($5.53 + $11.91), which exceeds the correct compensating variation by $.49 ($17.44 − $16.95).

In summary, the partitioning of benefits between existence and use is conceptually ambiguous when the same individuals derive both values from a policy change. More generally, policies that affect people's utilities in multiple ways are prone to overestimation of willingness-to-pay when each effect is valued independently as a separate benefit category.

Exercises for Chapter 9

1. Imagine a wilderness area of 200 square miles in the Rocky Mountains. How would you expect each of the following factors to affect people's willingness-to-pay for its preservation?
   a. The size of the total wilderness area still remaining in the Rocky Mountains.
   b. The presence of rare species in this particular area.
   c. The level of national wealth.
2. An analyst wishing to estimate the benefits of preserving a wetland has combined information obtained from two methods. First, she surveyed those who visited the wetland—fishers, duck hunters, and bird watchers—to determine their willingness-to-pay for these uses. Second, she surveyed a sample of residents throughout the state about their willingness-to-pay to preserve the wetland. This second survey focused exclusively on nonuse values of the wetland. She then added her estimate of use benefits to her estimate of nonuse benefits to get an estimate of the total value of preservation of the wetland. Is this a reasonable approach? (Note: In responding to this question assume that there was virtually no overlap in the persons contacted in the two surveys.)

Notes

1. John V. Krutilla, "Conservation Reconsidered," *American Economic Review*, 57, no. 4 (1967), 777–786 at p. 784.
2. Charles Plourde, "Conservation of Extinguishable Species," *Natural Resources Journal*, 15, no. 4 (1975), 791–797.
3. Bruce Madariaga and Kenneth E. McConnell, "Exploring Existence Value," *Water Resources Research*, 23, no. 5 (1987), 936–942.
4. K. G. Willis, "Valuing Non-Market Wildlife Commodities: An Evaluation and Comparison of Benefits and Costs," *Applied Economics*, 22, no. 1 (1990), 12–30.
5. For an overview, see V. Kerry Smith, "Nonmarket Valuation of Environmental Resources," *Land Economics*, 69, no. 1 (1993), 1–26.
6. Ronald J. Southerland and Richard G. Walsh, "The Effect of Distance on the Preservation Value of Water Quality," *Land Economics*, 61, no. 3 (1985), 281–291.
7. Raymond J. Kopp and V. Kerry Smith, "Benefit Estimation Goes to Court: The Case of Natural Resource Damage Assessment," *Journal of Policy Analysis and Management*, 8, no. 4 (1989), 593–612.
8. Bruce Madariaga and Kenneth E. McConnell, "Exploring Existence Value."
9. Douglas M. Larson, "On Measuring Existence Value," *Land Economics*, 69, no. 1 (1992), 116–122.
10. See, for example, David S. Brookshire, Larry S. Eubanks, and Alan Randall, "Estimating Option Prices and Existence Values for Wildlife Resources," *Land Economics*, 59, no. 1 (1983), 1–15;

Richard G. Walsh, John B. Loomis, and Richard A. Gillman, "Valuing Option, Existence, and Bequest Demands for Wilderness," *Land Economics,* 60, no. 1 (1984), 14–29; Kevin J. Boyle and Richard C. Bishop, "Valuing Wildlife in Benefit-Cost Analysis: A Case Study Involving Endangered Species," *Water Resources Research,* 23, no. 5 (1987), 943–950; K. G. Willis, "Valuing Non-Market Wildlife Commodities," and Thomas H. Stevens, Jaime Echeverria, Ronald J. Glass, Tim Hager, and Thomas A. More, "Measuring the Existence Value of Wildlife: What Do CVM Estimates Really Show?" *Land Economics,* 67, no. 4 (1991), 390–400.

11. See, for example, Donald H. Rosenthal and Robert H. Nelson, "Why Existence Value Should Not Be Used in Cost-Benefit Analysis," *Journal of Policy Analysis and Management,* 11, no. 1 (Winter 1992), 116–122; and Raymond J. Kopp, "Why Existence Value Should Be Used in Cost-Benefit Analysis," *Journal of Policy Analysis and Management,* 11, no. 1 (1992), 123–130.

Appendix Notes

1. A more formal treatment can be found in Alan Randall, "Total and Nonuse Values," in *Measuring the Demand for Environmental Quality,* John B. Braden and Charles D. Kolstad, eds. (New York: North-Holland, 1991), 303–321. The original analysis of the importance of the sequence of valuation can be found in J. R. Hicks, *A Revision of Demand Theory* (Oxford, United Kingdom: Clarendon Press, 1956), 169–179.

2. Though we use compensating variation as a measure of the dollar value of utility here because we find it most intuitive, equivalent variation, which measures welfare changes relative to the utility level after the price change, is generally considered a superior money metric for utility because it provides an unambiguous ordinal measure for ranking price changes. See George W. McKenzie, *Measuring Economic Welfare: New Methods* (New York: Cambridge University Press, 1983).

   If $U\sim$ is the utility after the price change, then the equivalent variation is:

   $$e(q_1, p_2, ..., p_n; U\sim) - e(p_1, p_2, ..., p_n; U\sim)$$

   where $e(q_1, p_2, ..., p_n; U\sim) = B$.

   Compensating and equivalent variation typically differ by a small amount due to income effects. In the case of quantity changes of public goods, however, the size of their difference also depends on the availability of close substitutes for the public good. See W. Michael Hanemann, "Willingness-To-Pay and Willingness-To-Accept: How Much Can They Differ?" *American Economic Review,* 81, no. 3 (1991), 635–647.

3. Of course, the value of *TV* will depend on whether it is measured in terms of compensating variation or equivalent variation.

4. John P. Hoehn and Alan Randall, "Too Many Proposals Pass the Benefit Cost Test," *American Economic Review,* 79, no. 3 (1989), 544–551.

5. If E is a public good, then we would interpret p_e as the tax per unit of E that the person pays. As everyone would have to consume the same quantity, the person would not be able to choose the value of E so that the optimization of utility would be over only X and Z.

6. The partial derivatives of L with respect to E, X, Z, and λ give four equations in four unknowns. Although these *first-order conditions* cannot be solved analytically, they can be rearranged so that E, X, and Z are each expressed as a function of λ and parameters. A solution can be found by guessing values of λ until a value is found that implies values of E, X, and Z that satisfy the budget constraint.

7. If we assume that E is fixed at its initial level, the more realistic case in evaluating an existing wilderness area, then the existence value equals only $5.47. It is smaller than in the example because the person does not have the opportunity to purchase more E when X is not available. This assumption changes neither the *TV* nor the existence value as estimated by the use-existence partition.

8. It may seem strange to partition in this way because one would normally think of existence as being a prerequisite for use. Some types of uses, however, could be provided without maintaining

existence value. For example, through stocking it may be possible to provide game fishing without preserving a stream in its natural form.

9. Using equivalent variation rather than compensating variation as the consumer surplus measure leads to the following:

$$e(p_e = \infty, p_x = \infty, p_z = 2; Q = 1; U\sim = 33.81) = 100.00$$

$$e(p_e = 0.5, p_x = 1, p_z = 2; Q = 1; U\sim = 33.81) = 84.10$$

$$e(p_e = \infty, p_x = 1, p_z = 2; Q = 1; U\sim = 33.81) = 89.00$$

$$e(p_e = 0.5, p_x = \infty, p_z = 2; Q = 1; U\sim = 33.81) = 94.68$$

$$TV_{ev} = 100.00 - 84.10 = 15.90$$

Existence-use partition:

existence value = $100.00 - 94.68$ = 5.32

use value = $94.68 - 84.10 = 10.58$

Use-existence partition:

use value = $100.00 - 89.00 = 11.00$

existence value = $89.00 - 84.10$ = 4.90

Independent summation:

existence value = $100.00 - 94.68$ = 5.32

use value = $100.00 - 89.00 = 11.00$

$$TB_{ev} = 16.32$$

10

THE SOCIAL DISCOUNT RATE

This chapter deals with theoretical issues pertaining to the selection of an appropriate *real* social discount rate (SDR).[1] When evaluating government policies or projects, analysts must decide on the appropriate weights to apply to policy impacts that occur in different years. Given these weights, denoted by w_t, and estimates of the real annual net social benefits, NB_t, the estimated net present value (*NPV*) of a project is given by:[2]

$$NPV = \sum_{t=0}^{n} w_t NB_t \tag{10.1}$$

Selection of the appropriate social discount rate is equivalent to deciding on the appropriate *set of weights* to use in equation (10.1). Sometimes the weights are referred to as *social discount factors*.

It is possible to do CBA without knowing the theoretical issues about the social discount rate in detail. Indeed, as we discuss later in this chapter, many government departments use prescribed discount rates. Many branches of the U.S. government use a real discount rate of 7 percent whereas in Canada many federal and provincial departments use 8 percent. Yet, without a strong conceptual foundation, you would not be able to give advice or answer questions about the choice of the discount rate.

Discounting reflects the generally accepted idea that a given amount of resources available for use in the future is worth less than the same amount of resources available today. This is because, through investment, one can transform resources that are currently available into a greater amount of resources in the future. Viewed somewhat differently, discounting is also needed because people prefer to consume a given amount of resources now rather than in the future. For these reasons it is generally accepted that the social discount weights decline over time; specifically, $0 < w_n \leq w_{n-1} \leq \cdots \leq w_1 \leq w_0 = 1$. There is not so much agreement about the values of the weights.

Equation (10.1) is a more general version of equations (6.8) and (6.9), the formulas for calculating the *NPV* of a project, which were introduced in Chapter 6. These equations are equivalent if:

$$w_t = \frac{1}{(1 + i)^t} \tag{10.2}$$

which implies $w_t = w_{t-1}/(1 + i)$, where $i \geq 0$. Thus, Chapter 6 implicitly assumed that the weights in one period are proportional to the weights in the previous period and that this relationship is constant over time. Put another way, Chapter 6 assumed the social discount weights declined at a constant rate, i, where i is the real social discount rate. In this chapter we relax this assumption and discuss situations in which it might be reasonable to assume that the weights do not decline at a constant rate.

Unfortunately, there is no agreement among experts about the weights or the relationship between the weights in different periods. However, some consensus is emerging. The key issue in discounting is to decide on the weights society should apply to consumption that occurs in future periods relative to the same amount of consumption in the current period. These weights represent how much current consumption society is willing to give up now in order to obtain a given increase in future consumption. It is generally accepted that society's choices, including the choice of weights, should be based on individuals' choices. But there are three fundamental unresolved issues. The first issue is whether market interest rates can be used to represent how individuals weight future consumption relative to present consumption. The second issue is whether the individuals in society should include individuals from unborn future generations in addition to individuals who are alive today. The third issue is whether society attaches the same value to a unit of investment as to a unit of consumption. Consideration of these issues means that there may not be a single discount rate that applies to all flows in all periods. Different assumptions will lead to the choice of a different *discount rate method.* In turn, choice of method leads to different discount factors or weights.

Some assumptions depend on the specifics of a particular project according, for example, to how it will be financed and whether it has long-term environmental impacts. Some methods are more appropriate than others in particular circumstances. Although there is still considerable disagreement about the most appropriate discount rate method, there is reasonable consensus about the discount rate that is most appropriate for each discount rate method. In short, there is greater disagreement among methods than among discount rates that are appropriate for a particular method.

The next section of this chapter shows that the choice of discount rate does matter: Different social discount rates lead to different policy recommendations. We then discuss the theory behind the social discount rate assuming perfect markets. In these circumstances the choice of social discount rate would be obvious. In the absence of perfect markets, there are a number of potential discounting methods that depend on the assumptions one makes. These methods vary according to the length of the project, whether intergenerational issues are a concern, whether there are large future environmental or health effects, and whether the costs and benefits affect consumption or investment. We discuss each method and present our best judgment about the most appropriate set of discount weights to use in each particular situation. Near the end of this chapter we discuss the social discount rate in actual practice.

One issue that invariably arises in the discussion of social discount rates is the treatment of risk and uncertainty. One approach is to add a risk premium to the discount rate. We do not favor this approach. In our view, the best way to handle risk is to use certainty equivalents, as discussed in Chapter 7. Throughout this chapter we assume that benefits and costs are measured in terms of certainty equivalents. Thus, the key issue is to determine how to discount certainty equivalents. However, when benefits and costs are not measured in certainty equivalents, which is often the case, we do believe that there is a case for adjusting the discount rates of projects depending on the correlation of the net benefits with national social income. Appendix 10A discusses this method of adjusting the social discount rate for systematic risk in more detail.

DOES THE CHOICE OF DISCOUNT RATE MATTER?

The choice of SDR is one of the most important topics in CBA. As Robert Lind points out, the SDR "has critical implications for the federal budget, for regional development, for technological choices, for the environment, and for the size of government."[3]

To see how the value of the SDR can change the ranking of projects, consider a government agency that has only $100,000 to spend on one of three potential projects. The annual net benefits of these projects are shown in Table 10.1. Choosing the lower discount rate (2 percent) would favor project C, whereas the higher discount rate (10 percent) would favor project B. Thus, the choice of project depends crucially on the choice of discount rate.

Generally, a low discount rate favors projects with the highest total benefits, irrespective of when they occur, because all of the social discount factor weights are close to one. Increasing the discount rate applies smaller weights to benefits (or costs) that occur further in the future and, therefore, weakens the case for projects with benefits that are back-end loaded (such as project C) and strengthens the case for projects with benefits that are front-end loaded (such as project B).

TABLE 10.1 Annual Net Benefits and Net Present Values for Three Alternative Projects

Year	Project A	Project B	Project C
0	−80,000	−80,000	−80,000
1	25,000	80,000	0
2	25,000	10,000	0
3	25,000	10,000	0
4	25,000	10,000	0
5	25,000	10,000	140,000
NPV ($i = 2\%$)	37,838	35,762	46,802
NPV ($i = 10\%$)	14,770	21,544	6,929

THE THEORY BEHIND THE APPROPRIATE SOCIAL DISCOUNT RATE METHOD IN PERFECT MARKETS

To understand the theoretical foundation of discounting, we must recognize that it is rooted in the preferences of individuals. As individuals, we tend to prefer to consume immediate benefits to ones occurring in the future. We also face an opportunity cost of forgone interest when we spend dollars today rather than invest them for future use. These two considerations of importance to individual decisions, the *marginal rate of time preference* and the *marginal rate of return on private investment,* provide a basis for deciding how costs and benefits realized by society in the future should be discounted so that they are comparable to costs and benefits realized by society today.

This section first introduces the concept of individual marginal rate of time preference. We then show that in a simple two-period model with perfect markets, individuals' marginal rates of time preference will equal the market interest rate. In this case the choice of the social discount rate is obvious. We then generalize the model to a small, isolated country and introduce production. The main results still hold in perfect markets: The *marginal social rate of time preference,* the marginal rate of return on investment, and the market interest rate would all be equal. Again, the choice of social discount rate would be obvious. Finally, we indicate that, due to taxes, risk, and transaction costs, the three rates of interest are unlikely to be equal in a real economy. In this circumstance, the choice of social discount rate is not clear.

An Individual's Marginal Rate of Time Preference

Most of us would be unwilling to lend someone $100 today in return for a promise of payment of $100 in a year's time, even if there were no inflation. We generally value $100 today more than the promise of $100 next year in real terms even if we are certain that the promise will be carried out. Perhaps $90 is the most that we would be willing to lend today in return for a promise of payment of $100 in a year's time. Economists refer to our preference to consume sooner rather than later as *time preference.* The rate at which an individual makes marginal trade-offs is called an individual's *marginal rate of time preference* (MRTP).

The concept of time preference can be easily understood in the context of borrowing and lending. Imagine that you are a graduate student who will receive a stipend of $5,000 this year and $9,000 next year. Your rich uncle offers to give you some money and asks if you would rather have $1,000 this year or $1,200 next year. Suppose that you are indifferent between the gifts; that is, you are just willing to sacrifice $200 additional consumption next year in order to consume the extra $1,000 this year rather than next year.[4] In this case, you would have an MRTP of 20 percent. Put another way, the MRTP tells us that you require 20 percent more next year in order to decrease your current consumption by a small amount.

Absent a rich uncle, you might be able to consume more today through borrowing. Although most banks may not be interested in lending you money because they fear you may not pay them back, let us assume that your local credit union will lend to you at an annual interest rate of 10 percent. That is, you can borrow $1,000 if you promise to pay back this amount plus $100 in interest next year. If you were willing to forgo $1,200 next year to get an additional $1,000 immediately from your uncle, then you would probably take advantage of the loan that requires you to give up only $1,100 in consumption next year in order to consume $1,000 more this year. Once you take the loan, you have $6,000 to spend this year and $7,900 to spend next year. Now that you have reduced the gap between what you have to spend this year relative to next year, you probably have an MRTP of less than 20 percent. After taking out the loan you may now, if given the choice, prefer a gift of $1,200 next year over a gift of $1,000 this year. If so, this indicates your MRTP is less than 20 percent. This example illustrates that your MRTP changes as you shift consumption from one year to another year.

Equality of Discount Rates in Perfect Markets

As long as you can borrow as much as you like, you can shift consumption from the future to the present until your MRTP falls to the rate of interest you must pay. If banks offer a rate of interest in excess of your MRTP, then you will happily save now and defer some consumption to the future. For example, if you are indifferent between an additional $1,000 today and an additional $1,050 next year but can deposit $1,000 for one year to obtain an additional $1,060 next year, then you would want to make the deposit. Only when the rate of interest you earn just equals your MRTP will you be indifferent between spending and depositing an additional dollar.

It is easy to show that in a perfectly competitive capital market an individual's MRTP equals the market interest rate. Suppose that an individual's utility is a function of consumption over two years: C_1 denotes consumption in this year (year 1) and C_2 denotes consumption in the next year (year 2). The consumer maximizes his or her utility, denoted by $U(.)$, subject to a budget constraint in which T denotes the present value of (total) income over the two years and i denotes the market interest rate:

$$\text{Max } U(C_1, C_2) \tag{10.3}$$

$$\text{s.t. } C_1 + \frac{C_2}{1 + i} = T \tag{10.4}$$

This problem is diagrammed in Figure 10.1. The curves labeled U^1 and U^2 are *indifference curves*. These curves represent an individual's preferences over combinations of current and future consumption. Each curve represents combinations of current and future consumption that provide the consumer with the same level of utility. Thus, the individual is indifferent between any two points on an indifference curve.[5] Points on the curve U^2 are preferred to points on the curve U^1; that is, the preference directions are north and east.

The slope of each indifference curve is negative, reflecting the fact that consumers require more in the next period in order to give up consumption in this period. Suppose, for example, that you are indifferent between an additional $1,000 today and an additional $1,050 next year. Then the slope of your indifference curve equals $-1,050/1,000 = -1.05$. The (absolute value of the) slope of the indifference curve measures the rate at which individuals are indifferent between substituting current consumption for future consumption and is called the consumer's *marginal rate of substitution* (MRS) between consumption this year and consumption next year.[6]

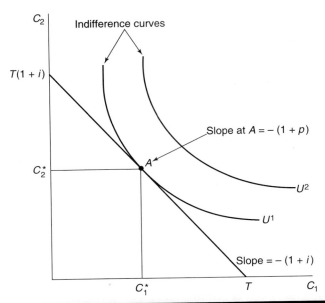

FIGURE 10.1 Equality of MRTP and the Market Interest Rate

Note that, in this example, the individual wants 5 percent more next year in order to defer consumption—her marginal rate of time preference equals .05. In general, if you require $1 + p$ more units in the future in order to give up one unit of current consumption, then the slope of the indifference curve is $-(1 + p)$, your marginal rate of substitution is $1 + p$, and your marginal rate of time preference is p. In the relevant range, $p > 0$, and the slope of the indifference curve is greater than 1 in absolute value.

As consumption in the current period increases, the indifference curve becomes flatter, indicating that the consumer requires relatively smaller additional amounts of future consumption in order to forgo a given amount of current consumption. Put another way, as current consumption increases, the consumer's marginal rate of substitution and the consumer's marginal rate of time preference decrease.

This utility maximization problem supposes that the individual receives all of his or her income in the first period and can invest all or part of it at interest rate i.[7] Thus, the individual could spend all of his or her income in year 1, which means $C_1 = T$ and $C_2 = 0$; the consumer could spend all of it in year 2 in which case $C_1 = 0$ and $C_2 = (1 + i)T$; or the consumer could consume at any other point on the budget constraint represented by the straight line with slope $-(1 + i)$. Each additional unit of consumption in period 1 costs $(1 + i)$ units of consumption in period 2, and each additional unit of consumption in period 2 costs $1/(1 + i)$ units of consumption in period 1.

To determine the optimal consumption levels, we find the point at which the budget constraint is tangential to an indifference curve. This occurs at point A in Figure 10.1 where the optimal consumption levels are denoted C_1^* and C_2^*. At this point the slope of the indifference curve, $-(1 + p)$, equals the slope of the budget constraint.

Now, rewriting the budget constraint, equation (10.4), thus:

$$C_2 = T(1 + i) - (1 + i)C_1 \qquad \textbf{(10.5)}$$

shows that the slope of the budget constraint equals $-(1 + i)$.[8] Thus at point A, the optimum, $p = i$, that is, the market interest rate equals the consumer's MRTP.[9]

This result holds generally for people without extreme preferences over consumption in the two periods.[10] Thus, every individual has an MRTP equal to the market interest rate. Because all consumers face the same market interest rate in an economy with a perfect capital market, all consumers have the same MRTP. Thus, everyone is willing to trade current and future consumption at the same rate. Consequently, it is natural to interpret this rate, which equals the market interest rate, as the social discount rate. Later we discuss the appropriateness of interpreting market interest rates as social discount rates when markets are not perfect.

Rate of Return on Private Investment Equals the Market Interest Rate Equals MRTP

We now present a more general two-period model that pertains to a group of individuals in a hypothetical country. We assume that this country does not trade with other counties. Moreover, as previously, we initially ignore taxes, risks faced by private-sector investors and lenders, and transaction costs associated with making loans. Consequently, anyone who wants a loan can borrow the desired amount at the market interest rate. In addition, except when explicitly indicated otherwise, we ignore market failures such as externalities and information asymmetry, which could cause private and social discount rates to diverge from one another.

The economy of this hypothetical country is depicted in Figure 10.2. As before, the horizontal axis indicates consumption during the current period and the vertical

FIGURE 10.2 The Optimal Levels of Consumption and Investment in a Two-Period Model

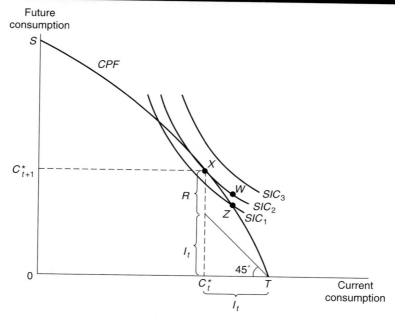

axis indicates consumption during the future period. The curve labeled *CPF* is a consumption possibility frontier that represents all the combinations of current and future consumption that are feasible if the economy utilizes its resources efficiently. A major difference between this model and the previous model is that this model incorporates production.

Suppose that at the beginning of the first period, the country has T units worth of resources, which can be allocated between current consumption and investment. As before, there are two extremes. The society could consume all T units in the current period, invest none and, therefore, have no future consumption, as represented by point T on the horizontal axis of Figure 10.2. At the other extreme society could consume no units in the current period, invest all T units, and consume S units in the future period. Note that $S > T$, implying a positive rate of return on all resources invested in the current period.

Point X represents a more realistic intermediate position where current consumption equals C_t^* and future consumption equals C_{t+1}^*. At this point society would relinquish $I_t = T - C_t^*$ units of potential current consumption for investment. But, in the future, it would consume $C_{t+1}^* = I_t + R$ units, where I_t represents the amount invested in the first period and R represents the return on this investment. This partitioning of future consumption into these two components is represented graphically on Figure 10.2 by drawing a 45° line from point T to the line between X and C_t^*. The lower segment corresponds to I_t and the higher segment corresponds to R.

Bearing in mind that this model pertains to a country, the investment, I_t, can be thought of as a number of smaller investments that sum to I_t. The average rate of return on these investments, r, equals R/I_t. This differs from the marginal return on (a small) investment at X, r_x. To see this, note that when viewed from below, the *CPF* is concave (i.e., it bows outward). This implies that as the economy moves along the *CPF* curve from T toward S, and more resources are invested in the current period, equal increments in investments engender successively smaller returns. In other words, the marginal return on investment falls as investment increases. Consequently, the marginal rate of return on investment at X, r_x is smaller than the average rate of return on investment between T and X, r.[11] This occurs because the best investments are made first.

The set of three curves labeled *SIC* in Figure 10.2 are social indifference curves. These curves represent society's preferences over combinations of current and future consumption. Like individual indifference curves, these social indifference curves slope downward. The slope of SIC_2 at X is $-(1 + p_x)$, where p_x is society's marginal rate of time preference or the *marginal social rate of time preference* at X.

Society would, of course, desire to reach the highest possible indifference curve. As can be seen in Figure 10.2, this curve is SIC_2 given an initial endowment of T units and the *CPF*. Although SIC_3 is preferable to SIC_2, the country's resources are insufficient to reach SIC_3. Indeed, the economy can only reach SIC_2 at a single point, X. At X, SIC_2 and the *CPF* curve are tangential and their slopes are equal. Consequently, at point X:

$$1 + p_x = 1 + r_x \text{ or } p_x = r_x$$

Accordingly, were the economy to operate at point X, the marginal social rate of time preference would equal the marginal rate of return on investment.

Furthermore, at point X, these rates would equal the economy-wide market rate of interest, denoted by i. As all of these rates would be equal, the choice of SDR would be obvious. To show why this rate would be appropriate, we need to establish first that at X all individuals in society have the same marginal rate of time preference, which equals i, and, second, that this rate would be the unanimous choice for the SDR.

Suppose that some individuals initially had a marginal rate of time preference in excess of i; in effect, they wanted to consume more now. These people could borrow at i, an interest rate below the rate they would actually be willing to pay, and thereby increase their current consumption at the expense of their future consumption. This increase in current consumption would increase the relative value of their future consumption, causing their personal marginal rates of time preference to decline until they eventually equaled i. Analogously, individuals with personal marginal rates of time preference initially below i would willingly postpone some current consumption in exchange for increased future consumption. By doing so their marginal rates of time preference would rise until they equalled i. Thus, at X every individual has the same marginal rate of time preference, one that is equal to the economy-wide market rate of interest.

Suppose now that a government project would reduce consumption by $1 today in order to produce a return of $\$(1 + y)$ next period. As every person's marginal rate of time preference equals i, individuals would value resources obtained next period at $1/(1 + i)$ times their value this period. Thus, everyone would calculate the present value of the future return of the project as $\$(1 + y)/(1 + i)$. As all individuals would discount at rate i, this is the only logical choice for the SDR. This result generalizes to many periods.

Real Economies: The Absence of Perfect Markets

Point X is the socially optimal point under the foregoing assumptions. However, unlike the hypothetical economy depicted in Figure 10.2, real economies are unable to operate at a point such as X. An actual economy with taxes, risk, and transaction costs would be more likely to function at point Z. Here, society would underinvest (actual investment $< I_t$), it would only be able to reach SIC_1, not SIC_2, and the marginal return on investment would exceed the marginal rate of time preference ($p_z < r_z$).[12]

To illustrate why there is a wedge between p_z and r_z, suppose individuals lend $100 to a corporation. Further suppose they have a marginal rate of time preference of 2 percent. Hence, in order to lend $100 to the corporation, they require at least $102 in the future. Assume that the corporation invests the $100 for one period and earns a return of 10 percent, or $10. If the corporate tax rate is 40 percent, then only $106 is available to repay the lenders. If, in addition, the individuals' marginal income tax rate is 50 percent and if they require $1 to cover the transactions cost and risk associated with making the loan, they will net only $2 on this loan. Hence, the corporation must earn a rate of return of 10 percent for the individuals to receive a return equal to their marginal rate of time preference of 2 percent.

Because different individuals and different corporations face different tax rates in practice, and the risk and transactions costs associated with loans vary across investment projects and across individuals, numerous values exist for both the marginal rate of time preference and the marginal rate of return on investment. Thus, there is no obvious choice for the SDR in practice.

ALTERNATIVE SOCIAL DISCOUNT RATE METHODS IN THE ABSENCE OF PERFECT MARKETS

This section discusses five potential discounting methods. Three methods assume that the social discount weights decline at a constant rate but differ in the rate of decline. One of these methods uses a social discount rate equal to the marginal rate of return on private-sector investments, r_z; a second uses a social discount rate equal to the marginal social rate of time preference, p_z; a third uses a social discount rate equal to a weighted average of p_z, r_z, and i, where i is the government's real long-term borrowing rate.[13] The weights should reflect the amount of the project's resources that are financed by consumption, investment, and foreign borrowing, respectively. A fourth method, which is called the shadow price of capital method, entails distinguishing between project impacts that affect investment and those that affect consumption. Changes in investment are weighted by a parameter, which is greater than one, called the shadow price of capital, denoted by θ. The resulting changes in "consumption equivalents" and the changes in consumption are then discounted at p_z. A fifth method uses a discount rate that declines over the time horizon of the project. A sixth method, which is discussed in Appendix 10B, discounts benefits and costs using s_G, a rate based on the growth in real per capita consumption.[14]

The key assumption behind the first four methods is that public-sector projects use resources that would otherwise be available to the private sector for consumption or investment. Thus, the resources have an opportunity cost. The key purpose of social discounting is to help determine whether it would be better to use the resources on the government project being evaluated or allow them to remain in the private sector. If the benefits of the project would exceed the opportunity cost of the resources, then it should be undertaken; otherwise, it should not. The key assumptions behind the other methods are discussed later.

Each method usually obtains a different value for the *NPV* of the same project. Hence, conclusions about whether a specific project should be undertaken often depend on the particular social discounting method selected. Thus, choice of method is important.

Using the Marginal Rate of Return on Private Investment

The argument for using the marginal rate of return on private investment as the social discount rate is that before the government takes resources out of the private sector, it should be able to demonstrate that society will receive a greater rate of return in the public sector than it would have received had the resources remained in the private sector. Therefore, the rate of return on the government project should exceed r_z, the marginal rate of return on private-sector investment.

The most compelling case for the use of r_z was made in an influential article by Arnold Harberger.[15] Harberger analyzed a closed domestic market for investment and savings, such as the one presented in Figure 10.3. In the absence of taxes and government borrowing, the demand curve for investment funds by private-sector borrowers is represented by D_0 and the supply curve of funds from lenders (or savers) is represented by S_0.

Now consider a corporate income tax and a personal income tax. The tax on corporate profits shifts the demand curve down to D_I because part of the returns from investments must now be paid to the government, whereas the tax on interest income shifts the supply curve up to S_S because part of the interest on savings must now be paid to the government. Thus, as Figure 10.3 implies, both taxes reduce investment.

Given these taxes, the market clearing interest rate would be i. That is, investors would pay an interest rate of i to borrow funds and savers would receive an interest rate of i prior to paying taxes. However, the marginal rate of return on investment before taxes (i.e., the opportunity cost of forgone private-sector investment) would be r_z, with the gap between r_z and i representing taxes paid by investors on profits. The marginal return on savings after taxes (i.e., the opportunity cost of forgone consumption or, equivalently, the marginal rate of time preference) would be p_z, with the gap between p_z and i representing taxes paid by savers on interest income. Thus, as previously discussed, taxes would cause r_z to exceed p_z.

Now consider the effects of a government project. Harberger assumes that the project would be financed entirely by borrowing in the closed domestic financial

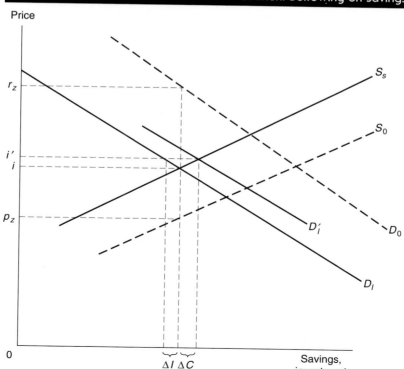

FIGURE 10.3 The Effects of Taxes and Government Borrowing on Savings and Investment

market. Suppose the demand for funds for the new project shifts the market demand curve to D_I'. The market rate of interest rises from i to i'. Private-sector investment falls by ΔI and private-sector savings increase by ΔC. As the increase in private-sector savings exactly equals the decrease in private-sector consumption, the project would "crowd out" both investment (by ΔI) and consumption (by ΔC).

Harberger suggests that the social discount rate should be obtained by weighting r_z and p_z by the respective size of the relative contributions that investment and consumption would make toward funding the project. That is, he suggests that the social discount rate, s, should be computed as follows:

$$s = ar_z + (1 - a)p_z \qquad (10.6)$$

where $a = \Delta I/(\Delta I + \Delta C)$ and $(1 - a) = \Delta C/(\Delta I + \Delta C)$.

Finally, Harberger asserts that savings are not very responsive to changes in interest rates. This assertion, which is strongly supported empirically, implies that the S_S curve is close to vertical and, as a consequence, ΔC is close to zero.[16] This, in turn, suggests that the value of the parameter a is close to one and the value of $(1 - a)$ is close to zero. In other words, almost all of the resources for public-sector investment are obtained by crowding out private-sector investment. Thus, Harberger suggests that the marginal rate of return on investment, r_z, is a good approximation of the true social discount rate.

Numerical Values of r_z   The value of r_z is, perhaps, best thought of as the rate of return on low-risk, private-sector investments before taxes but after correcting for inflation. To compute it, one might start with a market return such as the nominal rate of return on long-term corporate bonds. One possibility is to use the average monthly yield on Moody's AAA bonds from January 1947 to April 1999, which was 6.86 percent. However, this rate must be adjusted to account for corporate taxes and expected inflation. John Shoven and Michael Topper estimate the corporate tax rate in the United States was 0.38 in 1988.[17] This implies a nominal pretax return on bonds of about $[.0686/(1 - .38)] = 11.06$ percent. The average annual percentage change in the CPI (all items) between 1947 and 1999 was 3.92 percent. Using this percentage change in the CPI as the expected rate of inflation gives an estimate of the real expected pretax rate of return on investment of $[(.1106 - .0392)/(1 + .0392)] = 6.87$ percent. Accounting for the fact that historical estimates of the CPI typically overestimated inflation by about one percentage point per annum gives a real pretax rate of return of 7.9 percent. Rounding to the nearest whole number gives a real SDR of 8 percent.[18]

To illustrate discounting with r_z, we return to the library information example that was introduced in Chapter 6 and use a discount rate of 8 percent:

$$NPV = -325,000 + 80,000/(1 + .08)^1 + 80,000/(1 + .08)^2 + 80,000/(1 + .08)^3$$
$$+ 80,000/(1 + .08)^4 + 80,000/(1 + .08)^5 + 20,000/(1 + .08)^5 = \$8,028$$

Using this method, the NPV is positive and we would recommend the project.

Criticisms of the Calculation and Use of r_z   Several factors suggest that use of an SDR of 8 percent is too high. Some of these criticisms pertain to the estimation of r_z whereas others pertain to the strong assumptions made by Harberger. The first reason the 8 percent may be too high is that the return on private-sector investment incorporates a risk premium. If benefits and costs are measured in certainty equivalents, as we suggest, incorporating a risk premium would be double counting.[19] Second, the government project might be financed by taxes, rather than by loans, in which case consumption is more likely to be crowded out than investment. The reason is that most taxes are collected from individuals through income, payroll, and consumption taxes, which mainly affect consumption, especially if savings rates are fairly low. Third, the project may be partially financed by government loans obtained from foreigners at a lower rate. Fourth, private-sector rates of return may be pushed upward by distortions caused by negative externalities and monopolistic pricing. Fifth, there may not be a fixed pool of investment such that government investment replaces private investment dollar for dollar. Indeed, one can imagine cases in which a government project (e.g., a road, bridge, airport, or railway) actually creates private investment opportunities, raising the private return to capital. Moreover, if the economy is not fully employing all its resources, then complete crowding out is also unlikely. For all these reasons, using estimates of r_z, such as the 8 percent rate suggested here, should probably be viewed as the upper limit of the SDR.

Using the Marginal Social Rate of Time Preference Method (SRTP)

Many analysts hold that the SDR should be thought of as the rate at which individuals in society are willing to postpone a small amount of current consumption in exchange for additional future consumption (and vice versa). In principle, p_z represents this rate. Consequently, many believe that the SDR should equal p_z.

Note also that if a government project is financed entirely by domestic taxes and if taxes reduce consumption but not investment, it is appropriate to set $a = 0$ in equation (10.6), yielding an SDR equal to p_z.

Numerical Values of p_z   In practice, the best return that many people can earn in exchange for postponing consumption is the real after-tax return on savings. Therefore, one option is to use this rate as an estimate of p_z.

To compute this rate one might start with the interest rate on government bonds. The average monthly yield on 10-year U.S. treasury bonds for the period April 1953 to April 1999 was 6.77 percent. This nominal pretax rate of return must be converted to a real after-tax rate by adjusting for taxes and inflation. John Shoven and Michael Topper suggest the personal tax rate on savings is 30 percent, which implies the after-tax yield is $.0677(1 - 0.30) = 4.74$ percent.[20] Using the average annual percentage change in the CPI (all items) for this period as the expected rate of inflation, which equaled 3.98 percent, and substituting into equation (6.13), we obtain a real after-tax yield of $(.0474 - .0398)/(1 + .0398) = 0.73$ percent. Correcting for the upward bias in the historical CPI suggests $p_z = (0.0474 - 0.0298)/(1 + 0.0298) = 1.71$ percent, which we round to 2 percent. Calculations of this sort generally produce estimates of the marginal social rate of time preference that range from just below 0 to 4 percent.[21] Thus, this method suggests using an SDR equal to 2 percent with sensitivity analysis at 0 and 4 percent.

To illustrate discounting with the social marginal rate of time preference, we discount the costs and benefits of the library information system example at 2 percent:

$$NPV = -325{,}000 + 80{,}000/(1 + .02)^1 + 80{,}000/(1 + .02)^2 + 80{,}000/(1 + .02)^3$$
$$+ 80{,}000/(1 + .02)^4 + 80{,}000/(1 + .02)^5 + 20{,}000/(1 + .02)^5 = \$70{,}191$$

Therefore, using the marginal social rate of time preference implies the project should proceed. Because p_z is one of the smallest possible values for the SDR, its use tends to be favored by those who support government projects.

Criticisms of the Calculation and Use of p_z   There are several criticisms pertaining to the computation and use of p_z. First, individuals differ in preferences and opportunities: while some are saving, others are borrowing.[22] At the margin some save, in effect, by reducing their debt. Because consumer borrowing rates exceed savings rates and because reducing some debt is not taxed, consumers who save by reducing their debt earn a much higher real, after-tax return than 2 percent. However, it is not obvious how to aggregate different individual marginal rates of time preference into a single, marginal social rate of time preference. Second, many individuals simultaneously pay down mortgages, buy government and corporate bonds and stocks for retirement, and sometimes even borrow on their credit cards at very high interest rates.[23] Given this behavior, it is unclear whether each individual has a single marginal rate of time preference—a point we return to later in this section. Third, market rates of interest reflect rates of time preference of individuals currently alive. Some economists argue that current individuals fail to account appropriately for the effects of long-term infrastructure projects on the welfare of future generations—another point that we return to later.

Using the Weighted Social Opportunity Cost of Capital (*WSOC*)

Many economists have proposed that the social discount rate be calculated in terms of the social opportunity cost of the required resources with weights based on the relative contributions of the different sources of the resources.[24] They suggest that some of the resources for government projects come from crowding out domestic investment and that some of the resources come from crowding out current domestic consumption. Robert Lind and others argue that foreign borrowing is another potential source of the resources.[25] Thus, a government project need not crowd out domestic private consumption or investment on a dollar for dollar basis.[26] If a is the proportion of the project's resources that displace private domestic investment, b is the proportion of the resources that are financed by borrowing from foreigners, and $1 - a - b$ is the proportion of the resources displacing domestic consumption, then this method computes the social discount rate as the weighted average of these rates, called the weighted social opportunity cost of capital (*WSOC*):

$$WSOC = ar_z + bi + (1 - a - b)p_z \qquad (10.7)$$

where i is the government's real long-term borrowing rate. As $p_z < i < r_z$, it follows that $p_z < WSOC < r_z$. Obviously, the previous methods are special cases of this more general approach.

Numerical Values of *WSOC*   For projects partially funded by government borrowing, this method requires an estimate of the government's long-term borrowing rate. As mentioned earlier, 10-year U.S. treasury bonds have yielded 6.77 percent on average during the past 46 years. Adjusting for inflation during this period using the average annual increase in the CPI minus one percentage point, which equals 2.98 percent, gives a real bond yield of 3.7 percent per annum.[27] Rounding to the nearest whole number gives an estimate of i equal to 4 percent.

Estimates of a and b are harder to obtain. For Canada, Glenn Jenkins suggests $a = 0.75$, $b = .20$ and $1 - a - b = .05$, which implies $WSOC = .75 \times .08 + .20 \times .04 + .05 \times .02 = .069$, or rounding, 7 percent.[28] David Burgess argues that a is more likely to be between .26 and .32, b is more likely to be between .55 and .64, and $1 - a - b$ is more likely to be between .10 and .13.[29] Picking the low end of this range for a and the high end for b implies $WSOC = .26 \times .08 + .64 \times .04 + .10 \times .02 = .0484$ or, rounding, 5 percent. The average of these two rates is 6 percent. Discounting the library information system example using the $WSOC$ method and a discount rate equal to 6 percent gives the NPV equal to $26,934, which is between the two previous estimates.

Suppose, in fact, the project is financed by taxes rather than by issuing debt to domestic or foreign lenders; then $b = 0$. The parameter a should reflect the portion of taxes that reduces investment whereas $1 - a - b$ should reflect the portion of taxes that reduces consumption. A crude approximation for a is provided by the ratio of gross fixed investment to real GDP. For 1998, this ratio equaled 16.8 percent, which leads to an estimate of $WSOC = 3.0$ percent.[30]

Criticisms of the Calculation and Use of the *WSOC* Most of the criticisms pertaining to the calculation of r_z and p_z also apply to this method. There is, however, one other consideration. The previous methods each resulted in a single social discount rate. In contrast, the $WSOC$ method suggests that each project should be evaluated by its own discount rate, which depends on the sources of its resources. In practice, governments prefer a single social discount rate because of the difficulty of monitoring assumptions about the sources of resources required for specific projects and of explaining why different discount rates are used on different projects.

Using the Shadow Price of Capital (SPC)

If all the resources used in a project displace current consumption, and all the benefits produce additions to future consumption, then the social discount rate should reflect social choices in trading present consumption for future consumption, and p_z would be the natural choice for the discount rate. However, projects could produce costs and benefits in the form of consumption *or* investment. Due to market distortions, the rate at which individuals are willing to trade present for future consumption, p_z, differs from the rate of return on private investment, r_z, as previously discussed. Thus, flows of investment should be treated differently from flows of consumption. The shadow price of capital method converts investment gains or losses into consumption equivalents. These consumption equivalents, like consumption flows themselves, are then discounted at p_z.[31]

This method has strong theoretical appeal but is somewhat difficult to use in practice. Consequently, although there seems to be a growing consensus that, in principle, it is better than the previously discussed approaches, there are few instances of it actually being used in CBA.

The shadow price of capital method requires that discounting be done in four steps. First, the costs and benefits in each period are divided into those that directly affect consumption and those that directly affect investment. Second, flows into and out of investment are multiplied by the shadow price of capital, θ, to convert them into consumption equivalents. The term *shadow* emphasizes that the price of capital cannot be directly observed in a market but must be inferred. It is generally thought that the value of θ, which is explained later, lies between 1.5 and 2.5. Third, changes in consumption are added to changes in consumption equivalents. Fourth, the resultant flows are discounted at p_z, which measures how society values the cost of postponing consumption.

Consumption and investment are treated differently because consumption provides an immediate benefit whereas investment generates a stream of benefits that occur in future periods. To see this, suppose a dollar is invested in the private sector for an indefinite period. Suppose also that it earns a return of r_z each period and this return is consumed each period; the original dollar is reinvested. Thus, r_z is consumed each period in perpetuity. To obtain the present value of this consumption stream we discount the amounts received each period at p_z. Using equation (6A.3), the formula for the present value of a perpetuity, this reduces to:

$$\theta = r_z/p_z \tag{10.8}$$

The parameter, θ, is called the shadow price of capital. Because r_z is greater than p_z, its value is greater than one. Thus, displaced investment is more costly to society than displaced consumption.[32] The shadow price of capital represents the present value of the consumption resulting from investing one dollar in the private sector (under the preceding assumptions). By multiplying flows into and out of private-sector investment by θ, we convert them into their consumption equivalents.

To explore the shadow price approach a bit further, suppose that a project yields real annual benefits of B per year indefinitely. If all of these benefits are consumed as they arise, then the present value of this perpetual consumption flow discounted at p_z is B/p_z.

Now consider two extreme cases. If the project's capital cost, C, is paid in year 0 and all these funds are raised from consumption, then the *NPV* rule implies the project should be undertaken if $B/p_z > C$. Thus, in this extreme situation, the shadow price of capital method is equivalent to discounting benefits and costs at the marginal social rate of time preference.

Now suppose all the costs, which still occur in year 0, displace private investment. Under this assumption, the *NPV* rule implies the project should be undertaken if $B/p_z > \theta C = (r_z/p_z)C$, or, equivalently, if $B/r_z > C$. This condition is equivalent to discounting the benefits and costs at the rate of return on private investment, as suggested by Harberger.

The expression for the shadow price of capital in equation (10.8) is based on several simplifying assumptions. One is that the investment will not depreciate, but, of course, it will. Another is that the entire return from the investment will be consumed when it occurs. More likely, some of the return will be consumed when it is generated and some will be reinvested. Consideration of these possibilities leads to a more general expression for the shadow price of capital (SPC):

$$\theta = \frac{(r_z + \delta)(1 - f)}{p_z - r_z f + \delta(1 - f)} \tag{10.9}$$

where r_z is the *net* return on capital after depreciation, δ is the depreciation rate of the capital invested, f is the fraction of the gross return that is reinvested, and p_z is the marginal social rate of time preference.[33] Note that in the absence of reinvestment and depreciation (i.e., if $f = 0$ and $\delta = 0$) then this formula reduces to our initial expression for the shadow price of capital in equation (10.8).

Numerical Values of the SPC   To apply equation (10.9), we need values of f and δ. One way to estimate the fraction of the returns that are reinvested, f, is to use the real gross investment rate (i.e., the ratio of real gross investment to real GDP). The average quarterly real gross investment rate was 16.8 percent in 1998 and 13.3 percent for the longer period from Q1 in 1947 to Q1 in 1999. Thus, a reasonable estimate of the portion of the investment return that is reinvested, f, is 15 percent.

To obtain a value for δ, the depreciation rate, we are forced to go beyond readily available macroeconomic data to come up with even a rough estimate. Charles Hulten and Frank Wykoff have analyzed the relative prices of new and used equipment and structures to estimate *economic* depreciation rates.[34] Their analysis suggests that the annual depreciation rate for equipment used in manufacturing is 13.3 percent, and the annual depreciation rate for structures used in manufacturing is 3.4 percent. Weighting these rates by the relative proportions of equipment (67 percent) and structures (33 percent) in the capital stock gives an average depreciation rate of $[(0.67)(0.133) + (0.33)(0.034)] = 10$ percent.[35]

Using $r_z = 8$ percent, $\delta = 10$ percent, $f = 15$ percent, and $p_z = 2$ percent yields a value for the shadow price of capital of 1.65, which implies that an investment in the private sector of \$1 would produce a stream of consumption benefits with a present value equal to \$1.65. Thus, any government project that displaces private-sector investment by one dollar has an opportunity cost of \$1.65.

Table 10.2 shows the results of sensitivity analysis. It displays the shadow prices of capital for various values of the marginal social rate of time preference, p_z, for three different values of the net rate of return on private-sector investment, r_z, and for three

TABLE 10.2   Sensitivity Analysis on the Shadow Price of Capital

SRTP (p_z)	$\delta = .05$			$\delta = .10$			$\delta = .15$		
	$r_z = .06$	$r_z = .08$	$r_z = .10$	$r_z = .06$	$r_z = .08$	$r_z = .10$	$r_z = .06$	$r_z = .08$	$r_z = .10$
.00	2.79	3.62	4.64	1.79	2.10	2.43	1.51	1.69	1.89
.01	2.15	2.73	3.40	1.58	1.84	2.13	1.39	1.56	1.73
.02	1.74	2.19	2.68	1.42	1.65	1.89	1.29	1.44	1.60
.03	1.47	1.83	2.22	1.28	1.48	1.70	1.20	1.34	1.49
.04	1.27	1.57	1.89	1.17	1.35	1.55	1.13	1.26	1.39
.05	1.12	1.37	1.65	1.08	1.24	1.42	1.06	1.18	1.31
.06	1.00	1.22	1.46	1.00	1.15	1.31	1.00	1.11	1.23
.07		1.10	1.31		1.07	1.21		1.05	1.16
.08		1.00	1.19		1.00	1.13		1.00	1.10

Assuming the gross savings rate $(f) = 0.15$.

different values of the rate of depreciation, δ. Table 10.2 shows, for example, that the SPC ranges between 1.3 and 2.7 when $p_z = 2$ percent. This table assumes the gross savings rate is 15 percent. Higher values of the savings rate imply high values for θ and vice versa, as one can see from equation (10.9).

Applying the SPC in Practice   Once again using the library information system example, we illustrate how to use the shadow price of capital approach in practice. Because computing net present values with the shadow price method depends on the specifics of project funding, we compute the *NPV* under two alternative funding arrangements. We first assume that the $325,000 initial cost outlay is paid out of tax revenues collected at the beginning of the project. This gives an *NPV* of $49,461. We then assume instead that the $325,000 initial outlay would be funded by municipal bonds that would be paid for by local residents at 5 percent (real) interest through five equal annual installments of $75,067. The *NPV* in this case is $43,402. The key components of these analyses are summarized in Table 10.3.

Consider the case in which the $325,000 initial cost outlay is paid out of tax revenues. The first step in applying the shadow price of capital method is to determine the proportion of each benefit and cost that should be allocated to investment and the proportion that should be allocated to consumption. Suppose that 15 percent of the $325,000 in taxes required to pay for the initial cost outlay ($48,750) would displace private-sector investment, whereas the remaining $276,250 would displace consump-

TABLE 10.3   Computing the *NPV* of the Library Information System Using the Shadow Price of Capital

Year (1)	Changes in Private-Sector Investment (2)	Changes in Consumption (3)	Changes in Investment $\times \theta$ (4)	Sum (3) + (4) (5)
Assumption I: Initial outlay paid directly out of taxes				
0	−48,750	−276,250	−80,438	−356,688
1	3,000	77,000	4,950	81,950
2	3,000	77,000	4,950	81,950
3	3,000	77,000	4,950	81,950
4	3,000	77,000	4,950	81,950
5	6,000	94,000	9,990	103,900
NPV (with $p_z = .02$)				49,461
Assumption II: Funds raised through issuing bonds				
0	−325,000	0	−536,250	−536,250
1	52,995	27,006	87,442	114,448
2	55,494	24,506	91,565	116,071
3	58,119	21,881	95,896	117,777
4	60,875	19,125	100,444	119,569
5	66,767	33,233	110,166	143,399
NPV (with $p_z = .02$)				43,402

Assuming the shadow price of capital, θ, equals 1.65.

tion.[36] Similarly, suppose that the $20,000 annual costs would also result in increased taxes with 15 percent ($3,000) displacing private-sector investment and 85 percent ($17,000) displacing consumption. Turning now to project benefits, for purposes of illustration, we assume that $60,000 of the $100,000 in annual benefits can be viewed as pure consumption that would be enjoyed by library users, whereas the remaining $40,000 are cost savings to the library that would be used to reduce taxes. Again, 15 percent of the latter amount ($6,000) would *increase* private-sector investment and 85 percent ($34,000) would increase consumption. Similarly, in year 5, 15 percent of the liquidation benefits ($3,000) would be allocated to investment whereas 85 percent ($17,000) would be allocated to consumption. The annual net changes in investment and in consumption are summarized in columns 2 and 3 of Table 10.3.[37]

The second step multiplies the changes in investment by the shadow price of capital to compute their consumption equivalents. Using our estimate of $\theta = 1.65$, the results are given in column 4. The third step sums the changes in consumption (column 3) and the changes in consumption equivalents (column 4) to obtain the total changes in consumption, which are given in column 5. Finally, these amounts are discounted at $p_z = 0.02$ to obtain the $NPV = \$49,461$. As this NPV is positive, discounting using the shadow price of capital method suggests that the project should proceed *if* the initial cost outlay is funded through taxes paid at the time the project is initiated.

Calculating the annual changes in investment and consumption is more complicated when the project is financed through issuing bonds. The resulting amounts are presented in columns 2 and 3 in the second half of Table 10.3. Detailed description of computation of these amounts appears in Appendix 10C. Under the assumption that the project is financed by issuing bonds, the $NPV = \$43,402$, which is smaller than the previous estimate, although still positive.

Generally, using the shadow price of capital approach, the NPV is smaller if the project is financed by issuing a bond that is later repaid out of taxes than if the project is financed directly out of taxes. The main reason is that when the project is financed by borrowing, the entire amount borrowed is lost to investment until it is repaid, and displaced investment is more costly than is displaced consumption. The longer the repayment period, the smaller the NPV of a project financed through bonds will be relative to financing the project directly out of taxes.

Criticisms of Calculation and Use of the SPC   The shadow price of capital method accounts for increases and displacement of private investment and consumption in a theoretically appropriate fashion, which is an important advantage over other methods. Nonetheless, one can raise several objections. First, as opposed to just picking a discount rate and using it in the NPV formula, it is difficult to explain to policymakers how the NPV calculations are made, let alone why. Second, the information requirements are more formidable than for the other discounting approaches. For example, values for the reinvestment and depreciation rates must be obtained. Third, judgment plays an important role, especially in deciding how to allocate benefits and costs between investment and consumption. Hence, the procedure might be manipulated to meet political objectives. Of course, this objection is not unique to the shadow price approach. Whatever method of discounting is used, assumptions must be made and costs and benefits must be specified and estimated. These assumptions and estimates also involve judgment and can potentially be manipulated for political or other purposes.[38] Finally, as the *NPV* depends on θ, which in turn depends on r_z and p_z, the results are subject to the same criticisms that pertain to the calculation of these parameters.

Using Time-Declining Discount Rates

So far we have considered only constant (time-invariant) SDRs; thus, for example, the same discount rate is used to discount costs and benefits between years 50 and 51 as between years 0 and 1. There are at least three reasons to consider using a time-declining SDR—that is, to use lower rates to discount costs and benefits that occur further in the future than those that occur sooner.

The first reason is based on empirical evidence that individuals use lower discount rates for events that occur farther into the future.[39] Exhibit 10.1 presents evidence that individual MRTPs for saving lives now versus saving lives in the future decline as the time horizon extends further into the future. After reviewing the recent literature on counterexamples to constant discounting, George Loewenstein and Drazen Prelec conclude that "unlike the EU [expected utility] violations, which in many cases can only be demonstrated with a clever arrangement of multiple choice problems (e.g., the Allais paradox), the counterexamples to DU [constant discounting] are simple, robust, and bear directly on central aspects of economic behavior."[40]

EXHIBIT 10.1

Maureen Cropper and colleagues have conducted surveys to measure how participants are willing to trade off lives saved today with lives saved in the future. In round numbers, this research suggests that people are indifferent between one life saved today and two lives saved in five years' time, three lives saved in ten years' time, six lives saved in 25 years' time, 11 lives saved in 50 years' time, and 44 lives saved in 100 years' time. More precisely, and expressing the results in terms of MRTPs, the research found an implicit marginal rate of time preference of 16.8 percent over a five-year horizon, 11.2 percent over a ten-year horizon, 7.4 percent over a 25-year horizon, 4.8 percent over a 50-year horizon, and 3.8 percent over a 100-year horizon. These results suggest that individual MRTPs are significantly greater than zero, but they decline as the time horizon extends further into the future.

Source: Maureen L. Cropper, Sema K. Aydede, and Paul R. Portney, "Rates of Time Preference for Saving Lives," *American Economic Review: Papers and Proceedings,* 82, no. 2 (1992), 469–472.

David Laibson cites evidence from the psychology literature that individuals' discount functions are approximately hyperbolic; that is, they are characterized by relatively high discount rates over short time horizons and relatively low rates over long horizons.[41] He explains that individuals recognize that, if they cannot commit to saving, then on a day-to-day basis (using a high short-term discount rate) they will never save as much for the future as they know they should (using a low long-term discount rate). Recognizing their lack of self-control, individuals may commit themselves to savings plans with large penalties for early withdrawals, while using their available credit to otherwise maximize their current consumption. They may simultaneously save by purchasing an illiquid asset with a relatively low after-tax real return (such as a government savings bond), make predetermined monthly mortgage payments, and borrow on a credit card at a very high real interest rate. These observed patterns of saving and borrowing simply reflect individuals' recognition of their lack of self control and the time-declining discount rates that result from this. Borrowing on a credit card at a high interest rate reflects a high rate of discount for the near future, whereas purchasing a government savings bond or making monthly mortgage payments could result if individuals applied low discount rates to the more distant future and, hence, had strong commitments to save for their retirements.

The second reason for using a time-declining SDR pertains to evaluating decisions with impacts that occur far in the future, such as environmental effects, including climate change, the storage of nuclear waste, or reforestation. Consider, for example, the following two streams of benefits ($ millions), which are discounted at 10 percent:

Stream	2001	2002	2003	...	2036	2037	2038	...	∞	PV
A	100	100	100		100	100	100		100	1,000
B	151	100	100		100	0	0		0	1,014

Intuitively, one might think that stream A has higher benefits than stream B: It yields $100 million per year indefinitely, thereby being identical to stream B from 2002 to 2036 and is superior from year 2037 onward. It has lower benefits than stream B only in the first year. Nonetheless, at a discount rate of 10 percent, stream A has a lower *PV* than stream B (the *PV*s are in year 2000 dollars).

Using a constant market interest rate is particularly problematic when the rate exceeds the growth rate of the economy, as has recently been the case in many industrialized countries.[42] The use of a constant market rate implies that it never pays a society to spend even a tiny amount today in order to avert an environmental disaster that will destroy the economy's entire annual output, as long as that disaster occurs sufficiently far into the future. For example, if the U.S. economy produces $9 trillion of output this year and is growing at a real rate of 2 percent a year, and we use a real discount rate of 8 percent, then the PV of the economy's entire annual output in 300 years is only $321,490.[43] Many economists and other persons are uncomfortable with the implication that it is not worth spending more than $321,490 today to avert a total disaster in 300 years. In contrast, with a time-declining SDR, the *PV* of the future economy may remain "material," implying that it is indeed worth saving the economy that will prevail three centuries from now.

Even for less apocalyptic disasters, a large enough positive SDR gives negligible weight to costs and benefits that occur sufficiently far into the future.[44] Using a time-declining rate avoids having to choose between ignoring very long-term environmental or health consequences (with a time-invariant, nonzero SDR) and not discounting at all.

A third reason is that current market rates of interest or marginal rates of time preference reflect the preferences of individuals currently alive, not those not yet born. Some economists argue that current individuals fail to account appropriately for the long-term impacts of their actions, or of the government's actions, on the welfare of future generations.[45] Those yet unborn do not have a direct voice in current markets, yet we may believe that they should have standing in our (current) CBAs.[46] Some economic philosophers, most notably Frank Ramsay, have argued that the social discount rate should be zero, which, in effect, implies nondiscounting. According to this view, one that we do not share, society should be indifferent between, for example, $100 today and $100 in a century.[47] In other words, future impacts should have exactly the same weight as current impacts.

Charles Harvey and others have suggested that a potentially reasonable alternative is to use declining discount rates, that is, to use a lower discount rate for impacts that occur further in the future, with the discount rate tending to zero as the timing of the impacts tends to infinity.[48] For example, in *proportional discounting* the social discount factor in period t is given by:

$$w_t = \frac{b}{b + t} \qquad t \geq 0 \qquad\qquad \textbf{(10.10)}$$

for some parameter $b > 0$.

Martin Weitzman provides an environmental rationale for time-declining discount rates.[49] Two key assumptions in Weitzman's model are that the value of a clean environment will increase over time because of increasing incomes and the marginal return from spending money on the environment will decline over time due to diminishing marginal returns.

Recently, Weitzman conducted a survey of 2,160 economists.[50] On the basis of his survey he derives the following "sliding scale" SDRs: 4 percent for the near term (1 to 5 years), 3 percent for the medium term (6 to 25 years), 2 percent for the long term (26 to 75 years), 1 percent for the very long term (76 to 200 years), 0 percent for the distant future (over 200 years). He also argues that if one were forced to choose a single, constant-equivalent discount rate to represent the entire sliding scale, it would be less than 2 percent per year.

In summary, although there are some interesting arguments for the use of declining discount rates, analysts are not in agreement about how to resolve the issue of discounting impacts that occur far in the future. The case that has been made for the use of declining social discount rates is fairly recent. It has not yet been widely accepted.

Conclusion on Social Discounting Methods in the Absence of Perfect Markets

There are many alternative discounting methods. The choice among them can determine whether a project has a positive or negative net present value and, therefore, whether or not a government policy or project should be undertaken. The selection of a social discount rate method and the procedure used in discounting depend on the specific circumstances surrounding the project.

Several practical implications follow from accepting, as we do, the conceptual validity of the shadow price of capital approach to discounting. First, *if **all** costs and benefits are measured as increments to consumption, then they should be discounted at the marginal social rate of time preference.* We suggest using $p_z = 2$ percent with sensitivity analysis at 0 and 4 percent. Second, *if **all** costs and benefits are measured as increments to private-sector investment, then they should be discounted at the marginal rate of return on investment.* We suggest using r_z equal to 8 percent with sensitivity analysis at 6 and 10 percent. Note that in either of these cases the magnitude of the shadow price of capital is irrelevant. Third, *when some costs and benefits are measured as increments to consumption and others are measured as increments to private investment, apply the shadow price of capital to increments of investment and then discount at the marginal social rate of time preference.* Unfortunately, costs and benefits often cannot be definitively classified as increments to either consumption or private investment. In the absence of any other information, we suggest treating 15 percent of impacts as changes in investment and 85 percent as changes in consumption. We also suggest using a shadow price of capital of about 1.65 with sensitivity analysis at 1.3 and 2.7. If, for some reason, it is not possible to use the shadow price of capital method, we suggest using the weighted average social discount rate method using a discount rate of 3 percent with sensitivity analysis at 1 and 5 percent if the project is financed by taxes, or using a discount rate of 6 percent with sensitivity analysis at 5 and 7 percent if not.

For projects with large future (i.e., intergenerational) environmental or health effects there is some justification for applying lower discount rates, especially to impacts that occur far in the future. The discounting method based on the real growth rate suggests a discount rate of 3.25 percent, with sensitivity analysis at 2.1 percent and 5.25 percent (see Appendix 10B). Advocates of declining discount rate methods would probably suggest applying a slightly higher rate to impacts that occur within the next few years and would certainly suggest applying a lower rate to impacts that occur far in the future.

Our discussion of the issues should make clear that analysts are unlikely ever to have complete confidence in whatever discounting procedure they use. Even in the case of the more simple discounting methods, choice of the appropriate social discount rate requires judgment. Taking account of the shadow price of capital demands that even more parameters, which cannot be known with certainty, be specified. It is almost always desirable, therefore, for analysts to test the sensitivity of their results to changes in the parameters used in discounting.

THE SOCIAL DISCOUNT RATE IN ACTUAL PRACTICE

Current discounting practices in governments vary enormously. There is considerable evidence that, although they should, many government agencies do not discount at all.[51] For example, a survey of 90 U.S. municipalities with populations over 100,000 found that only 43 percent use discounting in evaluating projects.[52]

When governments do discount, they rarely use the shadow price of capital method. As mentioned earlier, this method is difficult to implement and it is difficult to explain to noneconomists. Also, governments do not use time-varying discount rates. Thus, the issue is largely one of describing what (positive) constant discount rate practitioners use. This rate varies from country to country and often from department to department.

As we discuss in Chapter 1, spenders, guardians, and analysts will tend to favor different discount rates. In general, guardians view government expenditures as crowding out private investment, or act as if they do; consequently, they tend to argue for a discount rate approximating the rate of return on private investment, a relatively high rate. Spenders view government expenditures as reducing current consumption or act as if they hold this view and, therefore, tend to argue for a discount rate approximating the social marginal rate of time preference, a relatively low rate.

When costs precede benefits, as is the case for most government projects, those who favor such projects may argue for a low rate whereas those who oppose them may argue for a high rate. In many practical situations, however, debate is ruled out because the discount rate is prescribed by government review and monitoring agencies. As these rates are set by guardians, they tend to be higher than social discount rates based on the theory presented in this chapter, but this is not always the case.

In North American jurisdictions, the prescribed discount rates for federal agencies have tended to be fairly high, but they have been trending lower.[53] For example, in the 1970s and 1980s, the U.S. Office of Management and Budget (OMB), which guides the cost-benefit analyses of all U.S. executive branch agencies, required most agencies to use a real discount rate of 10 percent. This rate was intended to approximate the opportunity cost of capital, measured as the real marginal before-tax rate of return on private investment. In 1992, the OMB revised this real rate downward to 7 percent (OMB A-94). This new rate was based on low-yielding forms of capital (e.g., housing) as well as high-yielding corporate capital.

The General Accounting Office (GAO) and the Congressional Budget Office (CBO), both of which are U.S. congressional oversight agencies, use lower rates that depend on the U.S. Treasury's borrowing rate. The CBO generally favors the use of a rate based on the marginal social rate of time preference. It has estimated the real historical yield on U.S. government securities at 2 percent and suggests the use of this rate plus or minus two percentage points.[54] Based on the Fisher model of interest rates, which was discussed in Chapter 6, the GAO uses the existing average nominal yield on treasury debt maturing between one year and the life of the project, less the forecast rate of inflation.[55] There are a number of exceptions for all agencies.[56]

A recent proposal by the U.S. Panel on Cost-Effectiveness in Health and Medicine recommends the use of a real 3 percent discount rate for cost-effectiveness studies, with sensitivity analysis at rates between 0 percent and 7 percent.[57] Similarly, U.S. municipalities that do discount also use a rate around 3 percent.[58]

Since 1976, the Federal Treasury Board Secretariat in Canada has recommended the use of a real discount rate of 10 percent, with sensitivity analysis at 5 percent and 15 percent.[59] The rationale for this rate draws extensively on research by Glenn Jenkins, which was discussed earlier. The Treasury Board sometimes allows much lower discount rates (0 percent to 3 percent) for health and environmental cost-benefit analyses, although this is not official policy. Provincial government guidelines in Canada have tended to follow federal guidelines.[60] Currently, the British Columbia Crown Corporations Secretariat recommends a real SDR of 8 percent.[61]

CONCLUSION

Discounting for time is fundamental to the proper practice of CBA. Most policy analysts realize the importance of discounting. Common practice, however, often does not reflect theory. Few analysts or bureaucrats employ the shadow price of capital approach. In view of the difficulties one faces in applying this method, we must not be too critical. Indeed, we should be humble about whatever procedure we use, presenting analysis of the sensitivity of our results to changes in parameter values.

For analysts who are unwilling or unable (for political or other reasons) to use the shadow price of capital method and are evaluating projects that do not have intergenerational implications, we believe that the appropriate real discount rate ranges between 1 percent and 7 percent. Using 4 percent would not be unreasonable. For impacts that occur far in the future, especially if they have large positive environmental impacts, one could use lower discount rates.

Appendix 10A

ADJUSTING THE SOCIAL DISCOUNT RATE FOR SYSTEMATIC RISK

In Chapter 7 we considered how to take account of uncertainty about the magnitude of costs and benefits that will be realized in future years. The basic notion is that costs and benefits can be estimated for each of a number of mutually exclusive contingencies. Assigning probabilities to each of these contingencies allows the analyst to calculate expected values (averages) for each period. If we assume risk neutrality (indifference between lotteries and certain payments equal to the expected values of the lotteries), then discounting these expected values for time in the standard way allows us to interpret the present value of expected net social benefits as the appropriate objective function for determining if policies are efficient.

As we discussed in Chapter 7, however, a complication arises because we generally assume that individuals are risk averse (i.e., they prefer guaranteed payments to uncertain amounts with the same expected value). Risk aversion among individuals raises the question of how to treat risky projects. As we suggested in Chapter 7, an appropriate way to take account of risk aversion is to use certainty equivalents. We can then discount using the methods suggested in this chapter.

This appendix focuses on whether and how the social discount rate for a project should be adjusted for the risk of the project *when the analyst does not compute certainty equivalent values*. Economists have expressed divergent views on whether the social discount rate should reflect project risk in these circumstances.[1] This controversy can be resolved to some extent by reference to the capital asset pricing model (CAPM). The basic idea of this model is that investors have to be compensated for risk. Individual investments are subject to two types of risk. One type of risk is *unique risk* (or *specific risk, residual risk,* or *unsystematic risk*), which pertains exclusively to a particular investment. This risk can be avoided by portfolio diversification, that is, by holding a fairly large number of different investments. The second type of risk is called *market risk* or *systematic risk*. This risk cannot be avoided by portfolio diversification. It arises because of economy-wide changes that affect all investments, including the market portfolio, to some extent. Stock prices, for example, tend to move in the same direction. The issue then is whether and how to take account of the systematic risk of a government project—the extent to which its returns are correlated with economy-wide changes.

Formally, the CAPM states that, in equilibrium, the expected rate of return on an asset equals the risk-free rate plus an amount that compensates for systematic risk:

$$E(r_i) = r_f + [E(r_m) - r_f]\beta_i \qquad \text{(10A.1)}$$

where $E(r_i)$ is the expected rate of return on individual investment i, $E(r_m)$ is the expected rate of return to the market portfolio, r_f is the risk-free rate of return or the rate of return on a risk-free asset, such as high-grade corporate bonds or T-bills, $E(r_m) - r_f$

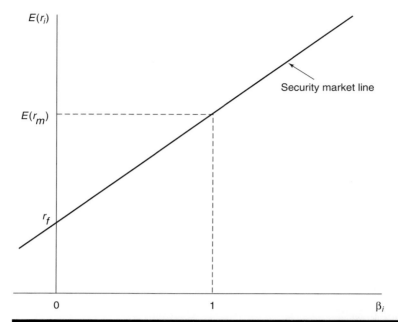

FIGURE 10A.1 The Capital Asset Pricing Model

is the market risk premium or equity premium, and β_i is a measure of systematic risk for individual asset i. Often the systematic risk for a security is called its beta.

This model is represented graphically in Figure 10A.1. In equilibrium, all investments lie on the security market line with the expected return of an investment varying in direct proportion to its systematic risk, β_i. It can be shown that:

$$\beta_i = \frac{\text{Cov } (r_i, r_m)}{\sigma_m^2} = \rho_{im} \frac{\sigma_i}{\sigma_m} \qquad \textbf{(10A.2)}$$

Thus, a security's systematic risk—its beta—equals the covariance of the security's own rate of return with the market portfolio divided by the variance in the market rate of return. Setting $r_i = r_m$ and substituting equation (10A.2) into equation (10A.1) indicates that the market portfolio has a beta of one. An investment that is uncorrelated with the market portfolio has a beta of zero and, as shown by equation (10A.1), has an expected return equal to r_f, the risk-free rate of return.

Private-Sector Capital Budgeting Implications of the CAPM

The private-sector capital budgeting implications of the CAPM are straightforward, at least in theory.[2] The first step is to ascertain a proposed investment's beta. This varies according to the correlation between the project's net benefits and the market portfolio, as shown in equation (10A.2). Indeed, a project's beta could be calculated using equation (10A.2) if the appropriate data were available. More likely, the analyst would use simple rules of thumb. Projects that tend to perform better than the market portfolio in good times and worse than the market portfolio in bad times (e.g., cyclical stocks) have betas greater than one. Investments that are highly correlated with the market portfolio have betas close to one. Investments that are weakly, positively correlated with the market portfolio have betas between zero and one. Investments that are uncorrelated with the market portfolio, so-called risk-free investments, have a beta equal to zero. Investments that are negatively correlated with the market portfolio, such as countercyclical stocks, have negative betas.

The second step is to estimate the right-hand side of equation (10A.1), which can be interpreted as the expected rate of return for an investment with the same systematic risk as the one under consideration or, more briefly, as the risk-adjusted rate of return. This requires knowing the risk-free rate, r_f, for which one can use interest rates on treasury bills or similar securities. It also requires an estimate of the market risk premium, $E(r_m) - r_f$. This premium has averaged six percentage points during the past century.[3] If, for example, an investment's beta equals 0.67, the risk-free rate equals 3 percent, and the market risk premium equals 6 percent, then the expected rate of return for an investment in this risk class is:

$$E(r_i) = 3 + 6(0.67) = 7 \text{ percent}$$

The third step is to compute the *NPV* of the proposed investment project by discounting its expected cash flows at the risk-adjusted rate of return, in this example 7 percent. If the resultant *NPV* is positive, then the investment should proceed; otherwise, it should not.[4] Formally, suppose the expected net benefits (cash flows) of a proposed investment all arise in one year's time and are denoted $E(NB)$. The expected *NPV* of the investment is:

$$E(NPV) = \frac{E(NB)}{1 + r_f + [E(r_m) - r_f]\beta_i} \qquad \textbf{(10A.3)}$$

Equation (10A.3) is referred to as the risk-adjusted present value formula. It is equivalent to equation (6.2), the formula for computing the present value of an amount received one period in the future, where $i = r_f + [E(r_m) - r_f]\beta_i$, the risk-adjusted discount rate.

Use of the CAPM in CBA

Now consider a potential government project as a possible new investment. Society may be risk averse and want to reduce the total risk associated with national social income. Consequently, it is appropriate to evaluate an investment using a discount rate that depends on the covariance of that investment with national social income or, more simply, national income. The rules developed previously can now be modified straightforwardly: *Government projects with expected net benefits that are negatively (or positively) correlated with national income should be discounted at a rate lower (higher) than the risk-free rate.* In practice, the CBO sometimes adjusts discount rates in this way.[5]

In general, the benefits and the costs of infrastructure projects, such as developing ports and building highways, are likely to be positively correlated with national income. Consequently, these projects should be discounted using a higher rate than normal. The benefits and costs of job-creation projects are likely to be negatively correlated with national income. These projects should be discounted using a lower rate than normal.

As a practical rule of thumb, some authors suggest that one should adjust the risk-free discount rate downward only when the expected net benefits of a project are likely to be highly negatively correlated with national income and the project has a long time horizon. If the correlation is not highly negative, then substantial adjustment is likely to be unwarranted; if the project has a short time horizon, then the lower discount rate is unlikely to affect the magnitude of the present value of net social benefits dramatically. *Worrying about adjusting discount rates for risk is probably only worthwhile in practice for clearly negative correlations and long time horizons.* So, for example, if we expect national income to be highly negatively correlated with the world price of oil, and we expect the net benefits of an oil stockpiling program to be positively correlated with the world price of oil, then the expected net benefits of the stockpiling program will probably be negatively correlated with national income. Therefore, if the time horizon of the stockpiling program is long, then downward adjustment of the risk-free discount rate would be justified. Unfortunately, the state of the art does not allow us to determine the exact magnitude of the adjustment.

Summary and Limitations of the CAPM for CBA

According to the CAPM, the variance of a project's net benefits (project risk) is not relevant to the choice of a discount rate. Systematic project risk matters, not unsystematic project risk, which can be diversified away. The contribution of a particular project to the total risk associated with national social income is essentially given by the beta of that investment, which depends on the covariance of that project with national income, not its variance. Projects whose returns are positively (negatively) correlated with national social income should be discounted at a higher (lower) rate than the risk-free rate. In practice, though, one might only make this adjustment for projects that are highly negatively correlated with national income and have long time horizons.

There are some limitations to these suggestions. First, for many projects it is hard to obtain accurate estimates of project betas. Second, it means applying different discount rates to different projects, which may encounter resistance in government agencies.

Appendix 10B

SOCIAL DISCOUNTING BASED ON THE REAL GROWTH RATE

Long-lived projects typically involve a sacrifice of consumption by the present generation in order to generate benefits for future generations. To decide whether the sacrifice is warranted, society must weight the current loss in consumption against the future gains. Some economists, including Frank Ramsey, Stephen Marglin, and Kenneth Arrow, have argued that market interest rates are inappropriate sources of weights for long-term projects that impact on future generations.[6] These authors argue that society should treat all generations' welfare equally but should consider that future generations will likely have higher per capita consumption than the current generation due to ongoing economic growth. Consequently, assuming that consumption has declining marginal utility, consumption by a future generation should have a lower weight than consumption by a present generation, where the rate at which the weights decline over time is proportional to the growth rate of per capita consumption—the higher the growth rate, the higher the SDR. Specifically, this method sets the SDR, denoted as s_G, equal to the long-run rate of growth in per capita consumption, g, multiplied by a non-negative constant, e, which is an elasticity that measures how fast the social marginal utility of consumption falls as per capita consumption rises:

$$s_G = ge$$

This discount rate is nonnegative as long as g is nonnegative. Industrialized market economies have seen periods during which per capita consumption has declined, some lasting as long as a decade or more. However, the overwhelming experience since the Industrial Revolution has been that average consumption rises over the long run; thus, $g > 0$ and $s_G \geq 0$.

The parameter e ($0 \leq e < \infty$) represents a social evaluation of the intergenerational distribution of income. It summarizes the key value judgment about how quickly the marginal utility of consumption declines as average consumption rises. When $e = 1$, the relative weight on each generation's consumption equals the inverse of its relative consumption per capita. This implies that a 10 percent reduction in the consumption of the current generation, for example, from \$20,000 to \$18,000, is an acceptable trade-off for a 10 percent increase in the consumption of a richer future generation, for example, from \$40,000 to \$44,000. In other words, society weights the poorer, current generation's loss of each dollar of consumption as twice as important as a gain of \$1 to the richer, future generation because the richer generation (initially) has twice the level of per capita consumption.

Setting e equal to zero would imply that there should be no discounting: Society should treat each unit of consumption received by future, richer generations as identical to a unit of consumption received by the present generation. Hence, a zero value for e signifies a complete lack of concern for intergenerational inequality in per capita consumption. At the opposite extreme, an infinite e would indicate that society cares only about the worst-off, current generation and would never sacrifice current consumption to increase the consumption of future generations.

If society wishes to give more weight to the current generation, it can add a pure rate of time preference, d, to the product of g and e:

$$s_G = ge + d$$

where d represents the rate at which society discounts future generations' welfare, even if all generations have equal consumption per capita (i.e., $g = 0$). There has been debate about assigning a positive value to d since Frank Ramsey argued in print that it was ethically indefensible.[7] However, Kenneth Arrow shows that the presumption that all generations' welfare should be weighted equally, although seemingly reasonable, can result in excessively high rates of savings being required of the current (or even of every) generation.[8] He demonstrates that, under reasonable parameter values, the current generation could be required to save approximately two-thirds of its income! To avoid this result, a positive pure rate of time preference should be employed. Arrow tentatively suggests a figure of around 1 percent for d, which we use in our calculations that follow.

Erhun Kula estimates the average growth rate in real per capita consumption was 2.3 percent in the United States between 1954 and 1976.[9] He treats e as representing the preferences of an "average" individual, and estimates it from an aggregate demand equation for food, arriving at a figure of 1.56. Finally, he views d as representing the "average" individual's expected annual mortality rate, which he estimates is 0.9 percent per year in the United States. Consequently, he estimates $s_G = (2.3)(1.56) + 0.9 = 5.3$ percent.

However, this estimate may be a bit high. We have updated and refined Kula's estimate of the growth rate, g. Regressing the logarithm of real per capita consumption on time gives an estimated U.S. growth rate of 2.25 percent per annum.[10] Second, we have modified e. Robert Brent suggests that e should be between 0 and 1, with 0.5 as a benchmark.[11] Kenneth Arrow and others argue that individuals reveal their own e's through their behavior with respect to risk and intertemporal choice.[12] They survey studies that indicate individual elasticities of marginal utility of consumption lie between 1 and 2. Thus, estimates of e vary between 0 and 2, with some consensus that setting $e = 1$ would not be unreasonable. With our estimate of $g = 2.25$ percent, $e = 1$ and, following Arrow et al., using $d = 1$ percent, $s_G = 3.25$ percent. Sensitivity analysis with e ranging between 0.5 and 2 implies s_G ranges from 2.1 percent to 5.25 percent.

There are several criticisms of this approach and of the particular estimated values. First, the estimate of g may be inaccurate. Using the national income accounts to measure the growth rate in real (aggregate) consumption expenditure per person may not accurately measure what economists mean by consumption. For example, this consumption measure includes purchases of consumer durables, which most analysts believe should be interpreted as investment. Also, it does not include the quantity and quality of public goods, which certainly affect consumers' welfare. An alternative plausible approach measures g as the average rate of growth of real per capita GDP because GDP includes both private-sector consumption and goods produced in the public sector. During the 1947–1998 period, real GDP per capita grew at 2 percent per annum, which is slightly lower than our previous estimate of 2.25 percent.[13] Using this growth rate and $e = d = 1$ percent gives $s_G = 3.0$ percent. But, as GDP includes investment and net exports as well as consumption, we prefer our previous estimate.

Second, the parameter e relies on a social value judgment about intergenerational equality. It may be even more difficult to aggregate individual preferences about equality than to aggregate individual marginal rates of time preference. Similarly, selecting a value for d also requires a value judgment.

Third, it is difficult to estimate the future long-run growth rate, g. The natural estimate is the recent historical growth rate, but this varies over time. Splitting our data into two time periods shows that the average growth rate was 2.33 percent from 1947 to 1972 but 1.88 percent from 1972 to 1998.[14] The growth rate may have picked up again recently.

The final criticism, which also applies to the marginal rate of time preference method, refers back to Harberger's argument. If s_G is less than r_z, this indicates that society is underinvesting (at point Z in Figure 10.2) relative to the socially best outcome (point X). If a government investment produces a one-period, real return greater than

s_G, then society should make this investment because it improves social welfare according to the explicit value judgments used in calculating s_G. However, if private investment yielded a higher return, then social welfare would improve even more if private investment increased instead of the government investment. Using the shadow price of capital approach and then discounting consumption and consumption equivalents at s_G provides a solution to this problem.

Appendix 10C

COMPUTING CHANGES IN INVESTMENT AND CONSUMPTION WHEN THE PROJECT IS FINANCED BY FUNDS RAISED THROUGH ISSUING BONDS

If the library information system project is financed by a $325,000 loan, following Harberger, we assume that the entire amount borrowed would displace private-sector investment.[15] Given that the loan is repaid with tax revenues over five years at 5 percent interest, the equal annual installments are $75,067. For the first year, $16,250 (0.05 × 325,000) is interest on the loan and $58,817 (75,067 − 16,250) is repayment of principal. Consequently, at the end of the first year, immediately after the first annual payment, the loan balance equals $266,183 (325,000 − 58,817). Extending this logic to the second and subsequent years, it follows that $61,758 (75,067 − .05 × 266,183) is paid toward the capital portion of the loan at the end of the second year, and $64,846, $68,088, and $71,491 are paid toward the loan at the end of years 3, 4, and 5, respectively. By the end of the fifth year the loan is completely paid off (58,817 + 61,758 + 64,856 + 68,088 + 71,491 = 325,000).[16] Again following Harberger, we assume that the full amount of each of the loan principal repayments goes toward increasing investment.

The first year's interest on the loan is $16,250, as just discussed. For years 2, 3, 4, and 5, the interest equals $13,309, $10,221, $6,979, and $3,576, respectively. Under the logic of the shadow price method, these payments should be treated symmetrically to taxes; that is, 15 percent is an addition to investment and 85 percent is an addition to consumption.

Now consider the $75,067 that is raised in taxes each year to pay for the loan. As before, we assume 15 percent ($11,260) of these annual payments displaces private-sector investment, whereas the remaining 85 percent ($63,807) displaces consumption.

Finally, the remaining annual benefits and costs—the $100,000 in annual project benefits, the $20,000 in annual maintenance cost required to support the library information system, and the $20,000 of terminal benefits—are treated exactly the same as before: Net changes to investment equal $3,000 in years 1 through 4 and $6,000 in year 5, and net changes to consumption equal $77,000 in years 1 through 4 and $94,000 in year 5.

In summary, under these assumptions, the net changes in investment each year, ΔI_t, are:

$$\Delta I_0 = -\$325,000$$
$$\Delta I_1 = \$58,817 - \$11,260 + \$3,000 + 0.15 \times \$16,250 = \$52,995$$
$$\Delta I_2 = \$61,758 - \$11,260 + \$3,000 + 0.15 \times \$13,309 = \$55,494$$
$$\Delta I_3 = \$64,846 - \$11,260 + \$3,000 + 0.15 \times \$10,221 = \$58,119$$
$$\Delta I_4 = \$68,088 - \$11,260 + \$3,000 + 0.15 \times \$6,979 = \$60,875$$
$$\Delta I_5 = \$71,491 - \$11,260 + \$6,000 + 0.15 \times \$3,576 = \$66,767$$

The net changes in consumption, ΔC_t, are:

$$\Delta C_0 = \$0$$
$$\Delta C_1 = -\$63,807 + \$77,000 + 0.85 \times \$16,250 = \$27,006$$
$$\Delta C_2 = -\$63,807 + \$77,000 + 0.85 \times \$13,309 = \$24,506$$
$$\Delta C_3 = -\$63,807 + \$77,000 + 0.85 \times \$10,221 = \$21,881$$
$$\Delta C_4 = -\$63,807 + \$77,000 + 0.85 \times \$6,979 = \$19,125$$
$$\Delta C_5 = -\$63,807 + \$94,000 + 0.85 \times \$3,576 = \$33,233$$

Exercises for Chapter 10

1. The following table gives cost and benefit estimates in real dollars for dredging a navigable channel from an inland port to the open sea.

Year	Dredging and Patrol Costs ($)	Saving to Shippers ($)	Value of Pleasure Boating ($)
0	2,548,000	0	0
1	60,000	400,000	60,000
2	60,000	440,000	175,000
3	70,000	440,000	175,000
4	70,000	440,000	175,000
5	80,000	440,000	175,000
6	80,000	440,000	175,000
7	90,000	440,000	175,000

The channel would be navigable for seven years, after which silting would render it unnavigable. Local economists estimate that 75 percent of the savings to shippers would be directly invested by the firms, or their shareholders, and the remaining 25 percent would be used by shareholders for consumption. The marginal social rate of time preference is assumed to be 2 percent, the marginal rate of return on private investment is assumed to be 10 percent, and the shadow price of capital is assumed to be 1.90.

Assuming that the costs and benefits accrue at the end of the year they straddle, calculate the present value of net benefits of the project using each of the following methods:

a. Discount at the marginal rate of return on private investment, as suggested by the U.S. Office of Management and Budget.

b. Discount at the marginal social rate of time preference, as suggested by the U.S. Congressional Budget Office.

c. Discount using the shadow price of capital method and assuming that all government expenditures come at the expense of private investment.

d. Discount using the shadow price of capital method and assuming that 90 percent of government expenditures come at the expense of private investment and 10 percent at the expense of private consumption.

2. An analyst for a municipal public housing agency explained the choice of a discount rate as follows: "Our agency funds its capital investments through nationally issued bonds. The effective interest rate that we pay on the bonds is the cost that the agency faces in shifting revenue from the future to the present. It is, therefore, the appropriate discount rate for the agency to use in evaluating alternative investments." Comment on the appropriateness of this discount rate.

3. Assume the following: Society faces a marginal excess tax burden of raising public revenue equal to METB; the shadow price of capital equals θ; public borrowing displaces private investment dollar for dollar; and public revenues raised through taxes displace investment at the savings rate, s, and consumption at the rate, $1 - s$. Consider a public project involving a large initial capital expenditure, C, followed by a stream of benefits that are entirely consumed, B.

a. Discuss how you would apply the shadow price of capital method to the project if it is financed fully out of current taxes.

b. Discuss how you would apply the shadow price of capital method to the project if it is financed fully by public borrowing, which is later repaid by taxes.

c. Discuss how you would apply the shadow price of capital method to the project if it is fully self-financed through fees charged to beneficiaries.

Notes

1. This chapter draws on parts of the first edition of this book; Anthony Boardman and David Greenberg, "Discounting and the Social Discount Rate," in Fred Thompson and Mark T. Green, eds., *Handbook of Public Finance* (New York: Marcel Dekker, 1998), pp. 269–318, especially pp. 296–316; and Mark A. Moore, Anthony E. Boardman, and David H. Greenberg, "The Social Discount Rate in Canada," in John Richards and Aidan Vining, eds., *Infrastructure* (Ottawa, Ontario: C. D. Howe, forthcoming). We would like to thank Mark for his contributions to this chapter and for computing the SDR estimates for the United States that are provided in this chapter.

2. Throughout this chapter we assume that impacts (costs and benefits) and discount rates are measured in real dollars.

3. Robert C. Lind, "A Primer on the Major Issues Relating to the Discount Rate for Evaluating National Energy Projects," in Robert C. Lind et al., *Discounting for Time and Risk in Energy Policy* (Washington, DC: Resources for the Future, 1982), pp. 21–94 at p. 8.

4. Assume here that, in order to reveal your true preferences, there is no arbitrage opportunity; that is, you could not borrow or lend money. Arbitrage means that you can simultaneously buy something in one market and sell it in another market and thereby make a guaranteed profit. If interest rates were less than 20 percent and arbitrage were allowed, you could say that you would rather have the $1,200 next year and then immediately borrow between $1,000 and $1,200 from the bank. Thus, you would say you would prefer to

have the $1,200 next year even though you would actually prefer to have $1,000 now.

5. Along an indifference curve, $dU = (\partial U/\partial C_1)dC_1 + (\partial U/\partial C_2)dC_2 = 0$.

6. Formally, $MRS = (dC_2/dC_1)\,|_{U=\text{constant}}$
$$= (\partial U/\partial C_1)/(\partial U/\partial C_2).$$

7. It would make no conceptual difference if the consumer received income in both periods.

8. The (absolute value of the) slope of the budget constraint exceeds 1, indicating that the consumer earns positive interest at rate i on the part of income saved this year.

9. To solve this problem formally we set up the following Lagrangian:

$$L = U(C_1, C_2) + \lambda\left(T - C_1 - \frac{C_2}{1+i}\right)$$

and then take derivatives with respect to C_1 and C_2:

$$L_{C_1} = \frac{\partial U}{\partial C_1} - \lambda = 0$$

$$L_{C_2} = \frac{\partial U}{\partial C_2} - \frac{\lambda}{1+i} = 0$$

Consequently, $(\partial U/\partial C_1)/(\partial U/\partial C_2) = 1 + i$. Now, by definition, $MRS = (\partial U/\partial C_1)/(\partial U/\partial C_2) = 1 + p$, where p = marginal rate of time preference. Therefore, $i = p$ at the optimum.

10. Formally, the result holds as long as the problem has an interior solution. A very impatient person has an $MRTP > i$ at all points on his indifference curve, which leads to a corner solution on the C_1 axis. For simplicity, we shall ignore this possibility.

11. By definition, $-(1 + r_x)$ equals the slope of the *CPF* at X, whereas the average slope of the *CPF* between T and X equals $-C_{t+1}/I_t = -(1 + r)$. Because of the concave shape of the *CPF*, the slope at X is not as steep as the average slope between X and T. Therefore, $r_x < r$.

12. In Figure 10.2, the absolute value of the slope of the *CPF*, $(1 + r_z)$, exceeds the absolute value of the slope of the *SIC*, $(1 + p_z)$.

13. In this section, we continue to use the subscript z on p and r to emphasize that we are discussing an economy that is at a point such as Z in Figure 10.2 (rather than at X) and, as a consequence, the marginal rate of time preference is smaller than the marginal rate of return on investment. Further-

more, it reminds us that we require marginal returns, not average returns.

14. For more information on this method see Mark Moore, Anthony Boardman, and David Greenberg, "The Social Discount Rate in Canada."

15. Arnold C. Harberger, "The Discount Rate in Public Investment Evaluation," *Conference Proceedings of the Committee on the Economics of Water Resource Development* (Denver, CO: Western Agricultural Economics Research Council, Report No. 17, 1969).

16. See, for example, Robert E. Hall, "Intertemporal Substitution in Consumption," *Journal of Political Economy*, 96, no. 2 (1988), 339–357 and, more recently, John Muellbauer and Ralph Lattimore, "The Consumption Function: A Theoretical and Empirical Overview," in M. H. Pesaran and M. R. Wickens, eds., *The Handbook of Applied Econometrics: Macroeconomics* (Cambridge, MA: Blackwell, 1995).

17. See John B. Shoven and Michael Topper, "The Cost of Capital in Canada, the United States and Japan," in J. Shoven and J. Whalley, eds., *Canada-U.S. Tax Comparisons* (Chicago: University of Chicago Press, 1992).

18. Using short-term, recent data gives a slightly higher estimate. The average monthly yield on Moody's AAA bonds was 6.53 percent in 1998 (7.26 percent in 1997). In 1998, the average quarterly ratio of nonfinancial corporate taxes to GDP was 0.365. Using the percentage change in the CPI (all items) in 1998 of 1.59 as the expected rate of inflation, gives a real expected pretax rate of return on investment of $[(.1028 - .0159)/(1 + .0159)] = 8.56$ percent.

19. Even if we measured benefits and costs in terms of their expected impacts, rather than certainty equivalents, one might argue that government projects are less risky than private-sector investments. Arrow and Lind argue that the government can improve on the social allocation of risks by holding a broader portfolio of assets than can any private agent. See Kenneth J. Arrow and Robert C. Lind, "Uncertainty and the Evaluation of Public Investment Decisions," *American Economic Review*, 60, no. 3 (1970), 364–378. We return to the issue of adjusting for risk in Appendix 10A.

20. As high-income individuals do most of the personal saving, the rates they face are likely to be the most appropriate ones to use.

21. For example, the average monthly yield on treasury bonds was 5.26 percent in 1998 (6.34 percent in 1997). Using a tax rate of 30 percent and the CPI (all items) for 1998 of 1.59 percent gives an estimate of p_z equal to 2.06 percent. This estimate is quite similar to our previous estimate, but it might not have been. Short-term estimates sometimes vary considerably from long-term estimates. In our view it would be inappropriate to use very short-term rates due to their potentially high variability.

22. If you think you have only a short time to live, then you will value the present very highly because, quite literally, there may be no tomorrow for you. Thus, it is reasonable to expect that older people have a higher MRTP rate than younger people. See Maureen L. Cropper, Sema K. Aydede, and Paul R. Portney, "Rates of Time Preference for Saving Lives," *American Economic Review,* 82, no. 2 (1992), 469–472, who found a positive relationship between age and the marginal rate of time preference but found no significant relationship between respondents' MRTP and their sex, education, marital status, or income.

23. An individual may have different marginal rates of time preference over different goods. For example, Jan Olsen suggests that it is possible that individual MRTPs for health differ from those for "ordinary consumption goods." See Jan Abel Olsen, "On What Basis Should Health Be Discounted?" *Journal of Health Economics,* 12, no. 1 (1993), 39–53. Paul Stern and others have suggested that we might have a high MRTP for mainframe computers but a low MRTP for clean air, clean water, or biological diversity. The differences in MRTPs may be partly due to different longevities of different goods: Computers have relatively short useful lives whereas environmental goods have long time horizons. See, for example, Paul C. Stern, "Blind Spots in Policy Analysis: What Economics Doesn't Say about Energy Use," *Journal of Policy Analysis and Management,* 5, no. 2 (1986), 200–227, especially pp. 207–209, for a discussion of differences in the implicit discount rates for different household appliances.

24. Agnar Sandmo and Jacques H. Dreze, "Discount Rates for Public Investment in Closed and Open Economies," *Economica,* 38, no. 152 (1971), 395–412.

25. See Lind, "A Primer on the Major Issues Relating to the Discount Rate for Evaluating National Energy Projects."

26. Under a flexible exchange rate regime, net exports may be reduced when increased government borrowing raises domestic interest rates relative to those abroad, causing a financial capital inflow and an appreciation of the exchange rate.

27. Similar results are obtained by taking the nominal bond yield on 10-year treasuries for 1998 of 5.26 percent and adjusting for inflation using the CPI of 1.59 percent to yield a real return of 3.6 percent.

28. See Glenn Jenkins, "The Measurement of Rates of Return and Taxation for Private Capital in Canada," in William A. Niskanen et al., eds., *Benefit Cost and Policy Analysis* (Chicago: Aldine, 1973), pp. 211–245; Glenn P. Jenkins, "Capital in Canada: Its Social and Private Performance 1965–1974" (Discussion Paper No. 98, Economic Council of Canada, Ministry of Supply and Services Canada, 1997); and Glenn P. Jenkins, "The Public Sector Discount Rate for Canada: Some Further Observations," *Canadian Public Policy,* 7, no. 3 (1981), 399–407.

29. David F. Burgess, "The Social Discount Rate for Canada: Theory and Evidence," *Canadian Public Policy,* 7, no. 3 (1981), 383–394.

30. $WSOC = (.168)(8) + (.832)(2) = 3.0$ percent.

31. This approach was first suggested by Otto Eckstein and was systematically developed by David Bradford. See Otto Eckstein, *Water Resource Development: The Economics of Project Evaluation* (Cambridge, MA: Harvard University Press, 1958), and David F. Bradford, "Constraints on Government Investment Opportunities and the Choice of Discount Rate," *American Economic Review,* 65, no. 5 (1975), 887–899. See also the *Journal of Environmental Economics and Management,* vol. 18S (1990).

32. Note that increments to investment are treated the same as displaced investments—they are also multiplied by θ. Thus, flows to investment are more beneficial than flows of consumption.

33. Proof of equation (10.9) is fairly straightforward. Understanding it clarifies the meaning of *f.* Suppose an investment of $1 yields a gross (before depreciation) return of ρ in the first period. Then, with a savings rate of $f, f\rho$ is reinvested and $(1 - f)\rho$ is consumed. With depreciation of δ in this period, the total amount invested in the second period equals $1 + f\rho - \delta$. Similarly, in the second period the return is $\rho(1 + f\rho - \delta)$ of which $f\rho(1 + f\rho - \delta)$

is reinvested and $(1 - f)\rho(1 + f\rho - \delta)$ is consumed. With depreciation of $\delta(1 + f\rho - \delta d)$ in the second period, the total amount invested in the third period equals $(1 + f\rho - \delta) + [f\rho(1 + f\rho - \delta)] - [\delta(1 + f\rho - \delta)] = (1 + f\rho - \delta)^2$, and so on. Consumption in period 1 is $(1 - f)\rho$, consumption in period 2 is $(1 - f)\rho(1 + f\rho - \delta)$, consumption in period 3 is $(1 - f)\rho(1 + f\rho - \delta)^2$, and so forth. This consumption stream is a perpetuity (with annual benefits of $(1 - f)\rho$ that grows at a constant rate, $f\rho - \delta$. Discounting this stream at p_z using equation (6A.7) gives:

$$\theta = \frac{\rho - f\rho}{p_z + \delta - f\rho}$$

In this formulation, r_z is the net return on capital after depreciation; that is:

$$\rho = r_z + \delta$$

Substituting for ρ in the preceding equation yields equation (10.9). For more information see Randolph M. Lyon, "Federal Discount Policy, the Shadow Price of Capital, and Challenges for Reforms," *Journal of Environmental Economics and Management*, 18, no. 2, part 2 (1990), S29–S50, Appendix I.

34. See Charles R. Hulten and Frank C. Wykoff, "The Measurement of Economic Depreciation," in *Depreciation, Inflation, and the Taxation of Income from Capital*, Charles R. Hulten, ed. (Washington, DC: Urban Institute Press, 1981), pp. 81–125. Note that we are concerned with real, economic depreciation—the reduction in the market value of capital invested—not accounting depreciation, which is of no relevance in CBA. It is perhaps important to note that the private sector does treat depreciation (capital cost allowance) as a cost (an expense) and deducts it from cash flows in order to arrive at net taxable income. But, because depreciation does not entail cash outlays, it is "added back" to net taxable income in order to obtain cash flows. Similarly, we add the depreciation rate to the net return on investment in order to obtain a gross rate of return. Here we assume implicitly that the average capital cost allowance rate equals the average physical rate at which assets depreciate. Although the accounting depreciation of the capital assets involved with any particular project may differ significantly from the economic depre-

ciation of these assets, it is probably reasonable to assume these rates are similar on average.

35. Bureau of the Census, *Statistical Abstract of the United States*, 1990 (Washington, DC: U.S. Government Printing Office, 1990), p. 743.

36. We assume that the proportion of the tax increase that displaces private investment equals the real gross investment rate, which we estimated earlier is 15 percent.

37. The net change in investment in year t, ΔI_t equals:

$$\Delta I_0 = 0.15(-325,000) = -48,750$$
$$\Delta I_t = 0.15(-20,000 + 40,000)$$
$$= 3,000 \ (t = 1, 2, 3, 4)$$
$$\Delta I_5 = 0.15(-20,000 + 40,000 + 20,000)$$
$$= 6,000$$

The net change in consumption in year t, ΔC_t, equals:

$$\Delta C_0 = 0.85(-325,000) = -276,250$$
$$\Delta C_t = 60,000 + 0.85(-20,000 + 40,000)$$
$$= 77,000 \ (t = 1, 2, 3, 4)$$
$$\Delta C_5 = 60,000 + 0.85(-20,000 + 40,000 + 20,000)$$
$$= 94,000$$

38. For a fascinating illustration of cost and benefit estimates that were politically influenced, see Steve H. Hanke and Richard A. Walker, "Benefit-Cost Analysis Reconsidered: An Evaluation of the Mid-State Project," *Water Resource Journal*, 10, no. 5 (1994), 324–329.

39. Put another way, the difference between the weights of successive periods in equation (10.1) is smaller for periods that are further into the future; that is, we have decreasing timing aversion.

40. George Loewenstein and Drazen Prelec, "Anomalies in Intertemporal Choice: Evidence and an Interpretation," *Quarterly Journal of Economics*, 107, no. 2 (1992), 573–597 at p. 574.

41. David Laibson, "Golden Eggs and Hyperbolic Discounting," *Quarterly Journal of Economics*, 112, no. 2 (1997), 443–477.

42. For example, analysis of *CANSIM* data shows that in Canada from 1992 through 1995, the real after-tax government long-term bond rate consistently exceeded the annual growth rate of per capita consumption.

43. $PV = [9,000,000(1 + 0.02)^{300}]/(1 + .08)^{300}$
    $= \$0.3214899$ million $= \$321,490.$

44. With constant discounting, impacts that arise in year n are weighted by the present value factor $a(n) = (1 + i)^{-n}$, which declines geometrically. Thus, impacts that occur far in the future have a low weight. For example, $1 in 100 years has an *NPV* of less than $0.01 using an SDR of more than 4 percent.

45. See, for example, Frank P. Ramsey, "A Mathematical Theory of Saving," *Economic Journal*, 38 (1928), 543–559, and Edmund Phelps, "The Golden Rule of Accumulation: A Fable for Growthmen," *American Economic Review*, 51, no. 4 (1961), 638–643.

46. For a discussion of this issue, see Daniel W. Bromley, "Entitlements, Missing Markets, and Environmental Uncertainty," *Journal of Environmental Economics and Management*, 17, no. 2 (1989), 181–194. Note, however, the willingness of people to pass inheritances to their children and to pay to preserve certain areas gives indirect standing to future generations.

47. Apparently, Ramsey did not share it either in practice.

48. The reasonableness of this is developed in Charles M. Harvey, "The Reasonableness of Non-Constant Discounting," *Journal of Public Economics*, 53, no. 1 (1994), 31–51. Harvey refers to declining discount rates as "slow discounting."

49. Martin Weitzman shows that $s = r_z[1 - Z(1 + 1/E)]$, where $s = $ the SDR; that is, the extra net consumption available at time $t + 1$ from a marginal decrease in consumption at time t, while keeping the costs of environmental damage at a constant fraction of GDP; $Z = $ environmental clean-up spending as a fraction of GDP; $E = $ the percentage reduction in environmental damage resulting from a 1 percent increase in clean-up spending; and r_z is the marginal return to private investment; see Martin Weitzman, "On the 'Environmental' Discount Rate," *Journal of Environmental Economics and Management*, 26, no. 2 (1994), 200–209.

50. Martin Weitzman, "Gamma Discounting," Harvard Institute of Economic Research Discussion Paper No. 1843, July (Revised December) 1998.

51. For a recent review of discounting in various U.S. government agencies, see Coleman Bazelon and Kent Smetters, "Discounting Inside the Washing-ton D.C. Beltway," *Journal of Economic Perspectives*, 13, no. 4 (1999), 213–228.

52. Richard O. Zerbe, Jr., and Dwight Dively, "How Municipal Governments Set Their Discount Rate: Do They Get It Right?" manuscript, University of Washington, October 1990.

53. Randolph Lyon provides an excellent review of U.S. federal discount rate policy to 1990. Interestingly, for water-related projects, which have been a focus of pork barrel politics for a long time, OMB required agencies to apply the estimated average cost of federal borrowing as determined by the Secretary of the Treasury—a nominal rate—to the *real* costs and benefits of water projects! See Office of Management and Budget, "Principles, Standards, and Procedures for Water and Related Land Resource Planning" and S.80-A of the U.S. Water Resources Development Act of 1974.

54. Robert Hartman indicates that when analysts at the CBO were considering how to estimate the marginal rate of time preference, they decided that they did not want a procedure that gave unstable estimates: "We did not want to have to explain why the MX missile was a good idea last month, but not now." See Robert W. Hartman, "One Thousand Points of Light Seeking a Number: A Case Study of CBO's Search for a Discount Rate Policy," *Journal of Environmental Economics and Management*, 18, no. 2, part 2 (1990), S3-S7, at S5.

55. In December 1998, the U.S. government's 10-year, constant-maturity bond was priced to yield 4.65 percent, whereas the rate of U.S. CPI inflation (all items) from December 1997 to December 1998 was 1.6 percent, yielding a 3 percent real discount rate. Source: bos.business.uuab.edu.

56. In the case of asset divestitures, both the OMB and CBO use comparable private-sector rates. If they did not do this, they would use a lower discount rate than the private sector, which would imply that the *NPV* of assets is higher in the public than in the private sector. Assuming no efficiency differences between public and private ownership, this would imply that the government would own all income-producing assets and never divest any of them; see Hartman, "One Thousand Points of Light Seeking a Number." For lease-purchase decisions, the OMB computes the *NPV* of leases using, in effect, the real rate on treasury bonds of

equal maturity to the lease payments (OMB A-11; OMB A-94). For projects with large intergenerational effects involving human life, the GAO uses an effective discount rate close to zero (GAO, 1991). Interestingly, as suggested in Appendix 10A, the CBO may use a higher discount rate if the net benefits of the proposed policy are highly correlated with GDP.

57. M. C. Weinstein, J. E. Siegel, M. R. Gold, M. S. Kamlet, and L. B. Russell, "Recommendations of the Panel on Cost-Effectiveness in Health and Medicine: Consensus Statement," *Journal of the American Medical Association,* 276, no. 5 (1996), 1253–1258.

58. Zerbe and Dively, "How Municipal Governments Set Their Discount Rate: Do They Get It Right?"

59. See Treasury Board Secretariat, *Benefit-Cost Analysis Guide for Regulatory Programs* (Ottawa, Ontario, 1976), Chapter 11: Discounting, available at the Web site: www.tbs-sct.gc.ca/tb/rad/english/cbgew11.html.

60. See, for example, Verne W. Loose, ed., *Guidelines for Benefit-Cost Analysis*, Environment and Land Use Committee Secretariat (Victoria, British Columbia: The Queen's Printer, 1977).

61. See British Columbia Crown Corporations Secretariat, *Multiple Account Evaluation Guidelines* (Victoria, British Columbia, 1993).

Appendix Notes

1. See, for example, Arrow and Lind, "Uncertainty and the Evaluation of Public Investment Decisions," who argue for using a risk-free rate, and Martin J. Bailey and Michael C. Jensen, "Risk and the Discount Rate for Private Investment," in *Studies in the Theory of Capital Markets*, Michael C. Jensen, ed. (New York: Praeger, 1972), pp. 269–293, who argue in favor of using a rate that varies with risk.

2. For the implications of the CAPM to private-sector capital budgeting, see Mark E. Rubinstein, "A Mean-Variance Synthesis of Corporate Financial Theory," *Journal of Finance*, 28, no. 1 (1973), 167–181.

3. The size of this premium is surprisingly large; see Rajnish Mehra and Edward Prescott, "The Equity Premium: A Puzzle," *Journal of Monetary Economics*, 15, no. 2 (1985), 145–161.

4. Alternatively, we may use the following decision rule. If the expected internal rate of return (IRR) of the proposed investment exceeds the expected rate of return for an investment in this risk class, then one should proceed with the investment. If the IRR is less than the appropriate risk-adjusted rate of return, then one should not proceed with the investment. In this particular example, we would proceed with the investment if its expected IRR is greater than 7 percent and would not proceed if its expected IRR is less than 7 percent.

5. See Coleman Bazelon and Kent Smetters, "Discounting Inside the Washington D.C. Beltway," p. 223.

6. See Frank Ramsey, "A Mathematical Theory of Saving"; Edmund Phelps, "The Golden Rule of Accumulation: A Fable for Growthmen"; Stephen Marglin, "The Social Rate of Discount and the Optimal Rate of Investment," *Quarterly Journal of Economics,* 77, no. 1 (1963), 95–111; and Kenneth J. Arrow," Intergenerational Equity and the Rate of Discount in Long-Term Social Investment," 1995, unpublished paper given to the IEA World Congress.

7. See Frank Ramsey, "A Mathematical Theory of Saving."

8. See Kenneth Arrow, "Intergenerational Equity and the Rate of Discount in Long-Term Social Investment."

9. Erhun Kula, "Derivation of the Social Time Preference Rates for the United States and Canada," *Quarterly Journal of Economics* (1984), 873–882.

10. Using quarterly data from DRI's CITIBASE on real consumption expenditures from 1947 to 1998, averaged to annual data and divided by the population, we estimated the following model (*t*-statistics in parentheses):

$$\ln(\text{real consumption expenditure/population})$$
$$= -35.05 + 0.0225 \text{ time}; R^2 = .99$$
$$(54.3) \quad (68.7)$$

11. Robert J. Brent, *Applied Cost-Benefit Analysis* (Brookfield, VT: Edward Elgar, 1994).

12. Kenneth J. Arrow, W. R. Cline, K.-G. Maler, M. Munasinghe, R. Squitieri, and J. E. Stiglitz, "Intertemporal Equity, Discounting and Economic

Efficiency," in James P. Bruce et al., eds., *Climate Change 1995* (Cambridge, United Kingdom: Cambridge University Press, 1995), pp. 128–144.

13. The estimated model (*t*-statistics in parentheses) is:

ln(real GDP/population)
$= -30.60 + 0.02$ time; $R^2 = .99$
(44.7)   (58.9)

14. An *F* test rejected the hypothesis that these two coefficients are the same.

15. If the loans for the project are obtained from persons residing outside the community, one might believe that benefits and costs accruing to these persons are irrelevant to its investment decisions and, therefore, ignore them in computing the project's net present value. Our computations do not allow for this possibility. Also, recall that the Harberger approach implicitly assumes a closed economy. If there is the possibility of borrowing from abroad, there will be less than complete crowding out of private investment. Private investment may also be less than completely crowded out if there are unemployed resources in the economy.

16. More precisely, the annual payments are $75,066.81. Rounding will result in slightly incorrect end-of-year balances.

CHAPTER

11

VALUING IMPACTS FROM OBSERVED BEHAVIOR

Demonstrations

Throughout this book, we have emphasized that the key concept in valuing the positive and negative outcomes (impacts) of a policy is willingness-to-pay as measured by changes in social surplus. To estimate changes in social surplus, we needed to know the shape of relevant supply and demand curves. Earlier, we typically assumed that these were known. In practice, however, these curves are usually unknown. The analyst has to either estimate them in order to give precise measures of benefits and costs or find an alternative means of valuing policy impacts.

Analysts in fact typically face a continuum of possibilities. At one end of this continuum are policy impacts on goods that are traded in well-functioning, competitive markets. At the other end are policy impacts on goods that are rarely traded in markets—impacts, for example, on health and safety, pollution levels, and access to scenic areas. In between are impacts on commodities that are traded in markets with important distortions such as monopoly power, information asymmetries, and externalities.

Where markets work well, analysts know at least one point on the demand and supply curves, represented by the observed intersection of market price and quantity exchanged, but still have to estimate these curves to measure either existing social surplus or changes in social surplus. Remember from Chapters 3 and 4 that changes in social surplus are approximated by areas, such as triangles, rectangles, and trapezoids. Conceptually, estimation can be done using relatively standard econometric techniques, but only when suitable data are available.

As we have seen, however, the rationale for much CBA is that markets are nonexistent or imperfect. In these situations, the analyst may not have even one point on the appropriate demand or supply curve, which makes it particularly difficult to estimate the impacts.

Nonetheless, as we show in this and the next four chapters, all is not lost! These chapters describe practical ways to estimate the impacts of a policy when estimates of the appropriate demand and supply curves are not readily available. In this chapter, we focus on estimating benefits and costs on the basis of *demonstrations* or *pilot programs*.

(We use the two terms interchangeably; both remind us that the purpose of the project is to learn whether the program "works.")

The chapter first presents a brief discussion of using demonstration projects to obtain estimates of benefits and costs. It then explores alternative ways in which these demonstrations might be structured. The remainder of the chapter shows the value of demonstrations by describing their use in cost-benefit analyses of employment and training programs. The observed impacts of employment and training demonstrations have been extensively used in conducting CBAs. The chapter concludes by examining actual CBAs of employment and training demonstration programs that were targeted at welfare recipients. The chapter provides numerous illustrations of how concepts developed earlier in this book can be used in actual cost-benefit analyses.

WHY CONDUCT DEMONSTRATION PROJECTS?

In Chapter 1, we noted that the fourth basic step in conducting a CBA is to predict impacts over the life of a project. Demonstration projects can help do this. They provide a straightforward method for measuring impacts in the case of proposed programs that provide services to people—for example, health, education, training, employment, housing, and welfare programs. The method works by setting up a small-scale replica or demonstration of the proposed program. To understand why demonstration projects are almost exclusively limited to testing programs that provide people-oriented services, just try to think about how to test a proposed physical investment, such as a new dam, on a small-scale, pilot basis.

The idea behind demonstration projects is to see if the tested program works before it is adopted on a widespread basis. *Ex post* findings from the demonstration, which are based on observing program impacts, can be plugged into an *ex ante* analysis that predicts benefits and costs for the full-scale program. For example, parameters estimated from the Seattle-Denver negative income tax experiment, a prominent demonstration program, have been used to predict the costs and benefits of proposed changes in the U.S. welfare system.[1]

An advantage of conducting a CBA of a demonstration project is that if it turns out that certain aspects of the program need adjustment, this can be done before the program is implemented on a widespread basis. Even more importantly, if it turns out that the program is a bad idea because costs exceed benefits, it can be scrapped before it is expanded and interest groups form to protect it.

Although the small scale of pilot projects offers important advantages, there are also potential disadvantages. First, the impacts of a small-scale demonstration program may not readily translate to a fully implemented large-scale program. For example, although it may be fairly easy to find jobs for graduates of a demonstration program that retrains unemployed workers as electricians if the program has only a few graduates, doing so may be far more difficult if large numbers of unemployed persons graduate from a full-scale program and seek employment in the same geographic area. Moreover, marketwide effects, such as those on the level of wages, may be missed by a small-scale demonstration.

More subtly, some policy innovations may cause changes in community attitudes and norms; and these changes, in turn, may result in feedback effects that influence the innovation's success. Furthermore, program success may depend on information diffusion. For example, a training program that is available to all unemployed persons in a particular community will become well known to both the unemployed and employers. As a result, the attitudes of the unemployed toward entering training and the decisions of employers concerning hiring the graduates of training programs could both be affected. Such effects are unlikely to occur if only a subset of the unemployed is allowed to participate. Thus, it has been suggested that feedback effects and information diffusion will not occur unless the innovation is adopted on a large scale and, hence, will be missed by small-scale pilot projects.[2] However, there is virtually no evidence on how important such effects are in practice.

A second and related disadvantage of small-scale demonstration programs is uncertainty concerning their *external validity*. That is, there is no assurance that findings from the evaluation, even though valid for the group of persons who participated in the demonstration program, can be generalized to any other group. The reason for this is that personal and community characteristics interact in complex ways with the services provided by a demonstration program. As a result, the program may more effectively serve some persons than others. For example, findings for a training program for unemployed, male, blue-collar workers who live in a community with low unemployment may provide little information concerning how well the program would work for unemployed female welfare recipients who live in a community with high unemployment. For this reason, some demonstration programs are tested on a variety of different groups in different locations.

ALTERNATIVE EVALUATION DESIGNS

CBAs of pilot projects require comparisons between alternatives: The existing environment is compared to the proposed program being tested by the demonstration, and impact is measured as differences in outcomes between the two situations.[3] The term *internal validity* refers to whether this measured difference can be accurately attributed to the program being evaluated. Internal validity, in turn, depends on the particular way in which the comparison between the existing environment and the proposed program is made. There are numerous ways in which this comparison can be made. Researchers usually refer to the specific scheme used for making comparisons in order to measure impacts as an *evaluation design*.

Diagrams that represent five commonly used evaluation designs,[4] as well as brief summaries of the advantages and disadvantages of each of these designs, appear in Table 11.1. In these diagrams, the symbol O represents an outcome measurement point, X represents a treatment point, and R indicates that subjects were assigned randomly to treatment and control groups.

The evaluation designs that are listed in Table 11.1 are not the only ones that exist. There are numerous others. But these designs provide a good sampling of the major alternatives. So that we can make our discussion of them as concrete as possible, we assume that they all pertain to alternative ways in which a pilot program for training the

TABLE 11.1 Five Commonly Used Evaluation Designs			
Type	*Structure*	*Major Advantages*	*Major Disadvantages*
Design 1: Comparison of net changes between treatment and true control groups	$R: O_1 \; X \; O_2$ $R: O_3 \qquad O_4$	Random assignment guards against systematic differences between control and treatment groups so highest internal validity	Direct and ethical costs of random assignment; as with all evaluations of demonstrations, external validity may be limited
Design 2: Comparison of posttreatment outcomes between true control and treatment groups	$R: \; X \; O_2$ $R: \qquad O_4$	Random assignment guards against systematic differences between control and treatment groups so high internal validity	Direct and ethical costs of random assignment; danger that a failure of randomization will not be detected
Design 3: Simple before/after comparison	$O_1 \; X \; O_2$	Often feasible and relatively inexpensive; reasonable when factors other than treatment are unlikely to affect outcome	Does not control for other factors that may cause change
Design 4: Comparison of posttreatment outcomes between quasicontrol and treatment groups	$X \; O_1$ O_2	Allows for possibility of statistically controlling for factors other than treatment	Danger of sample selection bias caused by systematic differences between treatment and quasicontrol groups
Design 5: Comparison of net changes between treatment and quasicontrol group	$O_1 \; X \; O_2$ $O_3 \qquad O_4$	Allows for possibility of statistically controlling for factors other than treatment; permits detection of measurable differences between treatment and quasicontrol groups	Danger of sample selection bias caused by systematic differences between treatment and quasicontrol group in terms of nonmeasurable differences

O—observation
X—treatment
R—random assignment

Source: Based on notation introduced by Donald T. Campbell and Julian Stanley, *Experimental and Quasi-Experimental Designs for Research* (Chicago: Rand McNally College Publishing Company, 1963).

unemployed might be evaluated. In this context, "being in the treatment group" means enrollment in the training program.

Design 1: Classical Experimental Design

Design 1 is a classical experimental design. The symbols indicate that unemployed persons are randomly allocated between a treatment group and a control (or comparison) group. Members of the treatment group can receive services from the pilot training program, whereas persons in the control group cannot. The way this might work in actual practice is that once the pilot program is put into place, unemployed persons are notified of its existence. Some of these persons apply to participate in it. A computer is used, in effect, to flip a fair coin: Heads the applicant is selected as a member of the treatment group and, consequently, becomes eligible to participate in the program; tails the applicant becomes a member of the control group. Controls are not eligible to participate in the program but can receive whatever other services are available for the unemployed.

The procedure just described for establishing treatment and control groups is called *random assignment*.[5] Random assignment evaluations of pilot projects of social programs—for instance, a training program—are often called *social experiments*.

To see how well the pilot program works, data on outcomes are collected for both the treatment group and the control group, both before the treatment is administered and afterward. Using the collected data, members of the experimental and control groups are compared. For example, the earnings of the two groups can be compared sometime after the training is completed to measure the size of the program's impact on earnings.[6]

Of the five design schemes summarized in Table 11.1, design 1 is the best for many types of evaluations. Its major advantage is the use of random assignment. Because of random assignment, the characteristics of people in the treatment and control groups should be similar, varying only by chance alone. As a result, random assignment helps ensure that the evaluation has internal validity; that is, members of the experimental groups can be directly compared in terms of such outcomes as earnings, and any differences that are found between them can be reasonably attributed to the treatment.

Sometimes, however, random assignment may be impractical or infeasible.[7] One reason for this is the resources required to assign individuals randomly to treatment and control groups. Generally, however, these resource costs are quite small.

A second reason concerns the notion of experimenting on human beings. For example, randomization implies that some persons—those assigned to the comparison group—will be denied services under the demonstration program. It is important to recognize, however, that if a program has only limited resources, some potential program participants will inevitably be denied services, and random assignment (which operates very much like a lottery) may be as fair a way to do this as any. A more serious ethical issue is raised by the possibility that some experimental treatments may actually harm some members of the treatment group. For example, as cost-benefit findings reported later in this chapter indicate, some training programs have actually been found to reduce the incomes of participants. However, this was not the intent of the program and there was no way to know in advance that this result would occur. Not knowing the impacts of a social experiment in advance would seem to constitute an ethical justification for conducting the experiment.

Design 2: Classical Experimental Design without Baseline Data

Design 2 is similar to design 1 in that random assignment is also used to assign individuals between the treatment and control groups, and both are referred to as *experimental designs*. The difference between the two designs is that collection of pretreatment, baseline information on members of the treatment and control groups is not part of design 2 but is part of design 1. The problem with not collecting pretreatment information is that there is no way of checking whether the treatment and control groups are basically similar or dissimilar.

For the comparison between the two groups to measure program effects accurately, the groups should, of course, be as similar as possible. But, as previously mentioned, they could be dissimilar by chance alone. This is more likely if each group only has a few hundred members, as is sometimes the case in social experiments. It is also possible that those running an experiment fail to implement the random assignment process correctly. If information is available on pretreatment status—for example, on pretreatment earnings—statistical adjustments can be made to make the comparison between the treatment and the control groups more valid. Hence, there is usually less certainty concerning internal validity with design 2 than design 1.

Design 3: Before and After Comparison

Design 3 is by far the worst of the five designs, relying as it does on a simple *before and after comparison* of the same group of individuals. For example, the earnings of a group of individuals that went through a training program are compared with their earnings before going through the program. The problem with this design is that there is no information on what would have happened without the program. Consequently, there is no way to ensure internal validity. For example, the average earnings of people going into a training program are likely to be very low if most of these people are unemployed at the time of entry. That, perhaps, is why they decided to go into the program in the first place. Even without the program, however, many of them might have found jobs eventually. If so, their average earnings would have gone up over time even if the program did not exist. With a before and after comparison, this increase in earnings would be incorrectly attributed to the program.

Before and after comparisons, however, do offer certain advantages. They provide a comparatively inexpensive way of conducting evaluations. Moreover, when valid information is not available for a control group, a before and after comparison may be the only feasible way of conducting an evaluation. Such a comparison is obviously most valid when nonprogram factors are not expected to affect the outcomes of interest (e.g., earnings) or can be taken into account through statistical adjustments.

Design 4: Nonexperimental Comparison without Baseline Data

Design 4 is based on a comparison of two different groups, one that has gone through a program and another that has not. Membership in the two groups is not determined by random assignment, however. For example, the comparison group could be made up of people who originally applied for training but ultimately decided not to participate. Because such a comparison group is not selected through random assignment, it is sometimes called a *quasicontrol group*. As previously discussed, use of a quasicontrol group may be necessary when obtaining a comparison group through random assignment seems to be costly, raises serious ethical issues, or would cause potentially important community effects to be ignored.

Unfortunately, with this design there is no means of controlling for those differences between the two groups that existed prior to the treatment and, hence, no way to ensure internal validity. Perhaps, for example, at the time of application for training, those who ultimately went through the program had been unemployed for a longer period of time than persons in the comparison group, suggesting that in the absence of training they would have fared worse in the job market than members of the comparison group. But if at the end of training, it is observed that they actually did just as well as persons in the comparison group, this suggests the training had an impact: It pulled the trainees up even with the comparison group. However, with design 4, there is no way to know the difference in the length of unemployment prior to training. As a result, it would just be observed that, after training, members of the treatment group were doing no better than people in the comparison group. This finding is attributable to a bias known as *sample selection bias* that results because systematic differences between the treatment and quasicontrol group are not, indeed cannot be, taken into account. In this instance, sample selection bias is quite important because it could lead to the incorrect conclusion that the training made no difference.

Design 5: Nonexperimental Comparison with Baseline Data

Design 5 utilizes both a treatment group and a control group. In addition, both pretreatment and posttreatment data are collected. This provides information on how the treatment group differed from the comparison group prior to the training. This information can be used in a statistical analysis to control for pretreatment differences between the treatment and control groups. For this reason, design 5 offers greater opportunity to obtain internal validity than either designs 3 or 4.

Even so, because this design does not randomly assign individuals to the treatment and control groups, a major problem occurs if people in the treatment and the comparison groups differ from one another in ways that cannot be measured readily. Then it becomes very difficult to adjust statistically for differences between the two groups. Perhaps, for example, unemployed persons who enter training are more motivated than unemployed persons who do not. If so, they might receive higher earnings over time even without the training. If analysts cannot somehow take account of this difference in motivation—in practice, sometimes they can, but often they cannot—they may incorrectly conclude that higher posttraining earnings received by the trainees are due to the training when, in fact, they are really due to greater motivation on the part of the trainees. In the evaluation literature, such a situation creates a threat to internal validity that is known as the *selection problem*.[8]

The occurrence of selection problems can be greatly reduced by using design 1 or 2. The reason is that when random assignment is used, people assigned to the treatment group should not differ from members of the comparison group in terms of characteristics such as motivation except by chance alone. Because of this advantage, an increasing number of demonstration projects that embody experimental designs have been conducted since the early 1960s.[9] Indeed, over $1 billion has been spent in conducting design 1 studies since the late 1960s.[10] However, large numbers of demonstrations that utilize nonexperimental designs, such as designs 3, 4, and 5, also continue to be conducted.

CBAs OF DEMONSTRATION PROJECTS

Although numerous demonstrations of programs that provide services to people have been conducted, formal CBAs have been carried out for only a minority of them. Sometimes the evaluations of particular demonstrations have focused instead on only one or two outcomes of interest. For example, demonstrations in the housing or health areas might be mainly concerned with whether the tested program can be administered effectively or whether housing or health status can be improved and, thus, no attempt may be made to measure other benefits and costs associated with the program. In a few relatively rare instances, demonstrations have been used to estimate demand and supply relationships. Though these estimates can be used in CBAs, the demonstrations themselves were not subjected to CBA. Two especially important examples of such demonstrations are described in Exhibits 11.1 and 11.2.

EXHIBIT 11.1

How the consumption of medical care changes as a function of the cost of care to those who use it is central to many public policy questions, especially those pertaining to universal health insurance. Between 1974 and 1977, the federal government funded a social experiment, the Rand Health Insurance Experiment, at six sites. Analysis of data from this experiment by Willard Manning and colleagues suggests that the price elasticity of demand for health care services is in the range of -0.1 to -0.2.

Source: Willard G. Manning, Joseph P. Newhouse, Naihua Duan, Emmett B. Keeler, Aileen Leibowitz, and Susan Marquis, "Health Insurance and the Demand for Medical Care: Evidence from a Randomized Experiment," *American Economic Review,* 77, no. 3 (1987), 251–277.

EXHIBIT 11.2

During the late 1960s and early 1970s, the U.S. government funded four income maintenance experiments, which focused on how income transfers affected the supply of labor (equivalently the demand for leisure) of low-income persons. Data from these experiments were used to obtain estimates of wage and income elasticities. Based on averages of separate estimates from the numerous studies that have relied on data from these experiments, Gary Burtless reported the following elasticity values:

	Married Men	*Married Women*	*Single Mothers*
Compensated Wage Elasticity	0.09	0.24	0.14
Uncompensated Wage Elasticity	−0.02	0.17	−0.04
Income Elasticity	−0.11	−0.07	−0.18

Source: Gary Burtless, "The Work Response to Guaranteed Income: A Survey of Experimental Evidence," in Alicia Munnell, ed., *Lessons from the Income Maintenance Experiments* (Boston: Federal Reserve Bank of Boston, 1986), 22–52.

CBAs OF EMPLOYMENT AND TRAINING DEMONSTRATIONS: AN INTRODUCTION

Almost all the demonstrations that have been subjected to CBA have tested programs that attempt to increase the employment or earnings of unemployed or low-skilled workers. In recent years, many of these demonstrations have focused on the welfare population. The services provided by these government-funded demonstration programs have varied considerably but have included job search assistance, remedial education, vocational training, subsidizing private-sector employers in exchange for hiring program participants, and the direct provision of public-sector jobs to participants. Although the individual programs that provide such services often differ greatly from one another, such programs are often referred to as *employment and training (E&T) programs.*[11]

E&T programs are often viewed as investments in the *human capital* of participants—that is, attempts to improve their skills and abilities. Thus, the major economic rationale for funding them revolves around assertions that E&T programs help correct market or institutional failures that cause underinvestments in human capital. For example, low-income people may not have the resources to invest in certain kinds of training, such as classroom vocational training. Their access to private financing may be limited by a lack of collateral and a high risk of default. Moreover, public training may be justified as compensating for inadequacies in the public education system or as providing a second chance to those who prematurely terminate formal schooling because of imperfect foresight or a high subjective rate of time preference. In addition, E&T programs may help correct imperfect information among participants about human capital investment opportunities by guiding them into activities that yield the highest payoff for them.

A quite distinct rationale for E&T programs results from a widely accepted value that all else equal it is better to receive income from employment than from transfer programs. To meet this goal, increasingly stringent requirements to participate in E&T programs have been imposed on welfare recipients in recent years.

THE CBA FRAMEWORK IN THE EDUCATION AND TRAINING CONTEXT

The basic CBA accounting framework has been described in previous chapters. However, different policy areas have developed variations of the basic CBA framework that address issues specific to each area. The particular accounting framework that is used today in conducting most CBAs of E&T programs was originally developed during the late 1960s and refined in the early 1980s. A stylized version of this framework appears in Table 11.2. Although details concerning the specifics of the framework vary somewhat from one E&T CBA to another, depending on the specific nature of the services provided, the table lists those benefit and cost components that are typically measured.

This framework offers several advantages: It is readily understandable to policymakers; by displaying benefits and costs from the perspectives of both participants and nonparticipants, it suggests some of the distributional implications of the program being evaluated; and, possibly most important, because measures of each cost-benefit component listed in Table 11.2 can actually be obtained from demonstration data, it is operationally feasible. Indeed, as will be seen, it is far easier to find shortcomings in the framework than to suggest practical alternatives to it.

Table 11.2 presents the benefit and cost impact categories of a stylized E&T demonstration. Plus signs indicate anticipated sources of benefits and minus signs indicate anticipated sources of costs from different perspectives. The first column (A) shows aggregate benefits and costs from the perspective of society as a whole. The remaining columns show the distribution of benefits and costs to the two groups that are typically relevant in assessing E&T programs: participants or clients served by the demonstration program (B); and nonparticipants, including taxpayers who pay for the program (C).

	TABLE 11.2 Stylized Cost-Benefit Framework of E&T Demonstrations		
	Society (A) (B + C)	Participant (B)	Nonparticipant (C)
Output produced by participant			
In-program output	+	0	+
Gross earnings	+	+	0
Fringe benefits	+	+	0
Participant work-related expenditures			
Tax payments	0	−	+
Expenditures on child care, transportation, etc.	−	−	0
Use of transfer programs by participants			
AFDC payments	0	−	+
Other transfer payments	0	−	+
Program operating costs	+	0	+
Use of support programs by participants			
Support services received by participants	−	0	−
Allowances received by participants	0	+	−
Program operating costs	−	0	−

Benefits and costs to society are simply the algebraic sum of benefits and costs to participants and to nonparticipants because society is the sum of these two groups. Hence, the table implies that if a demonstration program causes transfer payments received by participants (e.g., unemployment compensation or AFDC receipts) to decline, this should be regarded as a savings or benefit to nonparticipant taxpayers, a cost to program participants (albeit one that may be offset by earnings), and neither a benefit nor a cost to society as a whole but simply income transferred from one segment of the population to another.

This approach is consistent with the standard one used in CBA. As we have seen, in standard CBA "a dollar is a dollar," no matter to whom it accrues. Thus, in Table 11.2, a dollar gained or lost by an E&T participant is treated identically to a dollar gained or lost by a nonparticipant. Consequently, if an E&T program caused the transfer dollars received by participants to fall, this would be viewed as not affecting society as a whole because the loss to participants would be fully offset by benefits to nonparticipants in the form of reductions in government budgetary outlays.

Typically, however, E&T participants have much lower incomes, on average, than nonparticipants. For reasons that will be discussed in detail in Chapter 18, a case can sometimes be made for treating the gains and losses of low-income persons differently than those of higher-income persons. This is almost never done in CBAs of E&T demonstrations, however. Instead, as can be seen in Table 11.2, they simply lay out the results so that the distributional consequences of a particular program can be observed.

Table 11.2 divides the benefits and costs associated with E&T demonstrations into four major categories. The first two of these categories pertain to effects that result if a demonstration increases the work effort or productivity of participants—for example, by providing them work in a public-sector job where they perform useful services, providing them skill training, or helping them find private-sector employment through job search assistance. On the one hand, the value of the output they produce will rise, which in the private sector should be reflected by increases in earnings and fringe benefits. On the other hand, if hours at work rise, expenditures on child care and transportation will also increase. And if earnings rise, tax payments will also increase. The third major cost-benefit category in Table 11.2 pertains to decreases in dependency on transfer payments that may result from an E&T program. Such reductions in dependency should cause both the amount of payments distributed under transfer programs and the cost of administering these programs to fall. The fourth major category refers to expenditures on support services for program participants. Obviously, such expenditures increase when a demonstration program is implemented. However, this increase will be partially offset because participants in the demonstration programs no longer need to obtain similar services from existing programs.

Three of the subcategories listed in Table 11.2 pertain to job-related expenditures and require clarification: participant expenditures on child care, transportation, and so forth; support services received by participants; and allowances received by participants. The first of these subcategories refers to total job-required outlays by E&T participants on such items as child care, transportation, and uniforms. The subcategory of support services pertains to the direct provision of such goods by a government agency, and the allowances subcategory refers to government reimbursement of job-required expenditures by participants. Table 11.2 reflects the philosophy that *all* program-induced increases in job-required expenditures should be treated identically: as resource costs to society engendered in producing goods and services. Of course, to the extent the government directly provides support services to participants, client outlays for this purpose will be smaller. In a CBA, this would be reflected by a smaller dollar amount appearing under the participant expenditures on job-related outlays and a larger dollar amount appearing under the subcategory of support services received by participants. Job-required expenditures are further discussed later in the chapter.

Benefits and costs that are sometimes referred to as *intangible effects* but are rarely, if ever, actually estimated in evaluations of E&T programs do not appear in Table 11.2. Examples of intangible effects include the values of leisure forgone and satisfaction gained from substitution of work for transfer payments. Almost by definition, such impacts are very difficult to measure. In the next section, we examine the implications of not measuring them.

CONCEPTUAL ISSUES IN CONDUCTING CBAs OF EDUCATION AND TRAINING DEMONSTRATIONS

We now turn to a number of limitations of the accounting framework illustrated in Table 11.2. As will be seen, these arise from the fact that the framework is not completely consistent with the theoretical concepts discussed in Chapters 3 and 4. Because these limitations can result in incorrect policy conclusions, it is useful to compare some of the operational measures of benefits and costs typically used in conducting CBAs of E&T demonstrations with their conceptually correct counterparts. In doing this, it is helpful to examine measures of benefits and costs associated with E&T programs separately from the participant and the nonparticipant perspectives, keeping in mind that social benefits and costs are simply the algebraic sum of benefits received and costs incurred by these two groups.

The Participant Perspective

Two Alternative Measures The standard E&T framework, as Table 11.2 suggests, estimates participant net benefits as net changes in the incomes of program clients—that is, as increases in earnings that result from the program minus decreases in transfer payments and increases in work-related expenditures that result from the program. However, as Chapters 3 and 4 emphasize, the conceptually appropriate measure is net changes in the surplus of program participants, not net changes in their incomes. As will be seen, the difference between these two measures can be substantial.

The extent to which the two measures diverge depends on the precise mechanism through which E&T programs influence earnings. For instance, E&T programs may either increase the hourly wage rates of participants (e.g., by imparting new skills) or increase the hours they work (e.g., by aiding in job search or increasing the obligations that must be met in exchange for transfer payments). Numerous E&T demonstrations have been found to increase hours worked. Meaningful impacts on wage rates are more rare but have occurred. In the discussion that follows, we compare the two alternative measures of net benefits from the perspective of several different hypothetical E&T participants, each of whom is assumed to respond differently to the program.

The first participant is represented in Figure 11.1. Curve S is the labor supply schedule of this participant, an individual who is assumed to have successfully participated in an E&T program that increased her market wage from W_0 to W_1.[12] As a result, the individual increases her hours of work from h_0 to h_1. In the diagram, area A represents the increase in both participant surplus and earnings that would have resulted from the wage increase even if the participant had not increased her hours. Area B represents an additional increase in both participant surplus and earnings, one resulting from the increase in hours that actually takes place. Finally, area C represents a further increase in earnings that results from the hours increase. However, this last increase in earnings is fully offset by the individual's loss of leisure.[13] Hence, no change in participant surplus is associated with it. Consequently, although areas A, B, and C are counted as benefits when using the net income change measure of E&T effects, only A and B are counted in the conceptually more correct net surplus change measure.

In Figure 11.1, the first E&T participant was assumed to be in equilibrium both before entering the program and upon completing the program; that is, it was assumed that at both points she was able to work the number of hours she desired to work at her market wage. Many E&T participants, however, are not in equilibrium prior to entering a program. Indeed, many persons participate in E&T specifically because they are unemployed.

Such a situation is assumed to face the second participant, an individual who is represented in Figure 11.2. In this figure, the individual has a market wage of W_0 prior to

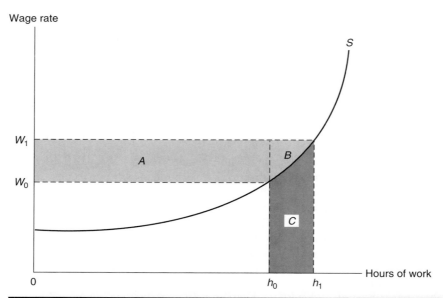

FIGURE 11.1 Welfare Change Resulting from an Induced Wage Increase

entering E&T but is able to obtain only h_0 hours of work instead of the desired h_1 hours. Assume now that, although participating in E&T does not affect the participant's market wage, it does permit him to increase his hours of work from h_0 to h_1. As a result of this hours increase, the participant enjoys an earnings increase equal to areas $A + B$ but a surplus increase equal to only area A. Thus, once again, the net income change measure of E&T benefits is larger than the conceptually more appropriate net surplus change measure.

Our findings for the first two E&T participants imply that although any earnings increases that result from wage increases should be fully credited to the program, only part of earnings increases resulting from hours increases should be credited. In Figure 11.3, we turn to a more complex situation facing a third E&T participant: a welfare recipient who, as a condition for receiving her welfare grant, is required to work at a public-sector job for h^* hours each month, where h^* is determined by dividing her grant amount by the minimum wage. Similar arrangements, which are often referred to as *workfare*, have frequently been used in administering welfare programs. The welfare recipient's market wage is assumed to equal W^m, the minimum wage, whereas curve S_0 represents her supply schedule in the absence of workfare. (Ignore curve S_1 for the moment.) Figure 11.3 implies that in the absence of workfare, W_0^r, the welfare recipient's reservation wage (i.e., the lowest wage at which she would be willing to work) would exceed her market wage. Thus, she would choose not to work.

Now imagine that the welfare recipient is enrolled in workfare in two distinct steps. In the first step, her welfare grant is withdrawn. This loss of income would cause her labor supply curve to shift to the right from S_0 to S_1. As a consequence, her reservation wage would fall from W_0^r to W_1^r, a value below the minimum wage. In the second step,

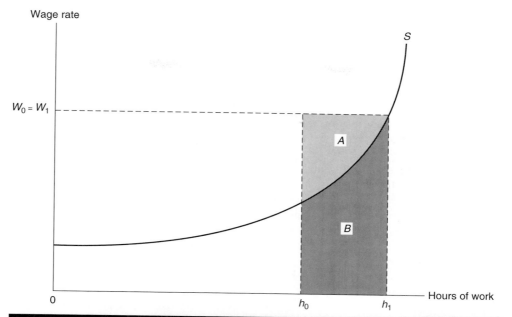

FIGURE 11.2 Welfare Change Due to an Induced Increase in Hours Worked

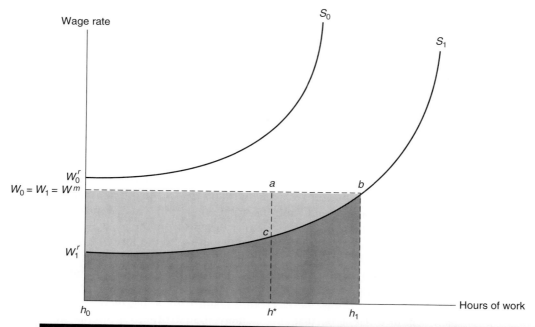

FIGURE 11.3 Welfare Change Due to Workfare

she is offered the opportunity to work h^* hours at a public-sector workfare job at a wage of W^m. In other words, she is given the opportunity to earn back her welfare grant, which in the diagram corresponds to the rectangular area $W^m a h^* h_0$.[14] Because W^m exceeds W_1^r, the participant represented in Figure 11.3 would prefer workfare to not working at all.

If the welfare recipient accepts the workfare offer, then the net income change and net surplus change measures of program impacts have quite different implications. Assuming she has no opportunities to work in addition to h^*, her net income would be unchanged from what it was prior to the program; consequently, the measure based on changes in net income would imply that she is no worse off. However, the net surplus change measure does imply that she is worse off. Specifically, her net surplus would decline by an amount represented by the area $W_1^r c h^* h_0$, an amount equal to the value that the recipient places on her lost leisure.[15]

So far, the focus has been on benefits received by and costs incurred by welfare recipients while they are participating in workfare. Now let us consider a different situation: the benefits and costs associated with a participant's move from welfare to a regular private-sector job. This is, of course, one of the major objectives of programs such as workfare, and Figure 11.3 implies that the program would in fact have the desired effect on the participant. Although in the absence of the workfare she would prefer not to work at all, given a choice between participating in workfare (point a) or working at a regular minimum-wage job (point b), the participant would select the latter. By restricting her hours to h^*, workfare causes the participant to be "off her labor supply curve." Only by finding a regular job can she work h_1 hours, the number of hours she would desire to work at the minimum wage. In actual practice, the participant might move directly from welfare to the job upon being confronted with the workfare requirement or, alternatively, she might first participate in workfare while seeking private-sector employment.

A comparison of the net income change measure of workfare's impact on a participant who moves directly to private-sector employment with the corresponding conceptually correct net surplus change measure yields an interesting finding. On the one hand, the net income change measure implies that the participant represented in Figure 11.3 enjoys a net gain. Her transfer payments fall from $W^m a h^* h_0$ to zero, but her earnings increase from zero to $W^m b h_1 h_0$, resulting in a net increase in income of $a b h_1 h^*$. On the other hand, the participant suffers a net loss of surplus because her gain from working, area $W^m b W_1^r$, is exceeded by the value of her lost transfer payments, area $W^m a h^* h_0$. Thus, under the circumstances represented in Figure 11.3, the net income change measure suggests a conclusion that is the diametrical opposite from that implied by the conceptually more correct net surplus change measure.

In measuring the impacts of E&T programs from the participant perspective, three rules can be drawn from the preceding analyses of the three illustrative E&T participants. First, the full value of reductions in transfer payments should be counted as a cost to E&T participants. Second, the full value of increases in earnings that result from wage rate increases should be counted as a benefit to E&T participants. Third, only part of the value of earnings increases that result from hours increases should be counted as a benefit to E&T participants; namely, the part that represents an increase in participant surplus should be counted, whereas the part that is offset by reductions in leisure should not.

In conducting CBAs of E&T demonstrations, the first two of these rules are straightforward to implement. Implementing the third rule, however, requires an estimate of the percentage of earnings changes attributable to increases in hours that should be counted. A procedure that can be used to obtain such an estimate has been developed by David Greenberg.[16]

Improvements in Self-Esteem   It is sometimes suggested that E&T programs can improve the self-esteem of E&T participants—for example, by imparting skills that are valued in the job market. If so, this is a program benefit that should, in principle, be included in CBAs of E&T programs, although it is obviously difficult to do so directly. However, to the extent an increase in the self-esteem of an E&T participant manifests itself as an increase in willingness-to-work (e.g., because he or she is less concerned about rejection when seeking employment), the participant's labor supply curve will shift to the right. The resulting gain in surplus is represented graphically as the gap between the old and new supply curves below the market wage upon completion of training. Program benefits that are measured as increases in participant earnings will also be larger than if the curve does not shift. However, the increase in earnings will not correspond very well to the increase in surplus. Moreover, at most, only part of the benefits from an improvement in self-esteem is likely to be reflected by a shift in the labor supply curve. Indeed, it is easy to imagine E&T participants who enjoy increases in self-esteem as a result of participating in the program but whose willingness-to-work does not change.

Job-Required Expenditures   As discussed earlier, in the framework traditionally used in cost-benefit analyses of E&T programs, increases in job-related expenditures such as child care and transportation that result from program participation are counted as a social cost of the program, regardless of whether paid for by E&T participants or the government. As discussed next, however, this approach can sometimes result in double counting.

For illustrative purposes, we focus here on child care, although a similar analysis could be made for other work-related costs such as transportation. Panel (a) of Figure 11.4 pertains to an individual who participated in an E&T program that increased her wage from W_0 to W_1. The supply curve, S, indicates the hours the individual would work if she must pay for child care. The diagram implies that, as a result of the program-engendered wage increase, she would go from not working to working h_1 hours. Thus, the program would engender an increase in earnings equal to area W_1ah_10 and a smaller surplus gain equal to area W_1aW_r. Panel (b) illustrates the E&T participant's demand for child care. P_0 represents the market-set price for child care. As indicated in the figure, the demand curve for child care would shift out from D_0 to D_1 as a result of the wage increase and the increased hours worked resulting from the E&T.

As the reader may have noticed, Figure 11.4 is very similar to the diagrams of primary and secondary markets that appear in Chapter 5. This is hardly surprising. The direct effects of E&T programs typically occur in labor markets, whereas a complementary relationship exists between work effort and child care. Hence, the primary market is the labor market for E&T participants, whereas the market for child care is a secondary market.

As discussed in detail in Chapter 5, effects in undistorted secondary markets should usually be ignored if program benefits in primary markets are measured in terms of

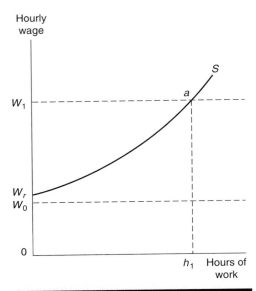

FIGURE 11.4(a) Labor Market Effects of E&T Program

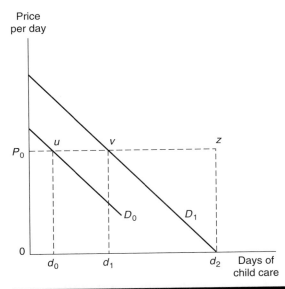

FIGURE 11.4(b) Child Care Market Effects of E&T Program

changes in surplus. Specifically, the individual represented in Figure 11.4 will presumably consider the child care expenses she will incur in determining the number of hours she would be willing to work at each wage rate. Thus, in using her labor supply curve to measure her surplus gain from participating in the E&T program, area $W_1 a W_r$, her child care expenditures are already fully taken into account. Consequently, her expenditures in the secondary market represented in panel (b)—that is, area $uvd_1 d_0$—should be ignored, as should the area between the two demand curves in panel (b). Not doing so will result in double counting.

As emphasized earlier, benefits to E&T participants are traditionally measured as changes in net income rather than as changes in surplus. To obtain this measure, expenditures on child care resulting from having participated in E&T would, of course, be subtracted from earnings increases. As indicated in Figure 11.4(a), the increase in earnings overstates the gain in surplus resulting from the E&T program by an amount represented by area $W_r a h_1 0$. Subtracting child care expenditures, area $uvd_1 d_0$, from the increase in earnings offsets this overstatement. However, area $uvd_1 d_0$ could be either larger or smaller than area $W_r a h_1 0$. Thus, the net income measure could be either larger or smaller than the more appropriate net surplus measure.

We next briefly consider benefits and cost if the government directly provides child care or reimburses individuals for their expenditures on child care. A rather natural way to examine such a policy is to compare the earnings increases that result from the government subsidizing child care with the government's cost. As will be seen, however, this approach is incorrect.

For illustrative purposes, we assume that child care is provided free to subsidized individuals, but the government pays the market price of P_0. As previously discussed, given a market wage of W_1, the demand curve for child care for the individual represented in Figure 11.4 would be D_1. Thus, if child care were provided to her free, she would consume d_2 units of child care.

Because the direct effects of the government's subsidy occur in the market for child care, it should now be viewed as the primary market for purposes of analysis, whereas the labor market should now be viewed as the secondary market. Thus, although the government's provision of subsidized child care would shift the labor supply curve and this, in turn, would affect earnings,[17] these effects should be ignored. Instead, the effects of the policy on individuals are best examined by measuring surplus changes in the primary market. For example, with free child care, the individual represented in Figure 11.4 would enjoy a surplus gain corresponding to area P_0vd_20. However, the cost to the government, which is represented by area P_0zd_20, would be considerably greater. Part of the cost to the government, P_0vd_20, is a transfer to the day care user. The remainder, vd_2z, is deadweight loss.[18]

The Nonparticipant Perspective[19]

This section discusses the following categories of benefits and costs that accrue to non-participants: intangible benefits, benefits from in-program output, and costs resulting from the displacement of public-sector and private-sector workers.

Intangible Benefits Received by Nonparticipants   The preceding section emphasized that in measuring the benefits and costs of E&T programs to participants it is changes in their surplus that should be estimated rather than changes in their money income. Thus, the effects on participant surplus of E&T-induced reductions in participant leisure time should be taken into account.

The same concept applies in measuring benefits and costs of E&T programs to nonparticipants. In particular, if at least some nonparticipants positively value the substitution of earnings for welfare payment in and of itself, then the increase in surplus received by nonparticipants will exceed any reductions in their tax obligations that might result from E&T programs that are targeted at welfare recipients. Thus, in principle, it is changes in the surplus of nonparticipants that result from E&T programs, rather than changes in their incomes, that should be measured. Given the practical difficulty of doing this, however, it has never been attempted.[20]

Benefits from In-Program Output   Many, although far from all, E&T programs involve the provision of public-sector jobs. Perhaps the best-known example of this is the Works Projects Administration (WPA), which operated in the United States during the Great Depression and was intended to absorb some of the massive number of workers who were unemployed during this period. More recently, the Comprehensive Employment and Training Act provided as many as 750,000 public-sector jobs for unemployed persons during the late 1970s. At present, as mentioned earlier, welfare recipients in some states are required to perform work at government and nonprofit agencies in exchange for their payments.

How should the value to taxpayers of the in-program output produced by E&T participants be assigned to public-sector jobs? Ideally, this would be done by determining what taxpayers would be willing to pay for this output. Typically, this is infeasible, however, because the output is not purchased in market transactions. Consequently, an alternative approach is used to determine what the labor resources required to produce the output would have cost if purchased on the open market. This is consistent with the procedures used for measurement of public-sector output in the national income accounts. However, in CBAs of E&T demonstrations, evaluation of output on the basis of resource cost is complicated by the fact that the agencies that "employ" E&T participants usually pay nothing for the services of these people. Therefore, the wage rate that would have been paid to similar workers hired in the open market to do the work performed by the participants is used instead. Once an appropriate wage rate is determined, the basic calculation involves multiplying the number of hours E&T participants work by this wage and perhaps adjusting to account for differences between the average productivity of the E&T workers and workers hired in the open market.

The procedure just described can result in an estimate that either overstates or understates the true value of the in-program output produced by E&T participants. The reasons for this can be seen by examining a key assumption that implicitly underlies this valuation method: The decisions of the public-sector agencies that employ E&T workers closely reflect the desires of taxpayers. More specifically, an analogy is implicitly drawn with the behavior of private-sector firms and consumers under perfect competition, and it is assumed that the amount that an agency would be willing to pay to employ an additional worker corresponds to the value that taxpayers would place on the additional output that the worker could potentially produce. Although this is not an appropriate place to assess the perfect competition analogy or discuss the extent to which bureaucratic behavior reflects taxpayer preferences, it should be obvious that a rather strong assumption is required to value output produced by E&T workers.

The implications of this assumption can be explored by use of Figure 11.5, which depicts the demand curve for workers by a public-sector agency that might potentially be assigned E&T participants and the supply curve the agency faces in hiring workers in a competitive labor market. In using this diagram, let us first examine a situation in which the assumption that bureaucratic behavior reflects taxpayer preferences is valid and then one in which it is not.

In Figure 11.5, the horizontal line, S, represents the supply curve, which is set at the level of the market-determined wage that must be paid to each regular worker hired by the agency; and the downward sloping line, D, represents the demand curve, which is assumed to slope downward as a result of diminishing returns and (as implied by the assumption about bureaucratic behavior) because the agency prioritizes its tasks so that, as its budget expands, successively less important services are performed. (Ignore curve D^* for the moment.) This demand curve reflects the willingness-to-pay for workers by the agency and, in keeping with the assumption concerning bureaucratic behavior, the area under this curve is presumed to measure the value to taxpayers of output produced by workers hired by the agency.

Figure 11.5 indicates that in the absence of E&T workers the agency would hire R regular workers; but if P E&T participants were assigned to the agency, a total of $R + P$ workers would be employed. Thus, if the bureaucratic behavior assumption is valid, the value to taxpayers of the output added by the E&T workers would equal area A.

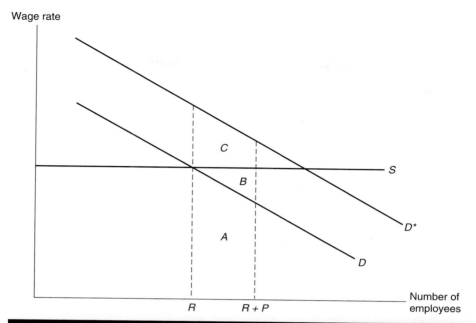

FIGURE 11.5 Demand for Workers by a Public-Sector Agency

Unfortunately, however, area *A* typically cannot be directly measured. The reason for this is that the output produced by public-sector agencies is rarely sold in market transactions and, consequently, the agency's demand curve, which is depicted in Figure 11.5, cannot actually be observed. However, even though government and nonprofit agencies that "employ" E&T participants pay nothing for the services of these people, the area under the supply curve between *R* and *R + P* can be valued by simply determining the wages that would have to be paid to similar workers hired on the open market to do the work performed by E&T participants. Consequently, it is the area under the supply curve—that is, area *A* plus area *B*—that is usually used in practice as the measure of the value of in-program participant output. As a glance at Figure 11.5 suggests, the size of the resulting overstatement of the value of the output produced by E&T participation, which is represented by area *B*, depends on the slope of the agency demand curve.

So far, we have assumed that agency bureaucratic behavior simply reflects the value that taxpayers would place on the agency's output. Let us now look at one of the numerous possible situations in which this is not the case.[21] The specific example we examine is one in which the agency, perhaps because of budget constraints resulting from the public goods characteristics of whatever services it provides, produces less output than taxpayers collectively desire. These circumstances are represented in Figure 11.5 by two demand curves. As before, curve *D* indicates *agency* willingness-to-pay for workers, but the value that *taxpayers* place on the output produced by the agency is now represented by the area under demand curve *D**. Consequently, the value of the additional output produced by the P E&T participants provided the agency now equals area A plus area B plus area C. Thus, under these circumstances, the measure based on the market supply curve for workers, which as previously indicated equals area A plus area B, understates the true value by an area equal to C.

Costs from Public-Sector Labor Displacement   So far, our discussion has been based on the assumption that the E&T workers made available to a public-sector agency would simply be added to the regular workforce that the agency would hire in the absence of the program. This need not be the case. The agency might instead substitute E&T workers for regular workers. In terms of Figure 11.5, this behavior on the part of the agency, which is usually referred to as *displacement,* would mean that agency employment would increase by less than the P number of workers provided by E&T. Indeed, with 100 percent displacement, the agency's workforce would remain at R, rather than increase to $R + P$. Consequently, at first blush, it would appear that displacement leads to overstatement of the value of output produced by E&T participants.

The issue is actually a bit more subtle and complex, however. If the displaced workers have a similar risk of joblessness as E&T participants, then increases in output produced by E&T participants assigned to public-sector agencies may be entirely offset by losses in the output formerly produced by the displaced workers. This need not be the case, however, if the E&T participants are exceptional in terms of lack of skills or if they face exceptional barriers to labor market access. Moving such persons directly into jobs under these circumstances will change the characteristics of the general pool of unemployed in ways that may allow a reduction in the net incidence of joblessness, especially if local labor market conditions are tight. Thus, to the extent that E&T participants are unskilled relative to those they replaced, the labor market consequences will differ from a simple one-for-one replacement.

Costs from Private-Sector Labor Displacement   A major objective of most E&T programs is to increase the unsubsidized private-sector employment of program participants. To the extent these efforts are successful, some participants undoubtedly end up in jobs that would otherwise have been held by nonparticipants. If, as a result, these nonparticipants become unemployed or accept lower-wage jobs, their earnings obviously fall. This earnings reduction, which is another type of displacement effect, is potentially a cost of E&T programs to nonparticipants. Because there is virtually no research quantifying the magnitude of private-sector labor displacement, it has not been taken into account in CBAs of E&T programs.

The failure to take account of private-sector displacement may not be very serious, however. CBA usually assumes that full employment is maintained. If it is, then it should be relatively easy for displaced nonparticipants to find alternative job opportunities and E&T programs will raise the feasible employment level. Nonetheless, if E&T programs add workers with a particular set of skills to the workforce, they may still depress the wages of workers with similar skills. Private-sector displacement is a more serious issue if unemployment is high. Even then, however, it is possible that E&T programs may impart skills that allow trainees to leave slack occupational labor markets for tight ones. If they do, then they will decrease the competition for job vacancies in the slack labor markets, making it easier for unemployed workers who remain in these markets to find jobs. To the extent this occurs, E&T programs will again raise feasible employment levels.

CHOOSING PREDICTION PARAMETERS

In using the cost-benefit framework illustrated in Table 11.2, it is necessary to take account of the fact that some benefits and costs of E&T programs are likely to extend beyond the demonstration period. For example, as a result of having participated in an E&T demonstration, some individuals could potentially enjoy increased earnings but pay higher taxes, incur greater job-required expenses, and receive fewer transfer payments over the remainder of their working lives. These streams of future benefits and costs must be incorporated into the CBAs of the demonstrations. Doing this requires that four important parameters be specified: the social discount rate, the time horizon, the decay rate, and the shadow price of capital. The social discount rate was discussed in detail in Chapter 10. The remaining three parameters are discussed in turn in the following three subsections.

The Time Horizon

As described in Chapter 6, the time horizon is the period over which benefit and cost streams are estimated. In CBAs of E&T programs, benefits and costs beyond the specified time horizon are assumed equal to zero, that is, to have zero terminal value. One procedure for determining the length of the period in CBAs of E&T programs is to subtract the age of program participants at the time they entered the program from the age at which they are expected to retire from the workforce. Often, however, a shorter, somewhat arbitrarily selected time horizon—for example, five years—is used instead. Doing this is simply an acknowledgment on the part of analysts that because they do not possess crystal balls, uncertainty increases the further one attempts to extrapolate beyond the demonstration period. Basing a CBA of an E&T demonstration on a short time horizon, however, is likely to understate E&T benefits relative to E&T costs, as at least one of the major potential benefits—earnings improvements—may persist well beyond five years, whereas the major cost—operating expenditures—does not.

This understatement of benefits relative to costs may be substantial. Table 11.3 shows the present discounted value of an improvement of $1 in annual earnings under alternative assumptions concerning the length of the time horizon over which

TABLE 11.3 The Sensitivity of the Present Value of a $1 Improvement in Annual Earnings to Alternative Time Horizons and Discount Rates		
	Discount Rate	
Time Horizon	**5%**	**10%**
5 years	$ 4.33	$3.79
10 years	7.72	6.15
20 years	12.46	8.51
30 years	15.37	9.43

the improvement persists and the value of the discount rate. The figures in the table have two important implications. First, it is evident that the magnitude of benefit and cost estimates is quite sensitive to the choice of the time horizon. For example, if a 5 percent discount rate and a five-year time horizon are used for extrapolation purposes, the present value of an improvement of $1 in earnings equals $4.33. But if a 5 percent discount rate and a 20-year time horizon are used instead, the present value equals $12.46, almost a threefold increase. Second, the longer the time horizon that is used, the more sensitive are projections of benefits and costs to the choice of the discount rate. Hence, if a short time horizon is used, cost-benefit findings are less likely to be sensitive to the choice of a discount rate than if a long time horizon is used.

The Decay Rate

A decay rate is necessary in extrapolating E&T effects that persist beyond the demonstration period in order to take account of the possibility that the size of these effects may change over time. For example, it is usually argued that programs that provide training or job placement for low-wage workers initially may give them a competitive advantage in the labor market, but this advantage may decay over time. In the case of training, however, one could alternatively argue that doors are opened on the job that allow participants to obtain additional training after leaving an E&T program and, consequently, the program's effects on earnings will grow over time.

Unfortunately, only very limited empirical evidence exists as to whether the earnings effects of E&T programs tend to grow or decay over time, let alone the magnitude of the actual rate of decay or growth.[22] Thus, the choice of an appropriate decay rate is one of the more problematic aspects of CBAs of E&T demonstrations.[23]

Once values for the discount rate, time horizon, and decay rate are chosen, equations (6A.5) and (6A.7) in Appendix 6A can be used to compute net present values. In using these formulas, care must be taken to use a negative value for g if it is determined that the effects of the E&T demonstration will decay over time and a positive value for g if it seems likely that these impacts will grow over time. For benefit and cost components that neither grow nor shrink over time, g should, of course, be set equal to zero.

The Shadow Price of Capital

As indicated in Chapter 10, in addition to the discount rate, the time horizon, and the decay rate, there is yet another parameter that should in principle be taken into account in projecting benefit and cost streams of E&T programs: the shadow price of capital. This parameter allows the benefits and costs of public-sector programs that cause additions or reductions in private-sector investment to be treated differently than those that result in additions or reductions in private-sector consumption. As discussed in Chapter 10, the reason this differential treatment is appropriate is that a dollar of program costs that would have been used for private-sector consumption in the absence of the program displaces only one dollar of consumption, but a dollar of forgone investment would have engendered a stream of future returns. If discounted at the social rate of time preference, then the present value of this stream of returns would have exceeded one dollar. Similarly, a dollar of program benefits that is directly consumed can only increase consumption by one dollar, but if the dollar is used instead for private-sector investment, the present value of the resulting stream of returns will also exceed one dollar. Thus, dollars of E&T costs that would have otherwise been used to make private-sector investments and dollars of E&T benefits that stimulate private-sector investments will be undervalued unless multiplied by the shadow price of capital. To the best of our knowledge, however, this has not been done in any CBAs of E&T programs. Later in this chapter, we demonstrate how sensitive findings from some actual CBAs of E&T demonstrations are to some alternative assumptions about the shadow price of capital.

A CASE STUDY: CBAs OF WELFARE-TO-WORK DEMONSTRATIONS

Since the 1970s, many states have conducted demonstrations that had the objective of reducing dependency on transfer payments among welfare recipients by enhancing their employability. Similar to other E&T demonstrations, the components of these *welfare-to-work* programs varied among the demonstrations but usually included one or more of the following: assessment of basic skills, structured job search, training and education, and subsidized employment in the public or private sector.

Many of the welfare-to-work demonstrations have been subjected to CBA. CBAs of a particular subset of demonstrations conducted during the 1980s, the Work/Welfare Demonstrations, exerted considerable influence on the Family Support Act of 1988, a major piece of welfare reform legislation. Much of this influence resulted from the fact that by 1988 many observers, particularly those in the policy-making community, had concluded on the basis of analyses of the Work/Welfare Demonstrations that welfare-to-work programs are cost-beneficial.[24] The Work/Welfare Demonstrations were targeted at participants in the Aid for Families with Dependent Children (AFDC) program, which at the time was the major cash welfare program in the United States. The Manpower Demonstration Research Corporation (MDRC), a well-known non-profit research firm, conducted the CBAs of these demonstrations, which were based on the classical experimental design denoted as design 1 earlier in the chapter.[25]

CBA Results

Table 11.4 presents summary results from MDRC's CBAs of the Work/Welfare Demonstrations. These estimates should be viewed as program impacts on a typical member of the treatment group in each of the listed demonstrations. The estimates in the table, which have been converted to 1999 dollar amounts using the U.S. consumer price index, are reported separately for one-parent (AFDC-R) and two-parent (AFDC-U) households and, when available, for new AFDC applicants and prior AFDC recipients. Parentheses are used to indicate when benefits or costs are in the opposite direction from that intended by the demonstration programs—for example, when net remuneration from employment declines or amounts of transfer payments increase.

The first three columns in the table present estimated benefits and costs from the participant perspective and the next four from the nonparticipant perspective. Columns A and D, respectively, report total net gains (or losses) from these two

TABLE 11.4 Summary of Cost-Benefit Estimates from MDRC Evaluations of Work/Welfare Demonstrations (in 1999 dollars)

	Participant Perspective			Nonparticipant Perspective				
	Net Present Value (A = B − C)	Net Gains from Employment	Loss in Transfer Payments	Net Present Value (D = E + F − G)	Value of In-Program Output	Tax-Transfer Gains	Program Service Costs	Net Social Gain (or Loss) (A + D)
	A	B	C	D	E	F	G	H

AFDC-R

APPLICANTS ONLY

San Diego EPP/EWEP

	A	B	C	D	E	F	G	H
Job search only	$1,077	$2,213	$1,135	$755	($5)	$1,614	$853	$1,832
Job search/ CWEP	1,335	3,134	1,800	$1,933	$342	$2,557	$967	$3,267
San Diego SWIM	(1,338)	1,732	3,070	2,482	274	3,272	1,064	1,145
Virginia	1,818	2,723	904	1,069	65	1,409	406	2,887
West Virginia	(772)	(653)	119	623	869	40	285	(148)

RECIPIENTS ONLY

	A	B	C	D	E	F	G	H
San Diego SWIM	1,103	4,800	3,698	2,582	274	3,931	1,623	3,684
Virginia	921	1,575	654	304	232	950	879	1,224
West Virginia	128	251	124	1,400	1,698	184	481	1,528
New Jersey	1,918	3,463	1,544	1,625	(13)	2,418	780	3,543
Maine	4,926	6,962	2,036	(648)	1,053	1,384	3,084	4,278

APPLICANTS AND RECIPIENTS

Cook County

	A	B	C	D	E	F	G	H
Job search only	(638)	221	858	722	1	914	193	84
Job search/ CWEP	(51)	473	524	551	152	639	240	500
Baltimore	2,788	3,109	321	119	625	823	1,330	2,907
Arkansas	(721)	657	1,378	1,514	32	1,734	252	793

TABLE 11.4 *(cont.)*

	Participant Perspective			Nonparticipant Perspective				
	Net Present Value (A = B − C)	Net Gains from Employment	Loss in Transfer Payments	Net Present Value (D = E + F − G)	Value of In-Program Output	Tax-Transfer Gains	Program Service Costs	Net Social Gain (or Loss) (A + D)
	A	B	C	D	E	F	G	H
AFDC-U								
APPLICANTS ONLY								
San Diego EPP/EWEP:								
Job Search only	($2,000)	$628	$2,628	$2,055	($8)	$2,972	$909	$55
Job search/ CWEP	(2,414)	216	2,630	2,364	592	2,896	1,124	(50)
San Diego SWIM	826	3,166	2,340	2,397	406	2,994	1,004	3,222
RECIPIENTS ONLY								
San Diego SWIM	(1,400)	3,310	4,710	3,776	406	4,928	1,558	2,376
APPLICANTS AND RECIPIENTS								
Baltimore	(1,977)	(3,234)	(1,257)	(2,976)	449	(2,564)	861	(4,953)

Notes: See text for detailed explanation of table.

*Separate estimates of the value of in-program output for applicants and recipients not provided for San Diego.

( ): The parentheses indicate negative net gains or increases in transfer payment amounts.

Sources: The following final reports on the individual Work/Welfare Demonstrations, all of which were published by the Manpower Demonstration Research Corporation, New York, New York: P. Auspos, G. Cave, and D. Long, *Maine: Final Report on the Training Opportunities in the Private Sector Program,* 1988; S. Freedman, J. Bryant, and G. Cave, *New Jersey: Final Report on the Grant Diversion Project,* 1988; D. Friedlander, G. Hoerz, J. Quint, and J. Riccio, *Arkansas: Final Report on the WORK Program in Two Counties,* 1985; D. Friedlander, G. Hoerz, D. Long, and J. Quint, *Maryland: Final Report on the Employment Initiatives Evaluation,* 1985; D. Friedlander, M. Erickson, G. Hamilton, and V. Knox, *West Virginia: Final Report on the Community Work Experience Demonstrations,* 1986; D. Friedlander, S. Freedman, G. Hamilton, and J. Quint, *Illinois: Final Report on Job Search and Work Experience in Cook County,* 1987; B. Goldman, D. Friedlander, and D. Long, *California: Final Report on the San Diego Job Search and Work Experience Demonstration,* 1986; G. Hamilton and D. Friedlander, *Final Report on the Saturation Work Initiative Model in San Diego,* 1989; J. Riccio, G. Cave, S. Freedman, and M. Price, *Virginia: Final Report on the Virginia Employment Services Program,* 1986.

perspectives, whereas columns B, C, E, F, and G provide information on the benefit and cost components that together account for these gains (or losses). For example, column B reports the estimated *net* gain by participants from employment under each demonstration program—that is, estimates of the sum of increases in earnings, fringe benefits, and any work-related allowances paid under the program less the sum of tax payments and participant job-required expenditures on child care and transportation. Column C indicates changes in AFDC and other transfer benefits received by participants. Column E presents MDRC's valuations of in-program output. Column F is the sum of tax increases paid by participants, reductions in transfer payments paid to participants, and reductions in transfer program operating costs, all of which may be viewed as benefits to nonparticipants. Column G shows the government's cost of operating the treatment programs. Finally, column H, which is computed by summing the benefit-cost components reported in columns B, C, E, F, and G, presents the overall CBA results.

As can be seen from column H, 16 of the 19 reported estimates indicate overall net gains and only three imply net losses. It is this preponderance of positive values that impressed the policy community. Taken at face value, these findings imply that the policies tested in the Work/Welfare Demonstrations generally resulted in positive social net gains. Yet, any final assessment depends on whether the estimates reported in column H are sensitive to the assumptions MDRC used to derive them. This issue is investigated later.

One of the most striking findings from Table 11.4 is that of the 19 reported sets of CBA estimates, 17 imply net gains for nonparticipants, but only 10 indicate net gains for participants. The reason for the nine instances of net losses among participants, which occur disproportionately among the two-parent AFDC-U households, is suggested by a comparison of columns B and C. Some of the demonstration treatments did not result in sufficiently large gains from employment to offset participant losses in transfer payments. Thus, as Table 11.4 implies, in eight of the nine instances, nonparticipants gained at the expense of participants. In one demonstration, that for Baltimore's AFDC-U population, both groups were apparently made worse off. Nine of the ten remaining sets of CBA estimates imply that the demonstration treatment made both participants and nonparticipants better off; the tenth, those for Maine, indicate that participants gained while nonparticipants suffered losses.

The total net gains and losses for participants and nonparticipants that are implied by columns A and D are not especially large. For example, a program that resulted in a net participant or nonparticipant gain of $2,000 per treatment group member (a figure that is larger than most of those appearing in either column A or D) and enrolled 1 million AFDC recipients each year, which was over a quarter of the AFDC caseload at the time the demonstrations were conducted, would have produced a total annual gain of $2 billion, a gain that was well under 10 percent of the annual budgetary cost of AFDC at the time the demonstrations were conducted.[26]

Extrapolations of Benefits and Costs: The Baltimore Options Program

As pointed out earlier, some of the benefits and costs of E&T demonstrations are likely to continue well after the demonstration has ended. To incorporate these future benefit and cost streams into CBAs, assumptions have to be made concerning the social discount rate, the time horizon, and the decay rate. Thus, in obtaining the findings reported in Table 11.4, MDRC used a 5 percent discount rate and a five-year time horizon. For the decay rate, MDRC often selected several alternative values and examined whether its findings were sensitive to these alternatives. The exact values used for this purpose varied among the studies but usually included a decay rate of zero, which implied no decay, and often also included a rate of infinity, which implied that no benefits or costs extended beyond the demonstration period. In addition, the actual rate of decay that was observed during the demonstration period was sometimes used,[27] as was an annual rate of 22 percent, which was obtained from a 1980 national study of the WIN program conducted by Ketron, Incorporated.[28] In no case did MDRC use a rate that implied that benefits or costs grow rather than decline over time. As discussed next, however, there is some evidence from MDRC's own data that growth rather than decay did in fact occur in at least one of the Work/Welfare Demonstrations: the Baltimore Options program.

Table 11.5 presents cost-benefit findings for the Baltimore Options program. These particular results were selected because they could be obtained from two separate sets of published estimates: one that appeared in MDRC's 1985 final report for the Baltimore Options program;[29] and one from a 1987 supplemental report that updated the original estimates by obtaining information on the earnings and transfer receipts of members of the treatment and control groups after the demonstration ended and,

TABLE 11.5 Six Alternative Estimates of Benefits and Costs per Baltimore Options Program Treatment Group Member: Reported from Participant Perspective (in 1999 dollars)

	Lower Estimates		Middle Estimates		Upper Estimates	
	Original Estimates	*Updated Estimates*	*Original Estimates*	*Updated Estimates*	*Original Estimates*	*Updated Estimates*
Earnings and fringe benefits	$787	$2,047	$1,451	$3,024	$2,040	$3,241
Tax payments	−130	−276	−396	−431	−550	−465
Out-of-pocket work expenditures	−34	−40	−39	−42	−39	−42
AFDC payments	−46	−84	−160	2	−237	20
Other transfer payments	−178	−279	−361	−338	−476	−341
Allowances and support services	305	353	341	375	341	375
Net gain	704	1,721	877	2,590	1,079	2,788

All estimates are based on a time horizon of five years. Lower estimates represent only observed program impacts and, thus, do not include estimates of future impacts. That is, there is no extrapolation. Middle estimates include estimates of future benefits and costs that are based on an assumed annual decay rate of 22 percent. Upper estimates include estimates of future benefits and costs that are based on an assumed zero decay rate. Original estimates are based on a demonstration period of around 1.5 years and an extrapolation period of about 3.5 years. Updated estimates are based on a demonstration period of around three years and an extrapolation period of about two years.

Source: Original estimates are from Table 6.7 in Daniel Friedlander, Gregory Hoerz, David Long, and Janet Quint, *Maryland: Final Report on the Employment Initiatives Evaluation* (New York: Manpower Demonstration Research Corporation, 1985). Updated estimates are from Table A.7 of Daniel Friedlander, *Maryland: Supplementary Report on the Baltimore Options Program* (New York: Manpower Demonstration Research Corporation, 1987).

hence, shortened the length of time over which extrapolation was required.[30] By comparing the two sets of estimates, one can obtain some sense of how sensitive the CBA results are to incorrect assumptions concerning the rate of decay.

The estimates appearing in Table 11.5 pertain to the participant perspective and are averaged over all members of the Baltimore Options AFDC-R treatment group. Three pairs of columns are displayed, one for each of the three alternative assumptions that MDRC made concerning decay rates. The left column in each pair is taken from MDRC's originally published estimates and the right column from the updated estimates.

In Table 11.5, some variation is apparent across the three pairs of columns, but much greater differences occur within each pair. These differences between the original and updated estimates are attributable to the fact that at least during the extended data collection period, even an assumption of a zero decay rate for the earnings impact of the Baltimore Options program was overly pessimistic. As it turned out, the earnings differences between the treatment and comparison groups in Baltimore continued to grow during the extended data collection period. This is one example of a *forecasting error*, a common CBA problem, which is discussed in some detail in Chapter 19.

Given the absence of good evidence concerning decay rates, MDRC's strategy of examining the sensitivity of its findings to alternative rates was a good one. It is important to recognize, however, that the amount of variance observed in these sensitivity tests was severely restricted by the very short five-year time horizon upon which they are all based. Nevertheless, as Table 11.5 attests, this variation is far from eliminated.

SENSITIVITY OF THE WORK/WELFARE FINDINGS TO ALTERNATIVE ASSUMPTIONS

As indicated earlier, numerous methodological issues arise in measuring the benefits and costs of E&T demonstrations. Consequently, measuring the benefits and costs of the Work/Welfare Demonstrations inevitably required MDRC to make a number of assumptions. In this section, we examine how sensitive MDRC's findings are to three of the more important of these assumptions. (In Chapter 18, we consider the sensitivity of the results to changes in assumptions about distributional weights.) By conducting these sensitivity tests, we hope to illustrate the role that some of the issues discussed earlier play in conducting actual CBAs of E&T programs, as well as provide some idea of how much confidence can be placed in MDRC's findings for the Work/Welfare Demonstrations.

Sensitivity to Alternative Assumptions about In-Program Output

For reasons discussed in detail earlier, MDRC's estimates of in-program output values could be either overstated or understated. Here we focus only on the implications of a possible overstatement, which is perhaps the more likely of the two possibilities.

Findings from a sensitivity test of this possibility are reported in the first two columns of Table 11.6. Column 1 simply duplicates the social net gain estimates reported in column H of Table 11.4. In keeping with the possibility that the in-program output values incorporated into column 1 are overstated, column 2 is based on the extreme assumption that in-program output should be valued at zero but is otherwise computed on the same basis as column 1. As suggested by a comparison of these two columns, except for the West Virginia demonstration, the estimates of social net gains and losses are insensitive to this assumption.

TABLE 11.6 Sensitivity Tests of Estimated Net Social Gains (or Losses) from the Work/Welfare Demonstrations (in 1999 dollars)

		Net Social Gain If Shadow Price of Capital = 2.0 and		
Unadjusted Net Social Gain (or Loss) $[B - C + E + F - G]$	*Net Social Gain (or Loss) if Value of In-program Output = 0* $[B - C + F - G]$	$S_c = S_n = .15;$ *Nonparticipant Tax-Transfer Gains Reduce Taxes; Program Service Costs Increase Taxes* $[1.15(B - C) + E + 1.15(F - G)]$	$S_c = 0,$ $S_n = .15;$ *Nonparticipant Tax-Transfer Gains Reduce Taxes; Program Service Costs Increase Taxes* $[B - C + E + 1.15(F - G)]$	$S_c = 0, S_n = .15;$ *Nonparticipant Tax-Transfer Gains Reduce National Debt; Program Service Costs Increase National Debt* $[B - C + E + 2.0(F - G)]$
1	2	3	4	5

AFDC-R

APPLICANTS ONLY

San Diego
EPP/EWEP

	1	2	3	4	5
Job Search Only	$1,832	$1,838	$2,109	$1,947	$2,594
Job Search + CWEP	3,267	2,925	3,707	3,508	4,859
San Diego SWIM	1,145	871	1,275	1,476	3,353
Virginia	2,887	2,822	3,311	3,038	3,892
West Virginia	(148)	(1,017)	(299)	(184)	(392)

RECIPIENTS ONLY

	1	2	3	4	5
San Diego SWIM	3,684	3,410	4,193	4,030	5,990
Virginia	1,224	992	1,374	1,237	1,297
West Virginia	1,528	(170)	1,502	1,483	1,229
New Jersey	3,543	3,530	4,046	3,790	5,182
Maine	4,278	3,225	4,764	4,024	2,580

TABLE 11.6 *(cont.)*					
			Net Social Gain If Shadow Price of Capital = 2.0 and		
	Unadjusted Net Social Gain (or Loss) $[B - C + E + F - G]$	Net Social Gain (or Loss) if Value of In-program Output = 0 $[B - C + F - G]$	$S_c = S_n = .15$; Nonparticipant Tax-Transfer Gains Reduce Taxes; Program Service Costs Increase Taxes $[1.15(B - C) + E + 1.15(F - G)]$	$S_c = 0$, $S_n = .15$; Nonparticipant Tax-Transfer Gains Reduce Taxes; Program Service Costs Increase Taxes $[B - C + E + 1.15(F - G)]$	$S_c = 0$, $S_n = .15$; Nonparticipant Tax-Transfer Gains Reduce National Debt; Program Service Costs Increase National Debt $[B - C + E + 2.0(F - G)]$
	1	2	3	4	5
AFDC-R *(cont.)*					
APPLICANTS AND RECIPIENTS					
Cook County					
Job Search Only	84	83	96	191	804
Job Search + CWEP	500	347	550	558	896
Baltimore	2,907	2,281	3,248	2,832	2,401
Arkansas	793	761	908	1,017	2,275
AFDC-U					
APPLICANTS ONLY					
San Diego EPP/EWEP					
Job Search Only	55	63	64	365	2,120
Job Search + CWEP	(50)	(642)	(144)	218	1,724
San Diego SWIM	3,222	2,817	3,644	3,522	5,213
RECIPIENTS ONLY					
San Diego SWIM	2,376	1,970	2,670	2,882	5,746
APPLICANTS AND RECIPIENTS					
Baltimore	(4,953)	(5,401)	(5,762)	(5,466)	(8,377)

S_c = Savings rate of clients.

S_n = Savings rate of nonparticipants.

( ): The parentheses indicate negative net gains or increases in transfer payment amounts.

Source: Table 11.4. (Letters in brackets in the column headings indicate the columns from Table 11.4 that were used in the computations.)

Sensitivity to Changes in the Shadow Price of Capital

Chapter 10 suggests that in principle dollars of program costs that represent forgone private-sector investment and dollars of program benefits that are used for investment purposes should be multiplied by the value of the shadow price of capital. Columns 3–5 of Table 11.6 test how sensitive the CBA findings for the Work/Welfare Demonstrations are to doing this. The value of the shadow price of capital that we use for this purpose is 2.0. The 2.0 figure, which seems reasonable given the analysis in Chapter 10, may be interpreted as implying that the forgone stream of returns from each dollar of private-sector investment displaced as a result of a public-sector program and each dollar of program benefits used for investment purposes have a present discounted value of $2.00.[31]

To use the shadow price of capital for CBA purposes, it is necessary to determine the fraction of each program benefit that is invested in the private sector and the fraction that is directly consumed. Similarly, it is necessary to determine the fraction of each cost that displaces private-sector investment and the fraction that displaces private-sector consumption. For the Welfare/Work Initiative Demonstrations, the values of these fractions are not self-evident. Thus, the estimates in columns 3–5 of Table 11.6 are based on three alternative sets of assumptions, each of which is described in turn.

For purposes of column 3, we begin by assuming that in-program output, which was mostly in the form of services, was entirely consumed. Consequently, this assumption implies that private-sector savings and investment were unaffected by in-program output. We further assume that, except for in-program output, 15 percent of any increases in income enjoyed by either participants or nonparticipants will be saved and, hence, invested in the private sector, and the remaining 85 percent will be consumed. Similarly, we also assume that 15 percent of any decreases in the incomes of either participants or nonparticipants will displace private-sector savings and investments, and the remaining 85 percent will displace private-sector consumption. These assumptions imply that, with the exception of in-program output, any increases or decreases in the incomes of either participants or nonparticipants should be multiplied by $[1(0.85) + 2.0(0.15)] = 1.15$. Finally, we assume that any increases in taxes paid by participants or reductions in transfers received by program participants as a result of the demonstration programs are used to reduce the taxes and, hence, increase the incomes of nonparticipants and that program service costs are paid by increasing the taxes of nonparticipants.

To compute column 4, we modify only one of the assumptions made in computing column 3. Rather than assuming that 15 cents of a dollar received by welfare participants is saved, we instead assume, somewhat more realistically we believe, that the entire dollar is consumed. In other words, we assume that, given their low incomes, the savings rate of welfare participants is zero; however, we continue to assume that the savings rate of nonparticipants is 0.15. Thus, although changes in the incomes of nonparticipants are multiplied by 1.15, changes in the incomes of participants are multiplied by 1.0.

With one important exception, column 5 is based on the same assumptions as column 4. It is assumed that rather than being used to reduce the taxes of nonparticipants, increases in taxes paid by participants and reductions in transfers received by participants are instead used to reduce the national debt. Similarly, it is assumed that rather than paying for program service costs by increasing taxes, the national debt is increased instead. This assumption should be viewed as somewhat unrealistic, if for no other reason than the fact that program service costs, reductions in participant welfare receipts, and increases in participant tax payments would affect state as well as federal budgets. However, the assumption is a useful one for conducting a sensitivity test, for it implies that if there is full employment in the economy and if the savings rate is insensitive to interest rates, each dollar increase in the national debt displaces one dollar of private-sector investment and that each dollar reduction in the national debt increases private investment by one dollar. Thus, instead of multiplying nonparticipant benefits and costs by 1.15, as we do in computing column 4, to compute column 5, we multiply by 2.0, the full shadow price of capital.

By now, it should be apparent that the estimates presented in columns 3–5 of Table 11.6 are based on a large number of assumptions, many of which are tenuous. Thus, these estimates should be considered as only illustrative. Nonetheless, a comparison of columns 3, 4, and 5 with column 1 strongly suggests that in most instances ignoring the shadow price of capital will cause the social net gains of programs such as those tested under the Welfare/Work Demonstrations to be understated. For example, 14 of the 19 estimates appearing in column 4, estimates that in our judgment are based on a more realistic set of assumptions than those reported in either column 3 or column 5, are more positive than their counterparts in column 1. Most of these differences, however, are small. Moreover, there is only one sign change. And that change is from a very small negative value to a small positive value. Thus, although estimates of the magnitude of social net gains from the Work/Welfare Demonstrations seem somewhat sensitive to using the shadow price of capital in their computation, conclusions concerning whether there is a positive payoff from such programs are not.

Sensitivity to Alternative Assumptions about Subtracting Losses in Leisure from Earnings Gains

An analysis presented earlier in this chapter implies that if participants value the time they must relinquish in order to either participate in E&T activities or take paid employment—time that economists usually refer to as *leisure*—then net gains for participants in E&T programs would be overstated (or, alternatively, net losses understated) by the results reported in the first column of Table 11.4. This possibility is explored in Table 11.7, which presents findings from a sensitivity analysis of the net social gains of a subset of the Work/Welfare Demonstrations that was conducted by David Greenberg.[32] The first column in this table shows the unadjusted net gain estimates that are also reported in column H of Table 11.4. The second column reports net gain estimates that have been adjusted to reflect the costs associated with reductions in the leisure time of program participants.[33]

A comparison of the two columns in Table 11.7 indicates that the estimates of net social gains and losses are quite sensitive to adjustments that account for losses of leisure, becoming substantially smaller. Nevertheless, like the unadjusted estimates, the adjusted estimates are positive in value, suggesting that the major implication of the unadjusted net gain estimates in the first column—that the programs listed in the table had positive impacts on society as a whole—is robust to adjustments for lost leisure.

In assessing the findings reported in Table 11.7, two additional points should be kept in mind. First, the net gain estimates that are reported in the table are only ad-

TABLE 11.7 Sensitivity of Findings from the Work/Welfare Demonstrations to Taking Account of the Value to Clients of Lost Leisure (in 1999 dollars)

	Unadjusted Net Social Gain	*Net Social Gain Adjusted for Lost Leisure*
	I	*II*
AFDC-R		
APPLICANTS		
San Diego SWIM	$1,145	$316
Virginia	2,887	1,586
RECIPIENTS		
San Diego SWIM	3,684	1,388
Virginia	1,224	473
APPLICANTS AND RECIPIENTS		
Baltimore	2,907	2,165
Arkansas	793	479

Source: David H. Greenberg, "The Leisure Bias in Cost-Benefit Analyses of Employment and Training Programs," *Journal of Human Resources,* 32, no. 2 (1997), Table 4.

justed for leisure that is lost through paid employment. The leisure of Work/Welfare participants was also reduced to the extent they participated in program activities, but data on time spent in these activities are not available. Thus, further adjustments to take these additional losses of leisure into account were not feasible.

Second, as pointed out earlier, it is likely that programs that reduce the leisure time of welfare recipients may, as a result, increase the utility of the nonrecipient taxpayers who support the welfare system. The dollar value of this increase in utility is also not taken into account in Table 11.7. However, although most nonrecipient taxpayers, if asked, would probably express a desire to see welfare recipients employed, the appropriate CBA question is how much they are willing to pay for this. It is less obvious that the collective willingness-to-pay of nonrecipients for reductions in the leisure time of recipients is of large magnitude.

One additional finding from Table 11.7 of considerable interest is that once the adjustment for the loss of leisure associated with program-induced increases in work hours is made, the largest estimated net social gains are associated with the Baltimore program. Of the programs listed in Table 11.7, this program was the only one oriented toward the goal of increasing enrollee employment in better-paying jobs and, in fact, it had some success in accomplishing this. The other programs were more oriented toward increasing hours at work and their effects on earnings are almost entirely attributable to increases in the hours worked by treatment group members.[34]

CONCLUSION

The analysis presented in this chapter suggests that CBAs of E&T demonstrations are more difficult both to conduct successfully and to interpret than they may first appear, even when the demonstrations utilize a classical experimental design. Nevertheless, they can provide useful insights. For example, MDRC's CBAs of the Work/Welfare Demonstrations suggest that the net social gains from the tested programs were generally positive but modest. However, because of the relatively short time horizons and the conservative assumptions concerning decay rates used in their computation, and the fact that the shadow price of capital concept was ignored, these estimated gains may well be understated. Moreover, the sensitivity tests presented in this chapter suggest that the finding that the Work/Welfare Demonstrations resulted in positive social gains is quite robust with respect to alternative assumptions. However, the sensitivity tests did indicate that the magnitude of the net social gains is quite sensitive to taking the value of reductions in the leisure time of demonstration participants into account.

Exercises for Chapter 11

1. Using the scheme shown in Table 11.1, diagram the evaluation design used in each of the following demonstration programs:
   a. To evaluate a government training program that provides low-income, low-skilled, disadvantaged persons job-specific training, members of the target population were randomly assigned to either a treatment group that was eligible to receive services under the program or to a comparison group that was not. Data were collected on the earnings, welfare receipts, and so forth of both groups during the training period and for two years thereafter, but not prior to training.
   b. To evaluate a government training program that provides low-income, low-skilled, disadvantaged persons job-specific training, members of the target population who live in the counties in the eastern half of a large industrial state were assigned to a treatment group that was eligible to receive services under the program, whereas members of the target population who live in the counties in the western half of the state were assigned to a comparison group that was not. Information was collected on the earnings, welfare receipts, and so forth of both groups for one year prior to the beginning of training, during the training period, and for two years thereafter.
   c. To evaluate a government training program that provides low-income, low-skilled, disadvantaged persons job-specific training, information is collected on the earnings, welfare receipts, and so forth of those persons who receive training. This information was collected for the year prior to the beginning of training, during the training period, and for two years thereafter.

2. Consider a government training program that provides low-skilled men job-specific training. To evaluate this program, members of the target population were randomly assigned to either a treatment group that was eligible to receive services under the program or to a comparison group that was not. Using this evaluation design, the following information was obtained:

   Members of the treatment group were found to remain in the program an average of one year, during which time they received no earnings but were paid a tax-free stipend of $5,000 by the program to help them cover their living expenses. During the program year, the average annual earnings of members of the control group were $10,000, on which they paid taxes of $1,000. During the program year, the welfare and unemployment compensation benefits received by the two groups were virtually identical.

Program operating costs (not counting the stipend) and the cost of services provided by the program were $3,000 per trainee.

During the two years after leaving the program, the average annual earnings of members of the treatment group were $20,000, on which they paid taxes of $2,000. During the same period, the average annual earnings of members of the control group were $15,000, on which they paid taxes of $1,500.

During the two years after leaving the program, the average annual welfare payments and unemployment compensation benefits received by members of the treatment group were $250. During the same period, the average annual welfare payments and unemployment compensation benefits received by members of the control group were $1,250.

a. Using a 5 percent discount rate, a zero decay rate, and a five-year time horizon, compute the present value of the net gain (or loss) from the program from the trainee, nonparticipant, and social perspectives. In doing this, ignore program impacts on leisure and assume that all benefits and costs accrue at the end of the year in which they occur.

b. Once again ignoring program impacts on leisure, recompute the present value of the net gain (or loss) from the program from the trainee, nonparticipant, and social perspectives, assuming that at the end of the two-year follow-up period program impacts on earnings and transfer payments begin to decay at the rate of 20 percent each year.

3. Perhaps the most careful effort to measure the effects of compensatory preschool education was the Perry Preschool Project begun in Ypsilanti, Michigan, in 1962. Children, mostly three years old, were randomly assigned to treatment (58 children) and control (65 children) groups between 1962 and 1965. Children in the treatment group received two academic years of schooling before they entered the regular school system at about age 5, whereas children in the control group did not. The project collected information on the children through age 19, an exceptionally long follow-up period. Using information generated by the study, analysts estimated that two years of preschool generated social net benefits (1988 dollars) of $13,124 at a discount rate of 5 percent. [For a more complete account, see W. Steven Barnett, "Benefits of Compensatory Preschool Education," *Journal of Human Resources,* 27, no. 2 (1992), 279–312.]

a. Before seeing results from the project, what would be your main methodological concern about such a long follow-up period? What data would you look at to see if the problem exists?

b. Benefit categories beyond age 19 included crime reduction, earnings increase, and reductions in welfare receipts. If you were designing the study, what data would you collect to help measure these benefits?

4. Five years ago a community college district established programs in 10 new vocational fields. The district now wants to phase out those programs that are not performing successfully and retain those programs that are performing successfully. To determine which programs to drop and which to retain, the district decides to perform cost-benefit analyses.

a. What perspective or perspectives should be used in the studies? Are there any issues concerning standing?

b. Using a stylized cost-benefit framework table, list the major benefits and costs that are relevant to the district's decision and indicate how each affects different pertinent groups, as well as society as a whole. Try to make your list as comprehensive and complete as possible, while avoiding double counting.

c. What sort of evaluation design should the district use in conducting its CBAs? What are the advantages and disadvantages of this design? Is it practical?

d. Returning to the list of benefits and costs that you developed in 4.b., indicate which of the benefits and costs on your list can be quantified in monetary terms. How would you treat those benefits and costs that cannot be monetized?

e. What sort of data would be required to measure those benefits and costs that can be monetized? How might the required data be obtained?

Notes

1. David H. Greenberg and Marvin B. Mandell, "Research Utilization in Policymaking: A Tale of Two Series (of Social Experiments)," *Journal of Policy Analysis and Management,* 10, no. 4 (1991), 633–656.

2. For a discussion, see Irwin Garfinkel, Charles F. Manski, and Charles Michalopoulos, "Micro Experiments and Macro Effects" in *Evaluating Welfare and Training Programs,* Charles F. Manski and Irwin Garfinkel, eds. (Cambridge, MA: Harvard University Press, 1992), pp. 25–75.

3. In practice, many of the services offered under a demonstration program may also be offered under the existing environment. For example, in the case of training programs, training of many types may already be available through community colleges and adult schools. Consequently, estimates of program effects on participants do not measure impacts of the receipt of service against the non-receipt of services. Rather such estimates usually pertain to the *incremental* effect of the demonstration program over the existing environment.

4. This method of diagramming evaluation designs was developed a number of years ago by Donald Campbell and Julian Stanley, *Experimental and Quasi-Experimental Designs for Research* (Chicago: Rand McNally, 1963).

5. On randomization problems, see Leslie L. Roos Jr., Noralou P. Roos, and Barbara McKinley, "Implementing Randomization," *Policy Analysis,* 3, no. 4 (1977), 547–559, and Larry L. Orr, *Social Experiments: Evaluating Public Programs with Experimental Methods* (Thousand Oaks, CA: Sage Publications, Inc., 1999).

6. Sometimes a problem occurs when some members of the two groups cannot be located for purposes of collecting postprogram information on outcomes or refuse to provide the information. This problem, which can occur with all five of the sample designs listed in Table 11.1 and which is known as *sample attrition,* can bias the impact estimates if those who can and cannot be located systematically differ from one another in terms of the postprogram outcome measures. For example, those who can be located may have higher earnings, on average, than those who cannot be located.

7. For discussions of issues and problems that arise in conducting social experiments, see Gary Burtless, "The Case for Randomized Field Trials in Economic and Policy Research," *The Journal of Economic Perspectives,* 9, no. 2 (1995), 63–84 and James S. Heckman and Jeffrey A. Smith, "Assessing the Case for Social Experiments," *The Journal of Economic Perspectives,* 9, no. 2 (1995), 85–110.

8. The name stems from the fact that in the absence of random assignment people select themselves to participate or not participate in a program on the basis of such unobservable characteristics as motivation. If appropriate statistical adjustments cannot be made to control for this—as the text indicates, sometimes this is possible, but sometimes it is not—then sample selection bias results. For further information on the selection problem and econometric techniques that are used to attempt to adjust for it, see G. S. Maddala, *Introduction to Econometrics* (New York: Macmillan Publishing Co., 1988); G. S. Maddala, *Limited-Dependent and Qualitative Variables in Econometrics* (New York: Cambridge University Press, 1983); and Christopher H. Achen, *Statistical Analysis of Quasi-Experiments* (Berkeley: University of California Press, 1986).

9. For a survey of the social experiments conducted between 1962 and 1996, see David Greenberg, Mark Shroder, and Matthew Onstott, "The Social Experiment Market," *Journal of Economic Perspectives,* 13, no. 3 (1999), 157–172. For two- to three-page summaries of each of the known 143

social experiments that were completed in the United States by the end of 1996, see David Greenberg and Mark Shroder, *Digest of the Social Experiments,* 2nd ed. (Washington, DC: The Urban Institute Press, 1997).

10. David H. Greenberg and Philip K. Robins, "The Changing Role of Social Experiments in Policy Analysis," *Journal of Policy Analysis and Management,* 5, no. 2 (1986), 340–362.

11. For recent summaries of findings from evaluations of E&T programs and methodological issues associated with these evaluations, see Robert J. La-Londe, "The Promise of Public Sector-Sponsored Training Programs," *Journal of Economic Perspectives,* 9, no. 2 (1997), 149–168; and Daniel Friedlander, David H. Greenberg, and Philip K. Robins, "Evaluating Government Training Programs for the Economically Disadvantaged," *Journal of Economic Literature,* 35, no. 4 (1997), 1809–1855.

12. The supply curve in Figure 11.1 should be viewed as a compensated supply curve. That is, it incorporates substitution, but not income, effects. For reasons discussed in Appendix 3A, this is the appropriate curve for measuring changes in worker surplus resulting from wage changes. However, as Exhibit 11.2 suggests, wage changes may engender substantial income, as well as substitution, effects. The implications of this possibility are mentioned later.

13. The word *leisure,* as commonly used by economists and as used here, refers to all activities that take place outside the labor market. Many of these activities (e.g., child care, home repair, and education) may, of course, be quite productive.

14. Because the hours the recipient is required to work are computed by dividing her welfare grant by the minimum wage (i.e., $h^* = \text{grant}/W^m$), her grant equals $W^m h^*$, a value that in Figure 11.3 is represented by area $W^m a h^* h_0$.

15. Notice that because the supply curve first shifts from S_0 to S_1, and then, in response to this shift the participant adjusts the number of hours she works, the surplus loss is measured using S_1 rather than S_0.

16. David H. Greenberg, "The Leisure Bias in Cost-Benefit Analyses of Employment and Training Programs," *Journal of Human Resources,* 30, no. 2 (1999), 413–439.

17. The specific manner in which the labor supply curve in Figure 11.4 may shift in response to subsidized child care is complex. The reservation wage of nonworkers, W_r in Figure 11.4(a), will clearly fall

as a result of subsidized child care. However, those who would work regardless of whether they receive a subsidy—for example, an individual at W_1 in Figure 11.4(a)—may actually work fewer hours as a result of the subsidy. This is due to the fact that the subsidy decreases their work-related expenditures and, hence, increases their discretionary income. The resulting income effect would tend to decrease hours of work. Hence, the earnings of these persons could actually fall as a result of the subsidy. Thus, the new supply curve may be below and to the right of the old supply curve at low market wage rates but above and to the left of the old supply curve at higher wage rates. [For a more detailed discussion, see Ronald G. Ehrenberg and Robert S. Smith, *Modern Labor Economics: Theory and Public Policy,* 6th ed. (Reading, MA: Addison-Wesley, 1997], Appendix 6A.

18. As mentioned earlier in the chapter, having as many able-bodied individuals work as possible is considered an important social goal by many U.S. citizens. Thus, even though subsidizing child care may be economically inefficient, it may still be justified if it helps meet this goal.

19. This section borrows heavily from David Greenberg, "Conceptual Issues in Cost-Benefit Analysis of Welfare-to-Work Programs," *Contemporary Policy Issues,* 10, no. 4 (1992), 51–63.

20. One approach that might be used to do this is contingent valuation, a topic that is taken up in Chapter 14.

21. For a review of what bureaucrats actually maximize, see David L. Weimer and Aidan R. Vining, *Policy Analysis: Concepts and Practice,* 3rd ed. (Upper Saddle River, NJ: Prentice Hall, 1999), pp. 183–190.

22. See Friedlander, Greenberg, and Robins, "Evaluating Government Training Programs for the Disadvantaged," p. 1836, for a summary of the scant evidence that exists.

23. Using five years of follow-up information on women who had received training under the Manpower Development and Training Act, Orley Ashenfelter found that the program's earnings effect decayed at an annual rate of 5 percent for black women but grew at an annual rate of 7 percent for white women [Orley Ashenfelter, "Estimating the Effects of Training Programs on Earnings," *Review of Economics and Statistics,* 60, no. 1 (1978), 47–57]. Not only are the divergent results for black and white women difficult to

reconcile, but in a reanalysis of Ashenfelter's data, Howard Bloom ["Estimating the Effect of Job Training Programs Using Longitudinal Data: Ashenfelter's Findings Reconsidered," *Journal of Human Resources,* 19, no. 4 (1984), 544–556] obtained quite different results.

24. For example, see Ron Haskins, "Congress Writes a Law: Research and Welfare Reform," *Journal of Policy Analysis and Management,* 10, no. 4 (1991), 616–632; Erica Baum, "When the Witch Doctors Agree: The Family Support Act and Social Science Research," *The Journal of Policy Analysis and Management,* 10, no. 4 (1991), 603–615; and Peter Szanton, "The Remarkable 'Quango': Knowledge, Politics, and Welfare Reform," *Journal of Policy Analysis and Management,* 10, no. 4 (1991), 590–602.

25. Summaries of each of the Work/Welfare Demonstrations, as well as more recent welfare-to-work demonstrations that have been evaluated using an experimental design, can be found in David Greenberg and Mark Shroder, *The Digest of the Social Experiments.* Detailed descriptions of the Work/Welfare Demonstrations, as well as the CBA findings from these demonstrations, can be found in the following reports published by the Manpower Demonstration Research Corporation, New York, NY: P. Auspos, G. Cave, and D. Long, *Maine: Final Report on the Training Opportunities in the Private Sector Program,* 1988; S. Freedman, J. Bryant, and G. Cave, *New Jersey: Final Report on the Grant Diversion Project,* 1988; D. Friedlander, G. Hoerz, J. Quint, and J. Riccio, *Arkansas: Final Report on the WORK Program in Two Counties,* 1985; D. Friedlander, G. Hoerz, D. Long, and J. Quint, *Maryland: Final Report on the Employment Initiatives Evaluation,* 1985; D. Friedlander, M. Erickson, G. Hamilton, and V. Knox, *West Virginia: Final Report on the Community Work Experience Demonstrations,* 1986; D. Friedlander, S. Freedman, G. Hamilton, and J. Quint, *Illinois: Final Report on Job Search and Work Experience in Cook County,* 1987; B. Goldman, D. Friedlander, and D. Long, *California: Final Report on the San Diego Job Search and Work Experience Demonstration,* 1986; G. Hamilton and D. Friedlander, *Final Report on the Saturation Work Initiative Model in San Diego,* 1989; J. Riccio, G. Cave, S. Freedman, and M. Price, *Virginia: Final Report on the Virginia Employment Services Program,* 1986.

26. U.S. House of Representatives, Committee on Ways and Means, *Overview of Entitlement Programs* (Washington, DC: U.S. Government Printing Office, 1993), p. 616, Table 1.

27. If the demonstration period were sufficiently long, then the decay rate could be determined on the basis of the pattern of changes in earnings actually observed. Typically, however, this period is only two or three years long, which is too short a time to establish a clear pattern.

28. Ketron, Incorporated, *The Long-Term Impact of WIN II: A Longitudinal Evaluation of the Employment Experiences of Participants in the Work Incentive Program* (Wayne, PA: Ketron, 1980).

29. Daniel Friedlander, Gregory Hoerz, David Long, and Janet Quint, *Maryland: Final Report on the Employment Initiatives Evaluation* (New York: Manpower Demonstration Research Corporation, 1985).

30. Daniel Friedlander, *Maryland: Supplemental Report on the Baltimore Options Program* (New York: Manpower Demonstration Research Corporation, 1987).

31. The 2.0 shadow price figure is based on the following assumptions: (1) the marginal rate of time preference is equal to 1.5 percent; (2) the gross pretax rate of return on capital in the private sector is equal to 19.6 percent; (3) the gross savings rate is equal to 15 percent; and (4) the depreciation rate of private-sector capital is 10 percent. The basis for each of these assumptions, as well as the formula used to compute the shadow price, can be found in Chapter 10.

32. Greenberg, "The Leisure Bias in Cost-Benefit Analyses of Employment and Training Programs."

33. Greenberg reported several sets of adjusted estimates based on alternative assumptions. The second column of Table 11.7 is based on the most conservative of these and, hence, differs the least from the unadjusted estimates in the first column. In making the calculations appearing in the second column of Table 11.7, Greenberg assumed that the income effect is equal to zero. However, Greenberg's analysis also indicates that this assumption is unlikely to cause large errors in the calculations.

34. Daniel Friedlander and Gary Burtless, *Five Years After: The Long-Term Effects of Welfare-to-Work Programs* (New York: Russell Sage Foundation, 1995).

CHAPTER

12

VALUING IMPACTS FROM OBSERVED BEHAVIOR

Direct Estimation of Demand Curves

The key concept for valuing policy impacts is change in social surplus. As discussed in Chapters 3 and 4, changes in social surplus are represented by areas, often as triangles or trapezoids, bounded by supply and demand curves. Measurement of changes in social surplus is relatively straightforward when we know the shape and positions of the supply and demand curves in the relevant primary market, before and after the policy change.

In practice, however, these curves are usually not known. Analysts have to estimate them or find alternative ways to measure benefits and costs. In the previous chapter, we discuss how such information can be gathered from demonstrations and social experiments. In this chapter, we discuss direct estimation of these curves.

We focus on estimating demand curves. The main reason is that, in practice, analysts are more interested in estimating changes in consumer surplus than changes in producer surplus. Many changes in producer surplus are either offset by changes in consumer surplus, and thereby constitute transfers, or are, in practice, negligible. There are three major exceptions. One pertains to unemployed labor, which we discuss in detail in Chapters 4 and 11. The second arises when the government intervenes in otherwise efficient markets for capital, foreign exchange, labor, and other productive assets. We discuss these issues in Chapter 16. The third concerns computation of the marginal excess tax burden, which is introduced in Chapter 3 and discussed later in this chapter.

For goods traded in well-functioning markets, we can usually observe at least one piece of information—the market clearing price. We may also be able to observe the aggregate quantity bought and sold so that we have the point of intersection of the demand and supply curves. Combining price and quantity provides expenditures (or revenues depending on your perspective). The next section discusses the use of revenues as an estimate of (gross) benefits. Often we have additional observations on price and quantity from different regions or different time periods. If the observed prices and quantities differ, we may be able to estimate the market demand curve using standard econometric techniques. (Appendix 12A contains an introduction to multiple regression analysis and ordinary least squares estimation.) The subsequent section discusses alternative ways to estimate demand curves and how to interpret the estimated coefficients. Finally, we discuss measurement of the marginal excess tax burden.

PROJECT REVENUES AS THE MEASURE OF (GROSS) BENEFITS

To private-sector producers of goods or services, project revenues are a natural measure of (gross) benefits. Revenues also feature prominently in the computation of producer surplus. But, as shown in Chapter 4, when there are no market imperfections, the social benefits of a project equal the revenues plus changes in social surplus. Considering only revenues omits changes in social surplus.

Of course, it is theoretically correct to treat revenues as benefits where changes in social surplus equal zero. Consider, for example, a publicly supported project that exports all of its output. In such projects, the consumer surplus accrues to foreigners and, therefore, should not be counted if the analyst takes a national perspective. The North East Coal Development Project, which we discuss in Chapter 6, provides an example. As this project would supply coal to Japanese customers only, Table 6.5 shows no consumer surplus benefits for Canadians. The primary beneficiaries (besides the Canadian federal government) were the mining and transportation companies that would benefit from increased revenues. Their producer surplus increase is legitimately computed as the differences between their (additional) revenues and their (additional) costs. Thus, when there are no domestic consumers, there are no changes in consumer surpluses so that benefits do equal revenues.

Another correct use of "revenues as benefits" occurs when the government sells a good in an undistorted market without affecting the market price. For example, a government may have surplus office equipment that it sells in sufficiently small quantities that the market price of office equipment does not change. This is just the reverse of the opportunity cost case discussed in Chapter 4 in which government purchases do not affect price in an undistorted market. The assumption of a negligible effect on price is more reasonable for goods traded in large national markets than for goods traded in small local markets. It is also more reasonable for homogeneous goods, such as surplus equipment, than for heterogeneous goods, such as land, which may differ from one parcel to another.

Unfortunately, the government often sells goods when markets are distorted or when the sale has a large impact on the price of the good. For example, electricity may not be available to residents of a remote town unless the government sponsors the construction of an electric power transmission line. Here introduction of electricity reduces the price from effectively infinity to the user fee charged. In these situations, revenues are a poor measure of social benefits.

DIRECT ESTIMATION OF THE DEMAND CURVE

It is sometimes possible to make inferences about the demand curve. We consider three possibilities. First, we know only one point on the demand curve, but previous research provides an estimate of either the elasticity or slope of the demand curve. Second, we know a few points on the demand curve that we can use to predict another point of relevance to policy evaluation. Third, we have a sufficient number of different observations of prices and quantities so that we can apply econometric methods to estimate the demand curve.

Knowing One Point on the Demand Curve and Its Slope or Elasticity

Many municipalities charge annual fees for household refuse collection that do not depend on the quantity of refuse disposed of by households. In such communities, the marginal private cost (MPC) of an additional unit of garbage is effectively zero, whereas the marginal social cost (MSC) of disposing of it is shared equally among all households.[1] This divergence between MPC and MSC leads to free riding and a socially excessive amount of refuse disposal. Raising the marginal private cost of refuse disposal would reduce the quantity of refuse disposed of by households and thereby reduce the social surplus loss from excess refuse disposal.

Imagine that you have been asked to measure the social benefits that would result if a town, Wasteville, which currently does not charge households by volume for refuse collection, imposes a fee of $1 per 30-gallon container. That is, households would be charged $1 for each such container put at the curbside for emptying by the sanitation department. As a 30-gallon container holds about 20 pounds of waste, the new policy implies a price increase from zero to about $0.05/lb, assuming the containers are full.

From the sanitation department's records, you find that the current refuse disposal rate is 2.60 pounds per person per day (lb/p/d) and the marginal social cost of each ton of refuse collected is approximately $120 per ton, or $0.06/lb. (One ton equals 2,000 pounds in North America.) This marginal social cost is the sum of the marginal collection costs of $40 per ton and the tipping fee at the landfill of $80 per ton. Though the fee still leaves the marginal private cost (price) below the marginal social cost, you expect it will produce a gain in social surplus by reducing the amount of waste generated.

To measure the social surplus gain, however, you require the demand curve for garbage disposal. You know only one point on the demand curve: 2.60 lb/p/d of garbage at a price equal to zero. To progress any further, you must find a way of estimating the rest of the demand curve. Usually demand curves are linear in logarithms. To begin, however, we assume the demand curve is linear.

Linear Demand Curve

A market demand curve for a good tells us how many units of the good consumers wish to purchase at each price. A linear functional form assumes that the relationship between the quantity demanded and the price is linear; that is, the demand curve can be written as:

$$q = \alpha_0 + \alpha_1 p \tag{12.1}$$

where q is the quantity demanded at price p, α_0 is the quantity that would be demanded when price is zero (the intercept), and α_1 indicates the change in the quantity demanded as a result of a one-unit increase in price (the slope). We expect demand curves to slope down; that is, $\alpha_1 < 0$. For Wasteville, we can assume $\alpha_0 = 2.60$ (the amount of garbage disposed at a price of zero). However, we do not know the slope, α_1. Two possibilities arise: We may obtain a direct estimate of the slope or we may estimate the slope using an estimate of the price elasticity of demand.

Using a Slope Estimate   If you went to a research library or used the bibliography at the end of this book, you might turn up a study that would give you an empirically based estimate of the slope of the demand curve for refuse disposal. Indeed, Robin R. Jenkins provides such a study.[2] Jenkins based her estimate on data from nine U.S. communities, which employed a variety of refuse fees linked to volume, ranging from zero in three communities to between $0.25 and $1.73 per 30- to 32-gallon container in the other six, over the period from 1980 to 1989. She estimated that each dollar increase in the price of a 30- to 32-gallon container reduces waste by 0.40 lb/p/d. Put another way, she estimated $\alpha_1 = -0.40$. Using this estimate leads to a prediction that if Wasteville imposed a fee of $1 per container ($0.05/lb), then residential waste disposal would fall by 0.40 lb/p/d from 2.60 lb/p/d to 2.20 lb/p/d.

Figure 12.1 shows the demand curve implied by Jenkins's slope estimate: $q = 2.60 - 0.4p$. This curve goes through the status quo point of 2.60 lb/p/d at zero dollars per pound (point *c*) and the predicted point of 2.20 lb/p/d at $0.05 per pound (point *d*).

We can use this curve to estimate changes in social surplus. Remembering that the socially optimal price is $0.06 per pound, the area of the triangle *abc*, $0.5(2.60 - 2.12)(.06 - 0.00) = $0.0144/p/d, is the social surplus loss at zero price, and the area of the small triangle *aed*, $0.0004/p/d, is the social surplus loss at the price of $0.05/lb. Thus, the area of trapezoid *debc*, $0.0140/p/d, is the gain in social surplus that would result from the price increase from zero to $0.05/lb. If the population of Wasteville is 100,000 people, then the annual gross benefit of imposing a container fee

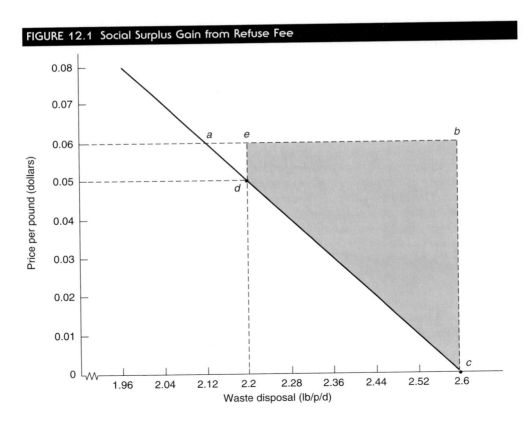

FIGURE 12.1 Social Surplus Gain from Refuse Fee

of $1 is ($0.0140/p/d)(365 days)(100,000 persons) = $511,000, the reduction in social surplus loss.

When using slope or elasticity estimates from previous research, it is important to consider issues of *internal validity* and *external validity*. Internal validity involves the sort of evaluation design issues discussed in Chapter 11, as well as issues related to the proper use of econometric techniques, which we discuss later in this chapter. External validity concerns the appropriateness of using estimates derived from data collected at other times, in other places, and with different populations. Applying estimates to circumstances similar to those under which they were obtained has high external validity. Specifically, the closer Wasteville is in economic, policy, demographic, and geographic characteristics to the communities in Jenkins's sample, the more confident we can be in the accuracy of our estimated change in waste disposal following the introduction of a volumetric user fee in Wasteville. We would be less confident if her estimate had been based on data from the 1960s or 1970s rather than the 1980s because there would have been more time for unmeasured variables, such as the level of environmental awareness or recycling infrastructure, to have changed.

Usually, demand curves are drawn with price on the vertical axis, not quantity. Demand curves in which price is a function of quantity are called inverse demand curves. Accordingly, rearranging equation (12.1) gives:

$$p = -\alpha_0/\alpha_1 + (1/\alpha_1)q \qquad (12.2)$$

The slope of the inverse demand curve equals $1/\alpha_1 < 0$. The intercept of the inverse demand curve, which indicates the quantity that would be demanded if the price were zero, is sometimes called the *choke price*. For the demand curve estimated previously and shown in Figure 12.1, the inverse demand curve is $p = 6.5 - 2.5q$, and the choke price is $6.50. We return to inverse demand curves later.

Using an Elasticity Estimate   The preceding section assumes that the demand curve for garbage disposal in Wasteville is linear and that we have a valid estimate of its slope. This section still assumes that the demand for garbage disposal in Wasteville is linear but supposes we have an estimate of the price elasticity of demand. We need to determine the slope.

The price elasticity of demand, ε_d, measures the responsiveness of the quantity demanded to changes in price—the more elastic, the more responsive. For a linear demand curve, equation (12.1), the price elasticity of demand equals:

$$\varepsilon_d = \alpha_1 p/q \qquad (12.3)$$

Thus, the elasticity is nonconstant—it varies with both price and quantity.[3] Notice that price elasticities of demand are *always* negative because $\alpha_1 < 0$, and p and $q > 0$. According to the preceding definition, the elasticity *increases* as the slope of the demand curve *decreases* (i.e., becomes more negative). As this is cumbersome, we follow the economist's usual practice of talking about elasticities as if they were positive, in effect taking the absolute value of the elasticity. Thus, we say that the elasticity *increases* as the slope *increases*. The noneconomist may find this a bit confusing at first, but everyone soon gets used to it.

Given an estimate of the price elasticity, we can use equation (12.3) to estimate the demand curve's slope if we also know the price and quantity at which the elasticity was estimated. Returning to our garbage example, suppose Jenkins did not provide an estimate of the slope but instead reported an estimate of the price elasticity of the demand for residential refuse disposal of -0.12 and the price and quantity at which this elasticity was calculated. Specifically, she estimated the elasticity at the average price charged by those communities in her sample that had nonzero fees, \$0.81/container, and the average residential waste disposed of by the communities in her sample, 2.62 lb/p/d.[4] Using this information, we can recover α_1 from equation (12.3), thus:

$$\alpha_1 = \varepsilon_d q/p = (-0.12)(2.62)/(0.81) \approx -0.40$$

The general point is that construction of a linear demand curve to measure changes in social surplus requires either a direct estimate of the slope itself or an estimate of the price elasticity of demand and the price and quantity at which the elasticity was estimated.

Constant Elasticity Demand Curve

The demand curve may not be linear. Economists have found that many goods have a *constant elasticity demand curve*; that is:

$$q = \beta_0 p^{\beta_1} \tag{12.4}$$

where q denotes quantity demanded and p is price, as before, and β_0 and β_1 are parameters. In order to interpret β_1 it is useful to take the natural logarithm, denoted by $\ln$, of both sides of equation (12.4), which gives:

$$\ln q = \ln \beta_0 + \beta_1 \ln p \tag{12.5}$$

We see immediately that the constant elasticity demand curve is linear in logarithms.[5] Furthermore, β_1, the slope of this logarithmic form of demand curve, equals ε_d, the price elasticity of demand.[6] As ε_d equals the slope of a linear curve, which is a constant, it follows that the price elasticity of demand is constant, hence, the name of this demand curve.

The slope of the constant elasticity demand curve is not constant; specifically, it equals $\beta_1 q/p$.[7] Clearly, it varies with q and p. Because $\beta_1 < 0$, generally, $q > 0$ and $p > 0$, the constant elasticity demand curve slopes downward (i.e., it has a negative slope). It is also asymptotic to both the price and quantity axes. That is, as price becomes infinite, the quantity demanded approaches zero, and as price approaches zero, the quantity demanded approaches infinity. As we are most often interested in the region of the demand curve where price is finite and greater than zero, and the estimates of elasticities are based on data in this range, these asymptotic extremes are usually not relevant to our analysis.

EXHIBIT 12.1

Erik Lichtenberg and David Zilberman wished to estimate the costs and benefits of government regulations that reduced pesticide use in agriculture. Their study covered three important crops: corn, cotton, and rice. There have been numerous empirical studies of price elasticities in agricultural markets. After reviewing this literature, they came up with "consensus values" for the elasticity of supply of 0.3 (corn), 0.5 (cotton), and 0.8 (rice), and for the elasticity of demand of -0.5 (corn), -0.41 (cotton), and -0.43 (rice). The supply and demand functions for all three crops were assumed to have constant elasticity forms.

Source: Erik Lichtenberg and David Zilberman, "The Welfare Economics of Price Supports in U.S. Agriculture," *American Economic Review*, 76, no. 5 (1986), 1135–1141.

As an illustration of how to use a constant elasticity demand curve, consider the following situation. A community (not Wasteville) currently charges a refuse collection fee of $0.05/lb and waste disposal is 2.25 lb/p/d. We have been asked to estimate the change in consumer surplus that would result if the collection fee were raised to $0.08/lb, assuming that the demand for refuse has a constant elasticity functional form.

After some research we find an applicable study that reports an estimate of the price elasticity of demand of -0.15. Using this estimate of β_1, equation (12.4), and our status quo point, which is labeled point a in Figure 12.2, we solve for β_0:

$$\beta_0 = (2.25)/(0.05)^{-0.15} \approx 1.44$$

which gives us $q = 1.44p^{-0.15}$ as the underlying demand curve for our application.[8] If fees were raised to $0.08/lb, waste disposal would fall to 2.10 lb/p/d.[9] This point is labeled as point b in Figure 12.2.[10]

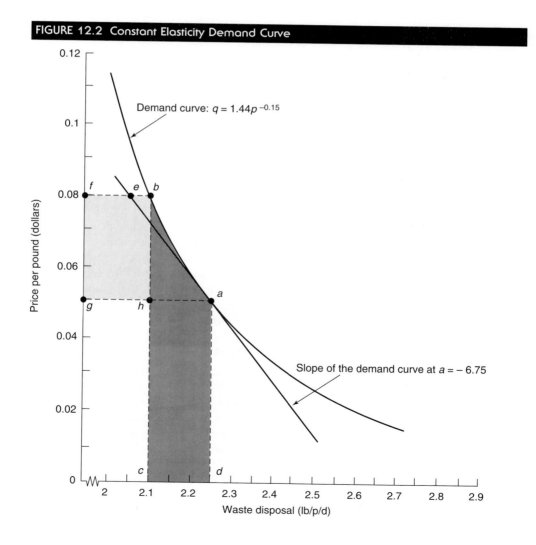

FIGURE 12.2 Constant Elasticity Demand Curve

Demand curve: $q = 1.44p^{-0.15}$

Slope of the demand curve at $a = -6.75$

Price per pound (dollars)

Waste disposal (lb/p/d)

The change in consumer surplus resulting from an increase in the price from $0.05 to $0.08 is represented by the area *fbag* in Figure 12.2. This can be broken down into two areas: *bah,* the consumer surplus lost on the garbage that was previously disposed of but is no longer generated after the price increase, and *fbhg,* the increase in fee payments on the remaining quantity.

To estimate the former area, *bah,* we need to calculate the darkly shaded area under the demand curve and then subtract the rectangle *hadc.* In general, the area under a constant elasticity demand curve from quantity q_0 to quantity q_1 is given (exactly) by:

$$\text{Area} = \left(\frac{1}{\beta_0}\right)^{1/\beta_1}\frac{(q_1 - q_0)^\rho}{\rho} \tag{12.6}$$

where $\rho = [1 + (1/\beta_1)]$.[11] Applying this formula to measure the area under the demand curve in Figure 12.2 where q ranges from 2.10 lb/p/d to 2.25 lb/p/d yields an area $0.0097/p/d. We could approximate the area as a trapezoid by assuming a straight line between the status quo point (point *a*) and the predicted point (point *b*), with *c* and *d* being the other corners of the trapezoid. This method would lead to an estimated area of $0.00975/p/d, a slight overestimation. In practice, imprecision in our empirical estimates of elasticities usually swamps the error resulting from linear approximation of areas. Thus, such approximations are usually reasonable.

Subtracting area *hadc,* which measures the reduction in fee payments due to the reduction in quantity [($0.05/lb)(2.25 lb/p/d − 2.10 lb/p/d) = $0.0075/p/d], from the area under the demand curve ($.0097/p/d) gives an estimate of area *bah* equal to $0.0022. Adding the increase in fee payments on the remaining quantity [($0.08 − $0.05)(2.10 lb/p/d) = $0.063/p/d] provides an estimate of overall loss in consumer surplus equal to $0.0652/p/d.[12] For a town with a population of 100,000, the consumer surplus lost annually would be $0.0652 × 365 × 100,000 = $2.38 million.

A complication arises when we wish to use an elasticity estimated with a constant-elasticity functional form to predict the effect of raising a price from zero to some positive level. As the constant-elasticity demand curve is inconsistent with an observation of zero price, there is no fully satisfactory way to make use of the elasticity estimate. We are forced to postulate some other functional form that goes through the status quo point and use the constant-elasticity estimate as a rough guide for specifying its parameters. This expediency should be thought of as an informed guess that can serve as the starting point for sensitivity analysis.

Extrapolating from a Few Points

Recent policy or other fortuitous changes (at least from the analyst's perspective) often provide a basis for predicting the impacts of future policy changes. For example, imagine that we wish to predict the effect of a fare increase on bus ridership. If the last fare increase of $0.25 resulted in 1,000 fewer riders per day, then it may be reasonable to assume that a further increase of $0.25 would have a similar effect. Here we are treating the observations as if they resulted from a simple before and after quasi-experimental design.

Two considerations are important in determining the appropriateness of extrapolating from the effects of a previous change.

The first consideration concerns the assumed functional relationship between the outcome and the policy variable. Linear functional forms can produce very different predictions than constant-elasticity functional forms, for instance. This is illustrated in Figure 12.3. Suppose that another municipality, Twopointsville, has been experimenting with waste disposal charges. When these residents were charged $0.01/lb for refuse, they disposed of 2.52 lb/p/d (point *a*), and when the fee was raised to $0.025/lb, they disposed of only 2.40 lb/p/d (point *b*). We would like to know how much waste disposal would occur in Twopointsville if the fee is raised further to $0.05/lb. If we fitted a linear demand curve to the two points, then we would predict that waste would fall by 0.20 lb/p/d to 2.20 lb/p/d (point *c*). If, instead, we fitted a constant-elasticity demand curve to the two points, then we would predict that waste would fall by a smaller amount, 0.09 lb/p/d to 2.31 lb/p/d (point *d*).[13] Note that each of these functional forms fits the two observed data points equally well—perfectly!

Note also that Figure 12.3 illustrates a very important general point: *The further we extrapolate from past experience, the more sensitive are our predictions to assumptions about functional form.* In the absence of theoretical guidance or other empirical evidence, we have no basis for choosing between the two widely different predictions shown in Figure 12.3.

FIGURE 12.3 Imputing a Demand Curve from Two Points

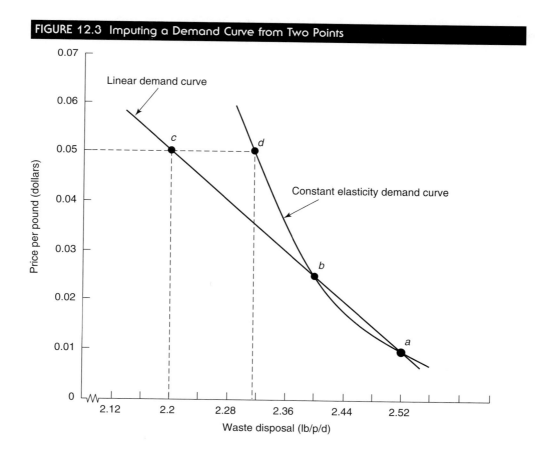

The second consideration concerns the validity of attributing the change in the outcome to the change in the policy variable. "History" poses threats to the internal validity of our quasi-experiment. In attributing the change in outcome to the policy change, we are implicitly assuming that no other variables of relevance to the outcome changed during the time period under consideration. For example, the fall in bus ridership might have resulted in part from the opening of a major new highway that reduced the effective price of driving a private vehicle, a substitute for riding the bus. If this were the case, then it is unlikely that a similar further change in fare would produce as large a reduction in ridership as did the previous fare change.

One way to control for changes in other variables and gain greater confidence about the appropriate functional form is to collect more observations on more variables and use econometric techniques to estimate key parameters.

Econometric Estimation with Many Observations

If many observations of quantities demanded at different prices are available, then it may be possible to use econometric techniques to estimate demand schedules. The linear regression model typically serves as the starting point for such efforts. We assume here that the reader is familiar with the basic concepts of linear regression. Readers unfamiliar with these concepts, or desiring to review them, should read Appendix 12A. Readers requiring a fuller treatment should consult a basic econometrics text.[14]

Model Specification[15]   The starting point for econometric estimation of demand functions is to specify the important explanatory, or independent, variables, such as price and income, that affect quantity demanded.[16] For example, we may have theoretical reasons to believe that the demand for a particular good, q, is a function of the price of that good, p, income, I, and temperature, T:

$$q = f(p, I, T) \tag{12.7}$$

Returning to waste disposal, a recent study by James Strathman, Anthony Rufolo, and Gerard Mildner assumes that the demand for waste disposal depends on the tipping fee, manufacturing income, and construction employment.[17]

The model should include all variables that theoretically affect demand. Even though we may not have a substantive interest in some of the explanatory variables, such as temperature or construction employment, they should be included in the model if they are theoretically related to demand. Including relevant explanatory variables enables one to "control" for their effects on the dependent variable and thereby isolate the *independent effects* of variables of interest, such as price and income.

In practice, however, the list of included explanatory variables is usually quite limited for three general reasons. First, measures of variables may not be available at reasonable cost. For example, the demand for waste disposal may depend on attitudes toward recycling that we cannot measure without specialized surveys, which may be too costly given available resources. Second, some variables may have relatively small effects. For example, temperature may have only a small effect on the demand for a good. Third, variables may be excluded because they are too highly correlated with other explanatory variables—the problem of *multicollinearity*. In this case, it may not be possible to estimate the parameters with precision, as we discuss in Appendix 12A.

The seriousness of excluding a theoretically important variable depends on the degree to which it is correlated with an included variable of interest—one whose coefficient we require for predicting policy effects. If an excluded variable is not correlated with an included variable, then excluding it will not bias the estimated coefficient of the included variable.[18] If an excluded variable is correlated with an included variable, then the estimated coefficient of the included variable will be biased because it incorporates part of the effect of the excluded variable with which it is correlated. The bias depends on both the degree of correlation between the included and excluded variables and the true coefficient of the excluded variable; if either is very small, then the bias is likely to be small.[19] But if neither is small, the bias may be large.

After identifying the theoretically important and practically available variables, the next task is to specify the functional form of the model. As previously discussed, linear and constant-elasticity forms are the most commonly used. Sometimes we have theoretical reasons for choosing between them; other times we simply see which fits the observed data better.

Assuming the model represented by equation (12.7) has a linear functional form gives the following model:

$$q = \alpha_0 + \alpha_1 p + \alpha_2 I + \alpha_3 T + \varepsilon \tag{12.8}$$

where ε denotes an error term. Note that although this is a linear model, it can contain nonlinear functions of the explanatory variables. For example, by adding the square of temperature as an explanatory variable along with temperature itself, we allow for a nonlinear relationship. Also we can allow for the possibility of different demand curves for different subgroups in our sample by introducing interaction terms. For example, if we have individual-level data and we suspect that men have a steeper demand curve than women, we could include a new variable that is the product of price and the dummy variable (or indicator variable) for sex (say, 0 for men and 1 for women). We would then interpret the coefficient of price as the slope of the demand curve for men, and the sum of the coefficient of the price variable and the coefficient of the price-sex interaction variable as the slope of the demand curve for women. The general point is that we can have quite complicated functional forms within the basic linear specification that can be estimated by ordinary least squares (OLS).

We can also use OLS to estimate the parameters of a constant-elasticity demand function. Imagine, for example, that we wish to estimate the price elasticity of demand for electricity using a random sample of households that face different prices because they are located in different jurisdictions. Let q denote the quantity of electricity consumed during some time period by each household, let p equal the price paid by each household during that time period, I equal each household's income, and S equal the number of individuals in the household. We could specify the following constant-elasticity functional form:

$$q = \beta_0 p^{\beta_1} I^{\beta_2} S^{\beta_3} e^{\varepsilon} \tag{12.9}$$

where the βs are parameters to be estimated, e is the base of the natural logarithm, and ε is the unobserved random error. Taking the natural logarithm of both sides of equation (12.9) gives:

$$\ln q = \ln \beta_0 + \beta_1 \ln p + \beta_2 \ln I + \beta_3 \ln S + \varepsilon \tag{12.10}$$

This constant elasticity specification can be estimated by OLS with $\ln q$ as the dependent variable and $\ln p$, $\ln I$, and $\ln S$ as explanatory variables. The parameters, β, can be interpreted in the standard way, noting that the intercept is an estimate of $\ln \beta_0$ rather than β_0. Thus, the coefficient of the variable $\ln p$ is the price elasticity of demand and the coefficient of the variable $\ln I$ is the income elasticity of demand.

Types of Data   The availability of data is usually the limiting factor in estimating demand schedules. Researchers sometimes have sufficient resources to assemble their own data through random sampling of observations across appropriate units, such as individuals or governmental jurisdictions, or over time, often by month, quarter, or even year. More often, however, resource limitations force researchers to rely on *convenience samples*, that is, data that happen to be available at acceptable cost. These include previously published data, data collected by researchers for other purposes, and samples of administrative records or program clients. Nevertheless, it is worthwhile to briefly review the major considerations in the choice of data and their implications for demand estimation.

The first major consideration is the *level of aggregation*. Individual-level data measure the behavior of persons, families, households, or other consuming units. Aggregate-level data measure the combined behaviors of groups of consumers, usually organized by geographic jurisdictions or demographic characteristics.

Consumer theory is based on models of individual utility maximization. Individual-level data are generally preferable because they provide a close congruence between data and theory. Furthermore, theoretically important variables, such as income, can often be measured directly with individual-level data. In contrast, when using aggregate-level data, a mean or median typically serves as the measure of income, possibly leading to less precise estimates of income elasticity because actual household incomes vary around the aggregate-level measure.

In using aggregate data, there is a risk of making serious errors about the effects of policy-relevant variables on demand. For example, suppose that we use individual-level data from different states to estimate the price elasticity of demand for each state. Further suppose, as expected, each of these price elasticity estimates is negative. Now suppose that another less fortunate researcher has only aggregate-level data that consist of one observation for each state (such as the average price and average quantity demanded in each state). He might hope that his estimated price elasticity is approximately a weighted average of the price elasticities of demand for each state. If so, using his estimate might lead to only slight over- or underestimation of the effects of price changes. It is possible, however, his estimated price elasticity, which is based on aggregate-level state data, is very different from the price elasticities that we estimate for each state. In fact, depending on the aggregate-level price and quantity observations, it could have the wrong sign.[20]

In practice, however, individual-level data are often not available. For example, in estimating the "demand" for criminal acts an important theoretical variable is the "price," which depends on the perceived probability of arrest. We cannot directly observe the probability of arrest perceived by an individual, but we can assume that it is related to the objective probability, which can be estimated as the fraction of crimes that result in arrest within a region or among a group of individuals.

The second major consideration in selecting data concerns the choice between *cross-sectional* data and *time series* data. Cross sections involve observations of variables for a number of comparable units at a particular time, whereas time series involve making repeated observations of variables for a particular unit over time. For example, if we wished to determine the price elasticity of demand for wine, we might take advantage of different excise tax rates across states. Using observations for each of the 50 states for a particular year, we would regress per capita consumption of wine on after-tax retail prices and other explanatory variables, such as average levels of income and education. Alternatively, if the real price of wine has varied over time, we might estimate an elasticity by regressing yearly national per capita consumption in each year on the real price of wine in each year and other variables, such as real per capita income in each year. Cross-sectional and time series data are prone to different types of econometric problems and yield coefficient estimates that have somewhat different interpretations.

Cross-sectional data generally provide estimates of long-run elasticities, whereas time series data usually provide estimates of short-run elasticities. In estimating elasticities from cross sections, we usually assume that the variations in demands across units reflect long-run adjustments to previous price changes. Thus, we obtain estimates of long-run elasticities. Only if we make our observations shortly after a major price change would we interpret the elasticity obtained from a cross section as a short-run elasticity. In estimating elasticities from time series, we observe responses to price changes occurring as frequently as the time unit of the observations. Thus, annual data provide estimates of annual elasticities, and monthly data provide estimates of monthly elasticities. For most goods, monthly elasticities would be interpreted as short run. Annual elasticities, however, may be either short run or long run, depending on the extent to which full adjustment to price changes requires changes in capital goods, location, and other factors that consumers alter gradually.

We would expect short-run price elasticities to be smaller in absolute value than long-run price elasticities because, by definition, there is less time for consumers to adjust to price changes. Indeed, based on a review of 120 empirical studies, Molly Espy found an average short-run price elasticity of demand for gasoline of −0.26 and an average long-run price elasticity of −0.58, with an average short-run income elasticity of 0.47 and an average long-run income elasticity of 0.88.[21] P. B. Goodwin reviewed 120 empirical studies and reports average elasticities of the demand for automobile "traffic" with respect to motor fuel prices based on time series studies: short run, −0.16; long-run, −0.33.[22]

Cross sections and time series tend to involve different econometric problems. Cross sections, especially when they consist of units of different sizes, often have error terms with different variances—the *heteroscedasticity* problem. For example, the variance in the number of accidental deaths from fire is likely to be larger in larger cities, such as New York City, than in much smaller cities, such as Utica, New York. If the variances of the error terms are unequal, then the OLS estimates of the coefficients are unbiased, but their calculated standard errors are smaller than the true standard errors. That is, the reported precision of OLS estimates would be overly optimistic. If the relative sizes of the variances of the error terms were known, then estimating the model by *generalized least squares* (GLS) would give more precise estimates of the coefficients and their standard errors. Discussions of tests for detecting heteroscedasticity and for alternative estimation procedures can be found in most econometrics texts.

Time series data also suffer from a common problem with the error term. Remember that the effects of excluded explanatory variables are incorporated into the error term. If an excluded variable tends to change gradually over time, then it may produce correlation between successive error terms. This is one example of the more general problem of *autocorrelation*, which often exists in one form or another in time series data. It has similar effects to heteroscedasticity: OLS coefficient estimates, though unbiased, are not as precise as reported. More precise estimates of the slope parameters and their standard errors can be obtained by using GLS if the pattern of the autocorrelation is known. The most widely used test for autocorrelation is the Durbin-Watson statistic, which should always be a component of time series analysis. Again, methods for detecting autocorrelation and correcting for it can be found in econometrics texts.

It is also possible to pool cross-sectional and time series data, say, by using data from each state for each of a number of years. Though modeling with pooled time series and cross-sectional data can be quite complex and cannot be discussed here, two points are worth noting. First, pooled data provide a rich source of information. Second, pooled data are vulnerable to the econometric problems encountered with both cross-sectional and time series data.

Identification   In a perfectly competitive market, price and quantity result from the simultaneous interaction of supply and demand. Changes in price and quantity can result from shifts in the supply curve, the demand curve, or both. In the absence of variables that affect only one side of the market, it may not be possible to estimate separate supply and demand curves. Indeed, if quantity supplied and quantity demanded depended only on price, then the equations for both the demand curve and the supply curve would look identical! How can we identify which is the demand curve and which is the supply curve? This is one example of the problem of *identification*. It occurs in multiple-equation models in which some variables, such as price and quantity, are determined simultaneously. Such variables are called *endogenous variables*. In contrast, variables that are fixed or are determined outside of the model are called *exogenous variables*.

In order to identify a demand curve we need to have a variable that affects supply but not demand. Consider a competitive and unregulated market for wheat. If rainfall affects the supply of wheat but not the demand for wheat, then including rainfall in the supply equation but not in the demand equation identifies the demand equation. The reason is that changes in rainfall result in systematic shifts in supply but not demand, which will trace out the demand curve. Similarly, if income affects demand but not supply, then including income in the demand equation but not in the supply equation results in systematic shifts in the demand curve, which will trace out the supply curve. In general, a two-equation model will be identified if there is one exogenous variable that belongs in the first equation but not in the second equation, and another exogenous variable that belongs in the second equation but not in the first equation. By "belong," we mean that it has a nonzero coefficient; and by "not belong," we mean that it has a zero coefficient. The zero coefficient conditions are most important. One cannot identify a model by excluding an exogenous variable from an equation that theoretically belongs in that equation.

Identification of demand curves tends to be less of a problem in the markets typically of interest to cost-benefit analysts than in markets generally. One reason is that

CBA often deals with markets that are subject to exogenous government interventions. For example, the demand for cigarettes is probably easily identified in cross-sectional analysis because differences in state excise taxes shift the supply curve by a different amount in each state.

Also, the identification problem does not arise in markets in which the model consists of only one equation, with quantity demanded as the dependent variable and all other variables are exogenous. In some markets, the government either provides the product or service, as is often the case with municipal waste disposal, or regulates the prices charged, as is the case with electricity. When government supplies a good or effectively sets price, there is no supply curve—price is exogenous. Thus, we avoid the identification problem. Indeed, some transportation researchers have begun to worry that the deregulation of the last decade will make identification of models more difficult in the future![23]

When should analysts worry about the identification problem? A key consideration is whether price can be reasonably treated as exogenous. If it can, perhaps because it is set by a government agency, then identification is unlikely to be a problem. If it is endogenous, then there is a potential identification problem. Information about this topic, as well as methods of simultaneous equation estimation, should be consulted in an econometrics text.

Confidence Intervals   The standard errors of the estimated coefficients of an OLS model can be used to construct confidence intervals for the coefficients. A 95 percent confidence interval is commonly interpreted as there being a 95 percent chance that the true value of the coefficient lies within the interval. Strictly speaking, this is an incorrect interpretation. The correct interpretation is that if we were to repeat our estimation procedure many times, with a new data sample each repetition, the estimated confidence intervals would contain the true value of the coefficient in about 95 percent of the repetitions. Nevertheless, the confidence interval provides some guidance for sensitivity analysis. Most analysts would consider it reasonable to treat the ends of a 95 percent confidence interval as best and worst cases.

Prediction versus Hypothesis Testing   As a final point on estimating demand curves, it is important to keep in mind the distinction between hypothesis testing and estimation. Social scientists are typically interested in testing hypotheses about one or more coefficients in a regression model. If the estimated coefficients are not statistically significantly different from zero, then social scientists do not reject the null hypothesis that the variables have no effect on the dependent variable. In other words, there is not a statistically convincing case that the variables have any effect.

As cost-benefit analysts, however, we have to make a prediction. For such purposes we should use the estimated value of the coefficient, even if it is not statistically significant at conventional levels. Although we may not be very confident that the true value of the coefficient is not zero, the estimated coefficient may be our best estimate of the true value. If so, it will give the best predictions. Sensitivity analysis should reflect the imprecision of our estimate. If we were to use only the statistically significant coefficients from an estimated model, we would bias our prediction. Eliminating these variables and reestimating the model may or may not be appropriate depending on the theoretical strength of their inclusion in the original model.

ESTIMATING THE MARGINAL EXCESS TAX BURDEN (METB)

Government projects are often financed using money raised through taxes. In Chapter 4, we indicate that a tax on a good, such as an excise tax, typically results in deadweight loss. Social surplus is lost in transferring the tax revenue from consumers and producers to the government. This loss (or leakage) occurs whenever there is a behavioral response to a tax—for example, an excise tax on a consumption good causes purchases of the good to fall somewhat or a tax on earnings causes workers to reduce their work hours somewhat. The marginal value of the forgone consumption or forgone hours of work is the deadweight loss of the tax. As a consequence of this loss, the social cost of raising a dollar of revenue through a tax is usually larger than one dollar, sometimes substantially larger.[24]

The social surplus lost from raising an additional dollar of tax revenue is known as the marginal excess tax burden (METB). As we discuss in Chapter 15, estimates of its average value for all taxes combined range from about 33 cents per tax dollar raised to 46 cents per tax dollar raised. As we discuss in Chapter 4, the revenues of government projects and the costs that are financed by taxation (expenditures) should be multiplied by about 1.40.

Estimating the METB is generally more complicated than estimating changes in consumer surplus in the primary market. In fact, it may be very complicated. Exhibit 12.2 presents a hypothetical, but not implausible, illustration of computing the average social cost of redistributing money from higher-income households to lower-income households. In this illustration, it costs $1.63 to transfer each dollar, on average.

EXHIBIT 12.2

The following table, which was adopted with modifications from a study by Edgar Browning, is based on a hypothetical society with only five households. The idea is to tax everyone to obtain $1,350 in additional revenue and then distribute this equally to everyone. The net effect,

The Marginal Cost of Redistribution

Household (1)	Initial (Gross) Earnings (2)	Change in Earnings (3)	Net Additional Tax Revenue* (4)	Transfer (5)	Net Transfer (6)	Change in Disposable Income (7)	Change in Real Income (8)
A	10,000	−25	90	270	180	155	170
B	20,000	−50	180	270	90	40	70
C	30,000	−75	270	270	0	−75	−30
D	40,000	−100	360	270	−90	−190	−130
E	50,000	−125	450	270	−180	−305	−230
Total	150,000	−375	1,350	1,350	0	−375	−150

*These figures are rounded to the nearest $10.

Source: Edgar K. Browning, "The Marginal Cost of Redistribution," *Public Finance Quarterly*, 21, no. 1 (1993), 3–32, Table 1 at p. 5. Reprinted by permission of Sage Publications, Inc.

as shown in column 6, is a total transfer of $270 from the two richest households to the two poorest households. The real incomes of the two poorest households increase by $240 in aggregate, whereas the real incomes of the three richest households decrease by $390. Thus, it costs $1.63 for every dollar transferred, ignoring administrative costs.

For purposes of the illustration, it is assumed that all households initially work 2,000 hours a year and face a marginal tax rate of 40 percent. Thus, as indicated in column 1, the gross before-tax hourly wage rate of household A is $5 ($10,000/2,000), but its after-tax net wage rate is only $3 ($5 × 0.6). The gross and net hourly wage rates for the remaining four households may be similarly computed. It is further assumed that the compensated labor supply elasticity for all households is 0.15, a value that is consistent with empirical estimates presented in Chapter 11. In other words, it is assumed that a 1 percent change in net wages, holding income constant, will cause households to change their hours worked by 0.15 percent.

Suppose now that the government introduces a separate income tax of 1 percent that increases each household's marginal tax rate from 40 percent to 41 percent. This reduces each household's net after-tax wage rate by 1.67 percent (i.e., 0.01/0.60 = 0.0167). As a consequence, hours worked fall by 0.25 percent (0.15 × 0.0167 = 0.0025), or 5 hours per year. Hence, as shown in column 3, earnings also fall by 0.25 percent.

Net additional tax revenue is given in column 4. For example, household A initially paid taxes of $4,000 ($10,000 × 0.4), whereas after the new income tax, it paid taxes of about $4,090 ($9,975 × 0.41), an increase of approximately $90. The total of $1,350 in additional tax revenue is divided equally and $270 is distributed to each household. The net transfer (column 5 − column 4) is given in column 6.

Column 7 presents the total change in disposable income, which is obtained by adding columns 3 and 6. The net incomes of the three richest households have been reduced by $570 in aggregate, whereas the net incomes of the two poorest families have been increased by a total of only $195. But all the families are now working less and enjoying more leisure. Assuming that the value of additional leisure equals the after-tax net wage rate, household A receives a leisure gain valued at $15 ($3 × 5 hours), household B receives a leisure gain valued at $30 ($6 × 5 hours), and so forth. The total change in real income (including the value of the gain in leisure) is given in column 8. The real incomes of households A and B increase by $240 in aggregate, whereas the incomes of households C, D, and E decrease by $390.

CONCLUSION

This chapter focuses on measuring changes in social surplus, especially consumer surplus, when the supply and demand curves are not known. It discusses the use of project revenues as a measure of benefits, direct estimation of the demand curve and estimation of the marginal excess tax burden. Using project revenues as a measure of benefits has relatively limited requirements: It requires the existence of a market for the primary outcome of the project and knowledge of expenditures in this market. In some situations, revenue is an appropriate measure of benefits, but often it is not. In these situations, we need to know more about the demand curve. Direct estimation of the demand curve is possible if we know a least one point on the demand curve, its functional form, and either its slope or the price elasticity of demand. In many practical situations we do not know the slope or the price elasticity of demand. Available data may enable analysts to use econometric methods to estimate the demand curve. It is important to consider the potential limitations of these methods. The final section discussed measurement of the marginal excess tax burden—the change in social surplus resulting from a tax.

Appendix 12A

AN INTRODUCTION TO MULTIPLE REGRESSION ANALYSIS

Linear regression provides a manageable way to control statistically for the effects of several explanatory variables.[1] Its use requires us to assume that the effects of the various explanatory variables on the dependent variable are additive. That is, the marginal effect of a unit change in any one of the explanatory variables on the dependent variable remains the same no matter what the values of the other explanatory variables are. We can express a linear regression model in mathematical form:

$$y = \beta_0 + \beta_1 x_1 + \beta_2 x_2 + \dots + \beta_k x_k + \varepsilon$$

where y is the dependent variable, $x_1, x_2, \dots, x_k$ are the k explanatory (or independent) variables, $\beta_0, \beta_1, \beta_2, \dots, \beta_k$ are parameters (coefficients) to be estimated, and ε is an error term that incorporates the cumulative effect on y of all the factors not explicitly included in the model. The basic model assumes that the explanatory variables are nonrandom and measured without error.

The intercept parameter, β_0, also called the *constant,* is the expected value of y if all the explanatory variables equal zero. The other parameters, $\beta_1, \beta_2, \dots, \beta_k$, which are called *slope* parameters, measure the marginal impact of an explanatory variable on the dependent variable. If, for instance, we were to increase x_1 by one unit while holding the values of the other explanatory variables constant, then y would change by an amount β_1.

Imagine that we set the values of all the explanatory variables except x_1 equal to zero. We could then plot y against x_1 in a two-dimensional graph. The equation $y = \beta_0 + \beta_1 x_1$ would represent the true regression line. The slope of this line is β_1; it measures the magnitude of the change in y that will result from a unit change in x_1, other things being equal. The actual observations will not lie exactly on the line. The vertical distances of the observed points from the line will equal the random error, represented in our model by ε. If the values of ε are small, the true regression line fits the data well in the sense that the actual observations are close to it.

Estimating the Parameters

The most commonly used procedure for fitting a line to the data is the method of ordinary least squares (OLS). When we have only one explanatory variable, so we can plot our data on a two-dimensional graph, the OLS procedure picks the line for which the sum of squared vertical deviations from the estimated line to the observed data is smallest.

Suppose we denote the OLS estimates of the parameters by "hats": $\hat{\beta}_0, \hat{\beta}_1, \dots, \hat{\beta}_k$. For the ith observation $(y_i, x_{i1}, x_{i2}, \dots, x_{ik})$, the predicted value of the dependent variable is:

$$\hat{y}_i = \hat{\beta}_0 + \hat{\beta}_1 x_{1i} + \hat{\beta}_2 x_{2i} + \dots + \hat{\beta}_k x_{ik} \qquad i = 1, \dots, n$$

and the *i*th *prediction error* or *residual* is:

$$\hat{\varepsilon}_i = y_i - \hat{y}_i \qquad i = 1, \ldots, n$$

Thus, the residual is the observed value of the dependent variable minus the value we would predict for the dependent variable based on our estimated parameters and the values of our explanatory variables. OLS selects the parameter estimates to minimize the sum of squares of these residuals.[2]

The square of the correlation between the actual and predicted values of the dependent variable, R^2, is commonly used as a measure of the goodness-of-fit of a regression. The R^2, which ranges between zero and one, measures the percentage of variation in the dependent variable that is explained by the estimated model. It can be used to help select between alternative model specifications when theory is ambiguous, or to test alternative theories.

Multicollinearity

As long as the number of observations in our sample exceeds the number of coefficients that we want to estimate, computer regression software packages will usually enable us to obtain the OLS estimates. However, when one explanatory variable can be written as a linear combination of the others, we have a case of *extreme multicollinearity*. A less severe but more common form of the problem occurs when the explanatory variables in the sample are highly correlated. This condition is called *multicollinearity*. If two or more variables are highly correlated, OLS has difficulty identifying the independent effect of each explanatory variable on the dependent variable. As a result, these parameter estimates are not very reliable or, in the extreme case, they cannot be estimated. When two explanatory variables are highly correlated, the sum of their estimated coefficients will be closer to the sum of their true coefficients than will either individual coefficient estimate be to its true value. Two possible ways to deal with multicollinearity problems include using ridge regression or combining collinear variables into indices using principal components analysis.[3]

Properties of OLS Estimators

The OLS estimator will generally have a number of very desirable properties. (Note: An *estimator* is the formula we use to calculate a particular estimate from the data.) If all of the explanatory variables are uncorrelated with the error term, ε, and if the expected value of the error term is zero, then the OLS estimators will be *unbiased*. To understand what it means for an estimator to be unbiased, we must keep in mind that a particular estimate depends on the errors actually realized in the sample of data. If we were to select a new sample, we would realize different errors and, hence, different coefficient estimates. When an estimator is unbiased, the average of our estimates across different samples will be very close to the true coefficient value. For example, if the price of gasoline had no true effect on the quantity of gasoline demanded, then we would almost certainly estimate its coefficient to be positive or negative rather than exactly zero. Repeating OLS on a large number of samples and averaging our estimates of the coefficient of gasoline price, however, would generally yield a result very close to zero. Indeed, by adding more and more samples, we could get the average as close to zero as we wanted.

The OLS estimator is also consistent, which means that its variance approaches zero as we increase the sample size.[4] Consequently, as the sample size increases, we become more confident about the accuracy of our estimates—the confidence intervals become narrower.

A problem arises, however, if an included variable is correlated with a variable excluded from the model that affects the dependent variable. Suppose, for example, that the weather (temperature) affects the quantity demanded and that temperature is also correlated with gasoline price. Now, gasoline price acts as a proxy for temperature. The coefficient of gasoline price will reflect both the effect of gasoline price on quantity demanded and the indirect effect of temperature for which it serves as a proxy. Other things being equal, the stronger the true effect of temperature on quantity demanded, and the higher the absolute value of the correlation between gasoline price and temperature, the greater will be the bias in the coefficient of gasoline price. This problem cannot be solved by increasing the sample size.

Statistical Significance and Hypothesis Testing

It is often important to determine whether an estimate deviates enough from zero for us to conclude that the true value of the parameter is not zero. If we make the reasonable assumption that the error term for each observation can be treated as a draw from a normal distribution with constant variance σ^2, then we can show that the OLS estimators will be distributed according to the normal distribution.[5] Specifically, we can interpret the particular numerical estimate of a coefficient, $\hat{\beta}$, as a draw from a random variable distributed with a normal distribution centered around the true value of the coefficient, β, with variance, $\sigma_{\hat{\beta}}^2$, which depends on σ^2. (The OLS estimator is the random variable; the actual estimate based on the data is a particular realization of that random variable.) Because we want to know how likely it is that we would observe a coefficient estimate as large as we did if the true value of the coefficient were zero, we now suppose that the true value of the coefficient is zero (the null hypothesis) so that the distribution of our estimator is centered around zero. We then standardize our distribution to have a variance of one by dividing our coefficient estimate by its *estimated standard deviation*. The resultant statistic, called a *t* statistic, or *t* ratio, has a *Student's t distribution*, or *t* distribution.[6] The *statistical significance* of our coefficient estimate can be determined by comparing the *t* statistic to the critical values in a table of the *t* distribution, which can found in the appendix of almost any statistics text. For example, we might decide that we will reject the null hypothesis that the true value of the coefficient is zero if there is less than a 5 percent probability of obtaining a *t* ratio (in absolute value) as large as we did if the null hypothesis is true.[7] If the sample size is large, we would reject this null hypothesis if the *t* statistic were larger in absolute value than 1.96.

The *t* distribution is tabulated by degrees of freedom. The OLS estimators have degrees of freedom equal to the total number of observations minus the number of coefficients being estimated. As the degrees of freedom increase, the Student's *t* distribution looks more like a standardized normal distribution.

Returning to our gasoline example, suppose that the analyst wants to test whether gasoline price has a statistically significant effect on gasoline demand at the 5 percent level of significance. She may specify a one-tailed alternative hypothesis test or a two-tailed alternative hypothesis test. For example, she may test the null hypothesis that the true coefficient value is greater than or equal to zero (the one-tailed alternative is that it is less than zero), which means that the *critical region* consists of the entire 5 percent in the negative tail. Alternatively, she may test the null hypothesis that the true coefficient value is equal to zero (the two-tailed alternative is that it is less than or greater than zero), which means that the critical region consists of the 2.5 percent in the negative tail and the 2.5 percent in the positive tail. Now suppose that the t statistic for the coefficient of gasoline price equals -1.84. Further suppose that the sample size was 122, and there was only one explanatory variable, so that only two parameters were estimated (the intercept and slope) and there were 120 degrees of freedom. The absolute values of the critical values of the t distribution with 120 degrees of freedom are 1.658 for the one-sided alternative and 1.98 for the two-sided alternative. Thus, at the 5 percent level of significance, the analyst would reject the null hypothesis if she had specified a one-sided alternative, but she would accept the null hypothesis if she had specified a two-sided alternative.

Most regression software saves us the trouble of looking up critical values in tables by directly calculating the probability under the null hypothesis of observing a t statistic as large as that estimated, assuming we want to test the null hypothesis that the true parameter equals zero against a two-sided alternative. To do this classical hypothesis test on the coefficient, we simply see if the reported probability is less than the maximum probability of falsely rejecting the null hypothesis that we are willing to accept. If it is smaller, then we reject the null hypothesis.

Exercises for Chapter 12

1. Consider the example presented in Figure 12.3. Imagine that the current price of waste disposal is $0.025/lb and the average waste disposal is 2.40 lb/p/d. As noted in the diagram, when the price was previously $0.01/lb, the average waste disposal was 2.52 lb/p/d. Assume that the marginal social cost of waste disposal is $0.06/lb, that marginal social costs are constant with respect to quantity, and that the town has a population of 100,000.
   a. Fitting a linear demand curve to the two observed points, calculate the annual net benefits of raising the price of waste disposal to $0.05/lb.
   b. Fitting a constant-elasticity demand curve to the observed points, calculate the annual net benefits of raising the price of waste disposal to $0.05/lb.
2. (Regression software recommended.) An analyst was asked to predict the gross social benefits of building a public swimming pool in Dryville, which has a population of 70,230 people and a median household income of $31,500. The analyst identified 24 towns in the region that already had public swimming pools. She conducted a telephone interview with the recreation department in each town to find out what fee it charged per visit (FEE) and how many visits it had during the most recent summer season (VISITS). In addition, she was able to find each town's

population (POP) and median household income (INCOME) in the most recent census. Her data are as follows:

	Visits	Fee	Income	Pop
1	168,590	0	20,600	36,879
2	179,599	0	33,400	64,520
3	198,595	0	39,700	104,123
4	206,662	0	32,600	103,073
5	170,259	0	24,900	58,386
6	209,995	0.25	38,000	116,592
7	172,018	0.25	26,700	49,945
8	190,802	0.25	20,800	79,789
9	197,019	0.25	26,300	98,234
10	186,515	0.50	35,600	71,762
11	152,679	0.50	38,900	40,178
12	137,423	0.50	21,700	22,928
13	158,056	0.50	37,900	39,031
14	157,424	0.50	35,100	44,685
15	179,490	0.50	35,700	67,882
16	164,657	0.75	22,900	69,625
17	184,428	0.75	38,600	98,408
18	183,822	0.75	20,500	93,429
19	174,510	1.00	39,300	98,077
20	187,820	1.00	25,800	104,068
21	196,318	1.25	23,800	117,940
22	166,694	1.50	34,000	59,757
23	161,716	1.50	29,600	88,305
24	167,505	2.00	33,800	84,102

a. Show how the analyst could use these data to predict the gross benefits of opening a public swimming pool in Dryville and allowing free admission.
b. Predict gross benefits if admission is set at $1.00 and Dryville has marginal excess tax burden of 0.25. In answering this question, assume that the fees are used to reduce taxes that would otherwise have to be collected from the citizens of Dryville to pay for expenses incurred in operating the pool.

Notes

1. More accurately, each household incurs a marginal private cost (MPC) of refuse disposal that is only $1/n$th of the marginal social costs (MSC); that is, $MPC = MSC/n$, where n is the number of households. The MPC equals zero for large n.
2. Robin R. Jenkins, *The Economics of Solid Waste Reduction: The Impact of User Fees* (Brookfield, VT: Edward Elgar Publishing Company, 1993).
3. Formally, $\varepsilon_d = \partial \ln q / \partial \ln p = (\partial q/\partial p)(p/q)$, where $\partial q/\partial p$ is the partial derivative of the quantity demanded with respect to price. For a linear demand curve, $\varepsilon_d = (\partial q/\partial p)(p/q) = \alpha_1 p/q$.
4. Jenkins, *The Economics of Solid Waste Reduction: The Impact of User Fees*, pp. 88–90, 101.
5. Some analysts call this functional form a *log-linear demand curve* whereas others call it a *log-log de-*

mand curve or a *double-log* demand curve. In order to minimize potential confusion, we will not use any of these terms.

6. As β_1 is the slope of the log-linear demand curve, $\beta_1 = \partial \ln q / \partial \ln p$. By definition, the price elasticity of demand $\varepsilon_d = \partial \ln q / \partial \ln p$. Consequently, $\varepsilon_d = \beta_1$.

7. The slope is given by

$$\partial q / \partial p = \beta_1 \beta_0 p^{\beta_1 - 1} = \beta_1 \beta_0 p^{\beta_1} / p = \beta_1 q / p.$$

8. Note that our estimate of $\beta_0 = 1.44$ will generally differ from the original estimate of β_0 obtained by the researchers from which we took our price elasticity estimate. This difference arises because we force the demand curve to pass through point *a*, our known data point, whereas the original estimated equation probably will not pass through point *a*.

9. The demand curve is $q = 1.44 p^{-0.15}$. If $p = 0.05$, then $q = 1.44 (.05)^{-0.15} = 2.1$.

10. An alternative, slightly easier way to predict the reduction in the quantity of waste disposal uses the estimated elasticity to approximate the slope of the demand curve. At point *a* the slope of the demand curve is $(-0.15)(2.25)/(0.05) = -6.75$. Therefore, a change in price from \$0.05/lb to \$0.08/lb would change the quantity of waste by approximately:

$$\Delta q = -6.75 (0.08 - 0.05) = -0.20 \text{ lb/p/d}$$

which would lead us to predict that waste disposal would fall to 2.05 lb/p/d due to the price increase (point *e* in Figure 12.2).

The discrepancy in the predicted levels of waste disposal at the higher price results because of the difference between *point elasticities* and *arc elasticities*. The point elasticity is the exact elasticity at a particular point, whereas the arc elasticity is an approximate elasticity for a finite change. For small changes in price, the two methods give approximately the same reduction. But for large price changes, such as the 60 percent price change in this example, the two methods can differ substantially. If we are fairly confident in the estimated demand curve, then we should recover its formula and use the first method to predict changes in quantities. The second method is a linear approximation to the first method. The more curvature in the demand curve, the worse the approximation becomes.

11. The area is calculated by integrating the inverse demand function from q_0 and q_1, that is, as $\int p\,dq = \int (q/\beta_0)^{1/\beta_1} dq$ with q_0 and q_1 as the limits of integration.

12. An easier way to estimate the change in consumer surplus (area *abfg*) is to integrate the demand curve between p_0 and p_1, that is, $\Delta CS = \int q\,dp = \int \beta_0 p^{\beta_1}$ with p_0 and p_1 as the limits of integration. For a constant elasticity demand curve, it can be shown that $\Delta CS = (p_1 q_1 - p_0 q_0)/(1 + \beta_1)$. Therefore, in this example $\Delta CS = (.08 \times 2.1 - .05 \times 2.25)/(1 - .15) = \$.0653$, which differs slightly from the number in the text due to rounding errors.

13. Solve for β_0 and β_1 as follows:

$$\beta_1 = \ln(q_0/q_1)/\ln(p_0/p_1) = -0.053,$$
$$\text{and } \beta_0 = (q_0/p_0^{\beta_1}) = 1.97.$$

14. For an excellent treatment of the econometric issues raised in this section, see William H. Greene, *Econometric Analysis,* 3rd ed. (New York: Macmillan, 1997). For a review of some major econometrics textbooks, see Clive W. J. Granger, "A Review of Some Recent Textbooks of Econometrics," *Journal of Economic Literature,* 32, no. 1 (1994), 115–122.

15. For an introduction to demand estimation, see William F. Barnett, "Four Steps to Forecast Total Market Demand," *Harvard Business Review,* 88, no. 4 (1988), 28–38. For examples of demand estimation in different industries, see Thomas F. Hogarty and Kenneth G. Elzinga, "The Demand for Beer," *Review of Economics and Statistics,* 54 (1972), 195–198, and Patricia L. Pacy, "Cable Television in a Less Regulated Market," *Journal of Industrial Economics,* 34, no. 1 (1985), 81–91.

16. Thus far this chapter has focused on demand curves that relate quantity demanded to price. Other variables also affect demand. A demand function relates the quantity demanded to price and other variables. Because a demand function is more general than a demand curve, this section focuses on demand functions. Sometimes we use the term *demand schedule* to refer to demand curves or demand functions.

17. They estimated an elasticity of disposal demand with respect to tipping fees of -0.11 for communities in the region around Portland, Oregon, over a seven-year period; see James G. Strathman, Anthony M. Rufolo, and Gerard C. S. Mildner, "The Demand for Solid Waste Disposal," *Land Economics,* 71, no. 1 (1995), 57–64.

18. Of course, if a theoretically important explanatory variable is excluded, then the overall fit of the model, measured by its R^2, will be poorer and the precision of the estimated coefficients will be lower.

19. If the regression equation contains more than one explanatory variable, then the bias in the coefficient of a particular variable depends on the *partial correlation* between that variable and the omitted variable, controlling for all other variables in the regression.
20. See, for example, Henri Theil, *Principles of Econometrics* (New York: Wiley, 1971), pp. 556–557.
21. Molly Espy, "Gasoline Demand Revisited: An International Meta-Analysis of Elasticities," *Energy Economics,* 20, no. 3 (1998), 273–295.
22. P. B. Goodwin, "A Review of New Demand Elasticities with Special Reference to Short and Long Run Effects of Price Changes," *Journal of Transport Economics and Policy,* 26, no. 2 (1992), 155–170 at pp. 158–159.
23. Tae Moon Oum, W. G. Waters II, and Jong-Say Yong, "Concepts of Price Elasticities of Transport Demand and Recent Empirical Estimates," *Journal of Transport Economics and Policy,* 26, no. 2 (1992), 139–154 at p. 153.
24. In this section, we continue to assume perfect competition. If prior to being taxed, however, a good was overconsumed from the social perspective, for example, as a result of a negative externality, then the introduction of a tax could increase efficiency by reducing the overconsumption. In this case, the marginal welfare cost of raising a dollar of taxes would be less than one dollar. More generally, the efficiency implications of interventions depend on the distortions already in the market. For example, Charles Ballard demonstrates that when labor markets for low-income groups are distorted by high effective marginal tax rates, redistributing through wage subsidies can actually result in efficiency gains. Charles L. Ballard, "The Marginal Efficiency Cost of Redistribution," *American Economic Review,* 78, no. 5 (1988), 1019–1033.

Appendix Notes

1. For clear introductions to regression analysis, see Eric A. Hanushek and John E. Jackson, *Statistical Methods for the Social Sciences* (New York: Academic Press, 1977); and Christopher H. Achen, *Interpreting and Using Regression* (Beverly Hills, CA: Sage Publications, 1982).
2. Formally, OLS minimizes $\sum_{i=1}^{n} \hat{\varepsilon}_i^2$.
3. See Greene, *Econometric Analysis,* pp. 423–427. For an application of ridge regression, which presents both OLS and ridge regression estimates, see A. E. Boardman, S. Miller, and A. P. Schinnar, "Efficient Employment of Cohorts of Labor in the U.S. Economy: An Illustration of a Method," *Socio-Economic Planning Sciences,* 13, no. 6 (1979), 297–302.
4. The OLS estimators are also *efficient*. Here, efficiency means that among all estimators whose formulas are linear in the dependent variable, the OLS estimator of a coefficient has the smallest variance. It, therefore, has the greatest "power" for rejecting the null hypothesis that a coefficient is zero.
5. The *central limit theorem* tells us that the distribution of the sum of independent random variables approaches the normal distribution as the number in the sum becomes large. The theorem applies for almost any starting distributions with finite variances. If we think of the error term as the sum of all the many factors excluded from our model and, furthermore, we believe that these excluded factors are not systematically related to one another or to the included variables, then the central limit theorem suggests that the distribution of the error terms will be at least approximately normal.
6. Student is the pseudonym of William Gosset, the quality control engineer at the Guiness Brewery in Dublin, who originally derived the *t* distribution.
7. The probability we choose puts an upward bound on the probability of falsely rejecting the null hypothesis. Falsely rejecting the null hypothesis is referred to as Type I error. Failing to reject the null hypothesis when in fact the alternative hypothesis is true is referred to as Type II error. We usually set the probability of Type I error at some low level, such as 5 percent. Holding sample size constant, the lower we set the probability of a Type I error, the greater the probability of a Type II error.

13

VALUING IMPACTS FROM OBSERVED BEHAVIOR

Other Revealed Preference Methods

The previous chapter discusses direct estimation of demand schedules for the purpose of measuring consumer surplus. It assumes there is a market demand curve for the good in question, such as garbage collection or gasoline, and we can observe some points along this demand curve. In practice, however, valuation is often more complicated. After all, the rationale for many public policies and the desirability of evaluating them with CBA are that either markets for certain "goods," such as human life or pollution, do not exist or are imperfect for reasons discussed in Chapter 3. In particular, in applying CBA to proposed but not yet implemented policies, we obviously have no track record on which to base our predictions and valuations of future effects. Indeed, we may have no experience with similar programs from which to draw guidance. The analyst may not have even one point on the appropriate demand or supply curve. In such situations it is particularly difficult to estimate the curves.

Generally, estimation of changes in social surplus requires knowledge of entire demand and supply schedules. Sometimes, though, the total change in surplus can be estimated from knowledge of the marginal social benefit or the marginal social cost of one more unit of the affected good or service. In a perfect market, the current price equals both the marginal social cost and the marginal social benefit of an additional unit of a good or service. When a market does not exist or market failure leads to a divergence between market price and marginal social cost, analysts try to obtain estimates of what the market price would be if the relevant good were traded in a perfect market. As we discuss in Chapter 4, such an estimate is called a *shadow price*.

The focus of this chapter is on various methods for estimating shadow prices based on observed behavior when markets for the primary good do not exist. Basing valuations on observed behavior is important because it means that people reveal their preferences without having to be asked. As we discuss in the following chapter on contingent valuation, survey methods are prone to a number of biases. When markets do exist but are imperfect due to government intervention, it is necessary to make adjustments to market prices. These methods are discussed in Chapter 16.

The following practical methods, which are based on revealed preferences, can be used to value impacts when primary markets do not exist. They are: (1) the market analogy method, (2) the intermediate good method, (3) the asset valuation method, (4) the hedonic price method, (5) the travel cost method, and (6) the defensive expenditures method. Some of these methods involve estimation of the whole demand or supply curve, whereas others provide only an estimate of the shadow price.

Similar to the previous chapter, this chapter focuses on measuring gross benefits and changes in consumer surplus rather than on changes in producer surplus. However, we cover the topics likely to be relevant to most CBA applications.

MARKET ANALOGY METHOD

Governments supply many goods that are also provided by the private sector. For example, campsites, university education, home care, and adoption services are often provided by both the public and private sectors. The government usually provides these goods and services free or at significantly below market prices. However, it may be possible to estimate the demand curve for a publicly provided good using analogous data for a good that is produced by the private sector and sold in a well-functioning market.

In some situations, the private market may not be legal. For example, there are no legal private-sector adoption services in some countries. Nevertheless, analysts may turn to the *black market* to obtain an estimate of the value of such services.

This section first discusses using prices of analogous goods as a measure of the value of a publicly provided good. Although this is relatively easy, it has its limitations. We then discuss estimation of the demand curve for the publicly provided good. Clearly, this is more informative. Subsequently, we discuss using the market analogy method to value time saved and lives saved.

Using Only Price or Market Expenditures of an Analogous Good

Consider, for example, a local government project that provides housing for 50 families. The local government may charge a nominal rent of $150 per month so that government revenue equals $7,500 per month (50 units at $150/month each). Clearly, using this expenditure would underestimate (gross) benefits. No occupying family would have a willingness-to-pay of less than $150 per month, but many of them would be willing to pay more than $150 per month and, therefore, the benefits of this project would be larger than $7,500 per month.

Suppose that comparable units in the private sector are rented out for $500 per month. If we took this market price as the shadow price for the publicly provided units, then the estimated total monthly benefits of publicly provided housing would be $25,000 per month (50 units at $500/month each).

The market price of a comparable good in the private sector is an appropriate shadow price for a publicly provided good if it equals the average amount that users of the publicly provided good would be willing to pay. In an efficient private market, those who buy units of the good unambiguously demonstrate a willingness-to-pay an amount greater than or equal to the market price. The willingness-to-pay for the marginal unit supplied is just equal to the market price. In the case of government allocation at a lower than market price, however, there is no guarantee that those who receive the good value it as highly as do purchasers in the private market. Families willing to pay the market price, or more, for comparable housing would probably have already found housing in the private sector. Those who occupy public units typically have lower than average incomes and are likely to be willing to pay less than the market price but more than the amount charged by government (i.e., somewhere between $7,500 per month and $25,000 per month).

The revenue for comparable private housing units would not necessarily be an upper bound of benefits if the publicly provided housing were poorly targeted. If the units were allocated to people with higher than average income who would have purchased similar private-sector units at market prices in the absence of obtaining publicly provided housing, then the market price would be a lower bound on their willingness-to-pay. Ironically, from the CBA perspective, in the absence of market failures, the more poorly targeted public housing units are, the higher their benefits! Such ironies have led some to suggest that benefits that accrue to low-income persons should be given greater weight than benefits that accrue to high-income persons, as we discuss in Chapter 18.

When willingness-to-pay values differ across different groups of users, it is useful to take such differences into account. Suppose, for example, an analyst wants to value a highway improvement that saves travel time. One estimate of the value of total time saved is obtained by multiplying the total time saved by an average shadow price for the value of travel time saved for all users. Yet, some people, such as business executives, value time savings more than other people, such as vacationers. To take account of these different valuations, an analyst could multiply the time saved by each group of travelers by the value of a unit of travel time for that group, and then sum these products across groups. Such a calculation generally gives a more accurate estimate of the aggregate value of time than simply applying a single shadow price to the total amount of time saved.

Using Price and Quantity of an Analogous Private-Sector Good to Estimate the Demand Curve for a Publicly Provided Good

Suppose a municipal government wants to measure the gross benefits of a swimming pool that it owns and operates. Currently, the municipality does not charge an admission fee and the pool receives 300,000 visitors per year, shown as point *a* in Figure 13.1. In a comparable municipality, a privately operated swimming pool, which charges $1 for admission, receives 100,000 visitors per year (point *b*). Assuming a linear demand curve that passes through these two points, we can estimate the gross benefits of the municipal pool as $(1.5)(300,000)/2 = $225,000.

Notice that using revenues at the private pool ($100,000) would underestimate benefits because it omits consumer surplus. This figure excludes the consumer surplus of those willing to pay more than the $1 admission fee, the area of triangle *bcd*, as well as the consumer surplus of those willing to pay something less than $1, the area of triangle *abe*.

How reasonable is it to interpret the observed price and quantity at the private pool as a point on the demand curve for the municipal pool? The answer depends on the similarity of the two facilities and their markets. Only if they are similar in terms

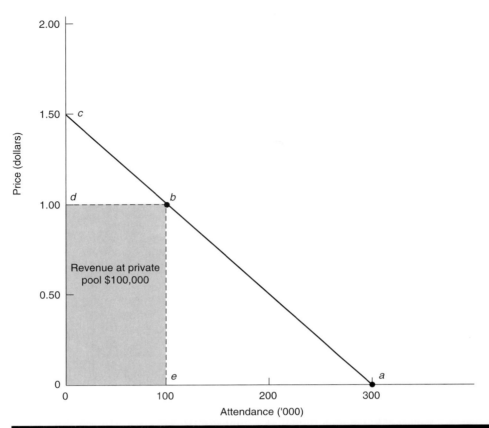

FIGURE 13.1 Demand Curve for Visits to a Municipal Swimming Pool

of such features as changing room facilities, hours of business, the friendliness of the staff, levels of crowding, and populations of potential users is the observed point on the demand curve for the private facility a reasonable prediction of a point on the demand curve for the municipal pool. If these assumptions do not hold, then adjustments should be made or other valuation methods should be used.

Using the Market Analogy Method to Value Time Saved

Researchers have used the market analogy method to obtain a shadow price for time saved, an important component of CBAs of transportation projects, such as highway improvements, and other projects that affect the amount of time people spend waiting in line, such as the hiring of more clerks in an unemployment insurance office. An obvious analogous market for time saved is the labor market, where people sell their time for wages. In the absence of market imperfections, the social value of an additional hour of work equals that person's wage rate. All other things being equal, when people can choose the number of hours they work, and there is no unemployment, the wage rate also equals the marginal value of their time. In other words, the value of an additional hour of leisure to the person enjoying it equals the wage rate. Thus, the value of a project that saves an hour for a person who earns $20 per hour, both to society and to that person, is $20. Setting the value of time saved equal to the wage rate is relatively easy. However, there are some serious problems in using the wage rate to value time saved by government projects.

First, wages ignore benefits. As benefits are a form of compensation for work, they should be added to wages.

Second, this method assumes that people do not work while they are traveling or standing in line. In fact, people often work and drive or work and fly at the same time. The notebook computer and the mobile phone facilitate working while flying or driving. If people do work while they are traveling or waiting in line, then an hour of such time saved is worth less than the wage rate. Of course, this does not apply to truck drivers who are obviously working while they are driving. For them, it does make sense to value their time saved at their wage rate plus benefits.

Third, we must take account of taxes. Although it is reasonable to view the value to society of an hour saved for a person who is working at the before-tax wage rate plus benefits, when deciding whether to work or not, individuals consider the after-tax wage rate plus benefits. Thus, the time saved of people who are not working should be valued at the after-tax wage rate plus benefits.

Fourth, people are willing to pay different amounts to save an hour traveling than they would to save an hour waiting in line. Some people like traveling, especially through spectacular scenery, such as along the Banff to Jasper highway. These people derive consumption benefits from traveling and are willing to pay for the experience of traveling itself. (Consider, for example, the "busman's holiday.") In contrast, many people really dislike waiting in line or in traffic jams and are willing to pay a lot to avoid it. Thus, the value of time saved depends on what one is doing. Because people generally do not dislike traveling, analysts value an hour of travel time saved for recreational travelers at a fraction (about 45 percent) of the *after-tax wage rate* plus benefits. In contrast, analysts value an hour of travel time saved for people who are working, such as truck drivers, at the *before-tax wage rate* plus benefits. (Estimates of the value of time saved are discussed in depth in Chapter 15.)

Fifth, people who work at dirty, dangerous jobs are generally paid more than people who work in clean, safe jobs, yet they may value a marginal hour of leisure time similarly. Therefore, the wage rate should be adjusted to take account of different job attributes.

Sixth, the wage rate may not be an appropriate shadow price for time saved because it assumes working hours are flexible. It ignores structural rigidities or market and government failures in the labor market. With an upward-sloping supply curve of labor, the more hours someone works, the more highly he or she values leisure. In practice, however, a person may not be able to easily adjust the number of hours worked. For example, a person who suffers from several weeks of unemployment or who involuntarily works overtime is off their labor supply curve. Other structural rigidities result in unemployment. Minimum wages and the monopoly power of unions or other factors may distort the labor market. Consequently, everyone who wants to work at the market wage may not be able to find work at that wage. Indeed, for some people, such as retirees, no wage rate can be observed.

Finally, firms may not pay their employees the marginal social value of their output for a number of reasons. For example, firms with market power may share their profits with employees in the form of higher than market wages. Of course, if an industry generated negative (positive) externalities, then the wage rate would exceed (be less than) the marginal social value of an hour saved.

Because of the serious nature of these problems, valuing time saved at the wage rate is only a first approximation to its social value. Later in this chapter we present better methods for valuing time saved.

Using the Market Analogy Method to Value a Life Saved

Valuing life is a highly contentious issue. Society often spends fortunes to rescue trapped miners or to give heart transplants to specific individuals. Yet it may not spend money to make obvious gains in mine safety or to reduce the risk of heart disease. In order to make efficient allocation of resources in the health care area, or to determine the benefits of projects that save lives, analysts require a monetary value of a life saved.

Forgone Earnings Method   Early efforts by economists to value life followed a similar method to the one discussed earlier concerning the value of time. Specifically, if one accepts that a person's value to society for one hour equals that person's wage, then one might reason that the value of that person to society for the rest of his or her lifetime equals the present value of his or her future earnings. One would, thus, conclude that the value of a life saved equals that person's discounted future earnings. This is the *forgone earnings method* of valuing a life saved.[1] It is currently used by the courts in some U.S. states and in some other countries to award compensation in cases involving death due to negligence. On average, this method generates a higher value for saving the life of people with higher incomes than for people with lower incomes. It also generates higher values for younger people than for older people and for men than for women.

The forgone earnings method provides an unsatisfactory shadow price for lives saved for reasons similar to those discussed previously concerning the value of time saved. It assumes full employment, although the method can easily be adjusted to reflect expected lifetime earnings given average employment expectations. It also assumes people are paid their marginal social product, while often they are not. The lives of full-time homemakers and volunteers, who are not paid at all for their services, are unreasonably valued at zero.

A fundamental problem with the forgone earnings method is that it ignores individuals' willingness-to-pay to avoid or reduce the risk of their own deaths. This point was made clearly by Thomas Schelling, who observed "[t]here is no reason to suppose that a person's future earnings . . . bear any particular relation to what he would pay to reduce some likelihood of his own death."[2]

Schelling also distinguished between the deaths of identifiable individuals and *statistical deaths*. A safety improvement to a highway, for example, does not lead to the saving of the lives of a few individuals who can be identified *ex ante* but rather to the reduction in the risk of death (or injury) to all users of the highway. *In order to value the benefit of proposed safety improvements, analysts should ascertain how much people are willing to pay for reductions in their risk of death that are of the same magnitude as the reduced risk that would result from the proposed safety improvements.* Such reasoning has led to a series of consumer purchase and labor market studies that have attempted to value life. We outline the general approach in the following sections and present a review of estimates of the value of life in Chapter 15.

Consumer Purchase Studies   Suppose airbags were not standard in new cars, but for $220 you could purchase and install an airbag at the time you purchased your new car.[3] The airbag would increase your survival rate from use of the car from p to $p + \omega$. Would you buy the airbag? This choice problem is represented diagrammatically as a decision tree in Figure 13.2. If a person is indifferent between the two alternatives, that is, between spending the $220 and increasing the probability of surviving by ω (the upper-branch alternative) and not spending the $220 (the lower-branch alternative), then:

$$(p + \omega)V(\text{life}) - \$220 = pV(\text{life})$$
$$(p + \omega)V(\text{life}) - pV(\text{life}) = \$220$$
$$\omega V(\text{life}) = \$220$$
$$V(\text{life}) = \$220/\omega$$

Suppose $\omega = 1/10,000$; that is, if 10,000 people buy airbags, then one statistical life will be saved. Then, for a person who is indifferent:

$$V(\text{life}) = (\$220)/(1/10,000) = \$2,200,000$$

This method of valuing a life saved has been applied not only to the purchase of airbags but also to the purchase of other safety-enhancing devices, for example, smoke detectors and fire extinguishers.

FIGURE 13.2 Decision Tree for Airbag Purchase

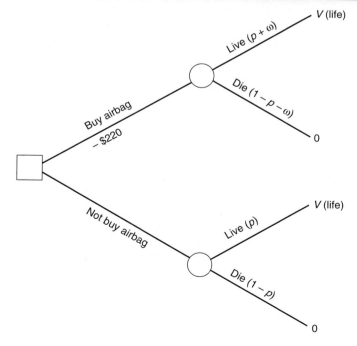

Labor Market Studies   Labor market studies examine the additional wage people require in compensation for exposing themselves to greater risk of death on the job. Suppose, for example, one type of construction job has a 1/1,000 greater chance of fatal injury in a year than another type of construction job. Further suppose that the riskier job offers a salary that is $2,000/year higher than the safer job. If workers are indifferent between the two types of job, this implies:

$$(1/1,000)V(\text{life}) = \$2,000$$

$$V(\text{life}) = \$2 \text{ million}$$

In general, the imputed values of life that are obtained from labor market studies vary according to the initial level of risk and the additional level of risk people are asked to assume. This reflects the fact that the value of additional amounts of safety declines as the level of safety increases, that is, people experience diminishing marginal utility for safety. When using an estimated value-of-life figure in a CBA, analysts should ensure that the risk level under which it was estimated corresponds to the risk level of the policy being investigated.

One problem with this method is that it assumes workers have full information concerning risks on their job. For example, in addition to knowing that the chance of dying in a risky type of job is 1/1,000 higher than in the less risky type of job, construction workers have to know what this means. Evidence, which we discuss in Chapter 14, suggests that people suffer from cognitive biases that limit their ability to make rational judgments and decisions in such situations. For example, some studies suggest that people overestimate the occurrence of low-probability "bad" events.[4] When people suffer from this cognitive bias, labor market studies may overestimate the value of life.

At the same time, however, people who are relatively less risk averse (more risk seeking) self-select into more risky jobs. This effect causes labor market studies to underestimate the value of a life saved.

Other problems with this method are that it assumes markets are efficient and that all other factors that influence wages are held constant. In practice, wage differences may depend partially on the relative bargaining power of unions, on the different characteristics of the different jobs, or on different characteristics (skills) of workers in different jobs. Indeed, this method suffers from many of the problems that affect the quality of the estimates obtained by using the market analogy method to value time saved.

INTERMEDIATE GOOD METHOD

Some government projects produce intermediate goods, that is, goods that are used as inputs to some other *downstream* activity. For example, a government irrigation project may provide water for farmers that is used as an input to the production of avocados. If the intermediate good—water—is sold in a well-functioning market, it may be possible to directly estimate the market demand curve for water by using econometric methods. But, if not, we have to impute its value. The intermediate good method estimates the (gross) benefit of a project that provides an intermediate good based on its *value added* to the downstream activity. Specifically, the value of the irrigation project can be measured by the increase in the incomes of avocado farmers. More generally, the annual benefit of a project equals the change in the annual incomes of the downstream businesses, thus:

Annual Benefit = Income (with the project) − Income (without the project)

The total benefit of a project can be computed by discounting these annual benefits over the project's life.

The intermediate good method is used to value the benefits of education and training programs. Investment in the skills and abilities of human beings improves the stock of *human capital*. Much of the economic successes of Japan and Switzerland, for example, both of which are relatively poor in terms of physical natural resources, can be attributed to their investments in human capital. The intermediate good method measures the benefit of such programs by comparing the average incomes of those who have been enrolled in them and the average incomes of those who have not. For example, the average annual benefit of a program to increase literacy equals the difference between the average income of people who participate in the program and the average income of similar people who do not. The total benefit of the program is found by discounting the annual benefits over the years people work after graduation and multiplying by the number of participants.

One problem with this method is that it assumes that differences in income capture all benefits of a project. Some intermediate goods, such as college education, may be partially "final" goods. That is, they may have consumption value in addition to having investment value. Some people may enjoy their college education so much that they would pay for it even if it had no impact on their expected earnings. People's willingness-to-pay for this consumption aspect should also be considered a benefit of a college education. Because the intermediate good method does not include this benefit, it underestimates (overestimates) the value of goods that have positive (negative) consumption benefits. Other problems with the intermediate good method are discussed in Exhibit 13.1.

EXHIBIT 13.1

Many studies have used the intermediate good method to value the social benefits from education. These studies usually measure the social benefits from a college education, for example, as the difference in before-tax earnings of college graduates and those whose education stopped after graduating from high school. These studies usually also estimate the cost of education—tuition fees, tax revenues, donations, and earnings that are forgone while in college. Similar to the benefits from education, forgone earnings are estimated by comparing the before-tax earnings of those with a high school education and those who are in college.

These estimates of benefits and costs are used to compute the internal rate of return to different additional amounts of education. For example, a recent summary found that the average rate of return to society from secondary schooling is 10 percent in developed countries, 18 percent in sub-Saharan countries, and 11 to 13 percent in other developing countries. The estimated average rate of return to society from investments in higher education is 9 percent in developed countries and 11 to 12 percent in developing countries. The rate of return to private individuals is higher than these estimates because they capture the benefits whereas the cost is often subsidized by the government or donors.

Use of the intermediate good method to value the benefits of education is subject to several potentially important biases. First, the higher earnings of those with more education may be at least partially attributable to their greater ability or motivation rather than to their greater education. Second, at least part of the higher earnings of the more educated may not be attributable to education imparting greater skill but due instead to a "credentials" or a "signaling" effect. That is, employers who are willing to pay premium wages to hire more able employees, but who otherwise would be uncertain as to whom these workers are, use possession of a high school or college degree to identify them. Third, by focusing on earnings, the intermediate good method ignores other benefits from education such as better citizenship, greater fringe benefits, more pleasant working conditions, more responsibility, more flexibility, and so forth. The first two of these biases tend to cause estimates of educational benefits and internal rates of return to be overstated, whereas the third causes them to be understated.

Source: George Psacharopoulos, "Returns to Investment in Education: A Global Update," *World Development,* 22, no. 9 (1994), 1325–1343.

Care must be taken in application of the intermediate good method to avoid *double counting.* If the value of an intermediate good has been measured in some other way, then its contribution to the value of downstream production should not be counted as an additional benefit. For example, if the benefits of an irrigation project were estimated based on the estimated demand curve for water, then including the increased income of avocado farmers as an additional benefit would be double counting.

ASSET VALUATION METHOD

Projects sometimes affect the prices of assets such as land, housing, and stocks. The impacts of these projects are said to be *capitalized* into the market value of the assets. Observed increases (decreases) in asset values can often be used to estimate the benefits (costs) of projects. For example, returning to the irrigation project to provide water to avocado farms, if the farms are the only users of the irrigation water and if the market for farm land is undistorted, then the full value of the irrigation project will capitalize into the market value of avocado farms.

Observing changes in asset values is a relatively quick and easy method for estimating benefits in *ex post* CBA. Changes in asset values resulting from similar, previously implemented projects can also provide the basis for estimating the benefits of a proposed project in an *ex ante* CBA.

A common application of the asset valuation method uses differences in housing prices to impute values of particular attributes of houses or the environment, including externalities such as noise.[5] For example, the difference in market price between a house with a view and a house with no view provides an estimate of how much households are willing to pay for a view. The difference between the average price of houses in a neighborhood with many parks and the average price of houses in neighborhoods with few parks provides an estimate of how much homeowners are willing to pay for parks.[6] Of course, similar to the other methods discussed earlier, this method assumes that houses are comparable in all other respects, and that no other factor affects differences in house prices. (Later we discuss how to control for such factors.)

Recently, *event studies,* which examine changes in stock prices, have become an important method for estimating the costs or benefits to shareholders of an event, including new programs, policies, or regulations.[7] The main advantage of using stock prices is that new information concerning policy changes is quickly and efficiently capitalized into stock prices. Changes in stock prices provide an unbiased estimate of the value of a policy change to shareholders. Also, stock price data are readily accessible in computer-readable form.

In an event study, researchers estimate the *abnormal return* to a security, which is the difference between the return to a security in the presence of an event and the return to the security in the absence of the event. Usually, researchers estimate daily abnormal returns during an *event window,* that is, for the period during which the event is assumed to affect stock prices. Because the return to the security in the absence of the event is unobservable, it is inferred from changes in the prices of other stocks in the market.[8] The estimated daily abnormal returns during the event window can be aggregated to obtain the *cumulative abnormal return,* which measures the total return to shareholders that can be attributed to the event. Cumulative abnormal returns provide an estimate of the change in producer surplus.

HEDONIC PRICE METHOD

The market analogy, intermediate good, and asset valuation methods have several potential limitations. Most importantly, these methods may suffer from *omitted variable* problems and *self-selection* bias. The *hedonic price* method, sometimes called the *hedonic regression* method, offers a way to overcome these problems.

The Omitted Variable Problem

Many benefit valuation methods suffer from omitted variable problems. Consider, for example, using the intermediate good method to value irrigation. Ideally, analysts would compare the incomes of farmers if the irrigation project were built with the incomes of the same farmers if the project were not built. In practice, if the project is built, analysts cannot directly observe what the farmers' incomes would have been if it had not been built. One way to infer what their incomes would have been without the project is to use the incomes of the same farmers before the project was built (a before-and-after design) or the incomes of similar farmers who did not benefit from an irrigation project (a nonexperimental comparison group design). The before-and-after design is reasonable only if all other variables that affect farmers' incomes remain constant. Often, however, important variables, such as weather conditions, crop choices, taxes, and subsidies, change from one year to another so that incomes observed before the project are not good estimates of what incomes would have been if the project had not been implemented. Similarly, the comparison group design is appropriate only if the comparison group is similar in all important respects to the farmers with irrigation, except for the presence of irrigation.

As mentioned in Exhibit 13.1, salary differences between those with a college degree and those with a high school degree may depend on ability, intelligence, socioeconomic background, and other factors in addition to college attendance per se. Similarly, in labor market studies of the value of life, differences in wages among jobs may vary according to the bargaining power of different unions in addition to different job risks. Again, the price of a house typically depends on factors such as its distance from the central business district and size, as well as whether it has a view. Analysts should take account of all important explanatory variables. If a relevant explanatory variable is omitted from the model and if it is correlated with the included variable(s) of interest, then the results will be biased, as discussed in Appendix 12A.

Self-Selection Bias

Another potential problem is self-selection bias. Risk-seeking people tend to self-select themselves for dangerous jobs. Or, put another way, because they like to take risks they may be willing to accept quite low salaries in quite risky jobs. Consequently, we may observe only very small wage premiums for dangerous jobs. Because risk seekers are not representative of society as a whole, the observed wage differential may underestimate the amount that average members of society would be willing to pay to reduce risks and, hence, may lead to an underestimate of the value of a life saved.

The self-selection problem arises whenever different people attach different values to particular attributes. Suppose, for example, we want to use differences in house prices to estimate a shadow price for noise. People who are not averse to noise, possibly because of hearing disabilities, naturally tend to move into noisy neighborhoods. As a result, the price differential between quiet houses and noisy houses may be quite small, which would lead to an underestimate of the shadow price of noise for the "average" person.

Hedonic Regression

Suppose, for example, that scenery can be scaled from, say, 1 to 10, and that we want to estimate the benefits of improving the quality ("level") of scenery in an area by one unit. We could estimate the relationship between individual house prices and the level of their scenic views. But we know that the market value of houses depends on other factors, such as the size of the lot, which are correlated with the quality of scenic view. We also suspect that people who live in houses with good scenic views tend to value scenic views more than other people. Consequently, we would have an omitted variables problem and a self-selection problem.

The hedonic price method attempts to overcome both of these types of problems.[9] It consists of two steps. The first step estimates the effect of a marginally better view on the value (price) of houses, a slope parameter in a regression model, while controlling for other variables that affect house prices. The second step estimates the willingness-to-pay for scenic views, after controlling for "tastes," which are proxied by income and other socioeconomic factors. From this information, we can calculate the change in consumer surplus resulting from projects that improve or worsen the views from some houses.

The hedonic price method can be used to value an attribute, or a change in an attribute, whenever its value is capitalized into the price of an asset, such as houses or salaries. The first step estimates the relationship between the price of an asset and all of the *attributes* (characteristics) that affect its value.[10] The price of a house, *P*, for example, depends on such attributes as the quality of its scenic view, *VIEW*, its distance from the central business district, *CBD*, its lot size, *SIZE*, and various characteristics of its neighborhood, *NBHD*, such as school quality. A model of the factors affecting house prices can be written as follows:

$$P = f(CBD, SIZE, VIEW, NBHD) \tag{13.1}$$

This equation is called a *hedonic price function* or *implicit price function*.[11] The change in the price of a house that results from a unit change in a particular attribute (i.e., the slope) is called the *hedonic price, implicit price,* or *rent differential* of the attribute. In a well-functioning market, the hedonic price can naturally be interpreted as the additional cost of purchasing a house that is marginally better in terms of a particular attribute. For example, the hedonic price of scenic views, which we denote as r_v, measures the additional cost of buying a house with a slightly better (higher-level) scenic view.[12]

Sometimes hedonic prices are referred to as *marginal hedonic prices* or *marginal implicit prices.* Although these terms are technically more correct, we will not use them in order to make the explanation as easy to follow as possible.

Usually analysts assume the hedonic price function has a multiplicative functional form, similar to equation (10.6), which implies that house prices increase as the level of the scenic view increases but at a decreasing rate. Assuming the hedonic pricing model represented in equation (13.1) has a multiplicative functional form, we can write:

$$P = \beta_0 CBD^{\beta_1} SIZE^{\beta_2} VIEW^{\beta_3} NBHD^{\beta_4} e^\varepsilon \tag{13.2}$$

The parameters, $\beta_1, \beta_2, \beta_3$, and β_4, are elasticities measuring the proportional change in house prices that results from a proportional change in the associated attribute. We expect $\beta_1 < 0$ because house prices decline with distance to the *CBD*, but β_2, β_3, and $\beta_4 > 0$ because house prices increase as *SIZE, VIEW,* and *NBHD* increase.

The hedonic price of a particular attribute is the slope of equation (13.1) with respect to that attribute. In general, the hedonic price of an attribute may be a function of all of the variables in the hedonic price equation.[13] For the multiplicative model in equation (13.2), the hedonic price of scenic views, r_v, is:[14]

$$r_v = \beta_3 \frac{P}{VIEW} > 0 \tag{13.3}$$

In this model, the hedonic price of scenic views depends on the value of the parameter β_3, the price of the house, and the view from the house. Thus, it varies from one observation (house) to another. Note that plotting the hedonic price against the level of the view provides a downward-sloping curve, which implies that the implicit price of scenic views declines as the level of the view increases.

The preceding points are illustrated in Figure 13.3. The top panel shows an illustrative hedonic price function with house prices increasing as the level of scenic view increases but at a decreasing rate. The slope of this curve, which equals the hedonic price of scenic views, decreases as the level of the scenic view increases. The bottom panel shows more precisely the relationship between the hedonic price of scenic views (the slope of the curve in the top panel) and the level of scenic view.

In order to estimate the hedonic price of an attribute with the multiplicative model given by equation (13.2), analysts usually take the natural logarithms, ln, of both sides to obtain the hedonic regression model:

$$\ln(P) = \ln \beta_0 + \beta_1 \ln(CBD) + \beta_2 \ln(SIZE) + \beta_3 \ln(VIEW) + \beta_4 \ln(NBHD) + \varepsilon \tag{13.4}$$

As we discuss in Chapter 12, the parameters of this equation, the βs, may be estimated by ordinary least squares. Substituting the estimated value of β_3, the price of a specific house, and the level of the view from this house into equation (13.3) provides an estimate of the hedonic price of the view for this house.

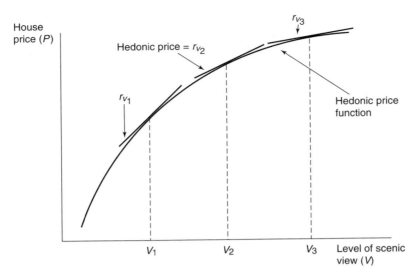

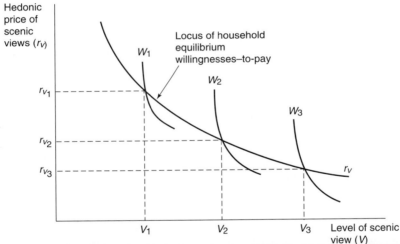

FIGURE 13.3 Hedonic Price Method

In a well-functioning market, utility-maximizing households will purchase houses so that their willingness-to-pay for a marginal increase in a particular attribute equals its hedonic price. Consequently, in equilibrium, the hedonic price of an attribute can be interpreted as the willingness of households to pay for a marginal increase in that attribute. The graph of the hedonic price of scenic views, r_v, against the level of scenic view is shown in the lower panel of Figure 13.3. Assuming all households have identical incomes and tastes, this curve can be interpreted as a household inverse demand curve for scenic views.

Yet, households differ in their incomes and tastes. Some are willing to pay a considerable amount of money for a more scenic view, whereas others are not. This brings us to the second step of the hedonic pricing method. To account for different incomes and tastes, analysts should estimate the following willingness-to-pay function (inverse demand curve) for scenic views.[15]

$$r_v = W(VIEW, Y, Z) \tag{13.5}$$

where r_v is estimated from equation (13.3), Y is household income, and Z is a vector of household characteristics that reflects tastes (e.g., socioeconomic background, race, age, and family size). Using the methods described in Chapter 4, it is straightforward to use equation (13.5) to calculate the change in consumer surplus to a household due to a change in the level of scenic view. These changes in individual household consumer surplus can be aggregated across all households to obtain the total change in consumer surplus.

Three willingness-to-pay functions, denoted W_1, W_2, and W_3, for three different types of households are drawn in the lower panel of Figure 13.3.[16] Equilibria occur where these functions intersect the r_v function. Thus, when incomes and socioeconomic characteristics differ, the r_v function is the locus of household equilibrium willingnesses-to-pay for scenic views.

In theory, the hedonic pricing method can be used to value incremental changes in the level of many goods that are not traded in markets, such as externalities and public goods; see, for example, Exhibit 13.2.[17] In practice, there are at least six potential problems. One is that people must know and understand the full implications of the externality or public good. For example, in order to use the hedonic pricing method to value pollution, families should know, prior to the purchase of their house, the level of pollution to which it is exposed and should also know the effect of different pollution levels on their health. Second, it is important that equation (13.4) includes attributes that households really do value, not more readily obtainable but incorrect proxies. For example, house values depend on the quality of construction, which is difficult to determine without inspection. Year of construction may or may not be a reasonable proxy. In econometrics, this problem is referred to as the *errors in variables* problem. Third, if the hedonic pricing model is in fact linear, then the hedonic price of each attribute is constant, which would make it impossible to estimate the inverse demand function, such as equation (13.5). Fourth, there should be many different houses so that families can find an optimal "package," that is, a house with just the right combination of attributes. In other words, there should be sufficient variety so that families can find a house that permits them to reach an "equilibrium." This would be a problem if, for example, a family wants a small, pollution-free house, but all of the houses in pollution-free areas were large. Fifth, there may be multicollinearity problems in the data. To use the same example, if expensive houses were large and located mainly in areas free of pollution, while inexpensive houses were small and located mainly in polluted areas, it would be difficult to estimate separate hedonic prices for pollution and size. Sixth, the method assumes that market prices adjust immediately to changes in attributes and in all other factors that affect demand or supply.

EXHIBIT 13.2

Dean Uyeno, Stanley Hamilton, and Andrew Biggs used the hedonic pricing method to estimate the cost of airport noise in Vancouver, Canada. They estimated the following hedonic price equation:

$$\ln H = \beta_0 + \beta_1 NEF + \sum_{j=2}^{k} \beta_k \ln X_j + \varepsilon$$

where ln H is the natural log of residential property value, *NEF* is a measure of noise level (ambient noise levels are in the *NEF* 15–25 range, "some" to "much" annoyance occurs in the *NEF* 25–40 range, and "considerable" annoyance occurs above *NEF*s of 40), the X_j are house characteristics ($j = 2, ..., k$), and ε is an error term.

Their results show that Vancouver International Airport generates noise costs that capitalize into residential house and condominium prices. The estimated coefficient of the noise variable implies that detached houses very close to the airport with *NEF*s of 40 are 9.75 percent cheaper than houses far from the airport with *NEF*s of 25. The estimated noise depreciation sensitivity is broadly consistent with previous studies, leading the authors to conclude that "the similarity of results spanning several decades and several Western countries would seem to suggest a broad and long-lived consensus on the issue (of the impact of airport noise on property values) . . . " (p. 14). In aggregate, the social cost of noise from Vancouver International Airport amounts to about $15 million in 1987 Canadian dollars.

Source: Dean Uyeno, Stanley W. Hamilton, and Andrew J. G. Biggs, "Density of Residential Land Use and the Impact of Airport Noise," *Journal of Transport Economics and Policy,* 27, no. 1 (1993), 3–18.

Using the Hedonic Price Method to Value a Life Saved

The relatively simple forms of consumer purchase and labor market studies to value life that we describe previously may be biased due to omitted variables or self-selection problems. For example, labor market studies to value life that examine *fatality risk* (the risk of death) often omit potentially relevant variables such as injury risks (the risk of injury). This problem may be reduced by using the hedonic pricing method. For example, a researcher might estimate the following regression model to find the hedonic price of fatality risk:

$$\ln(\text{wage rate}) = \beta_0 + \beta_1 \ln(\text{fatality risk}) + \beta_2 \ln(\text{injury risk}) \\ + \beta_3 \ln(\text{job tenure}) + \beta_4 \ln(\text{education}) + \beta_5 \ln(\text{age}) + \varepsilon \quad \textbf{(13.6)}$$

The inclusion of injury risk, job tenure, education, and age in the regression model controls for variables that affect wages and would bias the estimated coefficient of β_1 if they were excluded. Using the procedure demonstrated in the preceding section, the analyst can convert the estimate of β_1 to a hedonic price of fatality risk and can then estimate individuals' willingness-to-pay to avoid fatal risks. Most of the empirical estimates of the value of life that are reported in Chapter 15 are obtained from labor market and consumer product studies that employ models similar to the one presented in equation (13.6).

TRAVEL COST METHOD[18]

Most applications of the travel cost method (TCM) have been to value recreational sites.[19] If the "market" for visits to a site is geographically extensive, then visitors from different origins bear different travel costs depending on their proximity to the site. The resulting differences in total cost, and the differences in the rates of visits that they induce, provide a basis for estimating a demand curve for the site.

Suppose that we want to estimate the value of a particular recreational site. We expect that the quantity of visits demanded by an individual, q, depends on its price, p, the price of substitutes, p_s, the person's income, Y, and variables that reflect the person's tastes, Z:

$$q = f(p, p_s, Y, Z) \tag{13.7}$$

The TCM recognizes that the full price paid by persons for a visit to a recreational site is more than just the admission fee. It also includes the costs of traveling to and from the site. Among these travel costs are the opportunity cost of time spent traveling, the operating cost of vehicles used to travel, the cost of accommodations for overnight stays while traveling or visiting, and parking fees at the site. The sum of all of these costs gives the total cost of a visit to the site. This total cost is used as an explanatory variable in place of the admission price in a model similar to equation (13.7).

The clever insight of the TCM is that although admission fees are usually the same for all persons (indeed, they are often zero), the total cost faced by each person varies because of differences in the travel cost component. Consequently, usage also varies, thereby allowing researchers to make inferences about the demand curve for the site. It is worth emphasizing that when total cost replaces price in equation (13.7), this equation is not the usual demand curve that gives visits as a function of the price of admission. As we show, however, the TCM can be used to estimate the usual market demand curve.

Estimating the demand schedule for a particular recreational site with the TCM is conceptually straightforward. First, select a random sample of households within the market area of the site. Second, survey these households to determine their numbers of visits to the site over some period of time, all of their costs involved in visiting the site, their costs of visiting substitute sites, their incomes, and their other characteristics that may affect their demand. Third, specify a functional form for the demand schedule and estimate it using the survey data. An example is provided in Exhibit 13.3 on page 351.

Zonal Travel Cost Method

With the *zonal travel cost method,* researchers survey actual visitors at a site rather than potential visitors. This is often more feasible and less expensive than surveying potential visitors. Also the level of analysis shifts from the individual, or household, to the area, or zone, of origin of visitors—hence, the term *zonal travel cost method.*

The zonal TCM requires the analyst to specify the zones from which users of the site originate. Zones can easily be formed by drawing concentric rings or isotime lines around the site on a map. Ideally, households within a zone should face similar travel costs as well as have similar values of the other variables, including the price of substitutes, income, and tastes. If residents within a zone have quite different travel costs, then zones should be redrawn. In practice, analysts often use local government jurisdictions as the zones because they facilitate the collection of data on populations and demographic characteristics within zones.

Assuming a constant-elasticity functional form leads to the following regression model:

$$\ln\left(\frac{V}{POP}\right) = \beta_0 + \beta_1 \ln \bar{p} + \beta_2 \ln \bar{p}_s + \beta_4 \bar{Y} + \beta_5 \bar{Z} + \varepsilon \tag{13.8}$$

where V is the number of visits from a zone per period, POP is the population of the zone; and $\bar{p}, \bar{p}_s, \bar{Y},$ and $\bar{Z}$ denote the average values of $p, p_s, Y,$ and Z in each zone, respectively.

Note that the quantity demanded is expressed as a visit rate. An alternative specification is to estimate demand in terms of the number of visits, V, but to include population, POP, on the right-hand side of the regression equation. Although both specifications are plausible, the specification in equation (13.8) is less likely to involve heteroscedasticity problems (which we discuss in Appendix 12A) and is, therefore, more likely to be appropriately estimated by OLS.

Using estimates of the parameters of equation (13.8), it is possible to estimate the change in consumer surplus associated with a change in the admission price to a site, the total consumer surplus associated with the site at its current admission fee, and the average consumer surplus per visit to the site. We illustrate how to do this using an example for a hypothetical recreational wilderness area, assuming there are only five relevant zones from which people travel to the recreational site. To avoid unnecessary complications, we assume that demand depends directly only on total price, not on income, the prices of substitutes, or any other variable.

The basic data for the illustration are presented in Table 13.1. In this example, the value of time for residents from different zones varies considerably due to different income levels. Zone A is adjacent to the recreational area. Residents from zone A can, on average, pack up their equipment, drive to the site (2 kilometers on average), park, and walk to the entrance in approximately one-half hour. Assuming the opportunity cost of their time is \$9.40/hr and marginal vehicle operating costs are 15 cents/km, their total travel costs are \$10 per round trip. Adding the admission fee of \$10 per day yields a total cost of \$20 per visit. On average, these local residents make 15 visits each year. Zone B is about 30 km away, requiring two hours of total travel time (including driving, parking, walking, loading, and unloading vehicles) for a round trip. Assuming the value of time for residents of zone B is \$5.50/hr and they travel individually, total costs per visit are \$30. On average, zone B residents make 13 visits per year. Zone C is about 90 km away, requiring two hours of total travel time in each direction. Assuming the value of their time is \$10.35/hr on average, and that travel costs are shared between two people in each vehicle, total costs per person are approximately \$65 per visit. On average, zone C residents make six visits per year. Zone D residents live on the other side

TABLE 13.1   Illustration of the Travel Cost Method

Zone	Travel Time (hours)	Travel Distance (km)	Average Total Cost per Person ($)	Average Number of Visits per Person	Consumer Surplus per Person	Consumer Surplus per Zone ($ thousands)	Trips per Zone (thousands)
A	0.5	2	20	15	525	5,250	150
B	1.0	30	30	13	390	3,900	130
C	2.0	90	65	6	75	1,500	120
D	3.0	140	80	3	15	150	30
E	3.5	150	90	1	0	0	10
Total						10,800	440

of the metropolitan area and, on average, make three visits each year. Assuming that their average wage rate is $8/hr and that two persons travel per vehicle, their per person cost is $80 per visit. Zone E residents have to cross an international border. Though the distance is only slightly farther than from zone D, it takes almost one-half hour to get through customs and immigration. The average zone E wage is $8/hour. Assuming two persons per vehicle, the per person cost is $90 per visit.

The data for average total cost per person (TC) and average visits per person (V) are represented graphically in Figure 13.4 for zones A through E. The equation $TC = 95 - 5V$ fits these data perfectly. (In practice, ordinary least squares would be used to fit a line to data points that would not all lie exactly on the line.) This equation is the "representative" individual's inverse demand curve: It shows how much a typical person is willing to pay for a visit to the recreational area; specifically, $90 for the first visit, $85 for the second visit, . . . , $20 for the fifteenth visit.

Different individuals face different prices (costs) for their visits depending on their zone of origin. It is cheaper for those who live closer. Therefore, the individuals' consumer surplus varies according to the zone of origin. The consumer surplus for a

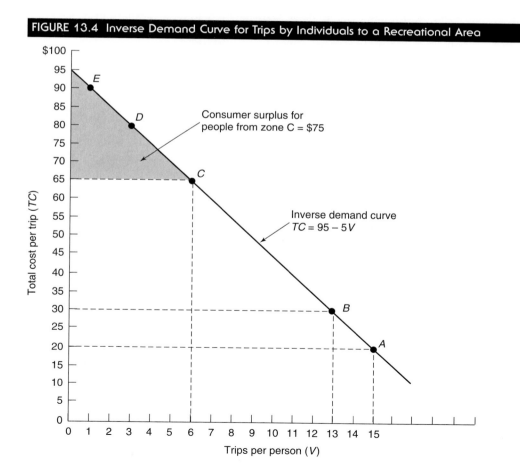

FIGURE 13.4 Inverse Demand Curve for Trips by Individuals to a Recreational Area

particular visit from a particular zone equals the difference between how much someone is willing to pay for that visit, given by the point on the individual inverse demand curve, and how much the person actually pays for a visit *from that zone*. For example, people from zone C are willing to pay $80 for their third visit, but they actually pay only $65 for that visit, yielding a consumer surplus of $15 for that visit.

The consumer surplus for someone from zone C is obtained by summing the consumer surpluses associated with each visit across all trips ($90 − $65 = $25 for the first visit, $85 − $65 = $20 for the second visit, and $15, $10, $5, and $0 for the third, fourth, fifth, and sixth visits, respectively), which equals $75. This amount is represented by the area of the shaded triangle in Figure 13.4.[20] Similarly, the consumer surplus is $525 per person for people from zone A, $390 for people from zone B, $15 for people from zone D, and $0 for people from zone E. These amounts are presented in column 6 of Table 13.1. Clearly, people who live closer to the recreational site enjoy a larger consumer surplus from it than people who live further away.

From this information and knowledge of the populations of each zone, we can calculate the total consumer surplus per year and the average consumer surplus per visit for the site. Suppose zones A, B, D, and E have populations of 10,000 people, whereas zone C has a population of 20,000 people. The consumer surplus per zone is obtained by multiplying the consumer surplus per person in a zone by the population of that zone, as shown in the second from last column in Table 13.1. Adding across all zones yields the total annual consumer surplus for the site of $10.8 million. Adding admission fees of $4.4 million indicates that the annual (gross) benefit of the site to all visitors equals $15.2 million. If the government decided to use the site for some completely different purpose, such as logging, this would be a measure of the lost annual benefits.

The total number of visits to the recreational area is 440,000, as shown in column 8 of Table 13.1. Dividing the total consumer surplus by the total number of visits gives an average consumer surplus per visit of $24.55. If we now add the admission fee of $10, then we obtain the *average demand price* per visit, which is the average maximum amount a visitor would pay for a visit to the site. In this example, the average demand price is $34.55.

Estimating the Market Demand Curve

It is possible to use the zonal TCM to construct an inverse *market demand curve* for the site, where the admission fee is a function of the *total* number of visits to the site. This curve can then be used to estimate total consumer surplus in the usual way. Unfortunately, as each point on the market demand curve has to be estimated separately, precise computation of consumer surplus is a bit more time consuming than the preceding approach.

To begin, we know two points on the market demand curve. At an admission price of $10, the current admission fee, there are 440,000 visits. Now consider how high admission fees can be raised until demand is choked off and falls to zero. We know from the individual inverse demand curve ($TC = 95 − 5V$) that the maximum willingness-to-pay (including all costs) is $95. Subtracting the travel cost of users from zone A (who have the lowest travel cost) implies that the maximum willingness-to-pay for admission is $95 − $10 = $85. This is the intercept (choke price) of the inverse market demand curve.

We can find other points on the market demand curve by assuming that the admission fee is increased or decreased and then predicting the visit rate from each zone at the new price. Suppose, for example, the admission fee were raised by $10 to $20, so that TC would increase by $10. Given that the *individual* demand curve can be written as $V = 19 - 0.2TC$ (the inverse of $TC = 95 - 5V$), a $10 increase in TC would reduce the number of visits per person by two. Thus, if the admission price were $20, then the predicted number of visits would be 13 for zone A, 11 for zone B, 4 for zone C, 1 for zone D, and -1 for zone E. As negative visits are not possible, we set the number of visits per person for zone E to zero. The total number of visits demanded at the new price is computed by multiplying the predicted visit rate for each zone by its population and summing these products $(13 \times 10,000 + 11 \times 10,000 + 4 \times 20,000 + 1 \times 10,000 = 330,000)$. Thus, at a price of $20 we would expect 330,000 visits. This is a second point on the market demand curve.

Other points on the market demand curve can be obtained in the same way. For example, we would expect 160,000 visits if the admission price were $40. With a sufficient number of points, the market demand curve can be sketched to any desired level of accuracy. A market demand curve for the site computed on the basis of $10 price increments is shown in Figure 13.5. The annual consumer surplus for the site is the area between the curve and the current admission fee from zero visits to 440,000 visits. Assuming for simplicity that the demand curve is linear between points *a* and *b*, and between points *b* and *c*, we estimate the annual consumer surplus of the site equals $12.6 million, and the annual (gross) benefit of the site is $17.0 million.[21] Due to the linear approximation and the relatively few points on the demand curve, we slightly overestimate the benefits.

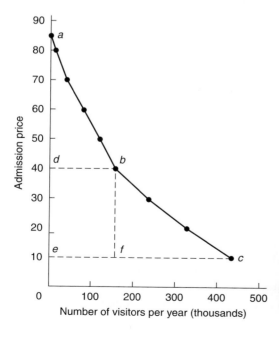

FIGURE 13.5 The Market Demand Curve for a Recreational Site Derived Using the Zonal Travel Cost Method

Limitations of the TCM

The usefulness of the TCM is limited in a number of ways. One limitation is that the TCM provides an estimate of the willingness-to-pay for the entire site rather than for specific features of a site. As we often wish to value changes in specific features of a site (e.g., improvements in the hiking trails), the basic TCM does not provide the needed information. However, if the residents of zones can choose from among a number of alternative recreational sites with different attributes, then it may be possible to use the *hedonic travel cost method* to find attribute prices.[22] This method treats the total cost of visiting a particular site from a particular zone as a function of both the distance from that zone to the site and various attributes of the site. Its application raises a number of issues beyond those previously discussed in the context of the basic hedonic pricing model. Therefore, before attempting to apply the hedonic pricing method in this context, we recommend consulting sources that deal with it specifically in the travel cost context.[23]

Another limitation of the TCM is that it is restricted to the analysis of sites to which people from different zones have quite different travel costs. If an analyst tried to use this method to value a civic theater where most attendees lived nearby, then it probably would not work well because there would probably be too little variation in travel cost among attendees and, hence, too little variation in total cost. Without variation in total cost, there is no leverage for estimating a demand curve.

Estimation of the market demand curve assumes that people respond to changes in price regardless of its composition. Thus, for example, people respond to a $5 increase in the admission price in the same way as a $5 increase in travel cost. This presumes that people have a good understanding of the impact of changes in the prices of fuel, tires, and repairs on their marginal travel cost.

The TCM also raises a number of analytical problems in its application, many of which concern measuring the price of a visit to the site.[24] Perhaps the most obvious problem is the estimation of the opportunity cost of travel time, which we have previously discussed.[25] Even defining and measuring travel costs raises some difficult issues. Some analysts include the time spent at the site, as well as the time spent traveling to and from it, as components of total price. If people from different zones spend the same amount of time at the site, and if the opportunity cost of their time is similar, then it does not matter whether the time spent at the site is included or not—both the height of the demand curve and total price shift by the same amount for each consumer so that estimates of consumer surplus remain unchanged. If, however, people from different zones have different opportunity costs for their time, or if they spend different amounts of time at the site, then including the cost of time spent at the site would change the price facing persons from different zones by different amounts and, thereby, change the slope of the estimated demand curve.

Another problem arises because recreation often requires investment in fairly specialized equipment such as tents, sleeping bags, wet-weather gear, canoes, fishing rods, and even vehicles. The marginal cost of using such equipment should be included in total price. Yet, estimating the marginal cost of using capital goods is usually difficult. As with time spent at the site, however, these costs can be reasonably ignored if they are approximately constant for visitors from different zones.

Multiple-purpose trips also pose an analytical problem. People may visit the recreational site in the morning and, for example, go river rafting nearby in the afternoon.

Sometimes analysts exclude visitors with multiple purposes from the data. Including visitors with multiple purposes is usually desirable if costs can be appropriately apportioned to the site being valued. If the apportionment is arbitrary, however, then it may be better to exclude multiple users.

A similar problem results because the journey itself may have value. The previous discussion assumes implicitly that the trip is undertaken exclusively to get to the recreation site and travel has no benefit per se. If the journey itself is part of the reason for the visit to the site, then the trip has multiple purposes. Therefore, part of the cost of the trip should be attributed to the journey, not the visit to the recreation site. Not doing so would lead to overestimation of site benefits.

A more fundamental problem is that the travel cost variable may be endogenous, not exogenous. One neighborhood characteristic some people consider when making their residential choices is its proximity to a recreational area. People who expect to make many visits to the recreational area may select a particular neighborhood (zone) partially on account of the low travel time from that neighborhood to the recreational area. If so, the number of trips to a particular recreational area and the price of these trips will be determined simultaneously. Under these circumstances equation (13.8) may not be identified, a problem which we discuss in Chapter 12.[26]

Another econometric problem is that the dependent variable in the estimated models is *truncated*. Truncation arises because the sample is drawn from only those who visit the site, not from the larger population that includes people who never visit the site. Application of ordinary least squares to the truncated sample would result in biased coefficients. However, there are more complicated estimation methods that overcome this problem,

Finally, there may be an omitted variable problem. If the price of substitute recreational sites varies across zones or if tastes for recreation vary across zones, then the estimated coefficients may be biased if the model does not control for these variables. As previously discussed, bias results when an excluded variable is correlated with an included variable.

EXHIBIT 13.3

Kerry Smith and William Desvousges used the travel cost method to estimate the average household value of a trip to recreational sites along the Monongahela River and the average household value of improving water quality. Their estimates of travel costs assumed the marginal cost of operating an automobile was $0.08 per mile in 1976. For the time cost component of travel cost, they set the value of time equal to the wage rate in a person's particular occupation, which ranged from $2.75 per hour for female farmers to $7.89 per hour for male professional, technical, and kindred workers in 1977 dollars. Smith and Desvousges estimated many models including the following relatively simple travel cost model (*t* statistics in parentheses):

$$\ln V = -3.928 - 0.051TC + 0.00001Y + 0.058DO \qquad (R^2 = 0.225)$$
$$(-3.075) \quad (-2.846) \quad (1.109) \qquad (3.917)$$

where V is the number of site visits, Y denotes income, and DO is the percent saturation of dissolved oxygen in the water. Based on this model, the authors estimated that the average annual value of improving the water quality from boatable to game fishing would be $7.16 in 1981 dollars (about $13 in 1999 dollars), and the average annual value of improving the water quality from boatable to swimming would be $28.86 in 1981 dollars (about $53 in 1999 dollars).

Source: V. Kerry Smith and William H. Desvousges, *Measuring Water Quality Benefits* (Boston: Kluwer Nijhoff Publishing, 1986), especially pp. 270–271.

DEFENSIVE EXPENDITURES METHOD[27]

If you live in a smoggy city, then you may find that the windows of your house often need cleaning. If you hire someone to clean your windows periodically, the cost of this action in response to the smog is termed a *defensive expenditure.* Suppose the city passes an ordinance that reduces the level of smog so that your windows do not get as dirty. You would now have to spend less on window cleaners. The reduction in defensive expenditures—the defensive expenditures avoided—has been suggested as a measure of the benefits of the city ordinance. Similarly, the costs of a policy change might be measured by the increase in defensive expenditures.

This method is an example of a broad class of *production function methods.* In these methods, the level of a public good or externality (e.g., smog) and other goods (window cleaners) are inputs to some production process (window cleanliness). If the level of the public good or externality changes, then the levels of the other inputs can be changed in the opposite direction, allowing the quantity of output produced to remain the same. For example, when the negative externality of smog is reduced, less labor is required to produce the same number of clean windows. The change in expenditures on the substitute input is used as a measure of the benefit of reduction of the public good or externality.

Suppose that the demand curve for clean windows is represented by the curve labeled D in Figure 13.6. Let S_0 represent the marginal cost of cleaning windows initially, that is, prior to the new ordinance. The initial equilibrium price and quantity of clean windows are denoted by P_0 and Q_0, respectively. The effect of the new ordinance is to shift the marginal cost of cleaning windows down and to the right: Because there is less smog, windows are easier to clean, so that more windows can be cleaned for the same price. At

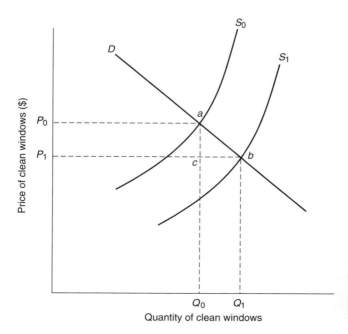

FIGURE 13.6 The Effect of an Ordinance Reducing Smog on Expenditures for Window Cleaning

the new equilibrium, the price of clean windows is P_1 and the quantity of clean windows is Q_1. The change in consumer surplus is represented by the area of the trapezoid $P_0 ab P_1$.

If households continued to consume the same quantity of clean windows after the price shift as they did before the price shift, Q_0, then the benefit of the ordinance would be represented by the rectangle $P_0 ac P_1$. This would be the amount by which consumers reduce their defensive expenditure. Consumers, however, would not maintain their consumption levels at Q_0, but would increase their consumption of clean windows to level Q_1. Individuals would spend area $b Q_1 Q_0 c$ on the purchase of $Q_1 - Q_0$ additional units of clean windows at a price of P_1. The net change in spending on window cleaning services equals the area of rectangle $b Q_1 Q_0 c$ minus the area of rectangle $P_0 ac P_1$. This net change in spending may be quite small. Indeed, if the demand curve were a constant-elasticity demand curve, with an elasticity equal to 1, there would be no change in total expenditure on window cleaning services at all! Yet, there are obviously positive benefits to consumers. In general, *the reduced spending on defensive expenditures will underestimate the benefits of cleaner air or whatever benefit is being estimated.*[28]

There are at least four additional problems with the defensive expenditures method. First, it assumes implicitly that individuals quickly adjust to the new equilibrium. It may actually take some time for individuals to adjust their purchases and return to equilibrium. Second, a defensive expenditure may not remedy the entire damage so that reductions in this expenditure do not fully measure benefits. For example, expenditures on window cleaning do not "avoid" the whole problem of smog. Smog also leads to dirtier shirts and to health problems. Defensive expenditures avoided on these items should also be included. Exhibit 13.4 illustrates that groundwater degradation may affect many different defensive expenditures. Third, the defensive expenditures may have benefits other than remedying damage. For example, the cleaning necessitated by the smog may result in cleaner windows than one would otherwise achieve. Fourth, not all of the defensive measures are purchased in markets. Some people clean their own windows—reductions in their opportunity costs should also be included as benefits.

EXHIBIT 13.4

Charles W. Abdalla, Brian A. Roach, and Donald J. Epp measured the costs of groundwater degradation in the small Pennsylvania borough of Perkasie (population 7,877) using the defensive expenditures method. They conducted mail and telephone surveys to gather information from a sample of residents on the actions they took in response to trichloroethylene (TCE) contamination of one of the borough's wells between December 1987 and September 1989. They estimated the total costs to the community's residents, including both monetary costs and time expenditures, of each of five defensive actions:

Category of Cost	*Cost Based on Value of Leisure Time Equal to Minimum Wage ($)[a]*	*Cost Based on Value of Leisure Time Equal to Individual Wage Rate ($)[a]*
Increased purchases of bottled water	11,100	11,100
New purchases of bottled water	17,300	17,300
Home water treatment systems	4,700	4,700
Hauling water	12,500	34,000
Boiling water	15,600	64,100
Total	61,200	131,200

[a]Costs in original rounded to nearest hundred dollars.

Note that the costs of hauling and boiling water are very sensitive to the assumed opportunity cost of leisure. The researchers interpreted these total costs as a lower-bound estimate of the true cost of the contamination to residents because of the generally conservative nature of the defensive expenditures method.

A specific factor suggesting that these defensive expenditures represent a lower bound is that only 43 percent of residents were aware of the TCE contamination despite notification laws! Moreover, not all residents who knew about the contamination took defensive measures. Nevertheless, those who had more information about the contamination, those who perceived the cancer risk due to TCE to be higher, and those who had children between 3 and 17 years old in the household were generally more likely to take defensive action than other residents. Among those who took defensive action, having a child under 3 years of age seemed to be the most important factor influencing the intensity of the defensive actions taken.

Source: Charles W. Abdalla, Brian A. Roach, and Donald J. Epp, "Valuing Environmental Quality Changes Using Averting Expenditures: An Application to Groundwater Contamination," *Land Economics,* 68, no. 2 (1992), 163–169.

CONCLUSION

This chapter and the last describe the major methods currently used in CBA for estimating benefits and costs by utilizing information on revealed preference that is obtained from sources other than demonstrations or social experiments. Some methods are not discussed because we believe that they are too advanced for this book. Perhaps most notably, we have not discussed the use of random utility models or probabilistic choice models to estimate demand, an approach that is quite important in the transportation area.[29] Also, we do not discuss recent methods that estimate demand curves by combining survey data with data on observed behavior.[30] Nevertheless, the methods covered here provide a rich set of tools for practical valuation of impacts.

Exercises for Chapter 13

1. Day care services in a small midwestern city cost $30 per day per child. The high cost of these services is one reason why very few mothers who are on welfare work; given their low potential wages, virtually no welfare mothers are willing to pay these high costs. To combat this problem, the city establishes a new program: In exchange for their welfare benefits, a group of welfare recipients is required to provide day care for the children of other welfare recipients who obtain private-sector employment. The welfare mothers who use these day care services are required to pay a fee of $3 per day per child. These services prove very popular; 1,000 welfare children receive them each day and an additional 500 welfare children are on a waiting list to receive them. Do the mothers of the 1,000 children who receive services under the program value these services at $30,000 ($30 × 1,000) a day, $3,000 a day ($3 × 1,000), or at a value that is greater than $3,000 but less than $30,000? Explain.

2. A worker, who is typical in all respects, works for a wage of $40,000 per year in a perfectly safe occupation. Another typical worker does a job requiring exactly the same skills as the first worker, but in a risky occupation with a known death probability of 1 in 1,000 per year, and receives a wage of $44,000 per year. What value of a human life for workers with these characteristics should a cost-benefit analyst use?

3. (Spreadsheet software required.) Happy Valley is the only available camping area in Rural County. It is owned by the county, which allows free access to campers. Almost all visitors to Happy Valley come from the six towns in the county.

Rural County is considering leasing Happy Valley for logging, which would require that it be closed to campers. Before approving the lease, the county executive would like to know the magnitude of annual benefits that campers would forgo if Happy Valley were to be closed to the public.

An analyst for the county has collected data for a travel cost study to estimate the benefits of Happy Valley camping. On five randomly selected days, he recorded the license plates of vehicles parked overnight in the Happy Valley lot. (As the camping season is 100 days, he assumed that this would constitute a 5 percent sample.) With cooperation from the state motor vehicle department, he was able to find the town of residence of the owner of each vehicle. He also observed a sample of vehicles from which he estimated that each vehicle carried 3.2 persons (1.6 adults), on average. The following table summarizes the data he collected:

Town	Miles from Happy Valley	Population (thousands)	Estimated Number of Visitors for Season	Visit Rate (visits per 1,000 people)
A	22	50.1	3,893	77.7
B	34	34.9	2,267	65.0
C	48	15.6	587	37.6
D	56	89.9	4,800	53.4
E	88	98.3	1,947	19.8
F	94	60.4	666	11.0
Total			14,160	

In order to translate the distance traveled into an estimate of the cost campers faced in using Happy Valley, the analyst made the following assumptions. First, the average operating cost of vehicles is $0.36 per mile. Second, the average speed on county highways is 50 miles per hour. Third, the opportunity cost to adults of travel time is 40 percent of their wage rate; it is zero for children. Fourth, adult campers have the average county wage rate of $9.25 per hour.

The analyst has asked you to help him use this information to estimate the annual benefits accruing to Happy Valley campers. Specifically, assist with the following tasks:

a. Using the preceding information, calculate the travel cost of a visit (TC) from each of the towns.

b. For the six observations, regress visit rate (VR) on TC and a constant. If you do not have regression software available, plot the points and fit a line by sight. Find the slope of the fitted line.

c. You know that with the current free admission, the number of camping visits demanded is 14,160. Find additional points on the demand curve by predicting the reduction in the number of campers from each town as price is increased by $5 increments until demand falls to zero. This is done in three steps at each price: First, use the coefficient of TC from the regression to predict a new VR for each town. Second, multiply the predicted VR of each town by its population to get a predicted number of visitors. Third, sum the visitors from each town to get the total number of predicted visits.

d. Estimate the area under the demand curve as the annual benefits to campers.

Notes

1. The *net output method* of valuing a life subtracts the value of a person's own consumption from his or her forgone earnings. It measures the benefit or cost the individual contributes to or imposes on the rest of society. The courts' use of this method to measure the loss to survivors of someone's death is somewhat arbitrary but perhaps reasonable. However, it is clearly inappropriate to use this method in CBA to value a life saved. One reason is that the value of the person's own consumption should be counted because the individual is a member of society. Another reason is that it ignores the life cycle of earnings: Although a typical person's net output will be slightly positive over his or her entire lifetime, it will be negative for a retired person. For an overview of the net output method, see John J. Lawson, "The Value of Transport Safety," Final Report (Transport Canada Report No. 10569, 1989).

2. Thomas C. Schelling, "The Life You Save May Be Your Own," in *Economics of the Environment: Selected Readings,* 3rd ed., Robert Dorfman and Nancy S. Dorfman, eds. (New York: W. W. Norton, 1993), pp. 388–408 at p. 402.

3. This was the case until a few years ago. If you do not like thinking about airbags, you could think about smoke detectors or any other device one pays for voluntarily that reduces the probability of death.

4. W. Kip Viscusi, "Perspective Reference Theory: Toward an Explanation of the Paradoxes," *Journal of Risk and Uncertainty,* 2, no. 3 (1989), 235–264. However, other studies suggest that people underestimate the probability of low-probability events, especially if they are in charge (e.g., driving a car) or when there are complex independent systems and the failure of one component causes failure in the whole system.

5. See, for example, Jon P. Nelson, "Airports and Property Values: A Survey of Recent Evidence," *Journal of Transport Economics and Policy,* 14, no. 2 (1981), 37–52.

6. See T. D. Schroeder, "The Relationship of Local Public Park and Recreation Services to Residential Property Values," *Journal of Leisure Research,* 14, no. 3 (1982), 223–234.

7. See, for example, Anthony E. Boardman, Ruth Freedman, and Catherine Eckel, "The Price of Government Ownership: A Study of the Domtar Takeover," *Journal of Public Economics,* 31, no. 3 (1986), 269–285; John C. Ries, "Windfall Profits and Vertical Relationships: Who Gained in the Japan-ese Auto Industry from VERs?" *Journal of Industrial Economics,* 61, no. 3 (1993), 259–276; Paul H. Malatesta and Rex Thompson, "Government Regulation and Structural Change in the Corporate Acquisitions Market: The Impact of the Williams Act," *Journal of Financial and Quantitative Analysis,* 28, no. 3 (1993), 363–379; and Anthony Boardman, Ilan Vertinsky, and Diana Whistler, "Using Information Diffusion Models to Estimate the Impacts of Regulatory Events on Publicly Traded Firms," *Journal of Public Economics,* 63, no. 2 (1997), 283–300.

8. For a discussion of different ways to estimate what the return would have been in the absence of the event, see Stephen J. Brown and Jerold B. Warner, "Measuring Security Price Performance," *Journal of Financial Economics,* 8, no. 3 (1980), 205–258.

9. Sherwin Rosen developed the theory for estimating hedonic prices; see Sherwin Rosen, "Hedonic Prices and Implicit Markets: Product Differentiation in Pure Competition," *Journal of Political Economy,* 82, no. 1 (1974), 34–55.

10. The basic idea behind hedonic regression was introduced in Kelvin L. Lancaster, "A New Approach to Consumer Theory," *Journal of Political Economy,* 74, no. 1 (1966), 132–157.

11. In general, the hedonic price function can be written $P = p(C_1, C2, ..., C_k, N_1, ..., N_m)$, where $C_i (i = 1, ..., k)$ denote k attributes of the house and $N_j (j = 1, ..., m)$ denote m neighborhood characteristics.

12. Formally, $r_v = \partial P / \partial VIEW$.

13. The hedonic price of C_i may be a function of all of the variables in the hedonic price function. Given the general hedonic regression model presented in note 11, $\partial P / \partial C_i = f(C_1, ..., C_k, N_1, ..., N_m)$.

14. Formally,
$$r_v = \partial P / \partial VIEW$$
$$= \beta_3 \beta_0 CBD^{\beta_1} SIZE^{\beta_2} VIEW^{\beta_3 - 1} NBHD^{\beta_4} e^\varepsilon$$
$$= \beta_3 (P / VIEW).$$

15. The functional form of this model may be linear, multiplicative, or have some other form.

16. These functions indicate households' willingness-to-pay holding household characteristics constant.

17. The seminal work on this topic, which actually preceded the formal development of the hedonic pricing method, is Ronald G. Ridker and John A. Henning, "The Determinants of Residential Property Values with Special Reference to Air Pollution," *Review of Economics and Statistics,* 49, no. 2

(1967), 246–257. For a review of studies that have attempted to use the hedonic method to estimate willingness-to-pay for reductions in particulate matter in air, see V. Kerry Smith and Ju-Chin Huang, "Can Markets Value Air Quality? A Meta-Analysis of Hedonic Property Value Models," *Journal of Political Economy*, 103, no. 1 (1995), 209–227. For an application to the value of life, see Paul Portney, "Housing Prices, Health Effects, and Valuing Reductions in Risk of Death," *Journal of Environmental Economics and Management,* 8, no. 1 (1981), 72–78.

18. This method is often referred to as the Clawson method, or the Knetsch-Clawson method. However, it is now attributed to Harold Hotelling; see Harold Hotelling, "Letter," *An Economic Study of the Monetary Evaluation of Recreation in the National Parks* (Washington, DC: National Park Service, 1949). For some of the earlier descriptions on this method, see Marion Clawson, "Methods of Measuring the Demand for and Value of Outdoor Recreation," Reprint No. 10 (Washington, DC: Resources for the Future, 1959); Marion Clawson and Jack L. Knetsch, *Economics of Outdoor Recreation* (Baltimore: Johns Hopkins Press, 1966); and Jack L. Knetsch and Robert K. Davis, "Comparisons of Methods of Recreation Evaluation," in *Water Research*, Allen V. Kneese and Stephen C. Smith, eds. (Baltimore: Johns Hopkins Press, 1966), pp. 125–142.

19. For an interesting and novel application of the TCM, see Charles J. Cicchetti, A. Myrick Freeman III, Robert H. Haveman, and Jack L. Knetsch, "On the Economics of Mass Demonstrations: A Case Study of the November 1969 March on Washington," *American Economic Review*, 61, no. 4 (1971), 719–724.

20. Note that computing the area of the triangle using the formula $(\$95 - \$65)(6)/2 = \$90$ provides a slight overestimate of the consumer surplus, whereas using the formula $(\$90 - \$65)(6)/2 = \$75$ provides the correct answer. In effect, if we treat the intercept as \$90 instead of \$95, we obtain the correct answer. The problem arises because the number of visits is a discrete variable, whereas the equation for the inverse demand function is continuous.

21. Area *abd* ≈ 3,600, area *dbfe* = \$4,800, area *bcf* ≈ \$4,200.

22. Gardner Brown, Jr. and Robert Mendelsohn, "The Hedonic Travel Cost Model," *Review of Economics and Statistics*, 66, no. 3 (1984), 427–433.

23. For more detail, see Nancy G. Bockstael, Kenneth E. McConnell, and Ivar Strand, "Recreation," in *Measuring the Demand for Environmental Quality*, J. B. Braden and C. D. Kolstad, eds. (Amsterdam: Elsevier, 1991), pp. 227–270, and V. Kerry Smith and Yoshiaki Kaoru, "The Hedonic Travel Cost Model: A View From the Trenches," *Land Economics*, 63, no. 2 (1987), 179–192.

24. Alan Randall, "A Difficulty with the Travel Cost Method," *Land Economics*, 70, no. 1 (1994), 88–96.

25. See also John R. McKean, Donn M. Johnson, and Richard G. Walsh, "Valuing Time in Travel Cost Demand Analysis: An Empirical Investigation," *Land Economics*, 71, no. 1 (1995), 96–105.

26. Also, the travel cost variable may not be independent of the error term, thereby leading to ordinary least squares estimates that are biased and inconsistent.

27. This method is also referred to as the avoided cost method. For a recent review of the use of this method to measure groundwater values, see Charles Abdalla, "Groundwater Values from Avoidance Cost Studies: Implications for Policy and Future Research," *American Journal of Agricultural Economics*, 76, no. 5 (1994), 1062–1067.

28. The accuracy of using changes in defensive expenditures on a substitute to measure the benefits of changes in the levels of externalities or public goods depends on how these goods enter the individual's utility function and on the relationship between these goods and the market for the substitute. For more discussion of this issue, see Paul N. Courant and Richard Porter, "Averting Expenditure and the Cost of Pollution," *Journal of Environmental Economics and Management*, 8, no. 4 (1981), 321–329. Also see Winston Harrington and Paul Portney, "Valuing the Benefits of Health and Safety Regulation," *Journal of Urban Economics,* 22, no. 1 (1987), 101–112.

29. These models are also referred to as qualitative response models. See, for example, G. S. Maddala, *Limited-Dependent and Qualitative Variables in Econometrics* (Cambridge: Cambridge University Press, 1983), and Kenneth Train, *Qualitative Choice Analysis* (Cambridge, MA: MIT Press, 1986).

30. See, for example, David A. Hensher and Mark Bradley, "Using Stated Preference Response Data to Enrich Revealed Preference Data," *Marketing Letters*, 4, no. 2 (1993), 139–152.

14

VALUING IMPACTS THROUGH SURVEYS

Contingent Valuation

Economists are generally much more comfortable observing individuals' valuations of goods and services through their behavior in markets than eliciting their valuations through survey questionnaires. They prefer to observe purchasing decisions because these decisions directly reveal preferences, whereas surveys elicit statements about preferences. Nevertheless, for some public goods there are simply no, or very poor, market proxies or other means of inferring preferences from observations. In such circumstances, many analysts have concluded that there may be no alternative to asking a sample of people about their valuations.

In CBA, questionnaires designed to elicit preferences are normally referred to as *contingent valuation* (CV) surveys, or sometimes hypothetical valuation surveys, because respondents are not actually required to pay their valuations of the good.[1] In this chapter we provide an overview of CV, review the major criticisms of its use, and consider some of the strengths and weaknesses of the most commonly used CV methods.

THE ROLE OF CONTINGENT VALUATION

The primary use of CV is to elicit people's willingness-to-pay (*WTP*) for changes in quantities of goods. Many kinds of goods, including water quality at recreation sites, trees near subdivisions, goose hunting, and outdoor recreation, have been valued with CV surveys.[2] Such agencies as the National Park Service and the U.S. Bureau of Reclamation commonly use CV surveys to value recreation and wildlife opportunities. CV surveys have also been used to value more complex and abstract "goods," such as hazardous waste reduction, spotted owl habitat protection, and lives saved.[3] Valuing the use, or potential use, of goods with CV is relatively uncontroversial. Valuing passive use (nonuse) with CV is highly controversial, both for the conceptual reasons discussed in Chapter 9 and for the practical reasons related to gathering valid information from surveys discussed later in this chapter.

In spite of the controversy, the use of CV as a method for estimating costs and, especially, benefits is growing rapidly. Indeed, the federal courts have held that surveys of citizens' valuations have "rebuttable presumption" status in cases involving the assessment of damage to natural resources.[4] A blue ribbon panel of social scientists convened by the National Oceanic and Atmospheric Administration (NOAA) further legitimized the use of CV by concluding that it could be the basis for estimating passive use values for inclusion in natural resource damage assessment cases.[5]

OVERVIEW OF CONTINGENT VALUATION METHODS

The general approach of all the CV methods is as follows. First, a sample of respondents from the population with standing is identified. Second, respondents are asked questions about their valuations of some good. Third, their responses provide information that enables analysts to estimate the respondents' *WTP* for the good. Fourth, the *WTP* amounts for the sample are extrapolated to the entire population. If, for instance, the respondents comprise a random sample of the population such that each member of the population had an equal chance of being in the sample, then the average *WTP* for the sample would simply be multiplied by the size of the population to arrive at the aggregate *WTP.*

As CV surveys are expensive to conduct, analysts may wish to extrapolate the results of existing surveys to different populations. The characteristics of these populations usually do not match those of the population that was previously sampled. For example, the populations may differ in terms of income, access to alternative goods, or other factors that may be relevant to their demands for the good. As we discuss in Chapter 15, reasonable extrapolation requires that these differences be controlled for statistically.[6] Therefore, analysts increase the chances that their CV surveys will have use beyond their own CBAs by collecting and reporting information about the characteristics of their samples, including *WTP* amounts for subsets of the sample, even when such information is unnecessary for their own studies.

The remainder of this section introduces particular methods that are used to elicit *WTP* amounts from survey respondents. We first briefly sketch three methods that have been used at various times: the *open-ended willingness-to-pay* method, the *closed-ended iterative bidding* method, and the *contingent ranking* method. We then turn to the *dichotomous-choice,* or *referendum, method,* which was advocated by the NOAA blue ribbon panel as the most appropriate method in most circumstances.[7]

Direct Elicitation (Nonreferendum) Methods

Several CV methods ask questions about preferences directly. The open-ended willingness-to-pay method and the closed-ended iterative bidding method seek to elicit the *WTP* amounts for each respondent. The contingent ranking method seeks to elicit a preference profile over a set of alternatives for each respondent. These methods contrast with the dichotomous-choice method, which is indirect in the sense that it relies on patterns of responses across a large number of respondents to make inferences about the preferences of respondents with particular characteristics.

Open-Ended Willingness-to-Pay Method   The earliest method to be used is the *open-ended willingness-to-pay question* approach. Here respondents are simply asked to state their maximum WTP for the good, or policy, that is being valued.[8] The question might be formulated as follows: "What is the most that you would be prepared to pay in additional federal income taxes to guarantee that the Wildwood wilderness area will remain closed to development?" This method had dropped out of favor because analysts feared "unrealistic" responses unless respondents were given some initial "guidance" on valuations. As evidence has mounted, however, that such "guidance" affects respondents' answers, open-ended questions have made a comeback.[9] Concerns that open-ended questions result in excessively large estimates of *WTP* seem unfounded.

Closed-Ended Iterative Bidding Method   In the *closed-ended iterative bidding* method, respondents are asked whether they would pay a specified amount for the good or policy that has been described. If respondents answer affirmatively, then the amount is incrementally increased. The procedure continues until the respondent expresses unwillingness to pay the amount specified. Similarly, if respondents answer negatively to the initial amount specified, the interviewer lowers the amount by increments until the respondent expresses a *WTP*.[10]

   The initial question for determining *WTP* typically starts with something such as the following: "Now suppose the costs to clean the Kristiansand Fjord were divided on [sic] all taxpayers in the whole of Norway by an extra tax in 1986. If this extra tax was 200 kronor for an average taxpayer, would you then be willing to support the proposal?"[11] In this CV survey the interviewer set the initial price at 200 kronor. If a respondent indicates a willingness to pay this initial price, then the interviewer raises the price by 200 kronor and asks the question again. The interviewer keeps going until the respondent gives a negative answer. Similarly, if the initial response is negative, then the interviewer incrementally drops the price by 200 kronor until the respondent gives a positive response. Although iterative bidding was at one time the most common method in use, it is rarely used now because of considerable evidence that its results are highly sensitive to the initially presented, or starting, value.

Contingent Ranking Method   In the *contingent ranking*, or *ranked choice,* method, respondents are asked to rank specific feasible combinations of quantities of the good being valued and monetary payments. For example, respondents choose on a continuum between a low level of water quality at a low tax price and a high level of water quality at a high tax price. The combinations are ranked from most preferred to least preferred.[12] The rankings provide a basis for estimating each respondent's *WTP* for various increments of quality. Contingent ranking implies an ordinal ranking procedure in contrast to the iterative bidding procedure, which requires cardinal evaluation. Typically, tasks that require only ordinal information processing—that is, a ranking rather than a precise specification of value—are considerably easier for respondents to perform.[13] This is a valuable attribute in the CV context where information processing complexity is often high. Of course, unlike the open-ended *WTP* method or the closed-ended iterative bidding method, the *WTP* of interest must be inferred from ordinal rankings rather than directly elicited. Additionally, responses appear to be sensitive to the order in which alternatives are presented to respondents.

Dichotomous-Choice (Referendum) Method

In the *dichotomous-choice,* or *referendum,* method respondents are asked whether they would be willing to pay a particular price to obtain a good or policy.[14] Each respondent receives one randomly drawn price. Respondents are then asked to state whether they would be willing to pay for the good or policy (e.g., closing the Wildwood wilderness area to development) at the offered price ("yes" means willing to pay and "no" means not willing to pay); in other words, they are made a "take it or leave it" offer of the sort that they face in many markets for private goods. The choice situation is also like that faced by referendum voters—hence, the label *referendum* method. The dollar amounts, often referred to as *bid prices,* that are presented to respondents vary over a range selected by the analyst.[15] Accept/reject respondent probabilities can then be calculated for each bid price.[16]

Figure 14.1 shows the distribution of responses to bid prices in the form of a histogram. Specific bid prices are shown on the horizontal axis ranging from the lowest dollar price offered ($X = \$0$) to the highest price offered ($X = \$100$) in \$5 increments. The vertical axis measures the percentage of respondents who answer "yes" to the bid price offered to them. In this example, almost all of the respondents who are offered

FIGURE 14.1 Histogram of Dichotomous-Choice Responses

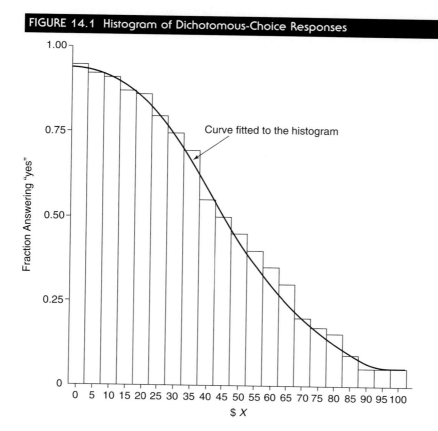

the specified outcome at $X = \$0$ state they would accept it. About 75 percent of respondents who are offered the outcome for $30 indicate that they would accept it at this price. We can interpret the response frequencies as estimates of the probability that a randomly drawn member of the sample of respondents is willing to pay a specific amount. For example, the probability a randomly drawn respondent would pay at least $30 for the specified outcome is about .75.

The fitted curve in Figure 14.1 may be viewed as the demand curve of a randomly drawn (i.e., average) member of the sample, whereas the histogram may be viewed as a rough approximation of this demand curve. The difference between the demand curve in Figure 14.1 and the more standard demand curve is that instead of the curve indicating the quantity of a good the individual would be willing to purchase at each price, the curve indicates the probability that the individual would be willing to pay for the specified outcome at each price.[17] As in the case of a standard demand curve, the area under the curve in Figure 14.1 provides an estimate of the individual's willingness-to-pay.

If the values of X are evenly spread, then the histogram can be readily used to obtain a rough estimate of the average individual's willingness-to-pay by applying a simple formula:

$$WTP = v \sum_{k=0}^{N} (\text{probability of acceptance at price } kv)$$

where v is the interval between prices (i.e., the width of the individual bars in the histogram) and N is the number of values of X (i.e., the number of bars). In other words, the area covered by the bars, the approximate WTP for an average member of the sample, can be computed by simply summing the heights of the bars and multiplying by the bar width.

Analysts rarely work directly from the histogram of accepted bids. Better estimates can usually be made by estimating a statistical model for predicting the probability that an individual with specific characteristics will accept a particular bid price. The estimated model, often a logistic regression with bid price as one of the explanatory variables, allows the analyst to sketch the relationship between bid price and the probability of acceptance.[18] The area under this curve approximates the mean willingness-to-pay for these individuals.[19] It can be estimated through numerical methods.[20] The statistical model can also be used to estimate a probability-of-acceptance curve for each identified group within the sample. It is, therefore, possible to estimate a WTP for an average member of each of these groups as the area under each group's probability-of-acceptance curve. *To find the aggregate WTP for the entire population, one multiplies the mean for each group by the size of that group in the population with standing and then sums across groups.*[21]

Because this method only tells one whether a given respondent's valuation is greater or less than the offered amount, sample sizes have to be large in order to achieve reasonable levels of precision. For small samples, the true value of WTP may be considerably different from the observed value of WTP. On the other hand, "take it or leave it" questions are very easy for respondents to answer, and they are the closest approximation to market-like transactions.

Some analysts have recently experimented with *double dichotomous-choice* questions to reduce the need for large samples. In this version of the method, depending on the answer to the first offer, a follow-up offer is made that is either double (if yes) or half (if no) the first offer. This provides considerably more information than the standard single-offer version. However, there is danger that the respondent's exposure to the first offer may affect the probability that he or she will accept the follow-up offer.[22] Recognizing that follow-up bids provide information to respondents that may change their perceptions of the likely price or quantity of the good being valued, Richard T. Carson, Theodore Groves, and Mark J. Machina suggest several ways that this information might affect their responses to the second bids:[23] First, those who initially rejected bids may take the lower follow-up bid as an indication that the bid price is negotiable and reject bids that they previously would have accepted. Second, those who initially accepted bids may believe that there is some possibility that the good could be provided at the lower price and reject the higher second bid even though it is below their *WTP*. Third, in responding to the follow-up bid price, respondents may base their responses not on that price but on some weighted average of the two bid prices they encountered. Whether the greater amount of information generated by the double dichotomous-choice method is worth the risk of such response behaviors remains an open research question.

PAYMENT VEHICLE

Almost all CV exercises specify a *payment vehicle,* which describes how the costs of providing the good will be paid. Payment vehicles include taxes paid into a fund specifically earmarked for the good, increased utility bills, higher income or sales taxes, and higher product prices. Specifying a payment vehicle, along with reminders that payments come at the expense of expenditures on other goods, helps ensure that respondents perceive the questions as "real." In order to increase the realism of CV surveys, researchers generally try to specify a payment vehicle that is as close as possible to the actual one that would be used were supply of the good to proceed.

The choice of payment vehicle can make a difference in the estimated *WTP*. In a recent study, for example, researchers found that respondents appeared to value watershed management plans differently depending on whether there was a guarantee that taxes imposed to pay for them would not be used for other purposes.[24] The presence or absence of such a guarantee also affected respondents' valuations of specific attributes of watershed plans.

There has been considerable debate in the CV literature as to whether differences in the *WTP* of respondents due to differences in payment vehicles should be treated as a bias. Kenneth Arrow and others argue that respondents are being asked to value all elements of a project, which include the method of payment; therefore, respondent preferences about payment methods do not imply bias.[25] Other analysts argue that if specific payment vehicles, such as taxes, introduce "protest" valuations, then such outliers should be excluded from the estimation of aggregate *WTP*. Currently, it is standard practice to eliminate protest outliers from estimation of *WTP*. Protest bidders can sometimes be screened out by their answers to specific questions designed to identify them.

GENERAL SURVEY ISSUES

Before turning specifically to CV surveys, it is useful to consider briefly some issues relevant to all survey contexts. One issue concerns the trade-offs among methods for administering surveys. Another issue is the extent to which the procedures for identifying and reaching respondents lead to an appropriate sample from which to estimate the distribution of attitudes within the population with standing.

Survey Administration: In-Person, Telephone, Mail, and Internet

Currently, there are three major technologies for administering surveys: in-person interviews, telephone interviews, and mail questionnaires. Each has strengths and weaknesses, and each raises different methodological issues. None of the three procedures is unequivocally superior to the others. It is quite possible that the Internet will eventually join the list as one of the major technologies for administering surveys.

Table 14.1 summarizes the characteristics of the survey administration alternatives. In-person interviews involve interviewers meeting face-to-face with respondents. Especially relevant in the CV context, they facilitate the provision of quite complex information to respondents through the presentation of maps, diagrams, photographs, and other visual aids by the interviewer. The interviewer can also clarify questions and provide additional information and otherwise interact with the respondent. This direct contact, however, also involves a high risk of interviewer bias, as respondents may react to the personal characteristics of the interviewer, perhaps slanting answers to gain the interviewer's approval. Unlike telephone interviews, which typically are conducted from a central location, in-person interviews are difficult to monitor. The greatest disadvantage, however, is that in-person interviews tend to be very expensive, especially

TABLE 14.1	Survey Administration Alternatives			
	Cost per Completed Interview	*Ease of Identifying and Reaching Respondents*	*Risk of Interviewer Bias*	*Maximum Complexity of Provided Information*
In-Person	Very high—depends on questionnaire length and geographic spread	Medium—depends on availability of lists and access	High—personal presence, monitoring difficult	Very high—interactive communication and visual aids possible
Telephone	High—depends on questionnaire length and call-backs	Very high—random digit dialing	Medium—interviewer cues	Low—verbal communication limits complexity of content
Mail	Low—depends on number of follow-ups	High—depends on availability of appropriate lists	Low—uniform presentation	High—visual aids possible
Internet	Low—marginal costs very small	Low—"spamming" restrictions require panels of willing respondents	Low—uniform presentation	Very high—visual aids and interactive questions possible

for geographically dispersed samples, because of the time spent traveling between interviews and the precautions that must be taken to ensure the security of the interviewers. As is the case with mail questionnaires, the capability for identifying a random sample of any population depends on the availability of lists of the individuals, families, or households that make up the population. In many locations, such as cities with guarded apartment buildings or suburbs with restricted-access housing developments, it may be very difficult to reach respondents randomly selected to be in the sample.

Telephone interviews have become the most common method of administering CV surveys. Telephone interviews have substantially lower cost than in-person interviews, even with a large number of call-backs to reach persons who are not at home or who use answering machines. They also have the advantage of allowing researchers to draw reasonable random samples through random digit dialing, obviating the need for address lists in surveys of households. Unfortunately, verbal communication limits the complexity of information that can be provided. It also opens up the possibility of interviewer bias, as respondents react to voice cues and perceptions of the characteristics of the interviewer.

Several trends are making telephone interviews more costly and difficult to implement effectively. One trend is the greater prevalence of telemarketing, often masquerading as surveys. More people are refusing to participate in surveys to avoid unwanted telemarketing solicitations. Others use answering machines and caller identification to screen out calls from strangers. Another trend is the growing complexity of the telephone system, which makes it increasingly difficult to draw good random samples through random digit dialing. Households more often have multiple telephone lines, some of which are dedicated to fax machines or teenagers. Cellular telephones are breaking down area codes, making it more difficult to sample geographically. Dealing with these problems will likely raise the costs of telephone surveys in the future.

Mail questionnaires, which allow the provision of visual aids to respondents, have the advantage of very low cost. The ease of identifying samples depends on the availability of appropriate lists. Accurate lists also make it easy to reach respondents, though response rates are typically low, often requiring multiple mailings to reach acceptable levels. As there are no interviewers, all respondents experience the same presentation and, therefore, there is no interviewer bias.

As more U.S. adults become Internet users, it becomes more feasible to use the Internet for conducting surveys. Internet surveys would have several advantages over the other methods. As interviewers are not needed, Internet surveys have extremely low marginal costs, perhaps even lower than mail surveys. Like mail surveys, they avoid the risk of interviewer bias, and they allow for the provision of very complex information. Indeed, one can imagine giving respondents access to huge quantities of information through menus and other interactive devices. Unfortunately, drawing random samples of populations remains a barrier. Not all members of most populations of interest are currently Internet users. This is changing, but even when Internet use has become ubiquitous, sampling is complicated by restrictions on "spamming," the broadcasting of messages, which prevent procedures analogous to random digit dialing in telephone surveys. Firms are beginning to develop databases of willing respondents, which may become sufficiently large and representative of populations of interest to allow scientifically valid CV studies to be administered through the Internet.

Sample and Nonresponse Biases

The essence of survey research is eliciting information about a population from a small sample drawn from the population. As summarized in Table 14.1, survey administration alternatives differ in terms of the ease with which they facilitate identifying and reaching respondents. How to identify individuals to be sampled from target populations is the topic of *sample design*.[26] The extent to which valid responses are obtained from those identified determines whether the sample design will actually produce data adequate for making valid inferences.

In almost all cases, the sample is selected by a probability mechanism, which produces a *random sample*. In a random sample, each individual has a known probability of being drawn from the population. *Simple random samples* give each individual in the target population the same probability of being sampled. *Stratified samples* give members of particular groups within a population the same probability of being sampled. In either case, knowing the selection probabilities allows researchers to base inferences about the characteristics of the population on the characteristics of the sample.

If a given sample is appropriately selected and administered, then sample biases can be avoided. Advances in probability sampling techniques have been such that findings based on samples of approximately a thousand people can be representative of the entire population of the United States. However, approximately the same sample size may also be necessary for much smaller populations—basically, the sample size needed to achieve any desired level of precision does not depend on the size of the population being sampled. Additionally, there is considerable evidence that the observed distributions of *WTP* in CV are skewed toward extreme values. For this reason, CV samples should be larger than samples drawn for many other purposes to obtain reliable estimates of population means. This is especially true for the dichotomous-choice method.

For CV purposes, *the relevant target population is usually all individuals with standing who are affected by the policy.* Unfortunately, this heuristic begs the question of who is affected. For many projects, this is apparent. But often it is not, especially in addressing environmental issues. In some contexts there is congruence between those who bear the cost of policies and those who are affected by them. In other contexts, however, these groups diverge, as when a state or province provides a wilderness area that is valued by people living in other jurisdictions. The greater such divergence, the more problematic it is to choose the correct population.[27]

Several major issues are involved in assessing who is affected. First, all those "users" directly affected by the project should be included. The term *users* is in quotes because we mean it in a specific way. Those who would directly utilize the good in question are, of course, users. But so too are individuals who suffer direct negative impacts that they would pay to avoid. For example, nearby residents of a duck hunting reserve who dislike the noise are as much users as the duck hunters. Potential users should also be included. As discussed in Chapter 8, in situations involving uncertainty, the option price that an individual would be willing to pay for a good may differ from his or her expected surplus. So even people who never actually consume the good may value it.

Second, it is important for survey respondents to understand whether they are being asked to estimate *WTP* just for themselves or as a representative for their whole household. This distinction is important in extrapolating from the sample to the target population.

Third, an explicit decision should be made concerning the inclusion of passive use benefits. As discussed in Chapter 9, either users or nonusers may derive existence value from a project. Conceptually, existence value should be included as a component of benefits. For environmental goods, CV surveys that either sample nonusers or estimate existence values of users typically yield much higher aggregate *WTP* estimates than those that include only use benefits. However, there is considerable disagreement on the validity of using CV surveys to estimate nonuse benefits.

Fourth, the geographic *spread* or *reach* of the sample should be wide enough to capture all affected individuals. There is increasing recognition that decisions concerning the geographic definition of the relevant "market" can drive the outcomes of many CBAs, especially if nonusers are included.[28] The importance of geographic definition is illustrated in Exhibit 14.1.

EXHIBIT 14.1

As part of a court case, the plaintiffs conducted a CV survey to estimate the natural resource damage caused by a mine. They surveyed residents of both the county (Eagle County) and the state (Colorado) in which the mine was located. Based on their surveys, they estimated past damages were $50.8 million and future expected damages would be between $15 and $45 million. The defendants sampled a much smaller group within Eagle County that they believed had been directly affected by pollution from the mine; they assumed that residents in the rest of Colorado did not bear costs from the mine. Although the per unit values of both sides were similar (e.g., on the value of a day's fishing), the defendants' estimate of total past and future expected damage was approximately $240,000, less than 1 percent of the plaintiffs' estimate. "The discrepancies in these respective aggregate estimates arise from the plaintiff's assumption that . . . there would be a much larger number of people experiencing gains with the restoration" (p. 605).

Source: Raymond J. Kopp and V. Kerry Smith, "Benefit Estimation Goes to Court: The Case of Natural Resource Damage Assessments," *Journal of Policy Analysis and Management,* 8, no. 4 (1989), 593–612.

An important sampling question relates to the exclusion of responses. It has been suggested that three categories of respondents should be excluded in estimating *WTP:* first, respondents who reject the whole notion of placing a value on the good in question, or of paying for the good in a certain way (this has already been discussed); second, respondents who refuse to take the exercise seriously; and third, respondents who clearly demonstrate that they are incapable of understanding the survey.[29] In the direct elicitation methods, all three types of respondents are usually assumed to provide either zero valuations or extremely high valuations. Sometimes such respondents can be directly identified by their answers to specific questions intended to screen them from the sample. Respondents who provide extreme values are known as *outliers.* Outliers are normally handled in CV by simply eliminating valuations that are above some specified threshold or that are above a specified percentage of the respondent's gross or discretionary income.

An appropriate sampling design can usually eliminate most sample bias if it is fully executed. Yet, bias can still remain if some individuals do not respond to the survey. Nonresponse bias is a serious problem in almost all survey research. Nonresponse problems have grown over the last 20 years as the public has been asked to give time to more surveys and has become suspicious of the motives of many who claim to be survey researchers. If nonresponse is purely random, then it can be dealt with by increasing the sample size. Unfortunately, nonresponse is often not random.[30]

There are two major types of nonresponse problems: refusal to respond and un-availability to respond. In CV contexts, the primary approaches for dealing with refusal to respond are to highlight the legitimacy of the exercise (e.g., by stressing government or university affiliations) or to offer various response incentives, such as donations to charities or entries into prize lotteries. Where unavailability biases the sample, researchers typically account for underrepresentation and overrepresentation in the sample when extrapolating to the target population.[31]

CRITICISMS OF CONTINGENT VALUATION

Some critics argue that CV has such serious weaknesses that it should only be used as a last resort. Other critics contend that it is so seriously flawed when used to value either complex goods or passive use impacts that it should not be used at all for these purposes.[32] It has been pointed out that the summation of average valuations over a broad range of projects to improve the environment would *exhaust* the budget of average individuals.[33]

The remainder of this chapter discusses specific problems relevant to CV. We then review the empirical evidence on the accuracy of contingent valuation methods. Finally, we present some heuristic checklists for analysts preparing or reviewing CV instruments.

CONTINGENT VALUATION PROBLEMS

Surveying opinions is not an exact science. The science of CV surveys is even less exact!

Specific CV survey difficulties stem from several sources. First, CV inevitably raises questions that are more novel and complex than those raised in other survey situations. This poses problems of *hypotheticality* (we use this as a catchall word to cover all problems of understanding, meaning, context, and familiarity). Hypotheticality appears to be particularly severe when respondents have not, and will not, "consume" the good in some way. That is, hypotheticality tends to be most severe in the valuation of passive use. Second, CV raises questions of neutrality in the presentation of information to respondents. Third, for certain methods, judgmental biases may arise in response to certain kinds of questions (including whether the question is framed as willingness-to-pay or as willingness-to-accept). Not all these problems necessarily create biases (i.e., a systematic tendency to overvalue or undervalue the goods in question), but all of them do raise questions about the validity and reliability of CV as a procedure. Some specific CV methods appear to be more prone to biases than others. Fourth, CV asks questions about *WTP*, raising the potential for biases related to strategic behavior (misstatements intended to influence some outcome) and the specified payment vehicle.

Hypotheticality, Meaning, and Context Problems

A major concern in CV design is whether respondents are truly able to understand and place in context the questions they are being asked and, consequently, whether they can accurately value the good in question. Issues relating to the valuation of the supply of many publicly provided goods are complex and highly contextual. CV questions can be contrasted to many other types of questions for which meaning is not an issue (for example, "For whom do you intend to vote in the next election?").

Questions of hypotheticality and meaning can be thought of as problems of specifying exactly what is the good in question. Understanding the good, or the policy that produces it, is difficult for respondents because they often are not familiar with either. Attitudes (as expressed in the CV survey) are unlikely to correspond to the behavior that would occur if the project were actually implemented when respondents are presented with questions about goods or projects that they really do not understand.[34] When a project (or the good itself) has multiple attributes, these all need to be explained to respondents: "Unless [an attribute is] specified explicitly (and comprehensively), evaluators must guess its value and, hence, what the offer really means. If they guess wrong, then they risk misrepresenting their values."[35]

This problem, however, has to be seen in context. Individuals also differentially value attributes of market goods: Some individuals may value a mountain bike mostly for prestige reasons and others for transportation purposes. The evidence also suggests that people find it difficult to value the attributes of new and unfamiliar products in market contexts.[36]

Additional problems arise in CV if the perceptions of the good by respondents are not independent of the quality or quantity of the information provided. The quantity and quality of information that could be provided when describing complex goods are unlimited. The quantity and quality of information, however, are limited in practice by the method of survey administration. Recently, several commentators have emphasized that there is hardly any evidence that hypotheticality per se introduces bias into CV.[37] But in the presence of hypotheticality certain kinds of bias may be more likely.

The potential for hypotheticality varies enormously across different CBA contexts. Unfortunately, CV is likely to be most useful in contexts in which goods are difficult to define, such as projects involving environmental impacts. When it is difficult to specify potential physical impacts, it is also likely to be difficult for respondents to understand what these impacts mean.

Hypotheticality and lack of realism can be reduced in a number of ways. *Clearly specifying the project and its impacts increases the likelihood of correspondence between attitudes and behavior; so too does providing explicit detail about the payment vehicle.* Visual aids such as photographs, maps, and diagrams often assist in understanding. One important class of visual aids useful in reducing hypotheticality is known as quality ladders. An example of a quality ladder is described in Exhibit 14.2. Quality ladders help respondents understand both what quality is under the status quo, and what particular increments of quality mean.

EXHIBIT 14.2

A "water quality ladder" has been used in several CBAs to help respondents understand how differing levels of toxins, dissolved solids, water clarity, and other factors affect water quality. In their CBA of water quality improvements to the Monongahela River, V. Kerry Smith and William Desvousges included a picture of a ladder with a 0-to-10 scale and the following interviewer instructions:

(*Interviewer: Read the following.*) Generally the better the water quality the better suited the water is for recreational activities and the more likely people will take part in outdoor recreation activities on or near the water. Here is a picture of a ladder that shows various levels of water quality. (*Interviewer: Give respondent water quality ladder.*)

The top of the ladder stands for the best possible quality of water. The bottom of the ladder stands for the worst possible water quality. On the ladder you can see the different levels of the quality of the water. For example: (*Interviewer: Point to each level—E, D, C, B, A—as you read the statements that follow*).

Level E (*Interviewer: Point.*) is so polluted that it has oil, raw sewage, and other things like trash in it; it has no plant or animal life and smells bad.

Water at level D is okay for boating but not fishing or swimming.

Level C shows where the water is clean enough so that gamefish like bass can live in it.

Level B shows where the water is clean enough so that people can swim in it safely.

And at level A, the quality of the water is so good that it would be possible to drink directly from it if you wanted to.

(*Interviewer: Now ask the respondent to use the ladder to rate the water quality in the Monongahela River on a scale of 0 to 10 and to indicate whether the ranking was for a particular site, and if so, to name it.*)

Source: V. Kerry Smith and William H. Desvousges, *Measuring Water Quality Benefits* (Boston, MA: Kluwer Academic, 1986), p. 87.

Baruch Fischhoff and Lita Furey have suggested a checklist for evaluating CV instruments in terms of the likelihood that respondents will understand the questions they are being asked.[38] It requires the analyst to assess the comprehensiveness of information with respect to the good, the specification of the payment vehicle, and the social context. In assessing the adequacy of information about the good, they stress the need to provide information on both substantive and formal components. The substantive aspect of the good deals with why someone might value it (basically its attributes), whereas the formal aspect of the good concerns how much they value it (once they understand its attributes).

In practice, *the only effective way to minimize hypotheticality and meaning problems in CV surveys is to devote extensive effort to developing detailed, clear, informative, and highly contextual materials and to pretest these materials extensively on typical respondents.*

Neutrality

Although the previous section indicated that lack of clear meaning does not necessarily pose a bias problem, lack of *neutrality* is certain to do so. As CBA deals with increasingly controversial and complex topics, the neutrality of the CV questionnaire becomes an increasingly important issue. Neutrality has come to the fore as litigants in (especially environmental) court cases have conducted their own CV surveys.

Meaning and neutrality issues often intersect in ways that are extremely difficult to disentangle. For example, in a recent study, Daniel Hagen, James Vincent, and Patrick Welle surveyed 1,000 U.S. households by mail concerning the value of preserving the spotted owl.[39] Of the total, 409 questionnaires were returned. Some of the information that respondents were given included the following: "... a scientific committee concluded that logging should be banned on some forest lands to prevent the extinction of the Northern Spotted Owl ... " and "a second group of independent scientists examined this study and agreed with these conclusions." The survey also included the comment that "the well-being of the northern spotted owl reflects the well-being of the entire old-growth forest eco-system" (p. 18).

In a review of spotted owl CV studies in general, and the Hagen et al. study in particular, William McKillop criticized this framing of the issue. He argues that the survey did not include many relevant facts that respondents should have been told.[40] For example, the "committee of scientists" focused almost exclusively on old-growth habitat for spotted owls and largely ignored the fact that many are found in second-growth timber stands. Respondents were also not told that logging was already prohibited on considerable areas of old-growth timberland, and these acres were likely to increase in the course of normal national forest planning. In sum, McKillop argues that the spotted owl issue was not presented accurately or neutrally to respondents. He further argues that this issue is simply too complicated to be addressed by CV surveys.

There are no simple answers to the neutrality problem. But an inevitable conclusion is that one has to be especially cautious in interpreting the results of CV surveys that have been prepared by either parties to litigation or advocacy groups. At a practical level, *neutrality can best be ensured by pretesting the survey instrument with substantive experts who have "no axe to grind" in terms of the specific project that is being considered.* If neutral experts cannot be found, then pretesting with opposing advocates is desirable.

Decision Making and Judgment Biases

Although it is reasonable to assume that individuals can make rational judgments about their valuations of goods in most market situations, evidence suggests that in certain circumstances they may not be able to do so readily. This is even more likely to occur in the context of CV surveys because judgment rather than decision making is involved, and because there are not opportunities to learn from "mistakes" (we discuss the evidence on this issue later in the chapter).[41] More formally, in such circumstances, there is a tendency for individuals to behave as if they are not maximizing utility, especially with respect to choices involving uncertainty. In the context of functioning markets, these behaviors appear as decision-making biases that can result in irrational purchases (or lack of purchases). These decision-making errors can be thought of as a type of market failure.[42] In the context of CV, the term *judgment bias* rather than *decision-making bias* is applicable because the respondent is not actually purchasing the good in question.

Both decision-making and judgment biases appear to be most serious for activities or projects that would generate small changes in the probabilities of (already) low-probability events that have "catastrophic" costs if they occur (e.g., activities that might cause a marginal change in the probability of a nuclear power plant accident).[43] As *WTP* depends on how likely respondents view such events, their perception of changes in probabilities is important in CV studies. Fortunately, researchers and analysts rarely have to rely solely on CV estimates in such contexts. For example, they can use value-of-life estimates derived from other methods in which these biases are less endemic (see Chapter 15).

Some of the major judgmental biases to which individuals are particularly prone include *availability bias,* whereby individuals estimate the probabilities of events by the ease with which occurrences can be recalled—more salient instances, such as those covered by the media, are more likely to be recalled; *representativeness* or *conjunction bias,* whereby individuals judge the probabilities of events on the basis of their plausibility—people perceive the probability of an event as being higher as more detail is added, even though the detail is irrelevant; *optimism bias,* whereby people believe that they can beat the objective odds; *anchoring bias,* whereby individuals do not fully update their probability assessments as new information becomes available; *hindsight bias,* whereby individuals believe, after an event occurs, that it was more predictable than it actually was; *status quo bias,* whereby individuals stick with the status quo even when it is inexpensive to experiment or when the potential benefits from changing are large; and *probability assessment biases,* whereby people tend to overestimate small probabilities and underestimate large probabilities.[44]

Many of these violations of the expected utility hypothesis can be explained by the fact that, when dealing with complex information, people tend to use simplifying (non-utility-maximizing) heuristics or "rules of thumb." Essentially, people "frame" problems consistently, but the framing does not correspond to maximization of expected utility.

One conceptual framework for explaining violations of the expected utility hypothesis is *prospect theory.*[45] Prospect theory, which is particularly relevant to CV issues, suggests that individuals deviate from expected utility maximization in the following ways: They value gains and losses from a reference point rather than valuing net wealth. Moreover, people are risk averse toward gains and risk seeking toward losses (known as *loss aversion*)—a loss and a gain of the same size would leave a person with loss aversion worse off. This may stem from an *endowment effect,* whereby individuals have a greater psychological attachment to things they currently possess.[46]

Several of these effects can be summarized in a prospect theory value function, which is illustrated in Figure 14.2. In this figure, the vertical axis measures value and the horizontal axis measures losses and gains. The figure is drawn to show three things. First, people start from a reference point from which changes are measured as losses or gains. Second, individuals are risk averse with respect to potential gains (i.e., they prefer a smaller certain gain over a larger probable gain, when the expected values of the two alternatives are the same). Individuals are also risk seeking with respect to potential losses (i.e., they prefer a larger probable loss to a smaller certain loss, when the expected values of the two alternatives are the same). In Figure 14.2 this is represented by the concave gain function and the convex loss function. Third, losses loom larger than gains of equal size. This is represented in the figure as the loss function being steeper for losses than for gains from the reference point.

The biases suggested by prospect theory are particularly relevant to CV for a number of reasons. Anchoring via reference points is always present. Even if open-ended questions are used to eliminate starting point bias, payment vehicles and other descriptive detail may introduce anchoring indirectly. Furthermore, detailed descriptions may evoke availability bias. Finally, as we discuss later, CV questions can sometimes be plausibly framed as either involving gains or losses.

Empirical research suggests that the most serious judgment problems actually found in CV results relate to *noncommitment bias, order effects* (sometimes described as sequencing effects), *embedding effects* (sometimes described as whole/part effects or inclusiveness effects), and *starting point bias.*

Noncommitment Bias[47]   It is well recognized in the marketing literature that respondents to surveys tend to overstate their willingness to purchase a product that is

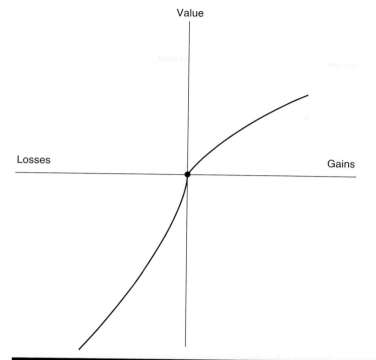

FIGURE 14.2 A "Loss Aversion" Value Function

described to them.[48] This may be a strategic response (an issue discussed later) but can also be thought of as a form of anchoring bias (e.g., "this product must be valuable because they are asking me about it and describing it in such detail") in a context in which potential consumers do not engage in any learning. It is likely to be quite unconscious. The bias can flourish, of course, because the respondent does not actually have to commit money.

One recent set of experiments has attempted to test for noncommitment bias. The researchers conclude that "hypothetical WTP is consistently and significantly higher than the WTP that reflects real economic commitments."[49]

It is very difficult to test for noncommitment bias when dealing with passive use values. One indirect way of testing for the bias is to introduce elements to the survey that encourage respondents to think more carefully about their income and their budget constraints. Michael Kemp and Christopher Maxwell have developed a "top-down disaggregation method" to do just this.[50] Top-down disaggregation attempts to mitigate noncommitment bias by raising awareness of budget constraints. After asking respondents to state initially their total *WTP,* they were questioned specifically about comparative valuations. For example, after respondents were asked about their *WTP* to avoid a specified oil spill, they were then asked about their valuations of environmental protection versus reduction in crime, homelessness, and other social problems. They were also asked about their valuations for different kinds of environmental protection (wilderness areas versus groundwater quality, rainforest protection, and other environmental goals). At the next level, they were asked to evaluate various kinds of wilderness area protection (reduction in harm from human-caused problems versus natural degradation and other destructive processes). At the end of this top-down disaggregation process, respondents were again asked their *WTP.* The result was *WTP* values several hundred times smaller than the *WTP* values from the initial open-ended questions.

In the more commonly used CV methods, it may be desirable to ask questions that require respondents to think more carefully about the budget constraints that they face.[51] For example, asking questions that encourage respondents to think about how much of their income is discretionary may help avoid noncommitment bias. The answers may also be useful in helping to assess whether the *WTP* values provided are subject to noncommitment bias.

Order Effects   George Tolley and Alan Randall found that survey respondents' statements of the value of improved visibility in the Grand Canyon were greatly affected by the order in which the issue was raised.[52] Other studies have also found important order effects. Consider, for example, a study that asked some respondents to value preserving seals and then whales, whereas others were asked to value preserving whales and then seals. Seal values were considerably lower when the seal question was asked after the whale question.[53]

These findings could be explainable in terms of either an income effect, a substitution effect, or a combination of both. The rationale for an income effect is as follows: If someone has expressed a positive *WTP* to pay for the first good in a sequence of goods, then that person has less income to spend on the second good in the sequence. Critics of CV, however, have observed that the steep declines in *WTP* as a good moves down in order cannot be fully explained by income effects as these should be relatively small.[54]

Substitution effects, as for example between seals and whales, could be quite large and consequently they can be important in CBA, especially in terms of assessing the aggregate impacts of projects. (That is, respondents may view one environmental improvement as a substitute for another quite different environmental improvement.) If people engage in extensive substitution, then the net aggregate benefits from a project may be smaller than predicted. For example, if a resident of Chicago agrees to contribute to a project that cleans the air in Chicago and is then offered a project that preserves visibility in the Grand Canyon, the value of the Grand Canyon project may be decreased because of the substitution effect.

The issue of whether substitution effects could account for much of the order inconsistency in CV surveys of passive use values is still undecided.[55] Critics argue that the phenomenon is explained neither by income nor by substitution effects, but it instead demonstrates that respondents cannot really understand these kinds of questions. Hence, they inevitably engage in judgment heuristics that usually cause them to overstate valuations. Thus, it seems unlikely that income and substitution effects provide a complete explanation for order effects.

Embedding Effects   A fundamental axiom in the standard economic description of preferences is that individuals value more of a good more highly than less of it. If CV respondents' valuations are only slightly higher for large changes in the amount of the good offered than for small changes, then the validity of their responses becomes a concern. But research indicates that individuals often do not readily distinguish between small and large quantities in their valuations of a good when the different quantities are *embedded* in one another. For example, William H. Desvousges and colleagues found that different samples of respondents value 2,000 migratory birds approximately the same as 200,000 birds, and small oil spills much the same as much larger oil spills (given that these are different samples, it does not directly test whether given individuals prefer more to less).[56] Two additional examples of embedding are described in Exhibit 14.3. It is unlikely that declining marginal utility can explain all or even most of the absence of different valuations for different quantities of goods.

EXHIBIT 14.3

Daniel Kahneman and Jack L. Knetsch report that residents of Toronto expressed a willingness to pay increased taxes to prevent a drop in fish stocks in all Ontario lakes that was only slightly larger than their expressed *WTP* to preserve fish stocks in a small area of the province. This is implausible.

The same researchers studied the impact of embedding by specifying a good very broadly to one sample of respondents (environmental services that included "preserving wilderness areas, protecting wildlife, providing parks, preparing for disasters, controlling air pollution, insuring water quality, and routine treatment and disposal of industrial wastes"), a considerably narrower subset to a second sample of respondents ("to improve preparedness for disasters" with a subsequent allocation to go to "the availability of equipment and trained personnel for rescue operations"), and an even narrower good to a third sample ("improve the availability of equipment and trained personnel for rescue operations"). Respondents in each sample were asked to express their willingness to pay for their "good." The differences in *WTP* among the three samples were not large.

Source: Daniel Kahneman and Jack L. Knetsch, "Valuing Public Goods: The Purchase of Moral Satisfaction," *Journal of Environmental Economics and Management,* 22, no. 1 (1992), 57–70. [For a critique of this study, see V. Kerry Smith, "Comment: Arbitrary Values, Good Causes, and Premature Verdicts," *Journal of Environmental Economics and Management,* 22, no. 1 (1992), 71–89.]

When dealing with passive use values, embedding is probably the most worrisome problem identified by critics of CV. It goes to the very heart of welfare economics. Critics argue that the empirical evidence suggests that in these contexts respondents are not actually expressing their valuations but instead are expressing broad moral attitudes to environmental issues—a "warm glow" or "moral satisfaction."[57]

Starting Point Bias   Prospect theory identifies anchoring as a common behavioral response to being asked to make complex judgments. A problem arises in CV when starting values are presented to respondents. The iterative bidding method is particularly prone to this problem because this method provides respondents with a specific initial starting "price."[58] Consider, for example, the Kristiansand Fjord study mentioned earlier in the chapter. It was found that a range starting at 200 kronor and progressing to 2,000 kronor produced different valuations than a range starting at 0 kronor and progressing to 2,000 kronor, even when there were no bids between 0 and 200 kronor.[59]

The dichotomous-choice question format is intended to eliminate starting point bias. It has been argued, however, that "responses to dichotomous-choice questions are very strongly influenced by starting-point bias, because respondents are likely to take initial cues of resource value from the solicited contribution amount (e.g., assuming it to be his/her share of the needed contribution)."[60] Moreover, there is at least some empirical evidence to support the contention that the dichotomous-choice method is subject to starting point bias,[61] though *WTP* estimated from dichotomous-choice responses appears to be less affected by the provision of information about the total cost of providing a good or the size of the group receiving it than does *WTP* estimated from open-ended surveys.[62]

Hypotheticality Bias versus Judgment Bias   In the last resort it is almost impossible to disentangle hypotheticality issues from various forms of judgment bias in nonuse contexts, as they are essentially two different sides of the same coin. Hence, the same approach is required to minimize both, an effort to present the project or good in question as concretely as possible, at the lowest level of disaggregation as possible, and with as much realism concerning budget constraints as possible. Neutrality problems also appear to be generic to CV. But this problem is less worrisome because it can be made reasonably transparent with good research protocols.

WTP versus *WTA*

Economic theory implies that if individuals behave rationally, and if markets are working efficiently, then in most circumstances it should make little difference whether respondents to a CV survey are asked their *WTP* for receiving a good or their willingness-to-accept (*WTA*) the loss of a comparable good.[63] Similarly, it should make little difference whether they are asked their *WTP* to prevent a loss or their *WTA* for a comparable loss.

As we have already discussed, considerable evidence suggests that individuals demand greater monetary compensation to give up things that they already possess than they are willing to pay to acquire the same exact item. In experiments that actually require people to trade goods for money, as well as in other contexts, it has been found that required *WTA* amounts range from a ratio of four to fifteen times greater than *WTP* amounts.[64] Similar differences have also been found in CV studies, even with a well-specified market good. There is some evidence that this difference between *WTP* and *WTA* is attributable to loss aversion.[65]

There is also considerable evidence, however, that as the subjects in experiments become more experienced, differences between *WTP* and *WTA* shrink considerably, usually as a result of decreases in *WTA* amounts.[66] Yet, other experimental evidence suggests that for nonmarket goods with imperfect substitutes the divergence between *WTP* and *WTA* persists even with experience.[67] In any event, CV survey contexts, which are typically "one-shot" affairs, do not present opportunities for learning. Moreover, they often involve nonmarket goods with no close substitutes.

Some commentators have argued that stated preferences are preferences and that, if respondents are actually being asked to give up something, then the relevant formulation is *WTA*. But even in a context in which something is being given up, analysts still have to decide whether to treat *WTA* as a judgment bias problem that requires "adjustments." In view of the fact that experiments show learning effects in some contexts and, as discussed later, *WTP* amounts are much closer to estimates derived from methods based on revealed preferences, the usual procedure is to use *WTP* estimates.[68] This rule is applied even in cases in which *WTA* questions fit the facts better than *WTP* questions—for example, as when the project involves the respondent giving up a good, such as a scenic view, that he or she currently consumes. The heuristic is, therefore, *that*

WTP question formats rather than WTA question formats should be used in CV in almost all cases.

In thinking about *WTP* and *WTA,* one additional point should be kept in mind: We are concerned only about differences between the two *for the same individual.* The fact that different individuals have differing *WTP*s and *WTA*s is what makes markets work and presents no problem to CV.

The Strategic Response (Honesty) Problem

Will respondents answer honestly when asked about their *WTP?* It is frequently argued that respondents in CV surveys have incentives to behave *strategically,* that is, to misrepresent their true preferences in order to achieve a more desired outcome than would result if they honestly revealed their preferences. An analogy is often drawn between strategic behavior in CV studies and free riding in the provision of public goods.[69] The potential for strategic behavior in CV, however, is actually more varied than the free-riding characterization suggests.[70]

The Carson-Groves-Machina Framework   In a recent paper, Richard T. Carson, Theodore Groves, and Mark J. Machina assess the nature of strategic responses to CV questions likely to be encountered in use of the major CV methods.[71] They begin by making the point that we should not expect respondents' answers necessarily to be consistent with economic theory and, hence, appropriate for inclusion in CBA unless respondents believe that the survey is *consequential* in the sense that it could potentially influence some outcomes about which they care. In contrast, if respondents believe that the survey will have absolutely no influence on outcomes about which they care, then it is *inconsequential* and economic theory offers no predictions about the nature of responses.

They next note that the design of consequential CV surveys falls under the theory of *mechanism design,* which deals with the problem of creating rules for collective choice based on signals sent by individuals. Mechanisms that provide incentives for individuals to reveal their preferences truthfully are called *incentive compatible.*

One of the central theorems of mechanism design is that, in the absence of restrictions on the domain of preferences,[72] no mechanism involving more than binary signals will always be incentive compatible.[73] Mechanisms employing binary signals will not always be incentive compatible, but, depending on the specific circumstances of choice, they may be. More complex signals always provide an opportunity for individuals to misstate their preferences in order to obtain a more desirable outcome.

As a brief illustration, return to the choice situation presented Chapter 2. Table 2.2 shows how the mechanism of pairwise majority rule voting could result in an intransitive social ordering. Consider a case in which the mechanism is being implemented by first putting X against Y in round 1 and then, in round 2, Z against the winner of round 1. Note that the signal sent by the voters in this situation is not binary—it consists of *two* binary signals, one for each round. If the voters send truthful signals about their preferences, then X beats Y in round 1 and Z beats X in round 2, so that the mechanism selects Z as the social choice, which is voter 1's least preferred outcome. Anticipating this, voter 1 has an incentive to misrepresent his preferences by voting for Y in round 1, so that Y would win and be put against Z in round 2 and win. This misrepresentation of preferences in round 1 would result in Y, an outcome more desirable to voter 1 than the one that resulted from sending a truthful signal about his preferences in round 1. Once the voters reach round 2, it is as if they are facing a new choice situation in which they send only a binary signal. In this last round, there is no incentive to misrepresent preferences.

One immediate implication of this theorem is that continuous response formats, as used in the open-ended *WTP* method, or multiple response formats, as used in the contingent ranking method, will always be vulnerable to strategic responses that misstate true preferences.

Consider the open-ended *WTP* method. We can imagine two types of misrepresentation of preferences. First, assume that respondents perceive having to make payments that do not depend on their stated *WTP*s, that they have true *WTP*s above their anticipated payments, and that they anticipate that the likelihood of the good being provided depends on the aggregate of stated *WTP*s. They would then have an incentive to overstate their *WTP*s, so that the estimated aggregate *WTP* would be too high. The possibility of such overstatement was widely anticipated by economists. Yet at least in comparison with the dichotomous-choice method, which, as we discuss later, can be incentive compatible, it does not appear that such overstatement is a major problem in the open-ended *WTP* method.[74] One explanation is that the assumptions that make overstatement a desirable strategy for respondents may not often hold. For example, respondents may fear that their shares of the cost of providing the good will be a positive function of their stated *WTP*s, and, hence, state *WTP*s that are as small as possible. However, they may also believe that the likelihood of provision depends on the fraction of respondents who state *WTP*s at or above the average cost of provision, rather than on aggregate *WTP*. If both of these assumptions hold, then a strategic respondent with a true *WTP* above the anticipated cost would state a *WTP* that is only slightly above the anticipated cost—above anticipated cost to increase the chances of provision but as little above as possible to minimize cost share.

Second, now consider respondents with true *WTP*s that are less than the costs that they anticipate would be imposed on them if the good were to be provided. Assume that they believe that the likelihood of provision depends on aggregate *WTP*. As they do not want the good provided, they have an incentive to state the smallest possible *WTP*, usually set to zero for goods researchers believe to be desirable. These strategic responses in the open-ended *WTP* method should lead to many zeros, and few *WTP* amounts under the respondents' perceived costs of provision. The larger the fraction of respondents following this strategy, the greater will be the underestimation of aggregate *WTP*.

As it involves a binary response, the dichotomous-choice method *may* be incentive compatible. Carson, Groves, and Machina note that incentive compatibility requires that payment for the good can be compelled and that the question deals only with a single issue. Table 14.2 summarizes the incentive properties of several circumstances in which the dichotomous-choice method has been used.

Using the dichotomous-choice method to elicit *WTP* for a new public (nonexcludable) good that will be funded with coercive payments by respondents meets the requirements for incentive compatibility. Respondents have no incentive to vote against their true preferences. As CV is often the only way analysts can estimate *WTP* for public goods, this is reassuring. Incentive compatibility also holds for comparison between two mutually exclusive public goods with the same cost. As long as respon-

TABLE 14.2 Incentive Properties of Dichotomous-Choice Questions Applied to Types of Goods

Type of Good	Incentive Property
New public good with coercive payment	Incentive compatible
New public good with voluntary payment	Not incentive compatible
Introduction of new private good	Not incentive compatible
Choice between two new public goods	Incentive compatible
Choice between an existing and an alternative private good	Incentive compatible, but choice does not reveal information about quantity demanded

Source: Adapted from Richard T. Carson, Theodore Groves, Mark J. Machina, "Incentive and Informational Properties of Preference Questions," Plenary Address, European Association of Resource and Environmental Economists, Oslo, Norway, June 1999. Reprinted with authors' permission.

dents place a positive value on both goods, they have no incentive to misstate their preferred good.

Incentive compatibility is lost in cases in which payment is voluntary because it introduces a second issue, whether to donate or to purchase, into the choice situation. In the case of a public good to be funded by contributions, respondents who place any positive value on the good have an incentive to accept bids above their *WTP*s to increase the chances that the good is provided, because they do not actually have to make a donation in that amount.[75] Similarly, respondents who have any probability of actually wanting a new private (excludable) good have an incentive to accept bids above their *WTP* to increase the chances that it will actually be provided because they can decline to purchase it if they decide that they do not want it. The problem is so severe for new private goods that dichotomous-choice CV has largely been abandoned for this purpose.

Questions that ask respondents to choose between an existing private good and an alternative are incentive compatible about that choice as long as only potential users are surveyed. (The question will not be consequential for those who are not potential users.) Answers to the questions, however, do not reveal information about how much of the selected private good will actually be demanded. For example, a town may ask a sample of residents to choose between the existing skating rink that is available only during daylight hours but has a small entrance fee and a new skating rink with electric lighting that would be available evenings but would have a higher entrance fee. The respondents have no incentive to misstate their true preferences over the choices, but the answers do not tell the town about how often residents will use the new facility.

Conclusion about the Importance of Strategic Responses   The danger that strategic responses to CV questions will bias estimates of aggregate *WTP* cannot be assessed without considering both the elicitation method and the nature of the good being valued. The dichotomous-choice method applied to the valuation of new public goods to be funded by taxes or other coercive payments can be designed to avoid strategic response bias. It is subject to an upward bias, however, if payments are voluntary. The open-ended *WTP* method will generally be subject to strategic response bias, most likely leading to aggregate *WTP* estimates that are too small if payments are coerced and too large if payments are voluntary.

HOW ACCURATE IS CONTINGENT VALUATION?

It is possible to test the accuracy of CV *WTP* estimates in a number of ways.[76] The first method is to compare CV values to those generated by other indirect methods. CV use values have been found to be approximately the same as those derived from travel cost studies.[77] They have also been found to be reasonably similar to prices derived from hedonic price regressions[78] and to the market prices of substitutes.[79] Wesley Magat and W. Kip Viscusi tested whether respondents' *WTP* for risk reductions associated with an insecticide and toilet bowl cleaner were consistent with standard economic theory or subject to the kinds of judgment biases described earlier. In general, they did not find strong evidence of bias.[80]

The second type of comparison, one that is more common and more appropriate, is between respondents' CV statements and their actual behavior when they participate in an experiment that utilizes a simulated or constructed market for the good in question.[81] Results from studies that have used experimental techniques to examine CV accuracy typically suggest that CV valuations of *WTP* relying on open-ended and dichotomous-choice methods approximate actual market transactions, although there is some tendency for overvaluation.[82] In assessing these experiments, it is useful to keep in mind that the simulated market only approximates the workings of a real market; for example, there is only one opportunity to buy the good. In addition, the experiments have been conducted only in contexts in which respondents clearly derive use value from the good. Richard Bishop and Thomas Heberlein at the University of Wisconsin have conducted a number of experiments along these lines. The example presented in Exhibit 14.4 is typical of these experiments.

EXHIBIT 14.4

A wildlife area in Wisconsin is periodically opened to hunting. Hunters require a special permit to participate in these hunts. The permits are issued free to the winners of a lottery. For the 1984 lottery, a large number of applications were received. As a result of the lottery, 150 permits to hunt were issued.

To measure *WTA*, half of these hunters also received a letter explaining the study and a check made out in their name. To cash these checks, the hunters had to relinquish their permits. The denominations of the checks, which ranged randomly from $18 to $518, corresponded to the dichotomous-choice method described earlier. The other half of the hunters received a similar letter with a hypothetical payment offer drawn from the same range as the first half. They were asked if they would have been willing to give up their permits for the hypothetical amounts stated in their letters.

To measure *WTP*, 150 unsuccessful lottery participants were selected at random. Again, 75 received a letter explaining that a hunting permit was available if they paid the amount specified in the letter. The amounts covered the same range as described previously. The other 75 were asked the same question hypothetically. That is, they were asked the CV question rather than given the opportunity to reveal their preferences through purchases.

Looking first at *WTP*, the results indicated that the CV valuations ($35) were only slightly higher than those measured through revealed preference ($31), a difference that was not statistically significant. These results suggest that noncommitment bias was not a major problem in this context. But, consistent with the findings discussed earlier, *WTA* valuations were much higher than *WTP* valuations. Furthermore, the CV valuations ($420) were considerably higher than those actually revealed by check cashing ($153).

Source: Richard C. Bishop and Thomas A. Heberlein, "The Contingent Valuation Method," in Rebecca L. Johnson and Gary V. Johnson, eds., *Economic Valuation of Natural Resources: Issues, Theory, and Application* (Boulder, CO: Westview Press, 1990), pp. 81–104.

John Loomis has investigated how consistent household CV valuations are over time. Though not a direct test of accuracy, his investigation is relevant because consistency is a prerequisite for accuracy. He surveyed both visitors and the general public's *WTP* for recreational, option, existence, and bequest values derived from Mono Lake in California. Identical surveys were administered to the same individuals eight or nine months apart. The results were virtually identical.[83]

Though the evidence tends to suggest that CV is plausible in "use" contexts, the jury is still out in terms of nonuse values, given the ordering, embedding, noncommitment, and starting point problems discussed previously. Obviously, given the nature of nonuse values, it is much more difficult to elicit *WTP* from observed behavior. Nonetheless, with sufficient cleverness researchers may be able to find ways to do so. For example, as noted in Chapter 9, voluntary contributions to environmental causes might serve as the basis for estimation. Market-like experiments might also be used.[84] For example, individuals who have expressed *WTP* for nonuse could be given the option of returning none, part, or all of the checks sent to them by experimenters. Successfully implementing such experiments would be extremely difficult with current levels of knowledge and typically available resources, however.

The Potential for Calibration

It has long been recognized in marketing research that it may be necessary to *calibrate* respondents' valuations of goods in various ways to get more accurate estimates of their *WTP*.[85] As noted earlier, noncommitment bias, which may also be interpreted as strategic response bias, is a well-recognized problem in marketing research when individuals are asked to express their valuations of market goods. Kenneth Arrow has concluded, "A hypothesis to be explored is that, if the results of CVs for nonuse values were suitably calibrated, they would provide useful and reliable estimates."[86] Testing Arrow's hypothesis may be one of the most valuable areas of future research on CV.

The Accuracy of Different CV Methods and Proneness to Biases

Richard Bishop and Thomas Heberlein have conducted experiments comparing the size of valuations from open-ended *WTP* questions and closed-end iterative bidding formats (again, this is in a "use" context). They conclude that:

> These experiments indicate that contingent values for willingness to pay may be somewhat high, but for open-ended and dichotomous-choice questions the difference was not large enough to be statistically significant . . . Bidding seems to introduce a substantial upward bias . . . Contingent compensation demanded tended to produce excessive values when an open-ended question was asked and values that were biased substantially upward compared to values obtained from actual cash transactions when dichotomous-choice questions were used.[87]

Other researchers have also addressed this issue. V. Kerry Smith and William Desvousges compared the valuations from four CV methods in their study of improvements in the quality of water in the Monongahela River. Their analysis suggests that starting point bias is important with iterative bidding: A low starting point ($25) generated lower valuations than other methods, whereas a high starting point ($125) produced valuations higher than other methods. Open-ended questions and payment card questions produced fairly similar valuations. Over all, mean valuations from different CV methods ranged from $7 to $36 for one water quality change, from $4 to $31 for another change, and from $11 to $51 for a third change.[88]

William Desvousges and his colleagues have compared open-ended question responses with dichotomous-choice responses to the same questions. They found that in some contexts the differences in the mean *WTP* valuations were not statistically significant, but in other contexts they were. They also found the dichotomous-choice method generated a considerable number of very high valuations.[89] This is consistent with the likely relative importance of strategic response bias discussed previously, as well as with the relatively lower precision of the dichotomous-choice method relative to direct elicitation methods.

HEURISTICS FOR THE DESIGN AND USE OF CV SURVEYS

Several experts in CV have suggested overall criteria for evaluating CV instruments. Ronald Cummings, David Brookshire, and William Schulze, for example, suggest five criteria for evaluating instruments. First, respondents should understand and be familiar with the good that is being valued. Second, respondents should have, or be given, experience in both valuation and the choice procedure. Third, there should be as little uncertainty as possible about the details of the project. All three of these concerns can best be addressed by attempting to reduce hypotheticality—for example, by employing quality ladders, by stressing realistically and concretely the substitution possibilities, and by presenting gains (benefits) in percentage terms as well as in absolute terms. Fourth, *WTP* rather than *WTA* should be used for valuation purposes. Fifth, attempts should be made to avoid anchoring and starting point bias.[90]

Heuristics for Using Estimates from Previous CV Studies

Because CV surveys are inevitably complex and expensive, many analysts will be more concerned with using values derived from existing CV studies than they will be in going out and doing CV surveys themselves. In a recent examination of alternative environmental regulatory policies for dealing with water pollution, Ralph Luken illustrates how existing CV estimates can be "plugged in" to a CBA. Specifically, he extrapolates previous CV valuations of benefits from the Monongahela River studies discussed earlier in this chapter. His analysis provides a useful example of how to use plug-in values and is described more fully in Chapter 15.[91] He is careful to specify which studies and which specific estimates he is using; the specific assumptions he makes in the extrapolations; the quality changes that are involved; the distinction between use and any nonuse components; and, finally, any potential remaining biases. He also performs sensitivity analysis.

Environment Canada, in cooperation with several international organizations, is developing a database of CV and other studies that value environmental impacts.[92] In order to facilitate the use of findings from these studies in CBA, it provides an abstract for each study describing the study area and its population characteristics, the environmental asset being valued, the research methods employed, and the monetary values that were estimated. Access to the on-line database is by subscription.[93]

CONCLUSION

Contingent valuation is now relatively uncontroversial in "use" contexts, although it may overestimate use values. Its accuracy in nonuse contexts is much more controversial, yet it is in this context where its potential usefulness is likely to be the greatest. Doubts about the accuracy of CV in nonuse contexts stem from the problems of hypotheticality and the attendant judgment biases that appear to flourish in this context. Strategic response bias, on the other hand, does not appear to be a major problem in the use of the dichotomous-choice method to value public goods with coercive payments, and neutrality bias can be minimized by use of appropriate survey techniques. Probably the most important topics for future CV research are the directional biases in particular methods and the development of techniques that allow reliable calibration.

Exercises for Chapter 14

1. The construction of a dam that would provide hydroelectric power would result in the loss of two streams: one that is now used for sport fishing; and another that does not support game fish but is part of a wilderness area.
   a. Imagine that a contingent valuation method is used to estimate the social cost of the loss of each of these streams. Would you be equally confident in the two sets of estimates?
   b. Consider two general approaches to asking contingent valuation questions about the streams. The first approach attempts to elicit how much compensation people would require to give up the streams. The second approach attempts to elicit how much people would be willing to pay to keep the streams. Which approach would you recommend? Why?
2. A number of residents of Dullsville have complained to the mayor that the center of town looks shabby compared to the centers of many other nearby towns. At the mayor's request, the parks department has put together a proposal for converting the town square parking lot into a sitting park with flower displays—it modeled the design on a similar park in the neighboring town of Flowerville. The annualized cost of installing and maintaining the park, and relocating parking to nearby Short Street, would be about $120,000. With about 40,000 households paying property taxes, the project would cost an average household about $3 per year. You have been asked to give advice about conducting a survey to measure the benefits of the project.
   a. The parks department proposes conducting a telephone survey. Does this seem like an appropriate survey vehicle?
   b. How might a random sample be drawn for a telephone survey?
   c. Write a statement that could be read by the interviewer to describe the project.
   d. Write questions to implement the open-ended *WTP* method.
   e. Propose a procedure for implementing the dichotomous-choice method.

3. Consider a project that would involve purchasing marginal farmland that would then be allowed to return to wetlands capable of supporting migrant birds. Researchers designed a survey to implement the dichotomous-choice method. They reported the following data:

Stated Price (annual payment in dollars)	Fraction of Respondents Accepting Stated Price (percent)
0	98
5	91
10	82
15	66
20	48
25	32
30	20
35	12
40	6
45	4
50	2

What is the mean willingness-to-pay for the sampled population?

Notes

1. CV overviews include Ronald G. Cummings, David S. Brookshire, and William D. Schulze, *Valuing Environmental Goods: An Assessment of the Contingent Valuation Method* (Totowa, NJ: Rowman & Allanheld, 1986); Robert C. Mitchell and Richard T. Carson, *Using Surveys to Value Public Goods: The Contingent Valuation Method* (Washington, DC: Resources for the Future, 1989); Richard C. Bishop and Thomas A. Heberlein, "The Contingent Valuation Method," in *Economic Valuation of Natural Resources: Issues, Theory, and Application,* Rebecca L. Johnson and Gary V. Johnson, eds. (Boulder, CO: Westview Press, 1990), pp. 81–104.

2. William H. Desvousges, V. Kerry Smith, and Ann Fisher, "Option Price Estimates for Water Quality Improvements: A Contingent Valuation Study for the Monongahela River," *Journal of Environmental Economics and Management,* 14, no. 3 (1987), 248–267; Richard C. Bishop and Thomas A. Heberlein, "Measuring Values of Extra-Market Goods: Are Indirect Measures Biased?" *American Journal of Agricultural Economics,* 61, no. 5 (1979), 926–930; M. W. Jones-Lee, M. Hammerton, and P. R. Philips, "The Value of Safety: Results of a National Survey," *Economic Journal,* 95, no. 377 (1985), 45–72.

3. For an example, see Gretchen J. Burger, "Application and Assessment of the Contingent Valuation Method for Federal Hazardous Waste Policy in the Washington, D.C. Area," Ph.D. dissertation, University of New Mexico, Albuquerque, 1984.

4. Raymond J. Kopp, Paul R. Portney, and V. Kerry Smith, "The Economics of Natural Resource Damages after *Ohio v. U.S. Dept. of the Interior,*" *Environmental Law Reporter,* 20, no. 4 (1990), 10,127–10,131.

5. Kenneth Arrow, Robert Solow, Paul Portney, Edward Leamer, Roy Radner, and Howard Schuman, "Report of the NOAA Panel on Contingent Valuation," *Federal Register,* 58, no. 10 (1993), 4601–4614.

6. On this point see, Daniel McFadden and Gregory Leonard, "Issues in the Contingent Valuation of Environmental Goods: Methodologies for Data Collection and Analysis," in *Contingent Valuation: A Critical Assessment,* J. A. Hausman, ed. (New York: North-Holland, 1993), pp. 165–208.

7. Arrow et al., "Report of the NOAA Panel on Contingent Valuation," p. 4608.

8. For an example of this approach, see J. C. Horvath, *Southeastern Economic Survey of Wildlife Recreation*, 2 vols. (Atlanta, GA: Environmental Research Group, Georgia State University, 1974).

9. One compromise between the open-ended format and the provision of "guidance" that has been used in in-person interviews is the *payment card* with a range of prices. For example, in the Nestucca oil spill CV survey, respondents were asked to specify the maximum amount their households would pay for particular programs to prevent oil spills. They were then shown a payment card with dollar amounts ranging from $0 to $5,000 and asked to circle the amount closest to their evaluation. Robert Rowe, William D. Schulze, W. Douglas Shaw, David Schenk, and Lauraine G. Chestnut, "Contingent Valuation of Natural Resource Damage Due to Nestucca Oil Spill," prepared for the Department of Wildlife, Ministry of the Environment, BC, and Environment Canada, by RCG/Hagler, Bailly Inc., June 1991.

10. For an example, see David Brookshire, Berry Ives, and William D. Schulze, "The Valuation of Aesthetic Preference," *Journal of Environmental Economics and Management,* 3, no. 4 (1976), 325–346.

11. James L. Regens, "Measuring Environmental Benefits with Contingent Markets," *Public Administration Review,* 51, no. 4 (1991), 345–352.

12. For an example, see V. Kerry Smith and William H. Desvousges, *Measuring Water Quality Benefits* (Boston, MA: Kluwer Nijhoff Publishing, 1986), Chapter 6.

13. Baruch Fischhoff and Louis A. Cox, Jr., "Conceptual Framework for Regulatory Benefits Assessment," in *Benefits Assessment: The State of the Art,* Judith D. Bentkover, Vincent T. Covello, and Jeryl Mumpower, eds. (Boston, MA: D. Reidel Publishing Co., 1986), pp. 51–84.

14. For an example using this method, see John Loomis, *Integrated Public Lands Management* (New York: Columbia University Press, 1993), pp. 276–279.

15. Selecting an appropriate set of bid prices is one of the most difficult tasks analysts face in applying the dichotomous-choice method. The bid prices must be spaced sufficiently far apart so that they show a range of acceptance rates, ideally from about .85 to about .15. Simply spreading bid prices over a very wide range, however, is unsatisfactory because, for a given sample size, statistical efficiency in estimating willingness-to-pay from the

pattern of acceptances is greater for fewer bid prices. These considerations suggest the importance of conducting pretest surveys to determine an appropriate set of bid prices. (Of course, in any survey study, pretests are important for ensuring that respondents understand questions.) See Hans Nyquist, "Optimal Design of Discrete Response Experiments in Contingent Valuation," *Review of Economics and Statistics,* 74, no. 3 (1992), 559–563; and Barbara J. Kanninen, "Bias in Discrete Response Contingent Valuation," *Journal of Environmental Economics and Management,* 28, no. 1 (1995), 114–125.

16. For more detail on this method, see Bishop and Heberlein, "Measuring Values of Extra-Market Goods," pp. 89–91. On the technical issues relating to interpreting the function as utility and how to deal with truncation, see W. Michael Hanemann, "Welfare Evaluations in Contingent Valuation Experiments with Discrete Responses," *American Journal of Agricultural Economics,* 66, no. 3 (1984), 332–341.

17. The formula for computing the *WTP* of the average member of the sample can be derived more formally if some additional notation is introduced. (Note that this derivation involves approximating the expected value of *WTP*.) Assume that the offer prices are 0, v, $2v$, $3v$, ... Nv, where v is the interval between prices, and Nv is the maximum price offered. For example, if the offer prices were 0, $10, $20, $30, ..., $200, then $v = \$10$ and $N = 20$. Let $F[X]$ be the fraction of respondents offered price X who accept the offer—this is the height of the bar in the histogram that sits above X. In order to calculate the expected value of *WTP*, we require the probability that each offer price is the *maximum* amount that a respondent would be willing to pay. We can approximate this for offer amount $\$kv$ with the expression: $F[kv] - F[(k+1)v]$ for $k = 0, 1, ..., N-1$, which is roughly the probability of a respondent accepting $\$kv$ minus the probability of accepting a larger offer price, $\$(k+1)v$. The mean *WTP* (i.e., the *WTP* of a randomly selected respondent) is then approximately the sum of the products of maximum payments times their probabilities:

$$E[WTP] = NvF[Nv]$$
$$+ (N-1)v\{F[(N-1)v] - F[Nv]\}$$
$$+ (N-2)v\{F[(N-2)v] - F[(N-1)v]\}$$
$$+ ... + 0\{F[0] - F[v]\}$$

Collecting terms yields the simple expression:

$$E[WPT] = v \sum_{k=0}^{N} F[kv]$$

18. For a thorough treatment of estimation issues, see W. Michael Hanemann and Barbara Kanninen, "The Statistical Analysis of Discrete Response CV Data," in *Valuing Environmental Preferences: Theory and Practice of the Contingent Valuation Method in the U.S., EC, and Developing Countries,* Ian J. Bateman and Ken G. Willis, eds. (Oxford, UK: Oxford University Press, 2000), pp. 302–441.

19. A complication arises because the statistical model usually assumes an infinite range for *x*. In practice, surveys use offer prices with a finite range, usually bounded from below at zero. Averaging over this finite range will miss some of the probability assumed by the statistical model. A correction to help account for this truncation bias involves rescaling the distribution to account for the missing areas in the tails of the distribution. See Kevin J. Boyle, Michael P. Welsh, and Richard C. Bishop, "Validation of Empirical Measures of Welfare Change: Comment," *Land Economics,* 64, no. 1 (1988), 94–98.

20. The area under the curve can be estimated through numerical integration. The procedure involves approximating the area with rectangles through the following steps. First, divide the range of *X* into equal segments of width *n*. Second, calculate the probability of acceptance at each of these points. Third, find the average acceptance value for adjacent pairs of points. Fourth, multiply each of these averages by *n*. Fifth, sum all these products to get the estimate of the area. Any desired degree of accuracy can be obtained by choosing a sufficiently small value of *n*.

21. For an overview of the statistical issues in estimating aggregate *WTP* from such models, see Timothy Park, John B. Loomis, and Michael Creel, "Confidence Intervals for Evaluating Benefits Estimates from Dichotomous Choice Contingent Valuation Studies," *Land Economics,* 67, no. 1 (1991), 64–73.

22. Joseph A. Herriges and Jason F. Shogren, "Starting Point Bias in Dichotomous Choice Valuation with Follow-Up Questioning," *Journal of Environmental Economics and Management,* 30, no. 1 (1996), 112–131.

23. Richard T. Carson, Theodore Groves, Mark J. Machina, "Incentive and Informational Properties of Preference Questions," Plenary Address, European Association of Resource and Environmental Economists, Oslo, Norway, June 1999.

24. Robert J. Johnston, Stephen K. Swallow, and Thomas F. Weaver, "Estimating Willingness to Pay and Resource Tradeoffs with Different Payment Mechanisms: An Evaluation of a Funding Guarantee for Watershed Management," *Journal of Environmental Economics and Management,* 38, no. 1 (1999), 97–120.

25. See "The Review Panel's Assessment," pp. 180–204, Kenneth Arrow, "Comments" at pp. 180–185, in Cummings, Brookshire, and Schulze, *Valuing Environmental Goods: An Assessment of the Contingent Valuation Method.*

26. For overviews, see Martin Frankel, "Sampling Theory," pp. 21–67, and Seymour Sudman, "Applied Sampling," pp. 145–194 in Rossi, Wright, and Anderson, *Handbook of Survey Research;* for issues specifically relevant to CV, see Steven F. Edwards and Glen D. Anderson, "Overlooked Biases in Contingent Valuation Surveys: Some Considerations," *Land Economics,* 63, no. 2 (1987), 168–178.

27. Richard T. Carson, "Constructed Markets," in *Measuring the Demand for Environmental Quality,* John B. Braden and Charles D. Kolstad, eds. (New York: Elsevier Science Publishers, 1991), p. 152.

28. For an example of an attempt to estimate the extent of a recreational market, see V. Kerry Smith and Raymond J. Kopp, "The Spatial Limits of the Travel Cost Recreational Demand Model," *Land Economics,* 56, no. 1 (1980), 64–72.

29. Desvousges, Smith, and Fisher, "Option Price Estimates for Water Quality Improvements."

30. F. L. Filion, "Estimating Bias Due to Non-response in Mail Surveys," *Public Opinion Quarterly,* 39, no. 4 (1975–6), 482–492.

31. For a review, see John B. Loomis, "Expanding Contingent Value Sample Estimates to Aggregate Benefit Estimates: Current Practices and Proposed Solutions," *Land Economics,* 63, no. 4 (1987), 396–402.

32. The most comprehensive criticisms of CV can be found in Hausman, ed., *Contingent Valuation: A Critical Assessment.*

33. William D. Schulze, Ronald G. Cummings, and David S. Brookshire, *Methods Development in Measuring Benefits of Environmental Improvements, Vol. II* (Washington, DC: Report to U.S. EPA, 1983).

34. For an extensive discussion of the attitude-behavior nexus, see Mitchell and Carson, *Using Surveys to Value Public Goods: The Contingent Valuation Method,* pp. 175–187.

35. Baruch Fischhoff and Lita Furey, "Measuring Values: A Conceptual Framework for Interpreting Transactions with Special Reference to Contingent Valuation of Visibility," *Journal of Risk and Uncertainty,* 1, no. 2 (1988), 147–184, at pp. 179–180.

36. In marketing, the technique called *conjoint analysis* is used to elicit consumer valuations for new, unfamiliar goods. For a review, see Daniel McFadden, "The Choice Theory Approach to Market Research," *Marketing Science,* 5, no. 4 (1986), 275–297.

37. For a discussion of this point, see Cummings, Brookshire, and Schulze, *Valuing Environmental Goods: An Assessment of the Contingent Valuation Method,* pp. 43, 253.

38. Fischhoff and Furey, "Measuring Values: A Conceptual Framework for Interpreting Transactions with Special Reference to Contingent Valuation of Visibility," Table 1, p. 156.

39. Daniel A. Hagen, James W. Vincent, and Patrick G. Welle, "The Benefits of Preserving Old-Growth Forests and the Northern Spotted Owl," *Contemporary Policy Issues,* 10, no. 2 (1992), 13–16. A second CV study of the spotted owl that can be critiqued on neutrality grounds is Jonathan Rubin, Gloria Heland, and John Loomis, "A Benefit-Cost Analysis of the Northern Spotted Owl: Results from a Contingent Valuation Survey," *Journal of Forestry,* 89, no. 12 (1991), 25–30.

40. William McKillop, "Use of Contingent Valuation in Northern Spotted Owls Studies: A Critique," *Journal of Forestry,* 90, no. 8 (1992), 36–37.

41. Ed Bukszar, "Does Overconfidence Lead to Poor Decisions? A Comparison of Decision Making and Judgment under Uncertainty," paper presented at the Annual Conference of Judgment and Decision Making, Washington, DC, November 7, 1993.

42. See David L. Weimer and Aidan R. Vining, *Policy Analysis: Concepts and Practice,* 3rd ed. (Upper Saddle River, NJ: Prentice Hall, 1999), pp. 124–125.

43. For a review of this issue, see Colin F. Camerer and Howard Kunreuther, "Decision Processes for Low Probability Events: Policy Implications," *Journal of Policy Analysis and Management,* 8, no. 4 (1989), 565–592.

44. For an extensive review of biases and the various theories behind them, see Camerer and Kunreuther, "Decision Processes for Low Probability Events: Policy Implications."

45. Daniel Kahneman and Amos Tversky, "Prospect Theory," *Econometrica,* 47, no. 2 (1979), 263–292. Many of the violations of expected utility hypothesis that can be explained by prospect theory can also be explained by assuming people maximize expected utility but employ Bayesian updating of probabilities; see W. Kip Viscusi, "Prospective Reference Theory: Toward an Explanation of the Paradoxes," *Journal of Risk and Uncertainty,* 2, no. 3 (1989), 235–263.

46. Richard H. Thaler, "Towards a Positive Theory of Consumer Choice," *Journal of Economic Behavior and Organization,* 1, no. 1 (1980), 39–60.

47. It may seem somewhat artificial to separate hypotheticality from noncommitment bias. However, as emphasized earlier, hypotheticality does not appear to generate upward or downward bias, while, as we will see, noncommitment does appear to bias valuations upward.

48. See, for example, Linda F. Jamieson and Frank M. Bass, "Adjusting Stated Intention Measures to Predict Trial Purchase of New Products: A Comparison of Models and Methods," *Journal of Marketing Research,* 26, no. 3 (1989), 336–345; F. Thomas Juster, *Anticipations and Purchases* (Princeton, NJ: Princeton University Press, 1964).

49. Helen R. Neill, Ronald G. Cummings, Philip T. Ganderton, Glenn W. Harrison, and Thomas McGuckin, "Hypothetical Surveys and Economic Commitments," *Land Economics,* 70, no. 2 (1994), 145–154; Kalle Seip and Jon Strand, "Willingness to Pay for Environmental Goods in Norway: A Contingent Valuation Study with Real Payment," *Environmental and Resource Economics,* 2, no. 1 (1992), 91–106.

50. For more detail, see Michael A. Kemp and Christopher Maxwell, "Exploring a Budget Context for Contingent Valuation Estimates," pp. 217–265, in Hausman, ed., *Contingent Valuation: A Critical Assessment.*

51. I. J. Bateman and I. H. Langford, "Budget-Constrained, Temporal, and Question-Ordering Effects in Contingent Valuation Studies," *Environment and Planning A.,* 29, no. 7 (1997), 1215–1228.

52. George Tolley and Alan Randall, "Establishing and Valuing the Effects of Improved Visibility in

the Eastern United States," (Washington, DC: Report to the U.S. EPA, 1983).

53. Karl C. Samples and James R. Hollyer, "Contingent Valuation of Wildlife Resources in the Presence of Substitutes and Complements," pp. 177–192, in Johnson and Johnson, eds., *Economic Valuation of National Resources: Issues, Theory, and Application.*

54. See Peter A. Diamond, Jerry A. Hausman, Gregory K. Leonard, and Mike Denning, "Does Contingent Valuation Measure Preferences? Experimental Evidence," pp. 43–85, in Hausman, ed., *Contingent Valuation: A Critical Assessment.*

55. See the heated argument between Peter Diamond and Richard Carson, in Hausman, ed., *Contingent Valuation: A Critical Assessment,* pp. 87–89.

56. William H. Desvousges, F. Reed Johnson, Richard W. Dunford, Sara P. Hudson, and K. Nicole Wilson, "Measuring Natural Resources Damages with Contingent Valuation: Tests of Validity and Reliability," in Hausman, ed., *Contingent Valuation: A Critical Assessment,* pp. 91–159.

57. Daniel Kahneman and Jack L. Knetsch, "Valuing Public Goods: The Purchase of Moral Satisfaction," *Journal of Environmental Economics and Management,* 22, no. 1 (1992), 57–70, 64–68.

58. Kevin J. Boyle, Richard C. Bishop, and Michael P. Walsh, "Starting Point Bias in Contingent Valuation Bidding Games," *Land Economics,* 16, no. 2 (1985), 188–194.

59. Regens, "Measuring Environmental Benefits with Contingent Markets," pp. 347–348.

60. Walter J. Mead, "Review and Analysis of State-of-the-Art Contingent Valuation Studies," pp. 305–332 in Hausman, ed., *Contingent Valuation: A Critical Assessment.*

61. See Trudy A. Cameron and D. D. Huppert, "Referendum Contingent Valuation Estimates: Sensitivity to the Assignment of Offered Values," *Journal of the American Statistical Association,* 86, no. 416 (1991), 910–918.

62. Alok K. Bohara, Michael McKee, Robert P. Berrens, Hank Jenkins-Smith, Carol L. Silva, and David S. Brookshire, "Effects of Total Cost and Group-Size Information on Willingness to Pay Responses: Open Ended vs. Dichotomous Choice," *Journal of Environmental Economics and Management,* 35, no. 2 (1998), 142–163.

63. But Michael Hanemann ["Willingness to Pay and Willingness to Accept: How Much Can They Differ?" *American Economic Review,* 81, no. 3 (1991), 635–647] has argued that there is no reason why *WTA* should not be considerably larger than *WTP* in certain circumstances. He points out, for example, that one cannot pay more than one's income year after year to save one's own life, but there may be no finite offer that could make one willingly give up one's life.

64. Jack Knetsch and J. S. Sinden, "Willingness to Pay and Compensation Demanded: Experimental Evidence of an Unexpected Disparity in Measures of Value," *Quarterly Journal of Economics,* 99, no. 3 (1984), 507–521; Shelby Gerking, Menno De Haan, and William Schulze, "The Marginal Value of Job Safety: A Contingent Valuation Study," *Journal of Risk and Uncertainty,* 1, no. 2 (1988), 185–199; Wesley Magat and W. Kip Viscusi, *Informational Approaches to Regulation* (Cambridge, MA: MIT Press, 1992).

65. Timothy McDaniels, "Reference Points, Loss Aversion, and Contingent Values for Auto Safety," *Journal of Risk and Uncertainty,* 5, no. 2 (1992), 187–200.

66. Don L. Coursey, John J. Hovis, and William D. Schulze, "The Disparity between Willingness to Accept and Willingness to Pay Measures of Value," *Quarterly Journal of Economics,* 102, no. 3 (1987), 679–690; Jason F. Shogren, Seung Y. Shin, Dermot J. Hayes, and James B. Kliebenstein, "Resolving the Differences in Willingness to Pay and Willingness to Accept," *American Economic Review,* 84, no. 1 (1994), 255–270; Wiktor L. Adamovicz, Vinay Bhardwaj, and Bruce McNab, "Experiments on the Difference between Willingness to Pay and Willingness to Accept," *Land Economics,* 64, no. 4 (1993), 416–427.

67. Shogren, Shin, Hayes, and Kliebenstein, "Resolving the Differences in Willingness to Pay and Willingness to Accept."

68. Arrow et al., "Report of the NOAA Panel on Contingent Valuation," p. 4608.

69. On free riding in the provision of public goods, see R. Mark Isaac, James Walker, and Susan Thomas, "Divergent Evidence on Free Riding: An Experimental Examination of Possible Explanations," *Public Choice,* 43, no. 2 (1984), 113–149; Oliver Kim and Mark Walker, "The Free Rider Problem: Experimental Evidence," *Public Choice,* 43, no. 1 (1984), 3–24; G. Marwell and R. Ames, "Economists Free Ride, Does Anyone Else? Experiments

on the Provision of Public Goods," *Journal of Public Economics,* 15, no. 3 (1981), 295–310; and Linda Goetz, T. F. Glover, and B. Biswas, "The Effects of Group Size and Income on Contributions to the Corporation for Public Broadcasting," *Public Choice,* 77, no. 2 (1993), 407–414.

70. Mitchell and Carson, *Using Surveys to Value Public Goods: The Contingent Valuation Method.*

71. Richard T. Carson, Theodore Groves, and Mark J. Machina, "Incentive and Informational Properties of Preference Questions," Plenary Address, European Association of Resource and Environmental Economists, Oslo, Norway, June 1999.

72. On the domain of preferences, see the discussion of Arrow's Possibility Theorem in Chapter 2.

73. Alan Gibbard, "Manipulation of Voting Schemes: A General Result," *Econometrica,* 41, no. 4 (1973), 587–601; and Mark Allen Satterthwaite, "Strategy-Proofness and Arrow's Conditions: Existence and Correspondence Theorems for Voting Procedures and Social Welfare Functions," *Journal of Economic Theory,* 10, no. 2 (1975), 187–217.

74. See Keven J. Boyle, F. Reed Johnson, Daniel W. McCollum, William H. Desvousges, Richard W. Dunford, and Sara P. Hudson, "Valuing Public Goods: Discrete versus Continuous Contingent Valuation Responses," *Land Economics,* 72, no. 3 (1996), 381–396.

75. A number of studies have found a large divergence between *WTP* as expressed in contingent-choice CV and actual donations. For a recent review, including a discussion of using follow-up questions on certainty of donation to adjust contingent donations, see Patricia A. Champ, Richard C. Bishop, Thomas C. Brown, and Daniel W. McCollum, "Using Donation Mechanisms to Value Nonuse Benefits from Public Goods," *Journal of Environmental Economics and Management,* 33, no. 2 (1997), 151–162.

76. For an overview of this issue and a listing of relevant studies, see V. K. Smith, "Nonmarket Valuation of Environmental Resources: An Interpretive Appraisal," *Land Economics,* 69, no. 1 (1993), 1–26, at pp. 8–14, and Table 1.

77. See William K. Desvousges, V. Kerry Smith, and Matthew P. McGivney, "A Comparison of Alternative Approaches for Estimating Recreation and Related Benefits of Water Quality Improvements" (Report to U.S. EPA, Research Triangle Institute, 1983); Christine Sellar, John R. Stoll, and

Jean-Paul Chavas, "Validation of Empirical Measures of Welfare Change: A Comparison of Nonmarket Techniques," *Land Economics,* 61, no. 2 (1985), 156–175; Smith and Desvousges, *Measuring Water Quality Benefits,* compare CV to "simple" travel cost methods.

78. David S. Brookshire, Mark A. Thayer, William D. Schulze, and Ralph C. d'Arge, "Valuing Public Goods: A Comparison of Survey and Hedonic Approaches," *American Economic Review,* 72, no. 1 (1982), 165–177.

79. Mark A. Thayer, "Contingent Valuation Techniques for Assessing Environmental Impacts: Further Evidence," *Journal of Environmental Economics and Management,* 8, no. 1 (1981), 27–44.

80. Magat and Viscusi, *Informational Approaches to Regulation,* Ch. 7.

81. For a listing of such studies, see Carson, "Constructed Markets," pp. 121–126.

82. Coursey, Hovis, and Schulze, "The Disparity between Willingness to Accept and Willingness to Pay Measures of Values"; Mark Dickie, Ann Fisher, and Shelby Gerking, "Market Transactions and Hypothetical Demand Data: A Comparative Study," *Journal of the American Statistical Society,* 82, no. 398 (1987), 69–75.

83. John Loomis, "Test-Retest Reliability of the Contingent Valuation Method: A Comparison of General Population and Visitor Responses," *American Journal of Agricultural Economics,* 71, no. 1 (1989), 76–84.

84. For a discussion of this possibility, see Douglas M. Larson, "On Measuring Existence Value," *Land Economics,* 69, no. 3 (1993), 377–388.

85. An example of such calibration is Donald G. Morrison, "Purchase Intentions and Purchase Behavior," *Journal of Marketing,* 43 (1979), 65–74. "It is possible to improve prediction accuracy by measuring and using perceptions that affect and modify the relationship between stated intentions and trial purchase for new products," in Jamieson and Bass, "Adjusting Stated Intention Measures to Predict Trial Purchase of New Products," p. 344.

86. Kenneth Arrow, "Contingent Valuation of Nonuse Values: Observations and Questions," pp. 479–483, p. 483 in Hausman, ed., *Contingent Valuation: A Critical Assessment.*

87. Bishop and Heberlein, "The Contingent Valuation Method," p. 97.

88. Smith and Desvousges, *Measuring Water Quality Benefits,* Table 105, p. 271.

89. Desvousges, Johnson, Dunford, Hudson, and Wilson, "Measuring Natural Resources Damages with Contingent Valuation: Tests of Validity and Reliability."

90. Summarized from "Comparison Studies: What Is Accuracy," pp. 71–109, and "reference operating conditions," Table 13.1, p. 230, in "Summary and Conclusions," pp. 205–236 in Cummings, Brookshire, and Schulze, *Valuing Environmental Goods: An Assessment of the Contingent Valuation Method.*

91. Ralph A. Luken, *Efficiency in Environmental Regulation: A Benefit-Cost Analysis of Alternative Approaches,* (Boston, MA: Kluwer Academic Publishers, 1990), pp. 45–53.

92. Richard T. Carson, "Contingent Valuation: A User's Guide," *Environmental Science and Technology,* 34, no. 8 (2000), 1413–1418.

93. The database address is www.evri.ec.gc.ca/evri/.

CHAPTER

15

SHADOW PRICES FROM SECONDARY SOURCES

Policy analysts typically face time pressure and resource constraints. They naturally wish to do cost-benefit analysis with the least redundant effort, at the lowest opportunity cost, and without getting into estimation issues beyond their competence. Anything that legitimately lowers the cost of doing CBA increases the likelihood that any particular CBA will be worth doing. In order to assess either existing or proposed policies and projects, analysts require credible measures of the social values of their impacts. As we see in Chapters 4 and 12, when these impacts occur in efficient markets, their impacts can be estimated from changes in market prices and quantities. The expected social cost of labor for environmental projects, for example, can usually be directly derived from local labor markets. However, when there are market failures or there is no market at all (so-called missing markets), then analysts need a shadow price. In order to obtain such estimates, analysts might conduct their own valuation studies. As we discuss in Chapter 13, there are many possible approaches, but many of these methods are time consuming and resource intensive. The most straightforward, low-cost method is to use *existing estimated shadow prices,* or *plug-ins*. Using plug-ins in a CBA is known as *benefit transfer* or sometimes *information transfer.*

Most CBAs involve some impacts that can be valued at current market prices and other impacts that can be valued using plug-ins. Transportation and infrastructure project analysts, for example, can use market prices for construction resources (materials, land, labor, and equipment) and ongoing operational costs (labor and maintenance materials) but require plug-ins for the value of lives saved, injuries avoided, accidents avoided, time saved, air quality changes, and noise level changes, to name only some.[1]

At least two kinds of plug-ins can be found in the literature. First, and most importantly, are the estimates of shadow prices when markets are missing. Examples include the value of a unit of time, the value of a statistical life, or the (negative) value of particular types of crime. After necessary adjustments, such as the conversion to current dollars, previously estimated values of these impacts can be directly used in new CBAs. This is the major focus of this chapter.

Second, economists have estimated price elasticities of demand, cross-elasticities, and income elasticities for a range of specific goods. Many elasticities have been summarized in survey articles.[2] Recently, meta-analyses have become more common.[3] As CBA analysts are frequently dealing with long-lived projects, long-run elasticities are usually more relevant than short-run elasticities. These elasticities can be used to project the policy impacts of proposed projects as we discuss in Chapter 12. As they are based on the responses of people to similar price changes in the past, they provide an empirically grounded basis for predicting the responses to proposed price changes. For example, how consumers responded to a price increase for water in New Mexico can be reasonably used to estimate how they will respond to a similar price increase in Arizona. In addition to own-price elasticities, estimates of cross-price elasticities, which identify changes in the demand for a good that are likely to result from changes in the prices of other goods, though less often available, are frequently very useful. For example, are transportation and various forms of communications (such as telecommuting and teleconferencing) complements or substitutes?[4] These cross-elasticities are important to transport planners and policy analysts who are estimating the costs and benefits of transport capital investments, assessing expected consumers' responses to price changes, or forecasting changes in demand for transportation. Existing estimates of income elasticities can also be very useful, especially when policies have strong distributional effects. Elasticity estimates are scattered widely throughout the academic literature, usually in the topic-specific journals. Therefore, analysts must garner them from the relevant economic and policy journals on an ongoing basis.

This chapter briefly surveys the relevant literature and provides a "best estimate" of the value of each impact. It focuses on impacts that occur in many CBAs: the value of life, the cost of various kinds of injuries (including those resulting from road crashes), the cost of crime, and the value of time.[5] We also review per-unit values of air pollution, water pollution, and recreational activities, and we briefly discuss empirical estimates of the marginal excess tax burden.

The plug-ins are summarized in Tables 15.1 through 15.6. In order to facilitate comparability and for ease of use, plug-in values are usually expressed in 1999 U.S. dollars using the consumer price index deflator obtained from Table 6.3. The units of each impact are usually dollars per person or per event. Other values are reported in terms of units produced, such as "per ton." We also report the relevant time unit, such as "per day," "per year," and so on.

People have varying preferences. Consequently, when using our best estimates in a particular CBA, they should be adjusted to take account of the preferences and profile of the affected population. After providing the plug-ins, we briefly address some of the information transfer issues related to adjusting plug-ins to new CBAs.

THE VALUE OF LIFE

Researchers have used several benefit estimation techniques to estimate the value of life. These techniques either indirectly estimate the "price" people must be paid to be willing to take, or accept, certain risks by observing their behaviors in markets for commodities that embody risks (Chapter 13), or directly elicit these amounts with hypothetical survey questions (Chapter 14). The most common and widely accepted of the market-based techniques are those that examine how much of a wage premium people working in risky jobs must be given to compensate them for the additional risks. Our purpose here is not to revisit methodological issues but to summarize the empirical estimates of the value of statistical life in the United States. We draw primarily on overviews of the evidence provided by Ted Miller, by Ann Fisher, Lauraine Chestnut, and Daniel Violette, and by W. Kip Viscusi.[6]

The Miller Survey of Value-of-Life Estimates

Ted Miller reviews 49 studies that estimated the value of life using criteria such as the quality of the survey design, sample size, and inclusion of appropriate risk variables. He then summarizes the value-of-life estimates from the 29 studies that best satisfied these criteria. All of Miller's estimates are in 1985 after-tax dollars and are computed with a consistent real discount rate of 2.5 percent.

The studies estimate the value of life in one of four ways based on (1) wage premia for risky jobs; (2) consumers' willingness to pay for safety features (safer cars and smoke detectors), houses in less polluted areas, or life insurance; (3) individual behavior with respect to decisions concerning the use of pedestrian tunnels and seat belts, choice of speed when driving, and driver travel time; and (4) contingent valuation methods to survey individuals about their willingness to invest in specific ways to increase health and safety. Consistent with our conclusions in Chapter 14, the contingent valuation studies produce somewhat higher values. The mean value of life across the 29 studies is $3.02 million in 1999 dollars, with a standard deviation of 0.77 in 1999 dollars. Miller concludes that there is enough consistency across the studies to suggest that this mean is quite plausible. He points out that the evidence also suggests that individuals value life similarly whether the risk is largely voluntary (e.g., auto driving behavior) or involuntary (e.g., the risk of a nuclear accident) and whether the potential death is slow and painful or sudden and quick.

The Fisher, Chestnut, and Violette Survey of Value-of-Life Estimates

These authors review 21 studies reporting estimates of the value of life. They provide both the range for each estimate of the value of life from each study and a best estimate. Additionally, they also report an estimate of the mean level of risk considered in each study. Knowing the mean level of risk is useful because individuals' valuation of risk reduction (or safety increase) tends to increase with the level of risk, as discussed in Chapter 13.

The authors divide the 21 studies that they review into five categories: early low-range wage-risk estimates, early high-range wage-risk estimates, new wage-risk estimates, new contingent valuation studies, and consumer market studies. They conclude that the most defensible empirical results indicate the range for the value-per-statistical-life estimates is $2.43 million to $12.92 million (in 1999 dollars) but place more confidence in the lower end of the range.

The Viscusi Survey of Value-of-Life Estimates

W. Kip Viscusi provides the most extensive review of both the conceptual framework and the empirical literature on the value of life. Here we concentrate on his assessment of the empirical literature, which is reported in 1990 dollars. He reviews three sets of studies: those concerning wage premia for risky jobs, other revealed preference approaches, and surveys. Viscusi reports the empirical results of 24 labor market studies. He observes that the value of life is not a constant but reflects the wage-risk trade-off pertinent to the preferences of the workers in a particular sample. The majority of these estimates are in the range of $3.82 million to $8.92 million (in 1999 dollars).

Viscusi reviews seven revealed preference studies based on behavior other than labor market behavior. As he points out, these studies are probably somewhat less reliable than labor market studies because the latter allow one to distinguish risk levels across individuals, whereas other revealed preference methods do not. For example, we normally do not know whether individuals purchasing smoke detectors live in apartments that are "firetraps" or modern apartments with built-in sprinklers. Additionally, some of these studies can only provide information on the lower bound of the value of life because discrete purchase decisions do not force individuals to reveal their total willingness-to-pay, only whether they will pay more than a given price.[7] These studies provide widely varying estimates of the value of life from $0.09 million to $5.10 million (in 1999 dollars). However, he argues that the study that provides the most reliable estimate is Scott Atkinson and Robert Halvorsen's analysis of the purchase of safety features on new automobiles.[8] This study includes the car purchase price (equivalent to the wage in the labor studies) and explanatory variables such as other product characteristics, characteristics of the purchasers, and the risk. The study estimates the value of life at the top of the range for this group of studies.

Finally, Viscusi reviews six survey, or contingent valuation, estimates of the value of life that have a wide range of values—from $0.13 million to $19.1 million (in 1999 dollars).

Conclusion on the Value of Life

As Table 15.1 shows, we suggest a plausible range for the value of a statistical life saved is between $2.5 million and $4.0 million in 1999 dollars. Although primarily based on Miller, this range is also quite close to Fisher and colleagues' lower-bound estimate, in which these authors expressed greater confidence. The upper end of the range corresponds to Viscusi's lower-bound estimate, which is the one in which he expresses the greatest confidence.

TABLE 15.1 Plug-Ins for Value of Life and Injury Costs (in 1999 U.S. dollars)

Plug-In Category (impact)	Shadow Price Value	Comments
VALUE OF LIFE	$2.5 million to $4.0 million per life saved	Based primarily on Miller (1989). See also Fisher, Chestnut and Violette (1989) and Viscusi (1993). Should adjust for risk level if known.
MONETARY INJURY COSTS 1) Eventually fatal 2) Hospitalized (nonfatal) 3) Nonhospitalized (nonfatal) 4) Average cost of an injury	1) $491,000 per injured person 2) $53,000 per injured person 3) $800 per injured person 4) $4,300 per injured person	Based on Rice, MacKenzie, and associates (1989). Includes monetary costs only, not pain and suffering.
A) Motor vehicle injury B) Falls C) Firearm injuries D) Poisonings E) Fire injuries and burns F) Drownings and near-drownings G) Other	A) $14,000 per injured person B) $4,700 per injured person C) $83,300 per injured person D) $7,800 per injured person E) $4,000 per injured person F) $100,600 per injured person G) $1,800 per injured person	
COST OF WORK-RELATED INJURY 1) Less serious 2) More serious	1) $31,000 per injured person 2) $64,000 per injured person	Based on Viscusi's (1993) survey of labor market studies; therefore, includes pain and suffering but not all social costs. Higher values involve loss of workdays.
SOCIAL COST OF MOTOR VEHICLE CRASH INJURIES 1) Spinal cord 2) Brain 3) Lower extremity 4) Upper extremity 5) Trunk/abdomen 6) Face, other head, or other neck 7) Minor external	1) $2,054,700 per victim (0.66) 2) $119,000 per victim (0.04) 3) $200,400 per victim (0.06) 4) $77,900 per victim (0.03) 5) $59,400 per victim (0.02) 6) $22,900 per victim (0.01) 7) $5,500 per victim (0.002)	Based on Miller's (1993) $2.8 million estimate of the value of life (in 1994 dollars). Attempts to measure total social cost, including pain and suffering. Numbers in parentheses measure cost as a fraction of the value of life.
A) Average for nonfatal crash B) Average for fatal crash	A) $56,200 per victim (0.02) B) $3,358,900 per victim (1.08)	
MONETARY COST OF FIREARM INJURIES 1) Eventually fatal 2) Hospitalized (nonfatal) 3) Nonhospitalized (nonfatal)	1) $578,400 per injured person 2) $51,400 per injured person 3) $700 per injured person	Based on Max and Rice (1993). Includes monetary costs only, not pain and suffering.

THE COST OF INJURIES

Table 15.1 also summarizes four sets of estimates for the cost of injuries in the United States, again updated to 1999 dollars. The first set of estimates, which is based on a major report prepared for Congress by Dorothy Rice, Ellen MacKenzie, and their associates, provides detailed estimates of costs for injuries from different causes and for three levels of severity.[9] The second set of estimates is based on a survey of labor market studies by V. Kip Viscusi that estimate the cost of injuries. The third set is based on Ted Miller's 1993 study of injury costs resulting from automobile crashes. The fourth set of estimates is based on Wendy Max and Dorothy Rice's study of the lifetime costs of firearm injuries.[10] We also discuss estimates of the cost of serious road injuries by the Transport Research Laboratory in the United Kingdom, although these are not summarized in Table 15.1.

The Rice-McKenzie and Associates' Estimates of the Cost of Injuries

The Rice-McKenzie estimates incorporate medical and rehabilitation costs and forgone earnings (including an imputed value for household labor) but, unfortunately, do not include pain and suffering and other dimensions of unhappiness that people would pay to avoid. They also do not include property damage losses and other related costs, such as court costs, as their study was only concerned with the monetary cost of injuries rather than with the social cost of any activity associated with the injury. Thus, the human capital approach adopted in the study leads to very conservative estimates of the social cost of injuries because it ignores disutility resulting from pain and suffering. (Methods for estimating this disutility are discussed in the section on using the market analogy method to value a life saved in Chapter 13 and in the discussion of quality-adjusted life-years in Chapter 17.) All estimates presented in Table 15.1 are updated to 1999 dollars and rounded.

The Viscusi Survey of Cost-of-Injury Estimates

W. Kip Viscusi has reviewed the evidence on the cost of nonfatal work-related injuries (in the same article as his value-of-life estimates, discussed earlier in this chapter). He computes cost-of-injury estimates from 14 labor market studies conducted between 1978 and 1991. These studies focus on individual willingness-to-pay; therefore, they include the disutility of pain and suffering. Unfortunately, the individual studies cover a wide range of nonfatal injury circumstances. For example, some studies only examine injuries that resulted in some degree of job interruption, whereas others include less serious injuries. Some studies use average injury risk rates for industries, whereas others use workers' (subjective) assessment of risk. Some studies control for wage differences due to loss-of-life risks, whereas others do not. Additionally, of course, mean injury risk rates vary considerably across the studies (from 0.03 to 0.10 per year). Because work-related injuries may be of different severity and type than other kinds of injuries, these estimates cannot be directly compared to estimates based on injuries in general. In Table 15.1, we divide these work-related injury estimates into a less serious estimate (item 1) and a more serious estimate (item 2).

The Miller Estimates of the Cost of Motor Vehicle Crashes

Reduced injuries and reduced automobile repair costs are common potential impacts of transportation projects, such as better road lighting, altered speed limits, or new vehicle safety features. Ted Miller has estimated the comprehensive costs of U.S. motor vehicle crashes.[11] The cost of motor vehicle crashes is not synonymous with the cost of injuries because motor vehicle crashes typically engender many costs, such as vehicle damage costs and additional time travel costs for other motorists, that the typical injury does not. Thus, one would expect the average cost of a motor vehicle crash to be higher than the average injury cost. Additionally, of course, vehicle crashes are also likely to have a distribution of injury severity that differs from the distribution of injuries from all causes.

Miller's cost estimates include medical and emergency services, lost wages and household production, workplace disruption, insurance administration costs, the cost of legal proceedings (but not the income transfers resulting from settlements), and the lost quality of life (including pain and suffering, which are inferred from individuals' willingness-to-pay to avoid injuries). Thus, these estimates differ methodologically from the cost-of-injury estimates calculated by Dorothy Rice and her colleagues, which only included "monetary" losses.

Miller first reports his estimates as a fully monetized "cost per crash" figure that can be directly plugged into a CBA. Nonfatal quality-of-life losses were calculated by first multiplying the value of fatal risk reduction by the ratio of the years of functional capacity lost through the injury to years lost in a fatality, and then subtracting the monetary component of this value, namely, the value of wages and household production that was lost due to the injury.

Miller also reports estimates quantitatively as years of life and functioning lost, which can be used in a cost-effectiveness ratio because they quantify but do not monetize the value of life or injuries. Thus, for example, crash injuries involving lower extremities, such as pelvis and hip, resulted in 6.5 years of functional loss, on average. This latter approach reflects the fact that some decision makers are uncomfortable monetizing the value of life or the cost of injuries. (Cost-effectiveness analysis is explained in detail in Chapter 17.)

Miller classifies crash injuries by region of the body in decreasing order of severity: spinal cord; brain; lower extremity; upper extremity; trunk/abdomen; other head, face, and other neck; and minor external. The summary findings by region of the body (rounded in 1999 dollars) are shown as items 1 through 7 in Table 15.1. He also simply divides injury costs into an average cost for nonfatal crashes and an average cost for fatal crashes (items A and B, respectively, in Table 15.1).

Miller points out that not using comprehensive cost measures (i.e., measuring incorrectly) can seriously distort public policy decision making. If injury costs are underestimated, then the benefits of safety-enhancing road improvements are lowered relative to the benefits of time-saving road improvements. It may, thus, appear that it is better to be dead than to be stuck in traffic![12] This is usually not the case when the numbers are estimated correctly.

The Max and Rice Cost of Firearm Injuries

Wendy Max and Dorothy Rice provide estimates of the cost of firearm injuries. We report these estimates here rather than under the cost-of-crime estimates because many firearm injuries are accidental. Their estimate of costs has two components: (1) direct costs such as medical and hospital, rehabilitation, medication, and transportation costs; (2) indirect costs resulting from lost productivity (including the value of household labor). Indirect costs include morbidity costs (estimated as the value of days lost from injury or as the years of life lost from injury-related disability) and mortality costs (estimated as either the monetary value of lost future output or the years of life lost from premature death).

The estimates are for three classes of firearm injury: those resulting in fatalities, those resulting in hospitalization, and those not requiring hospitalization. It is important to note that their method is likely to produce very conservative estimates of the cost of firearm injuries because they do not include psychological costs of injuries (which one would expect to be an important component of total individual costs) and they use forgone earnings (rather than willingness-to-pay) in estimating the (lost) value of life.

Max and Rice's estimates of the average total cost per injured person for firearm injuries are shown in Table 15.1. They also found that fatal injuries resulted in an average decrease in life of 35.7 years per injured person, nonfatal injuries that required hospitalization reduced the average longevity of the injured person by 2.87 years, whereas injuries that did not require hospitalization led to a 0.01-year reduction.

The Transport Research Laboratory Estimate of the Cost of Serious Road Injuries

In 1989, the United Kingdom Department of Transport commissioned a number of studies of the cost of serious road accidents. These studies adopted a *WTP* approach.[13] Two random samples of households were drawn: one using standard contingent valuation procedures and the other using "standard gamble" questions. The contingent valuation questions asked respondents how much they would be willing to pay for a hypothetical safety feature that would reduce the risk of given injuries by a specific amount and that had to be purchased annually.

In the standard gamble format, respondents were asked to suppose that they had suffered a road injury, which, if treated in the standard way, would have a given prognosis. They were then asked to suppose that an alternative treatment would return them to normal health if successful—a result that is better than that produced by the standard treatment—but which, if unsuccessful, would result in a prognosis worse than that associated with the standard treatment. As described in Chapter 17, the purpose of such questions is to determine the risk of treatment failure at which they would be indifferent between accepting and rejecting the treatment.

The researchers found that the contingent valuation questions produced estimates that were between 1.5 and 10.5 times higher than the standard gamble method. They conclude that, in this case, the standard gamble estimates are superior.[14] As a result of this work, the U.K. Department of Transport established a figure of £74,480 (in 1992 pounds) for the cost of a "serious" nonfatal road accident including all economic costs, which is about $145,000 in 1999 dollars.

Conclusion on Cost of Injuries

The Rice and MacKenzie estimates are least useful for injuries that eventually prove fatal, as monetary costs are likely to be only a small fraction of total social costs. However, their estimate of the cost of hospitalization for injuries is not much lower than Viscusi's upper-bound estimate in equivalent-year dollars.

In Table 15.1, motor vehicle crash injury costs are reported in dollars and as a fraction of the value of life. This illustrates the alternative method of reporting injury costs. The 1.08 coefficient for fatal crashes indicates that if a relatively conservative estimate of the value of life is used (in this case Miller's value of life), motor vehicle crashes resulting in death can produce costs that are higher than "average" value-of-life estimates.

THE COST OF CRIME

Many programs in criminal justice and education have as one of their projected impacts the reduction of crime among the "treated" population. In order to estimate the benefits of such programs, it is first necessary to estimate the number of crimes of each type that will be avoided during each time period. Suppose N_{it} denotes the number of crimes of type i avoided in period t and C_i denotes the value of each crime type avoided. The benefits of avoided crime are the sum of the discounted value of N_{it} times C_i. Ideally, N_{it} is estimated using an experimental design as described in Chapter 11, which is expensive because one is interested in the number of crimes avoided over an extended period. Additionally, one must estimate C_i. Here it is quite common to use estimates from secondary sources.

We provide evidence from two sources that are summarized in Table 15.2: estimates of victim costs of violent crimes by Ted Miller, Mark Cohen, and Shelli Rossman and estimates of the monetary costs of a variety of different crimes by David Long, Charles Mallar, and Craig Thornton.[15]

TABLE 15.2   Plug-Ins for Cost of Crime (in 1999 U.S. dollars)

VICTIM COST OF CRIME

1) Rape	1) $81,200 per rape ($63,700)	Based on Miller, Cohen, and Rossman (1993). Excludes criminal justice system costs. Pertains only to crimes that included some physical injury. Numbers in parentheses include attempted crimes and the cost of murder.
2) Robbery	2) $33,500 per robbery ($26,200)	
3) Assault	3) $30,000 per assault ($19,800)	
4) Arson	4) $66,700 per arson ($33,200)	
5) Murder	5) $3,207,100 per murder	

MONETARY COST OF CRIME

1) Robbery	1) $35,000 per robbery	Based on Long, Mallar, and Thornton (1981). Relatively old study but good methodology, although excludes productivity losses and reduction in quality of life.
2) Burglary	2) $16,200 per burglary	
3) Larceny	3) $7,200 per larceny	
4) Drugs	4) $7,200 per drug crime	
5) Assault	5) $7,500 per assault	
6) Murder	6) $68,100 per murder	

The Miller and Colleagues' Estimate of the Cost of Violent Crime

Ted Miller and his colleagues provide two sets of estimates of the cost of violent crimes. The first set in Table 15.2, pertains to actually *completed crimes* of rape, robbery, assault, and arson that result in injury but do not involve murder. Crimes that do involve loss of life (murder) are a separate category. These numbers are essentially victim costs per crime. The second set, which is in parentheses, includes *attempted crimes*, again for each crime category, but also allocates murders to each category (primarily to assaults). These numbers are also victim costs per crime.

Miller et al. focus on the injury costs that result from these crimes. Specifically, their estimates incorporate the following three components: (1) the direct costs of crime-related injuries such as medical care and emergency response services, (2) costs resulting from forgone productivity (estimated as forgone earnings, forgone fringe benefits, and the value of forgone housework), and (3) costs resulting from reductions in the quality of life (mental health problems, pain and suffering, etc.). Their estimates do not include property damage, legal costs, and employer costs. Focusing on injuries captures most of the social cost associated with rape, robbery, assault, and murder. However, it is unlikely to provide a realistic estimate of the social cost of arson because much of the cost of this crime is property damage (many arsons involve no physical injury).

Long, Mallar, and Thornton's Estimates of the Monetary Cost of Crime

David Long, Charles Mallar, and Craig Thornton estimated shadow prices for a wide variety of crimes, including murder, assault, robbery, burglary, larceny, motor vehicle theft, and drug violations. They estimated three major components of crime cost: criminal justice system costs, the costs of personal injury and property damage, and losses associated with stolen property. Criminal justice system cost estimates were based on the probability and cost of each arrested person passing through the various stages of the criminal justice system: police custody, arraignment, detention, trial, and incarceration. Personal injury medical costs and property damage costs were estimated from data collected in the National Crime Panel Survey. Specifically, the cost per victimization was multiplied by the ratio of victimizations to arrests to estimate a "per capita arrest cost." The value of stolen property was estimated as follows. The researchers found that thieves were only able to realize 35 percent of the value of stolen goods. The researchers, therefore, treated 35 percent of the value of stolen goods as a transfer (from property owners to thieves) and multiplied the dollar value of stolen property by 0.65 (1–0.35) to estimate the social cost of stolen property. One could certainly argue, however, that it is inappropriate to give thieves standing. Long, Mallar, and Thornton do not include pain and suffering, productivity losses, or victims' willingness-to-pay to avoid crime.

As can be seen in Table 15.2, the estimated cost of murder varies dramatically depending on methodology and included costs. Using the Long-Mallar-Thornton approach leads to a much lower estimate of the per victim cost of murder than that of Miller. The Long-Mallar-Thornton approach illustrates the weakness of including only monetary costs. Ironically, murder may have quite low monetary costs: Perpetrators often plead guilty, thereby reducing criminal justice costs, and the medical costs of murder are low compared to other crimes that can often result in long medical treatments.

Because the estimates of the cost of crime cover different crimes, we summarize both studies in Table 15.2. The only cases in which there is more than one estimate for the same crime are robbery and murder. The two estimates for robbery are extremely close in same-year dollars.

THE VALUE OF TIME

Time is a valuable commodity; as the saying goes, "time is money." Time spent traveling, which individuals would be willing to pay to avoid, is a cost. Change in travel time is an important component of many CBAs, most obviously those concerned with transportation. Though rarely a dominating cost or benefit, change in waiting time can nonetheless be important in many nontransportation projects. For example, queuing time is an important cost component of policies that ration goods such as gasoline or access to services such as motor vehicle registration, medical care, or social services.

Almost all of the empirical literature on the value of time has been concerned with estimating the value of travel time. This is normally referred to as the *value of travel time savings* (*VTTS*), reflecting the fact that many transportation projects save time. We use this terminology, even though in other CBAs time may be expended, not saved. Also keep in mind that travel time savings may only provide a rough guide to the value of other time savings; for example, people usually experience considerably greater disutility from waiting time than from "pure" travel time.[16]

The large body of empirical literature on *VTTS* has been reviewed by several authors, mostly on a country-specific or regional basis. Typically, these have been commissioned by the relevant government and have led to the adoption of a standard *VTTS* for a country. For example, there have been reviews of the *VTTS* evidence in the United Kingdom, Canada, New Zealand, the Netherlands, the United States, and for developing countries.[17] In most cases, *VTTS* is expressed as a proportion of the before-tax or after-tax wage rate, as we discuss later. This allows analysts to readily estimate travel time costs using local wage rates. This is the approach we adopt in Table 15.3.

We primarily rely here on a review of the literature by William G. Waters II.[18] Waters reviewed the estimates of *VTTS* from 56 empirical studies conducted between 1974 and 1990. These studies comprise both revealed preference approaches and contingent valuation studies. Revealed preference approaches include a wide range of situations: route choice decisions in which there are different costs (e.g., toll roads versus nontoll roads); mode choice decisions (bus or car travel versus faster, but more costly, airline travel); speed choice decisions (in which faster speeds involve higher operating costs); and location choice decisions (hedonic methods that isolate the

TABLE 15.3 Plug-Ins for Value of Travel Time Saved

1) Nonwork travel time (commuting)	1) 40% to 50% of the after-tax wage rate per hour saved	Based on Waters (1996). High variance among studies. Must adjust to apply to other uses of time.
2) Work travel time	2) 100% of the before-tax wage rate (plus benefits) per hour saved	

impact of commuting time on land values). Survey methods are increasingly being used to estimate *VTTS* because they allow researchers to gather data of direct relevance to determining willingness-to-pay.

As is the normal procedure in the *VTTS* literature, Waters presents the results as a percentage of the after-tax (hourly) wage rate rather than as a dollar figure. He found as much as a tenfold variation in estimates from his literature review. As with other estimates described in this chapter, the studies cover a wide range of circumstances. Waters partitions these studies in a number of ways. He aggregates the 32 studies that focus on commuting trips and (after eliminating some outliers) calculates the mean value at 48 percent of the after-tax wage rate with a median of 40 percent. When this is reduced to the 15 North American automobile commuting studies, Waters calculates a mean of 59 percent (54 percent with the elimination of outliers) and a median of 42 percent. The 17 non–North American auto commuting studies generate a mean of 38 percent. Waters concludes that a shadow price between 40 to 50 percent of the after-tax wage rate is appropriate for auto commuting.

This conclusion is broadly consistent with that of Herbert Mohring and his colleagues regarding all intracity transit travel time: "[W]age earners with annual incomes greater than about US$30,000 value an hour of time in intracity transit at about half their equivalent hourly wage rates."[19] Governments have usually mandated the use of rates of between 40 percent and 60 percent of the hourly wage rate in CBA. The U.S. Federal Highway Administration currently uses 60 percent as the *VTTS* for highway projects, whereas Transport Canada recommends 50 percent for nonwork time savings.[20] Based on Waters and Mohring, we suggest valuing commuters' time saved at 40 percent to 50 percent of the after-tax wage (item 1 in Table 15.3), although government agencies sometimes prescribe a higher ratio.

It is usually useful to separate travel time savings into work time, commuting time, and leisure time. *Work time is usually valued at the before-tax wage rate plus benefits, whereas leisure time is valued somewhat less than commuting time.* Again, Waters points out that valuations vary widely: The ratio of *VTTS* for work and nonwork ranges from 1:1 to over 5:1. In fact, travel for sightseeing purposes may involve no opportunity cost of time, or even provide net travel benefits, at least up to some level of travel.[21]

THE VALUE OF RECREATIONAL BENEFITS

Over the last 20 years there have been a vast number of studies that estimate the value of various kinds of recreation. These studies generally rely on the travel cost or the contingent valuation method. Recreational facilities almost always provide both use benefits and nonuse benefits. Within the category of use benefits, we include rivalrous consumption (such as hunting), direct nonrivalrous consumption (such as hiking), and indirect nonrivalrous consumption (such as watching a movie about hiking in the wilderness). Within the category of nonuse benefits, which are discussed in more detail in Chapter 9, we include pure existence value (valuing the "natural order") and altruistic existence value (such as valuing other people's use or nonuse value of wilderness).

A review of 93 recreational value studies was conducted by Cindy Sorg and John Loomis in 1984.[22] In 1992, Richard Walsh, Donn Johnson, and John McKean updated and extended this earlier study.[23] In total, Walsh and his colleagues summarized the values for 287 studies that were performed between 1968 and 1988, including the 93 earlier studies. Unfortunately, there has been no comprehensive review of studies since 1988, although there are a large number of more recent individual estimates based on more sophisticated estimation techniques. Sorg and Loomis reported all values in 1982 dollars per "activity-day." They excluded studies for which it was not possible to calculate such a value. They made several adjustments, which were approved by an expert panel, to facilitate comparisons. The major adjustments were the conversion of "value per trip" to value per activity-day; the addition of time travel costs to other travel costs for studies that had not included this element (a 30 percent upward adjustment); an adjustment for the fact that differences in travel costs alter the probability of participation—essentially the demand for specific recreational activities is more inelastic than actually estimated (the downward adjustment in predicted use ranged from zero for highly specialized activities to 30 percent for nonspecialized activities); an adjustment to include the value to out-of-state visitors, when this value had not been included and when it was deemed likely to be important as, for example, in the case of big game hunting (a 15 percent upward adjustment); and an adjustment to contingent valuation studies that had not excluded protest bids (a 15 percent upward adjustment).

In Table 15.4 we report the mean estimate for each recreational activity as estimated by Walsh and his colleagues (items 1 through 16), updated to 1999 dollars. Two notes of caution are necessary given the large number of studies reviewed: Some part of the differences between valuations of different recreational activities is due to differences in estimation methodology and some part is due to quality differences across sites. Hiking and fishing, for example, are likely to be more valuable if they take place at more beautiful sites. It is almost impossible in practice to control for such differences.

TABLE 15.4 Plug-Ins for Value of Recreational Activities (in 1999 U.S. dollars)

1) Big game hunting	1) $66 per recreational day	Based on Walsh, Johnson, and McKean (1992).
2) Small game hunting	2) $45 per recreational day	
3) Water fowl hunting	3) $52 per recreational day	
4) Cold water fishing	4) $45 per recreational day	
5) Warm water fishing	5) $351 per recreational day	
6) Salt water fishing	6) $107 per recreational day	
7) Motorized boating	7) $46 per recreational day	
8) Nonmotorized boating	8) $72 per recreational day	
9) Swimming	9) $34 per recreational day	
10) Winter sports (skiing)	10) $42 per recreational day	
11) Hiking	11) $43 per recreational day	
12) Camping	12) $28 per recreational day	
13) Sightseeing and off-road driving	13) $29 per recreational day	
14) Wilderness	14) $36 per recreational day	
15) Picnicking	15) $26 per recreational day	
16) Total average	16) $49 per recreational day	

EXISTENCE VALUE OF SPECIES

Literature surveys of existence value estimates are not yet available. Most studies provide estimates for specific activities or species, such as preservation of the bald eagle, the striped shiner, or the Californian condor.[24] Thomas Stevens, Jaime Echeverria, Ronald Glass, Tim Hager, and Thomas More provide relatively recent estimates of the average willingness-to-pay per person per year for four wildlife species reintroduced into New England.[25] These estimates are summarized in 1999 dollars in Table 15.5, along with other environmental values that are discussed later. The coyote is especially interesting because it has positive existence value to some persons (item 4, coyote preservation) and negative value to others (item 5, coyote control). Although we present these estimates of existence value, it is important to emphasize that both the concept of existence value and the methods used to estimate existence value (contingent valuation) have been seriously questioned.[26] On the other hand, there is no alternative.

TABLE 15.5 Plug-Ins for Value of Environmental Impacts (in 1999 U.S. dollars)

EXISTENCE VALUE OF SPECIES

1) Bald eagle	1) $26 per person per year	Based on Stevens, Echeverria, Glass, Hager, and More (1991).
2) Wild turkey	2) $16 per person per year	
3) Salmon	3) $10 per person per year	
4) Coyote preservation	4) $7 per person per year	
5) Coyote control	5) $6 per person per year	

WATER QUALITY IMPROVEMENTS

1) From unusable to boatable	1) $8 to $56 per year per household	Based on Luken, Johnson, and Kibler (1992).
2) From boatable to rough fishing	2) $12 to $48 per year per household	
3) From rough fishing to game fishing	3) $16 to $40 per year per household	
4) From game fishing to superior game fishing	4) $19 to $33 per year per household	
5) From unusable to superior game fishing	5) $40 to $144 per year per household	

COST OF NOISE

1) Residential properties	1) 0.65% reduction in value per NEF	Based on Uyeno, Hamilton, and Biggs (1993). Consistent with previous studies.
2) Condominiums	2) 0.90% reduction in value per NEF	
3) Vacant land	3) 1.66% reduction in value per NEF	

TABLE 15.5 *(cont.)*

COST OF AIR POLLUTION

1) PM10	1) $25 to $70 ($40) per person per year per microgram per m^3	Based on Krupnick's (1995) Monte Carlo simulations. Numbers in parentheses are central estimates directly computed from coefficient estimates.
2) Lead	2) $5.3 to $16.5 ($9.8) per person per year per .01 micrograms per m^3	
3) SO_2	3) $1.3 to $23.4 ($10.7) per person per year per microgram per m^3	
4) Ozone	4) $4.0 to $11.0 ($9.4) per person per year per .01 parts per million	

COST OF AIR POLLUTION

1) VOCs	1) $3,500 per ton per year	Based on Small and Kazimi (1995). Estimates reflect only health care costs of pollutants emitted by motor vehicles. These numbers are upper bounds for urban areas.
2) NO_x	2) $12,700 per ton per year	
3) SO_x	3) $130,500 per ton per year	
4) PM10	4) $121,100 per ton per year	

BENEFITS OF WATER QUALITY IMPROVEMENTS

A variety of methods has been used to estimate the benefits of improvements in water quality for recreational, drinking, or for other purposes, including contingent valuation surveys, the market analogy method, defensive expenditures, and the travel cost method.[27] Table 15.5 summarizes shadow prices (annual household willingness-to-pay) for water quality improvements made by Ralph Luken, F. Reed Johnson, and Virginia Kibler who drew on previous studies of the Monongahela River.[28] These estimates are based on local recreation use and, therefore, should be limited to the relevant recreational market. Luken-Johnson-Kibler argue for 30 miles as an upper bound in defining the relevant markets for such recreational sites. They also recommend using visitation rates for households within this distance that range from 50 percent for sites with few substitutes to 10 percent for sites with numerous substitutes.

EXHIBIT 15.1

Ralph Luken wished to estimate the costs and benefits of (technology-based) water pollution standards introduced by the Clean Water Act of 1972. However, there were no existing estimates of *WTP* for improvements in the water quality of the rivers in question. Therefore, he utilized *WTP* estimates from existing studies as a basis for his estimates of the value of improvements in water quality.

He initially considered eight existing studies that might provide plug-in values. Five of the existing studies used the contingent valuation method, two studies used the travel cost method, and the eighth study was a user participation study. Luken eliminated five of the studies because their focus was not similar to the sites he was considering. These five studies dealt with water systems, such as those on a large western lake and a western river basin. His sites, in contrast, were generally eastern rivers with local recreation usage. Therefore, he focused on three studies: one on the Charles River in Boston and two on the Monongahela River in Pennsylvania. The Monongahela studies estimated benefits for three levels of improvement in water quality (from boating to fishing, from fishing to swimming, and from boating to swimming), whereas the Charles River study only examined improvements in water quality from boating to swimming (i.e., the biggest "jump" in quality). The summarized values as annual *WTP* per household (1984 dollars) are as follows:

	Water Quality Change		
River	*Boat–Fish*	*Fish–Swim*	*Boat–Swim*
Monongahela (contingent valuation)	$25–40	$14–23	$40–64
Monongahela (travel cost)	$8	$10	$18
Charles (contingent valuation)	—	—	$74

Unfortunately, these benefit categories did not directly map into the benefit categories Luken was using, which covered five quality improvement levels: *U* = Unusable, *B* = Boatable, *R* = Rough fishing, *G* = Game fishing, and *G** = Superior game fishing. Luken assumed that the travel cost method estimates provided lower-bound estimates (because they include only use valuations) and the contingent valuation estimates provided upper-bound estimates (as they include nonuse as well as use valuations). As shown next, he also included intrause estimates to reflect smaller benefit improvements. His plug-in values for water quality benefits (willingness-to-pay per household per year in 1984 dollars) follow:

Initial Water Quality	*Final Water Quality*	*Lower Bound*	*Upper Bound*
U	U	$1–3	$9–18
U	B	$5	$35
U	R	$15	$50
U	G	$20	$80
U	G*	$25	$90
B	B	$2–4	$8–15
B	R	$8	$30
B	G	$15	$50
B	G*	$20	$60
R	R	$3–5	$6–13
R	G	$10	$25
R	G*	$15	$35
G	G	$3–6	$5–10
G	G*	$12	$20

Although the purpose of this exhibit is to illustrate the use of secondary sources, it is interesting to note that in using these values, Luken generally found that costs exceed benefits.

Sources: Frederick W. Gramlick, "The Demand for Clear Water: The Case of the Charles River," *National Tax Journal,* 30, no. 2 (1977), 183–195; Ralph A. Luken, *Efficiency in Environmental Regulation* (Boston: Kluwer Academic Publishers, 1990), pp. 45–50, pp. 88–90; V. Kerry Smith and William H. Desvousges, *Measuring Water Quality Benefits* (Boston: Kluwer-Nijhoff Publishing, 1986); V. Kerry Smith, William H. Desvousges, and Ann Fisher, "A Comparison of Direct and Indirect Methods for Estimating Environmental Benefits," Working Paper No. 83-W32, Vanderbilt University, Nashville, TN, 1984.

THE COST OF NOISE

Cost of noise estimates are mostly relevant in the evaluation of transportation projects. The dominant method for estimating the cost of noise is the hedonic pricing method using differences in property values, usually those of private residences. Noise is measured in units of *NEF*s (ambient noise is in the 15–25 *NEF* range, "some" to "much" annoyance occurs in the 25–40 *NEF* range, and "considerable" annoyance occurs above 40 *NEF*s).

Since a survey by Jon Nelson in 1980, there have been relatively few studies of the cost of noise.[29] We report more recent estimates from a study by Dean Uyeno, Stan Hamilton, and Andrew Biggs.[30] Uyeno-Hamilton-Biggs specify a semi-log hedonic price function in which the price of a house (in logarithms) is a linear function of noise (in *NEF*s) and other house quality characteristics. The estimated slope of this function with respect to noise (multiplied by -100) measures the "noise depreciation sensitivity index" (*NDSI*).[31] The *NDSI* can be interpreted as an estimate of the percentage reduction in the value of a house resulting from a one-unit increase in the noise level (measured in *NEF*s). Uyeno-Hamilton-Biggs estimate that the *NDSI* was 0.65 percent for detached houses with *NEF*s of 25 or higher. In other words, if the noise level increases by 1 *NEF*, then the price of an affected house decreases in value by 0.65 percent on average. Thus, houses adjacent to an airport with *NEF*s of 40 are priced 9.75 percent lower than houses further from the airport with *NEF*s of 25. This *NDSI* is broadly consistent with previous studies, leading the authors to conclude that "the similarity of results spanning several decades and several Western countries would seem to suggest a broad and long-lived consensus on the issue (of the impact of airport noise on property values) . . .".[32] Because of this consensus, Table 15.5 provides only the Uyeno-Hamilton-Biggs estimate.

THE COST OF AIR POLLUTION

Air pollution results in both health costs and nonhealth costs. The health cost of air pollution includes the costs of premature death and the costs of morbidity.[33] Nonhealth costs that result from air pollution include deforestation, retarded plant growth and reduced agricultural output, coastal erosion, damage to materials such as rubber, property losses, and losses of views. Air pollutants are emitted from many sources, especially motor vehicles, industrial plants, and power plants.[34] Important pollutants are volatile organic compounds (VOCs), nitrogen oxides (NO_x), sulfur oxides (SO_x), carbon oxides (CO_x), chlorofluorocarbons (CFCs), and particulate matter of less than 10 microns in diameter (PM10). VOCs combine with NO_x to produce ozone, which is a primary contributor to morbidity (illness). Through chemical reactions SO_x, VOCs, and NO_x produce PM10s, which cause both premature death and morbidity, especially respiratory diseases. The solution of SO_x and NO_x in cloud and rain droplets causes acid rain, which is known to damage pine and spruce forests, and is thought to damage tobacco, wheat, and soya crops. Acid rain also damages buildings, increases the acidification of lakes, and affects fish populations.[35] CFCs cause significant depletion to the ozone layer, which increases exposure to ultraviolet radiation and can damage crops and cause skin cancer as well as cataracts. The accumulation of carbon dioxide and other gases (including NO_x and CFCs) causes global warming.[36]

One approach to measuring the costs of damage associated with air pollution is to use dose response functions that relate unit increases in each pollutant to various health effects. They can, for example, be related to increases in the probability of premature death and increases in different types of respiratory problems. These effects are then weighted by dollar valuations, which are usually based on *WTP* estimates. A very different and frequently used approach involves the estimation of hedonic property value models.

We review three sets of estimates. Alan Krupnick provides recent estimates of the annual health costs per person attributable to PM10, sulfur dioxide, lead, and ozone, based on dose response functions.[37] In 1995, V. Kerry Smith and Ju-Chin Huang conducted a meta-analysis of 86 hedonic property value estimates based on 37 different studies conducted between 1967 and 1988.[38] Kenneth Small and Camilla Kazimi recently reported estimates of the annual costs of adding one ton of various pollutants for the Los Angeles area.[39]

The Krupnick Monte Carlo Estimates

Krupnick's estimates include both morbidity and mortality costs, except for SO_2, which includes only mortality costs. With the exception of ozone, mortality costs dominate. The per person per year ranges reported in Table 15.5 (items 1 through 4) may be viewed as 95 percent confidence intervals derived from Monte Carlo simulations, whereas the numbers in parentheses are point estimates directly computed from estimated coefficients.

The Smith and Huang Meta-Analysis

Each of the studies analyzed by Smith and Huang attempted to measure the impact of a one-unit change in total suspended particulates on the asset value of a typical house in one or more cities. The mean estimate is $183 per house per microgram per cubic meter (in 1999 dollars). However, Smith and Huang note that this value is substantially inflated due to a few outliers; the median value of the 86 estimates is only $37 per house per microgram per cubic meter. The variation in the estimates partially reflects the fact that they are for different cities, are estimated with different data, pertain to different time periods, and are based on different models and estimation techniques. Smith-Huang suggest that although the hedonic estimates partially reflect perceived health effects from pollution, they are probably more strongly influenced by "aesthetics, materials and soiling effects."[40] Indeed, they provide evidence that suggests that the dose response function approach results in much larger estimates of costs resulting from air pollution than does the hedonic property value approach. The Smith-Huang estimate is not presented in Table 15.5 as its hedonic value cannot be normally used directly as a plug-in.

The Small and Kazimi Estimates of the Health Care Costs of Pollutants from Vehicles

Unlike estimates of the value of a life or the cost of a crime, estimates of the cost of pollution on a per particulate unit basis are difficult to grasp intuitively and, for some purposes, may not provide a very convenient shadow price. Thus, Table 15.5 also presents estimates of the annual cost of adding one ton of various types of pollutants to the air.

The Small and Kazimi estimates are limited to health costs resulting from pollutants emitted by motor vehicles, costs that perhaps constitute the bulk of the costs engendered by air pollution in many urban areas. Their estimates imply that adding a ton of either SO_x or PM10 to the air is much more costly than adding a ton of either VOCs or NO_x. Moreover, consistent with Krupnick's estimates, Small and Kazimi's findings indicate that most of the costs of air pollution result from premature death rather than from illness. Because the locus of their study, the Los Angeles basin, is especially conducive to chemical reactions that produce pollutants and the area's mountain barriers are notorious for trapping pollutants, comparable values for other cities in the United States would be much smaller.

Like Krupnick's estimates, Small and Kazimi's estimates are based on dose response functions, dollar valuations of the various morbidity effects of pollution, and an estimate of the value of life. Their baseline cost estimates assume a value of life of about $5.6 million (in 1999 U.S. dollars). Earlier we suggested that a value about two-thirds as high may be more appropriate.[41] Use of this smaller value would cause the mortality cost estimates to fall proportionately. Small and Kazimi's estimates also require a value for the amount of ambient PM10 concentration in the air in Los Angeles. They use 57.8 micrograms per cubic meter, which is based on annual readings for downtown Los Angeles. As already suggested, this value is likely to be much higher for Los Angeles than for most other urban areas. Use of a smaller value would also cause Small and Kazimi's baseline estimates to fall proportionately.

Small and Kazimi also estimate the pollution cost of driving a motor vehicle one mile. Their baseline estimate is about 3 cents per vehicle-mile for a typical automobile (or roughly 53 to 63 cents per gallon) and 56 cents per vehicle-mile for a heavy-duty diesel truck driven in Los Angeles. These costs were predicted to fall to 1.9 cents and 42 cents (in 1999 dollars), respectively, by the year 2000 as newer, less polluting vehicles replaced older vehicles. Comparable costs in other cities would be much smaller.

THE COST OF TAXATION: MARGINAL EXCESS TAX BURDEN

Government projects often involve expenditures that have to be financed through taxes. As discussed in Chapter 4, taxes typically result in a deadweight loss—the marginal excess tax burden (METB). This loss or "leakage" occurs whenever there is a behavioral response to a tax—for example, an excise tax on a good causes purchases to fall or a tax on earnings causes workers to reduce their work hours. The marginal social value of the lost consumption or lost work is the deadweight loss of the tax. Important manifestations of the deadweight loss include the inefficient substitution of leisure for work, of barter for legal trade, and the search for tax loopholes. METBs vary according to the type of tax. In general, METBs are greater when the taxed activity is more elastic. The METBs from income taxes are higher than the METBs from property taxes and sales taxes.

Quite a few studies provide estimates of METB for specific taxes and countries, usually by assuming "reasonable" values of key parameters and then simulating the efficiency costs. Table 15.6 provides a range of estimates from the United States for a number of important tax "types": all taxes, income taxes, sales taxes, and property taxes. The ranges are derived from Charles Ballard, John Shoven, and John Whalley and from

TABLE 15.6 Plug-Ins for Marginal Excess Tax Burden per Dollar of Revenue		
1) All taxes	1) $0.33 to $0.46	Lower values generally drawn from Ballard, Shoven, and Whalley (1985); higher values from Jorgenson and Yun (1990).
2) Sales tax	2) $0.11 to $0.39	
3) Income tax	3) $0.31 to $0.56	
4) Property tax	4) $0.17	

Dale Jorgenson and Kun-Young Yun, with the former generally obtaining lower estimates than the latter.[42] Ballard-Shoven-Whalley estimate the METB for all taxes combined is 33 cents per dollar, assuming the uncompensated saving elasticity is 0.4 and the uncompensated labor supply elasticity is 0.15. Using similar assumptions, Jorgenson-Yun estimate the METB for all taxes is 46 cents per dollar.

W. Erwin Diewert and Denis Lawrence provide estimates of the METB for different sectors in New Zealand.[43] Their estimated METBs for 1991 were $0.14 for general consumption taxation and $0.18 for labor taxation, which are lower than the values obtained for the United States. Interestingly, they find that for automobiles the METB is positive, implying that taxing automobiles has a benefit. The intuition behind this result is that taxing automobiles reduces pollution and other negative externalities.

Which METB is relevant to CBA? With respect to federal projects in the United States, it is probably reasonable to view income taxes as the marginal tax source, suggesting that the appropriate METB would be about $0.40. With respect to local government projects, the marginal tax source is more reasonably viewed as the property tax, which has an METB of around $0.17.

TRANSFERRING AND ADJUSTING PLUG-IN VALUES

Most of the estimates discussed in this chapter are averages, based on many studies. For example, the per-day values of recreational activities are averages based on a survey of over 200 articles. Ideally, these values should be adjusted depending on the specifics of a particular application.[44] Here we briefly review four sets of relevant factors: (1) differences in socioeconomic and other personal characteristics of the population (e.g., income and age), (2) differences in physical and other characteristics of the jurisdiction (e.g., geographic characteristics), (3) differences in the characteristics of the project itself (e.g., project quality), and (4) temporal changes.

Income and Other Socioeconomic Factors

It is often important to make adjustments due to socioeconomic differences or preference differences among different populations. Perhaps the most important variable is income; higher-income people can and do place higher values on their lives and other goods. Thus, they value their travel time savings more than lower-income people[45] and people in wealthy districts value the effect of pollution on house prices proportionately more than those in poor districts.[46] Air travelers who, on average, have higher incomes place higher (implicit) value on their lives.[47]

Thus, both evidence and economic theory suggest that shadow price estimates should be adjusted upward for projects that affect people with higher than average incomes and should be adjusted downward for projects that affect people with lower than average incomes. On the other hand, arguments in favor of the use of distributional weights in cost-benefit analysis, as described in Chapter 18, suggest that the costs and benefits of people in lower income groups should receive greater weight than those of higher income groups. In view of these conflicting considerations, it is probably reasonable to use population values.

Waters has examined how estimates vary with income, time (year of study), country, and trip purpose (interurban versus commuting or "other").[48] He finds that *VTTS* increases with income but less than proportionately:

$$VTTS_Y = \left(\frac{Y}{\overline{Y}}\right)^{0.5} \overline{VTTS} \qquad \textbf{(15.1)}$$

where $VTTS_Y$ is the *VTTS* of a traveler with income Y, $\overline{Y}$ is the average income level, and $\overline{VTTS}$ is the average *VTTS*. He suggests that a convenient rule of thumb for the relationship is a square root rule. Using such a rule, the *VTTS* rises more slowly than does income. For example, if income goes up fourfold from the average, the *VTTS* only doubles.

The relationship between *VTTS* and other variables appears to be weak. Waters found that *VTTS* increases over time (drifting upward at one percentage point per year) and that interurban travel has a slightly higher value than trips for other purposes.

For the most part, the estimates discussed here are based on U.S. research (and, indeed, sometimes on specific regions). Differences in incomes and tastes bring into question the appropriateness of using these estimates to analyze projects in other countries. Although there are no established rules of thumb to provide guidance, analysts should consider modifying them to take account of differences in other countries that affect *WTP*. For example, it would be reasonable to assume that the cost of injuries or crime is lower in Spain than in the United States, given differences in incomes and, possibly, preferences.

Preferences may also differ from one region to another or from one occupational group to another. People who live near airports may object less than others to aircraft noise, people who live in polluted areas may not value changes in air quality as much as people who live in areas with better air quality, and people who work in dangerous jobs may have greater propensity for risk than the average worker. Such differences in preferences affect how much people are willing to pay for particular policy effects.

Physical Characteristics

The second set of factors that may affect the transferability of plug-in values is physical and other characteristics of a region. For example, the impact of air pollution varies widely geographically, depending on population density, climate, and topography. More people are affected in more densely populated areas. *Ceteris paribus,* the greater precipitation in Vancouver means that the morbidity costs of NO_x or particulate matter are lower there than in Los Angeles.

The current level of a good in a region may affect the value of changes in the amount of that good. In general, holding all other factors constant, people are willing to pay more (less) for safety-improving projects as the level of safety decreases (increases). Consequently, the value of life used in a project that saves lives in a "high-risk" area should be higher than the value of life used in a project that saves lives in a "low-risk" area, holding all other relevant factors constant.

Project Differences

The third set of factors pertains to the similarity between the policy under evaluation and the projects in the studies used to derive the plug-in values. For example, the value of water quality improvement obtained from studies involving small improvements in quality levels may not apply to a proposed policy that would involve a large change in the level of water quality. The magnitude of the error in the generalization depends on the degree of nonlinearity in the relationship between water quality improvements and willingness-to-pay. Additionally, there may be important differences in the price and availability of substitutes, which, if not accounted for, can cause biases.[49] In sum, policies or projects under evaluation should ideally be similar to the projects in the studies used to derive the plug-in values in terms of the availability and quality of alternatives.

Temporal Changes

The final set of factors that should be considered involves those relating to the fact that valuations may change over time. Technological change, as well as temporal changes in population characteristics or jurisdictional characteristics, may affect the plug-in estimates. For example, increasing incomes and declining supply of accessible recreational areas might increase the value of such activities, whereas increasing congestion at the sites might decrease the value of such activities. Implicitly, by updating all of the original estimates using the composite CPI index, we assume no change in the relative shadow price of each activity since the original study was performed.

CONCLUSION

By making use of the plug-in values presented in this chapter, analysts can apply CBA to a wider range of policies than would be feasible if all shadow prices had to be estimated firsthand. When resources are available, analysts can make their own estimates and check them against those reported here.

Exercises for Chapter 15

1. A 40-mile stretch of rural road with limited access is used primarily by regional commuters and business travelers to move between two major interstate highways. The legal speed limit on the road is currently 55 miles per hour (mph) and the estimated average speed is 61 mph. Traffic engineers predict that if the speed limit were raised to 65 mph and enforcement levels were kept constant, the average speed would rise to 70 mph.

   Currently, an average of 5,880 vehicles per day use the stretch of road. Approximately half are commuters and half are business travelers. Traffic engineers do not expect that a higher speed limit will attract more vehicles. Vehicles using the road carry, on average, 1.6 people. Traffic engineers predict that raising the speed limit on this stretch of road would result in an additional 52 vehicle crashes involving, on average, 0.1 fatalities annually. They also predict that operating costs would rise by an average of $0.002 per mile per vehicle.

The average hourly wage in the county in which the majority of users of the road work is $12.20/hour.

Estimate the annual net benefits of raising the speed limit on the road from 55 mph to 65 mph. In doing this, test the sensitivity of your estimate of annual net benefits to several alternative estimates of the value of time savings and the value of life that you have selected from the chapter.

2. Analysts estimate that the expansion of the capacity of the criminal courts in a city would require about 7,200 additional hours of juror time. The average wage rate in the county is $10/hour. A recent survey by the jury commissioner, however, found that the average wage for those who actually serve on juries under the present system, who are also currently employed, is only $6/hour. The survey also found that about one-third of those who actually serve on juries under the existing system do not hold jobs—for example, they are homemakers, retirees, or unemployed.

    a. What shadow price should the analysts use for an hour of jury time?

    b. About a quarter of jurors do not receive wages from their employers while on jury duty. How does this affect your choice of the shadow price?

Notes

1. This chapter draws upon Anthony E. Boardman, David H. Greenberg, Aidan R. Vining, and David L. Weimer, "Plug-In Shadow Price Estimates for Policy Analysis," *Annals of Regional Science*, 31, no. 3 (1997), 299–324.

2. For example, Tae Hoon Oum, W. G. Waters II, and Jong-Say Yong surveyed over 60 studies of own-price elasticities of transport demand, "Concepts of Price Elasticities of Transport Demand and Recent Empirical Estimates: An Interpretative Essay," *Journal of Transport Economics and Policy*, 26, no. 2 (1992), 139–154. A companion survey by Philip Goodwin reviews empirical estimates of public transit and auto usage, "A Review of New Demand Elasticities with Special Reference to Short and Long Run Effects of Price Changes," *Journal of Transport Economics and Policy*, 26, no. 2 (1992), 155–169.

3. For example, on gasoline demand, see Molly Espey, "Explaining the Variation in Elasticity Estimates of Gasoline Demand in the United States: A Meta-Analysis," *Energy Journal*, 17, no. 3 (1996), 49–60, and Molly Espey, "Gasoline Demand Revisited: An International Meta-Analysis of Elasticities," *Energy Economics*, 20, no. 3 (1998), 273–295.

4. For example, one recent study suggests that transportation and communications are substitutes. See E. A. Selvanathan and Saroja Selvanathan, "The Demand for Transport and Communication in the United Kingdom and Australia," *Transportation Research—B*, 28, no. 1 (1994), 1–9.

5. For our purpose, *value* and *cost* can be used interchangeably, but we stick with common nomenclature—that is, we refer to "the value of (a lost) life" and "the cost of injury."

6. Ted R. Miller, *Narrowing the Plausible Range Around the Value of Life* (Washington, DC: The Urban Institute, 1989); Ann Fisher, Lauraine G. Chestnut, and Daniel M. Violette, "The Value of Reducing Risks to Death: A Note on New Evidence," *Journal of Policy Analysis and Management*, 8, no. 1 (1989), 88–100; W. Kip Viscusi, "The Value of Risks to Life and Health," *Journal of Economic Literature*, 31, no. 4 (1993), 1912–1946.

7. This is analogous to the dichotomous-choice method discussed in Chapter 14. With the dichotomous-choice method, this problem is dealt with by offering different individuals different prices. This does not normally occur in markets.

8. Scott E. Atkinson and Robert Halverson, "The Valuation of Risks to Life: Evidence from the Market for Automobiles," *Review of Economics and Statistics*, 72, no. 1 (1990), 332–340.

9. Dorothy P. Rice, Ellen J. MacKenzie, and Associates, *Cost of Injury in the United States: A Report to Congress* (San Francisco, CA: Institute for Health and Aging, University of California and

Injury Prevention Center, The Johns Hopkins University, 1989).

10. Wendy Max and Dorothy P. Rice, "Shooting in the Dark: Estimating the Costs of Firearm Injuries," *Health Affairs*, 12, no. 4 (1993), 171–185.

11. Ted R. Miller, "Costs and Functional Consequences of U.S. Roadway Crashes," *Accident Analysis and Prevention*, 25, no. 5 (1993), 593–607.

12. Ascribed by Miller, *Narrowing the Plausible Range Around the Value of Life*, 1993, p. 605, to Ezra Hauer (no cite).

13. The studies are summarized in Deirdre O'Reilly, Jean Hopkin, Graham Loomes, Michael Jones-Lee, Peter Philips, Kate McMahon, Dawn Ives, Barbara Sobey, David Ball, and Ray Kemp, "The Value of Road Safety: U.K. Research on the Value of Preventing Non-Fatal Injuries," *Journal of Transport Economics and Policy*, 28, no. 1 (1994), 45–60.

14. For their reasoning, see O'Reilly et al., "The Value of Road Safety," pp. 52–53.

15. Ted R. Miller, Mark A. Cohen, and Shelli Rossman, "Victim Costs of Violent Crime and Resulting Injuries," *Health Affairs*, 12, no. 4 (1993), 186–197; David A. Long, Charles D. Mallar, and Craig V. Thornton, "Evaluating the Benefits and Costs of the Jobs Corps," *Journal of Policy Analysis and Management*, 1, no. 1 (1981), 55–76.

16. Herbert Mohring, John Schroeter, and Paitoon Wiboonchutikula, "The Values of Waiting Time, Travel Time, and a Seat on a Bus," *Rand Journal of Economics*, 18, no. 1 (1987), 40–56.

17. United Kingdom: C. Sharp, "Developments in Transport Policy, The Value of Time Savings and of Accident Prevention," *Journal of Transport Economics and Policy*, 22, no. 2 (1988), 235–238; Mark Wardham, "The Value of Travel Time: A Review of British Evidence," *Journal of Transport Economics and Policy*, 32, no. 3 (1998), 285–316. Canada: J. J. Lawson, *The Value of Passenger Travel Time for Use in Economic Evaluation of Transport Investments* (Ottawa, Ontario: Transport Canada, 1989); New Zealand: Ted Miller, "The Value of Time and the Benefit of Time Saving," presented to the National Roads Board, New Zealand, and the Federal Highway Administration, U.S. Dept. of Transportation (Washington, DC: Urban Institute, 1989); The Netherlands: H. F. Gunn and C. Rohr, "The 1985–1996 Dutch Value of Time Studies," paper presented at PTRC International Conference on the Value of Time, Wokingham, U.K., 1996); Norway: Farideh Ramjerdi, Lars Rand, and Kjartan Saelensminde, *The Norwegian Value of Time Study: Some Preliminary Results* (Olso: Institute of Transport Economics); United States: Texas Transportation Institute, "Value of Time and Discomfort Costs, Progress Report on Literature Review and Assessment of Procedures and Data," Technical Memorandum for NCHRP, pp. 7–12; Miller (this footnote); Developing countries: John Bates and Stephen Glaister, "The Valuation of Time Savings for Urban Transport Appraisal for Developing Countries: A Review," report prepared for the World Bank, 1990.

18. W. G. Waters II, "Values of Travel Time Savings in Road Transport Project Evaluation," in David Hensher, J. King, and Tae Hoon Oum, eds., *World Transport Research, Proceedings of the 7th World Conference on Transport Research*, Volume 3 (New York: Elsevier, 1996).

19. Mohring, Schoreter, and Wiboonchutikula, "The Values of Waiting Time, Travel Time, and a Seat on a Bus," p. 40.

20. Waters, "Values of Travel Time Savings in Road Transport Project Evaluation," Table 2.

21. Richard G. Walsh, Larry D. Sanders, and John R. McKean, "The Consumptive Value of Travel Time on Recreation Trips," *Journal of Travel Research*, 29, no. 1 (1990), 17–24. These authors found that travelers expressed *WTP* for up to 3 hours of scenic driving in the Rockies on weekends.

22. Cindy F. Sorg and John B. Loomis, *Empirical Estimates of Amenity Forest Values: A Comparative Review*, General Technical Report RM-107 (Fort Collins, CO: Rocky Mountain Forest and Range Experiment Station, Forest Service, USDA, 1984).

23. Richard G. Walsh, Donn M. Johnson, and John R. McKean, "Benefit Transfer of Outdoor Recreation Demand Studies, 1968–1988," *Water Resources Research*, 28, no. 3 (1992), 707–713.

24. For example, see Kevin J. Boyle and Richard C. Bishop, "Valuing Wildlife in Benefit-Cost Analysis," *Water Resources Research*, 23, no. 5 (1987), 943–950.

25. Thomas H. Stevens, Jaime Echeverria, Ronald J. Glass, Tim Hager, and Thomas A. More, "Measuring the Existence Value of Wildlife," *Land Economics*, 67, no. 4 (1991), 390–400.

26. For example, see Donald H. Rosenthal and Richard H. Nelson, "Why Existence Value Should *Not* Be Used in Cost-Benefit Analysis," *Journal of Policy Analysis and Management*, 11, no. 1 (1992), 116–122, and Jerry A. Hausman, ed., *Contingent*

Valuation: A Critical Assessment (New York: North Holland, 1993)

27. For a contingent valuation survey example, see Jeffrey L. Jordan and Abdelmoneim H. Elnagheeb, "Willingness to Pay for Improvements in Water Drinking Quality," *Water Resources Research*, 29, no. 2 (1993), 237–245. Charles W. Abdalla, Brian A. Roach, and Donald J. Epp, "Valuing Environmental Quality Changes Using Averting Expenditures: An Application to Groundwater Contamination," *Land Economics*, 68, no. 2 (1992), 163–169, use both the market analogy method (observations of bottled water expenditures) and defensive expenditures (expenditures incurred in boiling or hauling water or installation of household treatment systems). A study that estimates the benefits of water quality improvements on river segments using the travel cost method is V. Kerry Smith and William H. Desvousges, *Measuring Water Quality Benefits* (Boston: Kluwer-Nijhoff Publishing, 1986).

28. Ralph Luken, F. Johnson, and V. Kibler, "Benefits and Costs of Pulp and Paper Effluent Controls Under the Clean Water Act," *Water Resources Research*, 28, no. 3 (1992), 665–674.

29. Jon P. Nelson, "Airports and Property Values: A Survey of Recent Evidence," *Journal of Transport Economics and Policy,* 14, no. 1 (1980), 37–52. Two somewhat more recent studies are Patricia H. O'Byrne, Jon P. Nelson, and Joseph J. Seneca, "Housing Values, Census Estimates, Disequilibrium and the Environmental Cost of Airport Noise: A Case Study of Atlanta," *Journal of Environmental Economics and Management*, 12, no. 2 (1985), 169–178, and G. Pennington, N. Topham, and R. Ward, "Aircraft Noise and Residential Property Values Adjacent to Manchester International Airport," *Journal of Transport Economics and Policy*, 24, no. 3 (1990), 49–59.

30. Dean Uyeno, Stanley Hamilton, and Andrew J. G. Biggs, "Density of Residential Land Use and the Impact of Airport Noise," *Journal of Transport Economics and Policy*, 27, no. 1 (1993), 3–18.

31. Specifically, $NDSI = -100 (\partial \ln H / \partial NEF)$. In contrast, the hedonic price of noise or marginal implicit price of noise is the slope of the function relating house prices, H, to noise level; that is $(\partial H / \partial NEF)$.

32. Uyeno, Hamilton, and Biggs, "Density of Residential Land Use," p. 14.

33. Dallas Burtraw, Alan Krupnick, Erin Mausur, David Austin, and Deirdre Farrell, "Costs and Benefits of Reducing Air Pollutants Related to Acid Rain," *Contemporary Economic Policy*, 16, no. 4 (1998), 379–400.

34. For more on the sources of emissions in the United States, Germany, and the United Kingdom, see David W. Pearce and R. Kerry Turner, *Economics of Natural Resources and the Environment* (Baltimore: The John Hopkins University Press, 1990), p. 192. Also see Alan J. Krupnick and Paul R. Portney, "Controlling Urban Air Pollution: A Benefit-Cost Assessment," *Science*, 252, no. 26 (1991), 522–528.

35. Pearce and Turner, *Economics of Natural Resources and the Environment.*

36. Thomas C. Schelling, "Some Economics of Global Warming," *American Economic Review*, 82, no. 1 (1992), 1–14.

37. Alan Krupnick, "The Implementation and Enforcement of the Clean Air Act Amendments of 1990," Testimony before the Subcommittees on Oversight and Investigations and on Health and the Environment of the Committee on Commerce, U.S. House of Representatives, Thursday, November 9, 1995.

38. Kerry Smith and Ju-Chin Huang, "Can Markets Value Air Quality? A Meta-Analysis of Hedonic Property Value Models," *Journal of Political Economy*, 103, no. 1 (1995), 209–227.

39. Kenneth Small and Camilla Kazimi, "On the Costs of Air Pollution From Motor Vehicles," *Journal of Transport Economics and Policy*, 29, no. 1 (1995), 7–32.

40. Smith and Huang, "Can Markets Value Air Quality?" p. 223.

41. Indeed, Alan Krupnick and Paul Portney, "Controlling Urban Air Pollution," argue that smaller value-of-life estimates than those found in the literature should be used in estimating the costs of air pollution because air pollution mainly results in the premature deaths of older persons, that is, persons with considerably shorter life expectancies than average members of the population.

42. Charles L. Ballard, John B. Shoven, and John Whalley, "General Equilibrium Computations of the Marginal Welfare Costs of Taxes in the United States," *American Economic Review*, 75, no. 1 (1985), 128–138; same authors, "The Total Welfare Cost of the United States Tax System: A General Equilibrium Approach," *National Tax Journal*, 38, no. 2 (1985), 125–140; Dale W. Jorgenson and Kun-Young Yun, "Tax Reform and U.S. Economic

Growth," *Journal of Political Economy*, 98, no. 5 (1990), S151–S193. Other studies that provide U.S. estimates include Edgar K. Browning, "On the Marginal Welfare Cost of Taxation," *American Economic Review*, 77, no. 1 (1987), 11–23 and Charles E. Stuart, "Welfare Costs per Dollar of Additional Tax Revenue in the United States," *American Economic Review*, 74, no. 3 (1984), 452–462. Estimates for Sweden are from Charles E. Stuart, "Swedish Tax Rates, Labor Supply, and Tax Revenues," *Journal of Political Economy*, 89, no. 5 (1981), 1020–1038 and Ingemar Hansson and Charles E. Stuart, "Tax Revenue and the Marginal Cost of Public Funds in Sweden," *Journal of Public Economics*, 27, no. 3 (1985), 331–353; for Canada from Harry F. Campbell, "Deadweight Loss and Commodity Taxation in Canada," *Canadian Journal of Economics*, 8, no. 3 (1975), 441–446; for Australia from Harry F. Campbell and K. Bond, "The Costs of Public Funds in Australia," *Economic Record*, 73 (1997), 28–40, and Harry F. Campbell, "Deadweight Loss and the Cost of Public Funds in Australia," *Agenda,* 4, no. 2 (1997), 231–236.

43. W. Erwin Diewert and Denis Lawrence, "The Deadweight Costs of Taxation in New Zealand," *Canadian Journal of Economics*, 29, Part 2 (1996), S658-S673.

44. For further discussion of these issues, see Kevin J. Boyle and John C. Bergstrom, "Benefit Transfer Studies: Myths, Pragmatism and Idealism," *Water Resources Research*, 28, no. 3 (1992), 657–663; William H. Desvousges, Michael C. Naughton, and George R Parsons, "Benefit Transfer: Conceptual Problems in Estimating Water Quality Benefits Using Existing Studies," *Water Resources Research*, 28, no. 3 (1992) 675–683; Kenneth E. McConnell, "Model Building and Judgment: Implications for Benefit Transfers with Travel Cost Models," *Water Resources Research*, 28, no. 3 (1992), 695–700; John B. Loomis, "The Evolution of a More Rigorous Approach to Benefit Transfer: Benefit Function Estimation," *Water Resources Research*, 28, no. 3 (1992), 701–705; Mark Downing and Teofilo Ozuna Jr., "Testing the Reliability of the Benefit Function Transfer Approach," *Journal of Environmental Economics and Management*, 30, no. 3 (1996), 316–322.

45. Waters, "The Value of Travel Time Savings and the Link with Income."

46. Smith and Huang, "Can Markets Value Air Quality?"

47. W. Kip Viscusi, "The Value of Risks to Life and Health," *Journal of Economic Literature*, 31, no. 4 (1993), 1912–1946 and W. Kip Viscusi and William N. Evans, "Utility Functions That Depend on Health Status: Estimates and Economic Implications," *American Economic Review*, 80, no. 3 (1993), 353–374.

48. W. G. Waters II, "The Value of Travel Time Savings and the Link with Income: Implications for Public Project Evaluation."

49. Stephanie Kirchhoff, Bonnie G. Colbey, and Jeffrey T. LaFrance, "Evaluating the Performance of Benefit Transfer: An Empirical Inquiry," *Journal of Environmental Economics and Management*, 33, no. 1 (1997), 75–93.

16 ‖ SHADOW PRICES

Applications to Developing Countries

Why does this book contain a separate chapter on cost-benefit analysis in developing countries? CBA in developing countries has, in fact, much in common with CBA in industrialized countries. For the most part, therefore, the other chapters in the book are equally applicable to both. The major distinguishing characteristic of CBA in developing countries is the much greater emphasis on adjusting the market prices of project outputs and inputs so that they more accurately reflect their value to society. Consequently, examining CBA in developing countries is a good way to study shadow pricing.

The reason for the emphasis on shadow pricing in CBA in developing countries is that analysts in this field argue that markets are much more distorted in developing countries than in developed countries. They suggest, for example, that labor markets are segmented and labor mobility is limited by systems of land tenure; that official exchange rates do not accurately reflect the value of the national currency; that the price of goods exchanged in international markets is distorted by trade taxes, import controls, and high tariffs; and that credit markets are divided between formal and informal sectors. Consequently, the experts advocate that shadow prices, which are often called *accounting prices,* be used instead of market prices in conducting CBAs in developing countries. Just like shadow price adjustments used in industrialized countries for CBA, accounting prices may incorporate adjustments for market failures such as monopoly and externalities. Particular emphasis, however, is placed on adjustments for taxes (especially tariffs), subsidies, and quotas that affect the market prices of imports and exports.

Surprisingly, perhaps, there is not only agreement among the experts on using shadow prices but also on the basic methods to use in determining the values of these shadow prices, although there is considerable variation in the details of what is actually done in practice. These methods, which received much of their impetus from international organizations involved in the funding of projects in developing countries, were developed in the early 1970s by the United Nations Industrial Development Organization[1] and by I. M. D. Little and J. A. Mirrlees.[2] The ideas contained in these two publications were then synthesized by Lyn Squire and Herman G. van der Tak,[3] two employees of the World Bank. Squire and van der Tak especially emphasized the concepts developed by Little and Mirrlees. As a consequence, the resulting approach toward shadow pricing, which with some modification continues to enjoy wide acceptance, is sometimes called the *LMST accounting price method.*

This chapter describes the LMST method and discusses some of the key issues it raises. Because use of the method involves a large number of details and raises issues that can only be touched on in the space available for this chapter, readers who plan to use this method in a CBA are advised to consult sources that address its application in greater depth.[4]

THE LMST METHODOLOGY

The LMST methodology makes a basic distinction between tradeable goods and nontradeable goods. *Tradeable goods* include consumption goods and productive factors that are exported or imported, as well as products for which there might potentially be an international market—for example, close substitutes of the goods that are traded internationally. Thus, traded goods affect, or potentially can affect, a nation's balance of payments. *Nontradeable goods* include all other consumption goods and productive factors such as local transportation, electricity, services, and (most importantly) local labor. The key to the LMST project evaluation approach is in using world prices—the prices at which goods are actually bought and sold internationally—to shadow price all project inputs and outputs that are classified as tradeable.[5] As will be explained later, nontradeable goods are often produced with inputs that are tradeable so that world prices can also be used to value them. Even the labor for a project may be drawn from other sectors of the economy in which it was previously producing goods that are tradeable so that world prices can once more be used.

The rationale for using world prices is not that free trade prevails or that world prices are undistorted—although they are less distorted than the domestic market prices in many developing countries and are probably less distorted today than they were when the LMST methodology was initially developed—but that they more accurately reflect the opportunities that are available to a country and these opportunities should be recognized in evaluating projects. For example, if a project input has to be imported, it is reasonable to value it at its import price. Similarly, if project output is to be exported, it is reasonable to value it on the basis of its export price because this indicates what it would contribute to the nation's foreign exchange. Thus, the methodology is based on the principle of *trade opportunity costs.*

To see the rationale for using world prices to value project outputs and inputs more clearly, consider a developing country that is conducting a CBA of a proposal to build a steel plant with government funds. Although the country currently has a high tariff on imported steel, it nonetheless is dependent on steel produced in other countries. Because the tariff is incorporated into the domestic market price of steel, it can be viewed as a transfer between domestic steel buyers and the government. As will be seen, however, world prices do not incorporate tariffs. Thus, the world price for an export is often considerably lower than its market price. Consequently, a CBA that is based on domestic prices could indicate that the steel plant project should proceed, when, in fact, the real resource cost of importing steel (i.e., the cost net of the tariff) is smaller than the resource cost of producing it domestically. Similarly, if a project uses a locally produced (but potentially importable) input that has a price that is artificially inflated because of high tariffs or import quotas, the opportunity to purchase the input more cheaply on the world market should be recognized in determining the project's cost. As a third example, consider a project to increase the production and foreign sales of an agricultural crop. In some developing countries, national policies keep the domestic market prices of some agricultural crops artificially low. When this occurs, a crop production project might not pass the cost-benefit test if market prices are used but could if the analysis is based instead on world prices. Thus, it is argued that the values of imports and exports on the world market should be the basis for decisions about domestic projects.

ILLUSTRATIONS OF THE LMST METHOD IN PRACTICE

To describe how shadow pricing is done in practice, we discuss three illustrations: an import, an export, and a nontradeable good (electricity).[6] All three examples are assumed to pertain to a project being considered in a small, developing country. For simplicity, it is also assumed that the amount of imports and exports involved would not be large enough to affect world prices. This last assumption, which is sometimes called the "small country assumption," is the one usually made in conducting CBAs of projects in developing countries and is realistic except when a project will substantially affect a country's export of a good and the country has a large share of the world market for that good.[7]

As will be seen, shadow pricing in all three cases involves multiplying each market price by an *accounting price ratio* (APR). An APR can be defined as follows:

$$\text{Accounting price ratio for good } i$$
$$= \frac{\text{accounting price of good } i}{\text{market price of good } i}$$
$$= \frac{\text{shadow price of good } i}{\text{market price of good } i}$$

As the accounting price of a good or a productive factor is essentially synonymous with its shadow price, multiplying a domestic market price of a good by its accounting price ratio converts it to its shadow price. That is,

Shadow price for good i = accounting price ratio for good i × market price for good i

The ways in which accounting price ratios are obtained in practice will be described as we work through the examples.

An Import

Determination of the accounting price for an import that is being used as an input in our hypothetical project (or, alternatively, an output from the project that substitutes for a good that otherwise would have to be imported) is shown in Table 16.1. The *CIF price* of a unit of the good on the world market (i.e., the *c*ost of the item plus *i*nsurance and *f*reight expenses to the port of destination) is $40 U.S. This $40 price is sometimes

TABLE 16.1	Accounting Price for Imported Good			
Item	*Dollars (U.S.$)*	*Market Value (Pesos)*	*APR*	*Accounting Value (Pesos)*
CIF Price	40	80	1.00	80
Tariff	—	10	0.00	—
Transport	—	8	0.50	4
Distribution	—	5	0.80	4
Total	—	103	0.85	88

Exchange rate: 2 pesos = U.S. $1

Source: Adapted from Terry A. Powers, "An Overview of the Little-Mirrlees/Squire-van der Tak Accounting Price System," *Estimating Accounting Prices for Project Appraisal,* Terry A. Powers, ed. (Washington, DC: Inter-American Development Bank, 1981), Table 1.1.

called a *border price* because it corresponds to the amount of foreign currency needed to pay for the good at the border. To translate the $40 amount into the local currency, pesos, it would be multiplied by the country's exchange rate. In the example, a dollar is assumed to equal 2 pesos. Thus, the $40 *CIF* price is equivalent to 80 pesos. Because the 80 peso price is already a world price, its shadow price is also 80 pesos. Hence, the accounting price ratio equals 1.

As just indicated, the exchange rate is needed to translate foreign currency such as dollars into the local currency. Usually, the official exchange rate is used for this purpose. However, as the existence of black markets in currency exchange in many developing countries attests, a nation's official exchange rate may not accurately reflect the actual value of its currency. This would occur, for example, if the official exchange rate converts 1 dollar into 2 pesos, but a dollar can, on average, actually be used to purchase 3 pesos' worth of domestic output. This latter value is called the *shadow exchange rate.* In practice, the official, rather than the shadow, exchange rate is usually used in determining accounting prices because it is more easily obtained. This choice is not very important for CBA, however. In conducting a CBA using the LMST method, *all* project benefits and costs must be expressed in accounting prices. As just seen, some such as imports already are. As discussed later, others, such as nontradeables, must be converted into accounting prices. As a result, all benefits and costs are commensurable. Moreover, in essence each is the product of its value in dollars (or some other foreign currency) and a constant that equals whatever exchange rate is being used. Consequently, the choice between the official exchange rate and the shadow exchange rate affects the absolute size of benefits and costs—the shadow rate is usually larger than the official rate—but not their relative size. Thus, as long as it is consistently used, the choice determines neither whether net benefits are positive or negative nor the relative ranking of projects.[8]

As indicated in Table 16.1, in addition to its *CIF* price of 80 pesos, the domestic market price of the import also reflects a tariff of 10 pesos, local transportation costs of 8 pesos, and distribution costs of 5 pesos. Thus, a unit of the import would cost 103 pesos in the local market. However, only part of these additions to the market price reflects real resource costs to the economy. For example, as previously mentioned, the revenue from a tariff is simply a transfer between buyers and the government. Thus, its accounting price ratio is set equal to zero. Transportation and distribution do involve the use of real resources, but, in this example, their accounting price ratios are less than one. Consequently, their shadow or "accounting" prices are less than their market prices. (The reasons for this divergence will be discussed a bit later.) Hence, the shadow price of the import equals 88 pesos (80 + 4 + 4), considerably less than its market price of 103 pesos. The import's overall accounting price ratio is, therefore, less than one (.85 = 88/103), which is typically the case for imports.

An Export

Table 16.2 provides information for determining the shadow price of an export that is produced by the project (or, alternatively, a project input that otherwise would have been exported). The price of the export at the port of origin before insurance and freight charges to its ultimate destination are added, its so-called *free on board (FOB) price,* is assumed to equal $100 or 200 pesos. Because the $100 is the amount of foreign currency received at the border, it is the border price for an export. The FOB price includes the market price if purchased at the factory (148 pesos), as well as an export tax (50 pesos) and transportation costs to the port of origin (2 pesos). Only half the transportation costs are assumed to reflect real resource costs to the economy (the APR equals 0.5). The export tax is a transfer between foreign purchasers and the domestic government, but because foreigners typically would not be given standing in evaluating the project, the tax amount would be included in the shadow price. Therefore, if the good is produced by the project and exported, its shadow price would equal 199 pesos (148 + 50 + 1). Thus, the overall accounting price ratio for the export is greater than one (1.34 = 199/148).

It may be useful to point out that by shadow pricing the export, it is valued on the basis of each unit's contribution to the nation's foreign exchange. Thus, for example, although a tax on an export increases its shadow price (but possibly decreases sales), a subsidy on an export (perhaps to encourage sales), decreases its shadow price.

TABLE 16.2 Accounting Price for Export

Item	U.S. Dollars (U.S.$)	Market Value (pesos)	APR	Accounting Value (pesos)
FOB price	100	200	—	—
Export tax	25	50	1.0	50
Transport for export	1	2	0.5	1
Factory gate price	74	148	1.0	148
Transport for Domestic sale	—	4	0.5	2
Distribution in Domestic market	—	10	0.8	8

Exchange rate: 2 pesos = U.S. $1

Source: Adapted from Terry A. Powers, "An Overview of the Little-Mirrlees/Squire-van der Tak Accounting Price System," *Estimating Accounting Prices for Project Appraisal,* Terry A. Powers, ed. (Washington, DC: Inter-American Development Bank, 1981), Table 1.2.

Now imagine that rather than representing a product produced by the project for export, the good in question is a project input, one that would be exported if the project is not undertaken. Under these circumstances, the shadow price must include the additional costs incurred by diverting the good to domestic use, as well as revenue forgone and costs saved by not exporting the product. Thus, the net effects of not exporting the good must be determined. The revenue forgone is the 200 peso FOB price, whereas the cost saved is the 1 peso of transportation cost to the port of origin. The additional costs incurred by diverting the good to the project include local transportation costs of 4 pesos and distribution costs of 10 pesos. As previously mentioned, because only part of these additional costs reflects real resource costs to the economy, the additional costs must be adjusted to their shadow price equivalents by multiplying them by their accounting price ratios. Thus, the shadow price of the export when it is diverted to domestic use is 209 pesos (200 − 1 + 2 + 8).

A practical problem arises when project inputs are potential exports, such as the case just described, and also when project outputs are substituted for potential imports. The problem involves selecting the appropriate world price to use in shadow pricing, because often there will be several alternative world prices that are candidates as a result of similar products that may vary along different dimensions such as quality and ease of access. Obviously, a CBA that selects an export price from the low end or an import price from the high end of such a range is more likely to show that net benefits are positive than one that selects from the opposite end of the range. One reasonable approach is simply to use a value from the middle of the range if the good cannot be priced in terms of its specific characteristics.

A Nontradeable

Table 16.3 lists the costs of the various inputs needed to produce the additional electricity required by the project. These inputs would presumably be diverted by the project from other uses and, thus, represent opportunity costs associated with the project. The electricity itself is assumed to be produced domestically and, hence, is an example of a nontraded good. However, for cost-benefit purposes, it must be made commensurable with traded goods, which, as already discussed, are valued in terms of their world prices.

To make tradeable and nontradeable goods commensurable, the LMST approach involves determining the equivalent value of nontradeables in world prices. To do this, it exploits the fact that the production of nontradeables involves inputs that are tradeable. As the table indicates, for example, many of the inputs required to produce the needed electricity—the material required to construct the generating plant—are tradeable. Thus, using the LMST method to shadow-price a nontraded good involves breaking down the cost of the good into its traded, nontraded, and labor components. The nontraded components can then be further broken down into *their* traded, nontraded, and labor components, and so forth. These components and sub-components are listed in the table. By multiplying each of these components and subcomponents by their accounting price ratio, the opportunity cost of supplying an additional amount of a nontraded good to the project can be evaluated in terms of the tradeable goods required to produce the additional amount. Although the example pertains to electricity, a similar procedure would be used in the case of other nontraded goods such as the transport and distribution costs items listed in Tables 16.1 and 16.2.

TABLE 16.3 Accounting Price for Electricity Valued at Marginal Cost of Supply (in thousands of pesos)

Item	Cost in Domestic Prices	APR	Cost in Accounting Prices
Capital costs	**3,000**	0.89	**2,678**
Thermal generating unit (CIF)	1,800	1.00	1,800
Building and site construction	1,200	0.73	878
Imported materials (CIF)	500	1.00	500
Labor	250	0.60[a]	150
Industry taxes and tariffs	200	0.00	0
Other expenses	250	0.91	228
Imported materials (CIF)	180	1.00	180
Labor	40	0.60[a]	24
Other expenses	30	0.80[b]	24
Annual operating costs	**1,000**	0.83	**831**
Fuel oil (CIF)	800	1.00	800
Maintenance	40	0.78	31
Parts (CIF)	15	1.00	15
Labor	20	0.60[a]	12
Other	5	0.80[b]	4
Taxes and tariffs	160	0.00	0

[a]The accounting price ratio of labor is discussed later; here it is assumed to equal 0.6 for purposes of the example.

[b]The standard conversion factor (SCF), which is assumed to have a value of 0.8 for purposes of the example, is used to convert the domestic value to its accounting price.

Source: Adapted from Terry A. Powers, "An Overview of the Little-Mirrlees/Squire-van der Tak Accounting Price System," *Estimating Accounting Prices for Project Appraisal,* Terry A. Powers, ed. (Washington, DC: Inter-American Development Bank, 1981), Table 1.3.

The different accounting price ratios listed in Table 16.3 are derived by several different methods. As previously indicated, the accounting price ratio of a tradeable component that is expressed in CIF prices (e.g., imported materials) is 100, whereas the ratio for a domestic transfer (e.g., tariffs on tradeables and taxes on nontradeables) is zero. The accounting price ratio for domestic labor is complex to derive and will be discussed in some detail later. Those for nontradeable components are simply weighted averages of the APRs of their components, where the weights are the cost of each component expressed in shadow prices as a fraction of total cost. Sometimes these weighted averages are derived from calculations made by the project evaluators. For example, the APR for annual operating costs of .83, which is listed in Table 16.3, is computed as follows: $1.0(800/1,000) + .78(40/1,000) + 0(160/1,000)$. However, the weighted accounting price ratios that are used to obtain shadow prices for fairly small subcomponents (e.g., other maintenance expenses) are often *conversion factors* (*CF*s), which are obtained from previous studies and pertain to entire industries or national economic sectors, such as the electricity and gas industry, rather than to one specific input, such as the fuel oil used to produce the electricity needed by the project.

Except for pertaining to a broader segment of the economy, conversion factors are similar to APRs that are developed for a specific project evaluation. Like project-specific APRs, they are weighted averages of their components. Because conversion factors can be plugged into more than one CBA, they are obviously another example of a shadow price that is obtained from secondary sources, the topic covered in Chapter 15. Because the use of conversion factors saves time for evaluators, the extent to which they are used in a particular CBA depends on the resources available for the study and the accuracy required. In practice, as will be seen, the role of conversion factors is often of considerable importance.

A technique called *semi-input-output analysis* (SIO) is often used to derive conversion factors. SIO analysis utilizes national input-output tables, national censuses, household expenditure surveys, and other national data, such as information on tariffs, quotas, and subsidies. SIO analysis is particularly difficult to conduct if input-output tables are not already available because then the analyst must piece together the equivalent information. Given the required data, an SIO table is constructed that divides the economy into as many productive sectors as the data allow (e.g., corn and corn products, fishing, mining, hotels, electricity and gas, real estate, and so forth). Often 50 or more productive sectors are listed. Part of the output produced in each sector will, of course, be directly consumed and part will be used as inputs in the other sectors. The table indicates the percentage contribution of the output produced in each sector to the total market value of the output produced in each of the other sectors. In addition, primary factor inputs such as labor, capital, foreign exchange, and taxes and subsidies are also listed and their percentage contributions to the total market value of the output produced in each of the productive sectors is also indicated. Deriving conversion factors from the table constructed for SIO analysis essentially involves solving a set of simultaneous equations using matrix algebra.[9] In doing this, SIO analysis consistently treats interdependence between different sectors of the economy—for example, coal may be used to produce electricity, and electricity may be used in mining coal.

In addition to being used to obtain *CF*s for individual industries, SIO can be used to obtain *CF*s for skilled and unskilled labor and aggregate *CF*s. One such aggregate *CF* is the *consumption conversion factor* (*CCF*), which is a weighted average of accounting price ratios for a nationally representative market basket of consumption goods. The *CCF* plays several roles in shadow pricing that will be mentioned later. Another aggregate *CF* is the *standard conversion factor* (*SCF*), which is the ratio of the value of all production at accounting prices to the value of all production at market prices. In other words, the *SCF* is the weighted average of the *CF*s for the productive sectors of the economy, where the weights are the contribution that each sector makes to total national output. The *SCF* is used in computing the shadow prices of minor components of nontraded goods when more specific *CF*s are not available.

Although the *SCF* is usually derived by actually computing a weighted average of the *CF*s for the productive sectors of an economy, it is instructive to examine briefly the following formula, which has sometimes been used in the past to obtain a crude approximation of the *SCF*:

$$SCF = (M + X)/[(M + T_m - S_m) + (X - T_x + S_x)]$$

where M is the total value of imports in CIF border prices, X is the total value of exports in FOB border prices, T_m is total tariffs on imports, T_x is total taxes on exports, S_m is total subsidies on imports, and S_x is the total subsidies on exports. The numerator of this expression values imports and exports at their world prices, whereas the denominator values them at their market prices. The expression is only a crude approximation because it ignores transportation and distribution costs and nontraded goods in the economy and because it assumes that distortions in domestic market prices are entirely due to tariffs and import taxes and subsidies (thereby ignoring other distortions such as taxes on nontraded goods and import quotas, monopoly power, and externalities). What is interesting about the expression is that it implies that tariffs and export subsidies cause market prices to be larger than world prices, whereas taxes on exports and import subsidies have the opposite effect. As the former are usually more important in developing countries than the latter, the *SCF,* most *CF*s for specific sectors of the economy, and most APRs for specific goods have values that are less than one.[10] For example, Steve Curry and John Weiss examine separate studies of 13 different countries and find estimates of the *SCF* that range between .59 and .96, with an average value of about .8.[11]

SHADOW PRICING WHEN GOODS ARE IN FIXED SUPPLY

As indicated earlier, the LMST approach normally relies on the shadow prices of the inputs required to produce a good to convert its market price to a shadow price. There is an important exception to this procedure, however, which occurs when the supply of a good is fixed. This could happen, for example, if there is a quota on imports or the government exercises a monopoly over providing a particular good or service and has run out of funds needed to supply more.

A situation in which supply is fixed is illustrated in Figure 16.1 and pertains to the electricity that would be required for our project. The production of electricity is often characterized as having constant marginal costs up to a capacity level. Consistent with this, the supply curve in the figure is perfectly elastic to Q_1 and then becomes completely inelastic as the nation's generating capacity is exhausted. Say that D_a represents the demand curve for electricity without the project and D'_a represents the demand curve with the project. Under these circumstances, the fixed supply of electricity is not binding. As a result, the project would not affect the current consumers of electricity. However, it would require that additional inputs be used to produce the additional electricity needed by the project. Consequently, the method outlined earlier for deriving the shadow cost of the electricity used on the project would be appropriate.

Now suppose that without the project the demand curve for electricity is D_b and with the project it is D'_b. Thus, the project would increase the market price of electricity from P_1 to P_2 and reduce the consumption of electricity by current consumers from Q_1 to Q_2. Because of the price increase, current consumers lose surplus, whereas the producers of electricity gain surplus. As explained in Chapter 4, these changes in surplus can be appropriately taken into account in determining the cost of electricity to the project by simply using the average of the old and new prices, $(P_1 + P_2)/2$, as the market price. Thus, measured in market prices, the cost of electricity for the project would equal $[(P_1 + P_2)/2](Q_1 - Q_2)$ pesos.

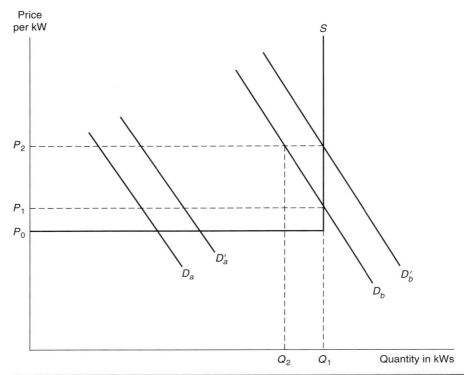

FIGURE 16.1 Shadow Pricing When Electricity Is Completely Elastic and Inelastic

To use the LMST method, however, this cost amount must be converted to its shadow price equivalent. In doing this, account must be taken of the fact that when the supply of electricity is fixed the opportunity cost of diverting some electricity from current consumers to the project is not additional inputs but the consumption forgone by current consumers. One way of doing this is to ask what consumers would purchase with $[(P_1 + P_2)/2](Q_1 - Q_2)$ pesos of additional income and then determine the shadow prices of each of these goods using the techniques discussed earlier. Of course, it is highly unlikely that the specific items that consumers would purchase would actually be known. Thus, in practice, $[(P_1 + P_2)/2](Q_1 - Q_2)$ would probably be converted to its shadow price equivalent by multiplying it by the consumption conversion factor, which as previously mentioned is a weighted average of accounting price ratios for a nationally representative market basket of goods.

THE SHADOW PRICE OF LABOR

A project in any country will use labor. In developing countries, increasing the employment of unskilled workers may, in fact, be an important part of the motivation for initiating many projects. Even when it is not, labor is still likely to be a major nontradeable input used in the project. Hence, shadow-pricing the cost of employing workers is of critical importance in conducting CBA in developing counties. Shadow-pricing labor raises some difficult special issues, however. In this section, we discuss these issues.

Like any input used in a project, labor has an accounting price ratio:

$$\text{Accounting price ratio of type } j \text{ labor} = \frac{\text{shadow wage of type } j \text{ labor}}{\text{the market wage of type } j \text{ labor}}$$

This expression implies that different types of labor (e.g., skilled and unskilled workers) may have different accounting price ratios. It also indicates that to determine the shadow price of labor it is first necessary to determine labor's market wage. Although doing this is fairly straightforward when skilled workers who are employed at a nation's business establishments are hired to work on a project, it is not so apparent when the project hires unskilled workers. We discuss the easier case first.

If a nation's labor markets for skilled workers are functioning reasonably well—for example, unemployment among such workers is not high—then, as seen in Chapter 4, the wage at which they are hired by a project provides a reasonable approximation of their market wage. Consequently, the project wage provides a reasonable approximation of their productivity elsewhere and, hence, represents the social opportunity cost (expressed in domestic prices) of hiring them for the project.[12] If a conversion factor is available for skilled workers, then the shadow wage can be obtained by multiplying it by the project wage. Alternatively, but less satisfactory, the project wage can be multiplied by sector-specific conversion factors to convert it to its foreign exchange equivalent. For example, if carpenters are hired, the project wage for carpenters can be multiplied by the conversion factor for the construction industry. Still less satisfactory, if neither a conversion factor for skilled workers nor an appropriate sector-specific conversion factor is available, then an estimate of the standard conversion factor can be used.

A special case occurs when a developing country does not have sufficient workers with the skills demanded by the project being evaluated and the required workers must be hired from abroad. These foreign workers would typically not be given standing. Nonetheless, they would spend some of their earnings within the country, while sending or taking the remainder out of the country. Thus, to determine the shadow cost of hiring foreign labor, the fraction of earnings sent abroad would have to be estimated. As these earnings would be a direct loss of foreign exchange, they would have an accounting price ratio of 1. In principle, the value of each item purchased within the country should be multiplied by its APR. Because the information to do this would probably not be available in practice, however, all earnings that remain in the country would probably be multiplied by the economy-wide consumption conversion factor (CCF).[13] Hence, the shadow wage for foreign workers, SW_f, would be computed as follows:

$$SW_f = [h + (1 - h)(CCF)](PW)$$

where PW is the project wage, h is the fraction of the project wage sent or taken home, and $(1 - h)$ is the fraction spent domestically.

Unskilled workers for a project in a developing country are ultimately likely to be drawn from the countryside. This will not only be true of projects in rural areas but also of projects in cities, even if the workers who are directly hired by the project currently reside in urban areas. The reason is that as employment increases in urban areas in developing countries, workers in rural areas are induced to migrate to the areas where employment has increased.

Why this migration occurs is suggested by a well-known model developed by John Harris and Michael Todaro.[14] Their model is based on two observations about developing countries: Unemployment is often very high in urban areas and earnings are typically considerably higher in urban than in rural areas. Harris and Todaro suggest that because of the higher urban wages workers will migrate from the countryside to the cities, even though some of them will not be able to find jobs. More specifically, they postulate that the probability that a rural worker will obtain employment upon migrating to a city equals $E/L = (L - U)/L$, where L is the size of the workforce in the city, U is the number of unemployed persons, and $E = (L - U)$ is the number of employed workers. Therefore, the model implies that workers will have an incentive to migrate from the countryside to the city as long as:

$$RMW < UMW(E/L)$$

where RMW is the rural market wage, UMW is the urban market wage, and $UMW(E/L)$ is the wage that migrating workers will receive on average (i.e., $UMW(E/L)$ is their expected wage). Thus, according to the model, rural-urban migration will cease when:

$$RMW = UMW(E/L) \qquad (16.1)$$

Two important implications of this model are that even when there is no incentive for further migration urban unemployment may continue to be high and urban wages will continue to exceed rural wages.[15]

We now use the Harris-Todaro model to examine the effects of locating a new project in a city. Assume that prior to initiating the project the equilibrium condition specified in equation (16.1) is being met. Now assume that ΔE unskilled workers are hired to work on the project. If ΔE is fairly small relative to the size of the workforce, then neither rural nor urban wage rates are likely to be affected. Consequently, the equilibrium can only be reestablished if:

$$E/L = (E + \Delta E)/(L + \Delta L) \qquad (16.2)$$

where ΔL is the number of workers added to the urban labor force.

There are two things to notice here. First, if there are no changes in urban wage rates, current residents of the city who are currently outside the labor force (i.e., not already employed or seeking employment) will not be induced to join it, except perhaps by the increase in the number of available jobs. Therefore, many, if not most, of the workers added to the urban labor force will be migrants from rural areas. Second, according to the model, the number of migrants is likely to exceed the number of jobs created by the project. This can be seen by first rearranging the terms in equation (16.2) to obtain:

$$L + \Delta L = L(E + \Delta E)/E \qquad (16.3)$$

And then by subtracting $L = L(E)/E$ from equation (16.3) and rearranging the terms to obtain:

$$L + \Delta L - L = L(E + \Delta E)/E - L(E)/E$$

or

$$\Delta L/\Delta E = L/E. \qquad (16.4)$$

Because the workforce consists of both workers and the unemployed (i.e., $L = E + U$), the ratio L/E must exceed 1 and, thus, as equation (16.4) implies, so will the ratio $\Delta L/\Delta E$.

The implications of this simple model can be illustrated with a numeric example. If the urban wage is 50 percent higher than the rural wage (i.e., if $RMW(L/E) = 1.5RMW = UMW$), then equation (16.1) implies that E/L equals .67. Hence, one-third of the urban workforce will be unemployed. Moreover, equation (16.4) implies that for each job created by a project, 1.5 workers will migrate to the city (i.e., $\Delta L = \Delta E(L/E) = 1(3/2) = 1.5$).

Because most or all of the unskilled workers employed by a government project would ultimately be drawn from the countryside, the output that is forgone is production in rural areas. If the project is located in a rural area, then rural-urban migration is not a consideration, and the shadow wage would be obtained by simply multiplying the rural wage by the most appropriate conversion factor that is available. (Some of the possible conversion factors that might be used were listed earlier when the shadow wage of skilled workers was discussed.) However, if the project is located in an urban area, then account must be taken of the number of workers who would leave the countryside for each job created. According to the Harris-Todaro model, if *all* the workers added to the urban work force as a result of the project are rural migrants, then this can be accomplished by multiplying the product of the rural wage and the conversion factor by the ratio, L/E. Notice, however, that equation (16.1) indicates that $RMW(L/E) = UMW$. In other words, the Harris-Todaro model implies that the shadow wage rate for evaluating projects in urban areas can be also obtained by multiplying the urban wage rate by the appropriate conversion factor.[16]

Although the Harris-Todaro model implies that for each job created by an urban project L/E rural workers will migrate, the actual number of migrants could be considerably less if, for example, workers are risk averse or there are monetary or psychic costs associated with migrating. If fewer than L/E workers per created job migrate, then the appropriate market wage to use in determining the shadow wage rate would be less than the urban market wage. Caroline Dinwiddy and Francis Teal demonstrate, in fact, that under a wide variety of assumptions, the appropriate market wage to use is likely to fall somewhere between the rural and the urban market wage.[17] Consequently, *if large numbers of unskilled workers will be employed on an urban project in a developing country, and there are wide differences between rural and urban wages, a sensitivity test should be conducted in determining the shadow wage rate by first using the rural market wage and then using the urban wage.*

Although urban market wage rates for unskilled workers can be obtained from survey data—for example, the average manufacturing wage can be used[18]—many rural workers produce homegrown crops. Hence, the market wage rate of these workers is more difficult to ascertain. One way to construct an estimate of the rural market wage is to first determine how a typical rural worker who is likely to be affected by the project being evaluated allocates his or her productive time and then estimate the value of the worker's output. Say, for instance, that the typical worker is employed on a cacao plantation for half the year and receives a daily wage of 40 pesos and food and transportation valued at 10 pesos a day, for a total of 50 pesos. Because the worker is only needed at the plantation for six months, he or she works at home during the remainder of the year, growing corn for three months and bananas for the remaining three.

Although the corn and bananas are mostly grown for home consumption, if they were brought to the local market, they could be sold for 910 pesos and 1,365 pesos, respectively. Dividing market value of corn and bananas by the 91 days during which the work to grow each was performed suggests that the worker earned a daily market wage of 10 pesos from growing corn and a daily market wage of 15 pesos from growing bananas. Given this information, the worker's daily wage can be computed as a weighted average of his or her daily return from each endeavor, where the weights are the fractions of time he or she devoted to each activity. That is:[19]

$$RMW = .5(50) + .25(10) + .25(15) = 31.25 \text{ pesos} \qquad \textbf{(16.5)}$$

In principle, at least two additional factors should be taken into account in determining the shadow wage rate of rural, unskilled workers, although in practice they rarely are because of the lack of adequate information.

First, it is possible that moving to the city requires the worker to work longer hours, places the worker under greater stress, and results in a less satisfactory lifestyle. If so, the shadow wage rate (which is a measure of opportunity costs) should, in principle, be adjusted upward to account for the resulting loss of utility.

Second, many rural workers live in large extended families. If a project induces a rural worker to migrate to the city, then the effects on the remaining family members should, in principle, be taken into account. The remaining family members lose the migrating worker's output, of course, but they gain because the worker no longer consumes the income available to the family. These two amounts are not necessarily offsetting; it is quite possible that the gain exceeds the loss. This would occur, for example, if the family shares its income, the total value of the output produced by all family members, equally among its members. Under these circumstances, each family member's consumption level would be equal to the average value of the output produced by the family. The family member's contribution to family output, however, would correspond to his or her marginal product. Because rural families typically produce much of their output at home on a fixed amount of land, it is quite likely that the family would be producing on the declining segment of its marginal product curve. If so, the value of a family member's marginal product will be smaller than the value of the output that he or she consumes. Thus, if a family member is induced by a project to migrate in such circumstances, the consumption levels of the remaining family members will increase.

ADDITIONAL TOPICS

As previously mentioned, with the exception of using world prices to shadow-price benefits and costs, conducting CBAs in developing countries is quite similar to cost-benefit analysis in industrialized countries. However, the literature concerning CBA in developing countries has evolved somewhat separately from the remaining CBA literature. As a result, there are a few additional topics that are treated somewhat differently in the former than in the latter. In this section, we briefly review these topics. The discussion is brief because these differences are mainly conceptual in nature; they appear to have had little effect on how actual cost-benefit studies are conducted.

Discounting

The points discussed in Chapters 6 and 10 concerning discounting are equally applicable to CBA in developing and industrialized countries. In Chapter 10, however, we presumed that funding for a public-sector project would displace private-sector investment, private-sector consumption, or both. The literature on developing countries often considers another possibility—that the governments in some developing countries are extremely reluctant or unable to borrow additional funds or increase tax revenues. In other words, it is suggested that government expenditures in some developing countries cannot or will not be increased even if such an increase would greatly benefit the public. By the same token, they cannot or will not be decreased even if the funds could be better used in the private sector. Given a fixed public-sector budget, a new project can only be funded if the funds are diverted from a current government project or program.[20] In other words, the opportunity cost of undertaking a project is not forgone private-sector investment or consumption but forgone public-sector investment, which results in a lower amount of some other government output or services being available.

We are skeptical that a government's budget would ever really be fixed, at least over the long run. Nonetheless, if this were the case, then private-sector interest rates would not be relevant to government investment decisions. Consequently, a discount rate would have to be obtained by conducting cost-benefit analyses of current government projects and determining their internal rates of return. The social discount rate could then be selected from among the positive internal rates of return at the lower end of the range, as funding for projects at this end of the range is among the more marginal of current public expenditures. Thus, existing projects with low internal rates of return are the best candidates for displacement by new projects that can reap a higher rate of return.

If government budgets are reasonably flexible, rather than fixed, then the social discount rate is appropriately determined on the basis of observed private-sector interest rates. The practical problems in doing this, however, are considerably more formidable in developing than in developed countries because of the high degree of fragmentation in domestic lending markets in developing countries. For example, Hoff and Stiglitz cite evidence that lending rates in the informal economy in some developing countries are up to six times higher than rates in the formal sector and that within the informal sector in many developing countries there is considerable variation in rates.[21]

Social Accounting in Project Evaluation

The literature on CBA in developing countries suggests that public expenditures have three somewhat conflicting goals: (1) increasing economic efficiency (i.e., maximizing net economic worth), (2) encouraging economic growth, and (3) redistributing income from the rich to the poor. In the literature, a sharp distinction is made between CBAs that focus solely on the first goal, economic efficiency, and CBAs that attempt to assess the contribution of a project to all three goals. This chapter has so far discussed only the first type of CBA. The second type of CBA is sometimes called *social project appraisal*.

In the LMST approach, social project appraisal is based on the following general framework:

$$SB = NPV - C(CCF) + C(\omega/\theta) \tag{16.6}$$

where *SB* is the total social benefit from a project, *NPV* is the net present value of benefits as they are usually estimated in cost-benefit analysis and is measured in accounting prices, *C* is the present value of the net change in private-sector consumption resulting from the project and is measured in domestic market prices, *CCF* is the economy-wide consumption conversion factor, θ is the shadow price of capital as it is defined in Chapter 10, and ω is a *distributional weight* parameter with a value that is greater than 1 if the change in consumption disproportionately accrues to persons with below average incomes and a value smaller than 1 if the consumption change disproportionately accrues to persons with above average incomes. The value of ω would equal 1 if the per capita consumption of all income groups changed by the same amount. Methods for obtaining values for the parameter ω are described in Chapter 18.

The first term in equation (16.6), *NPV*, reflects only the first of the goals listed earlier: economic efficiency. Most actual cost-benefit studies in developing as well as in industrialized countries simply stop at this point, thereby implicitly setting the second and third terms equal to zero. The second and third terms are meant to incorporate the other two goals: economic growth and income redistribution. For example, it is often suggested that savings rates are especially low in developing countries resulting in insufficient investment to sustain economic growth. Thus, the second term, *C(CCF)*, is subtracted from the first to reflect the notion that an increase in consumption has less social value than an equal increase in investment. In other words, the intent is to bias choices among projects toward those that do the most to increase investment. Because the benefits and costs that comprise the *NPV* estimate are all measured in shadow prices, but *C* is measured in domestic market prices, the consumption conversion factor is used to make the two terms commensurable. The third term in equation (16.6) offsets the second, as factoring out *C* to obtain $C(\omega/\theta - CCF)$ indicates, implying that although a reduction in investments is a social cost, an increase in consumption is a social benefit. The ratio, ω/θ, indicates that this benefit increases as a greater part of the increase in consumption accrues to persons with incomes below the national average (i.e., as ω becomes larger) but decreases as the amount of foregone investment becomes greater (i.e., as θ becomes larger).[22]

To get some flavor for how use of the framework summarized by equation (16.6) might affect a cost-benefit analysis in practice, consider a project that increases the per capita consumption of different income groups by a similar amount so that $\omega = 1$. Chapter 10 suggests that a reasonable range of values for θ is between 1.3 and 2.7. Thus, for purposes of illustration, we shall assume that $\theta = 2$. Finally, Curry and Weiss have assembled 14 different estimates of the value of the *CCF* from 12 studies of different developing countries.[23] These estimates range between 0.74 and 1.12, but all but four are between 0.79 and 0.94. For illustrative purposes, we assume that *CCF* = 0.85. Given these values, $(\omega/\theta - CCF) = (½ - .85) = -.35$. This implies that a one-peso increase in consumption as a result of a government project is around two-thirds as valuable as a one-peso increase in investment. Notice, however, that if most of the increase in consumption from the project accrues to the poor, it is conceivable that $(\omega/\theta - CCF)$ will have a positive value, implying that an increase in consumption has greater social value than a similar increase in investment. This would occur, for example, if $\omega = 2$.

Although the LMST framework for social project appraisal addresses important issues, it is somewhat ad hoc. In our view, the method that is described in Chapter 10 for incorporating the shadow price of capital into social discounting, which results in a direct adjustment of the *NPV* estimate, provides a more appropriate way to take account of the opportunity cost of consuming project output rather than investing it. The use of the parameter ω in equation (16.6) represents one particular approach to take account of the possibility that an increase in the consumption of lower-income persons is of greater social value than an equal increase in the consumption of higher-income persons. Alternative, and perhaps preferable, approaches that can be used to do this are described in some detail in Chapter 18, which discusses distributional weighting. These alternative approaches also directly adjust the net present value estimate.

IS THE LMST METHOD ACTUALLY USED FOR PROJECT EVALUATION?

Not surprisingly, international organizations such as the World Bank make regular use of the shadow pricing procedures discussed in this chapter in conducting CBA. However, the governments of many developing countries do not. Some time ago, the World Bank surveyed 27 developing countries about the project evaluations that they conduct.[24] All but three of these countries had one or more offices with specific responsibility for project evaluation. None of these offices conducted social project appraisals; that is, their formal analyses were concerned solely with whether the evaluated projects increased economic efficiency. However, some of the offices were not using appropriate methods to determine this. Although information was not available for several of the surveyed countries, only eight of the countries were found to use shadow pricing regularly in conducting project evaluations. In fact, seven of the remaining countries not only failed to shadow-price, they also did not discount benefits and costs.

CONCLUSION

A large fraction of economic activity in developing countries typically occurs outside of efficient markets. Consequently, the application of CBA in developing countries requires extensive use of shadow prices. The LMST accounting price method is the most commonly used framework for determining a consistent set of shadow prices. Implementing it often requires considerable skill in working with available information. Finding appropriate shadow prices for unskilled labor poses a particularly difficult problem. Thus, although the principles of CBA are readily transferable to developing countries, their application requires familiarity with a variety of complex shadow pricing issues.

Exercises for Chapter 16

1. A developing country is considering building a steel plant in its largest city. The estimated construction costs of this plant in domestic prices are listed in the table that follows. Fill in the missing values in this table and then:
   a. Compute the weighted accounting price ratio for the imported materials that would be used in constructing the plant.
   b. Compute the total construction cost of the plant in accounting prices.

Accounting Price for Steel Plant Construction
(in thousands of dubyas)

Item	Cost in Domestic Prices	APR	Cost in Accounting Prices
Imported materials			
CIF price	500		
Taxes and tariffs	100		
Transportation	50	.60	
Distribution	20	.80	
Local materials	600	.90	
Labor			
Skilled	300	.95	
Unskilled	800	.55	
Capital costs			
Equipment	250	.75	
Other	100	.90	

2. A certain developing country currently imports all its wheat but is considering funding an irrigation project that would allow domestic farmers to grow and sell wheat. The domestically grown wheat would be sold in competitive markets at an estimated price of 15 dubyas per bushel. The wheat the nation currently imports has a CIF price of U.S. $3 per bushel. The official exchange rate is 4 dubyas per dollar. The nation's tariff on imported wheat is 2 dubyas per bushel. Transportation and distribution charges from the port to a typical market are 2 dubyas and 1 dubya per bushel, respectively. The accounting price ratio has been estimated to be .6 for transportation and .8 for distribution.
   a. Calculate the market price of imported wheat.
   b. Calculate the shadow price of imported wheat.
   c. Should the irrigation project proceed?
3. Assume that a typical unskilled rural worker in a developing country would be paid 2 dubyas a week if he migrates to the city and finds a job. However, the unemployment rate for unskilled workers is 40 percent in the city.
   a. What does the Harris-Todaro model predict the worker's rural wage is?
   b. Assume now that the government is considering funding a project in the city that would use substantial numbers of unskilled workers. Using your answer to the preceding question, suggest a reasonable upper-bound estimate and reasonable lower-bound estimate of the market wage rate for unskilled workers that the government might use in conducting a CBA of the proposed project.

Notes

1. United Nations Industrial Development Organization (UNIDO), *Guidelines for Project Evaluation* (New York: United Nations, 1972).

2. I. M. D. Little and J. A. Mirrlees, *Project Appraisal and Planning for Developing Countries* (London: Heinemann Educational, 1974).

3. Lyn Squire and Herman G. van der Tak, *Economic Analysis of Projects* (Baltimore: The Johns Hopkins University Press, 1975).

4. An excellent concise summary of the approach can be found in Terry A. Powers, "An Overview of the Little-Mirrlees/Squire-van der Tak Accounting Price System," *Estimating Accounting Prices for Project Appraisal*, Terry A. Powers, ed. (Washington, DC: Inter-American Development Bank, 1981), pp. 1–59. Recent book-length treatments include Caroline Dinwiddy and Francis Teal, *Principles of Cost-Benefit Analysis for Developing Countries* (Cambridge, United Kingdom: Cambridge University Press, 1996); Robert J. Brent, *Cost-Benefit Analysis for Developing Countries* (Cheltenham, United Kingdom: Edward Elgar Publishing, 1998); and Steve Curry and John Weiss, *Project Analysis in Developing Countries* (London: Macmillan, 1993). The book by Curry and Weiss provides a particularly clear exposition of how to use the approach in practice. The Dinwiddy and Teal book focuses on the economic principles that underlie the approach.

5. There is an alternative to this approach, which is known as the UNIDO approach and is based on the United Nations Industrial Development Organization's 1972 guidelines. Instead of using world prices to shadow-price project inputs and outputs, it uses domestic prices to do this. In practice, the major focus of the LMST method is in adjusting nontradeables to world prices, whereas the major focus of the UNIDO approach is in adjusting tradeables to domestic prices. CBA can be conducting using either approach and, as demonstrated by Curry and Weiss (Chapter 6), the two approaches will produce similar results if equivalent assumptions are made in conducting analyses under them. Because the LMST method is much more widely used than the UNIDO approach, we focus on it in this chapter.

6. These examples are all adapted from Terry A. Powers, "An Overview of the Little-Mirrlees/Squire-van der Tak Accounting Price System," pp. 20–28.

7. If a project increases a country's exports of a good, and the increase reduces the world price for the good, a CBA must not only take account of the benefits to the country from the increased sales of the product but also the cost that results because previous exports of the product must now be sold at a lower price.

8. For a detailed discussion, see Dinwiddy and Teal, *Principles of Cost-Benefit Analysis for Developing Countries,* pp. 128–131, or Curry and Weiss, *Project Analysis in Developing Countries,* pp. 130–137.

9. For an introduction into using the semi-input-output approach to derive conversion factors, see Curry and Weiss, *Project Analysis in Developing Countries,* Chapter 11. For a detailed description of methods for computing conversion factors either directly with input-output tables or using the semi-input-output approach, as well as four case studies in which these methods are used to compute conversion factors for developing countries, see Terry A. Powers, ed., *Estimating Accounting Prices for Project Appraisal.*

10. The major exceptions usually occur among APRs for goods that are exported.

11. Curry and Weiss, *Project Analysis in Developing Countries,* pp. 264–266.

12. This will not be the case, of course, if labor markets are highly distorted by union contracts, by government wage controls, or for other reasons. Under these circumstances, the method described in Chapter 4 for determining the opportunity cost of hiring the unemployed to work on a project may have to be used.

13. Because the spending patterns of domestic and foreign workers are likely to differ, a *CCF* that is specific to foreign workers should ideally be used. Such a *CCF* is unlikely to be available, however. Thus, the *CCF* for the overall population would probably be used in practice.

14. John R. Harris and Michael P. Todaro, "Migration, Unemployment, and Development," *American Economic Review,* 60, no. 1 (1970), 126–142.

15. The Harris-Todaro model is, of course, only one explanation of these phenomena. For example, rural-urban differences in living costs, minimum wage legislation, and union contracts may also contribute. For a brief discussion of still other contributing factors, see Dinwiddy and Teal,

Principles of Cost-Benefit Analysis for Developing Countries, pp. 145–147 and p. 151.

16. The conclusion that the urban wage should be used was also reached by Christopher J. Heady, "Shadow Wages and Induced Migration," *Oxford Economic Papers,* vol. 33, no. 1 (1981), 108–121 on the basis of a model that incorporated more general and complex assumptions than the Harris-Todaro model. However, Heady also discussed certain circumstances under which a lower wage, but one that is probably higher than the rural market wage, should be used.

17. Dinwiddy and Teal, *Principles of Cost-Benefit Analysis for Developing Countries,* Chapter 9.

18. This particular measure is suggested by Heady.

19. If the rural market wage rate is being used to determine the shadow wage rate and a conversion factor exists for each crop, then the shadow wage can be directly computed by multiplying each of the terms in equation (16.5) by its conversion factor.

20. Little and Mirrlees, in particular, emphasize this possibility. The alternative possibility that is often also mentioned in the CBA literature on developing countries is that government investment will be funded through foreign borrowing. This latter possibility is discussed in Chapter 10.

21. K. Hoff and J. E. Stiglitz, "Imperfect Information and Rural Credit Markets: Puzzles and Policy Perspectives," *World Bank Economic Review,* vol. 4 (1990), 329–351.

22. In the framework represented in equation (16.6), the *NPV* would not be estimated by using the shadow price of capital method described in Chapter 10. Instead, the shadow price is incorporated into the third term of the equation.

23. Curry and Weiss, *Project Analysis in Developing Countries,* Table 11.5.

24. The findings are reported in Lyn Squire, "Project Evaluation in Theory and Practice," *Handbook of Development Economics,* Volume II, Hollis Chenery and T. N. Srinivasan, eds. (Amsterdam: North Holland, 1989), pp. 1126–1127.

CHAPTER 17

COST-EFFECTIVENESS ANALYSIS AND COST-UTILITY ANALYSIS

Cost-effectiveness analysis (CEA) and cost-utility analysis (CUA) are commonly used alternatives to CBA.[1] These methods are potentially useful when analysts seek efficient policies but face certain constraints that prevent them from doing CBA. Three constraints are common. First, analysts may be unwilling or unable to monetize the most important policy impact. This constraint arises frequently in the evaluation of alternative health policies; for example, many people are willing to predict the numbers of lives saved by alternative programs but are unwilling to place a dollar value on a life saved. The second constraint arises when analysts recognize that a particular effectiveness measure captures part but not all of the social benefits of each alternative, and some of these other social benefits are difficult to monetize. In using CBA, analysts face the burden of monetizing all impacts. If the effectiveness measure captures "most" of the benefits, it may be reasonable to use CEA to avoid the burden of conducting a CBA. The third constraint arises when analysts deal with intermediate goods whose benefits are not clear. For example, the exact contribution of different types of weapons systems to overall national defense is often unclear. In such situations, CBA is not possible, but CEA may give useful information concerning the relative efficiency of alternatives.

CEA compares (mutually exclusive) alternatives on the basis of the ratio of their costs and a single quantified but not monetized effectiveness measure, such as dollars per lives saved. Programs that cost less per life saved are more efficient than other programs. Cost-utility analysis also relates costs to a single benefit measure, but the benefit measure is a construct made up of several (usually two) benefit categories, reflecting both quantity and quality. For example, the benefit measure may be *quality-adjusted life-years* (QALY), which combines both the number of additional years of life and the quality of life during those years. Programs are compared on the basis of dollars per quality-adjusted life-year, $/QALY. Note that if analysts use only one benefit category, *either* dollars per additional year of life *or* dollars per quality of life, they are doing CEA, not CUA. As CUA measures both quantity and quality of impacts, it comes a step closer to CBA than CEA.

Even though both CEA and CUA have been widely used by analysts working in a number of policy areas, especially health and defense, they are not applied consistently. There is great variation in a number of practices, such as the specification of alternative policies, the justification of effectiveness measures, the inclusiveness of cost components, and the discounting of effectiveness over time.

This chapter first describes cost-effectiveness analysis and discusses some of its problems. We then turn to cost-utility analysis. Next, we discuss the application of CEA and CUA to the evaluation of pharmaceuticals. Finally, we consider the value of league tables.

COST-EFFECTIVENESS ANALYSIS

This section begins with a discussion of alternative ways to compute cost-effectiveness ratios. It then discusses the problems of omitted costs and of omitted (secondary) benefits and proposes a modified cost-effectiveness ratio to handle secondary benefits. In addition to these problems, using CEA ratios to make decisions can be problematic when alternative projects differ in scale. Imposing constraints facilitates decision making.

Cost-Effectiveness Ratios

As CEA does not monetize benefits, it inevitably involves two different metrics: Costs are measured in dollars whereas effectiveness may be measured in lives saved, tons of carbon monoxide reduced, children vaccinated, and so on. Because noncommensurable metrics cannot be added, it is impossible to obtain a single measure of net social benefits from the two metrics. However, it is possible to compute the ratio of the two measures, which can be used as a basis for ranking alternative policies. Obviously, this can be done in two ways.

First, one can measure cost-effectiveness in terms of cost per unit of outcome effectiveness, for example, dollars per life saved. To compute this cost-effectiveness (CE) ratio, one takes the ratio of the cost of each alternative i, denoted by C_i, to the effectiveness (or benefit) of that alternative, E_i:

$$CE_i = C_i / E_i \tag{17.1}$$

This CE ratio can be thought of as the average cost per unit of effectiveness. The most cost-effective project has the lowest average cost per unit of effectiveness. *Projects should be rank ordered from the most cost-effective (those with the smallest CE ratio) to the least cost-effective (those with the largest CE ratio).* Usually, costs are positive, effectiveness is positive, and CE ratios are positive. Sometimes, however, an option is really advantageous—it is both more effective and it costs less than the status quo. For example, bicycle helmet regulations are effective (they save lives) and they save the government money (they have negative cost). For such policies the CE ratio is negative. Even if some CE ratios are negative, we should still rank order projects from smallest to largest CE ratio.

Second, one can calculate the effectiveness-cost (EC) ratio, which is the ratio of the outcome effectiveness units to the cost, or:

$$EC_i = E_i / C_i \tag{17.2}$$

It is important to be aware that, rather confusingly, some authors call *this EC* ratio the cost-effectiveness ratio. This *EC* ratio can be thought of as the average effectiveness per unit of cost. The most cost-effective project has the highest average effectiveness per unit of cost. When using this measure, *projects should be rank ordered from the most cost-effective (those with the largest EC number) to the least cost-effective (those with the smallest EC number), as long as* $EC_i \geq 0$ *(for all i)*.

Both ratios involve computing the ratio of the input to the output (or vice versa) for each alternative. Thus, they measure technical efficiency. As we discuss in the following sections, differences across policy alternatives in terms of scales of project as well as the fact that cost-effectiveness measures often omit important social costs and benefits frequently make them poor measures of allocative efficiency.

In some situations, analysts are interested in whether a new alternative is preferable to the current policy. Thus, there are only two alternatives, which we denote as new (*N*) and old (*O*). Suppose C_N and C_O denote the costs of the new and old alternatives, and E_N and E_O denote the effectiveness of the new and old alternatives. Analysts may calculate the *incremental cost-effectiveness ratio:*

$$\text{Incremental } CE \text{ ratio} = \frac{C_N - C_O}{E_N - E_O} \tag{17.3}$$

When the new alternative is both more expensive and more effective, the numerator and the denominator are positive, and the ratio can be thought of as the average incremental cost per additional unit of effectiveness, for example, \$/life-year gained. Of course, incremental *CE* ratios can be used to compare two new alternative policies.

Measurement of Costs

The measurement of costs in CEA studies varies enormously. In the health care area, costs might only include the cost of treatment. Most narrowly, costs might consist only of the costs of medication. More broadly, costs might include other treatment costs, such as the doctor's time or hospitalization. This is important, for example, in the case of drugs for schizophrenia that may be expensive but may reduce the time in hospital, which is even more expensive. Even more broadly, costs might also include waiting time or time lost from work, which are borne by patients or employers.

Obviously, it is preferable to include all social costs. Costs that are constant across all alternatives can be omitted because this will not change the *CE* rankings, although it will change the *CE* ratios.

In practice, when CEA is conducted for a particular government agency, costs are usually measured as that agency's budgetary costs.[2] In the regulatory area, for example, analysts might measure only the agency's cost of enforcing compliance. It would be better to also include firms' costs of complying with the regulations.

Omitted Impacts: Technical versus Allocative Efficiency

CEA almost invariably omits impacts that would be included in CBA. Most CEA studies consider only budgetary costs. Relevant nonbudgetary opportunity costs are often omitted. Furthermore, CEA considers only one measure of effectiveness. In practice, however, projects often have multiple benefits. For example, regulations that save lives may also reduce injuries or illnesses. Similarly, new drugs may effectively cure a disease and also have fewer side effects than current drugs. To measure allocative efficiency, all costs and benefits should be taken into consideration. One way to get closer to doing this—that is, to reach a "halfway house" between standard CEA and CBA—is to compute the following *adjusted CE* ratio:

$$\widetilde{CE} = \frac{\text{social costs } - \text{ other social benefits}}{\text{effectiveness}} \qquad \textbf{(17.4)}$$

If the numerator can be fully valued and monetized, then this adjusted *CE* ratio incorporates all the impacts that would be included in a CBA. However, the inclusion or omission of a particular category of social cost or benefit from the numerator could very well alter the ranking of alternatives. The danger of obtaining an arbitrary ranking increases as alternatives become less similar in terms of the inputs they require and the outputs they produce. Moreover, the transparency of CEA is also reduced because costs may no longer have a simple interpretation, such as budgetary dollars. For these reasons, moving all the way to CBA with extensive sensitivity analysis is often a better analytical strategy than expanding the scope of measured costs and benefits in CEA.

It is important to emphasize that in CEA there may be a weak link between the measure of effectiveness and something that individuals are willing to pay for. It is quite reasonable to presume that individuals would be willing to pay for incremental units of "lives saved," an often used measure of effectiveness. But now consider the "number of addicts treated." This intermediate output may or may not be a good proxy for a final consumption good that individuals are willing to pay for, such as reductions in street crime. Analysts cannot avoid estimating the value of final consumption goods when doing CBA, even if they must rely on shadow prices from secondary sources. However, in CEA they may not make an explicit connection between the effectiveness measure used and benefits that individuals are willing to pay for. When analysts use an intermediate output as a measure of effectiveness, they should establish a link between the effectiveness measure and a final consumption good or show that the intermediate output has some value.[3]

CEA Where Scale Problems Are Irrelevant: Identical Program Budgets or Identical Program Effectiveness

Even if one ignores the problem of omitted costs and benefits, one may still feel uneasy about selecting policy alternatives on the basis of their cost-effectiveness ratios. This intuition is correct. Ratios do not take into account the different scales of projects, a reason discussed in Chapter 2 for avoiding benefit-cost ratios.

Scale is not a problem if all alternatives have the same cost. Table 17.1 compares three alternative projects (one of which might be the status quo) for saving lives. The only (measured) costs are budgetary costs (in millions of dollars) and the effectiveness criterion is the number of lives saved. The *CE* ratio reveals the average cost per life saved. Of course, in this simple example one does not even need to compute cost-effectiveness ratios: By "eyeballing" the table, one can readily observe that alternative C saves the most lives. Computing the cost-effectiveness ratio simply confirms this. It does not matter whether the ratio is calculated as cost per life saved or as lives saved per (million) dollars. Because all alternatives involve the same level of expenditure, they can be thought of as different ways of spending a *fixed budget*.

TABLE 17.1 Cost-Effectiveness Analysis with Fixed (Identical) Costs

	Alternatives		
Cost and Effectiveness	**A**	**B**	**C**
Cost measure (budget cost)	$10M	$10M	$10M
Effectiveness measure (number of lives saved)	5	10	15
CE ratio (cost per life saved)	$2.0M	$1.0M	$0.67M[a]
EC ratio (lives saved per million dollars)	0.5 life	1.0 life	1.5 lives[a]

[a]*CE* ratio or *EC* ratio of the most cost-effective alternative.

TABLE 17.2 Cost-Effectiveness Analysis with Fixed (Identical) Effectiveness Levels

	Alternatives		
Cost and Effectiveness	**A**	**B**	**C**
Cost measure (budget cost)	$5M	$10M	$15M
Effectiveness measure (number of lives saved)	10	10	10
CE ratio (cost per life saved)	$0.5M[a]	$1.0M	$1.5M
EC ratio (lives saved per million dollars)	2 lives[a]	1 life	0.66 life

[a]*CE* ratio or *EC* ratio of the most cost-effective alternative.

Similarly, scale is not a problem if the level of effectiveness is constant across all alternatives. This is illustrated in Table 17.2, which shows three alternatives for saving the same number of lives, namely, 10. Here, alternative A is best. Again, it does not matter whether the ratio is calculated as cost per life saved or as lives saved per (million) dollars. Situations in which the level of effectiveness is constant across alternatives, or is treated as constant, can be thought of as different ways of achieving a *fixed effectiveness*.

Note that in the case of fixed effectiveness, CEA corresponds to a simple cost-minimization problem (minimize dollars),[4] whereas in the fixed-budget case CEA corresponds to a simple effectiveness-maximization problem (maximize lives saved). Both tables contain examples of *dominated alternatives*—by holding one dimension constant, they ensure that the alternative with the best cost-effectiveness ratio dominates on one dimension and is exactly the same on the other dimension. It is possible that one alternative can dominate another even if they have neither the same cost nor the same effectiveness, as long as it is superior on both dimensions. Clearly, dominated alternatives should not be selected. If an alternative dominates all others, then it should be selected.[5]

Imposing Constraints to Deal with Scale Differences

Scale differences among alternatives may distort choice as illustrated in Table 17.3. If we used a cost-effectiveness ratio, then we would choose alternative A. Yet, if we look more closely at alternative B, we see that it would save a large number of lives at the relatively low "price" per life saved of $0.5 million per life, which is much less than the shadow prices reviewed in Chapter 15. It is, therefore, likely that a CBA would show alternative B has larger net social benefits. Given that CEA was probably proposed in

TABLE 17.3 The Problem with the *CE* Ratio When Scale Differs

Cost and Effectiveness	Alternatives	
	A	B
Cost measure (budget cost)	$1M	$100M
Effectiveness measure (number of lives saved)	4	200
CE ratio (cost per life saved)	$250,000[a]	$500,000
EC ratio (lives saved per million dollars)	4.0 lives[a]	2.0 lives

[a]*CE* ratio or *EC* ratio of the most cost-effective alternative.

the first place because analysts were unwilling to monetize lives saved, how can CEA be used sensibly as a decision rule without monetizing lives saved?

Before answering this question, it is helpful to remind ourselves that if we could replicate project A in 49 other locations (50 in total), the total cost would be $50 million and there would be 200 lives saved. This alternative, which we will call project C, would dominate project B. However, project C is not feasible. If it were feasible, it would have been included in Table 17.3. Implicitly, we always specify an *exhaustive* (i.e., complete) set of alternatives.

In order to use CEA for decision making, a common practice is to impose a constraint, either a minimum acceptable level of effectiveness, denoted $\overline{E}$, or a maximum acceptable cost, denoted $\overline{C}$.

If we impose a minimum level of effectiveness, we may either minimize costs, C_i, or the cost-effectiveness ratio, CE_i. Thus, we could select the project that meets a minimum level of effectiveness at the lowest cost:[6]

$$\text{Minimize } C_i$$

$$\text{s.t. } E_i \geq \overline{E}$$

In this specification, the decision maker is acting as if he or she does not value additional units of effectiveness. This might apply, for example, to alternative ways of ensuring that children receive minimum amounts of fluoride to protect their teeth. It might also apply to some national defense activities. Even in these examples, however, additional units of effectiveness above $\overline{E}$ are probably worth something to decision makers. Alternatively, and perhaps more appropriately, we could select the most cost-effective alternative that satisfies the effectiveness constraint:

$$\text{Minimize } CE_i$$

$$\text{s.t. } E_i \geq \overline{E}$$

This rule generally leads to higher levels of effectiveness and higher costs than the first rule.

If we specified a maximum budgetary cost, $\overline{C}$, we might select the project that yields the largest number of units of effectiveness, subject to the budget constraint:

$$\text{Maximize } E_i$$

$$\text{s.t. } C_i \leq \overline{C}$$

The problem with this rule is that it ignores incremental cost savings. In other words, cost savings beyond $\overline{C}$ are not valued. Alternatively, and perhaps more appropriately, we could select the alternative project that most cost-effectively meets the imposed budget constraint:

$$\text{Minimize } CE_i$$
$$\text{s.t. } C_i \leq \overline{C}$$

This rule places some weight on incremental cost savings and is more likely to result in the selection of a project with less than the maximum cost.

An Illustration of the Different *CE* Rules

Imagine that each of the 10 mutually exclusive and exhaustive projects shown in Table 17.4 is intended to save lives. The expected number of lives saved for each project is given in column 2, and the expected budgetary cost in millions of dollars for each project is in column 3. Dominated projects can be eliminated from the choice set at the outset to simplify the analysis: Project D can be eliminated because it is dominated by project C, and projects C and F can be eliminated because they are dominated by project A.

The cost-effectiveness ratio (cost per life saved) appears in column 4. The projects can be ranked from most cost-effective to least cost-effective using this ratio. Project E is most the cost-effective alternative with an average cost per life saved of $2.0 million. The next most cost-effective alternative is project B, followed by J, then I and A, which are equal, then G, and then H.

Note, however, that project E saves the fewest lives. Project B saves twice as many lives as project E and costs only $24 million more. Which project is better?[7] This question illustrates the problem of different scales. Preferably, we would like the option of performing 2.2 (or more) project Es, but this option is not feasible.

TABLE 17.4   Cost-Effectiveness Analysis with Constraints

				$E \geq 50$		$C \leq 250$	
	Lives Saved	Budget Cost ($M)	CE Ratio (cost per life saved) ($M/life saved)	Budget Cost of Projects That Save at Least 50 Lives	CE Ratio of Projects That Save at Least 50 Lives	Lives Saved of Projects That Cost No More than $250M	CE Ratio of Projects That Cost No More than $250M
Projects							
(1)	(2)	(3)	(4)	(5)	(6)	(7)	(8)
A	100	250	2.5	250	2.5[a]	100[a]	2.5
B	20	44	2.2	—	—	20	2.2
C	100	300	3.0	300	3.0	—	—
D	50	300	6.0	300	6.0	—	—
E	10	20	2.0[a]	—	—	10	2.0[a]
F	100	900	9.0	900	9.0	—	—
G	60	210	3.5	210	3.5	60	3.5
H	50	200	4.0	200[a]	4.0	50	4.0
I	40	100	2.5	—	—	40	2.5
J	45	110	2.4	—	—	45	2.4

[a]*CE* ratio, budget cost, or effectiveness of the most preferred alternative

Suppose the decision maker is willing to specify she will only adopt programs that save at least 50 lives. Which alternative that satisfies this constraint is preferable? The cheapest acceptable alternative is project H, whereas the most cost-effective acceptable alternative is project A. Note that project A costs $50 million more than project H, but it saves 50 more lives. The incremental cost-effectiveness ratio of project A relative to project H is $1 million per life saved, on average, which is very low. Indeed, spending the additional $50 million would be even more cost-effective than project E. However, the decision depends on the decision maker's willingness to trade additional lives saved for additional budgetary cost. Even though CEA is often proposed as a way of avoiding monetization of an important benefit category, analysts or decision makers must often make trade-offs between costs and a nonmonetized benefit in order to make decisions.

The same type of problem arises if a budget constraint is imposed. Suppose, for example, the decision maker indicates she wants to spend no more than $250 million. Subject to this constraint, project A saves the most lives, but project E is the most cost-effective. Again, to choose between projects A and E, the decision maker must consider trade-offs between additional lives saved and additional budgetary costs.

COST-UTILITY ANALYSIS

The greatest use of cost-utility analysis occurs in the evaluation of health policies. In CUA the (incremental) costs of alternative policies are compared to the health changes, usually measured in QALY, that they produce. CUA is most useful when a trade-off must be made between quality of life (morbidity) and length of life (mortality). In principle, however, CUA could be used with any two distinct dimensions of health status. CUA can be thought of as a form of CEA employing a more complex effectiveness measure; all of the previous discussion about decision rules thus applies. The reasons for discussing CUA is that considerable analytical effort has gone into the specific issues relating to measuring QALYs, and CUA is increasingly being used to make resource allocations decisions in health care.

The Meaning of Life—Quality-Adjusted Life-Years, That Is!

As QALYs involve two distinct variables—quality and quantity—the analyst must decide how these variables are to be defined and combined. This is a problem in *multiattribute decision making*. Consider, for example, the effects of three mutually exclusive alternative prenatal programs. Under the status quo, no babies with a particular condition are born alive. Prenatal alternative A will result in five babies being born alive per year but with permanent, serious disabilities. Prenatal alternative B will result in only two live births but with only low levels of disability. Before we can compare the costs of these alternatives to their effectiveness, we first have to combine quantity and quality.

The general form of the problem is shown in Table 17.5. The columns show additional years of life ranging from a low of Y_1 to a high of Y_5. The rows show health status ranging from the worst (health state H_1) to the best (health state H_5). For simplicity,

TABLE 17.5 The Basic QALY Format	Additional Years of Life (Y)				
Health Status (H)	Y_1	Y_2	Y_3	Y_4	Y_5
H_1	Y_1H_1 SQ	Y_2H_1	Y_3H_1	Y_4H_1	Y_5H_1
H_2	Y_1H_2	Y_2H_2	Y_3H_2	Y_4H_2 B	Y_5H_2
H_3	Y_1H_3	Y_2H_3	Y_3H_3 A	Y_4H_3	Y_5H_3
H_4	Y_1H_4	Y_2H_4	Y_3H_4	Y_4H_4	Y_5H_4
H_5	Y_1H_5	Y_2H_5	Y_3H_5	Y_4H_5	Y_5H_5

assume that alternatives A and B and the status quo (denoted SQ) involve the same costs and that there is no uncertainty about the longevities and health status they will yield. Suppose that the status quo gives Y_1H_1 (the fewest years of life in the worst health status), whereas alternative A achieves Y_3H_3 and alternative B achieves Y_4H_2. Clearly, the status quo is dominated, but how should we choose between alternatives A and B? Before answering this question, we must look more closely at the definition of health status.

Defining Health Status

Defining health status is complex. Health states are normally defined by CUA researchers in collaboration with clinicians familiar with variations in health—whether in relationship to particular diseases, injuries, and mental states, or to health in general. This reliance on experts is based on the assumption that neither the public nor potential treatment subjects are likely to have enough information and knowledge to formulate health states. Most often experts formulate health status indexes for specific diseases or illnesses.

George Torrance and his colleagues have developed a comprehensive four-dimensional classification system with the following dimensions: physical function (mobility and physical activity); role function (ability to care for oneself); social-emotional function (emotional well-being and social activity), and health problem (including physical deformity).[8] Paul Kind and his colleagues have developed a disability ranking based on two dimensions: disability level and the level of distress.[9] Their disability levels are no disability, slight social disability, severe social disability or slight work performance impairment, choice of work or work performance seriously limited, unable to work or continue education, confined to chair or wheelchair, confined to bed, and unconscious. Their distress levels are none, mild, moderate, and severe.

Formulating a Health Status Index and Measuring QALYs

How are different health states scaled to form an index? How are changes in the index traded against additional years of life? Obviously, the usefulness of CUA depends on the validity of the methods used to answer these two questions. In the CUA literature, efforts to answer these questions are referred to as measuring the *utilities,* or *utility values,* of individuals.[10]

Three common methods of deriving utilities of health status are the health rating method, the time trade-off method, and the standard gamble method. The methods vary in the extent to which they correspond to the economic concept of utility.[11]

Health Rating Method   Generally, analysts derive a *health rating* from questionnaires or interviews with health experts, potential subjects of treatment, members of society in general, or else on the basis of their own expertise. Respondents are presented with a scale with well-defined extremes. For example, the scale may assign "death" a value of 0 and "good health" a value of 1. Intermediate health states are described in detail to the respondents, who are then asked to locate each state between the end points, 0 and 1. If there are three intermediate health states described to an individual corresponding to "seriously disabled," "moderately disabled," and "minimally disabled," an individual might, for example, assign values of 0.15, 0.47, and 0.92 to these states, respectively.

This rating scale concerns only the health state dimension in Table 17.5. It does not directly provide a method for trading off health states with additional years. However, assuming that health status and longevity have independent effects on utility, the scale values can be directly merged with years of life to obtain QALYs. The two other methods we review scale the health index and can analyze trade-offs between the health states and years.

The Time Trade-Off Method   In the *time trade-off method*, respondents are asked to compare different combinations of length and quality of life. The typical comparison is between a longer life of lower health status and a shorter life with a higher health status. Figure 17.1 illustrates such a comparison. The horizontal axis measures additional years of life (Y) and the vertical axis measures health status (H). Respondents

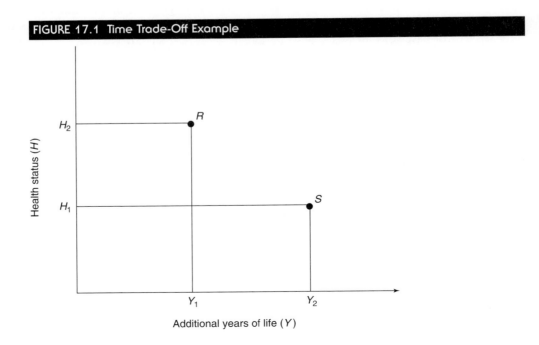

FIGURE 17.1 Time Trade-Off Example

Health status (H)

H_2 — R

H_1 — S

Y_1 Y_2

Additional years of life (Y)

might be asked to compare some status quo point, say R, representing health status H_2 and additional years of life Y_1, with an alternative point, say S, representing health status H_1 and additional years of life Y_2. If a respondent is indifferent between the two points, then he or she is willing to give up $H_2 - H_1$ units of health quality in return for $Y_2 - Y_1$ additional years of life. This pattern of trade-offs can provide a basis for rank ordering the cells in Table 17.5.

This method assumes implicitly that additional years of life are valued equally; that is, there is no discounting of health years.

The Standard Gamble Method   In the *standard gamble method,* respondents are presented with a decision tree along the lines described in Chapter 7. Respondents are offered a choice between two alternatives. Alternative C has two possible outcomes: either a return to normal health for n additional years (occurring with probability p) or immediate death (occurring with probability $1 - p$). Alternative C might be an operation that has probability $1 - p$ of failure (death), but which, if successful, will return the patient to normal health for n years. Alternative D guarantees the patient t additional years with a specified level of health impairment. This choice is shown in Figure 17.2. The probability p is varied until a respondent is indifferent between alternatives C and D. When using a health status index ranging from 0 (death) to 1 (normal health for n years), the p at which a respondent is indifferent can be interpreted as that respondent's utility from alternative D.

Some Caveats on CUA

The issues relating to QALYs are not all resolved. One problem is the issue of discounting additional years of life (the Y axis in Table 17.5). Clearly, it is problematic to discount costs but not to discount health years. The reason is that the cost-effectiveness

FIGURE 17.2 The Standard Gamble Method

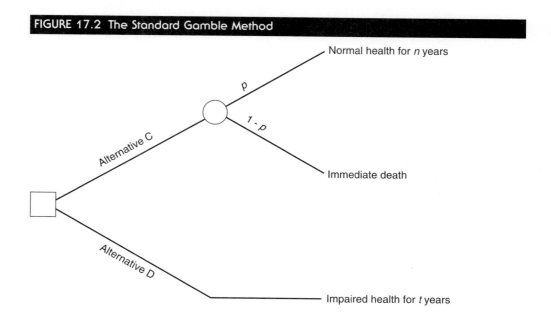

ratio would improve if we delayed the health expenditure until the following year.[12] The basic idea that individuals have positive discount rates relating to additional years is widely accepted, but there is considerable controversy over the theory, measurement, and level of the appropriate discount rate, as we discuss in Chapter 10.[13] One obvious problem when thinking about discounting health is that individuals cannot trade near (far) health years for far (near) health years.

EXHIBIT 17.1

Barbara McNeil and her colleagues conducted a study of laryngeal cancer treatment. First, the authors constructed a health status index for respondents in which 25 years of additional life (the full life expectancy for a 50-year-old male) with normal speech was assigned a value of 100 and immediate death was assigned a value of 0. Second, respondents were offered a choice between (1) a gamble with a 50 percent chance of survival for 25 additional years and a 50 percent chance of death in a few months (which we value as zero), and (2) a specified certain number of years of impaired survival (*t*) ranging between 0 and 25 years. The number of certain years offered with impairment (the lower branch in Figure 17.2) was varied until an individual was indifferent between the two branches. If an individual was indifferent when the value of the lower branch was seven years, for example, then seven additional years of certain life with impairment was assigned a value of 50 on the health status index. Additional gambles were offered to determine the periods of certain survival with impairment that would be assigned health status indexes of 25 and 75.

One of their findings was that executives and firefighters (males, with an average age of 40 years) would trade off 14 percent of their life expectancy to avoid artificial speech. Although most respondents would accept some decrease in life-years to avoid artificial speech, virtually none would accept any decrease in years when only five years or less of certain survival were offered.

Source: Barbara J. McNeil, Ralph Weichselbaum, and Stephen G. Pauker, "Speech and Survival: Tradeoffs Between Quality and Quantity of Life in Laryngeal Cancer," *New England Journal of Medicine,* 305, no. 17 (1981), 982–987.

As these preference elicitation methods are based on questionnaires, many of the issues discussed in Chapter 14 with respect to contingent valuation are also relevant to QALY methods. For example, samples drawn from the general public tend to be more prone to the hypotheticality problems described in Chapter 14—respondents simply have not thought very much about these kinds of issues. This problem can be ameliorated somewhat by providing detailed descriptions of the various health states and the expected changes in years of life. Additionally, in practice, convenience samples rather than random samples are often drawn from the general population. Unfortunately, respondents who are potential treatment candidates because they are already ill may have incentives to exaggerate the utility they would receive from better health states. Finally, of course, either type of sample may be subject to framing (and neutrality) effects inherent in the questionnaire approach. Therefore, a utility elicitation instrument should be subjected to the same kind of validity checks as a contingent valuation instrument. In spite of all these caveats, there is evidence that different samples—whether the general public, potential treatment candidates, or physicians—as well as different sexes, ages, and races, do not vary much in their responses, either in terms of ranking health states or making trade-offs.[14]

Another type of problem arises from the fact that different utility derivation techniques produce different weightings. One recent survey, for example, found that six different methods to assess preferences did not correlate well.[15]

COST-EFFECTIVENESS ANALYSIS IN PHARMACOECONOMICS

Pharmacoeconomics uses economic methodology to evaluate pharmaceutical products. In Canada, expenditures on drugs (including those administered in hospitals) equals 15.6 percent of total health care expenditures (about CDN $13 billion in 1999) and is growing in absolute and relative terms. Some industrialized countries, such as the United States, spend more on drugs per capita, whereas others spend less. In all countries, governments pay a significant portion of these costs. They need help deciding how to allocate scarce resources. CEA and CUA are particularly useful methods for this purpose.

Appropriate methodological procedures for conducting pharmacoeconomic evaluations are well documented. In Canada, for example, analysts are encouraged to follow the guidelines prepared by the Canadian Coordinating Office for Health Technology Assessment (CCOHTA).[16] Other countries have similar guidelines.[17] Most jurisdictions have independent bodies that make recommendations about whether governments should fund new pharmaceutical products on the basis of CEA and CUA studies. For example, in British Columbia, Canada, the Pharmacoeconomic Initiative Scientific Committee (PISC) reviews analyses of new drugs and makes recommendations about whether or not they should be included in the Provincial Formulary.[18] Similar independent bodies exist in other provinces and in other countries. Despite these bodies and clear guidelines for conducting CEA and CUA studies, however, many studies are of poor quality. Indeed, one recent review of the application of CEA and CUA to the evaluation of health policies found that approximately half of the studies examined were of less than adequate quality.[19] Some common problems include:

- No evidence of efficacy or effectiveness. For example, a study may focus on reduction of side effects but not address the issue of whether the drug is effective for its primary purpose.
- Inappropriate comparators. For example, studies fail to include relevant generic drugs in the analysis or they make comparisons to more expensive but inappropriate treatments.
- Exclusion of the cost of therapy.
- Exclusion of other costs (e.g., costs of hospitalization, time off work).
- Costs estimated on the basis of an expert panel without indicating the basis and qualifications of the panel.
- No comparison of the cost of courses of therapy for chronic problems. Some drugs may be more expensive but are taken for a shorter period.
- For short-duration, acute problems, costs are compared on a per-tablet basis rather than on a daily basis.
- Insufficient time horizon for clinical trials. When a drug is expected to be taken for a long time, for example, to maintain weight loss, the trial should be long enough to ascertain whether the drug is effective over a long period, or whether there are adverse side effects, such as gastrointestinal problems, which may not be noticeable in the short run. Trials should also have a long time frame if remission or relapse is possible.
- Different subgroups not studied, even though they may respond differently to treatment. For example, although children may benefit more than other subgroups

from a new delivery mechanism for an old drug, such as inhalers, they may not be studied separately.

Because these and other problems are so common, the PISC has developed a checklist, which appears in Exhibit 17.2. This report is provided to a pharmaceutical company after the committee has conducted a pharmacoeconomic review of its new drug. Such feedback may lead to improved CEA and CUA analyses in the future.

EXHIBIT 17.2

Pharmacoeconomic Assessment: Submission Feedback

Generic (Brand) Name: _____

Manufacturer: _____

Indication: _____

Review Date: _____

	Not Applicable	*Yes (Appropriate)*	*No (Inappropriate)*	*Pharmacoeconomic Initiative Scientific Committee (PISC) Comments*
Comparator				
Choice of drug/treatment comparators:	☐	☐	☐	
Selection criteria:	☐	☐	☐	
Dose equivalence clearly established:	☐	☐	☐	
Therapeutic equivalence and/or advantage established:	☐	☐	☐	
Resource Utilization				
Direct:	☐	☐	☐	
Indirect:	☐	☐	☐	
Cost Estimates				
Direct:	☐	☐	☐	
Indirect:	☐	☐	☐	
Economic Evaluation				
Target audience:	☐	☐	☐	
Study perspective:	☐	☐	☐	
Analytic horizon:	☐	☐	☐	
Discounting:	☐	☐	☐	
Outcome measurement:	☐	☐	☐	
Effectiveness analysis:	☐	☐	☐	
Incremental analysis:	☐	☐	☐	

Transparency of study

Objective:	☐	☐	☐
Hypothesis:	☐	☐	☐
Methods:	☐	☐	☐

Results

Replicable:	☐	☐	☐
Sensitivity analysis:	☐	☐	☐
Subgroup analysis:	☐	☐	☐
Limitations identified:	☐	☐	☐

Information

Listed all pertinent references:	☐	☐	☐
Provided data tables/ collection forms:	☐	☐	☐

Disclosure of Author Relationship	☐	☐	☐

Use of Standardized Submission Form for BC	☐	☐	☐
Compliant with CCOHTA/ Ontario Guidelines	☐	☐	☐

Further comments:

THE USE OF LEAGUE TABLES

CEA and CUA usually compare mutually exclusive alternatives. By definition, this means that the alternative projects address the same problems—for example, alternative methods of breast cancer screening. Yet, both CEA and CUA have been used to make rankings *across* policies that have the same broad purpose (e.g., save lives) but are not necessarily mutually exclusive. *League tables* rank multiple CEAs or CUAs that share the same cost-effectiveness measure. Tammy Tengs and her colleagues, for example, have developed a league table of 587 interventions intended to avert premature death (i.e., to save lives).[20] They found that, on average, the United States spent about $433,500 per life saved or $41,600 per year of life saved (in 1999 dollars). They also asked the question: How many lives would be saved if the same investment were focused on the most cost-effective interventions? They conclude that an additional 60,200 lives could be saved, or about twice as many lives as under the status quo allocation of funds. In an older study, John Morrall found that regulations ranged in their cost-effectiveness from a cost per life saved of $160,000 (steering column protection regulation) to a cost per life saved of $212 million (cattle feed regulation) in 1999 dollars.[21] CUA league tables are usually used to "compare" investments in different kinds of health treatments.[22]

How useful are league tables? Comparisons of mutually exclusive projects inherently control for some of the differences in the measurement of cost and effectiveness. There can be no such presumption when comparing studies across different authors, using different data, and somewhat different methodologies. Different studies may measure costs differently, they may omit different costs, some may include other social benefits, and they may differ considerably in scale. These problems apply even more so to CUA studies because different methodologies are used to calculate QALYs and, as discussed earlier, different QALY methodologies do not necessarily produce consistent results. Therefore, Karen Gerard's caution on the use of league tables is appropriate:

> [A]s more and more studies were read in the course of the investigation, it became striking how many not only placed their results in some standard QALY league table . . . but also purported to present their results as "favourable." It is unlikely to be the case that all of these studies can have "favourable" results.[23]

Thus, caution is warranted in using league tables as guides for policy choice.

CONCLUSION: WHEN IS CEA CLOSE TO CBA?

CEA measures technical efficiency, not allocative efficiency. It can rank alternative policies is terms of technical efficiency but cannot indicate whether something is worth doing. CEA is closest to CBA when all social costs are measured, when the effectiveness measure "captures" all of the social benefits, and when alternative projects are of similar scales. Under these circumstances, the most cost-effective alternative is the most allocatively efficient alternative. However, this does not necessarily imply that it should be adopted because it may not be worth doing. Unless we monetize or value units of effectiveness, we cannot answer this latter question.

When there are significant nonbudgetary social costs or other categories of benefits, CEA is not close to CBA. Analysts have three options. First, they can try to incorporate significant nonbudgetary social costs and other categories of benefits into an adjusted cost-effectiveness measure. Second, if they can also monetize effectiveness, they should, if they can, do CBA. Third, they can move to a more qualitative evaluation method.

Exercises for Chapter 17

1. A public health department is considering five alternative programs to encourage parents to have their preschool children vaccinated against a communicable disease. The following table shows the cost and number of vaccinations predicted for each program:

Program	Cost ($)	Number of Vaccinations
A	20,000	2,000
B	44,000	4,000
C	72,000	6,000
D	112,000	8,000
E	150,000	10,000

   a. Ignoring issues of scale, which program is most cost-effective?
   b. Assuming that the public health department wishes to vaccinate at least 5,000 children, which program is most cost-effective?
   c. If the health department believes that each vaccination provides social benefits equal to $20, then which program should it adopt?

2. Analysts wish to evaluate alternative surgical procedures for spinal cord injuries. The procedures have various probabilities of yielding the following results:
   • Full recovery (FR)—the patient regains full mobility and suffers no chronic pain.
   • Full functional recovery (FFR)—the patient regains full mobility but suffers chronic pain that will make it uncomfortable to sit for periods of longer than about an hour and will interfere with sleeping two nights per week, on average.
   • Partial functional recovery (PFR)—the patient regains only restricted movement that will limit mobility to slow-paced walking and will make it difficult to lift objects weighing more than a few pounds. Chronic pain is similar to that suffered under full functional recovery.
   • Paraplegia (P)—the patient completely loses use of legs and would, therefore, require a wheelchair or other prosthetic for mobility, and suffers chronic pain that interferes with sleeping four nights per week, on average. Aside from loss of the use of his or her legs, the patient would regain control of other lower-body functions.

   a. Describe how you would construct a quality-of-life index for these surgical outcomes by offering gambles to respondents. Test your procedure on a classmate, friend, or other willing person.
   b. Assume that the index you construct on the basis of your sample of one respondent is representative of the population of patients. Use the index to measure the

effectiveness of each of three alternative surgical procedures with the following distributions of outcomes:

	Surgical Procedures		
	A	**B**	**C**
FR	.10	.50	.40
FFR	.70	.20	.45
PFR	.15	.20	.10
P	.05	.10	.05

c. Imagine that the surgical procedures involved different life expectancies for the various outcomes. Discuss how you might revise your measure of effectiveness to take account of these differences.

Notes

1. For a discussion of other less comprehensive techniques, such as cost minimization, see Michael Drummond, Greg L. Stoddart, and George W. Torrance, *Methods for the Economic Evaluations of Health Care Programmes* (Oxford: Oxford University, 1987), pp. 7–9, 39–73.

2. Karen Gerard found that approximately 90 percent of the health studies she reviewed only looked at direct budgetary costs; see Karen Gerard, "Cost-Utility in Practice: A Policy Maker's Guide to the State of the Art," *Health Policy, 21*, no. 3 (1992), 249–279, at p. 263.

3. See Drummond, Stoddart, and Torrance, *Methods for the Economic Evaluations of Health Care Programmes,* especially p. 76.

4. See, for example, Karin V. Lowson, M. F. Drummond, and J. M. Bishop, "Costing New Services: Long-Term Domicilary Oxygen Therapy," *The Lancet*, no. 8230 (1981), 1146–1149.

5. Dominant alternatives tend to be rare but they can occur. For an example, see Russell D. Hall, Jack Hirsh, David L. Sackett, and Greg L. Stoddart, "Cost-Effectiveness of Primary and Secondary Prevention of Fatal Pulmonary Embolism in High-Risk Surgical Patients," *Canadian Medical Association Journal, 127*, no. 10 (1982), 990–995.

6. The term *s.t.* means "subject to."

7. This example illustrates that if we are prepared to monetize the value of a life saved, as in CBA, we can get closer to determining which alternative is the most allocatively efficient. From the cost and effectiveness estimates, we can see that if a life

saved is valued at more than $2.4 million, then project B is preferred to project E; if a life saved is valued at between $2.0 million and $2.4 million, then project E is preferred to project B; on the other hand, if a life saved is valued at less than $2.0 million, then no project at all is preferred to either project E or project B.

8. George W. Torrance, Michael H. Boyle, and Sargent P. Horwood, "Application of Multi-Attribute Utility Theory to Measure Social Preferences for Health Status," *Operations Research*, 30, no. 6 (1982), 1043–1069.

9. P. Kind, R. Rosser, and A. Williams, "Valuation of Quality of Life: Some Psychometric Evidence," in *The Value of Life and Safety*, M. W. Jones-Lee, ed. (Amsterdam: Elsevier/North Holland, 1982), pp. 159–170.

10. For a detailed review of this issue, see Debra G. Froberg and Robert L. Kane, "Methodology for Measuring Health-State Preferences—I: Measurement Strategies," *Journal of Clinical Epidemiology*, 42, no. 4 (1989), 345–354.

11. For an overview and discussion of this issue, see Debra Froberg and Robert L. Kane, "Methodology for Measuring Health-State Preferences—IV: Progress and a Research Agenda," *Journal of Clinical Epidemiology*, 42, no. 7 (1989), 675–685.

12. Emmett B. Keeler and Shan Cretin, "Discounting of Life-Saving and Other Nonmonetary Effects," *Management Science*, 29, no. 3 (1983), 300–306. However, this is not a paradox per se because, as we have shown, a *CE* ratio never tells us whether a project has positive social value and hence,

should be implemented—whether this year or next year.

13. Amiram Gafni, "Time in Health: Can We Measure Individuals' 'Pure Time Preference'?" *Medical Decision Making,* 15, no. 1 (1995), 31–37; Donald A. Redelmeier, Daniel N. Heller, and Milton C. Weinstein, "Time Preference in Medical Economics: Science or Religion?" *Medical Decision Making,* 13, no. 3 (1993), 301–303; Magnus Johannesson, Joseph Pliskin, and Milton C. Weinstein, "A Note on QALYs, Time Trade-off and Discounting," *Medical Decision Making,* 14, no. 2 (1994), 188–193.

14. David L. Sackett and George W. Torrance, "The Utility of Different Health States as Perceived by the General Public," *Journal of Chronic Diseases,* 31, no. 11 (1978), 697–704; Froberg and Kane, "Methodology for Measuring Health-State Preferences," p. 681.

15. See J. C. Hornberger, D. A. Redelmeier, and J. Peterson, "Variability Among Methods to Assess Patients' Well-Being and Consequent Effect on a Cost-Effectiveness Analysis," *Journal of Clinical Epidemiology,* 45, no. 5 (1992), 505–512. For more on the debate over how well different methods get at utility, see A. J. Culyer and Adam Wagstaff, "QALYs versus HYEs," *Journal of Health Economics,* 11, no. 3 (1993), 311–323; and Amiram Gafni, Stephen Birch, and Abraham Mehrez, "Economics, Health and Health Economics: HYEs versus QALYs," same issue, pp. 325–329.

16. Canadian Coordinating Office for Health Technology Assessment, *Guidelines for the Economic Evaluation of Pharmaceuticals in Canada* (Ottawa: CCOHTA, 1997). These guidelines can be downloaded from the CCOHTA Web site, www.ccohta.ca/body-e.html. The Web site also contains well-conducted CEAs and CUAs of pharmaceuticals.

17. See also Drummond et al., *Methods for the Economic Evaluation of Health Programs;* M. Gold, J. Seigel, L. Russell, and M. Weinstein, eds., *Cost-Effectiveness in Health and Medicine* (Oxford: Oxford University Press, 1996).

18. For more information about the PISC see www.pharmacoeconomic.ubc.ca.

19. Karen Gerard, "Cost-Utility in Practice," at pp. 271–275.

20. Tammy O. Tengs, Miriam E. Adams, Joseph S. Pliskin, Dana Gelb-Safran, Joanna E. Seigel, Michael C. Weinstein, and John D. Graham, "Five-Hundred Life-Saving Interventions and Their Cost-Effectiveness," *Risk Analysis,* 15, no. 3 (1995), 369–390. For more on their methodology and policy implications, see Tammy O. Tengs and John D. Graham, "The Opportunity Costs of Haphazard Social Investment in Life-Saving," in *Risks, Costs, and Lives Saved: Getting Better Results from Regulation,* Robert W. Hahn, ed. (New York and Oxford: Oxford University Press; Washington, DC: The AEI Press, 1996).

21. John F. Morrall III, "A Review of the Record," *Regulation* (1986), pp. 25–34.

22. See, for example, Alan Williams, "Economics of Coronary Artery Bypass Grafting," *British Medical Journal,* 291, no. 6491 (1985), 326–329.

23. Gerard, "Cost-Utility in Practice," p. 274.

18

DISTRIBUTIONALLY WEIGHTED COST-BENEFIT ANALYSIS

Government policies, programs, and projects typically affect individuals differently. Thus, in conducting CBAs, analysts often report benefits and costs for separate categories of people. The relevant classification of individuals into groups for this purpose depends, of course, on the specific policy under evaluation. Some examples include consumers versus producers versus taxpayers; program participants versus nonparticipants; citizens (of a nation or a state or a city) versus noncitizens; and high-income persons versus low-income persons.

Once individuals are divided into categories, the first issue that must be decided is whether each group will be given standing in the CBA.[1] For example, in conducting a CBA of U.S. regulatory policy on acid rain, a decision must be made as to whether to give standing to Canadians affected by acid rain resulting from manufacturing in the United States.

Given this decision, costs and benefits may be reported separately for each group receiving standing. But how is this information to be utilized in making a decision concerning the policy that has to be analyzed?

Throughout this book, we have emphasized use of the Kaldor-Hicks potential compensation test in reaching such decisions. In using this test, benefits and costs are simply summed across all groups with standing to determine whether total benefits are larger than total costs and, hence, whether the policy should be adopted. This test examines benefits and costs from the perspective of society as a whole, where "society" is composed of all groups with standing. Indeed, the implicit philosophy behind the Kaldor-Hicks potential compensation test is that, given standing, it does not matter who receives the benefits from a government program or who pays the costs ("a dollar is a dollar regardless of who receives or pays it"), as long as there is a net gain to society as a whole—in other words, as long as the program is efficient in terms of potential Pareto improvement. Strict use of the Kaldor-Hicks test means that information on how benefits and costs are distributed among groups is ignored in decision making.

In making actual policy decisions, however, the way in which benefits and costs are distributed among various groups is seldom ignored. In fact, this consideration can have a major influence over whether a policy is politically acceptable. Hence, in actual decision making, a dollar received or expended by a member of one group may not be treated as equal to a dollar received or expended by a member of another group.

In this chapter, we focus on the role of the distribution of benefits and costs among groups in using CBA for decision making.[2] We first examine the economic rationale for treating dollars received or expended by various groups differently in CBA. We then consider approaches for doing this in practice.

DISTRIBUTIONAL JUSTIFICATIONS FOR INCOME TRANSFER PROGRAMS

The rationale suggested by economists for treating dollars received or expended by various groups differently in CBA is mainly limited to situations in which low-income persons are helped (or hurt) by a program more than other persons.[3] Political decision makers may, of course, treat dollars received or expended by various groups differently, even if their income levels are similar. They may, for example, be influenced by differences among groups in voting behavior or campaign contributions. Economists, however, typically argue for treating dollars received or expended by various groups similarly unless they differ in terms of income or wealth.[4] Consequently, in this chapter, we focus on CBAs of policies that have differential effects on groups that differ by income—for example, projects that are located in underdeveloped regions or programs that are targeted at disadvantaged persons.

To illustrate such a policy, consider a hypothetical program that taxes high-income persons in order to provide income transfers to low-income persons. The tax component of this program is illustrated in Figure 18.1.[5] For purposes of discussion, assume that the market represented in this graph is for a luxury good, such as yachts, that is only purchased by the rich. In the absence of the tax, equilibrium in this market would occur at a price of P_1 and a quantity of Q_1. If an excise tax of t is levied against each unit of output, then the supply curve would shift up by this amount as suppliers attempt to pass along to consumers the additional cost the tax imposes on them.

Using the approach implied by the Kaldor-Hicks rule, a distributional analysis of the costs and benefits associated with this tax would look like this:

	Benefits	*Costs*
Producers		$C + D$
Consumers		$A + B$
Transfer recipients	$A + C$	
Society		$B + D$

Thus, a deadweight loss equal to areas $B + D$ would result from the tax. In addition to this deadweight loss, there are two off-graph social costs that also would result from our hypothetical transfer program:

1. Administering both the tax and the transfer parts of the program would require the use of social resources.
2. Some of those receiving the transfer would probably work less or stop working entirely, thereby reducing the goods and services available to society. In fact, there is

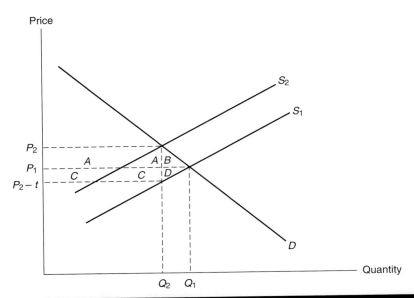

FIGURE 18.1 An Excise Tax on a Luxury Good

Source: Adapted from Arnold C. Harberger, "On the Use of Distributional Weights in Social Cost-Benefit Analysis," *Journal of Political Economy,* 86, no. 2, Part 2 (1978), S87–S120; Figure 1, p. S89.

considerable evidence that this is exactly what occurs under existing welfare programs.[6] Only part of this loss would be offset by the gains in leisure to transfer recipients (see Chapter 11). The remaining residual is a second source of deadweight loss.

It should be obvious that this program would never pass the Kaldor-Hicks test. It must instead be justified on distributional grounds. In other words, one would have to argue that giving a low-income person a dollar warrants taking more than a dollar away from a higher-income person. Apparently, this distributional argument has some force because programs such as AFDC (which is now called TANF) and food stamps, which transfer income from higher-income to lower-income persons, do in fact exist. Hence, it appears that society is willing to sacrifice some efficiency in order to provide assistance to low-income persons.

The importance of this for CBA analysis is that it implies that, in practice, a dollar of benefits received or a dollar of costs incurred by a low-income person is sometimes given greater weight in assessing government programs than a dollar of benefits received or a dollar of costs incurred by a higher-income person. How can this be justified?

THE CASE FOR TREATING LOW- AND HIGH-INCOME GROUPS DIFFERENTLY IN CBA

In the economics literature, there are at least three arguments for giving dollars received or paid by low-income persons greater weight in CBA than dollars received or paid by higher-income persons:

1. Income has diminishing marginal utility.
2. The income distribution should be more equal.
3. The "one person–one vote" principle should apply.

We discuss each of these arguments in turn.

Diminishing Marginal Utility of Income

The first argument is based on the standard assumption in economics that each additional dollar an individual receives provides less utility than the preceding dollar. A corollary of this assumption is that a dollar received or a dollar of cost incurred by a high-income person has less of an impact on his or her utility than it would on a low-income person's utility. For that reason, the argument suggests, it should count less in a CBA.[7]

This argument can be summarized algebraically as follows:

$$\Delta u_l / \Delta y_l > \Delta u_h / \Delta y_h \tag{18.1}$$

where $\Delta u_i / \Delta y_i$ is the marginal private utility (u) of income (y) of individual i, l indicates a low-income person, and h a high-income person.

Income Distribution Should Be More Equal

The second argument for giving dollars received or paid by the poor greater weight in CBA than dollars received or paid by the rich is premised on the assertion that the current income distribution is less equal than it should be and social welfare would be higher if it were more equal.[8] There are several possible bases for such an assertion. The first is that a highly unequal distribution of income may result in civil disorder, crime, and riots. More equality in income may reduce these threats to the general social welfare. Second, it can be argued that there is some minimum threshold of income that is so low that no one can (or, to preserve human dignity, should have to) live below it. This suggests that the income distribution be made more equal by truncating it at the minimum threshold through income floors. Third, some relatively well-off persons may receive utility if the circumstances facing the worse-off members of society improve. Certain types of charitable giving, such as contributions to the Salvation Army, provide some evidence for the existence of this form of altruism. Finally, it is possible that some persons value greater income equality in and of itself.[9]

If for any of these reasons society prefers greater income equality than currently exists, then a dollar increase in the income of a low-income person would result in a larger increase in the welfare of society as a whole than would a dollar increase in the income of a high-income person. Note that this would be true even if the marginal utility of income was not diminishing and, consequently, a dollar increase in the income of high- and low-income persons resulted in equal increases in the utilities of these persons. Each of the justifications listed in the previous paragraph suggests that society as a whole (or at least some relatively well-off members of society) becomes better off if those at the bottom of the income distribution gain relative to those in the rest of the distribution. Thus, the first and second arguments are quite distinct from one another.

Stated algebraically, the second argument implies that:

$$\Delta SW/\Delta y_l > \Delta SW/\Delta y_h, \text{ even if } \Delta u_l/\Delta y_l = \Delta u_h/\Delta y_h \qquad \textbf{(18.2)}$$

where ΔSW refers to the change in aggregate social welfare and $\Delta SW/\Delta y_i$ is the marginal effect on social welfare of a change in income that is received by individual i.[10]

This argument confronts the Kaldor-Hicks test quite directly. It implies that there are some projects and programs that fail the Kaldor-Hicks test but should nonetheless be adopted if they redistribute income in a way that makes the income distribution more equal. In other words, the argument suggests that some programs that are inefficient should be undertaken if they increase income equality sufficiently. This also implies, of course, that some projects that make the income distribution less equal should not be undertaken, even though the Kaldor-Hicks test implies that they are efficient.

The "One Person–One Vote" Principle

This argument begins by noting that the benefits and costs of government programs to consumers are appropriately measured as changes in consumer surplus. Then it goes on to point out that because high-income persons have more income to spend than low-income persons, the measured impacts of policies on their consumer surplus will typically be larger and, hence, will be of greater consequence in a CBA based strictly on the Kaldor-Hicks rule.

This is illustrated by Figure 18.2, which compares the demand schedules of a typical high-income consumer and a typical low-income consumer for a good. If the good is a normal good, that is, if demand for the good increases as income increases, then the demand schedule of the high-income consumer will be to the right of that of the low-income consumer, as the diagram shows. Now if a government policy increases the price of the good, say from P_1 to P_2, both consumers will bear the cost of that increase in the form of a loss in consumer surplus. However, the loss suffered by the high-income consumer (areas $A + B$) will be greater than the loss borne by the low-income

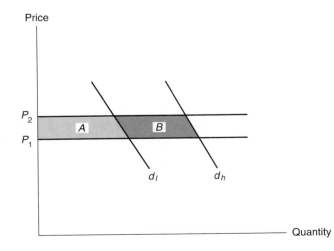

FIGURE 18.2 Changes in Consumer Surplus for High- and Low-Income Consumers

consumer (area *A* alone). As a result, a CBA will give more weight to the impact of the policy on the high-income consumer than to its impact on the low-income consumer.

The final part of the argument suggests that in a democracy, low-income persons should have as much influence over decisions on whether to undertake public projects as high-income persons. In other words, it is argued that "since the principle of 'one person, one vote' is deeply embedded in the concept of democracy," measures of changes in consumer surplus for different persons should be adjusted to what they would be if everyone had the same income.[11] For example, we would count the impact of the price change on the low-income person represented in the diagram at about double what we would count the impact on the high-income person, in effect, equalizing the "votes" of the two individuals.[12]

DISTRIBUTIONAL WEIGHTS

In principle, various groups can be treated differently in a CBA by using *distributional weights*. Distributional weights are just numbers, such as 1, 2, or 1.5, which are intended to reflect the value placed on each dollar paid out or received by each group. Table 18.1 compares a standard and distributionally weighted CBA for two projects affecting two income groups. In standard CBA, as shown in the upper panel of the table, both groups receive an equal weight of 1. In distributionally weighted CBA, group B (the highest-income group) is given a value of 1, whereas group A (a lower-income group) is given a value of 3, implying that a dollar received by a member of the low-income group is valued in the CBA at three times that of a dollar received by the high-income group.

TABLE 18.1 Standard versus Distributionally Weighted CBA

1. Standard CBA

Projects	Net Benefits Group A	Group B	Aggregate Net Social Benefits
I	10	50	60
II	20	30	50
Weights	1	1	Selection: Project I

2. Distributionally Weighted CBA

Projects	Net Benefits Group A	Group B	Aggregate Net Social Benefits
I	$10 \times 3 = 30$	50	80
II	$20 \times 3 = 60$	30	90
Weights	3	1	Selection: Project II

Given this weighting, as shown in the lower panel, project selection switches from project I to project II.

More formally, distributional weights can be incorporated into a CBA through a slight modification of the net present value (*NPV*) formula:

$$NPV = \sum_{j=1}^{m} \left[W_j \sum_{t=0}^{\infty} \frac{b_{tj} - c_{tj}}{(1 + s)^t} \right]$$

(18.3)

where W_j is the distributional weight for group j, b_{tj} are the real benefits received by group j in period t, c_{tj} are the real costs imposed on group j in period t, m is the number of groups, and s is the real social discount rate.

The idea behind this formula is simple. The persons affected by the government policy are divided into as many groups as seems appropriate. Each group is then given a distributional weight. The *NPV* for each group is then computed and multiplied by its weight. These weighted *NPV*s are then added together to obtain an overall *NPV*. Note that in CBAs that rely strictly on the Kaldor-Hicks rule, W_j is implicitly set equal to 1 for all groups.

DETERMINING DISTRIBUTIONAL WEIGHTS

The obvious difficulty with implementing this approach is determining appropriate weights for each group. The weights should, of course, be consistent with the rationale for using them. However, of the three arguments for using weights presented earlier, only the one based on the one person–one vote principle suggests an approach that could potentially be used in practice for valuing the weights of various groups, and even in this case, the information requirements are substantial. Among the required information is the average income level of each relevant group, an estimate of the *income elasticity of demand* for each good affected by the government policy being evaluated (i.e., the percentage change in the quantity demanded of each good that results from a 1 percent increase in income), and an estimate of the market demand curve for each affected good. Given this information, the consumer surplus of the average member of each group could then be computed. These estimates could, in turn, be used to derive distributional weights for each group that are consistent with the one person–one vote principle.[13]

To develop weights that are consistent with the remaining two arguments, information is needed on $\Delta u / \Delta y$ (the marginal private utility of income) and $\Delta SW / \Delta y$ (the marginal effect on social welfare of a change in income) for a typical member of each group of interest. For example, a set of distributional weights could be developed that is consistent with the diminishing marginal utility of income argument if we knew that a $100 increase in income increased the utility of rich people by, say, two units and the utility of poor people by three units by simply computing weights on the basis of the ratio of the marginal utility values. Thus, W_j would be set equal to 1 for rich persons and to 1.5 for poor persons. Similarly, a set of distributional weights that is consistent with the argument that the income distribution should be more equal could be developed if we knew that a $100 increase in the income of a typical poor person increased social welfare by two units, but the same increase in the income of a typical rich person increased social welfare by only one unit.

Unfortunately, such information is not available and there is no known way to obtain it. First, utility is a subjective concept that defies cardinal measurement.[14] Indeed, many economists eschew any explicit interpersonal comparisons of utility for this reason. But in the absence of interpersonal comparisons of utility, it is not possible to develop a system of relative distributional weights that is consistent with the diminishing marginal utility of income argument. Second, there is no general consensus among members of society concerning the specific relationship between a given change in the income levels of individuals and social welfare, except that most persons would, perhaps, agree that the relation is positive and its magnitude is larger for low-income than high-income persons. Without such a consensus, however, it is not possible to develop distributional weights that are consistent with the greater income equality argument.[15]

POLITICALLY DETERMINED WEIGHTS

Given these problems in deriving distributional weights, how can distributional issues be actually handled in CBA? One possibility is to use contingent valuation techniques to determine distributional weights. Distributional weights, after all, can be viewed as a type of shadow price, an effort to measure benefits and costs in terms of their true social value. To the best of our knowledge, however, no attempt has so far been made to do this. If such an attempt were made, it would, of course, be subject to the limitations of contingent valuation described in Chapter 14. Another approach is to derive distributional weights on the basis of revealed political behavior. For example, Otto Eckstein suggested that marginal income tax rates might be used to determine weights for different income classes.[16] For instance, families with annual incomes between $15,000 and $30,000 face a marginal tax rate of 15 percent under the U.S. income tax, whereas families with over $30,000 in income face a marginal tax rate of between 28 percent and 39 percent. One might infer that in establishing these tax rates society, or at least Congress, felt that at the margin, taxing away 15 cents from a low-income person was as painful as taxing away around 30 cents from a higher-income person. Taking this one step further, one could infer that the political process has implied that dollars paid out or received by moderate-income families under a government program should be weighted twice as heavily as dollars paid out or received by families at the top of the income distribution.

Although weighting schemes based on tax rates have been used in CBA,[17] such schemes raise serious issues. One problem is that tax rates do not only reflect what Congress thinks the relative value of a dollar to different income groups should be. For example, Congress may be afraid to set tax rates too high because of concern that high rates will create work and investment disincentives. In addition, Congress may use the progressive federal income tax to offset the fact that other taxes, such as state sales taxes, tend to be regressive. Indeed, it might be better to base weighting schemes on the total tax system than on the federal income tax alone. Finally, an implication of using tax rates to determine distributional weights is that distributional weights should decline as marginal tax rates decline.

An alternative to using marginal tax rates to derive distributional weights is to use public expenditure decisions instead.[18] To illustrate, consider two projects, A and B. If project A has a higher NPV than project B—that is, $NPV^A > NPV^B$—yet project A is rejected and *B* is undertaken, this suggests that decision makers must have viewed project *B* as at least as desirable as project *A* on nonefficiency grounds. One possible explanation is that project *B* provides greater net gains to low-income persons than does project *A* (i.e., $NPV_l^A < NPV_l^B$), whereas higher-income persons would be better off under project *A* $NPV_h^A > NPV_h^B$),

If these conditions hold and the values of NPV_l^A, NPV_l^B, NPV_h^A, and NPV_h^B are known, then it is possible to derive distributional weights by solving the following two simultaneous equations for W_l and W_h:[19]

$$W_l NPV_l^A + W_h NPV_h^A = NPV^A$$
$$W_l NPV_l^B + W_h NPV_h^B = NPV^A$$

(18.4)

The second equation is based on the premise that because decision makers selected project *B* over project *A*, even though NPV^A was actually larger that NPV^B, they must have implicitly used a set of weights that allowed them to treat project *B* *as if* it had an *NPV* that was *at least as* high as NPV^A. The weights are derived by treating the two projects as if, once weighted, they were of exactly equal value in the eyes of the decision makers.

The estimates of W_l and W_h should provide a reasonable approximation of the implicit weights that decision makers used in deciding between the two projects. Unfortunately, however, the estimates may reflect factors other than the concern of decision makers over the trade-off between efficiency and distributional equity. Considerations related to electoral prospects, for example, may very well have been more important in determining the decision.

A final approach to estimating weights is use experiments with real resources to test preferences for redistribution. One type of experimental game, which has been run, placed subjects behind a "veil of ignorance" where they had to decide the rules for allocating goods before they had any knowledge as to their share. Their ignorance was presumed to help produce "impartial reasoning" about their preferences for distributional weights. In one set of such experiments, most subjects preferred allocations that provided everyone with at least a minimum level of income, suggesting that they favored at least minimal redistribution.[20] Another type of experimental game that can be used to get a sense of distributional weights is dictator games. In this type of game, the first player unilaterally decides on the split of a fixed pie between the first player and a second player. Although allocations vary widely, depending on specific game contexts, the evidence suggests that fairness matters, but that it is complex: "Apparently, a player does not care about the other's welfare per se, but desires some kind of equity in the context of this particular interaction."[21]

A PRAGMATIC APPROACH TO WEIGHTING

Given the enormous practical problems with obtaining a defensible set of distributional weights, we suggest that their use be limited to only those CBAs in which distributional issues are of central concern—for example, CBAs of programs targeted at disadvantaged groups or at impoverished areas within countries, states, or cities. Even then, it may often be possible to use an approach that highlights the importance of the distributional implications associated with the policy being analyzed without requiring that any particular set of distributional weights be selected as the "correct" set.

To illustrate the particular approach that we suggest, return to the Work/Welfare Initiative Demonstrations that we first described in Chapter 11. As indicated there, these demonstrations were run in a randomized experimental setting during the 1980s to determine the impacts of various combinations of job search, training, and subsidized jobs for AFDC recipients.

Because these experimental programs were targeted at welfare recipients—an especially disadvantaged low-income group—both their distributional effects and their effects on economic efficiency are relevant. Thus, CBAs of the Work/Welfare Initiative Demonstrations should take both types of effects into account.

Displaying Unweighted Cost and Benefit Estimates

The first step in doing this is simply to display unweighted program impacts on society as a whole, as well as on pertinent subgroups. This is accomplished in the first three columns in Table 18.2, which simply duplicate total net present value estimates for the Work/Welfare Initiative Demonstrations that were originally reported in Table 11.4.[22] Column 1 reports these estimates from the perspective of program participants, column 2 from the perspective of nonparticipants, and column 3 (which is computed by summing the first two columns) from the perspective of society as a whole.

None of the estimates reported in the first three columns of Table 18.2 are weighted. *Even when distributional weighting is used, unweighted estimates of benefits and costs for society as a whole should always be provided in CBAs. In addition, whenever distributional considerations are important, benefit and cost estimates for relevant subgroups should also be provided,* if it is feasible to do so.

The unweighted *NPV* estimates reported in the first three columns of Table 18.2 have two especially important implications. First, they indicate that almost all the Work/Welfare Demonstration programs pass the Kaldor-Hicks test. Specifically, 16 of the 19 unweighted *NPV* estimates for society as a whole, which appear in column 3, are positive. Second, in 6 of the 16 cases that pass the Kaldor-Hicks test, program participants were apparently made worse off by the tested program, whereas nonparticipants—a group that, on average, enjoys substantially higher incomes than participants—were made better off. In these instances, a trade-off occurs between economic efficiency and distributional considerations. (A similar trade-off would also arise if a program failed the Kaldor-Hicks test but participants were made better off. However, this situation did not arise in any of the Work/Welfare Demonstrations.) It is only when such a trade-off occurs that distributional weighting is relevant.

Conducting Sensitivity Tests

Column 4 tests whether the estimates reported in column 3 of Table 18.2 are sensitive to the choice of distributional weights. Thus, in contrast to the unweighted figures appearing in column 3, which are based on the assumption that society values the gains and losses of AFDC recipients and nonrecipients equally, those appearing in column 4 assume that the gains and losses of AFDC recipients are valued by society at twice those of nonrecipients. In other words, participants are given a distributional weight of

TABLE 18.2	Sensitivity of the Work/Welfare Demonstration Estimates to the Use of Distributional Weights				
	NPV from Participant Perspective	*NPV from Non-participant Perspective*	*Unweighted Social NPV (Col 1 + Col 2)*	*NPV If Participant Distributional Weight = 2 (2 × Col 1 + Col 2)*	*Estimates of Internal Weights for Participants (Col 2/Col 1)*
	1	2	3	4	5
AFDC-R (ONE PARENT)					
APPLICANTS ONLY					
San Diego EPP/EWEP					
Job Search Only	$1,077	$755	$1,832	$2,909	NA
Job Search + CWEP	1,335	1,933	3,267	4,603	NA
San Diego SWIM	(1,338)	2,482	1,145	(194)	1.86
Virginia	1,818	1,069	2,887	4,705	NA
West Virginia	(772)	869	(148)	(921)	NA
RECIPIENTS ONLY					
San Diego SWIM	1,103	2,582	3,684	4,788	NA
Virginia	921	304	1,224	2,146	NA
West Virginia	128	1,400	1,528	1,656	NA
New Jersey	1,918	1,625	3,543	5,461	NA
Maine	4,926	(648)	4,278	9,204	NA
APPLICANTS AND RECIPIENTS					
Cook County					
Job Search Only	(638)	722	84	(554)	1.13
Job Search + CWEP	(51)	551	500	449	10.80
Baltimore	2,788	119	2,907	5,695	NA
Arkansas	(721)	1,514	793	72	2.10
AFDC-U (TWO PARENT)					
APPLICANTS ONLY					
San Diego EPP/EWEP					
Job Search Only	(2,000)	2,055	55	(1,945)	1.03
Job Search + CWEP	(2,414)	2,364	(50)	(2,464)	NA
San Diego SWIM	826	2,397	3,222	4,049	NA
RECIPIENTS ONLY					
San Diego SWIM	(1,400)	3,776	2,376	976	2.70
APPLICANTS AND RECIPIENTS					
Baltimore	(1,977)	(2,976)	(4,953)	(6,930)	NA

NA: not applicable.

( ): The parentheses indicate negative net gains or increases in transfer payment amounts.

Source for columns 1–3: Table 11.4 (pp. 290–291).

2 and nonparticipants a weight of 1. Although these weights are obviously arbitrary—as previously stressed, we do not know the actual relative values that society places on dollars received and paid out by participants and nonparticipants—in our judgment, it seems likely that they overstate society's generosity toward AFDC recipients and, thus, test whether the net social gain and loss estimates are sensitive to a rather extreme assumption.

A comparison of columns 3 and 4 indicates that this assumption causes ten of these estimates to become larger and nine smaller. More importantly, however, only three change sign. Although all three of these sign changes are from positive to negative, thereby turning a net gain into a net loss, in two cases, the originally estimated net gain was under $100. Hence, it appears that conclusions concerning whether most of the Work/Welfare Initiative Demonstrations listed in the table were cost-beneficial to society are not very sensitive to the choice of distributional weights.

Computing Internal Weights

Column 5 in Table 18.2 is based on the computation of *internal weights,* an alternative to the approach used in column 4 for distributional weighting. This scheme works best if there are just two pertinent groups, one of which is relatively disadvantaged (e.g., participants in the Work/Welfare Demonstrations) and the other relatively advantaged (e.g., nonparticipants in the demonstrations).

Internal distributional weights are derived by first setting the weight for the advantaged group equal to unity and then computing the weight for the disadvantaged group by dividing the estimated *NPV* for the advantaged group by the estimated *NPV* for the disadvantaged group. The idea is similar to that behind the computation of internal rates of return. Instead of somehow selecting weights, one finds the weights at which the program being analyzed would just break even, in other words, the weights at which the *NPV* for society as a whole would equal zero. Viewed a bit differently, the internal weight for the disadvantaged group indicates the dollars of costs incurred by the advantaged group per dollar of benefits received by the disadvantaged group, if the former is made worse off by the program and the latter better off, or the dollars of benefits received by the advantaged group per dollar of costs incurred by the disadvantaged group, if the former is made better off and the latter worse off.

In Table 18.2, we compute internal weights for Work/Welfare Demonstration participants by dividing column 2 by column 1. We do this, however, only when there is a trade-off between efficiency and distribution, that is, when column 1 and column 3 are of the opposite sign. In all other instances (i.e., when columns 1 and 3 are both positive or both negative), a trade-off between efficiency and distribution does not exist and, consequently, distributional weighting is not germane. As a trade-off between efficiency and distribution only occurred in six instances in the Work/Welfare Demonstrations, only six internal weights for program participants appear in column 5 of Table 18.2.

Each of these six values indicates the weight at which a demonstration program would just break even. Thus, if the "true" weight for participants is larger than their internal weight, programs with positive unweighted social *NPV*s would fail to break even once their distributional implications were taken into account and programs with negative unweighted social *NPV*s would more than break even. However, because the "true" weight for participants is unknown, policymakers would have to make a judgmental decision as to whether dollars of benefits or costs to participants should be given a higher or lower value than that implied by the computed internal weights. Indeed, a major advantage of internal weighting is that it makes the trade-off between efficiency and distribution explicit for policymakers.

For example, in all six of the cases for which internal weights are computed in Table 18.2, program participants were worse off under the demonstration programs, but the unweighted (standard) social *NPV* estimate was positive. Thus, all six programs pass the Kaldor-Hicks test, even though they make the distribution of income less equal. If policymakers believed that dollars lost to participants in the Work/Welfare Demonstrations should be valued at, say, 25 percent more than dollars gained by nonparticipants, this would imply that two of these six programs failed to break even and, hence, should be discontinued even though they passed the Kaldor-Hicks test. If they instead valued dollars lost to participants at three times more than dollars gained by nonparticipants, then this would imply that five of the six programs failed to break even. Thus, they would conclude that five of the programs that passed the Kaldor-Hicks test actually had a negative payoff once their adverse effects on the income distribution were taken into account. But is a weight for participants as high as 3 justifiable? We consider this issue next.

Obtaining Upper-Bound Values for Distributional Weights

It was pointed out earlier in this chapter that pure transfer programs inevitably fail the Kaldor-Hicks test because each dollar of transfer benefits costs nonrecipients more than a dollar. However, it has been argued that transfer programs can be used as a standard to which other types of programs that redistribute income can be compared.[23] Specifically, the argument suggests that if a nontransfer program makes the disadvantaged better off but results in a loss of efficiency, then it should not be accepted if a transfer program that results in a smaller loss in efficiency can potentially be used instead. By the same token, if a nontransfer program makes the disadvantaged worse off but results in gains in efficiency, then it should be accepted if there is a transfer program that can potentially compensate the disadvantaged for their losses without fully offsetting the gains in efficiency from the nontransfer program.

This approach requires that internal weights that are derived similarly to the six values that appear in the last column of Table 18.2 be obtained for transfer programs. This has been done by Edward M. Gramlich, who suggests that setting the internal weight for nonrecipients to unity, the internal weight for transfer recipients is on the order of 1.5 to 2. In other words, Gramlich found that it costs taxpayers around $1.50 to $2.00 to transfer a dollar to a recipient under a transfer program.[24] As Gramlich suggests, although these estimates should be considered tentative, if one accepts them as being of the right order of magnitude, then it can be argued that distributional weights for the disadvantaged should never be set above 1.5 or 2.

Consider, for example, a nontransfer program that costs the advantaged $2.50 for every dollar of benefits received by the disadvantaged. Gramlich's estimates imply that every dollar received by the disadvantaged under a transfer program would cost the advantaged only $1.50 to $2.00. Thus, in principle, a transfer program could be used instead to make the disadvantaged just as well off as the nontransfer program but at a lower cost to the advantaged. Thus, not only does the nontransfer program have a negative unweighted social *NPV*, it is inferior to a simple transfer program for redistributing income to the disadvantaged.

Now consider a program that provides the advantaged $2.50 of benefits for every dollar of costs incurred by the disadvantaged. Under these circumstances, each dollar lost under the program by the disadvantaged could, in principle, be reimbursed through a transfer program at a cost to the advantaged of only $1.50 to $2.00. Hence, this program not only has a positive unweighted social *NPV*, the disadvantaged also can be compensated for their losses without completely offsetting the gains in efficiency from the program. *The argument just presented implies that distributional weights assigned to the disadvantaged should not exceed 1.5 or 2 in value.* Larger weights would imply acceptance of inefficient programs that are also inferior to simple transfer programs for redistributing income and rejection of efficient programs that allow the advantaged to enjoy net gains even when the disadvantaged could be fully compensated through income transfers for losses they suffer.

This argument suggests that the two programs in Table 18.2 that have internal weights well in excess of 2 should definitely be accepted, whereas the two that have internal weights that are close to 2 should probably also be accepted, even though all four programs have adverse effects on the income distribution. (Note here we are switching from distributional weights to internal weights.)

Note, however, that this argument is very similar in spirit to the one underlying the Kaldor-Hicks rule. Both are based on the *potential* use of transfer payments to compensate losers under a policy, while leaving winners better off than they would be in the absence of the policy. Nothing, however, requires that these income transfers actually be made.

CONCLUSION

This chapter focuses on the use of distributional weighting to take account of the fact that many policies have divergent impacts on different income groups. Given the absence of generally accepted sets of distributional weights, we suggest that *the use of distributional weights should be limited to policies that meet both of the following conditions: (1) they are targeted at the disadvantaged; and (2) they result in reductions in overall social efficiency but make low-income persons better off or they increase social efficiency but make low-income persons worse off.*

There may, in fact, be relatively few policies that meet both of these conditions. Those policies that do might be subjected to sensitivity tests based on a plausible range of weights. Or alternatively, internal weights might be computed, thereby providing policymakers with information on which to base their choice of distributional weights. In either case, however, a cogent argument can be made for not allowing the distributional weights for low-income groups to be set much more than 50 percent to 100 percent above those for higher-income groups.

Exercises for Chapter 18

1. A city is about to build a new sanitation plant. It is considering two sites, one located in a moderately well-to-do neighborhood and the other in a low-income neighborhood. Indeed, most of the residents in the latter neighborhood live below the poverty line. The city's sanitation engineer is adamant that "the city needs the new plant and it has to go somewhere." However, he is indifferent as to which

neighborhood it is located in. The plant would operate at the same cost and as efficiently in either neighborhood, and about as many people would be affected by the air pollution emitted by the plant. The city hires an economist to study the two sites. The economist finds that the plant would cause a considerably larger fall in average property values in the well-to-do neighborhood than in the low-income neighborhood, given the more expensive homes that are located in the former. Consistent with this, a contingent valuation study that the economist conducts finds that willingness-to-pay to avoid the sanitation plant is substantially higher in the well-to-do neighborhood than in the low-income neighborhood.

The residents of the poor neighborhood strongly prefer that the plant be built in the well-to-do neighborhood. In the face of the economist's findings, what sort of arguments might they make?

2. Cost-benefit analyses have been conducted of six proposed projects. None of these projects are mutually exclusive and the agency has a sufficient budget to fund those that will make society better off. The findings from the CBAs are summarized here in millions of dollars:

	Net Social Benefits	Net Group I Benefits	Net Group II Benefits
Project A	$2	$2	$0
Project B	6	8	−2
Project C	4	12	−8
Project D	−1	−3	2
Project E	−2	−1	−1
Project F	−2	4	−6

Group I consists of households with annual incomes over $15,000, whereas group II consists of households with annual incomes under $15,000.

a. According to the net benefit rule, which of these projects should be funded?

b. For which of the projects might distributional considerations be an issue?

c. Compute internal distributional weights for the projects you selected in 2.b. Using these weights, indicate the circumstances under which each project might actually be undertaken.

d. Recompute social net benefits for the six projects using a distributional weight of 1 for group I and a distributional weight of 2 for group II. Using these weight-adjusted net social benefit estimates, indicate the circumstances under which each project might actually be undertaken. In doing this, assume that the distributional weight for group II is an upper bound—that is, it probably overstates society's true generosity toward low-income households.

Notes

1. For a further discussion of standing in CBA, see Chapter 2.
2. For a more general discussion of the role of distributional considerations in assessing policy initiatives, see Alphonse G. Holtmann, "Beyond Efficiency: Economics and Distributional Analysis" in *Policy Analysis and Economics,* David L. Weimer, ed. (Boston: Kluwer Academic Publishing, 1991), pp. 45–64.
3. It would be better to distinguish among the persons or families affected by government programs in terms of their wealth (i.e., the value of their

stock of assets) rather than in terms of their income (the observed flow of payments they receive in exchange for the labor, capital, and land that they provide the production process). For example, two households may have similar incomes, but if one owns a house and the other does not, their standard of living may be quite different. However, income is usually used instead of wealth in categorizing individuals or families because it is more readily measured.

4. As discussed in Chapter 16, however, an exception sometimes occurs in the case of less developed countries. Because of the paucity of funds for investment in such countries, some economists argue that each dollar of increase or reduction in savings that results from a project should count more heavily in conducting a CBA of the project than each dollar of increase or reduction in consumption. In principle, however, the relative importance of savings and consumption can be taken into account by using the shadow price of capital approach to discounting, which is described in Chapter 10.

5. This diagram was adapted from Arnold C. Harberger, "On the Use of Distributional Weights in Social Cost-Benefit Analysis," *Journal of Political Economy,* 86, no. 2 (1978), S87-S120.

6. See Robert Moffitt, "Incentive Effects of the U.S. Welfare System: A Review," *Journal of Economic Literature,* 30, no. 1 (1992), 1–61, and the references cited therein.

7. Martin Feldstein's discussion of technical issues in computing distributional weights is premised on this argument. See Martin S. Feldstein, "Distributional Equity and the Optimal Structure of Public Prices," *The American Economic Review,* 62, no. 1 (1972), 32–36.

8. Arnold Harberger's classical examination of distributional weighting ("On the Use of Distributional Weights in Social Cost-Benefit Analysis") can be viewed as a critical assessment of whether this assertion provides a basis for conducting distributionally weighted CBA.

9. These points are discussed in greater detail by Aidan R. Vining and David L. Weimer, "Welfare Economics as the Foundation for Public Policy Analysis: Incomplete and Flawed But Nevertheless Desirable," *The Journal of Socio-Economics,* 21, no. 1 (1992), 25–37. John Rawls, *A Theory of Justice* (Cambridge, MA: Harvard University Press, 1971), and others have provided a more

philosophical basis than the reasons listed here for greater income equality.

10. The first two arguments can be derived more formally by specifying a social welfare function. To illustrate, we specify a very simple social welfare function in which individual utility depends on income, total social welfare depends on a linear combination of individual utilities, and the possibility of interdependent utility (i.e., one person's utility being affected by the gains or losses of others) is ignored:

$$SW = f[u_l(y_l)\ldots, u_i(y_i)\ldots, u_n(y_n)]$$

where n is the total number of individuals in society. Totally differentiating the social welfare function yields the following expression:

$$dSW = \sum_{i=1}^{n} [(\partial SW/\partial u_i)(\partial u_i/\partial y_i)dy_i]$$

where dy_i represents the change in income resulting from a government policy. The first argument implies that $\partial u_l/\partial y_l > \partial u_h/\partial y_h$, whereas the second argument implies that $\partial SW/\partial u_l > \partial SW/\partial u_h$. Thus, together the two arguments imply that $(\partial SW/\partial u_1)(\partial u_l/\partial y_l) > (\partial SW/\partial u_h)(\partial u_h/\partial y_h)$.

11. D. W. Pearce, *Cost-Benefit Analysis,* 2nd ed. (New York: St. Martin's Press, 1983), pp. 64–66.

12. From the perspective of social choice theory, this is a somewhat naive view of democracy. See William H. Riker, *Liberalism Against Populism* (San Francisco: Freeman, 1982).

13. For an illustration of how this might be done in practice, see D. W. Pearce, *Cost-Benefit Analysis,* p. 71.

14. For a brief overview, see Amartya Sen, *On Ethics and Economics* (New York: Basil Blackwell, 1987). For a more detailed discussion, see Robert Cooter and Peter Rappoport, "Were the Ordinalists Wrong About Welfare Economics?" *Journal of Economic Literature,* 22, no. 2 (1984), 507–530.

15. In principle, a set of weights that is consistent with both the diminishing marginal utility of income and the greater income equality arguments could be derived by simply setting them equal to $(\partial SW/\partial u)(\partial u/\partial y)$ for the average member of each group of interest and then dividing the resulting values for each group by the value for the highest-income group. However, finding values for $(\partial SW/\partial u)(\partial u/\partial y)$ is subject to the same informational problems mentioned in the text. Moreover, the term itself was derived in note 10 by first arbi-

trarily specifying a simple social welfare function that did not allow for interdependencies in utility and in which social welfare depends on a linear combination of individual utilities. As noted in the text, general agreement on the form of the social welfare function does not exist. For example, utilities are probably interdependent and the social welfare function could very well be nonlinear.

16. Otto Eckstein, "A Survey of the Theory of Public Expenditure Criteria" in *Public Finances: Needs, Sources and Utilization,* James M. Buchanan, ed. (Princeton, NJ: Princeton University Press, 1961), pp. 439–494.

17. For example, see Robert H. Haveman, *Water Resource Investment and the Public Interest: An Analysis of Federal Expenditures in Ten Southern States* (Nashville, TN: Vanderbilt University Press, 1965); and V. C. Nwaneri, "Equity in Cost-Benefit Analysis: A Case Study of the Third London Airport," *Journal of Transport Economics and Policy,* 4, no. 3 (1970), 235–254.

18. This approach was first developed by Burton A. Weisbrod, "Income Redistribution Effects and Benefit-Cost Analysis" in *Problems in Public Expenditure Analysis,* S. B. Chase, ed. (Washington, DC: Brookings Institution, 1968), pp. 177–208.

19. The empirical analysis in Weisbrod's 1968 paper is actually somewhat more complex than suggested in the text. For example, Weisbrod analyzed four water resource projects considered by the U.S. Corps of Engineers. Of these projects, the one with the highest estimated *NPV* was rejected, whereas the other three were accepted. Thus, Weisbrod used four equations to estimate weights for four separate subgroups (rich whites, poor whites, rich nonwhites, and poor nonwhites).

20. Norman Frohlich, Joe A. Oppenheimer, and Cheryl L. Eavey, "Choices of Principles of Distributive Justice in Experimental Groups," *American Journal of Political Science,* 31, no. 3 (1987), 606–36.

21. Colin Camerer and Richard H. Thaler, "Ultimatums, Dictators and Manners," *Journal of Economic Perspectives,* 9, no. 2 (1995), 209–219.

22. Table 11.4 also provides estimates of the individual benefit and cost components of the various Work/Welfare Demonstrations.

23. This argument was apparently first made by Arnold C. Harberger, "On the Use of Distributional Weights in Social Cost-Benefit Analysis."

24. Edward M. Gramlich, *A Guide to Benefit-Cost Analysis,* 2nd ed. (Englewood Cliffs, NJ: Prentice Hall, 1990), pp. 123–127. Gramlich bases his conclusion on his own "simple analysis" and on findings from a general equilibrium computer simulation conducted by Edgar Browning and William Johnson ["The Trade-Off between Equality and Efficiency," *Journal of Political Economy,* 92, no. 2 (1984), 175–203]. Both analyses are examples of attempts to compute the marginal excess burden associated with taxes, which is discussed in Chapter 15.

CHAPTER

19 | HOW ACCURATE IS CBA?

Chapter 1 emphasizes that CBA can be useful as a public-sector decision-making tool. In practice, its usefulness depends on its accuracy. One way to examine the accuracy of CBA is to perform analyses of the same project at different times and to compare the results. We suggest in Chapter 1 that *ex ante/ex post* comparisons and *ex ante/in medias res* comparisons are most valuable for learning about the accuracy of CBA. However, that discussion provides few details. We now return to this subject in more detail.[1]

An *ex ante* CBA is performed when the decision is made about whether or not to proceed with a proposed project. We refer to this time as year 0 or $t = 0$. An *ex post* analysis is performed after all the impacts of the implemented project have been realized. This may take many years, even centuries. Suppose that, in fact, all impacts have occurred by year T, then an *ex post* analysis is one performed in year t, where $t \geq T$. Although an *ex post* analysis is conducted too late to influence a decision about this particular project, it offers insight into similar projects. An *in medias res* analysis is performed in some year t, where $0 < t < T$. An *in medias res* analysis may provide information about similar projects or about whether to continue or to terminate a particular project, if not yet completed. Both *in medias res* and *ex post* analyses are performed in the same way as *ex ante* analysis but use data actually revealed from the project. As time passes, there is usually less uncertainty about impacts and, therefore, it is possible to obtain more accurate estimates of the actual *NPV* of the project.

Accuracy of CBA depends on how well the analyst performs the nine steps presented in Chapter 1. Each step is subject to errors. The most important ones for analysts and decision makers relate to specifying the impact categories, predicting the impacts, and valuing the impacts and, for *in medias res* or *ex post* studies, measurement error. Difficulties associated with the other steps, although they occur frequently enough, should be avoidable by analysts with a good training in the concepts of CBA. In this chapter, then, we consider only omission errors, forecasting errors, measurement errors, and valuation errors.

In general, these errors decline as CBAs are performed later, but they never reach zero. Thus, CBAs performed toward the end of a project are more accurate than those performed earlier, but even later studies contain errors. This chapter illustrates these errors in CBA by providing a detailed example of the highway project discussed in Chapter 1. This project has been the subject of three separate CBAs performed at different times—one *ex ante*, one *in medias res,* and one *ex post*.

The estimates of net benefits differ considerably across the studies. Contrary to what might have been expected, the largest source of the difference was not errors in forecasts, nor differences in evaluation of intangible benefits, but from major differences in declared and actual construction costs of the project. Thus, the largest errors arose from what most analysts would have thought were the most reliable figures entered into the CBA.

SOURCES OF ERRORS IN CBA STUDIES

Errors in CBA studies may arise for many reasons. They may result from the manager's bureaucratic lens, as we discussed in Chapter 1.[2] Some errors in CBA studies appear to be disingenuous or strategic, that is, resulting from self-interest. There is considerable evidence that managers systematically overestimate benefits and underestimate costs; see, for example, Exhibit 19.1.[3] Strategic bias of this sort is widespread among managers and does not appear to be limited to the public sector.[4] For example, Nancy Ryan found that nuclear power projects experienced "awe-inspiring" cost overruns, some attributable to strategic underestimation of costs.[5]

EXHIBIT 19.1

Political and bureaucratic actors not only directly underestimate costs and overestimate benefits of their favored alternative, they also overestimate the costs and underestimate the benefits of alternatives they do not favor. John Kain documents the use of such "straw men" alternatives by Houston's regional transit authority in its consideration of a new urban light rail system. He shows how it made its preferred rail alternative appear better by "goldplating" the all-bus alternatives. For example, it overestimated the capital costs of the bus-way alternatives in one report by 70 percent.

Source: John F. Kain, "The Use of Straw Men in the Economic Evaluation of Rail Transport Projects," *American Economic Review: Papers and Proceedings,* 82, no. 2 (1992), 487–493.

When CBAs are performed by independent analysts, as was the case for our highway example, one would not expect to encounter strategic bias. Consequently, this section focuses on other potential causes of errors.

Omission Errors

Analysts may exclude some impact category completely because they think it is too unlikely to occur. This problem is quite likely when a project is highly technical and there are genuine disagreements about the physical impacts. There is, for example, still much uncertainty about the fundamental scientific relationships concerning global warming.[6] The scientific literature pertaining to many environmental issues, from dioxins to the marbled murrelet, is sparse or controversial. Analysts may find themselves in the middle of a "battle of the experts," not knowing with certainty what the impacts are of various policy alternatives. For our highway example, we would be surprised if there were significant problems of this sort.

Double counting is the converse of omission and, consequently, can be considered in this section. One way analysts double count benefits is by including benefits that arise in both the primary market and a secondary market, for example, including both time saved and increases in house prices. As we discuss in Chapter 5, benefits (or costs) in secondary markets should not be included when prices equal social marginal costs.

Although omission errors may be present in a CBA conducted at any time, we would expect these errors would decline over a project's lifetime. Undoubtedly, as a project progresses, more knowledge comes to light concerning the actual impact categories. Thus, omission errors are likely to be less frequent in CBAs performed later.

Forecasting Errors

Forecasting errors in CBA can arise from inherent difficulties (due, e.g., to the difficulty of predicting technological change), cognitive biases, changing project specifications as well as for strategic reasons. Forecasting beyond a few months is often inaccurate whatever the context.[7] The difficulty of accurate forecasting generally increases as projects are more complex, are unique, are further in the future, and involve unknown cause-and-effect relationships.[8]

The impacts of some government projects are relatively easy to predict because they are of low complexity, are not unique, and are easily comparable to previous projects. Small road improvements, for example, typically fall into this category. In contrast, major projects such as the Chunnel (the Channel tunnel between England and France) are complex, not easily compared to previous projects, and have impacts that extend far into the future.

Unknown cause-and-effect relationships frequently arise when there is uncertainty concerning fundamental scientific relationships, as discussed previously. They also arise when a government attempts a new project and analysts cannot be certain how affected individuals will respond. Evidence suggests, for example, that some individuals tend to react to new rules and regulations with "offsetting behavior," which attenuates the anticipated benefits of risk-reducing regulations.[9]

In the presence of uncertainty, both the people affected by policies and analysts of policies are potentially subject to cognitive biases. Evidence suggests that people systematically underweight low-probability "bad" events and overweight low-probability "good" events.[10] People who live on flood plains buy too many lottery tickets and not enough flood insurance! Analysts and decision makers are not immune from such biases. Indeed, there is a large literature concerning the importance of cognitive perceptions on decision making and information processing. Charles Schwenk provides a summary of the effect of cognitive biases on decision making, which one can reasonably assume also pertains to forecasting.[11] The main conclusion of this literature is that cognitive biases may lead analysts to make severe and systematic errors of forecast and judgment, with an overall tendency toward overoptimism.

Forecasting errors also arise due to changing project specifications. Large and complex projects are invariably modified when underway, often as a result of irresistible "evolutionary" adaption by front-line employees.[12]. Sometimes these changes are quite substantial. For example, changing regulatory requirements contributed significantly to construction cost overruns of nuclear power plants.[13] When projects are later modified, *ex ante/ex post* comparisons may, in effect, compare apples and oranges.

There is a tendency to assume that forecasting errors do not arise in *ex post* analysis because all impacts have been realized. But the analyst must still compare what did happen to what would have happened in the absence of the project—the counterfactual. Although analysts may know what did happen (subject to measurement error), they must estimate what would have happened if the project had not been implemented. In general, though, *ex post* forecasting error is likely to be smaller than *ex ante* forecasting error.

Measurement Errors

There is a tendency to assume that once an impact has occurred, all uncertainty associated with the impact is removed. But, in practice, impacts are often observed, recorded, or interpreted inaccurately. The extent of this problem depends largely on the quality of the measurement equipment (technology) and on the ability of statistical or econometric methods to make inferences in the presence of measurement errors (methodology). These problems have received little specific attention within the CBA literature. One possible explanation is that they are perceived as being of relatively little importance compared to other problems. Another reason is that current statistical methods for handling measurement error are complex, have stringent data requirements, or require strong underlying assumptions.

Valuation Errors

Accurate monetary estimates of the social value (i.e., shadow prices) of some impacts are scarce, as we discuss in Chapter 15. Until recently, even estimates of the value of such important categories as time saved and lives saved varied widely; many previous estimates were inaccurate. Valuation problems can be much greater in some CBA contexts than in others. For example, as we discuss in Chapter 16, obtaining appropriate shadow prices is particularly difficult for projects in developing countries.[14]

Valuation errors also arise due to unanticipated relative price changes. (This is a forecasting error rather than a valuation error.) This type of error can have significant impacts, especially on large infrastructure development projects.

THE DISTRIBUTION OF NET BENEFITS OVER TIME

Different types of error have different impacts on estimated net benefits. Furthermore, these errors have different impacts at different times. This section examines how the distribution of net benefits changes over time.

Suppose NB_t denotes the present value (in year 0 dollars) of the net benefits of a project at time t. NB_t is a random variable with a probability density function, $f_t(NB_t; \mu_t, \sigma_t)$, where μ_t is the mean and σ_t is the standard deviation. *Ex ante*, the distribution of the present value of net benefits, NB_0, typically has quite a large variance. Over time some impacts are realized—nature "rolls the dice" on some impact variable—for example, the initial volume of traffic. Consequently, the distribution of NB_t changes over time. The mean of the distribution, μ_t, may increase or decrease relative to the *ex ante* mean, μ_0. It may sometimes be above NB_t, the actual net benefits of the project, and sometimes below NB_T, but it will tend to approach NB_T over time. In contrast, the variance monotonically decreases over time, although it never equals zero.

These changes in the distribution of NB_t over time are represented graphically in Figure 19.1. Here, the present value of net benefits has an approximate normal distribution, which is a reasonable assumption for any project with many impacts. As t increases, the distribution of NB_t changes, its mean tends to move closer to NB_T and its variance decreases. As t approaches T, NB_t converges toward NB_T, which is represented by the vertical line in Figure 19.1.

Now consider the effects on omission, forecasting, valuation, and measurement errors when we vary the time in which a CBA is conducted. Omission errors will certainly decline over time as more is known about the project. Similarly, forecasting errors are likely to be reduced or eliminated as impacts are realized. Of course, as we mentioned earlier, even in an *ex post* study there may be some forecasting errors due to the problem associated with predicting the counter-factual events. Valuation errors are also likely to decline over the life of a project due to methodological improvements in valuing impacts. Although measurement errors may not change over time, this type of error is likely to be relatively small. Thus, in aggregate, as t increases, the variance of the estimate of the present value of net benefits will decrease. It will never equal zero: Uncertainty is reduced but never completely resolved.

Whether estimates of the present value of net benefits are consistently above or below NB_T, that is, whether estimators are systematically positively or negatively biased depends on whether omission, forecasting, measurement, or valuation errors are systematically biased (as well as on the size of these biases relative to other errors). Obtaining and comparing estimates of net benefits at different times provides clues about the magnitude of the different types of errors in a CBA and about the presence

FIGURE 19.1   Illustrative Probability Density Functions of the Present Value of Net Benefits at Time 0, Time *t*, and the Actual Net Benefits, NB_T.

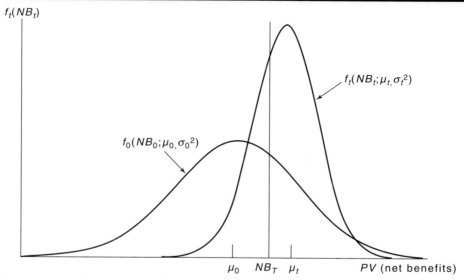

Source: Same as Table 19.1, page 479.

of systematic biases. With such knowledge, analysts may be able to provide better information about the precision of their estimates in similar situations.

SUMMARY OF THE CBAs OF THE COQUIHALLA HIGHWAY

The Coquihalla Highway is a four-lane toll road, which improves access to the interior of British Columbia (B.C.) from Vancouver; see Figure 19.2. Alternate routes are generally two lanes, with occasional sections of passing lanes. Congestion and safety concerns on alternate routes were important factors in the decision to build the new highway. Construction was performed in three phases. Phase I, which extends for 115 kilometers from Hope to Merritt, was completed in 1986. Phase II, which extends for another 80 kilometers from Merritt to Kamloops, was completed in 1987. Phase III extends east from Merritt for 108 kilometers to Peachland (near Kelowna) and was completed in 1990.

FIGURE 19.2 Map of the Coquihalla Highway and Nearby Routes

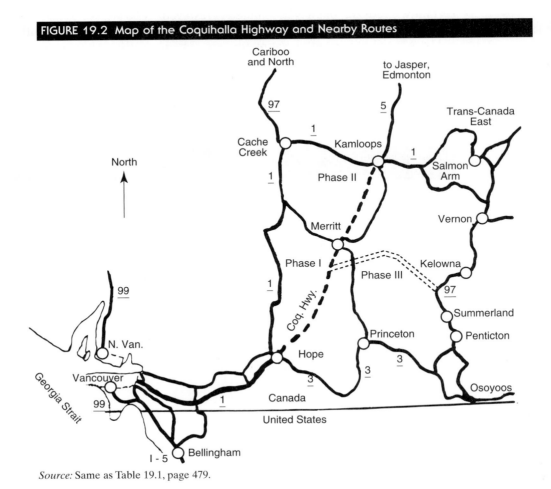

Source: Same as Table 19.1, page 479.

Three CBAs of the Coquihalla Highway are summarized in Table 19.1.[15] All were performed by independent analysts from the perspective of 1984 when the initial decision was made but used the information available at the time the CBA was conducted. Each study took a global perspective; that is, everyone had standing, including foreigners. All three studies assumed there would be tolls at the levels that were implemented initially. All CBAs were compared to the status quo (no new highway in this region) alternative. Furthermore, all used a 7.5 percent real social discount rate with a discounting period of 20 years, the assumed life of the project. Benefits and costs were expressed as present values in 1984 Canadian dollars. It is important to note that the *ex ante* study was performed on the first two phases only, whereas the other two studies were performed on all three phases.

The first CBA was conducted by Waters and Meyers, henceforth WM, in 1986.[16] This is essentially an *ex ante* study, although Phase I was just opening at that time. The authors used "information and forecasts developed before the highway was built as this is more relevant to assessing the original decision to build the highway."[17] The impact categories, which are listed in Table 19.1, are self-explanatory. Because the CBAs were performed from the global perspective, there is no impact category for toll revenues, which are transfers. WM calculated the present value of the net benefit of the project to be $40.2 million in 1984 dollars.

TABLE 19.1 Three CBAs of the Coquihalla Highway

	Waters and Meyers Phases I and II	Mallery Phases I, II, and III	Boardman, Mallery, and Vining Phases I, II, and III
	Ex Ante	**In Medias Res**	**Ex Post**
PROJECT BENEFITS:			
Time and operating savings	$290.7	$417.6	$900.3
Safety benefits	36.5	51.5	203.1
Reduced congestion on alternative routes	14.1	29.7	56.6
Terminal value after 20 years	53.3	140.6	147.8
Total Benefits	$396.6	$639.4	$1,307.8
PROJECT COSTS:			
Construction	$338.4	$702.6	$837.2
Toll collection	8.4	8.4	8.4
Maintenance and snow removal	7.6	56.6	67.9
Total Costs	$354.4	$767.6	$913.5
NET BENEFITS	$40.2	($128.2)	$394.3

Note: All figures are present values expressed in millions of 1984 Canadian dollars, discounted at 7.5 percent, assuming a project life of 20 years.

Source: Anthony E. Boardman, Wendy L. Mallery, and Aidan R. Vining, "Learning from *Ex Ante/Ex Post* Cost-Benefit Comparisons: The Coquihalla Highway Example," *Socio-Economic Planning Sciences,* 28, no. 2 (1994), 69–84, Table 2, p. 77. Reprinted with kind permission from Elsevier Science Ltd, The Boulevard, Langford Lane, Kidlington OX5 19GB, UK.

The second study was conducted by Wendy L. Mallery, hereafter MLY, in late 1987.[18] At that time, Phases I and II had been completed, but Phase III had not. MLY had access to actual traffic data (for 16 months for Phase I and for one month for Phase II) and published estimates of actual construction costs. Thus, MLY's study is an early *in medias res* CBA.

The most recent study by Anthony Boardman, Wendy Mallery, and Aidan Vining, hereafter BMV, was completed in 1993, although some impacts were estimated earlier.[19] Despite the fact that this study was conducted before the end of the project's life, we will treat it as an *ex post* study.

ANALYSIS OF THE DIFFERENCES AMONG THE CBAs

This section discusses the different types of errors that occurred in the Coquihalla Highway CBAs and the reasons for these errors. As the sources of many errors are unobservable, it is often impossible to disentangle the separate effect of each source. It is often virtually impossible to disentangle the degree to which errors result, for example, from optimism bias or from strategic bias.

Omissions

It could be argued that there were omission errors in all three studies. No study considered the opportunity cost of the land occupied by the highway. This land was owned by the provincial government. Even analysts have a tendency to treat publicly owned land as "free," which, of course, is incorrect. In fact, the land did not have a high opportunity cost and so excluding it did not have a large impact on the *NPV*s.

There is considerable controversy over the highway's environmental impacts. Though there is no separate impact category for environmental damage in any of the studies, the cost of constructing underpasses, which allow animals to safely cross underneath the highway, careful timing of construction activity, and special efforts to repair any encroachment of rivers were included in construction costs. All studies assumed implicitly that, after taking these actions, environmental impacts would be negligible. Environmentalists, however, contend the actual environmental impacts (e.g., wild animal road kills, wildlife and fish habitat destruction) are quite large.

None of the CBAs includes benefits associated with regional development. Such indirect, local benefits are generally viewed in CBA as transfers from other areas rather than real benefits. Yet, analysis of indirect effects becomes complicated in the presence of *network externalities* (also called *spillover benefits* and *agglomeration effects*). Since the construction of the highway, there has been an unexpected economic boom in Kelowna. These positive network externalities or agglomeration effects may be partially attributable to the highway.[20] If so, it would be legitimate to treat part of the regional development benefits as real benefits.

Forecasting Differences

Traffic Volume Data on the Coquihalla and Other Routes   Estimates of traffic volume are likely to be the most crucial forecast in a highway CBA because they directly affect many of the benefit categories. Traffic levels are difficult to predict. Furthermore, they may change over the life of the project as potential consumers "learn" about the advantages and disadvantages of the highway and alternative routes, as population distributions change, and as consumer tastes change.

WM obtained aggregate annual traffic forecasts by applying recent traffic growth patterns to a British Columbia Ministry of Transportation forecast for 1986, and allowing for an "EXPO 86" traffic bulge. They then disaggregated the data into different origin-destination groups for three categories of vehicles (trucks, passenger vehicles-work, and passenger vehicles-leisure). For each group, they estimated the proportion of diverted, undiverted, and generated traffic.[21] Price-sensitive diversion rates were used to account for the impacts of tolls on the Coquihalla Highway.

MLY used actual Coquihalla traffic counts from May 1986 (when Phase I opened) to September 1987 (when Phase II opened). For subsequent years, MLY produced three different *NPVs*, assuming a 1 percent, 3 percent, and 5 percent annual traffic growth. The 3 percent rate is used in Table 19.1. Under this assumption, total vehicle traffic (at the toll booth) in the years 2000 and 2005 was projected to be 2.85 million and 3.65 million, respectively. MLY estimated the annual average daily traffic allocations on alternative routes for 1984 to 1987 based on actual average summer daily traffic counts.[22] This historical information was used to estimate a diversion rate of 30 percent for Highway 3 traffic to the Coquihalla after the completion of Phase III.

BMV draw on four sources of data: (1) toll booth receipts for the years from 1986 to 1990, which were broken out by the following vehicle classes: motorcycles, passenger vehicles, trucks with two axles, three axles, four to five axles, or six axles or more;[23] (2) perusal of April 1991 traffic counts at the Coquihalla toll booth and on the Okanagan Connector (Phase III), which shows completion of Phase III increased Coquihalla traffic by about 40 percent; (3) counters on all alternative routes for 1985 to 1989. (When the summer traffic counts for each highway section were then adjusted to account for seasonality, summer traffic was 1.25 to 1.9 times the annual average daily traffic); (4) Ministry of Transportation origin-destination surveys, which suggested 90 percent of passenger vehicles were leisure travelers, whereas 10 percent were business travelers. Based on these data, and assuming a 5 percent annual growth rate (after completion of Phase III), BMV project annual Coquihalla traffic volumes of 4.03 million and 5.14 million vehicles for the years 2000 and 2005, respectively.

It is impossible to determine the accuracy of the traffic volume forecasts of WM's *ex ante* study because they did not present them, nor did they specify the growth rate. Backward induction suggests that WM only slightly overestimated initial use but seriously underestimated future traffic volumes. MLY used actual data for the initial year and then estimated a growth rate of 3 percent, whereas actual growth has been about 5 percent. MLY predicted that the opening of Phase III would increase the traffic base by 20 percent, but preliminary evidence suggests it increased by about 40 percent. BMV's *ex post* study projections for the years 2000 and 2005 are 41 percent higher than MLY's estimates.

Time and Distance Savings on the Coquihalla   One would expect that time and distance savings per trip would not vary by very much among the studies. In fact, they did vary, as shown in Tables 19.2 and 19.3. Differences in distance are due to changes in the final design as well as the use of different data to measure distance. Differences in time saved are due to differences in distance saved and different assumptions about the speeds traveled on different routes.

TABLE 19.2	Distance Saved per Coquihalla Trip (Kilometers)		
	Waters and Meyers	*Mallery*	*Boardman, Mallery, and Vining*
Trip	**Ex Ante**	**In Medias Res**	**Ex Post**
Phase I: Hope to Merritt	N/A[a]	87	112
Phases I and II: Hope to Kamloops	72	83	107
Phases I and III: Hope to Peachland	N/A	77	53

[a]N/A = Not available or not applicable.
Source: Anthony E. Boardman, Wendy L. Mallery, and Aidan R. Vining, "Learning from *Ex Ante/Ex Post* Cost-Benefit Comparisons: The Coquihalla Highway Example," *Socio-Economic Planning Sciences*, 28, no. 2 (1994), 69–84, Tables 3A and 3B, p. 79. Reprinted with kind permission from Elsevier Science Ltd, The Boulevard, Langford Lane, Kidlington OX5 19GB, UK.

TABLE 19.3	Time Saved per Coquihalla Trip (Minutes)		
	Waters and Meyers	*Mallery*	*Boardman, Mallery, and Vining*
Trip	**Ex Ante**	**In Medias Res**	**Ex Post**
Phase I: Hope to Merritt	N/A[a]	102	108
Phases I and II: Hope to Kamloops	72	89	120
Phases I and III: Hope to Peachland	N/A	100	79

[a]N/A = Not available or not applicable.
Source: Anthony E. Boardman, Wendy L. Mallery, and Aidan R. Vining, "Learning from *Ex Ante/Ex Post* Cost-Benefit Comparisons: The Coquihalla Highway Example," *Socio-Economic Planning Sciences*, 28, no. 2 (1994), 69–84, Tables 3A and 3B, p. 79. Reprinted with kind permission from Elsevier Science Ltd, The Boulevard, Langford Lane, Kidlington OX5 19GB, UK.

Reduced Congestion on Alternative Routes   WM estimated that, due to the Coquihalla, through traffic on the old routes would save 20 minutes during congested periods. They assumed local traffic would save less, proportional to the number of cars diverted to the new highway. MLY also used the 20-minute saving. BMV followed a different approach, assuming users of alternative routes would save 2 kph in 1986, and 5 kph from 1987 onward.

Accident Rates   WM calculated safety benefits resulting from both reduced distance traveled and from traveling on a safer highway. To estimate safety benefits from reduced distances, they multiplied the predicted 130 million vehicle-kilometers saved by the accident rates for fatal, injury, and property-damage-only accidents on two-lane highways determined by Radnor Pacquette and Paul Wright.[24] To estimate benefits resulting from a safer road, they multiplied the estimated 313 million vehicle-kilometers traveled on the Coquihalla by one-third of the accident rate—their estimate of the accident rate reduction due to using a four-lane divided highway versus the existing highway. MLY followed a similar approach but, for benefits due to a safer road, she used the higher accident rate reductions implied by Pacquette and Wright, which ranged from 35 to 50 percent, depending on the severity of accident. BMV obtained accident rate data by severity from the Ministry of Transportation.

The Coquihalla Highway does save lives. The fatal accident rate of the Coquihalla is about 50 percent lower than on alternate routes, a higher reduction than WM assumed but similar to MLY's estimate. Furthermore, actual fatal accident rates on all routes in British Columbia are higher than WM or MLY assumed. Consequently, more lives are saved due to reduced distance driving than either WM or MLY predicted. Relative to other routes, the Coquihalla has a lower injury rate but higher property-damage-only rate. Nonetheless, because both of these types of accident rates are also higher in British Columbia than anticipated, the shorter Coquihalla generates much higher safety benefits than projected.[25]

Estimation/Measurement Differences

Maintenance Expenses   At the time of the *ex ante* study, the Maintenance Services Branch estimated the cost of annual maintenance and snow removal ranged between $2,500 and $7,500 per lane-kilometer. WM selected a number near the low end of this range but interpreted the figures as per kilometer rather than per lane-kilometer, resulting in an estimate of $2,600 per kilometer. In contrast, MLY estimated $7,000 per lane-kilometer for Phase I, and $5,000 per lane-kilometer for Phases II and III. As the highway was 80 percent four-lane highway and 20 percent six-lane highway, MLY's maintenance and snow removal estimates are far higher than WM's estimates. BMV made a largely unsuccessful attempt to isolate actual maintenance expenses. One problem was that the ministry maintained appropriate data by district, not by highway. To complicate matters, in 1988, the ministry privatized highway maintenance. The two major contractors for the Coquihalla were reluctant to reveal their costs as they were bidding on new tenders. They did admit, however, that, due to poor quality control in construction, ditch cleaning costs were larger than expected and some older sections of the highway already required resurfacing. Ultimately, BMV used an estimate of $6,000 per lane-kilometer, the average of the two figures used by MLY. There was one difference, however, stemming from the record-breaking snowstorms over the 1990–1991 winter. To account for the "once in 10, 20, or 50 year" snowstorms that can severely affect the Coquihalla, maintenance and snow removal costs were arbitrarily increased in each of two randomly chosen years. Over all, this approach is not entirely satisfactory; but it highlights that, like *ex ante* analyses, *ex post* analyses can suffer from prediction error.

Construction Costs   WM performed their study after Phase I was completed. Consequently, forecasting construction costs was not an issue, but as we will see, they still encountered measurement problems. Based on the best available estimates, WM estimated the present value of construction costs for Phases I and II were equal to $338.1 million (in 1984 dollars).

Soon after completion of the highway, rumors circulated of higher costs. On November 7, 1987, the *Vancouver Sun* published estimates of undiscounted total costs of $570 million for Phases I and II and $270 million for Phase III. MLY discounted these estimates to obtain construction costs of $507.9 million for Phases I and II, and $194.7 million for Phase III. BMV's construction cost estimates are based on the MacKay Commission, a Commission of Inquiry which was formed when it became publicly known that the Coquihalla had cost much more than originally anticipated.[26] MacKay concluded that "differences between costs and estimates of the Coquihalla Highway . . . are due to . . . lack of proper budgeting, monitoring cost-control and reporting systems" (p. xi), and observed "[t]he current method of reporting highway capital spending . . . by individual contracts, by Electoral Districts, and on an annual basis . . . has served to disguise the true cost of major projects" (p. xi). MacKay also commented that "The Ministry's cost reporting system for capital works is fragmented and inconsistent" (p. xx). Based on the MacKay Commission report, BMV estimated that the present value of construction costs of the Coquihalla was $837 million, which is $135 million higher than MLY. The difference between BMV's estimate and the estimates in the earlier studies is probably mostly due to strategic biases.

During BMV's inquiries on actual construction costs, one ministry official estimated that MacKay's total Coquihalla construction cost figures were "out" (underestimated) by as much as 300 percent. Uncertainties undoubtedly remain even after the events. Doubling construction costs would be a rough way of accounting for work that was hidden or lost in general accounts and for increases in indirect ministry overhead costs due to the Coquihalla.

One should not go too far, however. Even if they ministry did overpay, these payments would be viewed as benefits by the recipients, such as construction workers. In so far as these overpayments are not associated with the use of incremental resources (there are no opportunity costs), the overpayments are transfers from the government to construction companies—they "cancel out." Furthermore, a significant part of the cost overruns for Phase I can be attributed to the political pressures to speed up completion in time for EXPO 86. These additional costs, although requiring real additional resources, should probably be attributed to the EXPO 86 project, not to the Coquihalla Highway.

Valuation Differences

Value of Vehicle Operating Cost Savings and Value of Time Saved   The three studies were quite similar in terms of how they valued time savings. Specifically, each assumed that business travelers value an hour of their time at the average gross wage for British Columbia hourly and salaried employees, whereas leisure travelers value their time at 25 percent of this rate. Each of the studies also made similar assumptions about the number of passengers in each vehicle. Based on a perusal of estimates from the ministry, BMV assumed 2.2 passengers per leisure vehicle and 1.2 passengers per business vehicle. As far as we know, the other studies used similar estimates.

The studies differed, however, in the estimated gross wage rates and in the vehicle operating costs. Consider, for example, the estimates pertaining to a trip from Hope to Kamloops. WM estimated vehicle operating cost savings per Coquihalla trip at $7.00 for automobiles and $33.50 for large trucks. Estimated time savings were $8, $14.40, and $16.80 per trip for leisure vehicles, business vehicles, and trucks, respectively. MLY calculated vehicle operating cost savings at $9.66 per automobile trip and at $46.73 per truck trip. Time savings were calculated as $6.58 per leisure trip, $20.25 per business-auto trip, and $22.35 per truck trip.[27] BMV's estimates were considerably higher. Based largely on data provided by Trimac Consulting Services, BMV estimated time *and* vehicle operating cost savings at $27.50 per leisure trip, $46.80 per business trip, and $86.50 for a five-axle semitrailer trip in 1987 dollars.[28]

Value of Safety Benefits   WM valued fatalities, injuries, and property-damage-only accidents at $500,000, $11,000, and $2,000, respectively. MLY used slightly higher valuations: Saved fatalities, injuries, and property-damage-only accidents were valued at $550,000, $12,000, and $2,000, respectively. Since 1984 there has been considerable research on this topic. As we discuss in Chapter 15, current valuations are considerably higher than was thought appropriate in 1984. Based on the most recent research at the time of their study, BMV used $2.2 million (1984 Canadian dollars) for the value of an avoided fatality.

Terminal Value   As we discuss in Chapter 6, with a discounting period of 20 years, the terminal value conceptually equals the present value of the net benefits of the project from the twenty-first year to infinity. The obvious difficulty is in making projections that far into the future. Future costs, for example, will depend critically on the actual depreciation rate of the highway, which is partially endogenous in so far as it varies with use.

The method used in all three studies was to base the terminal value on the initial construction cost. WM assumed the terminal value in the twenty-first year was 75 percent of the initial construction costs. MLY used 85 percent of initial construction costs, due partially to the high proportion of Coquihalla construction costs, such as rock cutting and sand blasting, that needed to be done only once. BMV used 75 percent.

CONCLUSIONS ARISING FROM THE COMPARISONS

Did the *Ex Ante* and *In Medias Res* Analyses Have Overall Predictive Capability?

Contrasting an *ex post* analysis with earlier CBAs of the same project provides an opportunity to assess the predictive capability of earlier analyses. This is a critical element in determining the value of *ex ante* CBAs. The *NPV* estimates of $40 million and −$128 million for the earlier studies are significantly lower than the *NPV* of $394 million for the *ex post* study. Given that total costs were under $1 billion, the overall order of magnitude of error in estimation is disconcertingly large.

Furthermore, the aggregate differences understate actual differences in the earlier studies for two reasons. First, some benefits and costs erred in the same direction, thereby tending to cancel each other. For example, the *ex post* study had higher construction costs but also had higher time and operating savings benefits than the previous studies. Second, some errors offset one another within an impact category. For example, concerning safety benefits, the Coquihalla accident rate was higher than predicted, but highway ridership and accident rates elsewhere were also higher than forecast.

One comparison study alone cannot tell us everything about the general accuracy of CBA. Are such aggregate prediction errors prevalent in other CBAs? If they are, it is troubling. One might argue that this particular project raises more problems than is typical, but we think not. This project is *relatively* straightforward; after all, it is a highway, not a high-tech, megaproject. Another possibility is that the cost underestimation problem (partly due to regional rather than project-specific budgeting) is specific to "wild and woolly" British Columbia. Again, we do not think so. Several non–British Columbia bureaucratic readers acknowledge that their agencies routinely hide project budget items in other accounts.

Other Lessons from This Comparison Study

This exercise is somewhat humbling. One lesson is that *ex ante* CBA is difficult to do precisely. Accuracy depends on omission, measurement, forecasting, and valuation errors (as well as other types of errors). In this study, there are examples of all four types of errors. As noted previously, some errors cancel out. Often, however, errors compound one another. For example, estimation of *ex ante* travel benefits requires estimates of both total time saved and the valuation of time. In turn, time saved depends on both the estimated number of vehicles and time saved per vehicle. When two or more terms with error are multiplied, the error in the resulting product can be quite large.

At least in other contexts, economists tend to anticipate forecasting errors, especially those associated with benefits. In this example, however, there were also large differences in measurement error (e.g., construction costs) and valuation (e.g., value of life). The *ex ante* CBA relied on announced estimates of total costs and did not attempt to reanalyze cost estimates. Although independent estimates of project costs are not easy to obtain, the *ex ante/ex post* comparison highlights the importance of not passively accepting announced cost estimates of projects. Analysts should attempt to generate at least rough independent estimates.

Of course, research on the value of life is independent of construction of the Coquihalla. We expect that future estimates of the value of life and of other impact categories to use in CBA will be more accurate. In general, valuation errors are less likely to occur as CBA matures and progresses technically.

Despite the difficulty of identifying the source of errors in *ex ante* studies, we found evidence of a variety of sources. Uniqueness and cognitive biases played a part. The highway is liable to extreme amounts of snow. The actual maintenance costs were underestimated. Other forecasting errors, for example, underestimation of the usage levels, are inherent and unavoidable. Project specifications also changed. Strategic biases by bureaucrats and politicians probably accounted partially for the low cost estimates in the *ex ante* study. And there were analysts' procedural errors; for example, WM erred in using maintenance costs per kilometer rather than maintenance costs per lane-kilometer.

In conclusion, the main lesson illustrated here is the importance of periodically conducting *ex ante/ex post* comparisons. This may seem trivial, but it is almost totally ignored in the cost-benefit analysis literature. If *ex ante* studies were mandatory, should one in ten be subject to *in medias res* or *ex post* follow-up and comparison to the *ex ante* analysis? If so, this chapter provides a template for how to do such comparisons.

Notes

1. The chapter draws on Anthony E. Boardman, Wendy L. Mallery, and Aidan R. Vining, "Learning from *Ex Ante/Ex Post* Cost-Benefit Comparisons: The Coquihalla Highway Example," *Socio-Economic Planning Sciences,* 28, no. 2 (1994), 69–84.

2. See also Anthony Boardman, Aidan Vining, and W. G. Waters II, "Costs and Benefits Through Bureaucratic Lenses: Example of a Highway Project," *Journal of Policy Analysis and Management,* 12, no. 3 (1993), 532–555.

3. For example, see Leonard Merewitz, "Cost Overruns in Public Works," in *Benefit-Cost and Policy Analysis, 1972,* W. A. Niskanen, A. C. Harberger, R. H. Haveman, R. Turvey, and R. Zeckhauser, eds. (Chicago: Aldine Publishing Company, 1973), pp. 277–295.

4. This bias has been found in a wide range of corporations by Stephen W. Pruitt and Lawrence J. Gitman, "Capital Budgeting Forecast Biases: Evidence from the Fortune 500," *Financial Management,* 16, no. 1 (1987), 46–51.

5. Nancy E. Ryan, "Policy Formation in a Politically Charged Atmosphere: An Empirical Study of Rate-Base Determination for Recently Completed Nuclear Power Plants," paper presented at the 14th Annual APPAM Research Conference, 1992, at p. 3.

6. William E. Colglazier, "Scientific Uncertainties, Public Policy, and Global Warming: How Sure Is Sure Enough?" *Policy Studies Journal,* 19, no. 2 (1991), 61–72; John Houghton, *Global Warming: The Complete Briefing,* 2nd ed., (New York: Cambridge University Press, 1997); and Robert Mendelsohn, *The Greening of Global Warming* (Washington, DC: American Enterprise Institute for Public Policy Research, 1999).

7. For recent reviews see, for example, Spyros Makridakis, "The Art and Science of Forecasting: An Assessment and Future Directions," *International Journal of Forecasting,* 2, no. 1 (1986), 15–39; Kenneth F. Wallis, "Macroeconomic Forecasting: A Survey," *Economic Journal,* 99, no. 1 (1989), 28–61; and K. Holden, D. A. Peel, and J. L. Thompson, *Economic Forecasting: An Introduction* (Cambridge: Cambridge University Press, 1990).

8. Jeffrey L. Pressman and Aaron Wildavsky, *Implementation* (Berkeley: University of California Press, 1973).

9. Robert S. Chirinko and Edward P. Harper Jr., "Buckle Up or Slow Down? New Estimates of Offsetting Behavior and Their Implications for Automobile Safety Regulation," *Journal of Policy Analysis and Management,* 12, no. 2 (1993), 270–296.

10. Howard Kunreuther, Ralph Ginsberg, L. Miller, Philip Sagi, Paul Slovic, B. Borkan, and N. Katz, *Disaster Insurance Protection: Public Policy Lessons* (New York: John Wiley, 1978); and Colin F. Camerer and Howard Kunreuther, "Decision Processes for Low Probability Events: Policy Implications," *Journal of Policy Analysis and Management,* 8, no. 4 (1989), 565–592.

11. Charles R. Schwenk, "The Cognitive Perspective on Strategic Decision Making," *Journal of Management Studies,* 25, no. 1 (1988), 41–55. See also J. E. Russo and P. J. Schoemaker, "Managing Overconfidence," *Sloan Management Review,* 33, no. 2 (1992), 7–17.

12. E. Hutchins, "Organizing Work by Adaption," *Organization Science,* 2, no. 1 (1991), 14–39.

13. Oak Ridge National Laboratory, *Prudence Issues Affecting the U.S. Electric Utility Industry,* Oak Ridge, TN, 1987.

14. I. M. D. Little and J. A. Mirrlees, "Project Appraisal and Planning Twenty Years On," *Proceedings of the World Bank Annual Conference on Development Economics* 1990, 1991, pp. 351–391.

15. For various reasons the summary benefit and cost figures of the *ex ante* CBA in Table 19.1 are not exactly the same as those presented in Table 1.3.

16. W. G. Waters II and Shane J. Meyers, "Benefit-Cost Analysis of a Toll Highway-British Columbia's Coquihalla," *Journal of the Transportation Research Forum,* 28, no. 1 (1987), 435–443.

17. Ibid.

18. Wendy L. Mallery, "A Cost-Benefit Analysis of the Coquihalla Highway," class paper for J. M. Munro, Simon Fraser University, December 1987.

19. Boardman, Mallery, and Vining, "Learning from *Ex Ante/Ex Post* Cost-Benefit Comparisons."

20. A positive network externality arises when the utility one person derives from the consumption of a good increases with the number of other people consuming the good. For example, the benefit of having a telephone increases with the number of other people who have telephones that are

connected to the same network; see Michael A. Katz and Carl Shapiro, "Network Externalities, Competition and Compatibility," *American Economic Review,* 75, no. 3 (1985), 424–440. In the context of regional development, positive externalities may arise when a region reaches a critical mass, or agglomeration, in terms of the nature, depth, and breadth of its economic activity. Michael Porter uses the related concept of clustering to explain the comparative advantage of nations in international competitiveness; see Michael E. Porter, *The Comparative Advantage of Nations* (New York: The Free Press, 1990).

21. Diverted traffic refers to traffic that would have gone on the old routes but now travels on the Coquihalla. Undiverted traffic refers to traffic that continues on the old routes despite the existence of the Coquihalla. Generated traffic refers to traffic that would not have made the trip by road at all without the Coquihalla but now does so because the effective price is lower. These travelers may have gone by air or train, or done something completely different.

22. These numbers were then adjusted by the estimated ratio of average summer to average annual traffic.

23. Total traffic data were obtained for 1986 to 1990. Traffic data by vehicle class were obtained for the period April 1987 to March 1991 and estimated for 1986 and part of 1987. The traffic data, thus, cover three full years of Phase II operation from

Hope to Kamloops and a few months of Phase III operation from Hope to Peachland. The *ex post* study excludes motorcycles, which comprise less than 1 percent of total annual Coquihalla traffic.

24. Radnor J. Pacquette and Paul H. Wright, *Highway Engineering* (New York: Wiley & Sons, 1979) at p. 73. In an earlier version of their paper, WM used an expected death rate of 0.027 per million vehicle-kilometers based on historical data for British Columbia.

25. MLY based her projections on Pacquette and Wright (p. 73), who estimated the accident rates on a divided highway are 0.0155, 0.168, and 0.304 (per million vehicle-kilometers) for fatalities, injuries, and property damage only, respectively.

26. Douglas L. MacKay, Commissioner, *Report of the Commission Inquiry into the Coquihalla and Related Highway Projects,* Province of British Columbia, December 1987.

27. MLY used the average April 1986 gross wage for all B.C. industries for hourly and salaried employees, from the Statistics Canada publication, *Monthly Employment Earnings and Hours,* as the business hourly wage.

28. Trimac Consulting Services Limited, *Operating Costs of Trucks in Canada,* 1988 and 1986 editions, prepared for the Motor Carrier Branch, Surface Transport Administration, Transport Canada (Ottawa, Ontario: Minister of Supply and Services, 1986, 1988).

A SELECTED COST-BENEFIT ANALYSIS BIBLIOGRAPHY

This bibliography provides representative CBA studies in a number of substantive areas. Instructors who adopt this book as a text can obtain a more comprehensive bibliography upon request to the publisher. Others may obtain an electronic copy by e-mailing Aidan Vining, Faculty of Business Administration, Simon Fraser University at vining@sfu.ca.

CONTENTS

1. Agriculture

Borcherding, T., and G. W. Dorosch, *The Egg Marketing Board: A Case Study of Monopoly and Its Social Cost.* Vancouver, B.C.: The Fraser Institute, 1981.

Graham, J. D., C. A. Webber, and R. J. MacGregor, "A Regional Analysis of Direct Government Assistance Programs in Canada and Their Impacts on the Beef and Hog Sectors," *Canadian Journal of Agricultural Economics*, 36, no. 4, part 2 (1988), 915–928.

Henze, A., and J. Zeddies, "EC Programmes, Economic Effects and Cost Benefit Considerations on Adjustments in EC Agriculture," *European Review of Agricultural Economics*, 15, no. 2/3 (1988), 191–210.

Klein, K. K., and F. P. Jeffer, "Economic Benefits from the Alberta Warble Control Program," *Canadian Journal of Agricultural Economics,* 35, no. 2 (1987).

Krystynak, R. H. E., "An Economic Assessment of 2,4-D in Canada: The Case of Grain," *Canadian Farm Economics*, 18, no. 1 (1983), 7–30.

McLeod, P. B., E. J. Roberts, and G. J. Syme, "Willingness to Pay for Continued Government Service Provisions: The Case of Agriculture Protection Services," *Journal of Environmental Management*, 40, no. 1 (1994), 1–16.

Norton, G. W., V. G. Ganoza, and C. Pomereda, "Potential Benefits of Agricultural Research and Extension in Peru," *American Journal of Agricultural Economics*, 69, no. 2 (1987), 247–257.

Parks, P. K., and I. W. Hardie, "Least-Cost Forest Carbon Reserves: Cost-Effective Subsidies to Convert Marginal Agricultural Land to Forests," *Land Economics,* 71, no. 1 (1995), 122–136.

Reichelderfer, K. H., "Externalities and the Returns to Agricultural Research: Discussion," *American Journal of Agricultural Economics*, 71, no. 2 (1989), 464–465.

Sampson, J. A., and C. D. Gerrard, "Government Interventions and the Production of Wheat in Saskatchewan and North Dakota: An Empirical Analysis," *Canadian Journal of Agricultural Economics*, 35, no. 1 (1987).

Spash, C. L., "Assessing the Economic Benefits to Agriculture from Air Pollution Control," *Journal of Economic Surveys,* 11, no. 1 (1997), 47–70.

Ulrich, A., W. H. Furtan, and A. Schmitz, "The Cost of a Licensing System Regulation: An Example From Canadian Prairie Agriculture," *Journal of Political Economy,* 95, no. 1 (1987), 160–178.

van Kooten, G. C., W. P. Weisensel, and E. de Jong, "Estimating the Costs of Soil Erosion in Saskatchewan," *Canadian Journal of Agricultural Economics*, 37, no. 1 (1989), 63–75.

2. Air Pollution

Adams, R. M., D. M. Adams, J. M. Callaway, C. Chang, and B. A. McCarl, "Sequestering Carbon on Agricultural Land: Social Cost and Impacts on Timber Markets," *Contemporary Policy Issues*, 11, no. 1 (1993), 76–87.

Adams, R. M., J. M. Callaway, and B. A. McCarl, "Pollution, Agriculture, and Social Welfare: The Case of Acid Deposition," *Canadian Journal of Agricultural Economics*, 34, no. 1 (1986), 3–19.

Adams, R. M., T. D. Crocker, and N. Thanavibulchai, "An Economic Assessment of Air Pollution Damages to Selected Annual Crops in Southern California," *Journal of Environmental Economics and Management*, 9, no. 1 (1982), 42–58.

Adams, R. M., S. A. Hamilton, and B. A. McCarl, "The Benefits of Pollution Control: The Case of Ozone and U.S. Agriculture," *American Journal of Agricultural Economics*, 68, no. 4 (1986), 886–893.

Adams, R. M., and B. A. McCarl, "Assessing the Benefits of Alternative Ozone Standards on Agriculture: The Role on Response Information," *Journal of Environmental Economics and Management*, 12, no. 3 (1985), 264–276.

Anderson, R. C., and B. Ostro, "Benefits Analysis and Air Quality Standard," *Natural Resources Journal*, 3, no. 3 (1983), 566–575.

Atkinson, S., and D. Lewis, "A Cost-Effectiveness Analysis of Alternative Air Quality Control Strategies," *Journal of Environmental Economics and Management*, 1, no. 3 (1974), 237–250.

Bailey, M. J., "Risks, Costs and Benefits of Fluorocarbon Regulation," *American Economic Review Papers and Proceedings*, 72, no. 2 (1982), 247–250.

Bayless, M., "Measuring the Benefits of Air Quality Improvement: A Hedonic Salary Approach," *Journal of Environmental Economics and Management*, 9, no. 1 (1982), 81–99.

Brady, G. L., B. T. Bower, and H. A. Lakhani, "Estimates of the National Benefits and Costs of Improving Ambient Air Quality," *Journal of Environmental Management*, 16, no. 3 (1983), 191–210.

Brown, D., and M. Smith, "Crop Substitution in the Estimation of Economic Benefits Due to Ozone Reduction," *Journal of Environmental Economics and Management*, 11, no. 3 (1984), 347–360.

Butraw, D., A. Krupnik, E. Mansur, D. Austin, and D. Farrell, "Costs and Benefits of Reducing Acid Rain Pollutants Related to Acid Rain," *Contemporary Economic Policy,* 16, no. 4 (1998), 379–400.

Cline, W. R., *The Economics of Global Warming*, Washington DC: Institute for International Economics, 1992.

Crocker, T. D., and J. L. Regans, "Acid Deposition Controls—A Benefit-Cost Analysis: Its Prospects and Limits," *Environment Science and Technology*, 19, no. 2 (1985), 112–116.

Farber, S., and A. Rambaldi, "Willingness to Pay for Air Quality: The Case of Outdoor Exercise," *Contemporary Policy Issues*, 11, no. 4 (1993), 19–30.

Fraas, A., and A. McGartland, "Alternative Fuels for Pollution Control: An Empirical Evaluation of Benefits and Costs," *Contemporary Policy Issues*, 8, no. 1 (1990), 62–74.

Freeman, A. M., III, "On Estimating Air Pollution Control Benefits from Land Value Studies," *Journal of Environmental Economics and Management*, 1, no. 1 (1974), 74–83.

Garcia, P., B. L. Dixon, J. W. Mjelde, and R. M. Adams, "Measuring the Benefits of Environmental Change Using a Duality Approach: The Case of Ozone Air Pollutants," *Journal of Environmental Economics and Management*, 13, no. 1 (1986), 69–80.

Gerking, S., and W. Schulze, "What Do We Know About Benefits of Reduced Mortality from Air Pollution Control?" *American Economic Review*, 71, no. 2 (1981), 228–234.

Giannias, D. A., "Consumer Benefit From Air Quality Improvements," *Applied Economics*, 21, no. 8 (1989), 1099–1108.

Haigh, J. A., D. Harrison Jr., and A. Nichols, "Benefit-Cost Analysis of Environmental Regulation: Case Studies of Hazardous Air Pollutants," *Harvard Environmental Law Review,* 8, no. 2 (1984), 395–434.

Harrison, D., Jr., and D. L. Rubinfeld, "Hedonic Housing Prices and the Demand for Clean Air," *Journal of Environmental Management*, 5, no. 4 (1978), 81–102.

Joyce, T. J., M. Grossman, and F. Goldman, "An Assessment of the Benefits of Air Pollution Control: The Case of Infant Health," *Journal of Urban Economics*, 25, no. 1 (1989), 32–51.

Kopp, R. J., and A. J. Krupnick, "Agriculture Policy and the Benefits of Ozone Control," *American Journal of Agricultural Economics*, 69, no. 5 (1987), 956–962.

Krewitt, W., M. Holland, A. Trukenmuller, T. Heck, and R. Friedrich, "Comparing Costs and Environmental Benefits of Strategies to Combat Acidification and Ozone in Europe," *Environmental Economics and Policy Studies,* 2, no. 4 (1999), 249–266.

Krupnick, A. J., "Costs of Alternative Policies for the Control of Nitrogen Dioxide in Baltimore," *Journal of Environmental Economics and Management*, 13, no. 2 (1986), 189–197.

Krupnick, A. J., and M. A. Walls, "The Cost-Effectiveness of Methanol for Reducing Motor Vehicle Emissions and Urban Ozone," *Journal of Policy Analysis and Management*, 11, no. 3 (1992), 373–396.

Maddison, D., "A Cost-Benefit Analysis of Slowing Climate Change," *Energy Policy,* 23, no. 2/3 (1995), 337–346.

McCorriston, S., and I. M. Sheldon, "The Welfare Implications of Nitrogen Limitation Policies," *Journal of Agricultural Economics*, 40, no. 2 (1989), 143–151.

Mendelsohn, R., "An Economic Analysis of Air Pollution from Coal Fired Plants," *Journal of Environmental Economics and Management*, 7, no. 1 (1980), 30–43.

Nelson, J. P., "Residential Choice, Hedonic Prices, and the Demand for Urban Air Quality," *Journal of Urban Economics*, 5, no. 3 (1978), 357–369.

Parks, P. K., and I. W. Hardie, "Least-Cost Forest Carbon Reserves: Cost-Effective Subsidies to Convert Marginal Agricultural Land to Forests," *Land Economics*, 71, no. 1 (1995), 122–136.

Perl, L. J., and F. C. Dunbar, "Cost-Effectiveness and Cost-Benefit Analysis of Air Quality Regulations," *American Economic Review*, 72, no. 2 (1982), 208–213.

Regens, J. L., and R. W. Rycroft, *The Acid Rain Controversy,* Pittsburgh, PA: University of Pittsburgh Press, 1988.

Repetto, R., "The Economics of Visibility Protection: On a Clear Day You Can See a Policy," *Natural Resources Journal*, 21, no. 2 (1981), 355–370.

Rowe, R. D., R. C. d'Arge, and D. S. Brookshire, "An Experiment on the Economic Value of Visibility," *Journal of Environmental Economics and Management*, 7, no. 1 (1980), 1–19.

Schulze, W. D., and D. S. Brookshire, et al., "The Economic Benefits of Preserving Visibility in National Parklands of the Southwest," *Natural Resources Journal*, 23, no. 1 (1983), 149–173.

Schwing, R. C., B. W. Southwark, C. R. von Buseck, and C. J. Jackson, "Benefit-Cost Analysis of Automobile Emission Reductions," *Journal of Environmental Economics and Management*, 7, no. 1 (1980), 44–64.

Smith, V. K., and J. Huang, "Can Markets Value Air Quality? A Meta-Analysis of Hedonic Property Value Models," *Journal of Political Economy*, 103, no. 3 (1995), 209–227.

Thomas, V., "Evaluating Pollution Control: The Case of Sao Paulo, Brazil," *Journal of Development Economics*, 19, nos. 1 and 2 (1985), 133–146.

Young, D., and S. Aidun, "Ozone and Wheat Farming in Alberta: A Micro-study of the Effects of Environmental Change," *Canadian Journal of Agricultural Economics*, 41, no. 1 (1993), 27–43.

3. Crime and Drug Abuse (Including Alcohol)

Anderson, D. A., "The Aggregate Burden of Crime," *Journal of Law and Economics,* 42, no. 2 (1999), 611–642.

Anderson, R. W., "Towards a Cost-Benefit Analysis of Police Activities," *Public Finance*, 29, no. 1 (1974), 1–17.

Coate, D., and M. Grossman, "Effects of Alcoholic Beverage Prices and Legal Drinking Ages on Youth Alcohol Use," *Journal of Law and Economics*, 31, no. 1 (1988), 145–171.

Cohen, M. A., "Pain, Suffering, and Jury Awards: A Study of the Cost of Crime to Victims," *Law and Society Review*, 22, no. 3 (1988), 537–555.

Cook, P., and G. Tauchen, "The Effect of Liquor Taxes on Heavy Drinking," *Bell Journal of Economics*, 13, no. 2 (1982), 255–285.

Grant, M. M., and A. W. Williams, eds., *Economics and Alcohol Consumption and Controls*. New York: Gardner Press, 1983.

Gray, C. M., *The Costs of Crime*. Beverly Hills, CA: Sage Publications, 1979.

Greenwood, P., ed., *Intervention Strategies for Chronic Juvenile Offenders*. New York: Greenwood Press, 1988.

Hakim, S., and Y. Shachmurove, "Social Cost-Benefit Analysis of Commericial and Residential Burglar and Fire Alarms," *Journal of Policy Modeling,* 18, no. 1 (1996), 49–67.

Kenkel, D. S., "Drinking, Driving, and Deterrence: The Effectiveness and Social Costs of Alternative Policies," *Journal of Law and Economics*, 36, no. 2 (1993), 3877–3914.

Kimbrough, J., "School-Based Strategies for Delinquency Prevention," in *Intervention Strategies for Chronic Juvenile Offenders*, ed. P. Greenwood. New York: Greenwood Press, 1987, pp. 193–206.

Lee, D. R., "Policing Cost, Evasion Cost, and the Optimal Speed Limit," *Southern Economic Journal*, 52, no. 1 (1985), 34–45.

Levy, D., and N. Sheflin, "New Evidence on Controlling Alcohol Use Through Price," *Journal of Studies on Alcohol*, 44, no. 6 (1983), 929–937.

Lipsey, M., "Is Delinquency Prevention a Cost-Effective Strategy? A California Perspective," *Journal of Research in Crime and Delinquency,* 21, no. 4 (1984), 279–302.

Miller, T. R., M. A. Cohen, and B. Wiersema, *Crime in the United States: Victim Costs and Consequences,* Final Report to the National Institute of Justice, 1995.

Pogue, T. F., and L. G. Sgontz, "Taxing to Control Social Costs: The Case of Alcohol," *American Economic Review*, 79, no. 1 (1989), 235–243.

Saffer, H., and M. Grossman, "Drinking Age Laws and Highway Mortality Rates: Cause and Effect," *Economic Inquiry*, 25, no. 3 (1987), 403–418.

Schweinhart, L. J., and D. P. Weikart, *Young Children Grow Up: The Effects of the Perry Preschool Pro-*gram on Youths Through Age 15, Monograph No. 7. Ypsilanti, MI: High/Scope Educational Research Foundation, 1980.

4. Economic Development and Industrial Policy

Grossman, G. M., "Promoting New Industrial Activities: A Survey of Recent Arguments and Evidence," *OECD Economics Studies*, no. 14 (1990), 88–125.

Hufbauer, G. C., and K. A. Elliot, *Measuring the Cost of Protection in the United States*. Washington, DC: Institute for International Economics, 1994.

Leff, N. H., "Externalities, Information Costs, and Social Benefit-Cost Analysis for Economic Development: An Example from Telecommunications," *Economic Development and Cultural Change*, 32, no. 2 (1984), 255–276.

Mynemi, G., J. Dorfman, and G. C. Ames, "Welfare Impacts of the Canada-U.S. Softwood Lumber Trade Dispute: Beggar Thy Consumer Trade Policy," *Canadian Journal of Agricultural Economics*, 42, no. 3 (1994), 261–271.

Warr, P. G., "The Jakarta Export Processing Zone: Benefits and Costs," *Bulletin of Indonesian Economic Studies*, 19, no. 3 (1983), 28–49.

5. Education and Employment/Training Programs

Ashenfelter, O., "Estimating the Effects of Training Programs on Earnings," *Review of Economics and Statistics*, 60, no. 1 (1978), 47–57.

Barnett, W. S., "Benefits of Compensatory Preschool Education," *Journal of Human Resources*, 27, no. 2 (1992), 279–312.

Bas, D., "Cost-Effectiveness of Training in Developing Countries," *International Labour Review*, 127, no. 3 (1988), 355–369.

Bloom, H. S., L. Orr, S. H. Bell, G. Cave, F. Doolittle, W. Lin, and J. M. Bos, "The Benefits and Costs of JTPA Title II-A Programs: Key Findings from the National Job Training Partnership Act Study," *Journal of Human Resources*, 32 (1997), 549–576.

Borus, M. E., "Assessing the Impact of Training Programs," in *Employing the Unemployed*, ed. E. Ginzberg. New York: Basic Books, 1980, pp. 25–40.

Cohn, E., and W. W. Hughes Jr., "A Benefit-Cost Analysis of Investment in College Education in the United States: 1969–1985," *Economics of Education Review*, 13, no. 2 (1997), 109–123.

Cooper, S. T., and E. Cohn, "International Rates of Return to College Education in the United States by Sex and Race," *Journal of Education Finance*, 23 (1997), 101–133.

Epp, D. J., "Unemployment and Benefit-Cost Analysis: A Case Study Test of a Haveman-Krutilla Hypothesis," *Land Economics*, 55, no. 3 (1979), 397–404.

Friedlander, D., D. Greenberg, and P. K. Robins, "Evaluating Government Training Programs for the Economically Disadvantaged," *Journal of Economic Literature*, 35, no. 4 (1997), 1809–1855.

Greenberg, D., and M. Wiseman, "What Did the OBRA Demonstration Do?" in *Evaluation Design for Welfare and Training Programs*, eds. I. Garfinkel and C. Manski. Cambridge, MA: Harvard University Press, 1992, pp. 25–75.

Gueron, J. M., *Reforming Welfare with Work*. New York: The Ford Foundation, 1987.

Gueron, J. M., and R. P. Nathan, "The MDRC Work/Welfare Project: Objectives, Status, Significance," *Policy Studies Review*, 4 (1985), 417–432.

Haveman, R. H., "The Dutch Social Employment Program," in *Creating Jobs: Public Employment Programs and Wage Subsidies*, ed. J. L. Palmer. Washington, DC: Brookings Institution, 1978, pp. 241–269.

Kemper, P., and P. Moss, "Economic Efficiency of Public Employment Programs", in *Creating Jobs: Public Employment Programs and Wage Subsidies*, ed. J. L. Palmer. Washington, DC: Brookings Institution, 1978, pp. 277–312.

Lalonde, R., and R. Maynard, "How Precise Are Evaluations of Employment and Training Programs: Evidence From a Field Experiment," *Evaluation Review*, 11, no. 4 (1987), 428–451.

Lane, J., and T. Berry, "A Multi-State Analysis of the Targeted Jobs Tax Credit Programme," *Applied Economics*, 21, no. 1 (1989), 85–94.

Long, D. A., C. D. Mallar, and C. V. D. Thornton, "Evaluating the Benefits and Costs of the Job Corps," *Journal of Policy Analysis and Management*, 1, no. 1 (1981), 55–76.

Psacharopoulos, G., "Returns to Education: An Updated International Comparison," *Comparative Education*, 17, no. 3 (1981), 321–341.

Psacharopoulos, G., "Returns to Education: A Global Update," *World Development*, 22, no. 9 (1994), 1325–1343.

Schiller, B. R., "Lesson from WIN: A Manpower Evaluation," *Journal of Human Resources*, 13, no. 4 (1978), 502–523.

Tines, J., et al., "Benefit-Cost Analysis of Supported Employment in Illinois: A State-Wide Evaluation," *American Journal on Mental Retardation*, 95, no. 1 (1990), 44–54.

Woodbury, S. A., and R. G. Spiegelman, "Bonuses to Workers and Employers to Reduce Unemployment: Randomized Trials in Illinois," *American Economic Review*, 77, no. 4 (1987), 513–530.

Zuidema, T., "Cost-Benefit Analysis in a Situation of Unemployment: Calculating the Decline in Unemployment as a Result of the Realization of a Government Project," *Public Finance Quarterly*, 15, no. 1 (1987), 105–115.

6. Energy and Energy Conservation

Anand, S., and B. Nalebuff, "Issues in the Application of Cost-Benefit Analysis to Energy Projects in Developing Countries," *Oxford Economic Papers*, 39, no. 1 (1987), 190–222.

Boyd, R., K. Krutilla, and W. K. Viscusi, "Energy Taxation as a Policy Instrument to Reduce CO_2 Emissions: A Net Benefit Analysis," *Journal of Environmental Economics and Management*, 29, no. 1 (1995), 1–24.

Burkhart, L. A., "Conservation Program Cost-Benefit Analysis—Choosing Among Options," *Public Utilities Fortnightly*, 125, no. 7 (1990), 41–44.

Burwell, C. C., and D. L. Phung, "On the Energy Cost-Effectiveness of Electric Home Heating," *Public Utilities Fortnightly*, 113, no. 6 (1984), 26–31.

Caves, D. W., L. R. Christensen, W. E. Hendricks, and P. E. Schoech, "Cost-Benefit Analysis of Residential Time of Use Rates: A Case Study for Four Illinois Utilities," *Electric Ratemaking*, 1 (1982–1983), 40–46.

Chao, H., and A. S. Manne, "An Integrated Analysis of U.S. Oil Stockpiling Policies," in *Energy Vulnerability*, ed. J. L. Plummer. Cambridge, MA: Ballinger Publishing Company, 1982, pp. 59–82.

Cicchetti, C. J., "The Trans Alaska Pipeline: A Benefit-Cost Analysis of Alternatives," in *Benefit-Cost and Policy Analysis, 1973*, eds. R. H. Haveman, et al. Chicago: Aldine Publishing, 1974, pp. 110–143.

Dixon, J. A., "Selected Policy Options for Fuelwood Production and Use in the Philippines," from materials prepared by E. L. Hyman in *Economic Valuation Techniques for the Environment*, eds. J. A. Dixon and M. M. Hufschmidt. Baltimore and London: The Johns Hopkins University Press, 1986, pp. 163–177.

Frieden, B., and L. Baker, "The Market Needs Help: The Disappointing Record of Home Energy Conservation," *Journal of Policy Analysis and Management*, 2, no. 3 (1983), 432–448.

Friedman, L., and K. Hausker, "Residential Energy Consumption: Models of Consumer Behavior and Their Implications for Rate Design," *Journal of Consumer Policy*, 11, no. 3 (1988), 287–313.

Hartman, R. S., "An Analysis of Department of Energy Residential Appliance Efficiency Standards," *The Energy Journal*, 2, no. 2 (1981), 49–70.

Hausman, J. A., and P. Joskow, "Evaluating the Costs and Benefits of Appliance Efficiency Standards," *American Economic Review*, 72, no. 2 (1982), 220–225.

Horwich, G., H. Jenkins-Smith, and D. L. Weimer, "The International Energy Agency's Mandatory Oil-Sharing Agreement: Tests of Efficiency, Equity and Practicality," in *Responding to International Oil Crisis*, eds. G. Horwich and D. Weimer. Washington, DC: American Enterprise Institute, 1988, pp. 104–133.

Horwich, G., and D. L. Weimer, *Oil Price Shocks, Market Response and Contingency Planning*. Washington, DC: American Enterprise Institute, 1984.

Kalt, J. P., "The Costs and Benefits of Federal Regulation of Coal Strip Mining," *Natural Resources Journal*, 23, no. 4 (1983), 893–915.

Khazzoom, J. D., "Economic Implications of Mandated Efficiency Standards for Household Appliances," *Energy Journal*, 4, no. 1 (1980), 27–40.

Levinson, M., "Alcohol Fuels Revisited: The Costs and Benefits of Energy Independence in Brazil," *Journal of Developing Areas*, 21, no. 3 (1987), 243–257.

MacAvoy, P. W., "The Regulation-Induced Shortage of Natural Gas," *Journal of Law and Economics*, 12, no. 1 (1971), 167–200.

Rosenfeld, A., C. Atkinson, J. Koomey, A. Maier, R. Mowris, and L. Price, "Conserved Energy Supply Curves for U.S. Buildings," *Contemporary Policy Issues*, 11, no. 1 (1993), 45–68.

Rowe, R., M. G. Shelby, J. B. Epel, and A. Michelsen, "Using Oxygenated Fuels to Mitigate Carbon

Monoxide Air Pollution: The Case of Denver," *Contemporary Policy Issues*, 8, no. 1 (1990), 39–53.

Sexton, R. J., and T. A. Sexton, "Theoretical and Methodological Perspectives on Consumer Response to Electricity Information," *Journal of Consumer Affairs*, 21, no. 2 (1987), 238–257.

Trane, K. E., "Incentives for Energy Conservation in the Commercial and Industrial Sectors," *The Energy Journal*, 9, no. 3 (1988), 113–128.

Walls, M. A., "Welfare Costs of an Oil Import Fee," *Contemporary Policy Issues*, 8, no. 2 (1990), 176–189.

Wenders, J. T., and R. A. Lyman, "An Analysis of the Benefits and Costs of Seasonal-Time-of-Day Electricity Rates," in Chapter 5 of *Problems in Public Utility Economics Regulation*, ed. M. A. Crew. Lexington, MA: D.C. Heath, 1979, pp. 73–91.

Wenders, J. T., and R. A. Lyman, "Determining the Optimal Penetration of Time-of-Day Electricity Tariffs," *Electric Ratemaking*, 1 (1982), 15–20.

7. Forestry

Anderson, F. J., "Ontario Reforestation Policy: Benefits and Costs," *Canadian Public Policy*, 5, no. 3 (1979), 336–347.

Hagen, D. A., J. W. Vincent, and P. G. Welle, "The Benefits of Preserving Old-Growth Forests and the Northern Spotted Owl," *Contemporary Policy Issues*, 10, no. 2 (1992), 13–26.

Hyde, W. F., R. G. Boyd, and B. L. Daniels, "The Impacts of Public Interventions: An Examination of the Forestry Sector," *Journal of Policy Analysis and Management*, 7, no. 1 (1987), 40–61.

Newcomb, K., "An Economic Justification for Rural Afforestation: The Case of Ethiopia," *Annals of Regional Science*, 21, no. 3 (1987), 80–99.

Rosenthal, D. H., and T. C. Brown, "Comparability of Market Prices and Consumer Surplus for Resource Allocation Decisions," *Journal of Forestry*, 83, no. 2 (1985), 105–109.

Rubin, J., G. Helland, and J. Loomis, "A Benefit-Cost Analysis of the Northern Spotted Owl: Results from a Contingent Valuation Survey," *Journal of Forestry*, 89, no. 12 (1991), 25–30.

Stone, M., and R. Reid, "Opportunity Costs of Spotted Owl Management Options for British Columbia," *Canadian Public Policy,* 23, no. 2, (1997), 69–82.

8. Hazardous Waste (Including Nuclear Power and Waste)

Gamble, H. B., and R. H. Downing, "Effects of Nuclear Power Plants on Residential Property Values," *Journal of Regional Science*, 22, no. 4 (1982), 457–478.

Grossman, P. Z., and E. S. Cassedy, "Cost-Benefit Analysis of Nuclear Waste Disposal: Accounting for Safeguards," *Science, Technology and Human Values*, 10, no. 1 (1985), 47–54.

Hageman, R. K., "Nuclear Waste Disposal: Potential Property Value Impacts," *Natural Resources Journal*, 21, no. 4 (1981), 789–810.

Nelson, J. P., "Three Mile Island and Residential Property Values: Empirical Analysis and Policy Implications," *Land Economics*, 57, no. 3 (1981), 363–372.

O'Donnell, E. P., and J. J. Mauro, "A Cost-Benefit Comparison of Nuclear and Non-Nuclear Health and Safety Protective Measures and Regulation," *Nuclear Safety*, 20, no. 5 (1979), 525–540.

Payne, B. A., S. J. Olshansky, and T. E. Segel, "The Effects on Property Values of Proximity to a Site Contaminated with Radioactive Waste," *Natural Resources Journal*, 27, no. 3 (1987), 579–590.

Sengupta, M., "The Choice Between Coal and Nuclear Power in India: A Cost-Benefit Approach," *Journal of Energy and Development*, 2, no. 1 (1986), 85–92.

9. Health and Health Regulation

Albritton, R. B., "Cost-Benefits of Measles Eradication: Effects of a Federal Intervention," *Policy Analysis*, 4, no. 1 (1978), 1–22.

Bartel, A., and P. Taubman, "Some Economic and Demographic Consequences of Mental Illness," *Journal of Labour Economics*, 4, no. 2 (1986), 243–256.

Bartel, A. P., and L. G. Thomas, "Direct and Indirect Effects of Regulation: A New Look at OSHA's Impact," *Journal of Law and Economics*, 28, no. 1 (1985), 1–25.

Berger, M. C., et al., "Valuing Changes in Health Risks: A Comparison of Alternative Measures," *Southern Economic Journal*, 53, no. 4 (1987), 967–984.

Birch, S., and C. Donaldson, "Applications of Cost-Benefit Analysis to Health Care: Departure from Welfare Economic Theory," *Journal of Health Economics*, 6, no. 3 (1987), 211–225.

Boyle, M. H., G. W. Torrance, J. C. Sinclair, and S. P. Horwood, "Economic Evaluation of Neonatal Intensive Care of Very-Low-Birth-Weight Infants," *New England Journal of Medicine*, 308, no. 22 (1983), 1330–1337.

Brown, R. A., and C. H. Green, "Threats to Health and Safety: Perceived Risk and Willingness-to-Pay," *Social Science and Medicine*, 15, no. 2, part D (1981), 67–75.

Bunker, J. P., B. A. Barnes, and F. Mosteller, eds., *Costs, Risks and Benefits of Surgery*. New York: Oxford University Press, 1977.

Butler, J. R., and D. P. Doessel, "Measuring Benefits in Health: A Clarification," *Scottish Journal of Political Economy*, 28, no. 2 (1981), 196–205.

Buxton, M. J., and R. R. West, "Cost-Benefit Analysis of Long-Term Haemodialysis for Chronic Renal Failure," *British Medical Journal*, 2, no. 5967 (1975), 376–379.

Cauley, S. D., "The Time Price of Medical Care," *Review of Economics and Statistics*, 69, no. 1 (1987), 59–66.

Chernickovsky, D., and I. Zmora, "A Hedonic Prices Approach to Hospitalization Costs: The Case of Israel," *Journal of Health Economics*, 5, no. 2 (1986), 179–191.

Smith, V. K., and W. H. Desvousges, "The Value of Avoiding a LULU: Hazardous Waste Disposal Sites," *Review of Economics and Statistics*, 68, no. 2 (1986), 293–299.

Churchill, D. N., B. C. Lemon, and G. W. Torrance, "A Cost-Effectiveness Analysis of Continuous Ambulatory Peritoneal Dialysis and Hospital Hemodialysis," *Medical Decision Making*, 4, no. 4 (1984), 489–500.

Clarke, P., "Cost-Benefit Analysis and Mammographic Screening: A Travel Cost Approach," *Journal of Health Economics*, 17, no. 6, (1998), 767–787.

Cummings, J., and F. Weaver, "Cost Effectiveness of Home Care," *Clinics in Geriatric Medicine*, 7, no. 4 (1991), 865–874.

Cummings, J., F. Weaver, et al., "Cost Effectiveness and Hospital-Based Home Care," in *Quality and Cost Containment in Care of the Elderly*, eds. J. Romeis and R. Coe. New York: Springer Publishing Company, 1991, pp. 159–174.

Dardis, R., S. Aaronson, and Y. Lin, "Cost-Benefit Analysis of Flammability Standards," *American Journal of Agricultural Economics*, 60, no. 4 (1978), 695–700.

Devaney, B., L. Bilheimer, and J. Schore, "Medicaid Costs and Birth Outcomes: The Effects of Prenatal WIC Participation and the Use of Prenatal Care," *Journal of Policy Analysis and Management*, 11, no. 4 (1992), 573–592.

Dewees, D. N., and R. J. Daniels, "The Costs of Protecting Occupational Health: The Asbestos Case," *Journal of Human Resources*, 21, no. 3 (1986), 381–396.

Disbrow, D., "The Costs and Benefits of Nutrition Services: A Literature Review," *Journal of American Dietetic Association*, 89, no. 4 (1989), supplements.

Evans, R. G., and G. C. Robinson, "Surgical Day Care: Measurements of the Economic Payoff," *Canadian Medical Association Journal*, 123, no. 9 (1980), 873–880.

Fisher, G. W., "Willingness-to-Pay for Probabilistic Improvements in Functional Health Status: A Psychological Perspective," in *Health: What Is It Worth? Measures of Health Benefits*, eds. S. Mushkin and D. W. Dunlop. New York: Pergamon Press, 1979, pp. 167–200.

Ginsberg, G. M., and D. Shouval, "Cost-Benefit Analysis of a Nationwide Neonatal Inoculation Programme against Hepatitis B in an Area of Intermediate Endemicity," *Journal of Epidemiology and Community Health*, 46, no. 6 (1992), 587–594.

Ginsberg, G., S. Sham, and B. Lev, "Cost-Benefit Analysis of Risperidone and Clozapine in the Treatment of Schizophrenia in Israel," *Pharmacoeconomics*, 13, no. 7 (1998), 231–241.

Goldman, F., and M. Grossman, "The Demand for Pediatric Care: A Hedonic Approach," *Journal of Political Economy*, 86, no. 2, part 1 (1978), 259–280.

Goodwin, P. J., R. Feld, W. K. Evans, and J. Pater, "Cost-Effectiveness of Cancer Chemotherapy: An Economic Evaluation of a Randomized Trial in Small-Cell Lung Cancer," *Journal of Clinical Oncology*, 6, no. 10 (1988), 1537–1547.

Grannemann, T. W., R. S. Brown, and M. V. Pauly, "Estimating Hospital Costs: A Multiple Output Analysis," *Journal of Health Economics*, 5, no. 2 (1986), 107–127.

Hagard, S., and F. A. Carter, "Preventing the Birth of Infants with Down's Syndrome: A Cost-Benefit Analysis," *British Medical Journal*, 1, no. 6012 (1976), 753–756.

Hagard S., F. Carter, and R. G. Milne, "Screening for Spina Bifida: A Cost-Benefit Analysis," *British Journal of Social and Preventive Medicine*, 30, no. 1 (1976), 40–53.

Harrington, W., and P. R. Portney, "Valuing the Benefits of Health and Safety Regulation," *Journal of Urban Economics*, 22, no. 1 (1987), 101–112.

Hartunian, N. S., C. N. Smart, and M. S. Thompson, "The Incidence and Economic Costs of Cancer, Motor Vehicle Injuries, Coronary Heart Disease and Stroke: A Comparative Analysis," *American Journal of Public Health*, 70, no. 12 (1980), 1249–1260.

Hellinger, F. J., "Cost-Benefit Analysis of Health Care: Past Applications and Future Prospects," *Inquiry*, 17, no. 3 (1980), 204–215.

Hull, R., J. Hirsh, D. L. Sackett, and G. L. Stoddart, "Cost-Effectiveness of Clinical Diagnosis, Venography and Noninvasive Testing in Patients With Symptomatic Deep-Vein Thrombosis," *New England Journal of Medicine*, 304, no. 26 (1981), 1561–1567.

Jerrell, J. M., and T. Hu, "Cost-Effectiveness of Intensive Clinical and Case Management Compared with an Existing System of Care, *Inquiry*, 26, no. 2 (1989), 224–234.

Johnson, L. L., *Cost-Benefit Analysis and Voluntary Safety Standards for Consumer Products*. Santa Monica, CA: Rand Corporation, 1982.

Joyce, T. J., M. Grossman, and F. Goldman, "An Assessment of the Benefits of Air Pollution Control: The Case of Infant Health," *Journal of Urban Economics*, 25, no. 1 (1989), 32–51.

Kutner, N. G., "Cost-Benefit Issues in U.S. National Health Legislation: The Case of the End-Stage Renal Disease Program," *Social Problems*, 30, no. 1 (1982), 51–64.

Levin, H. V., "A Benefit Cost Analysis of Nutritional Programs for Anemia Reduction," *World Bank Research Observer*, 1, no. 2 (1986), 219–245.

Logan, A. G., B. J. Milne, C. Achber, W. P. Campbell, and R. B. Haynes, "Cost-Effectiveness of Worksite Hypertension Programme," *Hypertension*, 3, no. 2 (1981), 211–218.

Ludbrook, A., "A Cost-Effectiveness Analysis of the Treatment of Chronic Renal Failure," *Applied Economics*, 13, no. 3 (1981), 337–350.

Mauskopf, J. A., C. J. Bradley, and M. J. French, "Benefit-Cost Analysis of Hepatitis B Vaccine Program for Occupationally Exposed Workers," *Journal of Occupational Medicine*, 33, no. 6 (1991), 691–698.

Neuhauser, D., and A. M. Lewicki, "What Do We Gain from the Sixth Stool Guaiac?" *New England Journal of Medicine*, 293, no. 5 (1975), 226–228.

Paterson, M. L., "Cost-Benefit Evaluation of a New Technology for Treatment of Peptic Ulcer Disease," *Managerial and Decision Economics*, 4, no. 1 (1983), 50–62.

Rosser, R., and P. Kind, "A Scale of Valuations of States of Illness: Is There a Social Consensus?" *International Journal of Epidemiology*, 7, no. 4 (1978), 347–358.

Ruchlin, H. S., et al., "The Efficacy of Second-Opinion Consultation Programs: A Cost-Benefit Perspective," *Medical Care*, 20 (1982), 3–20.

Schoenbaum, S. C., et al., "Benefit-Cost Analysis of Rubella Vaccination Policy," *The New England Journal of Medicine*, 294, no. 6 (1976), 306–310.

Schoenbaum, S. C., et al., "The Swine-Influenza Decision," *The New England Journal of Medicine*, 295, no. 14 (1977), 759–785.

Shukla, R. K., "ALL-RN Model of Nursing Care Delivery: A Cost-Benefit Evaluation," *Inquiry*, 20, no. 2 (1983), 173–184.

Stilwell, J. A., "Benefits and Costs of the Schools' BCG Vaccination Programme," *British Medical Journal*, 1, no. 6016 (1976), 1002–1004.

Strange, P. V. and A. T. Sumner, "Predictive Treatment Costs and Life Expectancy for End Stage Renal Disease," *The New England Journal of Medicine*, 298, no. 7, (1978), 372–378.

Torrance, G. W., "Measurement of Health State Utilities for Economic Appraisal: A Review," *Journal of Health Economics*, 5, no. 1 (1986), 1–30.

Warner, K. E., and R. C. Hutton, "Cost-Benefit and Cost-Effectiveness Analysis in Health Care: Growth and Composition of the Literature," *Medical Care*, 18, no. 11 (1980), 1069–1084.

Weisbrod, B. A., "Benefit-Cost Analysis of a Controlled Experiment: Treating the Mentally Ill," *Journal of Human Resources,* 16, no. 4 (1981), 523–548.

Weisbrod, B. A., "Costs and Benefits of Medical Research: A Case Study of Poliomyelitis," *Journal of Political Economy*, 79, no. 3 (1971), 527–544.

Williams, A. H., "Economics of Coronary Artery Bypass Grafting," *British Medical Journal*, 291, no. 2 (1985), 326–329.

Williams, A. H., "The Costs and Benefits of Surgery," in *Surgical Review I*, eds. J. S. P. Lumley and J. L. Craven. London: Butterworths, 1978.

Windle, R., and M. Dresner, "Mandatory Child Safety Seats in Air Transport: Do They Save Lives?" *Transportation Research Forum*, 31, no. 2 (1991), 309–316.

Zeckhauser, R., "Measuring Risks and Benefits of Food Safety Decisions," *Vanderbilt Law Review*, 38, no. 3 (1985), 539–569.

10. Housing

DeSalvo, J. S., "Benefits and Costs of New York City's Middle Income Housing Programs," *Journal of Political Economy*, 83, no. 4 (1975), 791–806.

Hammond, C. M. H., *The Benefits of Subsidized Housing Programs: An Intertemporal Approach.* Cambridge: Cambridge University Press, 1987.

Kraft, J., and E. O. Olsen, "The Distribution of Benefits from Public Housing," in *The Distribution of Economic Well-Being*, ed. F. T. Juster. New York: National Bureau of Economic Research, 1977.

Olsen, E. O., and D. M. Barton, "The Benefits and Costs of Public Housing in New York City," *Journal of Public Economics*, 20, no. 3 (1983), 299–332.

11. Industry Regulation (Not Professional or Safety)

Anderson, J. E., "The Relative Inefficiency of Quotas," *American Economic Review,* 17, no. 1 (1985), 178–190.

Bailey, E. E., D. R. Graham, and D. Kaplan, *Deregulating the Airlines.* Cambridge, MA: MIT Press, 1985.

Barnekov, C. C., and A. N. Kleit, "The Efficiency Effects of Railroad Deregulation in the United States," *International Journal of Transport Economics*, 17, no. 1 (1990), 21–38.

Barth, J. R., J. J. Cordes, and A. M. J. Yezer, "Benefits and Costs of Legal Restrictions on Personal Loan Markets," *Journal of Law and Economics*, 29, no. 2 (1986), 357–380.

Beck, R., C. Hoskins, and G. Mumey, "The Social Welfare Loss from Egg and Poultry Marketing Boards, Revisited," *Canadian Journal of Agricultural Economics*, 42, no. 2 (1994), 149–158.

Benston, G. J., "An Appraisal of the Costs and Benefits of Government-Required Disclosure: SEC and FTC Requirments," *Law and Contemporary Problems*, 41, no. 3 (1977), 30–62.

Bogen, K. D., "The Costs of Price Regulation: Lessons from Railroad Deregulation," *Rand Journal of Economics*, 18, no. 3 (1987), 408–416.

Boorstein, R., and R. C. Feenstra, "Quality Upgrading and Its Welfare Cost in U.S. Steel Imports, 1969–74," in *International Trade and Trade Policy*, eds. E. Helpman and A. Razin. Cambridge, MA: MIT Press, 1991, pp. 167–186.

Boyer, K., "The Costs of Price Regulation: Lessons from Railroad Deregulation," *Rand Journal of Economics*, 18, no. 3 (1987), 408–416.

de Melo, J., and D. Tarr, "Welfare Costs of U.S. Quotas in Textiles, Steel and Autos," *The Review of Economics and Statistics*, 72, no. 3 (1990), 489–497.

DeVany, A. S., W. Gram, T. Saving, and C. W. Smithson, "The Impact of Input Regulation: The Case of Costs and Input Use," *Journal of Law and Economics*, 25, no. 2 (1982), 367–382.

Dinopoulos, E., and M. E. Kreinin, "Effects of the U.S.-Japan Auto VER on European Prices and on U.S. Welfare," *Review of Economics and Statistics*, 70, no. 3 (1983), 484–491.

Feenstra, R. C., "How Costly Is Protectionism?" *Journal of Economic Perspectives*, 6, no. 3 (1992), 159–178.

Felton, J. R., "Costs and Benefits of Motor Truck Regulation," *Quarterly Review of Economics and Business*, 18, no. 2 (1980), 7–20.

Gomez-Ibanez, J., R. Leone, and S. O'Connell, "Restraining Auto Imports: Does Anyone Win?" *Journal of Policy Analysis and Management*, 2, no. 2 (1983), 196–219.

Gray, W., "The Cost of Regulation: OSHA, EPA and the Productivity Slowdown," *American Economic Review*, 77, no. 5 (1987), 998–1012.

Guash, J. L., and R. W. Hahn, "The Costs and Benefits of Regulation: Implications for Developing Countries," *The World Bank Research Observer*, 14, no. 1 (1999), 137–158.

Hahn, R. W., and J. A. Hird, "The Costs and Benefits of Regulation: Review and Synthesis," *Yale Journal of Regulation*, 8, no. 1 (1991), 233–278.

Hazilla, M., and R. Kop, "Social Cost of Environmental Quality Regulations: A General Equilibrium Analysis," *Journal of Political Economy*, 98, no. 4 (1990), 853–873.

Hufbauer, G. C., and K. A. Elliott, *Measuring the Cost of Protection in the United States*. Washington, DC: Institute for International Economics, 1994.

Ippolito, R. A., "The Effect of Price Regulation in the Automobile Insurance Industry," *Journal of Law and Economics*, 23, no. 1 (1979), 55–90.

Len, G. M., A. Schnitz, and R. D. Knutsen, "Gains and Losses of Sugar Program Policy Options," *American Journal of Agricultural Economics*, 69, no. 5 (1987), 591–608.

Luken, R. A., *Efficiency in Environmental Regulation: A Benefit-Cost Analysis of Alternative Approaches*, Studies in Risk and Uncertainty. Boston: Kluwer, 1990.

Moore, T. G., "U.S. Airline Deregulation: Its Effects on Passengers, Capital and Labor," *Journal of Law and Economics*, 29, no. 1 (1986), 1–2.

Morrison, S., and C. Winston, *The Economic Effects of Airline Deregulation*. Washington, DC: The Brookings Institution, 1986.

Mynemi, G., J. Dorfman, and G. C. Ames, "Welfare Impacts of the Canada-U.S. Softwood Lumber Trade Dispute: Beggar Thy Consumer Trade Policy," *Canadian Journal of Agricultural Economics*, 42, no. 3 (1994), 261–271.

Olsen, E. O., "An Economic Analysis of Rent Control in New York City," *Journal of Political Economy*, 80, no. 6 (1972), 1081–1110.

Peltzman, S., "The Effect of FTC Advertising Regulation," *Journal of Law and Economics*, 24, no. 3 (1981), 403–448.

Schmitz, A., and T. G. Schmitz, "Supply Management: The Past and Future," *Canadian Journal of Agricultural Economics*, 42, no. 2 (1994), 125–148.

Schneider, L., B. Klein, and K. M. Murphy, "Governmental Regulation of Cigarette Health Information," *Journal of Law and Economics*, 24, no. 3 (1981), 575–612.

Sloan, F. A., and B. Steinwald, "Effects of Regulation on Hospital Costs," *Journal of Law and Economics*, 23, no. 1 (1980), 81–110.

Smith, A., and A. J. Venables, "Counting the Cost of Voluntary Restraints in the European Car Market," in *International Trade and Trade Policy*, eds. E. Helpman and A. Razin. Cambridge, MA: The MIT Press, 1991, pp. 187–220.

Smith, J. K., "An Analysis of State Regulations Governing Liquor Store Licensees," *Journal of Law and Economics*, 25, no. 2 (1982), 301–319.

Smith, R. L., II, "Franchise Regulation: An Economic Analysis of State Restrictions on Automobile Distribution," *Journal of Law and Economics*, 25, no. 1 (1982), 125–157.

Treda, I., and J. Whalley, "Global Effects of Developed Country Trade Restrictions on Textiles and Apparel," *The Economic Journal*, 100, no. 403 (1990), 1190–1205.

Winston, C., "Welfare Effects of ICC Regulation Revisited," *Bell Journal of Economics*, 12, no. 1 (1981), 232–244.

Winston, C., T. M. Corsi, C. M. Grimm, and C. A. Evans, *The Economic Effects of Surface Rate Deregulation*. Washington, DC: Brookings Institution, 1990.

12. Information

Moffitt, J., R. L. Farnsworth, L. R. Zavaleta, and M. Kogan, "Economic Impact of Public Pest Information: Soybean Insect Forecasts in Illinois," *American Journal of Agricultural Economics*, 68, no. 2 (1986), 274–279.

Senauer, B., J. K. Kinsey, and T. Roe, "The Cost of Inaccurate Consumer Information: The Case of EPA Gas Mileage," *Journal of Consumer Affairs*, 18, no. 2 (1984), 193–212.

Sexton, R. J., "Welfare Loss from Inaccurate Information: An Economic Model with Application to Food Labels," *Journal of Consumer Affairs*, 15, no. 2 (1981), 214–231.

Sexton, R. J., and T. A. Sexton, "Theoretical and Methodological Perspectives on Consumer Response to Electricity Information," *Journal of Consumer Affairs*, 21, no. 2 (1987), 238–257.

13. Migration

Collier, V. C., and H. Rempel, "The Divergence of Private From Social Costs in Rural-Urban Migration: A Case Study of Nairobi, Kenya," *Journal of Development Studies*, 13, no. 3 (1977), 199–216.

Davies, G.W., "Macroeconomic Effects of Immigration: Evidence from CANDIDE, TRACE, and RDX2," *Canadian Public Policy*, 3, no. 3 (1977), 299–306.

Gerking, S. D., and J. H. Mutti, "Costs and Benefits of Illegal Immigration: Key Issues for Government Policy," *Social Science Quarterly*, 61, no. 1 (1980), 71–85.

Graves, P. E., and P. D. Linneman, "Household Migration: Theoretical and Empirical Results," *Journal of Urban Economics*, 6, no. 3 (1979), 383–404.

Greenwood, M. J., "Research on Internal Migration in the United States: A Survey," *Journal of Economic Literature*, 13, no. 2 (1975), 397–433.

MacMillen, M. J., "The Economic Effects of International Migration: A Survey," *Journal of Common Market Studies*, 20, no. 3 (1982), 245–267.

14. Noise Pollution

Alexandre, A., J. Barde, and D. W. Pearce, "Practical Determination of a Charge for Noise Pollution," *Journal of Transport Economics and Policy*, 14, no. 2 (1980), 205–220.

Gautrin, J. F., "An Evaluation of the Impact of Aircraft Noise on Property Values with a Simple Model of Urban Land Rent," *Land Economics*, 51, no. 1 (1975), 80–86.

Harrison, D., Jr., "The Problem of Aircraft Noise," in *Incentives for Environmental Protection*, ed. Thomas C. Schelling. Cambridge, MA: MIT Press, 1983, pp. 43–69.

Langley, J. C., Jr., "Adverse Impacts of the Washington Beltway on Residential Property Values," *Land Economics*, 52, no. 1 (1976), 54–65.

Mayeres, I., S. Ochelen, and S. Proost, "The Marginal External Costs of Urban Transport," *Transportation Reviews-D*, 1, no. 2 (1996), 111–130.

McMillan, M. L., et al., "An Extension of the Hedonic Approach for Estimating the Value of Quiet," *Land Economics*, 56, no. 3 (1980), 315–328.

Mieszkowski, P., and A. M. Saper, "An Estimate of the Effects of Airport Noise on Property Values," *Journal of Urban Economics*, 5, no. 4 (1978), 425–440.

Morrison, S., C. Winston, and T. Watson, "Fundamental Flaws of Social Regulation: The Case of Airplane Noise," *Journal of Law and Economics*, 42, no. 2 (1999), 723–743.

Nelson, J. P., "Airport Noise, Location Rent, and the Market for Residential Amenities," *Journal of Environmental Economics and Management*, 6, no. 4 (1979), 320–331.

Nelson, J. P., "Airports and Property Values," *Journal of Transport Economics and Policy*, 14, no. 1 (1980), 37–52.

Nelson, J. P., "Highway Noise and Property Values: A Survey of Recent Evidence," *Journal of Transport Economics and Policy*, 16, no. 2 (1982), 117–138.

O'Byrne, P. H., J. P. Nelson, and J. J. Seneca, "Housing Values, Census Estimates, Disequilibrium, and the Environmental Cost of Airport Noise: A Case Study of Atlanta," *Journal of Environmental Economics and Management*, 12, no. 2 (1985), 169–178.

Pearce, D. W., "Noise Valuation," in *The Valuation of Social Cost,* ed. D. W. Pearce. London: George Allen, 1978, pp. 31–53.

Pennington, G., N. Topham, and R. Ward, "Aircraft Noise and Residential Property Values Adjacent to Manchester International Airport," *Journal of Transport Economics and Policy*, 24, no. 3 (1990), 49–59.

Whitbread, M., "Measuring the Costs of Noise Nuisance From Aircraft," *Journal of Transport Economics and Policy*, 12, no. 2 (1978), 202–208.

15. Parks, Lakes, Rivers, and Other Recreation

Beasley, S. D., W. G. Workman, and N. A. Williams, "Estimating Amenity Values of Urban Fringe Farmland: A Contingent Valuation Approach: Note," *Growth and Change*, 17, no. 4 (1986), 70–78.

Brookshire, D. S., B. Ives, and W. D. Schultze, "The Valuation of Aesthetic Preferences," *Journal of Environmental Economics and Management*, 3, no. 4 (1976), 325–346.

Brown, W., C. Sorhus, B. Chou-Yang, and J. A. Richards, "Using Individual Observations to Estimate Recreation Demand Functions: A Caution," *American Journal of Agricultural Economics*, 65, no. 1 (1983), 154–157.

Burt, O. R., and D. Brewer, "Estimation of Net Social Benefits from Outdoor Recreation," *Econometrica*, 39, no. 5 (1971), 813–827.

Caulkins, P. P., R. C. Bishop, and N. Bouwes Sr., "The Travel Cost Model for Lake Recreation: A Comparison of Two Methods for Incorporating Site Quality and Substitution Effects," *American Journal of Agricultural Economics*, 68, no. 2 (1986), 291–297.

Clawson, M., and J. L. Knetsch, *Economics of Outdoor Recreation.* Baltimore: Johns Hopkins University Press, 1966.

Darling, A. H., "Measuring Benefits Generated by Urban Water Parks," *Land Economics*, 49, no. 1 (1973), 22–34.

Daubert, J. T., and R. A. Young, "Recreational Demands for Maintaining Instream Flows: A Contingent Valuation Approach," *American Journal of Agricultural Economics*, 63, no. 4 (1981), 666–684.

Dwyer, J. F., H. W. Schroeder, J. J. Louviere, and D. H. Anderson, "Urbanites' Willingness to Pay for Trees and Forests in Recreation Areas," *Journal of Arboriculture*, 15, no. 10 (1989), 247–252.

Gum, R. L., and E. W. Martin, "Problems and Solutions in Estimating the Demand for and Value of Rural Outdoor Recreation," *American Journal of Agricultural Economics*, 57, no. 4 (1975), 558–566.

Hanley, N. D., "Valuing Rural Recreation Benefits: An Empirical Comparison of Two Approaches," *Journal of Agricultural Economics*, 40, no. 3 (1989), 361–374.

Harris, B. S., and A. D. Meister, "The Use of Recreation Analysis in Resource Management: A Case Study," *Journal of Environmental Management*, 16, no. 2 (1983), 117–124.

Krutilla, J. V., and C. J. Cichetti, "Evaluating Benefits of Environmental Resources with Special Application to Hells Canyon," *Natural Resource Journal*, 12, no. 2 (1972), 1–29.

Loomis, J. B., "Balancing Public Trust Resources of Mono Lake and L. A.'s Water Right: An Economic Approach," *Water Resources Research*, 23, no. 8 (1987), 1449–1456.

Loomis, J. B., C. S. Sorg, and D. M. Donnelly, "Evaluating Regional Demand Models for Estimating Recreation Use and Economic Benefits: A Case Study," *Water Resources Research*, 22, no. 4 (1986), 431–438.

McConnell, K. E., "Congestion and Willingness to Pay: A Case Study of Beach Use," *Land Economics*, 53, no. 2 (1977), 185–195.

Menz, F. C., and J. K. Mullin, "Expected Encounters and Willingness to Pay for Outdoor Recreation," *Land Economics*, 57, no. 1 (1981), 33–40.

Morey, E. R., "The Demand for Site-Specific Recreational Activities: A Characteristic Approach," *Journal of Environmental Economics and Management*, 8, no. 4 (1981), 345–371.

Richer, J., "Willingness to Pay for Desert Protection," *Contemporary Economic Policy,* 13, no. 4 (1995), 93–104.

Schroeder, T. D., "The Relationship of Local Public Park and Recreation Services to Residential Property Values," *Journal of Leisure Research*, 14, no. 3 (1982), 223–234.

Schulze, W. D., and D. S. Brookshire, "The Economic Benefits of Preserving Visibility in the National

Parklands of the Southwest," *Natural Resources Journal*, 23, no. 1 (1983), 124–133.

Smith, R. J., "The Evaluation of Recreation Benefits: The Clawson Method in Practice," *Urban Studies*, 8, no. 2 (1971), 89–102.

Walker, J. L., "Tall Trees, People, and Politics: The Opportunity Costs of the Redwood National Park," *Contemporary Policy Issues*, no. 5 (1984), 22–29.

Willis, K. G., and J. F. Benson, "A Comparison of User Benefits and Costs of Nature Conservation at Three Nature Reserves," *Regional Studies*, 22, no. 5 (1988), 417–428.

Willis, K. G., and G. D. Garred, "Valuing Landscape: A Contingent Valuation Approach," *Journal of Environmental Management*, 37, no. 1 (1993), 1–22.

16. Professional Regulation

Begun, J. W., *Professionalism and the Public Interest: Price and Quality in Optometry*. Cambridge, MA: MIT Press, 1981.

Benham, L., "The Effect of Advertising on the Price of Eyeglasses," *Journal of Law and Economics*, 15, no. 2 (1972), 337–352.

Caroll, S. L., and R. J. Gaston, "Occupational Restrictions and Quality of Service Received: Some Evidence," *Southern Economic Journal,* 47, no. 4 (1981), 959–976.

Feldman, R., and J. W. Begun, "The Effects of Advertising Restrictions: Lessons From Optometry," *Journal of Human Resources*, 13, supplement (1978), 248–262.

Haas-Wilson, D., "The Effect of Commercial Practice Restrictions: The Case of Optometry," *Journal of Law and Economics*, 29, no. 1 (1986), 165–186.

Leffer, K. B., "Physician Licensure: Competition and Monopoly in American Medicine," *Journal of Law and Economics*, 21, no. 1 (1978), 165–186.

Shepard, L., "Licensing Restrictions and the Cost of Dental Care," *Journal of Law and Economics*, 21, no. 1 (1978), 187–201.

White, W. D. "The Impact of Occupational Licensure of Clinical Laboratory Personnel," *Journal of Human Resources*, 8, no. 4 (1978), 91–102.

White, W. D., *Public Health and Private Gain: The Economics of Licensing Clinical Laboratory Personnel.* Chicago: Maaroufa Press Inc., 1979.

17. Public Works (Nontransit)

Blackorby, C., G. Donaldson, R. Picard, and M. Slade, "Expo 1986: An Economic Impact Analysis," Chapter 13 in *Restraining the Economy: Social Credit Economic Policies for B.C. in the Eighties*, eds. R. C. Allen and G. Rosenblath. Vancouver: New Star Books, 1986, pp. 254–278.

Conrad, K. and H. Seitz, "The Economic Benefits of Public Infrastructure," *Applied Economics*, 26, no. 4 (1994), 303–311.

Graves, S. C., M. Horwitch, and E. H. Bowman, "Deep-Draft Dredging of U.S. Coal Ports: A Cost-Benefit Analysis," *Policy Sciences*, 17, no. 2 (1985), 153–178.

Muller, R. A., "Some Economics of the Grand Canal," *Canadian Public Policy*, 14, no. 2 (1988), 162–174.

Shaffer, M., "The Benefits and Costs of Two B.C. Hydro Construction Projects," Chapter 14 in *Restraining the Economy*, eds. R. C. Allen and G. Rosenblath. Vancouver: New Star Books, 1986, pp. 279–296.

Viscencio-Brambila, H., and S. Fuller, "Estimated Effects of Deepened U.S. Gulf Ports on Export-Grain Flow Pattern and Logistics Costs," *Logistics and Transportation Review*, 23, no. 2 (1987), 139–154.

Yochum, G. R., and V. B. Agarwal, "Economic Impact of Port on a Regional Economy: Note," *Growth and Change*, 18, no. 3 (1987), 74–87.

18. R&D

Bozeman, B., and A. N. Link, "Tax Incentives for R&D: A Critical Evaluation," *Research Policy*, 13, no. 1 (1984), 21–31.

Fox, G., "Is the United States Really Underinvesting in Agricultural Research?" *American Journal of Agricultural Economics*, 67, no. 4 (1985), 806–812.

Griliches, Z., "Research Cost and Social Returns: Hybrid Corn and Related Innovations," *Journal of Political Economy*, 66, no. 1 (1958), 419–431.

Mansfield, E., and L. Switzer, "How Effective Are Canada's Direct Tax Incentives for R&D?" *Canadian Public Policy*, 11, no. 2 (1985), 241–246.

Nagy, J. G., and W. H. Furtan, "Economic Costs and Returns From Crop Development Research: The Case of Rapeseed Breeding in Canada," *Canadian Journal of Agricultural Economics*, 26, no. 1 (1978), 1–14.

Nelson, R., "Government Support of Technical Progress—Lessons from History," *Journal of Policy Analysis and Management*, 2, no. 4 (1983), 499–514.

Norton, G. W., and J. S. Davis, "Evaluating Returns to Agricultural Research: A Review," *American Journal of Agricultural Economics*, 63, no. 4 (1981), 685–699.

Norton, G. W., V. G. Ganoza, and C. Pomereda, "Potential Benefits of Agricultural Research and Extension in Peru," *American Journal of Agricultural Economics*, 69, no. 2 (1987), 247–257.

Stranahan, H. A., and J. S. Shonkwiler, "Evaluating the Returns to Postharvest Research in the Florida Citrus-Processing Subsector," *American Journal of Agricultural Economics*, 68, no. 1 (1986), 88–94.

Terleckyj, N., "Direct and Indirect Effects of Industrial Research and Development on the Productivity Growth of Industries," in *New Developments in Productivity Measurements*, eds. J. W. Kendrick and B. Vaccara. Chicago: Chicago University Press for NBER, *Studies in Income and Wealth,* no. 44 (1980), 359–377.

Widmer, L. R., G. Fox, and G. L. Brinkman, "The Rate of Return to Agricultural Research in a Small Country: The Case of Beef Cattle Research in Canada," *Canadian Journal of Agricultural Economics*, 36, no. 1 (1988), 23–35.

Zentner, R. P., "Returns to Public Investment in Canadian Wheat and Rapeseed Research," in *Economics of Agricultural Research in Canada,* eds. K. K. Klein and W. H. Furtan. Calgary: University of Calgary Press, 1983, pp. 169–188.

19. Recreational and Commercial Fisheries

Anderson, D. M., S. A. Shankle, M. J. Scott, D. A. Neitzel, and J. C. Chatters, "Valuing Effects of Climate Change and Fishery Enhancement on Chinook Salmon," *Contemporary Policy Issues*, 11, no. 4 (1993), 82–94.

Anderson, L. G., "The Demand Curve for Recreation Fishing with an Application to Stock Enhancement Activities," *Land Economics*, 59, no. 3 (1983), 279–286.

Cauvin, D., "The Valuation of Recreational Fisheries," *Canadian Journal of Fishing and Aquatic Sciences*, 37, no. 8 (1980), 1321–1327.

Hufschmidt, M. M., and J. A. Dixon, "Valuation of Losses of Marine Produce Resources Caused by Coastal Development of Tokyo Bay," adapted from materials prepared by Y. Hanayama and I. Sano in *Economic Valuation Techniques for the Environment*, eds. J. A. Dixon and M. M. Hufschmidt. Baltimore and London: Johns Hopkins University Press, 1986, pp. 102–120.

Layman, R. C., J. R. Boyce, and K. R. Kriddle, "Economic Valuation of the Chinook Salmon Sport Fishery of the Gulkana River, Alaska, Under Current and Alternative Management Plans," *Land Economics,* 72, no. 1 (1996), 113–128.

Loomis, J. B., C. Sorg, and D. Donnelly, "Economic Losses to Recreational Fisheries Due to Small-

Head Hydro-Power Development: A Case Study of the Henry's Fork in Idaho," *Journal of Environmental Management*, 22, no. 1 (1986), 85–94.

McConnell, K. E., "Values of Marine Recreational Fishing: Measurement and Impact of Measurement," *American Journal of Agricultural Economics,* 61, no. 5 (December 1979), 921–925.

McConnell, K. E., and V. Duff, "Estimating Net Benefits of Recreational Fishing," *Journal of Environmental Economics and Management*, 2, no. 3 (1976), 224–230.

McConnell, K. E., and I. Strand, "Measuring the Cost of Time in Recreation Demand Analysis: An Application to Sportfishing," *American Journal of Agricultural Economics*, 63, no. 1 (February 1981), 153–156.

Meyer, P. A., "Publicly Vested Values for Fish and Wildlife: Criteria in Economic Welfare and Interface with the Law," *Land Economics*, 55, no. 2 (1979), 223–235.

Russell, C. S., and W. J. Vaughan, "The National Recreational Fishing Benefits of Water Pollution Control," *Journal of Environmental Economics and Management*, 9, no. 3 (1982), 328–354.

Samples, K. C., and R. C. Bishop, "Estimating the Value of Variations in Anglers' Success Rates: An

Application of the Multiple-Site Travel Cost Method," *Marine Resource Economics*, 2, no. 1 (1985), 55–74.

Schwindt, R., A. Vining, and S. Globerman, "Net Loss: A Cost-Benefit Analysis of the Canadian Pacific Salmon Fishery," *Journal of Policy Analysis and Management,* 19, no. 1, (2000), 23–45.

Sorg, C., et al., "The Net Economic Value of Cold and Warm Water Fishing in Idaho," Resource Bulletin, Rocky Mountain Forest and Range Experiment Station, U.S. Forest Service, Fort Collins, Colorado, 1985.

Vaughan, W. J., and C. S. Russell, "Valuing a Fishing Day: An Application of a Systematic Varying Parameter Model," *Land Economics*, 58, no. 4 (1982), 450–463.

Weithman, S., and M. Haas, "Socioeconomic Value of the Trout Fisheries in Lake Taneycomo, Missouri," *Transactions of the American Fisheries Society*, 111 (1982), 223–230.

20. Redistribution Programs

Ballard, C., "The Marginal Efficiency Cost of Redistribution," *American Economic Review*, 78, no. 5 (1988), 1019–1033.

Browning, E. K., "On the Marginal Welfare Costs of Taxation," *American Economic Review*, 77, no. 1 (1987), 11–23.

Caniglia, A. S., "The Economic Evaluation of Food Stamps: An Intertemporal Analysis with Nonlinear Budget Constraints," *Public Finance Quarterly*, 16, no. 1 (1988), 3–30.

Gramlich, E., and M. Wolkoff, "A Procedure for Evaluating Income Distribution Policies," *Journal of Human Resources*, 14, no. 3 (1979), 319–350.

Hu, S. T., and N. L. Knaub, "Effects of Cash and In-Kind Welfare on Family Expenditures," *Policy Analysis*, 2, no. 1 (1976), 71–92.

Jorgenson, D. W., and K. Yun, "The Excess Burden of Taxation in the United States," *Journal of Accounting, Auditing, and Finance*, 6 (1991), 487–508.

Knaub, N. L., "The Impact of Food Stamps and Cash Welfare on Food Expenditures, 1971–1975," *Policy Analysis*, 7, no. 2 (1981), 169–182.

Lermer, G., and W. T. Stanbury, "The Cost of Redistributing Income by Means of Direct Regulation," *Canadian Journal of Economics*, 28, no. 1 (1985), 190–207.

Lewis, H. G., and R. J. Morrison, *Income Transfer Analysis.* Washington, DC: The Urban Institute, 1989.

Mead, L. W., "The Potential for Work Enforcement: A Study of WIN," *Journal of Policy Analysis and Management*, 7, no. 2 (1988), 264–288.

Moffitt, R. A., and K. C. Kehrer, "The Effect of Tax and Transfer Programs on Labor Supply," *Research in Labor Economics*, 4 (1981), 103–150.

Tullock, G., *Economics of Income Redistribution.* Hingham, MA: Kluwer Boston, 1983.

21. Transportation/Transit (Including Safety)

Alexander, D. A., "Motor Carrier Deregulation and Highway Safety: An Empirical Analysis," *Southern Economic Journal*, 59, no. 1 (1992), 28–36.

Beggs, S., S. Cardell, and J. Housman, "Assessing the Potential Demand for Electric Cars," *Journal of Econometrics*, 17, no. 1 (1981), 1–20.

Binder, R. H., "Cost-Effectiveness in Highway Safety," *Traffic Engineering*, 46, no. 12 (1976), 26–30.

Blomquist, G., "Economics of Safety and Seat Belt Use," *Journal of Safety Research*, 9, no. 4 (1977), 179–189.

Brems, H., "Light Rail Transit: Cost and Output," *Journal of Urban Economics*, 7, no. 1 (1980), 20–30.

Brent, R. J., "Imputing Weights Behind Past Railway Closure Decisions Within a Cost-Benefit Framework," *Applied Economics*, 7, no. 2 (1979), 157–170.

Castle, G., "The 55 MPH Speed Limit: A Cost-Benefit Analysis," *Traffic Engineering*, 46, no. 1 (1976), 11–14.

Chalk, A. J., "Market Forces and Commercial Aircraft Safety," *The Journal of Industrial Economics*, 36, no. 1 (1987), 61–80.

Claybrook, J., and D. Bollier, "The Hidden Benefits of Regulation: Disclosing the Auto Safety Payoff," *Yale Journal of Regulation*, 3, no. 1 (1985), 87–132.

Clotfelter, C., and J. Hahn, "Assessing the 55 MPH Speed Limit," *Policy Sciences*, 9, no. 3 (1978), 281–294.

Conybeare, J. A. C., "Evaluation of Automobile Safety Regulations: The Case of Compulsory Seat Belt Legislation in Australia," *Policy Sciences*, 12, no. 1 (1980), 27–39.

Crandall, R. W., and J. D. Graham, "Automobile Safety Regulation and Offsetting Behaviour: Some New Empirical Estimates," *American Economic Review Papers and Proceedings*, 74, no. 2 (1984), 328–331.

Crandall, R. C., H. W. Gruenspecht, T. E. Keeler, and L. B. Lave, *Regulating the Automobile*. Washington, DC: The Brookings Institution, 1986.

Davidson, B. R., "A Benefit-Cost Analysis of the New South Wales Railway System," *Australian Economic History Review*, 22, no. 2 (1982), 127–150.

de Rus G., and V. Inglada, "Cost-Benefit Analysis of the High-Speed Train in Spain," *Annals of Regional Science*, 31, no. 3 (1997), 175–188.

Dodgson, J. S., "Benefits of Changes in Urban Public Transport Subsidies in Major Australian Cities," *Economic Record*, 62, no. 177 (1986), 224–235.

Dodgson, J. S., and N. Topham, "Benefit-Cost Rules for Urban Transit Subsidies: An Integration of Allocational, Distributional and Public Finance Issues," *Journal of Transport Economics and Policy*, 21, no. 1 (1987), 57–71.

Forester, T., R. McNown, and L. Singell, "A Cost-Benefit Analysis of the 55 MPH Speed Limit," *Southern Economic Journal*, 50, no. 3 (1984), 631–641.

Gardner, B. M., and R. O. Goss, "Lifeboats vs. Inflatable Liferafts: A Comparison of Costs and Benefits," in *Advances in Maritime Economics*, ed. R. O. Goss. New York: Cambridge University Press, 1977, pp. 247–287.

Gomez-Ibanez, J. A., and G. R. Fauth, "Downtown Auto Restraint Policies: The Costs and Benefits for Boston," *Journal of Transport Economics and Policy*, 14, no. 2 (1980), 155–168.

Goodman, A. C., "Willingness to Pay for Car Efficiency: A Hedonic Price Approach," *Journal of Transport Economics and Policy*, 17, no. 3 (1983), 247–266.

Goss, R. O., and A. H. Vanags, "The Costs and Benefits of Navigational Aids in Port Approaches," in *Advances in Maritime Economics*, ed. R. O. Goss. New York: Cambridge University Press, 1977, pp. 213–256.

Graham, J. D., and S. Garber, "Evaluating the Effects of Automobile Safety Regulation," *Journal of Policy Analysis and Management*, 2, no. 2 (1984), 206–224.

Graves, S. C., M. Horwitch, and E. Bowman, "Deep-Draft Dredging of U.S. Coal Ports: A Cost-Benefit Analysis," *Policy Sciences*, 17, no. 2 (1984), 153–178.

Greene, D., and K. G. Duleep, "Costs and Benefits of Automotive Fuel Economy Improvement: A Partial Analysis," *Transportation Research-A*, 27, no. 3 (1993), 217–235.

Hanke, S. H., and R. A. Walker, "Benefit-Cost Analysis Reconsidered: An Evaluation of the Mid-State Project," *Water Resources Research*, 10, no. 5 (1974), 898–908.

Hansen, B., and K. Tourk, "The Suez Canal Project to Accommodate Super-Tankers," *Journal of Transport Economics and Policy*, 8, no. 2 (1974), 103–121.

Hartunian, N., C. N. Smart, T. R. Willemain, and P. Zander, "The Economics of Safety Deregulation: Lives and Dollars Lost Due to Repeal of Motorcycle Helmet Laws," *Journal of Health Politics, Policy and Law*, 8, no. 1 (1981), 76–98.

Hettich, W., "The Political Economy of Benefit-Cost Analysis: Evaluating STOL Air Transport for Canada," *Canadian Public Policy*, 9, no. 4 (1983), 478–498.

Horowitz, A. J., "Assessing Transportation User Benefits With Maximum Trip Lengths," *Transportation Planning and Technology*, 6, no. 3 (1980), 175–182.

Jara-Diaz, S. R., "On the Relation Between Users' Benefits and the Economic Effects of Transportation Activities," *Journal of Regional Science*, 26, no. 2 (1986), 379–391.

Jara-Diaz, S. R., and T. L. Friezz, "Measuring the Benefits Derived from a Transportation Investment," *Transportation Research-B*, 16, no. 1 (1982), 57–77.

Jonah, B. A., and J. L. Lawson, "The Effectiveness of the Canadian Mandatory Seat Belt Use Laws," *Accident Analysis and Prevention*, 16, no. 5/6 (1984), 433–450.

Jones-Lee, M. W., M. Hammerton, and P. R. Philips, "The Value of Safety: Results of a National Sample Survey," *Economic Journal*, 95, no. 377 (1985), 49–72.

Joray, P. A., and P. A. Kochanowski, "Inter-Urban Rail Passenger Service—Social Benefits of Retaining the South Shore Railroad (Chicago)," *Logistics and Transportation Review*, 14, no. 1 (1978), 81–89.

Kamerud, D. B., "The 55 MPH Speed Limit: Costs, Benefits, and Implied Trade-Offs," *Transportation Research-A*, 17, no. 1 (1983), 51–64.

Kamerud, D. B., "Benefits and Costs of the 55 MPH Speed Limit: New Estimates and Their Implications," *Journal of Policy Analysis and Management*, 7, no. 2 (1988), 341–352.

Kanemoto, Y., "Cost-Benefit Analysis and the Second Best Land Use for Transportation," *Journal of Urban Economics*, 4, no. 4 (1977), 483–503.

Kanemoto, Y., "General Equilibrium Analysis of the Benefits of Large Transportation Improvements," *Regional Science and Urban Economics*, 15, no. 3 (1985), 343–363.

Keeler, T. E., "Public Policy and Productivity in the Trucking Industry: Some Evidence on the Effects of Highway Investments, Deregulation, and the 55 MPH Speed Limit," *American Economic Review*, 76, no. 2 (1986), 153–158.

Kim, J., and D. S. West, "The Edmonton LRT: An Appropriate Choice?" *Canadian Public Policy*, 17, no. 2 (1991), 173–182.

Krupnick, A. J., and M. A. Walls, *The Cost-Effectiveness of Methanol for Reducing Motor Vehicle Emissions and Urban Ozone Levels*. Washington, DC: Resources for the Future, 1990.

Lave, C. A., "Speeding, Coordination, and the 55 MPH Limit," *American Economic Review*, 75, no. 5 (1985), 1159–1164.

Lave, L. B., and W. E. Weber, "Benefit-Cost Analysis of Auto Safety Features," *Applied Economics*, 2, no. 4 (1970), 265–275.

Loeb, P. D., "The Efficacy and Cost-Effectiveness of Motor Vehicle Inspection Using Cross-Sectional Data—An Econometric Analysis," *Southern Economic Journal*, 52, no. 2 (1985), 500–509.

Loeb, P. D., and B. Gilad, "The Efficacy and Cost-Effectiveness of Motor Vehicle Inspection: A State Specific Analysis Using Time Series Data," *Journal of Transport Economics and Policy*, 18, no. 2 (1984), 145–164.

Mackie, P. J., and D. Simon, "Do Road Projects Benefit Industry? A Case Study of the Humber Bridge," *Journal of Transport Economics and Policy*, 20, no. 3 (1986), 377–384.

McBride, M. E., "An Evaluation of Various Methods of Estimating Railway Costs," *Logistics and Transportation Review*, 19, no. 1 (1983), 45–66.

Mohring, H., "Maximizing, Measuring and Not Double Counting Transportation Improvement Benefits: A Primer on Closed- and Open-Economy Cost-Benefit Analysis," *Transportation Research-B*, 27, no. 6 (1993), 413–424.

Muller, A., "Evaluation of the Costs and Benefits of Motorcycle Helmet Laws," *American Journal of Public Health*, 70, no. 6 (1980), 586–592.

Nelson, D. E., T. D. Peterson, T. L. Chorba, O. J. Devine, and J. Sacks, "Cost Savings Associated with Increased Safety Belt Use in Iowa, 1987–1988," *Accident Analysis and Prevention*, 25, no. 5 (1993), 521–528.

Obeng, K., "Fare Subsidies to Achieve Pareto Optimality: A Benefit-Cost Approach," *Logistics and Transportation Review*, 19, no. 4 (1983), 367–384.

Obeng, K., "The Economics of Bus Transit Operation," *Logistics and Transportation Review*, 20, no. 1 (1984), 45–65.

Olson, D. D., "A Benefit-Cost Analysis of Improving Alaska's Dalton Highway," *Logistics and Transportation Review*, 22, no. 2 (1986), 141–157.

Orr, L. D., "Incentives and Efficiency in Automobile Safety Regulation," *Quarterly Review of Economics and Business*, 22, no. 3 (1982), 43–65.

Peaker, A., "The Economics of VTOL Aircraft," *Journal of Transport Economics and Policy*, 8, no. 1 (1974), 48–57.

Peltzman, S., "The Effect of Automobile Safety Regulation," *Journal of Political Economy*, 83, no. 4 (1975), 677–725.

Sagner, J. S., "Benefit/Cost Analysis: Efficiency-Equity Issues in Transportation," *Logistics and Transportation Review*, 16, no. 4 (1980), 339–388.

Sawicki, D. S., "Break-Even B-C Analysis of Alternative Express Transit Systems," *Journal of Transport Economics and Policy*, 8, no. 3 (1974), 274–293.

Schwing, R. C., B. Southwark, C. von Buseck, and C. J. Jackson, "Benefit-Cost Analysis of Automobile Emission Reductions," *Journal of Environmental Economics and Management*, 7, no. 1 (1980), 44–64.

Small, K. A., "Estimating Air Pollution Costs of Transport Modes," *Journal of Transportation Economics*, 11, no. 2 (1977), 109–132.

St. Seidenfus, H., "European Ports in the Context of the World Economy and the European Economy: Changes in Sea Transport," *International Journal of Transportation Economics*, 14, no. 2 (1987), 133–138.

Swoveland, C., "Benefit-Cost Analysis of a Proposed Runway Extension," *Management Science*, 27, no. 2 (1981), 155–173.

Talley, W. K., and E. E. Anderson, "An Urban Transit Firm Providing Transit, Paratransit and Contracted-Out Services: A Cost Analysis," *Journal of Transport Economics and Policy*, 20, no. 3 (1986), 353–368.

Taylor, S., and R. Wright, "An Economic Evaluation of Calgary's North-East Light Rail Transit System," *Logistics and Transportation Review*, 19, no. 4 (1983), 351–365.

Viscencio-Brambila, H., and S. Fuller, "Estimated Effects of Deepened U.S. Gulf Ports on Export-Grain Flow Pattern and Logistics Costs," *Logistics and Transportation Review*, 23, no. 2 (1987), 139–154.

Vitaliano, D. F., "An Economic Assessment of the Social Costs of Highway Salting and the Efficiency of Substituting a New De-icing Material," *Journal of Policy Analysis and Management*, 11, no. 3 (1992), 397–418.

Viton, P. A., "On the Economics of Rapid-Transit Operations," *Transportation Research-A*, 14, no. 4 (1980), 243–253.

Wabe, S., and O. Coles, "The Short and Long Run Cost of Bus Transport in Urban Areas," *Journal of Transport Economics and Policy*, 9, no. 2 (1975), 127–140.

Walters, A. A., "The Benefits of Minibuses: The Case of Kuala Lumpur," *Journal of Transport Economics and Policy*, 13, no. 3 (1979), 320–334.

Waters, W. G., II, and S. J. Meyers, "Benefit-Cost Analysis of a Toll Highway: British Columbia's Coquihalla," *Journal of the Transportation Research Forum*, 28, no. 1 (1987), 434–443.

Watson, G. S., P. L. Zador, and A. Wilks, "The Repeal of Helmet Use Laws and Increased Motorcyclist Mortality in the United States, 1975–1978," *American Journal of Public Health*, 70, no. 6 (1980), 579–585.

Wheaton, W. C., "Residential Decentralization Land Rents and the Benefits of Urban Transportation Investment," *American Economic Review*, 67, no. 2 (1977), 136–143.

Wilson, H. G., "The Cost of Operating Buses in U.S. Cities," *Journal of Transport Economics and Policy*, 11, no. 1 (1977), 68–91.

Woolley, P. K., "C-B Analysis of the Concorde Project," *Journal of Transport Economics and Policy*, 6, no. 3 (1972), 225–239.

22. Waste Disposal

Bingham, T. M., "Allocative and Distributive Effects of a Disposal Charge on Product Packaging," in *Resource Conservation: Social and Economic Dimensions of Recycling*, eds. D. Pearce and I. Walter. London: Macmillan, 1977.

Dewees, D. N., and M. J. Hare, "Economic Analysis of Packaging Waste Reduction," *Canadian Public Policy*, 24, no. 4 (1998), 453–470.

Dinan, T. M., "Economic Efficiency Effects of Alternative Policies for Reducing Waste Disposal," *Journal of Environmental Economics and Management*, 25, no. 3 (1993), 242–256.

Jenkins, R. R., *The Economics of Solid Waste Reduction: The Impact of User Fees*. Brookfield, VT: Edward Elgar Publishing Company, 1993.

Judge, R., and A. Becker, "Motivating Recycling: A Marginal Cost Analysis," *Contemporary Policy Issues*, 11, no. 3 (1993), 58–68.

Palmer, K., H. Sigman, and M. Walls, "The Cost of Reducing Municipal Solid Waste," *Journal of Environmental Economics and Management*, 33, no. 2 (1997), 128–150.

Porter, R. C., "A Social Benefit-Cost Analysis of Mandatory Deposits on Beverage Containers," *Journal of Environmental Economics and Management*, 5, no. 4 (1978), 351–375.

Rose, D., "National Beverage Container Deposit Legislation: A Cost-Benefit Analysis," *Journal of Environmental Systems*, 12, no. 1 (1982), 71–84.

Strathman, J. G., A. M. Rufolo, and G. C. S. Mildner, "The Demand for Solid Waste Disposal," *Land Economics*, 71, no. 1 (1995), 57–64.

23. Water

Boyle, K., G. L. Poe, and J. C. Bergstrom, "What Do We Know About Groundwater Values? Preliminary Implications from a Meta-Analysis of Contingent Valuation Studies," *American Journal of Agricultural Economics*, 76, no. 5 (1994), 1055–1061.

Crouter, J. P., "Hedonic Estimation Applied to a Water Rights Market," *Land Economics*, 63, no. 3 (1987), 259–271.

Decooke, B. G., J. W. Buckley, and S. J. Wright, "Great Lakes Diversions: Preliminary Assessment of Economic Impacts," *Canadian Water Resources Journal*, 9, no. 1 (1984), 1–15.

Gibbons, D. C., *The Economic Value of Water*. Washington, DC: Resources for the Future, 1986.

Kanazawa, M., "Pricing Subsidies and Economic Efficiency: The U.S. Bureau of Reclamation," *Journal of Law and Economics*, 36, no. 1 (1993), 205–234.

Kulshreshtha, S. N., et al., "Economic Impacts of Irrigation Development in Alberta Upon the Provincial and Canadian Economy," *Canadian Water Resources Journal*, 10, no. 2 (1985), 1–10.

MacRae, D., Jr., and D. Whittington, "Assessing Preferences in Cost-Benefit Analysis: Reflections on Rural Water Supply Evaluation in Haiti," *Journal of Policy Analysis and Management*, 7, no. 2 (1988), 246–263.

McGuckin, J. T., and R. A. Young, "On the Economics of Desalination of Brackish Household Water Supplies," *Journal of Environmental Economics and Management*, 8, no. 1 (1981), 79–91.

Renzetti, S. "Evaluating the Welfare Effects of Reforming Municipal Water Prices," *Journal of Environmental Economics and Management*, 22, no. 2 (1992), 147–163.

24. Water Pollution

Ashworth, J., J. Papps, and D. J. Storey, "Assessing the Impact Upon the British Chlor-Alkali Industry of the EEC Directive on Discharges of Mercury into Waterways," *Land Economics*, 63, no. 1 (1987), 72–78.

Beck, M. B., and B. A. Finney, "Operational Water Quality Management: Problem Context and Evaluation of a Model for River Quality," *Water Resources Research*, 23, no. 11 (1987), 2030–2042.

Bockstael, N. E., W. M. Hanemann, and C. L. Kling, "Estimating the Value of Water Quality Improvements in a Recreational Demand Framework," *Water Resources Research*, 23, no. 5 (1987), 951–960.

Cohen, M. A., "The Costs and Benefits of Oil Spill Prevention and Enforcement," *Journal of Environmental Economics and Management*, 13, no. 2 (1986), 167–188.

Dasgupta, A. K., and M. N. Murty, "Economic Evaluation of Water Pollution Abatement: A Case Study of Paper and Pulp Industry in India," *India Economic Review*, 20, no. 2 (1985), 231–267.

Desvousges, W. H., V. K. Smith, and A. Fisher, "Option Price Estimates for Water Quality Improvements: A Contingent Valuation Study for the Monongahela River," *Journal of Environmental Economics and Management*, 14, no. 3 (1987), 248–267.

Feenberg, D., and E. S. Mills, *Measuring the Benefits of Water Pollution Abatement*. New York: Academic Press, 1980.

Gardner, R. L., and R. A. Young, "An Economic Evaluation of the Colorado River Basin Salinity Control Program," *Western Journal of Agricultural Economics*, 10, no. 1 (1985), 1–12.

Greenley, D. A., R. G. Walsh, and R. A. Young, "Option Value: Empirical Evidence From a Case Study of Recreation of Water Quality," *Quarterly Journal of Economics*, 96, no. 1 (1981), 657–673.

Grigalunas, T. A., et al., "Estimating the Cost of Oil Spills: Lessons from the *Amoco Cadiz* Incident," *Marine Resource Economics*, 2, no. 3 (1986), 239–262.

Harris, B. S., "Contingent Valuation of Water Pollution Control," *Journal of Environmental Management*, 19, no. 3 (1984), 199–208.

Hufschmidt, M. M., "Systematic Analysis of Water Pollution Control Options in a Suburban Region of Beijing, China," from a report prepared by F. Guowei, Z. Lansheng, C. Shengtong, and N. Guisheng in *Economic Valuation Techniques For the Environment*, eds. J. A. Dixon and M. M. Hufschmidt. Baltimore and London: Johns Hopkins University Press, 1986, pp. 178–192.

Hufschmidt, M. M., "The Nam Pong Water Resources Project in Thailand," from a paper prepared by R. Srivardhana in *Economic Valuation Techniques For the Environment*, eds. J. A. Dixon and M. M. Hufschmidt. Baltimore and London: Johns Hopkins University Press, 1986, pp. 141–162.

Kitabatake, Y., "Welfare Costs of Eutrophication-Caused Production Losses: A Case of Aquaculture in Lake Kasumigaura," *Journal of Environmental Economics and Management*, 9, no. 3 (1982), 199–212.

Lichtengerg, E., and D. Zilberman, "Efficient Regulation of Environmental Health Risks: The Case of Groundwater Contamination in California," *Recherche Economics*, 39, no. 4 (1985), 540–549.

Mitchell, R. C., and R. T. Carson, "Option Value: Empirical Evidence from a Case Study of Recreation of Water Quality: Comment," *Quarterly Journal of Economics*, 100, no. 1 (1985), 291–294.

Montgomery, M., and M. Needelman, "The Welfare Effects of Toxic Contamination in Freshwater Fish," *Land Economics,* 73, no. 2 (1997), 211–223.

Peshin, H. M., and E. P. Seskin, eds., *Cost-Benefit Analysis and Water Pollution Policy*. Washington, DC: The Urban Institute, 1975.

Raucher, R. L., "A Conceptual Framework for Measuring the Benefits of Ground Water Protection," *Water Resources Research*, 19, no. 2 (1983), 320–326.

Raucher, R. L., "The Benefits and Costs of Policies Related to Ground Water Contamination," *Land Economics*, 62, no. 1 (1986), 33–45.

Russell, C. S., and W. J. Vaughan, "The National Recreational Fishing Benefits of Water Pollution Control," *Journal of Environmental Economics and Management*, 9, no. 3 (1982), 328–354.

Smith, V. K., and W. H. Desvousges, "The Generalized Travel Cost Model and Water Quality Benefits: A Reconsideration," *Southern Economic Journal*, 52, no. 2 (1985), 371–381.

Smith, V. K., and W. H. Desvousges, *Measuring Water Quality Benefits*. Boston: Kluwer Nijhoff Publishing, 1986.

Sutherland, R. J., "A Regional Approach to Estimating Recreation Benefits of Improved Water Quality," *Journal of Environmental Economics and Management*, 9, no. 3 (1982), 229–247.

Sutherland, R. J., and R. G. Walsh, "Effects of Distance on the Preservation Value of Water Quality," *Land Economics*, 61, no. 3 (1985), 281–291.

25. Wilderness/Wetlands/Wildlife

Batie, S. S., and C. C. Mabbs-Zeno, "Opportunity Costs of Preserving Coastal Wetlands: A Case Study of a Recreational Housing Development," *Land Economics*, 61, no. 1 (1985), 1–9.

Batie, S. S., and L. A. Shabman, "Estimating the Economic Value of Wetlands: Principles, Method, and Limitations," *Coastal Zone Management Journal*, 10, no. 3 (1982), 255–278.

Brouwer, R., and L. Slangen, "Contingent Valuation of the Public Benefits of Agricultural Wildlife Management: The Case of Dutch Peat Meadow Land," *European Review of Agricultural Economics,* 25, no. 1 (1998), 53–72.

Clayton, C., and R. Mendelsohn, "The Value of Watchable Wildlife: A Case Study of McNeil River," *Journal of Environmental Management*, 39, no. 2 (1993), 101–106.

Danielson, L. E., and J. A. Leitch, "Private vs. Public Economics of Prairie Wetland Allocation," *Journal of Environmental Economics and Management*, 13, no. 1 (1986), 81–92.

Farber, S. C., "The Value of Costal Wetlands for Protection of Property Against Hurricane Wind Damage," *Journal of Environmental Economics and Management*, 14, no. 2 (1987), 143–151.

Guldin, R. W., "Wilderness Costs in New England," *Journal of Forestry*, 78, no. 9 (1980), 548–552.

Guldin, R. W., "Predicting Costs of Eastern National Forest Wildernesses," *Journal of Leisure Research*, 13, no. 2 (1981), 112–128.

Hyde, W. F., "Developments Versus Preservation in Public Resource Management: A Case Study from the Timber-Wilderness Controversy," *Journal of Environmental Management*, 16, no. 4 (1983), 347–355.

Jaworski, E., and C. N. Raphael, "Economics of Fish, Wildlife, and Recreation in Michigan's Coastal Wetlands," *Coastal Zone Management Journal*, 5, no. 3 (1979), 181–200.

Lakhani, H., "Benefit-Cost Analysis: Substituting Iron for Lead Shot in Waterfowl Hunting in Maryland," *Journal of Environmental Management,* 14, no. 3 (1982), 201–208.

Loomis, J. B., and R. G. Walsh, "Assessing Wildlife and Environmental Values in Cost-Benefit Analysis: State of the Art," *Journal of Environmental Management*, 22, no. 2 (1986), 125–131.

Lynne, G. D., P. Conroy, and F. Prochaska, "Economic Valuation of Marsh Areas for Marine Production Processes," *Journal of Environmental Economics and Management*, 8, no. 2 (1981), 175–186.

McKillop, W., "Wilderness Use in California: A Quantitative Analysis," *Journal of Leisure Research*, 7, no. 3 (1975), 163–178.

Peterson, G. L., and A. Randall, *Valuation of Wildland Benefits*. Boulder, CO: Westview, 1984.

Porter, R. C., "The New Approach to Wilderness Preservation Through Benefit-Cost Analysis," *Journal of Environmental Economics and Management*, 9, no. 1 (1982), 59–80.

Rafsnider, G. T., M. D. Skold, and R. J. Sampath, "Range Survey Cost Sharing and the Efficiency of Rangeland Use," *Land Economics*, 63, no. 1 (1987), 92–101.

Rausser, G. C., and R. A. Oliveira, "An Econometric Analysis of Wilderness Area Use," *Journal of American Statistical Association*, 71, no. 354 (1976), 276–284.

Simpson, R. D., R. A. Sedjo, and J. W. Reid, "Valuing Biodiversity for Use in Pharmaceutical Research," *Journal of Political Economy*, 104, no. 1 (1996), 163–185.

Wetzstein, M. E., R. D. Green, and G. H. Elsner, "Estimation of Wilderness Use Functions for California: An Analysis of Covariance Approach," *Journal of Leisure Research*, 14, no. 1 (1982), 16–26.

NAME INDEX

A

Abdalla, Charles W., 353–354, 357n27, 415n27
Achen, Christopher H., 302n8, 328n1
Adamovicz, Wiktor L., 388n66
Adams, Miriam E., 455n20
Alston, Julian M., 66n7
Ames, R., 388–389n69
Anderson, Glen D., 386n26
Anderson, Robert J., Jr., 212n18
Anderson, Roy M., 190n14
Arrow, Kenneth J., 33, 35, 47n4, 48n10, 191n17, 212n23, 212n24, 254, 255–256, 260n19, 264n1, 264n6, 264n8, 264–265n12, 381, 384n5, 384n7, 386n25, 388n68, 389n86
Ashenfelter, Orley, 303–304n23
Atkinson, Scott E., 394, 413n8
Auspos, P., 291, 304n25
Austin, David, 415n33
Aydede, Sema K., 246, 261n22

B

Bailey, Martin J., 264n1
Balintfy, Joseph L., 191n1
Ball, David, 414n13
Ballard, Charles L., 328n24, 409–410, 415–416n42
Barnett, W. Steven, 301
Barnett, William F., 327n15
Bass, Frank M., 387n48, 389n85
Bateman, Ian J., 386n18, 387n51
Bates, John, 414n17
Baum, Erica, 304n24
Bazelon, Coleman, 263n51, 264n5
Becker, Gary S., 211n8

Behn, Robert D., 23n29, 189n5
Bentkover, Judith D., 385n13
Bergson, Abram, 48n9
Bergstrom, John C., 416n44
Berliant, Marcus C., 48n20
Berndt, Charles R., 152n12
Berrens, Robert P., 388n62
Bhardwaj, Vinay, 388n66
Biggs, Andrew J. G., 343–344, 404, 407
Birch, Stephen, 455n15
Bishop, J. M., 454n4
Bishop, Richard C., 209, 224–225n10, 380, 381, 384n1, 384n2, 385n16, 386n19, 388n58, 389n75, 389n87, 414n24
Biswas, B., 388–389n69
Blackorby, Charles, 47–48n5–7
Blais, Andr, 23n25
Bloom, Howard, 303–304n23
Boadway, Robin W., 66n7
Boardman, Anthony E., 4, 8, 18, 20, 23n22, 152n1, 191n20, 259n1, 260n14, 328n3, 356n7, 413n1, 479, 480, 482, 487n1–2, 487n19
Bockstael, Nancy G., 357n23
Bohara, Alok K., 388n62
Bond, K., 415–416n42
Borins, Sanford, 23n24
Borkan, B., 487n10
Boskin, Michael J., 136, 153n18
Boulding, Kenneth E., 12
Boyle, Kevin J., 224–225n10, 386n19, 388n58, 389n74, 414n24, 416n44
Boyle, Michael H., 454n8
Braden, John B., 225n1, 357n23, 386n27
Bradford, David, 261n31
Bradley, Cathy J., 162, 190n13
Bradley, Mark, 357n30

Brent, Robert J., 256, 264n11, 435n4
Briggs, Andrew J. G., 415n30, 415n32
Bromley, Daniel W., 48n13, 48n16, 263n46
Brookshire, David S., 224–225n10, 382, 384n1, 385n10, 386n25, 386n33, 387n37, 388n62, 389n78, 390n90
Brown, Gardner, Jr., 357n22
Brown, Stephen J., 356n8
Brown, Thomas C., 389n75
Browning, Edgar K., 320, 321, 415–416n42, 472n24
Bruce, James P., 264–265n12
Bruce, Neil, 66n7
Bryant, J., 291
Buchanan, James M., 101–102n22, 472n16
Bukszar, Ed, 387n41
Burdick, Donald S., 191n1
Burger, Gretchen J., 384n3
Burgess, David F., 241, 261n29
Burtless, Gary, 273, 302n7, 304n34
Burtraw, Dallas, 415n33

C

Camerer, Colin F., 210–211n2, 387n43, 387n44, 472n21, 487n10
Cameron, Trudy A., 388n61
Campbell, Donald T., 269, 302n4
Campbell, Harry F., 415–416n42
Carson, Richard T., 363, 377, 378, 379, 384n1, 386n23, 386n27, 387n34, 388n55, 389n70–71, 389n81, 390n92
Cave, G., 291, 304n25
Champ, Patricia A., 389n75
Chase, S. B., 472n18
Chavas, Jean-Paul, 389n77

SUBJECT INDEX

518

521